The Modern Middle East
and North Africa

The Modern Middle East and North Africa

LOIS A. AROIAN
UNIVERSITY OF MICHIGAN

RICHARD P. MITCHELL
Late of UNIVERSITY OF MICHIGAN

MACMILLAN PUBLISHING COMPANY
NEW YORK

COLLIER MACMILLAN PUBLISHERS
LONDON

To
Marlyn Steinmetz Garfinkel
and
Patricia Richmond

Macmillan Publishing Company
866 Third Avenue, New York, New York 10022

Collier Macmillan Canada, Inc.

Library of Congress Cataloging in Publication Data

Aroian, Lois A.
  The modern Middle East and North Africa.

  1. Near East—History. 2. Africa, North—
History.
I. Mitchell, Richard P. (Richard Paul),
II. Title.
DS62.A76   1984   956   83–18785
ISBN 0–02–304200–1

Printing: 1 2 3 4 5 6 7 8   Year: 4 5 6 7 8 9 0 1 2

ISBN   0-02-304200-1

Preface

First and foremost, this book is about the Middle East and North Africa, its peoples and their history. The area has long served as a focus of international interest and has maintained close ties with other parts of the world. In this book, we consider the region's involvement in international affairs as well as the interests there of foreigners and foreign countries. But we turn that consideration around to view the international arena from the area perspective. Too often, westerners writing about the Middle East and North Africa have acted as though the area was the passive recipient of attentions from others. We try to show how those governments and peoples have often taken the initiative in dealing with indigenous concerns, although both successes and failures frequently involved foreign interference. By treating the various countries as actors in their own right, we portray dynamic rather than static relationships in earlier as well as in more recent times.

We stress the integration of Southwest Asian and North African political and economic life regionally. We have also chosen to discuss not only European-United States relations with the area but also interactions with nearby regions. Among our most important aims is to demonstrate the extent to which North Africa and Southwest Asia have been incorporated into the world economy and international finance, a critical factor in the restraints placed on local initiatives and goals. In that context, we raise questions about the militarization of the region, foreign aid to and from the area, and the various instances of international intervention. While our readers may feel we devoted undue attention, proportionately speaking, to the Palestine question and the Arab-Israeli conflict, these questions have become central determinants in the unfolding of the area's recent history. More crucial, however, is the fact that the area has significant historical dynamics apart from this very recent issue. Our overall goal was to help the reader gain an appreciation of the texture of Middle Eastern and North African history and to provide a framework of analysis that will both encourage exploration of these issues in greater depth and give coherence to the daily unfolding of the Middle Eastern and North African drama.

We have written this history with both college students and general readers in mind. We believe that our colleagues also will find our book easy to use, regardless of their course structure and teaching styles. We ourselves have taught not only highly specialized courses at a major university but also more general courses at a small college and at a small university abroad.

Several factors have influenced the style, structure, and content of this book. Both of us have resided in the area several times and have traveled widely. We have exchanged ideas with our fellow scholars working in the field on a regular basis. As Americans who have roots in the Middle East, we have focused on writing a history with empathy and balance. A history ought to view the peoples about whom it is being written as subjects, not as objects. Moreover, in light of recent research, it is not enough to write political history. We pay special attention to economic, social, and cultural history. Our own involvement in interdisciplinary courses has influenced our decision to give these other types of history relatively greater emphasis than is usual.

In a work of geographical and topical breadth, one inevitably makes choices about what in the past is worth noting and remembering. Our book uses both chronological and thematic approaches, and we have chosen our chapter titles and internal headings accordingly. We have tried to strike a balance between the need for detail and the importance of explaining broad themes and trends. Students should not have to comb libraries in search of basic information. We also have paid more attention to issues of contemporary importance that interest general readers and students. We have incorporated recent reinterpretations of both Middle Eastern and Western scholars. Be-

cause of constraints on length, we have synthesized many complex topics like the Palestine question and the Arab-Israeli conflict. We regard history as an exercise of critical inquiry, transcending partisanship and sensitivities, and demanding either analysis or interpretation. Our readers should feel that they, too, are interpreters of history. We have provided a generous up-to-date bibliography for further reference.

Originally, we planned to write a book about the Middle East. Based on Lois Aroian's teaching experience in Nigeria, however, we decided to include North Africa, too. We hope that our decision has made our book a more versatile teaching tool for colleagues who would like to incorporate North Africa into their Middle East courses. Instructors and students will find our book most useful if they supplement it with documentary selections, novels, short stories, interviews, memoirs, photographs, and films. We have provided such resources in our bibliography. To make our book widely accessible to those outside our country, we have avoided American colloquialisms. Our publisher made recommendations which resulted in a more formal, less conversational book. We also added selected footnotes at the request of our publisher.

All specialists who deal with foreign languages appreciate the difficulties of transliteration, weights and measures, and dates. For the most part, we followed the Library of Congress system of transliteration. Although we assume that our teaching colleagues will introduce students to correct pronunciation, we have in special cases provided a guide. Words and concepts in the languages of the region are generally defined when they first appear in the text. For Arabic, we have retained only the medial 'ayn. Because of common usage, we kept it in the personal name Sa'ud but deleted it in the adjective form Saudi. Weights and measures are those commonly used in our field today. Currency equivalents generally appear in U.S. dollars, British pounds, or currencies of the region. Although Muslims utilize the lunar calendar beginning in 622 C.E., we refer to the more universal Gregorian calendar.

During the various stages of research and writing, many people helped us. Both specialist and general readers examined and evaluated the text. Richard Mitchell tested it in his classes for three semesters in 1982–83. Several early chapters were read in 1980 by Herbert Bodman of the University of North Carolina, Darrell Dykstra of Western Illinois University, and Wil Rollman of the University of Michigan. Professors Bodman and Dykstra, along with Professor Brice Harris, Jr. of Occidental College also read the revised and shortened manuscript at Macmillan's request. In addition to these, Louise Baldwin, Joel Beinin, Brenda Bickett, Vernon Egger, and Kira Stevens made suggestions that we incorporated. Richard Mitchell would like to thank all of the students with whom he interacted over the years for their great share in shaping his perceptions of the area.

Among our nonspecialist friends who read parts of the text, we would like to thank Arminé and Leo Aroian, Jeanie Droddy, Jo Holmes, Peachy Johansen, Esther Langworthy, and Ann Macomber. Derwin Bell of the University of Michigan spent hours drawing maps to our specifications; the maps are extremely helpful in clarifying events described in the text. Lois Aroian would like to thank Sandra, Kjell, and Marc Johansen for their cheerful countenances during the two summers they opened their home in Ann Arbor to her. Our thanks also go to Louise and Dikran Dingilian for their hospitality to Lois during numerous trips to New York for editing and consultation. Janet Rose, Mary Foster, and Polly Berry assisted Lois Aroian in typing the final manuscript. Numerous friends and colleagues facilitated our progress by carrying text from Nigeria and Egypt to the United States for posting. Thanks, finally, to the scores of the unnamed who bore with us during the course of this project.

Throughout our association with Macmillan, Clark Baxter and Gene Panhorst proved both patient and helpful. We would like to thank our production editor Eileen Schlesinger for her role in assuring a smooth transition from manuscript to bound book. Westinghouse Health Systems in Cairo, the Institute of Industrial Administration (especially Mary Woods) at Union College in Schenectady, New York, and the Department of History at the University of Michigan gave us access to facilities used in producing the text. The Center for Near Eastern and North African Studies at Michigan was especially helpful, and we thank its directors, especially the late Ernest Abdel Massih, and its staff.

Lois Aroian is dedicating this book to the college classmate who encouraged her to study in Lebanon in 1965 and to the professor there who most inspired her to pursue an academic career. She would also like to thank her professors, students, and colleagues, all of whom have helped to shape her ideas.

In the end, we are responsible for this book. We hope that you, our readers, will assist us in making the next edition even better by letting us know your thoughts and reactions.

L.A.A.
R.P.M.

Contents

Maps

CHAPTER ONE

The Geography and Ecology of the Middle East and North Africa

What constitutes the Middle East? The terms *Middle East* and *Near East* are employed in many recent and not-so-recent works, most often interchangeably. When we speak of any *"east"* in that area, we are doing so from a European perspective that arose when various explorers were trying to reach the sources of the extensive trade in luxury items: East Asia and Southeast Asia. Eventually, colonial penetration reinforced the use of European-oriented terminology. The fact is that the area has its own history and dynamics apart from its former colonial status.

In a strict geographic definition, the area is most accurately termed *Southwest Asia and North Africa*, although parts of Europe, particularly Greece and the Balkans, will fall within our scope due to their inclusion in the former Ottoman Empire. Although both terms obscure cultural variables, they are perhaps a bit more precise. The term *maghrib* presents similar problems since it means the west, the place or time of the sunset, just as *mashriq* means the east. Only from the lands to the east is the Maghrib west, but at least it and Mashriq are terms which people in the area have applied to themselves. The Moroccans use Maghrib as the Arabic name for their country. The terms Northwest Africa and Maghrib will be employed synonymously. Northeast Africa will apply to Egypt and Sudan. We may refer to Libya in both contexts.

Most books about the Middle East or Near East examine countries of the eastern Arabic-speaking world, as well as Iran, Israel, and Turkey. Sometimes the scope of these terms is broadened to embrace Afghanistan, Greece, Cyprus, the Balkans, and North Africa. By Middle East, we mean Egypt, Arabic-speaking Asia, Israel, Iran, Cyprus, Turkey, and occasionally Libya and Sudan. We apply the term *Levant* and its adjective *Levantine*, derived from a French term meaning East, to the eastern Mediterranean coastal areas and their hinterlands in Pales-

1

tine/Israel, Syria, Lebanon, and Cilicia (southeast Mediterranean Anatolia/northern Syria). Anatolia and Asia Minor are used for present-day Asiatic Turkey. The Arab Republic of Egypt, or just Egypt, is most often treated as part of Southwest Asia, but is equally significant as an African and North African nation. By including both Northwest and Northeast Africa in our study, we emphasize the links with the Middle East rather than the separate regional identities which have led most authors to treat them independently of one another (see Map 1).

Historical Ties Between North Africa and Southwest Asia

What are some of the historical characteristics shared by North Africa and Southwest Asia? From the most ancient times, these two regions have been in contact. The earliest known Mediterranean empires, those of the Phoenicians, Hellenes (Greeks), and Romans, encompassed settlements in three continents: Europe, Asia, and Africa. Roman Africa corresponded roughly to inhabited parts of North Africa today.

Arab armies consisting primarily of Arabians began their conquests of North Africa in the name of Islam circa 640 C.E. However, North African Berbers played a significant military role in expeditions which brought the Iberian peninsula (Spain and Portugal) under their control to form al-Andalus or Muslim Spain. The conquests did not immediately Arabize and Islamize the populations of these areas. These processes in North Africa took several centuries but were never completed. The incorporation of North Africa into the Muslim world created special bonds among their respective peoples, bonds derived from shared aspects of Islamic culture and civilization, trade and urban life, religious belief and practice, government, and military activity. The east-west movement of Arabic-speaking peoples and dynasties as well as the west-east Muslim pilgrimages reinforced these ties. In the twentieth century, bonds have tightened due to individual nations' struggles against European occupiers, and the formation of regional and international organizations (including those based on religion and language) to coordinate economic, political, and social policies.

Principal Topographical Features

The physiography of Southwest Asia and North Africa displays elements of diversity. The mountain ranges, deserts, and waterways shown on Map 2 have influenced historical developments in the region. Our discussion here will call attention to regional similarities and differences since the prominent features in each area are visible on the map.

The Middle East and North Africa

land area consists of mountain ranges, plains, and plateaus. In the Maghrib, the Atlas Mountains run from southwest to northeast, dominating parts of the interior. Morocco's major parallel ranges in the Atlas system, named from south to north, are the anti-Atlas, High Atlas, Middle Atlas, and Rif mountains. Waters from these sources make fertile the Atlantic plains. The ranges of Algeria, which extend into Morocco and Tunisia, are called the Tell Atlas, Saharan Atlas, Dorsal Atlas, and Aures mountains. The principal mountainous areas elsewhere are in Iran and Turkey, though important ranges are found in the Levant, in the two Yemens of southwest Arabia, in Egypt east of the Nile, in Sudan, and in the Jabal al-Akhdar of eastern Libya.

In Turkey the dominant topographical feature is the presence of two great mountain ranges, the Pontus in the north and the Taurus in the south. Passes such as the Cilician Gates in the Taurus have facilitated invasions from time to time. Both the Taurus and the Elburz mountains in northern Iran have also proved to be formidable obstacles to human movement throughout history. Iran's other major mountain range is the Zagros in the west; this system extends from south to north. These mountains of Turkey and Iran have contributed to the evolution of Muslim, non-Arab nations in the areas sheltered by them. The movement of geological plates in mountainous regions of Iran and Turkey has caused devastating earthquakes in recent years.

Two peaks of Turkey and Iran are especially noteworthy. Mount Ararat in eastern Turkey (5,165 m.) is both a symbol for the Armenians across the border in the Soviet Union (U.S.S.R.) and the alleged site of Noah's Ark, and Mount Damavand in Iran is the highest mountain in the Middle East, standing at 5,610 meters or nearly 19,000 feet.

Mountains play a major role in the history of other areas, too. The elevated areas, though not the whole of present-day Lebanon, sheltered Middle Eastern minority groups, notably the Maronite Christians and the Druze, adherents to an offshoot of Shi'i Islam (see Chapter 3). The Anti-Lebanon mountains on the eastern side of the Biqa Valley form the boundary between Lebanon and Syria. Control of the Julan (Golan) Heights of Syria, occupied in 1967 and annexed in 1981 by Israel, has been a major issue of the Palestine-Arab-Israeli conflict. Equally important are the mountains of the Arab Republic of Yemen (North Yemen); their presence accounts for the relative isolation of its people, despite commercial activities on its coast resulting from its location on the trade routes involving the Mediterranean, the Red Sea, and the Far East.

The land area of Middle East consists primarily of plains and plateaus. The vast desert areas of the Middle East and North Africa have often hindered but not entirely obstructed the advances of migrants and armies. While the Sahara effectively divided Africa into two broadly defined culturally and ethnically distinct areas, the deserts for centuries were inhabited and traversed by nomads and traders. While the Syrian desert did not prevent incursions into Syria by invaders from the east and north, the size of the Arabian desert protected the innermost parts of the peninsula from external invasion, though long-distance traders crossed it. Deserts, like mountains, have isolated various portions of the middle Eastern and North African land mass from each other.

The avenues of invasion, north–south and east–west across valleys and plains, have been well-traveled throughout history. At the seaside cliffs near the Dog (Kalb) River in Lebanon, north of Beirut, an observer will find plaques chiseled over the centuries by invading armies. The Crusader and Muslim fortifications of the Levant, incuding Qal'at al-Husn (Krak des Chevaliers) in Syria, the Beaufort Castle in Lebanon, and the Karak fortress in Jordan, towered over the valleys that served as gateways for military expeditions but on which the agricultural livelihood of the resident population depended.

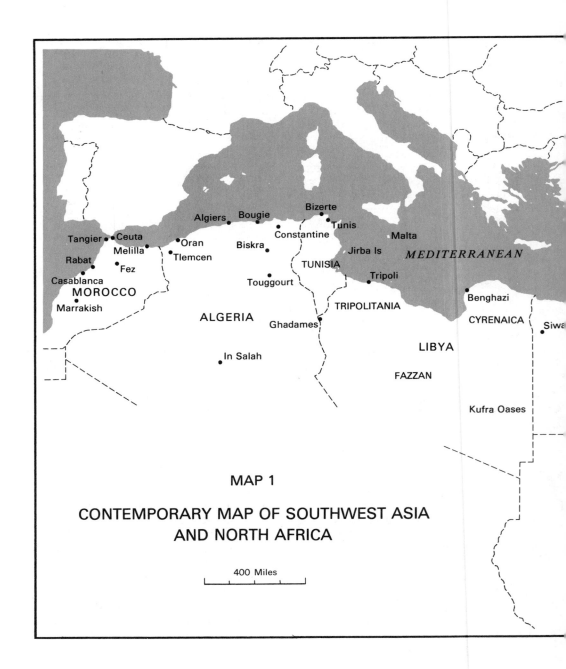

MAP 1

CONTEMPORARY MAP OF SOUTHWEST ASIA
AND NORTH AFRICA

400 Miles

5

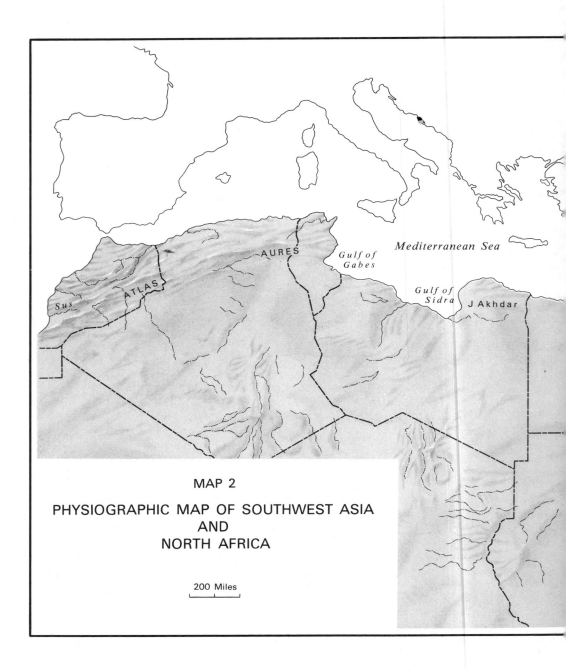

MAP 2

PHYSIOGRAPHIC MAP OF SOUTHWEST ASIA
AND
NORTH AFRICA

200 Miles

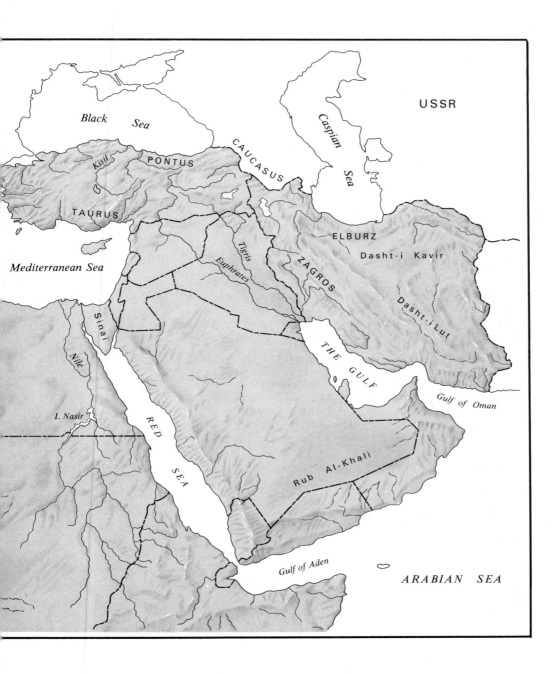

Soils

In soil composition, Southwest Asia and North Africa contain a variety of agriculturally productive lands. Alluvial soils predominate in the Nile Valley of Egypt and Sudan, the lower Tigris-Euphrates Valley of Iraq and Southwest Iran, the Caspian Sea coast in northern Iran, and along the Algerian coast. The *terra rossa* and reddish soils of Syria, northern Iraq, the Levantine coast, the Sudan, the northern Maghribian plains, and small parts of Libya and Turkey are best employed for cereal production. Soils suitable for dry farming, that which can be accomplished without irrigation and which may require field rotation, are located in the Maghrib, parts of Syria, the Iranian highlands, and on the Anatolian plateau which today constitutes most of Turkey.

Most of the land mass of the Middle East and North Africa, however, consists of soils that are not highly suited for cultivation. The major salt and sand deserts of North Africa, Iran, and the Arabian peninsula hold little potential for vast land reclamation, though such efforts have been made, especially in Libya and Egypt. Saudi Arabia is the home of the world's largest sand sea, the Rub' al-Khali. Winds have contributed to the rocky nature of the Sahara, the area that comprises well over 90 percent of the land in Egypt, Libya, and Algeria.

The Sudan, Africa's largest nation in land area, consists both of very rich land in its *Jazira* (island) between the White and Blue Niles, and of infertile land in the vast Saharan and Nubian deserts of the north. The Sudan also has North Africa's only tropical areas. It forms, as do Morocco, Algeria, and Libya to a lesser extent, an important bridge between the northern and sub-Saharan parts of Africa. For this reason, despite its historical ties to the Middle Eastern and Muslim worlds, the Sudan has evolved a unique identity that embraces both northern Arab and southern sub-Saharan African cultures.

In sum, the only countries relatively free of deserts are Turkey, Lebanon, Tunisia, and Morocco, each of which has large mountain ranges limiting the land available for agricultural activity. Only in Tunisia and Morocco, two of the smallest countries, do fertile plains cover a large section of the total territory.

Climate

The Middle East and North Africa tend to be very dry areas. What causes this aridity? The most obvious answer lies in the scarcity of rainfall throughout the region. Only a few areas receive sufficient annual precipitation to sustain agriculture that does not require special conservation or irrigation. Some sections of Turkey, Iran, Lebanon, Israel, Tunisia, Sudan, and Morocco are not suitable for agriculture; their ample rainfall therefore does not translate into crop production. In particular, precipitation in Morocco, Lebanon, Turkey, and Yemen occurs not primarily in valleys but high in the mountains. In the Sudan, much of the rainfall takes place in the tropical south where dense forests have made large-scale cultivation difficult.

Some types of air-mass movement, such as cyclones, contribute to Middle

Eastern and North African rainfall. In autumn and spring, these movements also bring hot, dry winds that carry fierce sandstorms and dust. The winds are known as *khamsin* in Egypt, *shlur* in Syria and Lebanon, *sharqi* in Iraq, *simun* in Iran, and *ghibli* in Libya. So, soil and climate deprive the region of high-yielding agricultural lands like those in Europe and the Americas.

The aridity of the Middle East, however, cannot be explained solely by the scarcity of rainfall and the presence of distinctive winds. The dry conditions result from weather and solar factors as well. Southwest Asia and North Africa, like the rest of that band of land masses and oceans at 30° parallel north all around the world, experience a high rate of evapotranspiration—moisture lost by vegetation through evaporation and transpiration. High solar heat rates, higher than those found either to the north or to the south, are attributed to the axis of the earth and to the changing relationship between the positions of the earth and the sun at different times of the year. In some parts of the Middle East, for example Egypt, Kuwayt, the Red Sea, and most of Saudi Arabia, the rate of evapotranspiration is so high that extreme aridity persists at all times. Desalination plants convert water from the sea, and water-deficit tables aid governments in assessing the amount of water needed to insure adequate supplies throughout the year.

A consequence to the sun's heat in Southwest Asia and North Africa is the tendency toward high summer temperatures, especially at midday. The hottest areas—the Sahara region, eastern Arabia and the Red Sea coast, the Gulf states, central and southwestern Iran, and most of Iraq, as well as the Syrian deserts—constitute much of the Middle Eastern land mass. Rare exceptions to this excessive heat occur in the mountainous regions of Turkey, Iran, and along the Mediterranean Sea, the Black Sea, the Caspian Sea, and the Indian Ocean.

In winter, the temperatures vary much more with a rough division between the mountainous lands of Turkey and Iran, on the one hand, and the areas to the south (also east and north in Iran) on the other. Except for the cold mountains and inland areas, where temperatures can be quite severe, winter in the Middle East and North Africa tends to be mild, with the least variation occurring along the coasts.

Management of Water Resources

How have the peoples of the Middle East and North Africa coped for so many millenia under these inhospitable circumstances? First of all, the area contains two major river systems and a number of minor ones. These waters sustained some of the earliest and most highly developed civilizations known to humankind. Sophisticated systems of irrigation supplied communities with the surplus needed for the building of their civilizations. From earliest times, the Egyptians used elaborately designed drains and basins. These were planned, constructed, and regulated by centralized bureaucracies to assure the harvest from year to year. Though much less easily regulated, the Tigris and Euphrates Rivers also provided for the sustenance of large populations and for the creation of surplus rather than subsistence agriculture. Today, these river systems support even larger populations and provide for the electrification of rural areas through the construction of large dams such as the High Dam on the Nile in Egypt and the Tabqa Dam on the Euphrates in Syria.

Some of the smaller rivers, including the Litani (Lebanon), the Orontes and Barada (Syria), the Jordan (Lebanon, Jordan, and Israel), the Sebou (Morocco), the Sakarya and Kizil (*Red*) Rivers

(Turkey), and the Majarda (Tunisia), to name but a few, have attracted and sustained agriculturalists through the centuries. As small rivers in fragmented terrain, they have become known outside their region today primarily because of political struggles or religious history. For example, the Jordan, Yarmuk, and Litani rivers play prominent roles in the Palestinian and Lebanese questions. These rivers, too, have been dammed and diverted to expand agricultural production in the countries through which they flow. Today, the National Water Carrier canal in Israel transports much of the Jordan's water to Israel's main populated areas, providing about 90 percent of Israel's water needs.

Basin irrigation has aided farmers in utilizing water from small as well as large rivers. A farmer floods the field and then lets the ground soak up the water, a useful process for cultivating cereal crops. Another type of irrigation employs furrows to channel water in trenches along each row of produce or fruit. The ancient Egyptians developed three devices, still in use today for lifting and transporting water from the Nile to their fields—the Archimedean screw (a spiral device in a cylinder), the *shaduf* (a weighted pole with a bucket), and the water wheel. Animal manpower has driven water wheels like those in the Fayyum region. The famous huge water wheels of the type found along the Orontes River in Hama, Syria, have channeled for centuries that city's notably pure

water into elevated aqueducts. Power-driven pumps are replacing these traditional mechanisms, although in a few cases the new efficiency has exhausted local water resources.

From ancient times, resourceful Middle Easterners have practiced another method for transporting water. Complex networks of underground canals (called *qanats* in Iran and Syria, *ghattara* in Morocco, and *fuqqara* in Tunisia) make use of slopes to transport water from one area to another. Sometimes the canals extend for 30 miles (50 km.) or more, but usually their lengths range from less than one to three miles (1–5 km.). Workers dig these canals by drilling or digging holes in the ground at intervals to provide air for their work and routes for repairing the channels when necessary.

Finally, the Middle East has some springs and subterranean lakes. Where such springs are located in the desert, oases emerge. Egypt's major oases—Fayyum, Kharga, and Siwa—as well as the smaller ones, served as important centers for the caravan trade across Africa. The same is true for Ghadames and Kufra in Libya, of Tadmur (Palmyra) in Syria, of Makka and Madina in Arabia, and of Sijilmasa in Morocco, especially notable examples of the Middle East's numerous oases. Makka's original water source, the famous well of Zam Zam, has been supplemented by the drilling of many other wells that transport water via aqueducts.

Towns and Cities

The Middle East is among the world's most highly urbanized and urbanizing regions. Towns and cities have always overshadowed the rural areas in history books because history has generally been written, invented, used, and abused by and for the benefit of people in cities, not in villages. Since so many Middle Eastern cities date from ancient times, or were founded during the period of Islamic domination,

we need to consider among other important questions, the roots of cities (how and why they were founded), the reasons for their location, the factors contributing to their periods of ascendancy and decline, and the causes of their survival or demise.

Some of the most ancient Middle Eastern towns grew up by the major rivers in Egypt and Iraq. From archeological remains, and even from written records, we

Southwest Asia and North Africa, Selected Statistics

Country	1983 Estimated Population	Area (Sq. km.)	Percent Urban Population, 1977	Land Use[e]			
Afghanistan	17,500,000	647,497	11	22% A	12% C	and	10% P
Algeria	20,487,000	2,381,741	55	3% A	3% C		16% P
Bahrayn	433,000	622,000	78	5% A	5% C		
Chad[a]	4,944,000	1,384,000	18	17% A			35% P
Cyprus	699,000	9,251	53	47% A			10% P
Egypt	46,067,000	1,001,449	44		2.8% C		
Gaza[c]	468,000		N.A.	N.A.			
Iran	40,444,000	1,648,000	47	14% A	16% C		8% P
Iraq	14,650,000	434,924	66		18% C		10% P
Israel[d]	4,144,000	20,770	87		20% C		40% P
Jordan[d]	3,571,000	97,740	42		11% C	and	P
Kuwayt	1,624,000	17,818	56		0		
Lebanon	2,658,000	10,400	60		27% C	and	P
Libyan Arab Jamah.	3,353,000	1,759,540	60		6% C	and	P
Mauritania[a]	1,775,000	1,030,700	23		1% C		10% P
Morocco	22,248,000	446,550	42		32% C	and	P
Oman	854,000	212,457	5		0		
Qatar	291,000	11,000	69		0		
Saudi Arabia[f]	8,888,000	2,149,690	24		1% C	and	P
Sudan	19,751,000	2,505,813	20	37% A	3% C	and	15% P
Syria[d]	10,041,000	185,180	49	48% A			29% P
Tunisia	7,221,000	163,610	50	28% A			23% P
Turkey	48,410,000	780,576	45	35% A			25% P
United Arab Emir.	1,124,000	83,600	65		0		
Western Sahara[b]	224,000	266,000	N.A.				
A.R. (North) Yemen	6,205,000	195,000	11	1% A			
P.D.R. (South) Yemen	2,156,000	332,968	33		20% C	and	P

[a]Saharan countries noted in the text.
[b]Occupied by Morocco.
[c]Under Israeli occupation since June 1967.
[d]Population and area figures based on pre-June 1967 claimed boundaries.
[e]A = area under cultivation (arable); C = total cultivable area; P = grazing and pasture land.
[f]Estimates vary between 5 and 10 million.
N.A. = not available.

Sources: The Europa Yearbook 1982: A World Survey (London, 1982); *World Population Trends and Prospects by Country. 1950–2000: Summary Report of the 1978 Assessment* (UN); *National Intelligence Basic Factbook* (CIA), January, 1980; Ruth Leger Sivard, *World Military and Social Expenditures* 1980 (World Priorities, July 1980).

have learned that stratified, sophisticated societies existed in such urban environments as Damascus, Syria's capital today. On the Lebanese coast, Phoenician traders established Byblos, Tyre, and Sidon (known today as Jbayl, Sur, and Saida). Carthage was their center in North Africa. The Alexandrian conquests of the fourth century B.C.E. led to the foundation of many cities in Southwest Asia and North Africa, the largest of which today is Alexandria, Egypt, still a major port city. After the Romans took over the Mediterranean world, they too built many cities, often for reasons of defense. Amman, capital of Jordan today, owes its existence to the Romans, but other Roman towns such as Jarash in northern Jordan and Leptis Magna in Libya, were later deserted. Only their ruins remain to remind us of their former splendor.

During the Islamic period, new cities rose up, especially in the Maghrib, hitherto somewhat isolated, and in Mesopotamia. Qayrawan in Tunisia, established by the Umayyad conqueror Uqba ibn Nafi in 670 C.E. served as a garrison town. A similar settlement, Fustat, Egypt, built by Muslim conqueror Amr ibn al-As in 642, was superseded by another Muslim city built after 969 to the north—Cairo. Baghdad, Fez, Marrakish—all of these prominent cities were founded by Muslims before the twelfth century. Even towns that did not result from the location of garrisons were usually walled, both for defense and for the protection of their inhabitants from sand blown off the desert.

The medieval Muslim walled city usually had several main roads leading from its gates. Many alleys and small roads sheltered inhabitants from the hot sun. Usually the most important mosque and a central market (*suq* or *bazaar*) were located near each other, with supportive and related activities like schools and storehouses close by. The old markets and mosques remain vital centers of Muslim cities with different sections reserved for particular trades or businesses, for example, goldsmiths and carpetmakers. New markets and supermarkets have supplanted other market districts in many cities today.

Muslim cities were divided characteristically into residential quarters (*hara*), often occupied by distinct ethnic and religious groups. Especially in hot climates, urban village houses usually included a courtyard onto which opened both public and private sections. In accordance with customs regulating public and private life, houses consisted of both public areas for entertaining guests and private rooms reserved for the family. Houses were built close together on narrow alleys, with most windows opening onto the courtyard to protect against noise and dust. Cairo's Fatimid city is a living illustration of the effectiveness of this type of construction, with ventilation in most houses provided by decorative wooden screens called *mashrabiyya*. Residential areas, especially those of the affluent, included fountains and wind catchers, too, to counteract oppressive heat. In Turkey, by contrast, houses were built to conserve rather than to keep out heat.

Today, many of the cities built in the Islamic period that were beautiful, useful, and clean, with sewers and running water, have become the victims of modern superstructures and overcrowding. Population growth in Middle Eastern cities, however, is again a recent phenomenon. Prior to the nineteenth century, many formerly great cities had undergone severe depopulation. For example, the city of Alexandria is estimated to have had in the year 1800 less than one tenth of its population of one thousand years earlier. Natural disasters, invasions, taxation, disease, and changes in the trade routes seem to have accounted for much of the decline. Only recently, then, in the nineteenth and twentieth centuries, has a new type of Middle Eastern city emerged.

Modernization in Middle Eastern and North African cities arose mainly from pressures related to foreign penetration of one sort or another, mostly either commercial or colonial. Broad boulevards contrast with narrow streets. Modern office buildings in major cities stand beside medieval schools or houses. High-rise apartment buildings for all income levels have gone up as population pressures have increased the demand for urban housing. Where possible, though, the concept of reserving a special room for welcoming visitors has been retained by apartment dwellers. Mass transportation and private automobiles have also contributed to changes in the layouts of Middle Eastern cities, requiring wide streets or railroad tracks, bridges, and sometimes traffic signals.

In the most crowded cities—Istanbul, Cairo, and Tehran—the contrast between the prosperous and not-so-properous sections of town is great. The harmony which prevailed in earlier centuries has been replaced by dissonance, noise, congestion, urban pollution, and tensions arising from contrasts between rich and poor. Nevertheless, Middle Eastern cities tend to be relatively safe when compared with those of similar size in Europe, Latin America, the United States, or sub-Saharan Africa. Many neighborhoods retain elements of the cohesion found in villages. Often, members of individual families still live close to one another once they have settled in cities. These city dwellers usually return frequently to their birthplaces. The elements of alienation are thus mitigated somewhat by the retention in the cities of rural associations and relationships.

Even in cities that owe their existence

to nineteenth- and twentieth-century trade or industry, for example, Ismailia on the Suez Canal or Abadan in southern Iran, social elements of the old Islamic cities remain amidst the European-style streets and buildings. Mediterranean port cities like Beirut and Algiers grew faster in modern times because of increasing European trade. The city of Tel Aviv, though established as a Jewish town early in the twentieth century, does not differ appreciably from large cities in predominantly Muslim Middle Eastern and North African countries, perhaps because so many of its people emigrated from these areas.

Modern Middle Eastern cities function much like other large cities that require goods and services. Urban life is accordingly characterized by the same kind of hustle and bustle. Both men and women occupy all types of jobs. Women in Middle Eastern countries today occupy ministerial and legislative positions. They teach in universities, work in offices, and serve as doctors and lawyers. The possibilities for women working outside the home are enhanced by the opportunity to leave young children with relatives or servants. Poor women employed in factories or as servents must rely on friends and relatives or occasionally bring children to work with them. In today's Middle Eastern cities, one even finds women working as auto mechanics.

Agriculture and Village Life

As many Middle Easterners live in villages, we need to address the question: what is a village? A place is defined as a village on the basis of certain characteristics as well as by its size per se. In general what distinguishes a village from a city or town is the absence of attributes associated with urban life. Urban services such as paved roads, street lights, electricity and water in the home, public transportation, restaurants, telephones, theaters, department stores, hospitals, and higher educational facilities may also be absent. Unlike a town or city, a village can be self-sustaining, thereby reducing the need for substantial cash earnings among its inhabitants. This is because, unlike in the West where farmers may live isolated in country homes, Middle Eastern agriculturalists have for protection lived in villages adjoining their fields. In the village, many goods which would have to be bought in a town or city may be acquired by barter using local produce or manufacture.

What characterizes village life? Throughout the Middle East, an individual's identity has depended on family, locality, and religious affiliation. The concept of modern nation-states was superimposed on traditional Middle Eastern and North African societies, often at the behest of ruling elites, regardless of whether or not its form provided the most appropriate social framework for the particular area involved. The identity crisis is an urban phenomenon in the sense that people in villages generally have a clear idea of who they are and how their daily lives should be conducted.

Since by definition most Middle Eastern villagers are involved in labor-intensive agriculture, much of their daily and yearly existence is controlled by the growing cycle. Until fairly recently, people living in the most fertile areas often cultivated land belonging to someone else, often a large landholder, who was either absentee or present. In parts of North Africa and Southwest Asia heavily colonized during the last 150 years, foreigners owned huge tracts of land and hired villagers to farm in exchange for a small share of the crop. In Iraq, Iran, Egypt, and Syria, however, other Middle Easterners have been the main exploiters of peasant labor. Ownership, especially during the nineteenth century, derived from land registration—communally owned land became the property of one individual who had registered it in his own name. The owner then forced the tenants to work for him. Sharecropping, a type of labor-intensive system, is still very widespread throughout the Middle East, but machines are being substituted for people in many areas. In addition, land reforms from time to time, especially since World War II, have modified the former power of landlords and have allowed individual cultivators greater freedom despite problems associated with marketing in a world system and the task of feeding growing populations.

Grains, especially wheat, barley, sorghum, and rice, provide the bulk of the food crop in the Middle East and North Africa today, but countries have recently become net importers of grain due to population growth and the cultivation of export crops such as cotton, sugar, and tobacco. Egypt's long-staple (long-fibre) fine cotton has acquired fame throughout the world and is still the country's most important export crop. Turkey, Sudan, Syria, and Iraq also produce cotton for export.

Cultivators grow many tree crops, specifically fruits and nuts, as well as vegetables. Olive trees and grape vines, both of which require peaceful conditions and a steady water supply, have long been cultivated in the area. The Middle East leads the world in producing dates, most of them originating in Iraq, although some are exported from Algeria, Iran, and Arabia. The ancient citrus groves of Palestine, supplemented by those planted by the Israelis, provided a substantial portion of Israel's hard currency earnings in the 1950s prior to the growth of industry. Citrus fruits are also important export crops in the rest of the Levant and North Africa. Turkey supplies figs and hazelnuts, in addition to its cereals and cotton. Although the Egyptians grow a wide variety of fruits and vegetables, they lament because they lack the apples found in Lebanon, available only at high prices!

Despite our previous use of masculine terminology, we should emphasize that village women in the Middle East often own land and participate in the growing and harvesting of crops. Even if they have responsibilities outside the home, women do the main work within the home, too—they prepare food and clothing, the spin, weave, and care for the children. Some village women operate businesses.

Village houses vary in form from place to place as do the materials for building them. Yemen, for example, is noted for its multistoried stone structures. Stone is also a common building material in mountainous areas such as Lebanon. Two-story houses are found in villages in Egypt, Iraq, Arabia, and Turkey. Middle Eastern villagers utilize different styles and materials for roofs. Barrel-vaulted or conical roofs are seen especially in Syria, Turkey, Arabia, Iraq, and Yemen. A typical lowland house is rectangular and made of mud brick with a flat roof. Usually the house has a courtyard and may form part of a compound. Relatives often share their compounds with each other and with their animals. Since houses are usually small for the number of people living in them, many daily chores are performed outdoors. Although villagers often possess furniture, many families own a minimum of a few mats or carpets. Men may remain away from home for the entire day, working in the shop or field or visiting with friends. Women, too, spend a lot of time together, but more often than not while they are doing their chores.

One of the most fundamental characteristics of village life is that people know and are often related to each other. Lives tend to be closely integrated. Issues affecting individual families can easily become matters of importance to the entire community. Rites of passage such as circumcisions, in addition to holidays, weddings and funerals, are usually shared by entire villages. Due to interdependence, villagers often settle their disputes through arbitration or negotiation. When two or more large groups within a village are at odds, the disruption of the local social, political, and economic environment can be very great. The village as a whole may also become involved with other villages over questions relating to marriage, property, herds, or water.

People from villages in close proximity to each other still intermarry. Formerly, marriages in the area were arranged by families, often when their children were quite young. Young girls might have to marry prosperous older men who already had one or more wives. With the decline of polygyny today, young women in the villages have far more opportunities than in the past to gain some measure of control over their own lives. Polygyny, however,

gave women a chance to divide household responsibilities and to enjoy daily companionship. The extended family was part of the economic system which provided security and a livelihood for its members. Today's village girl, like her city counterpart, is likely to choose her own spouse with parental approval. The participation of village women in the Algerian struggle for independence and in Palestine liberation movements of recent years illustrates the potential for women to be recognized not just as wives, mothers, and daughters, but as important contributors to the historical development of the area.

Pastoralism

Although farming provides the main agricultural activity in the Middle East and North Africa today, much of the land is used by pastoralists: settled, transhumant, or nomadic. The most important animals are sheep, goats, and camels. While the former two predominate due to their minimal food demands, camels still provide desert nomads with most of the requirements for daily living. Since camels can travel for several days without water, they serve as ideal transportation for long-distance travelers. Today, however, they are used mainly as a source of milk, hides, and meat. Sheep and goats, however, must remain near water. Their mobility and versatility make them well-suited for the climates and terrrains. Unfortunately, goats also cause devastation in grazing areas, leading to widespread soil erosion and deforestation.

Although many pastoralists live in villages, the region has long been inhabited by various people who move around, though their numbers are decreasing. The transhumant pastoralists include those who have a home base which they leave in the dry season in order to graze their animals at desert oases or at well-watered

river valleys. Other transhumants migrate long distances from highlands to lowlands and back again. Some patterns, for example, those of Iran's Bakhtiari, have for centuries involved fixed routes, locations, and times. Because the transhumants have regular patterns, they can usually be located and made subject to control by a central authority, especially in this era of improved communications and transportation.

A few genuine nomads, though, still move about from place to place with no single home base. Libya and southern Arabia contain many such nomads. Ever since the advent of the modern nation-state in the Middle East and North Africa, the numbers of people following the nomadic lifestyle have been declining, for both internal and external reasons, economic pressures, and governmental policies.

In some cases, for example Morocco, it has been argued that the periphery, or the so-called less civilized areas inhabited by pastoralists, has controlled historical developments in the urban centers far more then these centers have influenced life in the frequently remote hinterlands.

Entire areas have been altered by nomadic invasions; the incursion of the Banu Hilal in the Maghrib in the eleventh century, for example, was a development said to have completed the Arabization of Tunisia. Other historians argue that the initial Islamic conquests were nomadic invasions, although the invasions were organized and led by Muslims from urban Arabia. The interrelationships among urban, rural settled, rural pastoralist, and rural nomadic groups have influenced the course of Southwest Asian and North African history. Many questions remain regarding the dynamics of such contacts and their consequences.

CHAPTER TWO

Peoples and Cultures of Southwest Asia and North Africa

Looking at the current demographic situation in the Middle East and North Africa with the perspective of long centuries of human activity there, we observe that the land area has embraced many peoples and cultures. Oft-invaded, the peoples of the Middle East and North Africa have usually absorbed their conquerers as much as the various invaders have influenced them. Today, the region seems to be united culturally but with broad variations of ethnicity, language, and local identity. How did this diversity come about?

The Middle Easterners and North Africans of Antiquity

Egyptians

The ancient Middle East and North Africa are well known to us due to the brilliant civilizations which flourished there in antiquity. Over five thousand years ago in the Nile Valley, kings united Egypt and ruled an area from the Mediterranean to the first Nile cataract at Elephantine (an island opposite Aswan). Ancient Egyptians lived in a peaceful, tolerant society. They assumed that Egypt was the gods' chosen

17

land, and they viewed their own king as a god. Egyptians found deities in many manifestations of nature and prayed to both individual and widely recognized gods for prosperity and security. When their rulers died, the ancient Egyptians buried them in a way designed to assure their safe passage in the underworld. We know little about the origin of the ancient Egyptians beyond the fact that historians call them *Hamites,* due to the kinship of their language to North African Berber and to the Kushitic language of Ethiopia, Kenya, and Sudan. This ancient Egyptian language, known to us through hieroglyphs found on temples and tombs throughout Egypt, evolved into Coptic and is still used in the religious rites of the Coptic Orthodox Church in Egypt. Until Semitic Asiatic peoples invaded Egypt circa 1750 B.C.E. the Egyptians felt fairly secure. After that, they began to worry about protecting themselves against invasion, especially via Sinai and the Palestine corridor. From that time on rulers of Egypt have followed as a major facet of their foreign policy the informal or formal control of as much of greater Syria as possible, especially of the Palestine corridor (the site of Israel today).

It was under Thutmose III who ruled from about 1490–1436 B.C.E. that the first Egyptian empire embracing Syria was created. Although the Hittites of Anatolia succeeded in temporarily ending that hegemony, Ramses II (1290–1224 B.C.E.) regained control over Palestine. During these imperial centuries, Egyptians and Asiatics developed close cultural and commercial ties with a resultant population transfer, especially that of Asiatics into Egypt.

The concept of *mu'at* or ultimate truth, made it possible for Egyptians to preserve the integrity and continuity of their civilization and rule despite invasions by Semites, Ethiopians, Persians, Greeks, and Romans. The ancestors of the Copts (a word related to the Greek name for Egypt), developed and retained, then, a sense of national identity which survived intact despite subsequent invasions and supranational interests in the Arabic-speaking and Muslim worlds.

Tradition has it that St. Mark (Arabic: *Murqus*) introduced Christianity into Egypt. Monophysite rather than Roman Christianity ultimately took hold and withstood the later pressures of Greek Orthodox Byzantium. It survives today as the Coptic Orthodox Church. When the Arab invasion of Egypt began in 639, its population was predominantly Coptic. Only after several hundred years of Arab-/Muslim rule did the Copts become a minority, mostly as a result of conversion to Islam. Today, Egypt's Coptic population constitutes about 7 percent of the total. Copts still retain pride in their direct descent from the ancient Egyptians.

Mesopotamians

Inhabitants of that other cradle of civilization, the Tigris-Euphrates Valley (Mesopotamia or Iraq) have a more varied history of cultures and civilizations. As in Egypt, hunters and farmers inhabited this valley thousands of years before the rise of cities. The first known dynasty, like that in Egypt, arose circa 3000 B.C.E. in southern Iraq and established a general model that assimilated subsequent peoples and states. The peoples living in this land, Sumer, spoke a language neither Semitic nor Indo-European. Their city-states often fought among themselves, thereby allowing political hegemony to pass to the Semites of Akkad, a city to the north. Although Akkad itself passed from history and the Sumerians experienced a brief revival, the movement of other Semites into Mesopotamia produced a united kingdom with Babylon as its capital and a Babylonian form of Akkadian as its administrative and commercial language. Mesopotamians wrote their language in *cuneiform,* a wedge-shaped writing system in which shapes represented combinations of sounds.

The religious beliefs of the ancient Mesopotamians were based on the idea that they and their cities were earthly counterparts of divine models. Each city belonged to a god who owned it and whose statue resided in a central temple. Certain lands supported the temple cults, but most lands were cultivated by individuals for their own use. After the rise of kings in Mesopotamia, the institution of kingship was said to be based on cosmic models. Originally, the king was regarded as only a representative of the city-god, but under the Akkadians and Babylonians, he acquired a certain divinity, though his former status was ultimately restored.

Unlike the Egyptians, who felt secure in their religion and society, the Mesopotamians were not at all confident about their gods. Since the gods acted so arbitrarily, the Mesopotamians devised law codes such as the Twelve Tables of Hammurabi (1700 B.C.E.) to regulate human behavior. They also engaged in divination and prayer to please and placate the gods. While the Egyptians believed that life and death were happy and harmonious states, the Mesopotamians expected both to be a continuum of gloom and doom. This world view was passed on to the many invaders of Mesopotamia through mythical literature and traditions preserved by linguistic and cultural continuity. Though the Sumerians were eclipsed by the Akkadians, Kassites, Hurrians, Assyrians, Chaldeans, and others, these successors absorbed attitudes about religion, society, and government that appeared not only in Mesopotamia but elsewhere in the Middle East, especially in the cultures and peoples of the eastern Mediterranean. Ongoing and recent excavations in eastern Arabia are shedding new light on the nature and extent of the ancient Mesopotamian states.

Semitic Peoples

Today, most Middle Eastern peoples speak languages related to those of the ancient Akkadians and the later Assyro-Babylonians. We call these languages and the people who use them Semitic or Semites. The modern-day heirs of the label

"Assyrian" speak Syriac, a form of Aramaic, and follow Nestorian Christianity. Although decimated in numbers, small pockets remain in Iraq, Syria, and Iran. Asiatic Semites formed some of the earliest states in the Middle East, migrated to the eastern Mediterranean, and even invaded Egypt, all in ancient times.

Canaanites and Phoenicians

The societies of the Canaanites and Phoenicians brought Semitic languages and traditions to the eastern Mediterranean and embraced a highly developed religious syncretism as a result of Egyptian influences. It was by virtue of the meeting of Phoenicians, Canaanites, and Semites from Egypt that alphabets replaced cuneiform and hieroglyphics. This facilitated the spread of literacy among the ancient Semitic peoples. All Middle Easterners use alphabets—Arabic, Armenian, Coptic, Hebrew, and Greek writing systems—whose origins may be traced to an eastern Mediterranean source. European alphabets also originated with the Phoenicians. Semitic alphabets exclude vowels, thus allowing for regional development of pronunciation. Today, the major Semitic languages spoken in the Middle East and North Africa are Arabic and Hebrew.

Hebrews

Although their ancestors migrated from Mesopotamia to the western Mediterranean, and then to Egypt, the ancient Hebrews began their national history as contemporaries of the Philistines (non-Semites from whom Palestine takes its name), Canaanites, and Phoenicians. Although it was the Phoenicians who established cities throughout the Mediterranean in Asia, Europe, and Africa, it was the ancient Hebrews who evolved a religion that acquired international influence and significance as the first of the monotheistic Middle Eastern religions, Judaism: a religion whose god acted not only in nature but also in history. The Hebrew scriptures (the Torah, Psalms, and prophetic books) which Christians call the Old Testament, are at the same time historical, legal, and religious documents. They supplied the major bond for Jews over the centuries and preserved the Jewish tie to Palestine.

The only large state ever established by the ancient Hebrews lasted from about 1000–900 B.C.E. under the kings David and Solomon. It encompassed at its height territories extending almost from the Nile to the Euphrates. The Hebrews consolidated themselves into the Jewish people as they developed the synagogue as a learning and worship center following the Babylonian exile in the sixth century B.C.E. Thereafter, their sole independent period occurred only in the wake of the Macabeen (Hasmonean) revolt against the Seleucids (successors of Alexander) in 167 B.C.E. With the Roman conquest of Palestine in 63 B.C.E., these vestiges of Jewish national independence were wiped out.

The Jewish religion did not depend on a local god, and had its preserved scriptures. Even in the people's exile elsewhere in the Middle East, North Africa, and Europe, Jews maintained their religious observances and institutions of learning. There, they compiled law books and commentaries. Because their holiest days were associated with events recorded in their scriptures—events which had taken place in Palestine and elsewhere in the Middle East—the Jews were constantly reminded of their origins. The persecution of Jews throughout the ages by Christians, especially in Europe where Jews were thought responsible for the crucifixion of Jesus, kept alive the idea of an eventual return to the "promised land." Although Hebrew ceased to be used except as a language of religious learning, and although Jews in the Middle East and North Africa became Arabized after the Islamic conquests, groups of Jews in Europe nearly nineteen hundred years after the Roman exile succeeded in reviving the idea of a homeland in Palestine.

Arabs

Arabs were also among the ancient Semitic peoples inhabiting the Arabian peninsula and speaking various dialects of Arabic. From archeological sites in Arabia and records of other peoples, we know that Arabs were active in sea trade during the second millenium B.C.E. and that they began using camels for overland trade before 1000 B.C.E. Kinda was an important pre-Islamic kingdom in fifth and sixth century Arabia. The Arab Nabateans established a kingdom in Jordan after 300 B.C.E., founding the carved cliff city of Petra. Their representatives traded extensively in the eastern Mediterranean. Later Arabs established a kingdom in the Syrian oasis of Palmyra (Tadmur today), leaving magnificent tower and subterranean tombs as well as majestic temples. Both Palmyra and Petra stand today. Excavations now being conducted in Arabia should shed more light on other ancient Arabs and their communities, especially those in southern Arabia. Long before Muslim Arabs poured out of Arabia into the northern, eastern, southern, and western lands, other Arabs had left Arabia and had interacted with a wider world. Like other Middle Easterners, their existence as a people predated their formation of large states and empires.

Just before the Islamic conquests of the seventh century, two Arab states dominated the lands north of Arabia. The Ghassanids controlled most of present-day Jordan and the eastern areas of Syria. Although they practiced Monophysite Christianity, the Ghassanids allied themselves with the Greek Orthodox Byzantines, providing a buffer between the latter and their eastern rivals, the Sassanids of Iran (224–651). The other Arab kingdom, that of the Lakhmids based at al-Hira in southern Iraq, ruled for several hundred years as a Sassanid client. While the subjects of the Lakhmids tended to practice Syrian Nestorian Christianity, only the last Lakhmid ruler ever adopted the religion. At the time of the Arab conquest, the Persians had replaced these Arab rulers with Persian governors.

Indo-Europeans

Armenians

In addition to the ancient Sumerians, Semites, and Egyptians, a variety of Indo-Europeans were also known in the Middle East of antiquity. In Anatolia and Syria, Indo-European Hittites created an empire, often fighting Egypt for control of Syria. The Hittites disappeared with the invasions of the Philistines, sea peoples from Europe. Another group of Indo-Europeans, the ancient Armenians, entered eastern Anatolia and Transcaucasia around 1100 B.C.E. They practiced paganism until about 301 C.E., at which time they became the first people to adopt Christianity as their group religion. Located on a major invasion route, the Armenians preserved their national identity over the centuries by tenaciously maintaining their language, a unique branch of the Indo-European family, and their religion, Monophysite Christianity, realized in the Armenian Orthodox (Gregorian) Church. Eventually the Armenians spread to other parts of Anatolia and the Middle East. Linguists consider Armenian to be among the oldest of the Indo-European languages.

Iranians

Although they appeared after the Hittites and the Armenians, the Iranians (called Persians by the Greeks) and Medes—both Indo-Europeans—established even greater empires in the Middle East. In the seventh century B.C.E., the Medes took over a territory embracing Anatolia and the Iranian plateau. The Iranians under Cyrus the Great defeated them in the mid-sixth century. Cyrus and his successors also conquered Egypt and Asia Minor. Within a few years, the Iranians ruled a vast empire from the Mediterranean to India. Willing to borrow culturally from conquered peoples, the Persians constructed a state that employed an Egyptian calendar, Aramaic as an administrative language in the western areas, and art and architecture from Babylon, Assyria, and Egypt.

The Persians adopted as their official religion Zoroastrianism, a form of dualistic monotheism which later influenced post-exilic Judaism. A highly intellectual religion, Zoroastrianism proclaimed the supremacy of one god, Ahura Mazda, who was responsible for all good and true forces. Juxtaposed against truth and goodness was evil. Individuals were considered free and responsible for their own fates. Zoroastrianism remained the primary religion of Iran for over a thousand years. Its imagery of light and dark, of good and evil, of truth and falsehood, of heaven and hell, and of reward and punishment, influenced later mystery cults that competed with Christianity during its first few centuries. However, two other religious ideologies arose during the Sassanid dynasty. Like Zorastrianism, Manichaeism used dualistic imagery to reject material aspects of life, emphasizing instead the spirit. Both the Manichaens and their offshoot, the followers of Mazdak in the fifth and sixth centuries, reacted against class and economic disparities increasingly characteristic of Sassanid rule. Historians have viewed the egalitarian and communistic focus of Mazdaism as well as the spiritual anti-worldly thrust of Manichaeism as examples of pre-Islamic social protest. Shi'ism, the form of Islam dominant in Iran today, is said to have incorporated into its world view certain aspects of Zorastrianism, Manichaeism, and Mazdaism. Despite Islam's protection of these groups as monotheists, few adherents remain in Iran today. All of the successor states to Cyrus' Achaemenids—Alexander and the Seleucids, the Parthians, the Sassanids—tried to restore the ancient glory of Iran. The now-defunct Pahlavi dynasty of Iran, which looked back to the Achaemenid state for its roots, illustrates the influence of ancient Iranian history even today.

Other Indo-Europeans in the Iranian Region

Various peoples who were related to the ancient Iranians never formed significant political entities, but established distinct identities which survive today. The first of these are the Kurds. In antiquity they were described by Xenophon, historian of the fifth century B.C.E., as living in the Zagros Mountains, and as indigenous peoples who were absorbed by Indo-Europeans and who adopted an Indo-European language. Another Indo-European-speaking people now in southeastern Iran and Pakistan, the Baluchis, may be equally ancient. The Bakhtiaris of Iran, who trace their origins to the later Sassanid period, also speak an Indo-European language but claim Mongol ancestors. From time to time, strong central governments in Persia brought these distinct peoples within their scope, providing a basis for Iran's current boundaries.

Greeks

Often at conflict with the Persians in ancient times were the Greeks. An Indo-European people, the Greeks began to move into the Aegean area sometime before 1600 B.C.E. At the time, the area was dominated by Minoan civilization on the island of Crete. By about 1100 B.C.E. Greeks had taken control of the Aegean area, including Crete, the coast of Asia Minor, coastal areas of Thrace and Macedonia, and the European peninsula which we now call Greece. By about 800 B.C.E., the Greeks organized their city-states and consolidated their hold over captured areas. During the eighth and seventh centuries B.C.E., the Greeks, well-established as a seafaring people in the Aegean, founded settlements at Massilia (Marseilles) and Byzantium (Constantinople and Istanbul) in the Mediterranean and Black Sea regions. Greek civilization was at its zenith from about 600–400 B.C.E.

During the fourth-century decline, Alexander the Great of Macedonia (who ruled from 336–323) conquered most of Southwest Asia from Greece to India, and Northeastern Africa from Cyrenaica to Egypt. In the process, Alexander spread Hellenistic or Greek-like culture throughout the area. Greeks emigrated to the successor states that arose after Alexander's death. They established a significant presence in communities which he had founded, among these were Alexandria in Egypt, capital of the Ptolemies, and Antioch in Asia Minor, the center of the Seleucid successor state.

After Rome had absorbed the Greek cities of southern Italy; the Romans fought three wars with the Phoenicians (264–146 B.C.E.) which destroyed the Carthaginian state. Rome also absorbed the Mediterranean territories that were under the Ptolemies and the Seleucids. In so doing, they absorbed much of Greek civilization. Greek influences again predominated when the Roman state moved its capital east to Byzantium under Emperor Constantine, who introduced tolerance of Christianity.

The Byzantine empire began in 330 when Constantine established an administrative center in Byzantium. Situated at the entrance of the Bosporus to the Sea of Marmora, the new Constantinople became the capital of what with the gradually emerging East-West schism became known as the Eastern Roman or Byzantine empire. Under the emperor Justinian (who brought North Africa under Byzantine in place of Western Roman rule), Roman law was codified in Latin, but new laws appeared in Greek. Roman influences were gradually moderated by local custom. Greek replaced Latin as the imperial language. Constantinople became the seat of the Greek Orthodox Church which spread into Russia and the Balkans in the ninth and tenth centuries. The Byzantine empire became Christianity's eastern flank, resisting attacks from the east and south until the Ottomans finally captured Constantinople in 1453.

During later centuries under Muslim rule, Greeks played an important commercial role and retained their identity through their language and the Greek Orthodox religion. Between the final collapse of the Byzantine empire in 1453 and the emergence of an independence movement in the nineteenth century, no independent Greek state existed on the mainland. Today's Greeks inhabit some of their ancient Mediterranean communities as well as the territory of Greece.

Berbers

The ancient inhabitants of north-western Africa were a nation called the Berbers. Like the Egyptians, the Berbers used to be regarded as among the Hamitic peoples, but recent research suggests that they originated from diverse groups in North Africa. The various names by which Berbers have been known, including *Berber,* were applied to them by conquerors. They called themselves either *imazighen* (Berber-language plural of *amazigh,* meaning free man) or tribal confederacy names such as Zanata, Masmuda, and Sanhaja. Since a majority of the Berbers remained in the hinterland, they survived most ancient incursions relatively intact.

The first colonizers, the Phoenicians, established bases for trade on the North African coast. Carthage, near present-day Tunis, was their most important Maghribian city, but they also settled as far away as Cadiz in Spain. Somewhat later than the Phoenicians, Greeks and Jews also emigrated to North Africa. As a result of Greek colonization, Cyrenaica (eastern Libya today) became the object of both Greek and Phoenician designs. Conflicts arose among the colonizers as well as between them and the native populations. Eventually Carthage became Hellenized and stopped fighting with the Greeks. Its trans-Saharan caravans traded via bases in present-day Tunisia. Expeditions were also undertaken by sea north to Britain and south to Guinea.

Towards the waning years of Carthage's existence, three Berber kingdoms emerged in the western Maghrib. These nations spoke Punic and worshipped Phoenician gods. The Berber chief Masinissa aimed to establish a united Maghribian Berber kingdom. When he allied with Rome to eliminate the Carthaginians, however, he brought in a new foreign power. As Masinissa died in the war against the Carthaginians, the Romans appointed his sons as local governors. The Romans, to preserve their rule, favored localized rather than unitary government in North Africa. Masinissa's goal of Berber unity was left unfulfilled.

Because the Romans did not require the Berbers to change their religion and did not generally discriminate against them, the Berbers cooperated with Roman rule. Historians still debate the extent to which North Africa became Romanized or Christianized. It is known that the spread of Christianity into North Africa, which began in the first century, resulted in persecution by Rome. Conflicts arose between Christians who favored martyrdom and those who preferred apostasy to death. As persecution gave way to official toleration early in the fourth century under the Roman Emperor Constantine, North African Christians became involved in the various controversies of the Christian Church.

North Africans resisted the idea of control by the hierarchical church that, under Roman influence, divided Christians into clergy and laity. The central question of the Donatist heresy, propounded in the fourth century by Donatus, Bishop of Carthage, maintained that a sinful priest could not administer a valid sacrament. Donatism attracted many followers because of insecurity resulting from the sack of Rome in 410, but the orthodox hierarchy led by St. Augustine, Bishop of Hippo (354–430) opposed it because it emphasized the person of the priest rather than the supremacy of God. Despite Augustine's suppression, Donatism survived in parts of North Africa until the Arab conquest. This apparent Berber tendency to take up heterodox religious positions continued during much of the Islamic period as well. Some historians use this evidence to support a disputed theory that religious dissidence was used for many centuries by the Berbers to assert national identity and to resist foreign rule.

When the Vandals of Europe conquered the Maghribian coast in 430, they tried to replace Catholicism with the Arian heresy which claimed that Jesus was human only. Outside attempts at religious control, however, the Vandals allowed Berber confederacies to arise in the western Maghrib and brought commercial and agricultural prosperity to the eastern Maghrib. The Vandals were succeeded by the Byzantines under Justinian (527–565).

The Byzantines met with Berber opposition when they tried to exert control over the Berber hinterlands. Opposition was eliminated when the Byzantines changed their policies and paid subsidies to Berber chiefs. However, they continued to alienate local populations by involving them in religious controversies, especially those pertaining to Monophysite Christianity which by that time had become heretical from the viewpoint of the Orthodox Church.

During these periods of conquests the Berbers in the interior of North Africa were only periodically in close contact with invaders and colonizers. Most cultural penetration occurred in the coastal areas where the conquerors and traders set up their governments and commercial activities. Although fortresses were often constructed in remote areas, the garrisons did not represent attempts at permanent settlement. The Arab conquest of North Africa initially was just another in a long series of foreign invasions that substituted one set of foreigners along the coast with a new set. The Berber identity was not automatically and rapidly subsumed by that of the Arabs. The question remains an issue in present-day Morocco and among the Kabyles of Algeria.

Peoples and Cultures of the Middle East Since the Coming of Islam: Linguistic Transformation

It is sometimes assumed that the advent of Islam in Southwest Asia and North Africa brought about an immediate demographic transformation of these areas. Nothing could be farther from the truth. Since the conquerors did not initially encourage conversion, Islamization proceeded rather slowly by design. Even after Muslim rulers began to allow non-Arabians to adopt Islam, some areas retained their previous religious beliefs for centuries. Some nations that adopted Islam, for example, Persia and the western Maghrib, retained their local languages. The three largest linguistic groups in the region today are the Arabs, the Turks and the Persians.

Spread of Arabic

The influence of Arabic may be attributed to two facts: (1) the Qu'ran, the Holy Book of the Muslims, was revealed in Arabic; and (2) it was, therefore, essential to memorize the Qu'ran in Arabic since translation at that time was not permitted. Although Arabic spread as the language of the Muslims, it took hold in areas that did not already have a strong national tradition, such as Syria, or which, like Egypt, were very close to Arabia. Southwest Asian and North African peoples gradually became Arabized.

When we use the term *Arab*, then, we do not refer to a distinct racial or ethnic group. The Arabs of greater Syria (Syria, Lebanon, Palestine/Israel, Jordan), for example, have descended not only from Arabians but from Greeks, Jews, Armenians, Circassians, Turks, and miscellaneous Europeans, many of whom arrived during the Crusades. Egyptian Arabs represent the same combination, with the additions of native Copts and Nubians. Many of the Arabs of North Africa trace their ancestry to Spanish Andalusia where Visigoths, Slavs, Arabs, Jews, and Berbers created a brilliant civilization. Most North African Arabs, however, for the reasons we mentioned earlier, are the descendants of Berbers or black Africans who at some point began speaking Arabic instead of their local language.

Who, then, is an Arab? Roughly speaking, an Arab is someone who identifies as one. The most common point of identification is that of language. The word *Arab* originally meant a desert nomad, but in the early modern world it was used pejoratively by urban Arabs to mean uncivilized desert wanderer. The current usage of the word *Arab* as a positive political concept, as in *Arab nationalism,* is a phenomenon that began only in the late nineteenth century. Although Arabs read and write literary Arabic, they speak their own local dialects. Had it not been for the influence of Quranic education in preserving a literary language, Arabic might have gone the way of Latin by dividing itself into variations which became languages in their own right. In today's dialects, the most common expressions and vocabularies are likely to differ, so that a compliment in one country might be an insult in another. Pronunciation of Moroccan and Syrian dialects usually differs so much that the two are almost mutually unintelligible. Today, Arabic is the primary language spoken by the peoples in most of the areas covered in this work except Iran, Israel, and Turkey. Berber is spoken most notably in Morocco and Algeria. Arabic speakers exist in southwest Iran. In the Gulf states, Arabic and Persian exist side by side.

Although most Arabs are Muslims, Christian Arabs are found throughout the Middle East, especially in Lebanon where until the mid-twentieth century they outnumbered the Muslims. The significant Coptic minority of Egypt is of course Arabic-speaking. The Maronite Church of many Lebanese Arabs which has its own cardinal is affiliated with the Roman Catholic Church. Arab Christians outside Egypt, however, most often belong to the Greek Orthodox, Greek Catholic, Roman Catholic or Anglican churches. Smaller numbers adhere to the many evangelical Protestant churches, notably the Coptic Evangelical Church of Egypt and the Evangelical Synod of Syria and Lebanon, products of early Congregational and Presbyterian missionary activities. Besides the several million Arab Christians, there are scattered communities of Arab Jews, that is, Arab-speaking natives who practice Judaism and who are citizens of predominantly Arabic-speaking countries. They constitute a small remnant of the once substantial and influential Jewish communities of the Middle East. Due to this religious mosaic, very few Arab countries maintain Islam as a state religion or try to implement Islamic law in all its dimensions. Moreover, Islam institutionalized pluralism from the outset, unlike Judaism and Christianity.

With this variety of race, religion, nationality, and even language, the so-called Arab world is really a rich and vital mosaic composed mainly of people who have chosen to identify themselves as Arabs. To present the Arab world as a monolithic entity is to deny to the citizens of the individual countries those aspects of their heritages which make them Syrians rather than Iraqis or Moroccans rather than Algerians. Although the widespread use of radio and television, of rapid transportation, and of the cinema has brought Arabic-speakers into much closer contact and mutual understanding than ever before, the likelihood that the entire Arabic-speaking world will ever choose to form a single nation-state is perhaps as remote as that of the French or Spanish-speaking peoples throughout the world doing so.

It is not for outsiders either to disparage or commend the idea of Arab national unification. We aim to understand the dynamics of inter-Arab relations and of Southwest Asian and North African societies, not to impose preconceived ideas about their destinies. As Frithjof Bergmann said in *On Being Free:* "That man forms a self, that he creates an image of his own identity and acts this out—nothing less than this is the foundation of his freedom."[1] For the people of the Middle East and North Africa to be free, then, they must evolve their own systems.

Turks

The Turks and Turkic-speaking peoples (such as the Azeris) constitute, next to the Arabic speakers, the largest ethnolinguistic group in the area today. They are the only group which did not exist in the Middle East of antiquity. Linguistically, they belong to the Ural-Altaic peoples among whom are also found the Hungarians, Finns, and Mongols. The earliest Turks known to Europe were the Huns who invaded in the fifth century. Chinese records, however, mention them some eight hundred years earlier. Turkish penetration into the Middle East came via Transoxania, between the Amu Darya (Oxus) and Syr Darya (Jaxartes) rivers (which are part of Soviet Central Asia today).

In the sixth century, a large Turkish confederation existed in this area; the people called themselves the *Oguz*. Most of them practiced nomadism, but they also founded settled communities along trade or migration routes. Their leaders were called *khans*. Before they came into contact with Muslims, they held onto their native shamanistic beliefs or had adopted one of the religions which they encountered—among them Nestorian Christianity, Buddhism, Zorastrianism, Judaism, Hinduism, and Manichaeism. Their native religion focused on the present life but also held some belief in the hereafter. As the Oguz spread across Asia to eastern Europe, south to China, and southwest to the Middle East, they began to supplant the indigenous populations.

When they reached the borders of present-day Iran, the Oguz tended to assimilate so long as the Muslim Abbasid empire remained strong. In Turkish tradition, males usually left home once they had

learned to fight, to ride horses or to hunt. As the Muslims became familiar with Turkish military skills, they purchased or captured many of the Oguz for service in Muslim armies. The prestige and prosperity that often resulted from the "enslavement" of these Turkish soldiers caused many poor parents to give up their children willingly for military training or service under the Muslims. By the ninth century, long before the Turks were pushed out of Mongolia, they comprised most of the military and many of the political leaders of the Abbasid state. Before the first independent Turkish Muslim state came into being, an Abbasid govenor of Turkish origin, Ahmad ibn Tulun, established an autonomous Egypt. After the demise of the Tulunids, another Turk, Muhammad ibn Tughj, built a dynasty there as well (935–969).

The first states that were ruled independently by Turkish Muslims were those of the Ghaznavids (977–1186) in Afghanistan and Khurasan, and the Karakhanids (tenth and eleventh centuries) in Transoxania. The first Middle Eastern Turkish empire came about through the descendants of one Saljuk, an Oguz from the Aral Sea region who moved to Central Asia and converted to Islam later in life. His grandsons served the Karakhanids and then became vassals of the Ghaznavids.

In the mid-eleventh century, a Saljuk named Tughrul-Beg began his conquest of the Muslim and Byzantine-ruled territories to the west: Iran, Mesopotamia, Armenia, Azerbayjan, and Anatolia. Baghdad submitted in 1055. Defeat of Byzantine forces at Mantzikert, Armenia (1071) opened Christian Anatolia to the Saljuk armies. A decentralized Saljuk empire with centers in Khurasan, Iraq, and Anatolia resulted from his successes. Although the Anatolian state, based in Konya, lasted until 1304, the Saljuks ended up contesting for control of the central regions with another Turkish group, the Danishmendids, who were based in northern Anatolia.

During the first two centuries after the Saljuk penetration into Anatolia, a

---

[1] Frithjof, Bergmann, *On Being Free.* (Notre Dame: University of Notre Dame Press, 1977), p. 102.

gradual migration of Turks into the area occurred. Some of them intermarried with Armenians, Georgians, or Greeks, but they nevertheless remained Muslims. Both the Saljuks and the Danishmendids began as nomads but settled in towns. The Armenian cities of Erzurum and Erzinjan resisted both Turkish and Kurdish influences. Prior to the Mongol invasions, Anatolia still remained predominantly non-Turkish and non-Muslim.

With the Mongols in the mid-thirteenth century came new Turkic groups as well as Persians, Mongol settlers, and more Kurds. Although the actual distinctions among the various Turks are not clear, sufficient numbers of them were present along the Anatolian frontier and within Anatolia itself to provide the nucleus of both the Ottoman state in Anatolia (circa 1300–1923) and the Safavid state of Persia (1501–1722). Until the rise of separatist nationalism among the original inhabitants—Armenians, Greeks, and Kurds—in the last 250 years, all of these peoples continued to coexist with Turks, though not always in complete harmony, in Asia Minor.

With the massacre and deportation of the bulk of the Armenian population and the population exchange of Greeks and Turks after the first World War, Anatolia under the Turkish Republic became a land of Turks and Kurds. Along with the Azeris of northern Iran, these Turks and a small group in Syria comprise the Turkic-speaking population of the Middle East today. We mentioned the Kurds as an ancient Middle Eastern people. They are still spread throughout southeastern Turkey and northern Iran, Iraq, and to a lesser extent Syria, and are still aspiring to establish a Kurdish national state.

Ongoing Ethno-Linguistic Diversity

In considering the third large linguistic group in the Middle East, the Persians, it is important to recognize that present-day Iran is actually a political entity in which people who regard themselves as ethnic-ally Persian are a minority. Though the Pahlavi dynasty looked back to the Achaemenids for its inspiration as well as for its aspiration, the new republic in Iran confronts non-Persian minorities—smaller than the dominant Persian minority—many of whom desire some form of autonomy or independence. Most prominent among these groups are several that were mentioned earlier: the Azeris, the Kurds, the Baluchis, the Bakhtiaris, and the Arabs. The smallest non-Persian groups are the Turkomans, Armenians, and Assyrians.

We also stressed the fact that virtually all contemporary Middle Easterners and North Africans have some connection with peoples who were known in antiquity. The Turkic peoples constitute, aside from the Europeans and Americans, the only major outside group to have entered the area since the advent of Islam. Some ancient peoples, for example, the Armenians, no longer live in their area of antiquity, but have relocated elsewhere in the Middle East, in Syria, Lebanon, Egypt, and Iran, as well as in Europe and the United States. The Armenian Soviet Socialist Republic, located now on the eastern frontier of Turkey, has a population made up of eastern Armenians whose language differs slightly from that of the decimated western Armenians. Despite their nationalist movements, many Armenians elsewhere will be assimilated and lost in another generation.

In this sense, the present fact of Israel and of the immigration of large number of Jews from eastern and western Europe and from the United States in the mid-twentieth century is a startling demographic phenomenon within the Middle Eastern context. Jewish communities in the Arab world and in the Muslim Middle East and North Africa as a whole constituted a small but significant presence throughout the Islamic era. These Arabic Jews remained scattered until after the creation of Israel in 1948. Israel's founders were Jews from Europe who, inspired by secular Zionism and European discrimination and persecution, sought to establish some form of national entity in Arab

Palestine. The immigrants were foreign, not indigenous Jews. Unlike the Jews of the Middle East and North Africa, the culture and customs of these early arrivals derived from their experiences in Europe, although their religious practices were basically the same as those of Middle Eastern Jews. While Eastern European Jews included both those who had tried to assimilate with the populations of their home countries and those who had tried to preserve a Jewish identity, the Jews who came from Western Europe and the United States—certainly a minority among the founders—were much like their fellow Westerners in culture.

Due to their unfamiliarity with the Middle East and North Africa in general, Israel's founders faced a great challenge as the post-independence influx of Jews from the Arab world began. Today, the *Oriental* Jewish population of Israel exceeds that of the European founders, but political power remains concentrated in the hands of the latter. One potential equalizer of the future is the training of the younger generation in Hebrew, the ancient language revived by the Zionist settlers.

The largest non-Arab population in North Africa still consists of Berbers. During the French protectorate in twentieth-century Morocco, Berbers were accorded special administrative laws designed to encourage separation from the Arabic-speaking population. The Kabyles faced the same sorts of policies under the French in Algeria. Yet Berbers fought against French colonial occupation. In Algeria, they were among the most vigorous leaders of the revolution. Berbers today continue to react strongly to Arabizing policies often viewed as threatening to their unique identity.

This brings us to our final but peripheral ethnic division in the part of Africa included in our study: the unique and diverse Nilotic populations of the Sudan who represent an ethnic transition between northern and sub-Saharan Africa. While the Sudan was under joint British and Egyptian administration after 1899, the southern part of the country was deliberately isolated from the Muslim north because of British fears of national unity. For this reason, the south still tends to look to southern countries for its cultural models, rather than to the northern capital city of Khartum. As long as the Sudanese government continues to identify with the Arab Middle East, however, the history of the Sudan ought to be incorporated into that of the dominant culture.

CHAPTER THREE

The Islamic Heritage

To a great extent, the forces that have molded the modern Middle East have been associated with its Islamic heritage. Islam today is rapidly gaining adherents, and it remains a powerful influence in Middle Eastern and North African societies among both Muslims and non-Muslims. About 90 percent of the people of the region identify themselves as Muslims. By exploring their roots, we gain a better appreciation of the relationship between the Muslim past and present.

Muhammad and the Rise of Islam

Islam began when the Prophet Muhammad received Allah's (God's) revelation (compiled as the Quran or recitations). He transmitted it through preaching, teaching, and example in his home city of Makka in the section of western Arabia called the Hijaz. Muhammad ibn Abd Allah ibn Abd al-Muttalib (570–632) belonged to the clan of Hashim, a branch of the Quraysh tribe that ruled Makka and that continued to do so through the early twentieth century. Orphaned as a child, Muhammad grew up in the homes of his grandfather and his uncle Abu Talib, a trader. Following his uncle, Muhammad became a merchant. He entered the service of a wealthy widow, Khadija, who was fifteen years his senior, and prospered as a merchant. They soon married and enjoyed a happy life although of their four daughters and two sons, only the daughters survived.

Despite his professional success and prosperity, Muhammad was disturbed by the spiritual malaise and social injustice of Makkan society. Great disparities of wealth arose from Makka's location on the caravan routes and its position as a pilgrimage center. Despite the presence of Jews and Christians (mainly Monophy-

29

sites but also some Orthodox), the dominant religious beliefs in pre-Islamic Makka centered around a variety of gods whose main shrine, the Ka'ba attracted pilgrims from all over Arabia. Many of the old gods had begun to be consolidated in a supreme diety enmeshed in superstition. Muhammad spent many hours seeking solutions to the problems facing his community. In the year 610 during the month of Ramadan, while meditating in a cave near Makka, he heard a voice calling him to recite. Muslims believe that voice belonged to Allah (God), speaking through the angel Gabriel. He was frightened because he did not know how to read, and could not identify who was calling him.

The voice commanded Muhammad to preach the supremacy of Allah, the only God—unique and indivisible. Muhammad was to be God's final messenger in the prophetic tradition. He explained that Allah was fully transcendent. Ninety-nine names described Allah's all-encompassing nature, for example, *al-Karim* (the generous) and *al-Rahim* (the compassionate). Both the Christian idea of the Trinity and the Makkan notion of many gods were rejected. The Arabic word *Islam* means submission; those who have submitted are Muslims.

Muhammad also warned Makkans that a day of judgment would come on which the wicked would be punished. The just would receive their reward in paradise. Shi'i Muslims as well as some Sunni—the two main divisions within Islam—much later evolved a non-Quranic idea that the day of judgment would be heralded by the coming of a *Mahdi,* a pious Muslim who would exhort Muslims and non-Muslims alike to vow allegiance to Allah. This messianic expectation gave rise to *Mahdist* movements from time to time. The most recent of these began in late nineteenth-century Sudan, where it is still influential.

A more important aspect of Muhammad's warnings about the last judgment is that they condemned Makka's elite for promoting class distinctions based on wealth, for exacerbating the gap between rich and poor, and for propagating social injustice. Makkans rejected the warnings as threatening to their privileged social and economic position, and they organized a boycott of the Hashimite clan. Some Makkans, however, listened and accepted: among them the dispossessed, the disenchanted, the hopeful, and the inspired. Muhammad's cousin Ali, Abu Talib's son, accepted Islam. So did Muhammad's associate Abu Bakr. Uthman of the wealthy Makkan clan of Umayya, and Umar, a dynamic leader, became Muslims, too. The issue of social justice in Islam has become a focus of twentieth-century Muslim thought.

Although Abu Talib never accepted Islam, he protected Muhammad from persecution. When Abu Talib and Khadija both died in 619, the Muslim community in Makka became more vulnerable. Because of Muhammad's reputation as an upright, just man, a delegation from Yathrib, (a prosperous commercial and agricultural city north of Makka), asked Muhammad to move there to mediate their disputes. He accepted on condition that they submit to his leadership and welcome his community of Muslims. After the move, Yathrib became known as *Madinat al-Nabi, city of the prophet,* or just *Madina.*

Islam's Evolution as a Comprehensive Social System

Muhammad's migration or *hijra* to Madina in 622 marked a decisive point in Islamic history. For this reason, the Muslim or Hijri calendar began in that year.

The hijra established the basis for the Muslim umma as a comprehensive social, political, economic, and religious entity. Muhammad continued, however, to receive revelations. These provided specific guidance for governing individual and communal relations and were longer than those given to him in Makka.

Based on his ongoing revelations, Muhammad set up a just society that could be extended to urban Makka and to Arabia's rural and nomadic clan groups. He hoped that Madina's citizens, mainly Jews and worshippers of local dieties, would accept his authority not only as arbitrator and governor but as Allah's final messenger. The divine revelations referred to Hebrew prophets and incorporated Jewish religious practices. Muslims prayed facing Jerusalem and fasted on Yom Kippur, the Jewish Day of Atonement. The Jews of Madina rejected these new teachings but were protected until they conspired with Muhammad's opponents.

The Institutionalization of Pluralism

Although Jews who conspired were expelled or killed, the Quran accorded protected (*dhimmi*) status to fellow monotheists with revealed prophecy (Jews, Christians, Zoroastrians, and others). Their own revealed laws administered by their own religious leaders governed them because Muslim law did not apply. The Quran required non-Muslims to pay the *jizya* (special head tax) and *kharaj* (land tax applied to all conquered peoples), but exempted them from military service. In early Islamic history, the tolerance of Islam contrasted favorably with Byzantine oppressive taxation and persecution of non-Orthodox Christians and with Sassanian persecution of Manichaeans and followers of Mazdak. Throughout the centuries, Islamic polities institutionalized this system of pluralism. Non-Muslims were classified according to religious rather than ethnic or linguistic identity. The system worked until the eighteenth century, when individual religious groups moved toward greater autonomy. Influenced by European notions of nationhood, citizenship,

and equality, these groups began to demand recognition of national status apart from the larger Islamic entities, especially throughout the Ottoman Empire in Europe, Asia, and Africa. The reassertion of Islamic identity today has again raised the question in Southwest Asian and North African Muslim majority states. Former President Anwar al-Sadat of Egypt said in May 1980: "The best protection for the Christians of Egypt is an Islamic system"[1]—the Quranic idea of communal rights, incorporating minority status for non-Muslims among the *umma* rather than the idea of individual rights inherent in equality of citizenship in a nation-state.

The rise of the nation-state raises two major issues of contemporary importance in Islam. The insistence on an uncompromising monotheism means that the greatest sin in Islam is to suggest that God has partners. This is known as *shirk*. Muslim traditionalists insist that if there is a community (*umma*) united in loyalty to God transcending political boundaries, Muslims cannot also pay allegiance to a nation-state.

If the rise of the nation-state disrupted the Islamic consensus on pluralism the problem was further confounded by the fact that traditional religious loyalties often paralleled ethnic and/or tribal divisions. Even the later development of Arab nationalism, although it was intended to address the problem of pluralism, never fully resolved the tension between the idea of the *umma,* on the one hand, and the nation-state, on the other. Arab nationalism always tried to reach a modus vivendi with the Islamic factor without making it central. Perhaps the most dramatic example of this unresolved issue is Lebanon today.

The Victory over Makka

Muhammad gradually led non-monotheists in Madina to accept Islam.

---

[1] Speech to People's Assembly, Egypt, 14 May 1980.

He then used economic and military warfare—attacking Makkan caravans—to challenge those who had oppressed him and his followers. Because of a later truce with Makka, Muhammad undertook a new Allah-centered pilgrimage (*hajj*) to Makka in 629. In 630, he conquered Makka with only minimal opposition but continued to base his rule at Madina. His unified rule enhanced conditions for Makka's merchants; they were absorbed as leaders and administrators into his government. He then began subduing the Arabs of Arabia; many submitted voluntarily. Before he died in 632, he made a final pilgrimage to Makka. His followers carefully observed it and made it the model for the Muslim *hajj* of today. Similar reports of Muhammad's sayings (*Hadith*) and behavior were used to establish traditions (*Sunna*) that supplemented the Quran as a source of guidance for Muslim behavior.

Authority and Legitimacy in Early Islam: Sunnism, Shi'ism, and Kharijism

Muhammad's death in 632 produced the first enduring crisis in Islam. The Muslim community recognized Muhammad's father-in-law Abu Bakr as his *khalifa* (successor). Often rendered as caliph, the position granted the possessor comprehensive authority over territories under the rule of Islam. The caliph did not, however, have the power to interpret revelation. Muhammad's companions Umar and Uthman succeeded Abu Bakr. The main criterion for this position, besides piety and leadership, was membership in the Quraysh tribe. Only men could hold the position.

Some Muslims, the partisans (*Shi'a*) of Ali, Muhammad's cousin and son-in-law, felt that the succession resided exclusively in Ali and his heirs, Muhammad's grandsons Hasan and Husayn. Many *Hadith* supported their case. Initially, the Shi'a accepted the largely political content of successorship, but they subsequently introduced the concept of *Imams* (distinguished from the imams who lead Friday prayers in mosques). The Imams were divinely inspired charismatic figures who held authority in matters of theology and doctrine. Belief in the *Imams'* interpretive authority contrasted with the Sunni idea of caliphal leadership, with its implied emphasis on consensus. Although the Muslims chose Ali as the fourth khalifa, his Shi'a continued to view the first three as usurpers. They considered election as inappropriate to the Imamate.

Another Muslim faction, the Kharijites or *khawarij* (seceders), carried charismatic leadership to the point of accepting any pious Muslim as khalifa. They also believed that an unjust khalifa could be deposed. They repudiated and later murdered Ali for having agreed to subject his Imamate to arbitration and usurpation. Although the Kharijites achieved widespread influence in North Africa during the early centuries of Islam, their polities tended to be local and were beset with internal squabbles. Remnants of the Kharijite Ibadi sect are found today in Oman, on the island of Jirba off the Tunisian coast, and in the Mzab oasis of Algeria. Most Kharijite principalities, however, disappeared in the ninth and tenth centuries.

The primary historical influence of Kharijism lies in its insistence on 1) the Quranic injunction to exhort men to do good and to enjoin them from doing evil, even by force; and 2) their perception of the role of the community to select leaders and to make decisions of communal importance. Muslims in the organized fundamentalist movements of today, such as the Muslim Brothers, resemble the Kharijites in their moral focus and ideas about organization. Saudi Arabia, for example, has taken up the idea of a moral police force to assure that Muslims pray, do business properly, and observe Quranic injunctions.

Sunni Muslims consider the first four khalifas (632–661) as the *Rashidun* or rightly guided. Despite ongoing disputes with Ali's party, the era of these khalifas witnessed the consolidation by Abu Bakr

(632–34) of Muslim rule in Arabia and its expansion by Umar (634–44) and his generals to greater Syria, Egypt, Mesopotamia, and Persia (see Map 3). Under Uthman (644–56), the abode of Islam (*Dar al-Islam*) expanded to the edges of Armenia and to present-day Afghanistan and Soviet Central Asia. Governors in Egypt and Syria built fleets to extend and then protect Muslim-ruled Mediterranean lands. The Rashidun preceded the evolution of Sunna. Indeed, it was Uthman who saw to the standardization of the Quran. Modern Muslim fundamentalists seek to return to the essentials of the Quran and the traditions of the prophet and his companions. They assign three periods to Islamic history: 1) the period of Muhammad; 2) the era of the Rashidun; 3) the decline.

The Rashidun caliphate ended precisely because of troubles which arose during it, especially under the khalifa Uthman. Trying to establish centralized control through better tax collection, he appointed his relatives as governors of the provinces. His cousin Mu'awiya built the fleet that in 649 conquered Cyprus. Mu'awiya regarded himself as a strong candidate to succeed Uthman. However, when Uthman was murdered by rebels from Egypt, the Muslims turned to Ali, whose piety still commanded respect. But Mu'awiya (who with Muhammad's young widow Aisha felt that Ali had not sufficiently prosecuted the murderers) refused to submit to Ali's authority. From 660, he claimed the caliphate for himself. To avoid his rivals, Ali moved the capital to Kufa in southern Iraq, but at the battle of Siffin (657) he acceded to Mu'awiya's call for arbitration of the dispute. The Kharijites objected to Ali's decision and decided to oppose him, too. In 661, they assassinated him in Kufa. Though the Kufans elected Ali's son Hasan as khalifa, Mu'awiya's supporters pressured him to relinquish his claim.

The Umayyads, ruling from Damascus (661–749), abandoned elections in favor of dynastic rule characterized by hereditary succession. After Mu'awiya's death, Ali's other son Husayn, supported by descendants of Muhammad's companions, took up the fight against Mu'awiya's son Yazid. On a day now commemorated by Shi'i Muslims throughout the world, *Ashura* or 10 Muharram 61 (10 October 680), Husayn and his small band were killed by Yazid's forces at Karbala. One of Husayn's sons survived, though, to carry on the Imamate, and southern Iraq has remained committed to Shi'ism to the present day.

The Shi'a continued to revere the Imams, hoping that one of them would gain power if the Umayyads could be overthrown. When the Abbasid revolt succeeded in 749, though, khalifas were chosen from other Qurayshis. Divisions within Shi'ism took place after this time. The most Sunni-like Shi'a were the Zaydis who revered Zayd instead of his brother Muhammad al-Baqir as the fifth Imam. Zaydis do not hold the Imams to be infallible. Today, this group predominates in the Arab Republic of Yemen.

The Isma'ilis (Seveners) accepted Isma'il as the seventh khalifa. They then continued to recognize several lines of living Imams, including that of the Agha Khans. Isma'ilism became especially influential in the ninth–twelfth centuries when the Isma'ili Qarmatians adopted a socialist system and the Fatimids contested for rule over much of North Africa and Western Asia. The Druze of the Levant today are an eleventh-century offshoot of Fatimid Isma'ili Shi'ism; they deified the third Fatimid khalifa, al-Hakim (996–1021). From late in the eleventh through the thirteenth century, an Isma'ili sect known as Assassins (from *hashishiyun*—those who use hashish), based in Persia, created havoc among Sunni Muslims in Western Asia.

The Ithna-Asharis, or Imamis, accepted twelve Imams. They evolved the belief that the twelfth, who disappeared as a baby, went into hiding (occultation) and will return as the Mahdi. They more or less coexisted with Sunni rulers, unlike the Isma'ilis. Imami Shi'ism became a state religion in sixteenth-century Iran after which it acquired a more overt hostility to Sunni Islam.

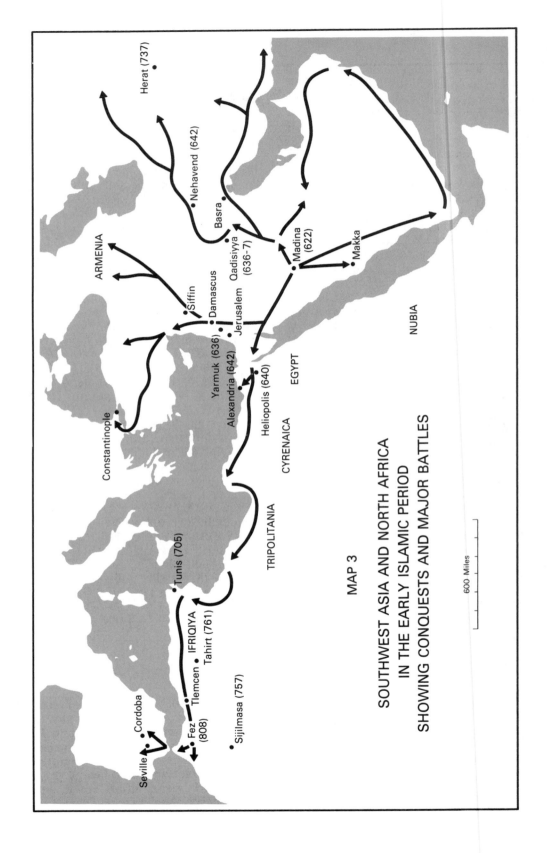

Herat (737)

Nehavend (642)

Basra

Madina (622)

Makka

Qadisiyya (636-7)

ARMENIA

Siffin

Damascus

Jerusalem

Yarmuk (636)

Alexandria (642)

Heliopolis (640)

EGYPT

NUBIA

Constantinople

CYRENAICA

TRIPOLITANIA

Tunis (705)

IFRIQIYA

Tahirt (761)

Sijilmasa (757)

Fez (808)

Tlemcen

Seville

Cordoba

MAP 3

SOUTHWEST ASIA AND NORTH AFRICA
IN THE EARLY ISLAMIC PERIOD
SHOWING CONQUESTS AND MAJOR BATTLES

600 Miles

The Shari'a

All revelations given to Muhammad in Makka and Madina were compiled in the 114 chapters of the Quran. Except for the short opening (*fatiha*) which alone makes Allah the addressee rather than the addressor, the Quran's chapters are arranged according to length, with the longest first. The Quran is both a path for reaching heaven and a guide for living on earth. God-given law rather than theology or philosophy is central to Islamic society. The Arabic word meaning law in the sense of proper Muslim behavior subject to legal sanction is *al-shari'a*, literally the path. Its first and most important source has always been the Quran.

The Quran includes many safeguards for the health and protection of Muslims. Muslims are required to wash frequently in addition to performing ritual cleansing before prayer. Practices involving social injustice—such as gambling and usury—or antisocial behavior such as theft, murder, drinking alcoholic beverages or ingesting drugs—are strictly forbidden. Stiff penalties are clearly stipulated. As in Jewish law, the Quran prohibits the eating of pork or unconsecrated flesh. Both men and women are provided for in inheritance matters, women receiving half of a man's share.

Marriage is set forth as a contractual relationship in which each party has rights and responsibilities. Extramarital relations are heavily penalized. Islam has contributed to the security of marriage by giving women financial guarantees in case of divorce and by limiting the number of wives to four. Muhammad, though he had multiple spouses after Khadija's death, enjoined his followers not to marry more than one woman unless they could treat them equally. Contemporary scholars have begun to interpret this as meaning that a man should take only one wife since no ordinary man could treat two or more women with complete equality. Polygamy has never been widespread in parts of the Muslim world such as Iran. Though polygamy is declining in many areas, Muslim jurists have maintained the legal limit of four wives, and some predominantly Muslim countries actively discourage the custom. Shi'i Muslims permit temporary or *mut'a* marriage under certain circumstances to legitimize temporary sexual relationships.

Muhammad intended that women should be respected. His own wives covered themselves completely, but other women were told just to dress modestly. Only later in Islamic history were women in some Muslim lands expected to veil themselves and restrict their activities to home and family. The model of Khadija, the urban businesswoman, faded away in a social milieu often based more on patriarchal pre-Islamic customs than on the Quran and Sunna of Muhammad, though verses from the Quran were found to support these older customs. In rural Muslim society, women have rarely practiced seclusion or veiling. These have been urban phenomena.

Sources of Shari'a

After Muhammad's death, the community adopted the Hadith and Sunna as the second most important source for the Shari'a after the Quran. In the early days of Islam, traditions about the prophet abounded. In later years, the Muslims developed elaborate systems for determining which Hadith were legitimate. Each report had to be traced to the prophet through a chain of reliable authorities, preferably through the prophet's companions. Biographical studies became essential to those Muslims determining the authenticity of individual Hadith. The traditions that achieved acceptance were much fewer in number than those originally circulated. The compilation of Hadith was not isolated from politics; disputes over this issue constituted a fundamental aspect of the Sunni-Shi'i split. Each group accepted the Hadith supporting its case. In the 1970s, Libya's leader Muammar al-Qadhdhafi challenged the acceptability of Hadith as a source of Shari'a, claiming that the literature contained too much questionable and contradictory material. He took only the Quran as a proper source of Muslim law.

Other sources for Shari'a have aroused even greater controversy. The Sunni, Islam's main body, accepted analogy (*qiyas*) and consensus of the community (*ijma*), the latter based on the hadith, "My umma will not agree upon an error." Ijma, which came to mean the consensus of Muslim scholars (*ulama*), became the principal means by which Sunnism determined practice not resolved by other sources. Shi'i Muslims rejected ijma and qiyas, and adhered more closely to the Quran and their own collections of Hadith. After the infallible Imams went into occultation, Shi'i Islam accepted *ijtihad* (independent judgment) through which a qualified but fallible individual (*mujtahid*) could introduce revolutionary change. Because each judgment could be followed only if pronounced during the believer's lifetime, the law was constantly refreshed through contemporary interpretation based on present realities. Ijtihad was a powerful force in implementing the 1978–79 Iranian revolution. Although they initially practiced ijtihad, Sunni ulama more or less abandoned it after the consolidation in the tenth century of four equally acceptable Sunni legal systems—Hanbali, Hanafi, Shafi'i, and Maliki—each named after a prominent jurist. Twentieth-century Muslim reformers view ijtihad as the key device for implementing social change.

In neither Sunni nor Shi'i Islam, though, was there a clergy serving as a medium between God and the believers. Equality of all Muslims remained a fundamental tenet of the faith. Prayer leaders have always been religious functionaries, not ordained men set apart from the rest of the community.

Acts of Devotion

Early in Islamic history, Muslims isolated from the Shari'a five acts of devotion essential to the life of a pious Muslim. The affirmation (*shahada*)—"There is no God but Allah and Muhammad is his Messenger (Apostle)"—causes one to be recognized as a Muslim. The shahada expresses the supremacy of God, and declares Muhammad to be the final prophet in the apostolic tradition of Jewish and Christian scriptures as well as of the Quran.

The other four pillars of Islamic devotion which every devout Muslim incorporates into his or her life are ritual prayer (*salat*), community tax (*zakat*), fasting (*sawm*), and pilgrimage (*hajj*). The Quran enjoins Muslims to pray regularly but sets forth no particular ritual. Most Muslims, based on Muhammad's example, pray facing Makka at daybreak, noon, midafternoon, sunset, and at night. Five prayers are performed, but Shi'a combine them and pray only three times a day. Since the purpose of prayer is to remind the believer of God's sovereignty throughout the day, an individual may pray alone or in a group. In the act of prayer itself, the believer repeats the words "God is the greatest" (*Allahu akbar*) while bowing, kneeling, and prostrating himself. The essence of Muslim prayer is worshipping God. Repeated acknowledgment of God's omnipotence is inherent in this act of submission. No special location is required for prayer, but early in Islamic history, the mosque, called in Arabic either a *masjid* (place of worship) or a *jami* (gathering place) became the location for the weekly community prayer on Friday at noon. Since a Muslim must be in a pure state in order to pray, mosques have always contained facilities for washing (ablutions) although the believer may use sand in their absence. In the congregational prayer, the sexes pray in different parts of the mosque, and a sermon (*khutba*) is preached. Since the sermon has traditionally been delivered in the name of the ruler, Muslims in earlier times often learned about changes in leadership through the insertion of a new name in the prayer. Because of the importance of this prayer, Friday is a weekly holiday in most predominantly Muslim countries.

The significance Islam accords to the community (the umma), mandates the giving of zakat, a specific percentage of an individual's wealth or income to the community for support of the poor. The central government collected the zakat in early Islamic times, but as the umma grew, collection became more localized. Muslims were also encouraged to give of their resources in the form of additional cash or contributions (*sadaqat*). Donations of property, known as *waqf* (charitable endowments), support particular endeavors such as schools, hospitals, and mosques. During the period of the Islamic conquests, one fifth of the spoils also helped to sustain the needy.

Muslims focus on God even more intensely in the month of Ramadan, the month in which Muhammad received his first revelations. During this joyful fast, Muslims may not eat, drink, smoke, or have sexual intercourse from dawn to sunset. When Ramadan occurs in the hot summer months, as it does regularly because of the advance of the Muslim lunar calendar each year, fasting imposes considerable discipline and hardship on even a healthy Muslim. During Ramadan, Muslim countries institute reduced work and study schedules. Pregnant women, soldiers, travelers, young children, and the ill are exempted from fasting. Each night, after sunset is celebrated with special festivities and the eating of particular sweets made for the season. A holiday atmosphere prevails. Religious lectures are often delivered as well.

Finally, any physically and financially able Muslim should, at least once in his or her lifetime, follow the example set by Muhammad in his last days by joining other Muslims from all over the world in the hajj to Makka, which takes place in Dhu al-Hijja, the twelfth month of the Muslim calendar. During the hajj, all distinctions of class or wealth are subsumed as each Muslim dresses in identical white cloths. Near the end of the pilgrimage, Muslims gather on the plain of Arafat where Muhammad made his last speech. The communal prayer of these multitudes at Arafat displays God's supremacy and underscores the spiritual unity of Allah's people, and the universalism and brotherhood of the umma. At the height of the pilgrimage, the believers sacrifice a lamb commemorating the substitution of this animal for Ishmael (Isma'il), son of Abraham and Hagar. The sacrificial act takes place on Id al-Adha (feast of the sacrifice), the longest and most important Muslim festival or *bayram* (a four-day holiday in most Muslim countries).

In the twentieth century, Muslims have questioned the compatibility of some of the acts of devotion with the requirements of the modern age. For example, is prayer five times a day compatible with assembly lines in factories? Is the change of routines during Ramadan too disruptive? This issue has been most directly confronted in Tunisia.

Muslims are also told to struggle against unbelief. Each individual must guard against unbelief through a moral *jihad* (striving). The call to jihad, often interpreted as holy war, has led to a distorted belief that Muslims are warlike. But jihads have often resulted from threats to Islamic lands or to Muslims in lands not under the rule of Islam. Although some Muslim scholars consider jihad a sixth act of devotion required of Muslims, there is no unanimity on this point.

We have emphasized the aspects of early Islam that became part of Shi'i and Sunni orthodoxy as approved by religious scholars and as practiced by Muslims. As with other revealed religions, the degree of adherence by Muslims to practices or theological positions laid down by scholars has varied enormously. The spiritual dimension of individual believers' responses is even harder to pin down. Both Shi'i and Sunni Muslims from the early days of Islam believed in a deep personal relationship with a transcendent God. As official Islam expressed by Ulama became more elaborate, both scholars and people without legal training intensified their search for a path that would allow for open expression of an individual response not fully satisfied by the acts of devotion. A broad dimension of Islam which gave full rein to these emotions was Sufism.

Sufism

The Arabic word *sufi* is thought to have been derived from *suf* (wool) because of a simple woolen garment worn by early Sufis. The course and direction of popular Islam molded by ordinary people as well as through introspection by religious scholars led to the widespread acceptance of the sufi or mystical path as one way of knowing and serving God. By Islam's second century, the Sufi path had arisen. Small groups met for prayer. Ritualistic practices, sometimes derived from those of local pre-Islamic cults, were designed to produce religious ecstasy. Motions, rhythmic and ritualistic spontaneous movements, and repetition (*dhikr*) of the name of God created an atmosphere and a means to reach and become one with God. The ceremonies came to be known as *dhikr*, too.

This combination of the human and the divine, found also in the notion of sainthood, is absolutely forbidden in Islam. Uncompromising monotheism insists on the unity of God who has no partners. At first inspired by the fear of God and his wrath in the last judgment, Sufism gradually took on a basic characteristic that is true in the end of all mysticisms, the concept of love, not human love, but divine love—union with, identification with God.

The emotional heights of Sufism were often combined with personal asceticism. The Quran and traditions condemned celibacy. Official Islam incorporated neither priests nor monks nor nuns who would deny the needs of the flesh. But from the earliest days, ascetics shunned ritual practice in favor of the discipline of the soul, although they did not necessarily repudiate acts of devotion. That is how monasticism and celibacy, disdained by Islamic orthodoxy, became a way of life for many Sufis. By avoiding sex and mar-

riage, they removed obstacles to a direct relationship with God.

The Sufi ideal was to gain esoteric truth (inward knowledge) through studying with a master who had already achieved it. The teacher initiated the student gradually. Sufi educators often addressed problems encountered by individuals in daily life at home or in public. Muslims began forming fraternal orders (*tariqas*) to follow the teachings of particular saintly figures. Pilgrimages to the tombs of these brotherhood-founders led to a sort of saint worship which, though strictly forbidden as a form of *shirk*, has been practiced in much of the Muslim world to the present day. Teaching often took place at a *zawiya, tekke* or *khaniqa* where teachers and students, mainly men, lived and studied. The *futuwwa* (fraternal orders of young men; also their codes of behavior) of the medieval Muslim world included a chivalrous dimension not necessarily present in Sufism, but many of the orders were at the same time Sufi organizations. Both futuwwa and Sufi brotherhoods could be associated with particular trades or guilds. Many tariqas were international fraternities. Tariqas still exist, which on a local scale have political and economic power. Because of their control at the popular level, indigenous and colonial rulers alike have co-opted them from time to time.

Sufis played a critical role in the spread of Islam. They wandered through towns, villages, and the countryside, transmitting the message of Islam. Like Muslim merchants, the Sufis were Islam's missionaries. In Africa, these two groups spread Islam where no Muslim armies had gone already or were to follow later. In parts of North and West Africa especially, Sufis have been central figures in politics. Sufi orders also supplied the major inspirational and ideological power that motivated the great infantry of the Ottoman Empire, conquerors of almost all of eastern Europe.

Despite repression from time to time, Sufism even to this very day is the means whereby the masses express their religious emotions. It in no way precludes, though, attendance at congregational prayer in mosques. Sufism has been particularly influential in Sunni Islam because Shi'i Islam from the outset provided for personal engagement with God. There are also Shi'i Sufis.

Conclusion

Islam appealed to the peoples of Arabia because it provided a comprehensive solution to genuine social and psychological needs. In addition it preserved the religious symbolism of the Arabs while using its features in a new frame of reference. The Muslims' new frame of reference was Allah's supremacy and will revealed in the Quran and extended through Shari'a. Looking at the historical context, the rise of an Islamic polity in Arabia has also been analyzed in the context of state formation on the periphery of two exhausted empires, the Byzantine and the Sassanian.

But was the Shari'a a fixed, unchanging ideal sanctioned by revelation or a flexible system applicable and appropriate for all times and places? Among the revealed religions, only Judaism and Islam provide this kind of total ethic expressed in a set of laws. Muslims have never felt it necessary to agree on a single Shari'a nor have fully tried to apply it in all its facets except in rare cases, such as in Saudi Arabia of today. Some Muslims claim that the ideal Islamic polity ruled by Shari'a never existed. The question of imposing a comprehensive Shari'a has become controversial and central to the Muslim revival of the twentieth century. It is analogous to the earlier question of *shirk* and the nation-state.

Because Islam spread rapidly, the legal and social institutions of converts could not be abolished all at once. Berbers, for example, retained their customary law, as did others on Islam's periphery in India, Southeast Asia, and sub-Saharan Africa. Stipulations in penal and commercial realms, and laws protecting women's rights, were often disregarded. Later, Islamic polities derived laws not only from legal opinions (*fatwas*) issued by qualified scholars called *muftis* but also from decrees (*qanuns*) promulgated by rulers in the name of Islam and from customary law (*urf*). Most often, qanuns related to political or administrative matters. During the last 250 years, nation-states have evolved that increasingly have restricted the scope of Shari'a, substituting for it civil laws based on European models and applied to Muslims and non-Muslims alike.

But can Muslims accept a government that relegates the Shari'a to an inferior role? Even if jurists reinterpret and codify Shari'a as the law of the land, does the system offer the same flexibility as laws based on distinctions between the religious and the secular? Muslims today are facing these questions because the Shari'a, after thirteen centuries, continues to express the principles by which most Muslims hope to live. In the twentieth century, the social-justice component of Shari'a has come again to the fore. Islam always embraced a dynamic, a means of addressing contemporary realities, and of seeking solutions to complex problems in a variety of linguistic and ethnic milieus. Three questions summarize concerns of early Muslims still being debated:

1. How to resolve discrepancies between ideals and practices.
2. How to define accepted boundaries of diversity in belief and practice of those united by Islam.
3. How to incorporate necessary change while maintaining continuity.

CHAPTER FOUR

State, Economy, and Society in the Islamicate Age To About 1500

Students of the modern Middle East and North Africa should have some idea of historical developments between the demise of the Rashidun khalifas and the emergence between 1500 and 1550 of the Ottoman Empire as the major regional power. This chapter provides a brief historical outline of concepts and processes that developed during the period and are most relevant to gaining an understanding of modern history.

Arabization, Islamization, and the Expansion of the Dar al-Islam

The expansion of lands under Muslim rule continued for centuries. After the Rashidun conquests, the Umayyads extended and consolidated their position in North Africa. Early in the eighth century, they crossed into Spain. Although Muslim armies entered France and were defeated at Poitiers in 732 by the Frankish leader Charles Martel, there is little evidence that they intended to conquer rather than just to raid northern Europe. By 1200, Muslim rule had reached northern India, present-day Somalia, and Central Asia. Within another three hundred years, the

Dar al-Islam included southern India, parts of Indonesia, Madagascar, broad expanses of today's Soviet Union (U.S.S.R.), the East African coast through Tanzania, all of Anatolia, and southeastern Europe to the Danube. In 1492, however, Muslims lost their last foothold in Spain.

The act of expansion differs, of course, from that of either conversion to Islam or of taking on a new ethnolinguistic identity. In the early years of Muslim expansion, the Muslims discouraged conversion, and the religion retained a strong Arab identity. Non-Arabs who accepted Islam were forced to become clients of Arab tribes. Gradually, Arab Muslims allowed non-Arabs to become Muslims without having first to become Arabs. Why did Christians, Jews, Zoroastrians, and others accept Islam? Initially, one can point to the straightforwardness of Islam and to the justice, tranquillity, and prosperity brought by Muslims to conquered lands. Conversion was also prompted through social and psychological pressures, especially through the inherent inferiority of dhimmi status exemplified by legal restrictions, occasional persecution, and rigid rules against apostasy. Finally, many converts viewed Islam and Islamic culture as superior to their own. The process took centuries and was never fully completed in many areas of Muslim rule, especially in greater Syria, Egypt and Anatolia.

Arabization also occurred gradually. Kurds, Iranians, and many Berbers maintained their old ethnolinguistic identities. Others—Copts, Jews, and some Greek Orthodox—kept their religion but adopted Arabic as their native language. Of the Middle Eastern Asians conquered by the Arabs, only the Armenians and Greeks retained both their native language and their religion in large numbers. The Turks, who entered the area after Islam had arrived, kept their ethnolinguistic identity, but with the international culture that spread from the tenth century on, they often wrote in Arabic or Persian. The institutionalization of pluralism in Muslim-governed states thus accommodated religious and linguistic diversity.

Periodization in the History of Muslim-Ruled Lands

How do historians approach the history of Southwest Asia and North Africa following the rise of Islam? Back-to-basics Muslims would classify the period after the Rashidun as a unity called "the Decline." Mainly because most Muslim polities after the Rashidun were dynastic, many historians have adopted a dynastic framework for both North Africa and the central Muslim lands between Egypt and the boundaries of Central Asia.

A rigid framework focusing on the Rashidun's successors—the Umayyads (661–750) and Abbasids (750–1258)—is inappropriate for this study because it obscures major political, social, religious, and economic developments. A dynastic exploration does not explain processes such as urbanization, evolution of art and architecture, the changing relationships and struggles over authority and legitimacy, militarization and secularization of Muslim polities, the rise of the ulama, the development of international trade, and the consolidation of Muslim social organizations. Broad movements such as Sufism, Mu'tazilism, or the Shi'i revival transcended dynasties. Finally, a multiplicity of dynastic and other polities cropped up during the Abbasid period in lands supposedly under Abbasid authority.

Authority and Legitimacy After the Rashidun

The types of government that evolved in Islam were related to the concept of the umma united under the khalifa. Disputes among Muslims arose from the presumed usurpation of the caliphate by the Umayyads. In Damascus, the Umayyads adopted the administrative apparatus of Byzantine rule. The egalitarianism of the Rashidun was subsumed in a new tradition of an expanding, somewhat decentralized empire under the Makkan ruling commercial elites.

Mu'awiya and his successors divided their territories into provinces administered by Arab governors (often merchants) who controlled the administration, the army, and justice. Initially, the khalifas employed local bureaucrats who used their own languages for record-keeping. After a protracted civil war in the 680s and 690s Abd al-Malik (685–705) decided instead that solely Arab officials should keep records, in Arabic. Despite the efforts of Umar II (717–720) to implement Shari'a, a cleavage developed between the theoretical society of the ulama and the increasingly secular state. Madina, Makka, and Kufa remained the centers of Muslim learning. The study of tradition, philology, history, and the law developed relatively undisturbed.

Although Damascus later became the heart and soul of the Arab nationalist movement, only under the Umayyads was it the capital of an empire. Syria became the hinterland of the three real power centers—Anatolia, the Tigris-Euphrates river systems, and the Nile Valley. Today, the Arabian peninsula has re-emerged as a fourth locus of power.

After the Abbasid revolt, which originated among Arab settlers in the eastern Iranian plateau but which was co-opted by non-Arab converts (mainly Turks and Persians), the caliphate instituted a centralized bureacracy dominated by Persian administrators. The most important officials were the khalifas' chief advisors or *vizirs* (Arabic: *wazir*). As khalifas retreated to luxurious courts modeled after those of the Sassanids, vizirs held more real authority than the khalifas. Subsequent Muslim governments retained this institution. Caliphal prestige, partly because of efficient vizirs, reached its height internally in the late eighth century under al-Mansur (754–775),al-Mahdi (775–785), Harun al-Rashid(786–809), and Ma'mun (813–833).The seeds of decentralization, though, had already been sown. *Amirs* (princes), usually generals of the Abbasids, were allowed to form autonomous dynasties that paid tribute to and acknowledged the authority of the khalifa. The Aghlabids (800–909) of Tunisia, Tahirids (821–873) in Khurasan, and the Tulunids (868–905) and Ikhshidids of Egypt (935–969) offer such examples.

Early Abbasid rulers were also faced with rivals for power. After their success in 749–50, an Umayyad survivor Abd al-Rahman I made his way to Spain to continue the Umayyad dynastic state. He claimed the title *amir*, signifying acceptance of the authority of the Abbasid khalifa. This shows the reluctance of early Sunni Muslims to challenge formally caliphal authority. The Kharijites, who rejected Sunni khalifas, won a broad following in the Maghrib for their egalitarian and charismatic ideals. Leaders in the main Kharijite principalities of Tahirt, Tlemcen, and Sijilmasa were elected, and members of the same family were consistently chosen in Tahirt. The Sijilmasa and Tahirt principalities lasted until the early tenth-century Fatimid conquests. Until that time, they too avoided confronting Abbasid power directly. In late eighth-century Morocco, one Idris, great-grandson of Ali and therefore a *sharif* (descendant of Ali), founded the Idrisid dynasty that had Shi'i leanings. The combination of Alid descent and charismatic leadership (but not Shi'ism) became a model for later Moroccan rulers such as today's Alawi dynasty. Idris' followers recognized him as Imam. His successors divided his state into small principalities.

In the ninth century, Turkish body-guards of the Abbasid khalifa began assuming the title *sultan* (signifying temporal sovereign authority). Many rulers adopted the title in later centuries. Noncaliphal rulers also called themselves *amir al-umara* (commander of the commanders, or prince of the princes), *malik* (king), and *amir al-muslimin* (commander of the Muslims). *Amir al-mu'minin* (commander of the faithful) remained a caliphal title only. When the khalifas in Baghdad found their scope as rulers curtailed, they occasionally tried to consolidate their religious authority and ties with the ulama. Scholars tried to reconcile the idea of a ruling khalifa with the reality of nonreligious amirs, especially in later centuries.

The Shi'i Century

The tenth century brought about a Shi'i revival in Islamdom, partially reflected in the assumption of power by Shi'a. In part a result of the decline of caliphal power at home and in the provinces, each Shi'i polity ensued from particular circumstances in its area and in no way represented a coordinated or united effort. Shi'ism rather than Kharijism gained adherents in the tenth century because protest movements of the ninth century had crystalized around it. Intellectually, the movement may have originated with a need to consolidate Shi'i belief after 940 when the twelve Imams' last representatives died. The greatest power, though, was assumed by Isma'ili rather than Im-

ami Shi'is. The failure of Shi'is to convert the masses during their era of supremacy accounts for their political demise.

Where were these Shi'i states? A Zaydi Imamate took root in the interior of northern Yemen the late ninth century. It survived until 1962 despite loss of power to various local dynasts and to big polities such as Egypt and the Ottoman Empire. A short-lived (ninth and tenth century) Zaydi state south of the Caspian Sea won that region for Shi'ism, a development of long-lasting impact. The Isma'ili Qarmatians in the late ninth century founded an egalitarian state extending along the eastern Arabian coast. Now called al-Hasa province in Saudi Arabia, it remains an area of Shi'i concentration.

The Isma'ili Fatimids (909–1171) succeeded in conquering Tunisia from the Aghlabids because of missionary successes in converting the Kutama Berbers to their cause. The Fatimid leader Ubayd Allah claimed to be both Mahdi and khalifa. Though the Fatimids contested with the Spanish Umayyads and local polities for control of the Maghrib, they could not sustain their position. Because of Fatimid-Umayyad rivalry, the Umayyad amir Abd al-Rahman III in 929 also claimed the title khalifa. This gave the theoretically united Muslim world a total of three khalifas. After taking Egypt in 969, the Fatimids built Cairo as their new capital, leaving in the Maghrib two successor states ruled by relatives of their general Ziri: the Zirids and Hammadids. Both of these dynastic polities renewed their allegiance to the Abbasid khalifas prior to the Fatimid demise in Egypt. Originating among Syrian beduin and acknowledging Fatimid authority, the Hamdanids of Aleppo and Mosul (tenth century) ruled over parts of southern Turkey, northern Syria, and northern Iraq.

Meanwhile, the Abbasid caliphate from 945 to 1055 came under the domination of Imami Buyid (Buwayhid) amirs from the southern Caspian coast. They restricted the khalifa's governing power. The three founding amirs, with their Turkic military supporters, set up a decentralized state based in Baghdad, Isfahan, and Shiraz. Though briefly united, authority became increasingly fragmented until the Sunni Saljuk Turks took Baghdad in 1055.

Resurgence of Sunnism

The Saljuk leader Tughrul-Beg legitimized his position in Baghdad through an agreement with the khalifa al-Qa'im (1031–75); he co-opted the latter's vizir. Al-Qa'im soon found himself subjected to a new temporal power, but at least the Saljuks promoted Sunni Islam. Under Alp Arslan (1063–72) and Malikshah (1072–92), the vizirate achieved paramount importance. A Persian, Nizam al-Mulk (d. 1092), aimed to restore a universal empire based on a Persian tradition of centralized rule and bureaucracy. His *Siyasat Name* (Book of Government) set forth guidelines which later Muslim rulers used.[1] If Nizam al-Mulk's plans had succeeded, he would have subjected the Turkish military to the bureaucracy, but they refused to submit. But under his leadership, the Saljuks consolidated their military conquests in Anatolia, the Hijaz, Yemen, and Central Asia.

In the twelfth century, the Saljuk empire became fragmented and Saljuk princes became subservient to and were finally replaced by their tutors (called *atabegs*). These began to clash with the European crusaders who reached the area in 1097 because of distorted reports of Saljuk rule in Jerusalem, 1071–98. The Fatimids recaptured the city in 1099, but lost it to the Crusaders later that year. Crusader principalities endured for two hundred years mainly because of the relative weakness and differences among their neighbors—Abbasids, Fatimids, and Saljuks. Their most long-lasting impact was to give traders from the Italian city states a firm foothold in eastern Mediterranean commerce.

The Christians' first main rivals, the atabeg Zangi of Mosul and his son Nur al-Din (d. 1174) began challenging them in the mid-twelfth century. The Fatimid khalifa enlisted Nur al-Din's aid against the Crusaders, too. The Kurdish generals sent by Nur al-Din notably Salah al-Din al-Ayyubi, ended the Fatimid caliphate and restored permanent government support of Sunni Islam in Egypt. Although Salah al-Din expanded into southern Arabia, Syria, and northern Iraq, civil wars followed his death in 1193. Turkish and Circassian "white slave" troops—*mamluks*—seized control of Egypt in 1250. The importation of such troops was a widespread phenomenon in the Middle East. Since such slaves were manumitted in the first generation, individuals continuously imported military slaves for their private armies.

The Saljuks at Konya experienced ups and downs until the Mongol attacks of 1243. In Abbasid domains, the khalifa al-Nasir (1180–1225) reasserted caliphal authority for the last time, exploiting futuwwa organizations to win support of the Shi'i in southern Iraq. When the Mongol leader Hulegu (grandson of Jingis Khan) arrived in Mesopotamia, his advisor the learned Shi'i Nasir al-Din Tusi (author of *The Nasirean Ethics*) advised him to seek an agreement with the Khalifa al-Musta'sim. The khalifa's refusal sealed the fate of the dynasty. In 1258, the Mongols defeated and killed him. Though the Mamluks in Egypt gave refuge to an Abbasid survivor after defeating the Mongols at Ayn Jalut in Palestine in 1260, no other Muslims recognized him. The Abbasid caliphate was dead.

Berber States of the Maghrib

Meanwhile, in eleventh-century northwest Africa, after Shi'i predominance had waned and the Spanish Umayyad state had collapsed, Berbers from Mali inspired by their Maghribi leader moved into Morocco and Spain. Historians call the new dynasty established by his successor the Murabitun (those of the *ribat* or fortified

---

[1] Nizam al-Mulk, *The Book of Government or Rules for Kings*. Trans. Hubert Dark. (London: Routledge and Kegan Paul), 1978.

religious retreat), known as Almoravids. Although the Murabitun lost their original zeal for a Shari'a-state advised by ulama, historians credit them with having cemented the predominance of Maliki Sunni Islam in Morocco. Their declining spiritual commitment to Islam and their excessive legalism brought on in the early twelfth century a new movement with Shi'i overtones—the Muwahhidun (Almohads) or Unitarians led initially by their charismatic Berber Mahdi, Ibn Tumart (who died in 1128). Translating the Quran into Berber, he fostered Islamic education among the masses. After again reuniting much of the Maghrib and Spain, his successors by the early 1200s had also fallen victim to ideological erosion.

Three new Berber dynasties arose in the Maghrib: the Marinids based in Fez; the Zayyanids based in Tlemcen; and the Hafsides based in Tunis. Of these, only the Hafsids were the heirs of Ibn Tumart's ideology, and they eventually abandoned it. The demise of the Abbasid khalifas in 1258 led to proclamation of a Hafsid caliphate whose religious leadership was recognized by the remaining Spanish Muslim polity, the Nasrids of Granada (1230–1492), and by other African Muslim leaders.

Between the mid-thirteenth and mid-sixteenth centuries, along with the Mamluks of Egypt, the Mongol states in Iraq-Iran, and the growing Ottoman Empire, these Berber entities constituted the main North African and Southwest Asian polities. In the absence of a universally recognized khalifa, they ceased to rely on religious authority for recognition of their legitimacy, or on religious legitimacy for recognition of their authority.

Evolution of Political Theory and Legal Systems

From the demise of the Rashidun, Muslim apologists evolved rationalizations for legitimizing authority. Influenced by Greek philosophy and Manichaeism, Mu'tazilism, a ninth-century Muslim movement, promoted the idea that Allah was a just, rational God who had given man a searching mind to exercise free will. Like man, God had to act in accordance with natural law and could not be blamed for injustice in the world. The Quran and Islamic doctrines could be subjected to rational scrutiny, too. For about fifty years until the mid-ninth century, the khalifas favored Mu'tazilism, but circa 847, the khalifa al-Mutawakkil repudiated it. The ulama then rallied around a more theologically oriented view later elaborated by the *alim* (singular of *ulama*) al-Ash'ari (d. 941). All causation was attributed to God and to Allah's justice. Although theology replaced philosophy as the focus of the Muslim mainstream, Mu'tazilism, with its emphasis on justice, remained influential in Shi'i Islam.

What does the Mu'tazilite debate tell us about the evolution of Muslim polities? First of all, the ulama at an early date functioned as potential rivals to be co-opted by rulers as allies if possible through patronage. The khalifas became associated with factionalism, and their powers eroded. Secondly, though more tolerant of speculation, Mu'tazilism, like Kharijism, could be used to justify overthrowing an unjust ruler. Ash'arism tended to support the status quo as based on Allah's will; it was used by ulama from the tenth century on to rationalize historical developments in the Dar al-Islam. Not coincidentally, the four Sunni systems of jurisprudence were consolidated at about the same time although other systems still existed.

The system of Abu Hanifa, a scholar based in Kufa and Baghdad, came to predominate in the Ottoman Empire, Central Asia, and parts of India. The Maliki system, named after Malik ibn Anas of Madina, prevailed in North and West Africa, Spain, and eastern Arabia. Al-Shafi'i, who studied in Madina but who lived mostly in Cairo (where he is buried) and Baghdad, gave his name to the system that claimed more adherents than any except the Hanafi; they are found in northern Egypt, parts of greater Syria, East Africa, and much of Arabia (though not

Saudi Arabia) India, and Indonesia. The last and most basic school was that of Ibn Hanbal. He rejected all sources of law except the Quran and Hadith. Few believers followed this system until its revival by the Wahhabis of eighteenth-century Arabia, but it was an important influence in establishing Sunni orthodoxy.

With caliphal authority in retreat and the ulama absorbed in Shari'a, the spiritual initiative in the tenth century passed to the Sufis and to the more mystically oriented Shi'is. This remained so until the ulama integrated the Sufi path along the lines favored by the Khurasanian alim al-Ghazzali (d. 1111). By 1250 scholars and Sufis, bolstered by rulers and institutions that had evolved through Islamic jurisprudence and custom, were equipped for ongoing promotion of Islam in the absence of a khalifa.

Economic Organizations and Institutions

Islamic polities had from the beginning relied on a combination of agrarian wealth, trade, and booty for their economic well-being. The early Abbasids in particular tried to create a stable environment in outlying areas so that agriculture could prosper. They maintained and developed waterworks throughout their domains. The land-tenure system that had evolved by the late tenth century encompassed four main types of property: (1) property belonging to the ruler; (2) land grants (Arabic: *iqta*; Persian: *tuyul*; Turkish: *timar*) given to military or administrative officers during their lifetimes; (3) private property; and (4) religious endowments (*waqf* or *habus*).

Peasants farmed the land on behalf of the owners or administrators. Often, tribes or clan groups also received the right to cultivate particular areas. In this way, individual peasants or groups secured cultivation rights which endured for centuries although they did not actually own or control the land.

Because demand for iqta was always expanding and therefore was threatening to private property, many Muslims put their property into waqf, theoretically making it untransferable. Since iqta reverted to the state after the holder's death, it could not be made into waqf. The family or *ahli* waqf provided heirs with the benefit of residual income. The institution of waqf resulted in the building and maintaining of numerous hospitals, mosques, and schools. Although one might assume that waqf, as inalienable property, could only expand, periodic confiscations prevented steady accumulation. A fifth type of property holding was the tax farm (*iltizam*). Agents of the state would collect taxes from cultivators in exchange for a share, but would not require military obligations. The distribution of agrarian-based wealth in Southwest Asia and North Africa periodically created disaffection among peasants and the rural working population who received such small rewards for their labor. The Zanj (black slave) movement in ninth-century Iraq has been cited as an example of an economically rooted social protest.

As the Dar al-Islam expanded, large-scale commerce continued, promoting the rapid spread of technological improvements. What did Muslims manufacture? Arts and crafts—textiles, metalwork, ceramics, glass, carpets, leatherwork, paper, perfumes, inlaid and enamel-decorated wood—flourished throughout Muslim states long before their development in non-Muslim Europe. Guilds or craft organizations evolved to protect the interests of local artisans. Public observation of the Shari'a in the marketplace was regulated by a *muhtasib* (moral police). In times of shortages or famine, the government tried to control prices to prevent gouging or hoarding, but enforcement was

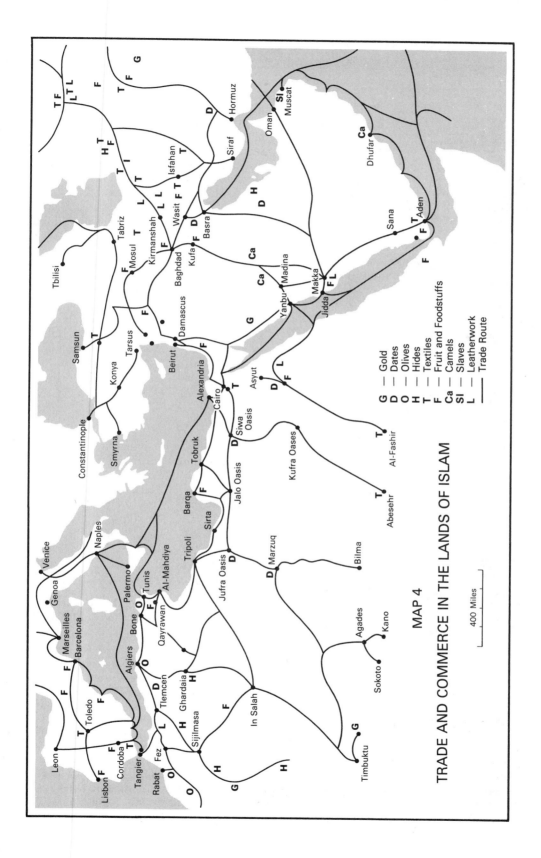

MAP 4

TRADE AND COMMERCE IN THE LANDS OF ISLAM

G — Gold
D — Dates
O — Olives
H — Hides
T — Textiles
F — Fruit and Foodstuffs
Ca — Camels
Sl — Slaves
L — Leatherwork
— Trade Route

400 Miles

generally left to the muhtasib so long as governors or rulers received the appropriate fees and taxes.

In large central markets, merchants grouped themselves by trade and constructed buildings (*wikala* or *khan*) for shops and temporary housing. Occasionally, closed markets that could be locked were built for housing luxury goods. Out-of-town merchants might reside in apartments above their rented shops in the khan. Goods from caravans were inventoried, stored, and assessed customs duties. In the countryside, rulers provided lodgings for travelers in caravansarais located on principal routes. Scholars have determined travel times and trade routes through discovery of these former stopping points. In remote areas, tribes often set up their own customs stations. Map 4 shows some of the important trade routes that crisscrossed Africa and Asia. While the Abbasid state was land-based, the Fatimids and Mamluks built up navies to control sea-borne trade. Historians have attributed Portuguese efforts to circumnavigate Africa partly to the high customs duties collected on the Red Sea by the Mamluks. The same tariffs helped to revive land routes through Persia and Syria.

Besides contributing to economic well-being, trade was also associated with the spread of plagues. In the mid-fourteenth century, the Black Death or bubonic plague spread along Middle Eastern and Asian trade routes into Europe, Western Asia, and North Africa. As in Europe, the Black Death created a labor shortage in the Middle East, especially in rural areas. But instead of leading toward a wage-labor based economy as in Europe, the shortage created movement toward agricultural feudalism. In contrast to Europe, which experienced bubonic plague with a focused impact limited in time, the Middle East continued to undergo highly infectious pneumonic plagues with such regularity that mortality was always very high. Famine and other epidemics also decimated both urban and rural populations. A somewhat feudal relationship was one way of inhibiting rural-urban migration.

The Mongol invasion of Hulegu circa 1240–1260 and the Turkish-Mongol invasion of the Muslim leader Timur Leng (Timur the Lame) beginning late in the fourteenth century have been blamed for vast destruction and renewed nomadization of the central Islamic lands. The Il-khanid Buddhist ruler Ghazan Khan, who in 1295 adopted Islam, tried to reverse the initial consequences of his people's invasion. While inter-Mongol rivalries contributed to the collapse of the Il-khanid state between 1335 and 1380, a major factor weakening the region was the onset of plague at the same time. What the Timurids found in the Middle East was an area already in decline; their invasion did not cause it. However, Timur's devastating conquests of Baghdad, Isfahan, Aleppo, Damascus, Ankara, and Smyrna left Mamluk Egypt as the Middle East's strongest polity. In the sixteenth century, the major production centers in Southwest Asia were losing the initiative to European merchant capitalists, partly because of the lack of incentives among Middle Eastern working populations.

Intellectual and Cultural Life in the Dar al–Islam: Maslaha and Patronage

The economic structure of the Dar al-Islam brought vast revenues to the rulers (often commercial and later military elites). In accordance with the concept of social welfare (*maslaha*) and the desire to leave records of their achievements, individuals endowed not only hospitals, schools, khans, and caravansarais but also intellectual endeavors of the ulama.

Education

From the outset, education occupied a premier place in Muslim communities. Its emphasis was based on a popular but not fully established Hadith that declared "Seek knowledge even unto China." The basis of education was memorization of the Quran in Arabic. Both boys and girls could also learn arithmetic, rudimentary reading, and writing. A *hafiz* (one who had memorized the Quran) could then teach others or be hired to recite on special occasions. Education took place in homes or in mosques, and was arranged privately. Higher studies in jurisprudence were required of those who would implement Shari'a. Wealthy Muslims endowed mosque-colleges (Arabic, *madrasa*; Turkish, *medrese*; North African, *medersa*). Nizam al-Mulk's Nizamiyya in Baghdad, the University of Granada, and al-Azhar in Cairo arose from such patronage. Brilliant students of jurisprudence could rise to positions of *qadi* (judge) and *mufti* (giver of *fatwas* or legal opinions on particular cases). The division of labor between qadis and muftis was an important characteristic of Muslim legal practice. In the Ottoman Empire, students may have spent six or seven years qualifying as a Friday prayer leader, fourteen years becoming a qadi, and twenty-one years preparing to be a teacher or mufti. Students did not take a degree from a corporate entity or university, as in the West, but rather received a permission (*ijaza*) from a teacher qualifying them to teach particular works. The European notions of fixed curricula, degree programs, and the university as corporation were incorporated into Muslim higher education only in the nineteenth and twentieth centuries when nation-states took over education from individual patrons.

Arabic and Islamic studies developed hand-in-hand because knowledge of Arabic was a prerequisite to Quranic education. Early Muslim scholars, such as the eighth-century grammarian Sibawayh, looked to pre-Islamic poetry to determine fine points of grammar. The Quran influenced styles of public speaking and literature. Arabic-language education is still taught as part of Islamic studies in many parts of the world. Though Islamic education as it evolved focused increasingly on law and theology, theoretically and from time to time it embraced all areas of human endeavor. We pointed out in Chapter 3 that the mystical tradition of education differed from that in mosque-colleges, though both systems relied on a teacher-pupil relationship. Sufi education, catering to the psychological needs of the masses, promoted spiritual rather than juridical knowledge. Some ulama sought both madrasa and Sufi education to enhance their Muslim experience.

Literature

Sufi and Madrasa traditions were reflected in the evolution of literature, too. After the advent of Islam, secular poetry extolling the virtues of pleasure remained, but religious and especially mystical poetry such as that of Jalal al-Din Rumi (d. 1273) and Muhiyy al-Din ibn al-Arabi (d. 1240) also developed. Elaborate phraseology and rhyme were important characteristics. In Muslim Spain, the singing of poetry led to the rise of the troubadour tradition. Tenth-century literature included collections such as the *Book of Songs* (Kitab al-Aghani) and the *Thousand and One Nights*. The two best-known Persian works of poetry are the *Shahnameh* of Firdawsi (d. 1020), viewed today as the Persian national epic but written for the Turkish ruler Mahmud of Ghazna, and Umar al-Khayyam's *Rubaiyat* (d. 1123). However, the pre–sixteenth-century poets Sa'di, Nizami, Hafiz, and Jami have equally prominent reputations among Persians.

In the fifteenth- and sixteenth-century Ottoman Empire, an imperial or *diwan* tradition developed on Persian and Arabic models, producing the *ghazal* (short lyric poem), *qasida* (long, often panegyric poem), and the multirhyming couplet *mesnevi* (used for epic, didactic poems). Among the less educated circles of society, a Turko-Anatolian tradition evolved that was more purely Turkish and more relevant to everyday Ottoman society. Its practitioners had usually studied only in a Quran school. Although local patrons occasionally recorded samples, this type of poetry remained largely oral. Finally, mystical Ottoman poetry drew from diwan and Turko-Anatolian traditions. Ulama often wrote in both mystical and diwan styles. Mystical poetry focused on love of God and spiritual ecstasy, usually in ghazal form. It offered an alternative to the rigid formality prevailing in official Muslim circles.

Prominent Intellectuals

Who were some of the intellectuals who flourished in the Muslim world during the Islamicate age? The Arab philosopher Yaqub al-Kindi (800s) was equally at home in chemistry, medicine, music and optics. Umar al-Khayyam improved on the mathematical work of al-Khawarizmi (source of the word *algorithm*) who was also a geographer. Nasir al-Din Tusi composed brilliant works in trigonometry. Through activities of Muslim scholars, many Arabic mathematical terms such as *algebra* and *cipher* entered European languages. Arithmetical tasks were simplified through use of Arabic numerals of local or Indian origin. Mathematical discoveries of Muslims were transmitted to Europe mainly through Spain and Sicily.

Ibn Sina (Avicenna) (d. 1037) along with Ibn Rushd (Averroes) (d. 1198) developed a school of philosophy using Aristotelian ideas that later influenced Thomas Aquinas (d. 1274) and other Europeans. But Ibn Sina also wrote a famous medical treatise, *al-Qanun*, which became the main source of medical knowledge in Southwest Asia, North Africa, and Europe until the seventeenth century. His work developed beyond Greek traditions of medicine that had circulated in the Umayyad period, incorporating mystical theology. Because of Sufi influences, an

even more psychologically oriented medical culture existed among slaves, peasants, and craftsmen in rural and urban areas.

Historians and geographers were also among those who found patrons in the Muslim world and influenced later scholars in Europe. One of the earliest chroniclers was al-Tabari (d. 923), whose works are still a major source for studying early Islamic history. Widespread travels of traders and scholars helped to expand geographical knowledge. Al-Idrisi (d. 1154) in Norman Sicily wrote a geographical manual while Yaqut (d. 1229) drew up compendia treating all known countries. Ibn Battuta (d. 1377) documented his journeys to East Asia.

Probably the most famous of all Muslim scholars in the Islamicate age was the historian, philosopher, and founder of modern sociology Ibn Khaldun (d. 1406). An alim and bureaucrat, he served at various times the Nasrids of Spain and all of the North African dynasties of his day, ending his career as a qadi in Mamluk Egypt. Expounding his cyclical theory of history, Ibn Khaldun concluded that ideological movements often originate with nomads desiring to purify a corrupt, urban society. But they, too, become corrupt through contact with the urban movement, thus paving the way for the emergences of new polities and movements. The basic concept binding society together is group cohesion (*asabiyya*). When it is lost, society collapses. Curious about the world around him, Ibn Khaldun used his position as Mamluk emissary to Timur to interview the Turkish Muslim leader during his invasion of Southwest Asia. Ibn Khaldun not only proposed a philosophy of history that integrated social and economic factors but also wrote the first study of the Berbers.

The involvement of ulama with all levels of society made them the principal moral and social guardians. Their importance increased after the demise of the khalifas. During the ongoing plagues after the mid-fourteenth century, ulama guided the umma to continue caring for the living and observing rituals of birth and death.

Whereas in Europe, minorities (especially Jews) were blamed and persecuted for the onset of plagues, no group was held responsible in the Middle East. The Ash'ari idea of Allah's supremacy in causation led to acceptance of plague as God's will. Even though, as in Europe, between one third to one half of the population died during the Black Death, Middle Easterners guided by the ulama held fast to communal and social values, thereby avoiding exacerbation of the crisis.

Art and Architecture

Maslaha and patronage produced the spectacular monuments of Middle Eastern art and architecture in the Islamicate age. Between 1250 and 1517, the Mamluks endowed Cairo with its most beautiful public buildings—mosques, schools, hospitals, fountains. Arches and columns were common features of mosque architecture, along with the presence of a prayer niche to show the direction of Makka. Geometric art and calligraphy developed to an elaborate plane because most Muslims viewed portraying images of humans or animals as a violation of the Quranic prohibition against idolatry. Miniature manuscript painting developed between the fourteenth and eighteenth centuries in non-Arab Muslim polities—notably the Timurids, Ottomans, and Safavids (the sixteenth–eighteenth century Shi'i dynasty in Iran). Chinese influences penetrated Muslim manuscript art. Ottoman paintings often depicted important political and military events. Travelers today can still view some of Islamdom's most prominent mosques and public buildings: the great mosque of Makka, the Dome of the Rock and al-Aqsa mosque in Jerusalem, the great mosque of Cordoba and the Alhambra at Granada in Spain, the Umayyad mosque in Damascus, the mosques of Ibn Tulun and Sultan Hasan in Cairo, the Friday and Shah mosques in Isfahan, the Qayrawan mosque in Tunisia, the Sulaymaniyya and Sultan Ahmad mosques in Istanbul, the Green Mosque in Bursa, the madrasa of Ulugh Beg in Samarkand, the mausoleum of Isma'il Samanid in Bukhara, and the most famous and recent of them all the Taj Mahal built in eighteenth-century India by the Moghul emperor Shah Jahan for his wife. One example of the relationship between building-construction, economic policies, and social crisis is Sultan Hasan's mosque college—it was funded in the 1350s by the influx of death duties arising from the Black Death.

CHAPTER FIVE

The Ottoman Age

Both the Ottoman and Shi'i Safavid states originated with Sunni Sufi brotherhoods of nomadic Turkic Muslim warriors (*ghazis*) in Anatolia. In the late thirteenth century, the Ottomans (Anglicized *Osmanli;* from Osman, the dynasty's founder) were a small Turkish confederation located east and south of Constantinople. Their earliest acquisitions were along the Asiatic coast of the Sea of Marmora. Though historians are still defining the nature of a tribe, it appears that Osman was a charismatic ghazi who rallied nomadic Turks to his leadership. *Ghazi* became the first and most important title of early Ottoman sultans.

In 1326, the Ottomans conquered Bursa, making it their capital and familial burial place. Though Adrianople (Edirne) was taken in 1361, it began functioning as the main seat of government only in the early fifteenth century after the Timurids had captured Sultan Bayezid I in Anatolia and carried him off. Campaigning mainly in Europe, the Ottomans by 1451 held more territory there than in Asia. In 1453, Mehmed II (*Fatih* or Conqueror) took Constantinople, the last major Byzantine stronghold and symbol of Eastern Orthodox Christianity. As Istanbul, it remained the Ottoman capital until 1923.

Mehmed II defeated the rival Shi'i Turkoman Ak Koyunlu (White Sheep) confederation based in Diyarbakir. This league, by virtue of its victory over the Kara Koyunlu (Black Sheep) confederation, ruled over Armenia, eastern Anatolia, the Caucasus and northwestern Iran. Allying with the Sunni Safavid brotherhood, the Ak Koyunlu made it an instrument of a mystical, eclectic Shi'ism. By 1501, from his capital at Tabriz, the Safavid leader Isma'il proclaimed himself Shah and declared Shi'ism the official doctrine of his state. Historians have attributed the rise of both the Ottomans and the Safavids to the renomadization of Anatolia, Iraq, and Iran that followed the disasters of the thirteenth–fifteenth centuries. The two polities (see Map 5) came into increasing conflict in the sixteenth–seventeenth centuries. Both states expanded and consolidated their power through adoption of gunpowder for their armies.

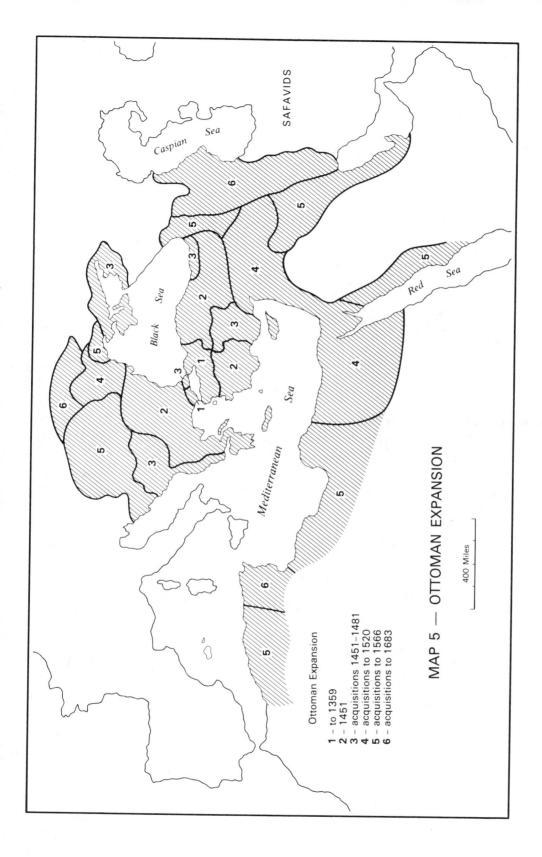

MAP 5 — OTTOMAN EXPANSION

Ottoman Expansion

1 – to 1359
2 – 1451
3 – acquisitions 1451–1481
4 – acquisitions to 1520
5 – acquisitions to 1566
6 – acquisitions to 1683

400 Miles

SAFAVIDS

Caspian Sea

Black Sea

Red Sea

Mediterranean Sea

Institutional Bases of Ottoman Power

As a ghazi state, the Ottomans strove for expansion of the Dar al-Islam. Despite the exemption of dhimmis from military service, the Ottomans developed a *Yeni Cheri* (new soldier) corps (known to Europeans as janissaries) based on previous models of non-Muslim mercenary and slave armies. The rapid expansion of the Ottoman state gave it a slave surplus. In the fourteenth century, the janissary standing army amounted to several thousand men. Besides captives, the Ottomans also instituted a collection (*devshirme*) of predominantly Greek Orthodox (Greeks, Albanians, Serbs, Bulgars) boys aged twelve through twenty. These boys were converted to Islam, given special training in Istanbul, forbidden marriage while on active duty, and attached to the person of the sultan. Parents increasingly gave up their sons willingly in hopes of future favors since bright boys could rise to the highest ranks of state administration including to the position of grand vizir, chief advisor to the sultan. Murad II (1421–51) placed the best janissaries in administrative-training classes with his own children, but it was Mehmed II who founded a palace school with a ten-year rigorous course for captured and levied boys. Studying arts, sciences, physical training, and a trade, graduates usually emerged with loyalty to both the sultan and their classmates.

Until recently, scholars judged the devshirme as having placed the state in Christian hands during its era of strength. Erosion was blamed on the entry of freeborn Muslims into the corps and administration. Historians now acknowledge that the empire was governed by a ruling class that was Ottoman rather than Christian or Muslim. The sultans themselves were representative of their subjects' ethnic diversity, as they intermarried with women from all segments of the population. The janissaries, of Christian origin, often married Muslim women after leaving active service. Freeborn Muslims of Turkish or non-Turkish origin served as advisors or as teachers in the palace school and constituted the Muslim establishment. The legal authority of the grand mufti paralleled the administrative authority of the grand vizir. The janissary corps was supplemented by a freeborn Muslim regular army of cavalry (*sipahis*), who served in exchange for land grants (*timars*) or who were sent by holders of such grants. A *za'im* (leader; plural is *zu'ama*) was a particularly large landholder responsible for provisioning more troops. High military and administrative officers of the state held iqta grants. All of the above constituted the Ottoman oligarchy which controlled, regulated, and sustained Ottoman society and government for centuries.

A second institution of importance was the Ottoman system of succession. Before the accession of Mehmed II, sultans assumed that their most able son, usually groomed in provincial governorships, would succeed them, but this practice sometimes involved bitter civil wars between rival brothers. Mahmud II authorized his successors to execute rival claimants, but this made his sons more protective of their persons. After his death, his son Bayezid II defeated his brother Jem who escaped but spent his days as a hostage of various European rulers, finally dying in Naples. Early in the seventeenth century, the sultans resorted to a system whereby the oldest members of the dynasty would be installed, but to eliminate discord they imprisoned possible successors in the palace. Instead of putting into power dynamic, experienced leaders, the new system of accession led to sultans who lacked training and who suffered from varying degrees of mental illness, dissipation, depression, or susceptibility to manipulation because of years of isolation and confinement. Their mothers, eunuchs and others living in the *harim* (women's quarters) were able to exercise great influence.

A third important Ottoman institution was the *millet* (nation) system confirmed for dhimmis by Mehmed II after his conquest of Constantinople. From the outset, pluralism was a feature of Ottoman rule. Bayezid II was to lead to Ottoman cities some 100,000 Jews expelled from Christian Spain in 1492. Mehmed II gave the chief leaders of the Greek Orthodox, Armenian, and Jewish communities authority to establish educational, religious, and cultural institutions for their respective communities, and he allowed them use of their own languages. Except in matters involving Muslims or state security and crime, these non-Muslims fell under jurisdiction of their own religious courts. Millet leaders collected taxes and paid them to the sultan. Theoretically, the religion-based autonomy of communities made Muslims a millet, too, but they were a ruling millet protected by the sultan and the Muslim religious establishment.

Zenith of Ottoman Power

The age of greatest Ottoman domination was brought about in the sixteenth century by sultans Selim I (1512–20) and Sulayman the Lawgiver (1520–66). After Jem's death, Bayezid II had pursued a more aggressive European policy, defeating a Venetian fleet at Navarino in 1499. But the Ottoman Empire faced rivals in Mamluk Egypt and in Eastern and Southern Anatolia. Bayezid II attacked Turkic dissidents in Kayseri; he also fought the *kizilbash* (or redhead, based on their red caps) supporters of Shah Isma'il. Selim I continued the anti-kizilbash campaign, killing an estimated 40,000 in 1513. Then, in August 1514, he inflicted a severe defeat on Shah Isma'il's retreating army at Chaldiran near Lake Van, thereby establishing Ottoman hegemony in eastern Anatolia and pushing the Safavids into Iran.

Egypt's Mamluks miscalculated by backing Isma'il against Selim. In 1516, using firearms shunned by the Mamluks, Selim defeated them in Syria and Palestine. Early the next year, he marched into Cairo and executed the reigning Mamluk. Although this action ended official Mamluk rule in Egypt, Mamluk influence endured to the early nineteenth century. Selim II's conquest brought him control over the holy cities of Makka and Madina and allowed him to capture the surviving Abbasid who was brought with the Prophet's standard to Istanbul. Islamic authority was transferred thus to the Ottomans, the major Muslim power in North Africa and Southwest Asia for the next four hundred years. The conquests of Selim II changed the nature of the Ottoman Empire from that of a Turkish-based ghazi state oriented toward Europe to a more broadly Islamic polity with responsibilities in the Arabic-speaking Muslim world.

Sulayman brought the empire almost to its territorial zenith (see Map 6). He consolidated Ottoman power in Southwest Asia, North Africa, the Balkans, and the Crimea, while threatening Europe's Mediterranean flanks. Campaigns in Hungary led the Ottomans to attempt seizure of Europe's gateway, Vienna. On the verge of capturing it in 1529, Sulayman had to withdraw his forces who were disgruntled by a long campaign delayed by bad weather. Not until 1683 did the Ottomans again attempt to capture Vienna, the northernmost point of penetration. Sulayman died on his seventh campaign to Hungary in 1566. Though focusing on Europe, he also achieved recognition of Ottoman authority in Asia and Africa.

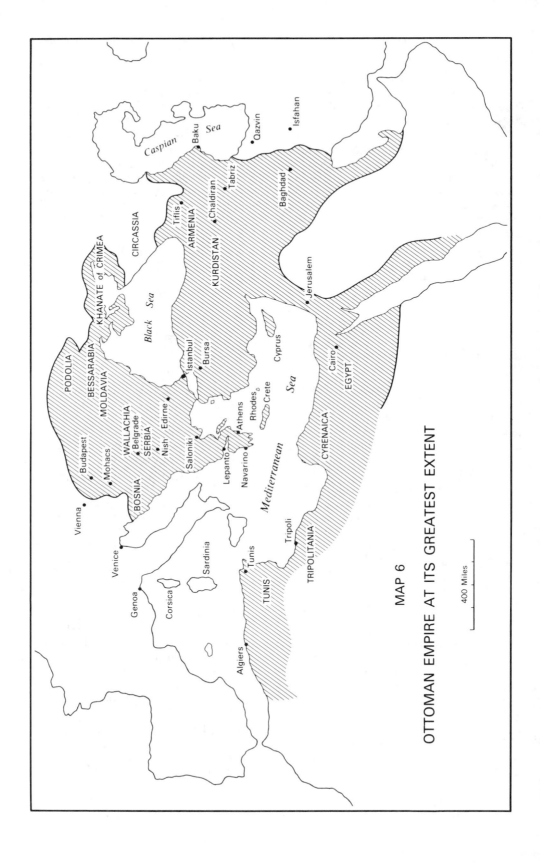

MAP 6

OTTOMAN EMPIRE AT ITS GREATEST EXTENT

400 Miles

Although he sent an army to southern Arabia in 1525, another fifty years passed before the Ottomans could establish a position in both Yemen and Aden. By the sixteenth century, the Portugese had gained such a secure foothold in the Gulf and around Africa that the extension of Ottoman power throughout the Red Sea did not lead to new trade advantages. Ottoman-Safavid rivalry brought the Ottomans a tenuous hold over Mesopotamia in the 1550s and forced the Safavids to move their capital from Tabriz to Qazvin.

Wars and boundary changes between the Ottomans and rulers of Iran on their shared frontier persisted into the nineteenth century. Between 1603 and 1623, after the Ottomans had broken the peace, the Safavid armies won back their former capital of Tabriz, parts of eastern Anatolia, and all of Mesopotamia. In 1639, though, another war forced the Safavids to return Mesopotamia and Anatolia to the Ottomans but confirmed their own hold over Azerbaydjan.

Evolution of the Safavid State

Ottoman-Safavid rivalry led to the eventual definition of Iran's present frontiers, and helped to shape the distinctive characteristics of Safavid Iran. Historians agree that in 1501, Iran was still predominantly Sunni and that the Imami (as opposed to Isma'ili) Shi'is and Sunnis coexisted in relative harmony. The Safavids turned Iran into a more militantly Shi'i polity, thereby giving themselves a dynastic identity clearly distinguished from that of fellow Turks, the Sunni Ottomans in the west, and Sunni Uzbeks in the northeast. In seeking a more orthodox Shi'i following in Iran, the Safavid rulers began patronizing the Persian ulama and bureaucracy at the expense of the Sufi Turkoman kizilbash who had brought them to power.

Both Isma'il and his son Tahmasp (1524–76) sought to erode kizilbash influence. Isma'il focused on placing more Persians in his administration, while Tahmasp imported Georgian and Circassian wives as well as slaves for the army and government service. As Sufi beliefs of the kizilbash were denigrated, Iranian Shi'ism began emphasizing the following doctrines: cursing the first three khalifas, accepting Ali as ("friend of God," acknowledging ruler's prerogative, incorporating customary law into legal practice, and imposing non-Quranic

taxes. Tahmasp's efforts to diminish kizilbash influence failed miserably. He was too weak to expropriate their lands, the basis of their economic and political power. When his non-Turkish wives tried to gain favor for their sons, the kizilbash refused to support them. Tahmasp was succeeded first by his son Isma'il II (soon poisoned after he killed all but one of his brothers) and then by his son Muhammad Khoda Banda (killed in 1587 by kizilbash). The Safavid state survived mainly because of the administrative apparatus with its three principal officers: the *vakil* (chief assistant to the ruler), the *vizir* (in charge of taxes), and the *sadr* (responsible for converting the population to Shi'ism).

The era of Safavid glory and greatness came under Khoda Banda's son Abbas I (1587–1629) who came to power when both the Uzbeks and Ottomans were threatening the frontiers. Abbas I solidified his rule through warding off external threats, strengthening political and economic structures, and avoiding religious struggles. The ideological focus that had inspired the Safavid kizilbash ghazis was dropped with this consolidation of dynastic power. Abbas' military and administrative forces included many *ghulams,* white slaves who paralleled the status of the Ottoman janissaries and the

Mamluks in Egypt. Abbas divided Iran into provinces ruled by governors responsible to him.

Early in his reign, Abbas aimed at invigorating both internal and external trade. He restored older communications networks, caravansarais, and security of roads. To encourage the silk trade, he brought a large community of Armenian silk dealers from Julfa in Azerbayjan to a new community, New Julfa, across the river from his capital at Isfahan. In exchange for tax-relief benefits and political autonomy, the Armenian merchants organized the shah's silk monopoly and from that time on constituted a significant economic and political presence in Iran. An astute observer of market trends, Abbas supported other local industries and created new ones. He brought Chinese potters to Isfahan to adjust the Persian craft to European tastes and inaugurated workshops at the court for other luxury items, notably carpets. Besides exporting raw silk, the Persians developed high-quality brocades and velvets. Enamel work, miniature paintings, engraved plates, glassware, and jewelry contributed to the fame of Persian craftsmanship. Abbas' commissioning of his mosque, pavilions, and the huge market in Isfahan promoted local artisans and led to the city's fame as *nisf-i jihan,* or *half the world.*

To promote external trade, Abbas proved amenable to negotiation of trade concessions for representatives of the British East India Company who during the seventeenth century established themselves in the Gulf, Iran, Yemen, and southern Mesopotamia. In exchange for preferential agreements, the British helped Abbas to expel the Portuguese from their base at Hormuz, guarding entry into the Gulf. Abbas then eliminated the Portuguese position on Bahrayn. By the early nineteenth century, long after Abbas' death, the British controlled maritime trade in the Gulf and frequently intervened in Gulf politics. They also began to view the lands from Mesopotamia to the east as being within the scope of Indian affairs, a perspective that had

significant consequences during World War I.

The Safavid state declined much more rapidly than did the Ottoman, partly because of Abbas' fear of potential rivals. Though they lasted another one hundred years, the Safavids' rule in the provinces deteriorated as local officials secured offices through purchase with funds extracted from peasant cultivators. Instead of investing in the economy, Abbas' successors used the money for extravagant projects. Tribal resurgence accompanied the localization of authority, and with no large standing army like that of the Ottomans, the Safavids were hard put to restore a strong central government. Decentralization prevailed.

In Kandahar, oppressive taxation policies led to revolt expressed in the form of increased Shi'i-Sunni conflict. In 1722, Sunni Afghan forces attacked and took the city of Isfahan. This precipitated an exodus of Shi'i ulama to Karbala and Najf in Iraq. This eighteenth-century development led to a debate within Shi'ism that produced the ascendancy of the mujtahids as sole interpreters of the faith. The Afghans were driven out in 1730 by a Turkoman of the Afshar tribe, Tahmasp Kuli Khan, who took the name Nadir Shah. Although he briefly restored a child of the Safavid dynasty to the throne, the dynasty ended with the child's death in 1736. From his capital at Mashhad, Nadir Shah waged war with the Moghuls of Delhi, in the course of which he carried off the famous Peacock Throne and other jewels now stored in the National Bank at Tehran. The conquest helped to compensate for the disruption of trade and continued internal resistance to oppressive taxation.

Nadir Shah failed to co-opt the Iranian ulama with a new religious policy designed to cut down on Ottoman-Iranian hostility. Dropping the cursing of the khalifas and an end to the denial of their legitimacy did not promote the absorption of Shi'ism into the Sunni mainstream. Nadir Shah had intended to retain Shi'i Shari'a as the Ja'fari system. The Ottomans, too, refused to accept a Ja'fari *madhhab.* Ottoman-Iranian religious antagonism increased, but Nadir's effort allowed for the liberation of Shi'ism from state control in Iran.

After Nadir's assassination in 1747, Karim Khan Zand emerged to bring about a measure of internal peace, but the economy remained in a state of collapse.

The ulama and mujtahids bound themselves more closely to the Iranian people, serving as intermediaries with the decentralized state. Passion plays showing the martyrdom of Husayn became more common as expressions of political dissent.

The Ottoman Expansion into North Africa

The Ottoman expansion into North Africa represented a new stage in the evolution of European-North African-Middle Eastern relations, though elements of the past still remained. A significant event was the final success of the Spanish *reconquista* at Granada in 1492, under the unified rule of Ferdinand and Isabella. Historians have attributed the long-range Spanish success to the failure of the tenth-century Umayyads to impose full Arab-Muslim rule in conquered lands; they preferred instead to preserve old feudal relationships, thereby perpetuating the power of local Christian rulers. When by the mid-thirteenth century Christian Spaniards had taken all but the small Nasrid kingdom, Christian rulers on the Iberian peninsula, especially in Aragon and Castile, continued to gain strength through playing off the Nasrids and the North African rulers (Hafsids, Zayyanids, and Marinids-Wattasids) with whom they carried on a lively trade. The Spanish Inquisition, which from the 1480s was placed directly under the united crown was related to the *reconquista,* with both aimed at imposing religious conformity and loyalty to the new Catholic Spain. Jews and Muslims converted to Christianity to avoid persecution, but suspicions about their sincerity led many converts to flee Andalusia rather than face possible death. During the sixteenth century, they and nonconverts took refuge in North Africa, the Ottoman Empire, and Egypt, practicing their Andalusian cultural traditions. The Sephardic or Spanish Jews played a

significant role there, especially in Morocco. Muslim influences persisted in Andalusia for centuries, and the European offensive against Mediterranean Islamdom, as in the Middle East after the Crusades, did not end with the Spanish *reconquista.* The combination of fear and fascination with the Muslims world continued to be an important theme in European literature. Europe's advance eventually culminated in the nineteenth and twentieth-century occupation of most of the Muslim world.

Economic warfare of the sixteenth century focused on control over Mediterranean trade as technological improvements in astronomy, navigation, shipbuilding, and warfare allowed European countries to venture farther afield. Travelers could circumvent Mamluk and later Ottoman-controlled routes while discovering new markets in the East and sources of wealth in the West. But the English and French began to challenge the Italian, Spanish and Portugese naval power for a share of Mediterranean trade. With the joining of Spain and Austria under Hapsburg monarchs, the land-based Austrian-Ottoman struggle over the Balkans could easily be extended to the Mediterranean. Often independent European, North African, and Ottoman corsairs preyed on rival ships and then collected ransoms on captives. The nonreligious character of Mediterranean warfare is clearly exemplified in the flexible, even fluid alliances arranged by European powers for advancing their individual goals. Ottoman-European collaboration was as common as Ottoman-European rivalry.

During the late fifteenth and early sixteenth centuries, Spain and Portugal took over major North African ports, centers for Mediterranean and trans-Saharan trade. North Africans organized corsairing corporations to attack Spanish and Portuguese ships. Following the conquest of Egypt, Selim I and Sulayman I secured the services of two skilled Muslim corsairs, Aruj and Khayr al-Din Barbarossa, to lead the Ottoman navy in order to protect their western flank. By placing themselves in Ottoman service, the Barbarossa brothers gained both control over a powerful navy and the prestige of the Ottoman association. With Khayr al-Din as admiral of the fleet from 1533 until his death in 1546, the Ottoman navy won Algiers, making it the principal Ottoman beylicate in the Maghrib. Tripoli became the second Maghribian governorate in 1551. Its conqueror and governor to 1565 was Dragut, a Muslim captain who had been ransomed by Khayr al-Din in 1544. Though Khayr al-Din temporarily seized Tunis from the Hafsids, the Hapsburgs of both Spain and Austria recovered it twice and restored the compliant Hafsid ruler. Only in 1574 did the Ottoman forces led by Algiers' governor Ulj Ali and the famous Ottoman architect Sinan capture Tunis and send the last Hafsid into exile at Istanbul.

Evolution of Ottoman Rule

Ottoman rule in the sixteenth-century era brought economic security and prosperity to areas that had previously been in decline. The presence of a strong central authority tended to reduce local outlays for military purposes, and security was improved along both land and maritime trade routes. The forces of Selim II, son of Sulayman, added Chios (from Genoa), Cyprus (from Venice), and firmer control over Yemen to the realm. Tax collection by the Ottomans was regularized. Sulayman I is known in Ottoman history as "the lawgiver" for having arranged the codification of law.

Socioeconomic Change

Nonruling Muslim Ottoman circles in Anatolia included peasant tenant farmers who were economically self-sufficient but responsible for supplying the government with troops and food. Historians until recently attributed the rising inflation in the Ottoman Empire and Europe to the influx of silver from the Americas. New-world bullion caused the Ottoman Empire to suffer more than Europe because Spain tried to stabilize prices by smuggling gold and silver into countries that had rates of inflation lower than its own.

Historians now give greater weight to the failure of food supplies to keep up with population increases in Anatolia. Food prices rose in the seventeenth century while rural wages remained stable. Despite the lack of resources to maintain them, both the *sipahi* and janissary corps ballooned in comparison with their former sizes. Free-born Muslims entered the corps, and janissaries were allowed to marry while on active duty. By 1600, there were second and third generation janissaries serving. The devshirme ceased temporarily in the mid-seventeenth century, was briefly revived, and finally was dropped by 1700.

Instead of being an elite force as before, united in loyalty to sultans, the janissaries became a motley assortment of married men and tradesmen focusing on outside obligations. Occasionally they lacked military training. The sipahis also suffered. With the declining value of their products, timar-holders could no longer meet their state obligations. This led to sipahi unemployment and to expropriations of peasant land. Revolts broke out in Anatolia in response to economic dislocation, exacerbated by the empire's ongoing demand for resources to fuel the military machine in Eastern Anatolia and especially in Europe.

The transfer of janissary troops to Anatolia to quell these disturbances gave some janissaries the opportunity to establish themselves as landowners. They gradually joined the local notables or *ayan* as a regional counterforce to the centrally based Ottoman bureaucracy. Decentralization became a feature of Ottoman rule as an *iltizam* system gradually replaced the timar system, giving rise as in Egypt to a class of tax-farmers who had only a financial obligation to an increasingly remote state. Growing complexity within the state increased the frequency of bribery to gain office in place of the merit-based system that had provided a strong internal foundation for the Ottoman government. Observant Ottomans criticized these developments as early as the late sixteenth century. Turkish-speaking pastoral peoples in Anatolia constituted the largest nonsettled indigenous group; they raised flocks and engaged in seasonal migrations. Nomadic groups with no fixed bases were most often Kurds.

The bearer of Ottoman authority in the provinces generally was a governor (*pasha*) appointed by the sultan for a limited time period, backed by janissaries and supported by local levies. Ottoman administrators preferred postings in the wealthier European provinces, especially those near the Danube and Maritza rivers. Governors in predominantly Christian Europe tried to establish harmonious relations with locals in order to avoid harassment. Greater involvement with the European provinces led to more rapid evolution of decentralized rule in distant parts of the empire.

In urban areas, guilds were responsible for distributing resources and raw materials, and were widespread among the crafts and professions. Historians have viewed the monopolistic character of Ottoman guilds as one reason for the erosion of Ottoman craft industries despite the sixteenth and seventeenth-century influx of Andalusians, especially Jews, who had expertise in metal and textile production. Guild pressures forced up wages, adding to inflationary pressures and making products less competitive with imports. Though Ottoman society was theoretically polygamous and male-dominated, most men could afford only one wife who then managed the household. Ottoman sultans after the sixteenth century were heavily under maternal influence due to confinement in the women's quarters or *harims*.

The Ottomans in Southwest Asia

What were the distinctive characteristics of Ottoman Southwest Asia? The main local authority in southern Syria was the Druze family of Fakhr al-Din Ma'an (1590–1635). His castle above Tadmur in central Syria still stands. From the seventeenth–nineteenth centuries, the Shihabi family dominated political life. Officially amirs of the Druze, these Sunni Muslims became Maronite Christians in the nineteenth century, thereby effecting a balance-of-power shift in the Lebanon. Alliances, as elsewhere, did not always coincide with religious affiliation. Aleppo and Damascus also took on the appearance of city-states, although they were still under Ottoman hegemony. Power in Aleppo was contested between the *ashraf* or sharifs (notables descended from Muhammad) and the janissaries. In early eighteenth-century Damascus, where the al-Azm family predominated, the Ottomans attempted to restore centralized rule. The Azms were co-opted as Ottoman governors.

A major duty of governors in Damascus was to organize the annual Western Asian pilgrimage caravan to Makka. This required careful tax collection as well as the making of arrangements for security and provisions. Gifts for the Hashimite sharifs ruling Makka and for the poor

Ottoman International Relations to the Mid-Eighteenth Century: Ottoman Europe

In both the seventeenth and eighteenth centuries, the European pressure almost constantly placed the Ottoman Empire at war or in danger of war. The first five sultans of the seventeenth century died before reaching the age of thirty-five. During this period, leaders relied heavily on officials such as the historian Kochu Bey who even told Ibrahim (1640–48) the kind of clothing to wear. After mid-century, Ottoman strength was renewed under the firm leadership of vizirs from the Köprülü family. In this period, Ottoman reformers attributed ills of the state to disintegration of old institutions rather than to changing world realities that would require substantial restructuring of state, economy, and society. The first of the Köprülüs, Mehmed (1656–61) physically eliminated some 30,000 officials for misconduct in affairs of state, hoping to end corruption and mismanagement. His son Ahmad (1661–76) followed in his footsteps. Sultan Mehmed IV (1648–87) remained fairly steadfast in supporting the Köprülüs. In 1663, the army under Ahmad's leadership moved north against the Hapsburgs but lost the Battle of St. Gothard. The island of Crete was finally conquered in 1669. Ottoman armies in the 1670s forced the Poles to agree to cede the Ukraine and Podolia and to pay annual tribute. Ahmed Köprülü was succeeded in 1676 by Kara Mustapha, who led the last Ottoman campaign against Vienna in 1683. After failing to take the city, the Ottomans between 1683 and 1689 faced Venetian attacks against their possessions in present-day Greece (the Venetians damaged the Parthenon). Armies of the Hapsburgs took Budapest. Due to these losses, Mehmed IV stepped down as sultan in favor of his brother Sulayman II (1687–91) who had spent most of his life confined in the palace. Sulayman II, after more losses in what is now Yugoslavia, called on Ahmed Köprülü's brother Mustafa who recouped them. In the Muslim Crimea, however, Peter the Great of Russia defeated the Ottoman defenders despite the renewed zeal of Ottoman leadership under sultan Mustafa II (1695–1703).

Mustafa appointed yet another Köprülü, Husayn, as grand vizir. The Ottomans were quickly caught up in European squabbles preceding the War of Spanish Succession (1701–14). The English hoped to take the Ottomans away from war with the Austrian Hapsburgs so that the latter could defend the Hapsburgs in Spain. In Ottoman-European negotiations, Husayn agreed to the presence of nations that had not been involved in the wars, thereby acknowledging the interest of nonbelligerents in Ottoman affairs. This was to be a harbinger of the future conduct of Ottoman-European relations.

The Peace at Karlowitz

In a peace conference held at Karlowitz in 1699 each power was allowed to keep territories already in its possession. Much of the negotiation was carried on through Ottoman Greek translators. Because of the concern of the European conferees—Austria, Britain, the Netherlands, Poland, Venice, and Russia—the Ottoman sultan was obliged to make a special point of promising to protect Christians in his empire. Thereafter, Europeans used the issue of Christian minorities as a pretext for intervention.

Probably the greatest impact of the treaty was psychological. Europe, after many decades of warfare against Ottoman invaders, had taken the offensive at the expense of the empire. The territorial extent of the Ottoman Empire, after it reached its height in the 1690s, had begun what was to be a more or less irrevocable but slow attrition. With the uncertain condition of the Ottoman army, territorial integrity was a tribute to the institutions and individuals who believed in their state and did what they could to preserve it in the face of growing determination on the part of individual European nations to destroy it. Inter-European rivalries prevented a more concerted effort.

Military Modernization

Some Ottoman rulers of the seventeenth and eighteenth centuries recognized the need for Ottoman military modernization to keep up with technological change in Europe and to counteract the scarcity of tin that put Ottoman armaments factories at a disadvantage. Osman II (1618–22) provoked a janissary revolt by trying to create a new army. All Ottoman rulers after 1703 employed European military advisors because of a perceived need for military modernization.

Educational improvement was sought through book printing, initially by minorities. Jewish refugees from Spain had circa 1493 introduced the first press. Like the later presses of the Armenians (1567) and Greeks (1627), it could not print books in Arabic or Turkish. However, during the reign of Ahmed III (1703–30)—an age recognized for modernization—the grand mufti issued a fatwa allowing the printing of nonreligious books (history, geography, mathematics, and others) in Turkish. From 1729 to 1742, the press printed seventeen books, including a Turkish grammar in French. Though shut down from 1742–84, it led to the development of not only books but also newspapers. The decision to distinguish nonreligious from religious works represented a recognition by ulama of a division between religious and secular subjects, preceding by years the French Revolution which some historians have credited with introducing secularism and openness to technological change.

Ahmed III's awareness of the need for reform, especially in military matters, was heightened by Russian and Austrian offensives during much of his reign. At Pruth in 1711, the victorious Ottoman army passed up a chance to annihilate the Russian army under Peter the Great, though Crimean losses were regained by the victory. The Ottoman armies then recovered parts of Greece ceded to Venice at Karlowitz and began to challenge the Austrians with raids along the Adriatic. The Austrians reacted to the Ottoman victories by moving against Ottoman possessions around Belgrade. In the Treaty of Passarowitz of 1718, Austria gained what it had conquered, but the Ottomans kept their own Venetian conquests. After Russia and Austria launched a combined attack during the reign of Mahmud I (1730–54), the Treaty of Belgrade (1739) ensued. The Ottomans recovered Belgrade, lost in 1718, but gave Russia permission to trade on Ottoman ships in the Black Sea. Finally, the Ottomans entered a period of quiescence that was not broken until 1768.

Rise of the Sa'dians and Alawis in Morocco

Morocco never came under Ottoman rule. New leaders (the Sa'dians), claiming Sharifian descent and aided by zawiya-based holy men, launched a jihad in 1511 against the Portuguese base at Agadir. By the mid-1540s their efforts to chase out the Portuguese in Agadir and Safi met with success. The early Sa'dians adopted a policy of confrontation with the neighboring Ottomans who sided with the weak but still reigning Wattasids at Fez. The first Sa'dian ruler, Muhammad al-Shaykh, finally defeated his rivals in 1554, and then moved the capital to Marrakish. The aggressive anti-Ottomanism of the Sa'dians brought about the ruler's assassination in 1557 by Ottoman agents. His successors continued his policies but without unanimity. The pro-Ottoman Abd al-Malik deposed his nephew Muhammad al-Mutawakkil who fled first to Spain and then to Portugal. With aspirations of his own in Morocco, the Portuguese ruler Sebastian backed Muhammad against Abd al-Malik, sending a huge army into Morocco.

At the Battle of the Three Kings or al-Qasr, all three rulers died, leaving Abd al-Malik's brother Ahmad al-Mansur (*the victor*) with a huge booty obtained from spoils and ransoms. This booty was to provide the basis for Sa'dian wealth during Ahmad's reign (1578–1603). A period of Ottoman-Moroccan tranquillity began.

Europeans sent ships to Morocco's ports, hoping to borrow or share in Ahmad's riches through trade. Purchasing guns and the services of mercenaries, Ahmad raised an army that with superior weapons easily conquered the Songhai of present-day Mali and Mauritania in 1591, giving him control of salt mines and gold in the western Sudan. This is among the historical developments that account for recurrent Moroccan claims to Saharan territory. Though early Moroccan governors remitted slaves as well as profits, the wealth did not compare with that gained at Ahmad's accession. This unearned money led Ahmad to neglect taxation. The decaying of his military power led his governors in Sudan to stop forwarding tribute. He also lost the British sugar trade to Brazil through refusal to grant special trading privileges.

Ahmad is generally credited with establishing a central government system, the *makhzen* (literally, *treasury*), whose rules and structure endured to the twentieth century. After his death, two of his sons divided his kingdom, ruling at Fez and Marrakish as Sa'dian power waned. Regional authorities, with their own sources of arms, took over effective control. Subsequent Moroccan rulers encountered difficulty in perpetuating their control outside major cities. Tensions between the *blad al-makhzen* (areas under government control) and *blad al-siba* (areas of dissidence) were to characterize modern Moroccan history.

In the mid-seventeenth century, the Alawis—charismatic Sharifians who still rule Morocco—easily triumphed over the Sa'dian principalities. Their greatest early ruler was Isma'il (1672–1727) a half-Black who based his regime on a strong makhzen and on an army of descendants of black slaves whose training was like that of the early Ottoman janissaries. With makhzen unity and the ensuing social stability, people prospered and had adequate food despite high taxes. Isma'il built up his capital at Meknes, with a special quarter for Jews outside the city, but Fez remained important for northerners. Lacking his charisma, few of his successors could hold the country together.

European Resurgence and the Middle Eastern Response: Militarization and Centralization

Between the sixteenth and mid-eighteenth centuries, the balance of power between Europeans and the rest of the world shifted in Europe's favor. While the population of the Middle East in the sixteenth century was increasing by perhaps 40 percent, that in Europe doubled to reach an estimated 100 million. The discovery of new territories, the importation of mineral wealth, and rising demands for food affected Europe as well as Southwest Asia and North Africa. Europe's location and its possession of fertile land gave it an advantage in developing industry and trade. Recent research indicates that New-World silver followed not only a west-east route but also an east-west route though the Spanish Philippines to India and China. European efforts to control East and South Asia as well as other lands should be viewed at least partially in this context.

In the seventeenth century, it was the Dutch Republic that derived the greatest benefit through provision of credit and banking facilities, control over the Baltic grain trade and fisheries in Newfoundland, its inroads into Latin American commerce, its expertise in shipbuilding and trade, and its offering of religious freedom to persecuted minorities. Dutch prosperity, fueled by the successes of the Dutch East India and West India Companies, led to war with England and France. Although the Thirty Years War (1618–48) involving nearly every continental European power temporarily invigorated trade, international commercial activity declined thereafter. Most nations then turned to mercantilism, a system in which the state regulated trade to expand exports while restricting imports. By the end of the War of Spanish Succession in 1714, Dutch commercial supremacy had disappeared. In the eighteenth century, Britain became supreme in international trade.

Several developments seem to have influenced Southwest Asian and North African history. Included among them were the rise in European demand for tropical products such as sugar, coffee, cocoa, and tobacco; the growth of finance and shipbuilding; the establishment of colonies in the Americas; the early Industrial Revolution; the founding of trading bases in Asia and Africa; and perhaps most important, the extremely profitable, largely British-controlled slave trade that promoted the development of sugar and cotton plantations in the Americas.

As trade expanded, European nations moved away from mercantilism and toward free trade. With their ability to exercise more control, most of it informal, over their trading outposts overseas, European nations could build up large industries based on competition, capitalism, and the supply of inexpensive raw materials from overseas. It was capitalism that contributed most to the alteration of European economic relations with North Africa and Southwest Asia.

Capitalism is a mode in which the owner or owners of the means of production are not the laborers who make the products. Commodity exchange, wage labor, and the generation of profits for the owner(s) characterize capitalism, with people regarded primarily as a labor force. State capitalism—a system found in contemporary Southwest Asia and North Africa (especially in the 1960s)—replaces individual or private ownership with state ownership, and private decision-making with state planning. Determination of prices and wages, however, remains the same; the goal is still to maximize profits by reducing production costs, thereby permitting the accumulation of capital.

In capitalism, the production of goods for consumption is closely linked to the production of the products required for making these goods. Whereas capitalism developed in milieu in which the state could choose to regulate capital and labor in order to achieve some measure of equilibrium, the rise of transnational corporations in the twentieth century has created a new situation in which production of a single product may take place under corporate sponsorship in different countries, while labor and capital remain within the jurisdiction of national governments.

Eighteenth-century western Europe was characterized not only by industrial growth but by an improvement in agricultural technology and the expansion of land under cultivation (this led to greater crop yields). The pace of population growth accelerated with the increased food supply, better health and nutrition, and a general rise in prosperity, but eventually population increases surpassed food availability. Demand for manufactured goods also rose, providing an additional impetus for newly expanding textile industries, especially in northern Europe. Cotton and silk, which began to make inroads into wool production, were factors in the improvement of health because these materials were easier to keep clean.

The largest state in Europe from 1500 on was Russia, but this nation did not challenge the Ottoman Empire until the eighteenth century. The principality of Moscow had in the fifteenth and sixteenth centuries made alliances with the various Mongol confederations, and the government took on trappings of Byzantine rule. The demise of Constantinople in 1453 led to the rise of a Russian Orthodox Church whose first patriarch took office in 1589. The emergence of this Church as separate from the Middle Eastern Greek Orthodox led to the idea of Moscow as the "third Rome," just as Constantinople had been the "second Rome." In the seventeenth century, Peter the Great brought the Church under supervision of a council chaired by a state-appointed layperson. Russian diplomacy in the Ottoman Empire referred increasingly to the protection of Ottoman Orthodox Christians and to control of the holy places in Palestine, especially Jerusalem. The main architects of Russia's land and sea military might were Peter the Great (1672–1725) and

Catherine the Great (1762–96). Funds were provided by a successful mercantile policy that increased the value of Russian exports.

Rise of Capitulations in Southwest Asia and North Africa

While Europe practiced mercantilism, the Ottoman Empire provided readily accessible though regulated markets by extending and expanding commercial and other extraterritorial privileges later known as *capitulations*. Bayezid I (1389–1402), Mehmed I (1402–21), and Murad II (1421–51) concluded agreements with a few Italian city-states, among them Venice and Genoa. By the time of Selim I, Hungary and the Knights of St. John in Rhodes were also among the signatories.

In general, these treaties allowed the Europeans concerned to send representatives to Istanbul. Each representative was given limited travel and residence privileges in other cities of the empire. The representative was allowed to settle all cases involving his nation's citizens. The Ottomans promised to treat such citizens fairly in cases that involved Ottomans or that concerned criminal offenses. A treaty with Hungary in 1503 stated that other states could be included as long as each nation's sovereign agreed to the terms. The intention of such treaties was to provide means of legal treatment for Christians who were not Ottoman subjects.

Much has been made of a commercial treaty between Sulayman I and Francis I of France in 1536 following an alliance (1535) between the two. This treaty with France was not a great departure from previous treaties, and indeed, the French did not actually ratify it. Its real significance lay in the fact that of all the nations with whom the Ottomans had contracted treaties previously not one was destined to become a lasting power in Europe. The treaty with France, reaffirmed in 1569, 1581, 1597, 1604, and 1673, began a rivalry among the larger powers of Europe. Husayn ibn Ali of Tunis made treaties with not only the French but also with England, Spain, Holland, and Austria. In 1740, the French signed a much longer treaty with the Ottomans, allowing for far greater European penetration into the affairs and lands of the Ottoman Empire.

Consisting of eighty-two articles, it exempted French subjects from all taxation except for a 3 percent export and import duty. Frenchmen could be arrested by Ottoman officers only in the presence of a French consul. Through the treaty, the French extended their protection over Roman Catholics within the empire. French clergy were free to build new churches and had special privileges in the Holy Land. Through French actions, independent churches such as that of the Maronites in Lebanon recognized the authority of the Pope in Rome but retained their own hierarchies. The French and other nations that had special clauses in their treaties were also allowed to sell special papers called *barats* to indigenous Ottoman subjects, thereby giving them the same trading privileges and legal immunity as foreigners. Eventually, much of the trading activity within the empire was excluded from Ottoman control, and many non-Muslims had come under the protection of foreign powers.

The 1535–36 agreements with the Ottomans led Henry VIII of England to strengthen his sources of information about the Ottoman Empire. He was interested in economic and political rapprochement. Only in the 1580s, though, did the English Levant Company (which, however, fell apart early in the eighteenth century) succeed in obtaining a commercial agreement similar to that of the French. British-French commercial rivalry continued after the treaty of 1740 and culminated in the Seven Years War, with Britain emerging victorious in India and parts of the Americas in 1763. The Mediterranean contacts that France had been developing for years began to absorb far more of France's attention. The extravagances of Louis XIV and frequent warfare contributed to social and economic disintegration. By the 1780s, France's agricultural decline and the need for grain made Egypt a significant source of foodstuffs. As early as 1774, French merchants asked their government to occupy Egypt in order to control the trade of Sudan, too. The success of French merchants in penetrating the Egyptian market thus produced important social, economic, and political ramifications in Egypt, the Ottoman Empire, and elsewhere in Europe.

The ascendancy of European economic penetration leading to political interference was the crucial factor that in the second half of the eighteenth century altered the relations of the Ottoman Empire with the population of its hinterlands in North Africa and Southwest Asia. In Ottoman domains, trade became more firmly consolidated in the hands of Christians and Jews, who were often under foreign protection, and who then demanded a political role commensurate with their economic power. It was in the name of capitulations that almost the entire world was conquered by western Europe, from China through Africa and throughout the Muslim world. In the mid-nineteenth century, these privilages served as the *casus belli* for the Crimean War. Yet, from the sixteenth through the mid-eighteenth centuries, such consequences seemed rather remote and unlikely. Southwest Asia and North Africa remained remarkably strong and stable in an era of aggressive European expansion. Commercial treaties constituted part of the normal conduct of international relations.

Consolidation of the New International Order and Its Impact in the Middle East

European interference in Ottoman affairs grew in the second half of the eighteenth century. Under Catherine II, Russia made an alliance with Austria that resulted in the partition of Poland. Fearing further expansion in his direction and despite lacking adequate preparation, the Ottoman sultan Mustafa III (1757–74) decided to fight the Russians. His army was unprepared for the task, though his European military advisor Baron de Tott shored up the capital's defenses before the Russians could attack there. The Russians were induced to forego further conquest of Ottoman territory in exchange for a tripartite partition of Poland, an action that had great consequence for the nineteenth-century rise of Zionism.

In the peace treaty signed at Kuchuk Kaynarja in 1774, Russia received broad powers of interference in the Ottoman Empire, including the privilege to construct a new church in Istanbul, the right to advise the sultan on matters pertaining to Christians in the empire, and the right to station diplomatic representatives wherever the czar deemed it appropriate. Russian pilgrims were given unhindered access to the holy sites of Palestine. Moreover, having freed navigation on the Danube, Russia was allowed to represent populations there as well as in Bessarabia.

The Muslim Crimean Tatars, however, remained under Ottoman religious authority despite their political incorporation into the Russian state—they were the first Muslims ceded to European Christian control, with the full annexation of the Crimea coming in 1783.

Russia and Austria continued to plan the dismantling of the Ottoman state. They included the major interested European parties in their machinations, intending to give Egypt and Syria to France. Austria would gain most of present-day Yugoslavia while a large section of Greece as well as Crete and Cyprus would revert to Venetian control. Russia aimed to reconstitute the old Byzantine Empire. To achieve these goals, Austria and Russia again went to war against the Ottomans. At Sistova, the Austrians concluded a peace with the Ottomans that changed nothing while the Russians at Jassy in 1792 slightly extended their boundary. The partition plans exemplified a radical change in European perspectives of the Muslim world, for the Ottoman Empire formerly had been regarded with awe. Europeans assumed that their own resurgence was indicative of the superiority of Christianity and of European culture.

European Pressure on Ottoman North Africa

European activity had broad consequences in Ottoman domains. Pressures of plague, civil disturbances, and corsair crimes led the population of Ottoman Tripolitania to demand restoration of direct Ottoman rule during the latter years of the Qaramanli "golden age" under Ali Qaramanli (1754–93). The Qaramanlis temporarily preserved their status through gifts and support from the neighboring Husaynids. Yusuf Qaramanli (1795–1832) entered into new disputes with European governments and the United States over payment of tribute; his actions led to the birth of the U.S. Navy and Marines. Alawi rulers in Morocco coped with European and Ottoman

pressures by accommodating their demands but trying to restrict foreign activities to coastal cities. Europeans managed to bypass Moroccan officials, though, and exerted considerable influence on the interior, gaining access to Moroccan produce and supplying local *qa'ids* (leaders) with modern arms. Quite possibly the combination of the Napoleonic wars, the wave of Muslim expansion that established the powerful Sokoto Caliphate in northern Nigeria, and the penetration by European coastal traders also rerouted some former trans-Saharan trade, including the slave trade, to the coast of West Africa. A more modest salt and hide trade continued on the old routes.

Mamluk Centralization in Egypt

Egypt's Mamluks re-established a strong central government from the mid-eighteenth century. They viewed commercial contacts with Europeans favorably. Extracting high bribes and taxes from merchants and traders, Mamluk policies harmed indigenous Muslim traders more than they did foreigners and minorities protected by capitulations. Many independent craftsmen found themselves forced into wage labor. Significant segments of the population turned to religious brotherhoods for psychological support and social and economic protest. To avoid incurring the wrath of the rulers, ulama concealed social protests in glosses on old texts.

The first eighteenth century Mamluk to insert his own name into the Friday prayer (thus emphasizing his autonomy from the Ottomans) was Ali Bey al-Kabir (*the Great*) who ruled from 1760–73. Though briefly overthrown in 1766–67, and though he had a reputation for ruthlessness, Ali Bey tried to restore Egypt's former Syrian empire. Even when he supposedly helped the Ottomans by restoring their authority in the Hijaz port of Jidda, he appointed as officials men loyal to him.

In January 1772, Ali Bey exiled and tried to murder his own Mamluk general and brother-in-law Muhammad Bey Abu al-Dhahab, who had suddenly withdrawn Egypt's troops from Syria. The popular Abu al-Dhahab, though, overthrew Ali Bey and then defeated him in battle. Ali Bey died later from wounds received there and was respectfully buried by his Mamluk. Abu al-Dhahab renewed allegiance to the Ottoman Empire but at the same time more firmly established his autonomy. He died in 1775 while invading Palestine to suppress the ruler of Akka and its hinterland, Zahir al-Umar al-Zaydani (1693–75). Zaydani, originally from Tiberias, had been the dominant figure of eighteenth-century Palestine, ignoring financial obligations to Ottoman governors based in Damascus and Sidon. Zaydani had restored just government and economic prosperity but had backed Ali Bey and the Russian Baltic fleet that had tried to incite revolts in the Levant against the Ottoman Empire.

After Abu al-Dhahab's sudden death, his own mamluks Murad and Ibrahim struggled for power with one Isma'il Bey. After 1784, these two beys ruled Egypt jointly, resisting the obligatory payment of tribute to the Ottomans. Egypt became their personal tax farm, and they continued to pursue trading policies that excluded Egyptians from control of foreign trade. Moreover, the export of foodstuffs exacerbated local shortages caused by low Nile floods early in the 1780s. Popular discontent became evident in 1785–86.

The Ottoman sultan learned about developments in Egypt from Ali Bey's former mamluk, Ahmad al-Jazzar (*the butcher*), governor of Syria who gave him a solicited report. Jazzar concluded that misrule and tyranny in Egypt were so severe that Egyptians would rally to the support of any Ottoman army. Based on his recommendations, the Ottomans sent exploratory forces to Gaza and Ramla, ostensibly to quell the revolt by Zahir al-Umar's sons. The full July 1786 expedition met with an enthusiastic reception from Egyptians as well as mamluks. Ibrahim and Murad had to flee to upper Egypt. Because of a new war with Russia in October 1787, however, the Ottoman troops were forced to leave Egypt before having captured the rebels. After the Ottoman appointee, the beys' rival Isma'il died in 1791, Murad and Ibrahim returned to Cairo and re-established their rule over Egypt. They were still in power when Napoleon's army invaded in 1798.

The Impact of the Napoleonic Wars in the Middle East

The Napoleonic wars from 1792 to 1815 engulfed virtually all of Europe, including the Ottomans, and influenced developments worldwide. The wars helped American colonists in North and Latin America break free from the colonial powers of Britain, Spain, and Portugal, but they also made Britain Europe's strongest power, based on its formidable navy and colonial wealth. Britain expanded into southern Arabia and the Gulf, initially establishing a base at Perim, a small island off the coast of Aden. Because of poor conditions there, the British sought and obtained permission of Aden's ruler, the sultan of Lahej, to set up a mainland base. Then they pressured the sultan of Oman, a major Gulf and East African power, to cease dealing with the French until the conclusion of the wars. Eventually the British extended a protectorate over most Gulf and Red Sea rulers. Through the East India Company, the British curtailed piracy (caused by the same forces that led to Mediterranean corsairing) originating in Bahrayn and Oman. Local rulers managed to retain a large measure of internal independence because British strategic and commercial interests focused on Arabia's coasts.

France Occupies Egypt

Considering European involvement in the world market, the fact of widespread economic disruption during the wars was no surprise. Bread riots in France in 1788 and 1789 preceded the French Revolution. The wars of the 1790s began cutting France off from world trade. The takeover of Venice's Ionian Islands in 1797 brought France close to its Ottoman allies but was not a major factor in the French decision to invade Egypt. A good harvest in 1793 brought grain prices down. Thus, when Ibrahim Bey cooperated in 1794 with British boycotts against French grain merchants, one such merchant complained to the French government. The French Directorate, in power from 1795, considered this protest in deciding to send an expedition to Egypt to set up a colony that would secure French food supplies. Napoleon, aiming perhaps at creating an oriental empire such as that of Alexander the Great, also hoped to block Britain's communications with India.

The extent of French colonization plans is further substantiated by the presence on their expedition in 1798 of archeologists, architects, chemists, engineers, historians, and mathematicians. Plans were formulated to build a canal across the Suez Isthmus to promote designs in India. The French invasion ensued as a consequence of Egypt's incorporation into the world market, not as a prelude to it. The later policies of Muhammad Ali represented continuity with the past rather than a break with it.

The invasion of Egypt began at Alexandria. Within a few weeks, the French force had defeated the atrophied Mamluk army in the Battle of the Pyramids at Giza (see Map 7). Again, the Mamluk rulers escaped to Upper Egypt where they organized resistance. The French then invaded Palestine but failed in their attack on Akka due to a spirited defense led by Jazzar and Ottoman troops of the new-order (*nizam al-jadid*) military force founded by Selim III (1789–1807). They had accompanied a British force sent to defend the city against the French. It was part of Selim III's attempt at a more comprehensive restructuring of the empire. After the British admiral Nelson destroyed the French fleet at Abuqir near Alexandria (at the Battle of the Nile) on 1 August 1798, the French force was stranded in Egypt. Napoleon left his deputy Kleber in Egypt and escaped via Syria to France, apparently gaining provisions on the way from Tripoli's Qaramanlis.

In Egypt, the French claimed to be both saviors of Islam and liberators. They appealed to al-Azhar's ulama, hoping to influence the general population to support the occupation and revolt against the Mamluk aristocracy. Stranded by Nelson's victory, French forces needed to find suitable allies and revenues to maintain their position. They instituted more efficient tax collection and even raided waqf revenues. French soldiers disrupted caravans from the Sudan. Instead of making allies, the French alienated the Egyptians. Only a small but significant elite was influenced positively by French economic policy, political and administrative institutions such as governing councils, and the idea of an Egyptian rather than an Ottoman identity. Few Egyptians read the materials printed on their Arabic presses.

The long-range significance of the invasion was that European attention was drawn to Egypt. French academicians prepared the multivolume *Description de l'Egypte* that remains a major source of information. Scholars also unearthed a tablet (later called the Rosetta Stone) near the town of Rashid (Rosetta). It provided the key to understanding Egyptian hieroglyphic writing and revived not only European interest but also Egyptian curiosity about ancient Egypt. The invasion, in the context of growing Russian imperialism directed southward toward British possessions in Asia, also aroused British suspicions about France's intentions in Egypt. On the whole, however,

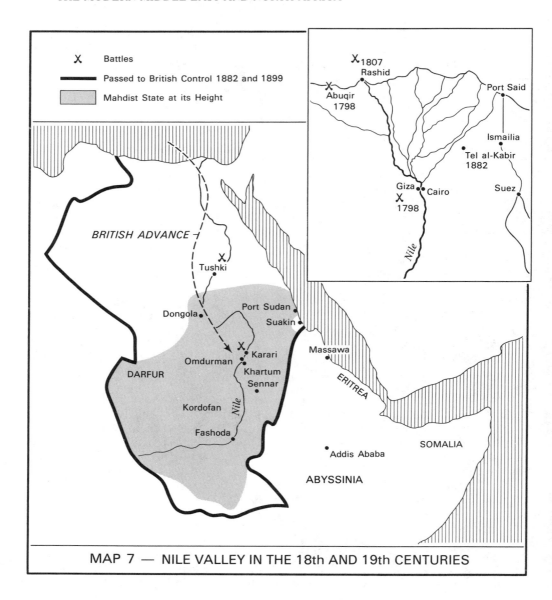

X	Battles
▬	Passed to British Control 1882 and 1899
▨	Mahdist State at its Height

X 1807
Rashid
Port Said
X
Abuqir
1798
Ismailia
Tel al-Kabir
1882
Giza • Cairo   Suez
X
1798
Nile

BRITISH ADVANCE ⌐

X
Tushki

Port Sudan
Dongola •   Suakin

X
Omdurman • X Karari   Massawa
DARFUR   Khartum
Sennar   ERITREA

Kordofan   Nile

Fashoda   SOMALIA

• Addis Ababa

ABYSSINIA

MAP 7 — NILE VALLEY IN THE 18th AND 19th CENTURIES

the expedition represented only a brief disruption of Egyptian society. It undermined but did not destroy the power of the Mamluks. The coming of a combined Ottoman-British force into this unstable atmosphere in August 1801 provided the opportunity for the assumption of authority by Muhammad Ali who had arrived with an Ottoman force in 1799 and was to rule for over forty years. The French occupation ended in 1802, and the British invaders left the following year. French political influence in the Ottoman Empire waned, though amicable French-Ottoman relations were restored except for brief periods. The Congress of Vienna in 1815 inaugurated the *pax Britannica* that prevented full-scale though not local wars from breaking out in Europe until World War I.

Introduction of New Orders in Southwest Asia and North Africa

The rise of Muhammad Ali in Egypt was preceded by two other Middle Eastern developments of later consequence. In the Ottoman capital, Selim III's new order was accompanied by efforts to renovate the Janissary corps. He introduced improved weapons and training, supervision of pay, and a new militarily capable hierarchy. With this updated military program, the Ottoman armies should have been able to meet external threats, but the janissaries resented the new force and refused to serve in the field with its members. The new soldiers were wiped out in a coup d'état carried out against Selim III in 1807. But the way charted by Selim was not ignored. After his deposition and replacement by Mustafa IV (1807–08), supporters tried to restore him to the throne. He was killed before they could succeed. Thus, the only remaining Osmanli, Mahmud II (1808–39), became sultan; he was to proceed cautiously with recentralization and rejuvenation of the Ottoman state. Introduction of new orders was to be a major characteristic of nineteenth-century Southwest Asian and North African rule from Iran to Morocco.

The Wahhabi Movement: Internal Islamic Revitalization

The second development was the rise in mid–eighteenth-century east and central Arabia of the Wahhabi movement. Taking its name from a religious reformer Muhammad ibn Abd al-Wahhab (1703–92), the Wahhabis aimed to purify Arabia and to restore Islam on the Hanbali model. Opposed to Sufism and other additions to Islamic practice, they wanted to return to the early Islam of the Quran and its traditions. Rather than being a response to European culture or penetration, the Wahhabi movement was indicative of an internal dynamic of periodic revitalization that characterized Islam from the outset. Wahhabi ideology and the movement itself inspired Muslims in many parts of the Middle East and North Africa to re-examine their societies on the basis of Islamic criteria at that time. The idea of rigorous purification, as distinct from its manifestation in the modern Saudi state, remains central to the contemporary Islamic movement. Abd al-Wahhab's ideas were adopted by a tribal leader Muhammad ibn Sa'ud (see also Saud) from whom the name of present-day Saudi Arabia is derived. Early in the nineteenth century, leaders of this religio-political movement led their forces to attack Baghdad, Damascus, and Aleppo. They also occupied the holy cities of Makka and Madina. At the same time, then, that Southwest Asian and North African governments were turning to westernization, exemplified by their hiring of foreign consultants and their adoption of Western models, Arabians isolated from European penetration sought a purely Islamic remedy to contemporary problems.

National Formation and Imperialism

Today the idea of a nation as a fixed territorial entity based on a common history, symbols, language, and ethnicity (or *race*) is commonly accepted, although many formerly colonized countries are beset with problems arising from the fact that colonial boundaries ignored these shared bases. In the nineteenth-century Middle East, locality, family, religion, and perhaps linguistic group were more important identities. Though government policy affected peoples' lives, they did not choose their leaders and were subjects with obligations to their rulers rather than to states. The nation-state idea gave rise to the transformation of national consciousness—the awareness of being a distinct people—into nationalism, the desire for the political independence of a group, usually in a specific territory. Germany and Italy came into being only in the mid-nineteenth century, although "Germans" and "Italians" had existed prior to that time. The nation-state required loyalty to a national government by citizens who had rights as well as duties. Nineteenth-century romanticism fueled this idea in Europe. Race was an important ingredient in identity. Benjamin Disraeli (English politician of Jewish origin) described it as "being universally recognized as the key to history."[1] Movements today by peoples who failed to secure a state, for example, the Kurds, Palestinians, and Armenians, illustrate both the fragility and the attractiveness of the nation-state as a universally applicable political construct. Problems arising from the nation-

state, with its focus on territory, have led to a revival of political ideologies such as those of early Islam. The ongoing dilemma of Lebanon illustrates the weakness of the territorially-based definition of nation.

Secularism played a prominent role in the nineteenth-century evolution of Middle Eastern nation-states, but secular movements rarely received support or acquiescence of most Muslims and Christians though intellectuals found it attractive. European pressures to improve the status of Christians led to greater emphasis on religious identities. National elites perceived the nation-state as a basis for unity transcending religious differences. In the nineteenth century, efforts to introduce new orders brought about a socioeconomic transformation that included the emergence of new elites, especially Muslim elites. Often educated in newly introduced state schools, they stood to gain from institutional changes that displaced or threatened old elites, particularly the ulama and other religious hierarchies. Some traditional Ottoman elites discovered ways of perpetuating their status, often by nullifying the impact of threatening laws.

From Persia to Morocco, rulers looked to centralization of their own power as a means to protect their positions. Military modernization continued, enabled by access to new technologies affordable to states but not usually to smaller groups. As the pace of technological advances quickened, though, the Middle Easterners, principally the Ottomans, simply could not keep up with Europeans in whose countries these advances were taking place. Capitalism helped to promote national formation by requiring closer governmental supervision over population migration and market integration. It

---

[1] Quoted in Thom Braun, *Disraeli the Novelist*. (Boston: George Allen and Unwin, 1981, p. 113. Braun gives his source as the preface to the 1870 edition of *Tancred*, the third volume in a trilogy. The theme of race was also prominent in the first two novels, *Coningsby* and *Sybil*.

also promoted imperialism, though not necessarily colonialism. The establishment of European colonies in Southwest Asia and North Africa usually ensued from causes other than deliberate colonization schemes such as that of Italy in Libya. Strategic motivations, as in Persia and Egypt, gave impetus to formal and informal imperialism. Yet the long-range integration of the area into the world market was perhaps the most important factor that led to direct European control where indirect control no longer sufficed.

Egypt and Muhammad Ali's New Order

Muhammad Ali came to power with the support of Egypt's Arabic-speaking elite—the ulama—led by Umar Makram. Three internal revolts had taken place during the foreign occupation to 1805, led by ulama. The last of these resulted in acceptance of Muhammad Ali as *wali* (viceroy), a position later confirmed by the Ottomans. He was apparently an attractive, charismatic individual. The ulama anticipated that Muhammad Ali would not impose the heavy taxation that had characterized Mamluk rule and French occupation policies. The new viceroy, however, entertained ambitious plans that required even greater revenues than previous rulers had collected. Divided among themselves, the ulama undermined each other so that when Muhammad Ali, who had unsuccessfully sought their opinions, began to tax them, they could not protest effectively. Makram, who did attempt to rally the ulama against the new policies, was exiled. Muhammad Ali in 1809 gained control of waqf revenues, further eroding the power base of the ulama. Despite the ending of the ulama alliance, he continued to maintain them financially, to employ them in his administration, and to generally uphold their traditional religious and teaching functions. At the same time, he created a new educational and administrative elite into which a few young ulama were co-opted.

Intellectuals such as Abd al-Rahman al-Jabarti and Hasan al-Attar (d. 1835) infused Egyptian cultural life with dynamism. Known for his poetry and numerous works in medicine, language sciences, natural sciences, literature, history, philosophy, logic, and religious sciences such as Hadith and *kalam* (speculative theology), al-Attar played a leading role in the neoclassical revival that supported the rise of secular positivism and utilitarianism, two currents that helped to provide the intellectual underpinnings of capitalism in Egypt. Only a few students, notably the more famous Rifa'a Rafi al-Tahtawi (d. 1873) carried on his work. Tahtawi, under Muhammad Ali, achieved recognition as a translator and as director from 1836 of the School of Languages founded in 1835 as part of the ruler's new order; he was also an early advocate of improving the status of women.

The Monopoly System

What was the new order? Muhammad Ali's new order represented the first consolidated program of military modernization in its broadest definition. He perceived that his military forces required not only new weapons, new uniforms, new training, and new schooling facilities but also systematic organization of national resources for supportive goods and services. In conjunction with plans for a new army and navy, Muhammad Ali instituted his monopoly over the nation's productive resources, thereby implementing a sort of state capitalism in which he personally constituted the state. Commerce, industry, and agriculture were all under his direction. Among the commodities that fell under the monopolies were olive oil from Crete, coffee in the Yemen, products from Sennar in Sudan (including ivory, henna, gums, hides), and Egyptian industrial and agricultural products—wheat, tobacco, maize, sugar cane, beans, barley, rice, and cotton.

Muhammad Ali organized agricultural production systematically. Ending the iltizam system, Muhammad Ali instituted a government tax-collection bureaucracy. Since he had distributed lands to his family and retainers but kept ultimate control over all state lands, he could tell farmers which crops to plant and then assure them of a market through his monopolies. Agricultural production flourished under Muhammad Ali's administration because he never lost sight of the need for an overall support system. In order to increase productivity, he organized a comprehensive set of waterworks: canals, pumps, basins, dams. Perennial irrigation replaced basin irrigation in the Nile Delta region, permitting farmers to produce three crops per year on the same land. Birseem, a type of clover eaten by animals, replenished nutrients lost to the other two crops and enabled the development of cattle breeding.

The improvement in the agricultural support system produced an expansion of cash crops that tied Egypt even more firmly to the world market economy. Muhammad Ali's introduction of long-staple (long fiber) cotton, the most prized in the world, made Egypt more important to European spinning and weaving industries. Factories for textile production, tanning, food processing, and munitions provided support for military services, but they also threatened to make Egypt an industrial power that could eventually compete with Europe. Although lack of metals, fuels, and sufficient numbers of trained personnel to repair and replace parts more severely undermined his industrialization schemes, it is also true that Europeans, other than those employed by Muhammad Ali, preferred to see Egypt as a producer of raw products rather than finished goods. Pressures from European representatives in Egypt forced the end to the monopoly system that funded all of these projects.

Besides developing agriculture and industry, Muhammad Ali also expanded transportation and communications, with both military and economic applications. He built the Mahmudiyya Canal connecting Alexandria and Cairo to bring increased import-export trade to both cities. His monopoly of all boats using the canal was among the first targets of European merchants. When the French proposed constructing a canal connecting the Mediterranean with the Red Sea, Muhammad Ali resisted, perceiving accurately that the canal would jeopardize Egypt's autonomous status by greatly increasing its already noticeable strategic value. Early in the 1830s, French followers of the positivist Saint Simon arrived in Egypt, intending to cut a canal through the Suez Isthmus. Their survey showed that the heights of the Mediterranean and Red Seas were about the same; this removed what had been considered a technical obstacle. Muhammad Ali's reign also marked the beginning of an overland postal route. The postal company, started by an Englishman, soon began to transport passengers overland. With its success, Muhammad Ali took it over in the 1840s. Later, it was superceded by the opening of a railway built by a British firm under a concession granted by his successor, Abbas Hilmi Pasha (1849–54).

Expansion of the State: Toward a New Bureaucracy

Muhammad Ali's new order also changed health and education. He made the state, not the religious institutions, responsible for at least some education. Two kinds of schools were founded at the highest levels: strictly military schools, on the one hand, and support schools,—engineering, medical, veterinary, administrative services, and technical—on the other. Students trained as officers generally came from the non-Egyptian population in Egypt, but the second category was dominated by native Egyptians. Students at the preparatory school, Military Staff College, and Naval School all founded in 1825, were at first almost entirely non-Egyptian. Within a few years, however, about 15 percent of the students were ethnic Egyptians. The emphasis in Muhammad Ali's system was on higher education, most of it designed for non-native Egyptians, and all of it part of his military modernization program. Even the music school was intended to fulfill military needs.

Because Egypt could not provide educational opportunities early in Muhammad Ali's governorship, he later began to send Egyptians abroad for specialized training. A member of the 1844–45 group, Ali Mubarak, was a native Egyptian who went on to become the most durable Egyptian bureaucrat of the nineteenth century. His companions in the group included four princes, two future prime ministers (Nubar and Muhammad Sharif), and other future civil servants in the Egyptian and Ottoman governments. Muhammad Ali's successor Abbas continued the missions, but he directed them away from strictly military education and toward a greater variety of European countries instead of to France alone.

Muhammad Ali in 1837, based on earlier French models, organized the government into departments or ministries, including a schools department. The end to the monopoly system brought about the closing of most schools in the 1840s. The ideas set in motion by Muhammad Ali's programs persisted through the personnel who had been trained in and influenced by them. The Bulaq Press, founded in 1822, had made available to literate Egyptians a wide variety of books written in Arabic. In a twenty-year period, over two hundred books were published. An official gazette, *al-Waqa'i al-Misriyya*, also began appearing in Arabic. Despite the preponderance of miscellaneous Ottomans in the special schools, native Egyptians began to dominate the lowest administrative ranks and to aspire to higher positions. The frustration of these aspirations among the military was to fuel discontent late in the 1870s and contribute to the movement led by an Egyptian officer named Ahmad Urabi.

Muhammad Ali's Role in Middle Eastern Affairs

In the early years of his viceroyalty, Muhammad Ali consolidated his power, eliminated rivals, kept Ottoman interference to a minimum, and kept out European armies. When Mahmud II called upon him to send an expedition to Arabia to suppress the Wahhabis and bring an end to economic and pilgrimage disruption, he obeyed. In 1811, before sending his new army abroad, Muhammad Ali disposed of his major internal military threat, the Mamluks, by inviting them to a banquet in the Cairo citadel and having them massacred. The lesson was not lost on Mahmud II in regard to his own problem with the janissaries. Muhammad Ali's army, led first by his son Tusun and then by his son Ibrahim, defeated the Wahhabis in 1818 at the Saudi capital Dar'iyya in the Najd. The withdrawal of the Egyptians from the Najd in 1824 permitted a much later resurgence of Saudi Wahhabi power. The immediate result was to restore the holy cities to nominal Ottoman control, although Muhammad Ali's campaign established him as the real paramount power in Hijaz and Yemen.

The Establishment of Egyptian Power in Sudan

In his next campaign, Muhammad Ali on his own decided to send his son Isma'il to conquer the areas of Darfur, Sennar, and Kordofan in what is now the Sudan but then was the three-hundred-year-old but weak Muslim Funj sultanate. Muhammad Ali hoped to restore the disrupted southern trade, to find the famous mines which produced Sudan gold, and to recruit slaves for his new-order army, intended to replace his Albanian troops. Although his army fought and won a few battles in an 1820–21 campaign, Isma'il met with little resistance because the rudimentary weapons of the Sudan tribes were no match for the Egyptian artillery. The army that entered the Funj capital at Sennar after the last sultan had submitted found it in decay. A second force that left Egypt under Muhammad Ali's son-in-law Muhammad Khusraw subjected Kordofan but not Darfur. At his base in Sennar, Isma'il was joined by his brother Ibrahim. Sudan's petty rulers resisted the attempts of the Egyptians to take slaves. Isma'il tried to lower the taxes which his officials had established but his army was ravaged by disease. When he moved his headquarters to Shendi (one hundred miles north of present-day Khartum), he and his companions were killed. The revolt spread, but the Egyptians continued to maintain superiority of arms and military experience over the poorly organized and disunited Sudanese. Muhammad Khrusraw commanded the troops who by the fall of 1825 ended the uprising. Muhammad Ali's plans for a slave army had to be abandoned, but he decided to employ Sudanese troops in his garrison.

The new governor Uthman established a fort at the confluence of the White and Blue Niles; this became Khartum. Subsequent governors after 1825 decided to conciliate the population by helping alleviate famine and by consulting with local notables. Refugees were encouraged to return home. By the 1830s, Khartum was a well-established town with permanent buildings. By the 1840s, governors had expanded their area of control to Suakin and Massawa on the Red Sea and had sent three exploratory expeditions up the White Nile. Gradually, though, they stopped exercising authority. European traders made direct approaches to Sudanese who assisted them in acquiring slaves and ivory. By the mid-1860s, most of these had left because of the harsh climate, and control of the Bahr al-Ghazal trade passed to Egyptians and Syrians. Many Sudanese regard the Egyptian presence in nineteenth-century Sudan as an extension of Ottoman power and call it "the Turkiyya."

The Greek Revolt in Ottoman–Egyptian Relations

Based on his success against the Wahhabis and the reputation of his new army of Mamluk officers, slave recruits, and peasants, Muhammad Ali was called upon again by Mahmud II, this time to quiet the Greek Revolt, the first major rebellion among the empire's non-Muslim subject peoples. This second expedition began an era of Ottoman-approved Egyptian autonomy. Egypt's rulers continued to make obeisance and seek approval of sultans while acting independently and even against them. Profits won by sea captains during the Napoleonic wars helped provide funding for the Greek revolt. In 1814, Greeks at Odessa, Ukraine, organized the first secret society aimed at Greek independence. Following the Napoleonic wars and the ensuing depression, the independence movement grew to several hundred thousand. In 1821, a revolt led by Alexander Ypsilanti began. Although he deserted his followers and fled to Hungary, many Greeks in the Morea took up the spirit of the revolt, massacring Turkish officials and entire families, even in cities like Tripolitsa where Turkish populations surrendered.

Mahmud II's military preoccupation at this time with the revolt of Ali Pasha of Janina in Ottoman Macedonia allowed the revolution among the Greeks to spread, though not all Greeks supported it. Turks in the Morea tried to fight back, and Mahmud II hanged the Greek patriarch in Istanbul as a suspected revolutionary. Rather than risk losing Crete, Mahmud II promised it to Muhammad Ali on condition that the Egyptian viceroy restore order there, an action accomplished by 1824. The Greeks meanwhile set up a government-in-exile that received its first bank loan from Britain in 1824, with support from European admirers of Greek culture. The English poet Byron did much to popularize the Greek struggle.

In 1823–24, Mahmud II called again on Muhammad Ali. Ibrahim was thus appointed governor of the Peloponnesus (Morea) in exchange for subduing the revolutionaries. Ibrahim landed in 1825 and achieved such great success that the British, French, and Russians intervened to impose a settlement. Russia in 1826 pressured Mahmud II to evacuate the Danubian provinces, to grant Serbia autonomy, and to give up parts of eastern Anatolia. By the Treaty of London in 1827, the three European powers promised to force an armistice between the Greeks and the Ottomans. When Mahmud II refused to accept the treaty, the Europeans launched a blockade to prevent delivery of supplies to Ibrahim. At the naval battle of Navarino in October 1827, their combined fleet so severely defeated the Ottomans that Ibrahim was forced to withdraw. The Russians inaugurated a new war and advanced both in eastern Anatolia and Rumelia, reaching Edirne. In 1829, Mahmud II signed the Treaty of Edirne which retained the old frontiers but left the Ottomans with only tributary payments among their former sovereign privileges in Moldavia and Wallachia. The Russians filled the void. Weakened by this warfare, Mahmud II agreed to a second London treaty between Russia, England, and France. This created a small Greek state in the Morea.

With the setting up of an independent state in the Morea, the governorship promised by the sultan to Ibrahim failed to materialize. Therefore, Muhammad Ali tried to obtain jurisdiction over an area traditionally within the sphere of Egypt's rulers: Syria. Having already established good relations with two local rulers there, Muhammad Ali felt justified in requesting the addition of Syria to his viceroyalty. The official pretext for his invasion lay in his accusation that the governor of Akka was protecting Egyptians fleeing conscription.

Ibrahim commanded the Egyptian forces that invaded Syria in the fall of 1831. While besieging Akka in 1832, he heard that Mahmud II had declared the Egyptians rebels. Neverthless, the Egyptain army continued to push north through Damascus, Aleppo, and Alexandretta (Iskenderun), all the way to Konya where it inflicted a severe defeat on the Ottoman army in December 1832. Adhering to Muhammad Ali's policy of trying to avoid European intervention, Ibrahim had to weigh the cost of trying to depose the Ottoman sultan, perhaps in favor of his father.

The presence of the Russian navy at Istanbul, however, fueled rumors of the possibility of Russian intervention. The French and British pressured the parties to end hostilities. According to the Kutahya Convention of April–May 1833, Muhammad Ali gained as a lifetime fief requiring tribute the district of Adana in Cilicia and the province of Syria. As in the case of his Greek success, Ibrahim had won for his father a pyrrhic victory.

The Egyptian Interlude in Syria

Ibrahim's initial success derived from implementation of orderly government, elimination of foreign abuses, provision of safeguards for all religious communities, and promotion of education and communications. Ibrahim eliminated the former division of the country into pashaliks. In its place, he appointed a subgovernor who would have representatives, usually local Arabs, in each district. Sustained by his large military forces, Ibrahim put down the opposition of notables to the new scheme. The army curtailed the nomadic beduins' disruptive activities. Although local leaders were displaced, most of the population of Syria enjoyed greater security of property and life, promoted by new secular courts and supervision of the religious courts as well as by less arbitrary taxation. The Egyptians brought agricultural experts to Syria to provide peasants with supplies and advice that allowed them to introduce better methods of grow-

later as the Ottomans increased efforts to bring the area more fully under their authority.

During the frequent Kurdish uprisings, individual Kurdish leaders tried to extend the amount of territory under their control. Some hoped to achieve recognition of independence from the Ottomans and Qajars, and like other minorities, tried to enlist the support of European powers such as Britain. In the end, all of these leaders failed because of their inability to transcend personal rivalries and unite against non-Kurdish forces. Moreover, the Kurdish revolts of the nineteenth century lacked political programs and goals because the social organization did not promote formation of an intelligentsia. Only after Kurds began to participate in educational opportunities offered to their elites late in the century did a Kurdish national movement begin to catalyze.

Although Mahmud II judiciously avoided a direct attack on the janissaries during the early years, and even courted their leaders, he accurately perceived that they would never again be an effective fighting force. With the poor performance of troops fighting in the early Ottoman campaigns, Mahmud II disposed of many politicians and notables who supported the janissaries, and he brought most of the Balkans, Anatolia, and the Arab provinces back under the direct control of the Empire through appointment of loyal cadres and occasional police actions. He also enlisted the support of the ulama for his programs. Slowly and carefully, Mahmud II laid the foundations for what Ottomans called the "auspicious event." Finally, Mahmud II secured the acquiescence of his officials to a comprehensive program of military modernization that included a new force made up of janissaries. Mahmud II guessed that the janissaries would resist, but he was ready to fight any rebels.

Before he had completely finished with the Greek issue, Mahmud II decided that the time for striking against the janissaries had arrived. Arming his loyal forces with artillery, he quelled the janissary re-volt of 1826 by sending an artillery barrage against them. His loyal troops then moved into Anatolia and the provinces to eliminate or scatter the rest of the janissaries. Mahmud II's new troops were not sufficiently ready by 1828 and 1829 to combat Russian assaults effectively, and were in fact demoralized by the defeats, but at least he had done away with a powerful barrier to change.

Provincial Consolidation Efforts

Once Mahmud II had rid himself of this major obstacle, he initiated further measures to consolidate and centralize his hold over the Ottoman provincial administration. The first census was taken, land surveys were instituted, communications were improved, and a postal system was set up. Mahmud II established quasi-ministries like those of Muhammad Ali. He also did away with the timar system. Instead of maintaining sipahi service, he intended to have taxes collected by government officials directly from the landowners, but he met with opposition. Even though Mahmud II tried to erode the popularity of the Sufi orders, especially the Bektashi order with whom the janissaries had been associated, they recovered most of their properties and resources after Mahmud II's death and still survive in Turkey.

Da'ud Pasha's New Order in Mesopotamia

In Mesopotamia, the destruction of the janissaries brought Da'ud to institute a new order fighting force to supplement his own mamluks. He also decided to follow Muhammad Ali's lead toward greater autonomy. In 1830, after he killed Mahmud II's emissaries, the Ottomans appointed Ali Rida new governor of Mesopotamia (including Mosul and Aleppo). Again disease, this time plague, intervened. An outbreak in Baghdad prevented Da'ud from mounting a strong defense, though the population upheld him. Ali Rida destroyed both Da'ud's mamluk and new-order armies in the aftermath, though Da'ud lived to old age in exile at Madina.

Mir Muhammad's New Order in Kurdistan

The Ottomans, however, never controlled outlying areas in Iraq. The Kurds and others retained their autonomy and parochial loyalties. In 1834, the Baghdad governors ended Jalili rule in Mosul. Kurdish leader Mir (Prince) Muhammad, based in nearby Rawanduz, decided that the time was ripe for an independent Kurdistan. Based on Muhammad Ali's model, Muhammad began a military industrialization program to help build a modern, standing army.

By mid-1833, he controlled southern Kurdistan, thereby encroaching on other Kurdish territory under Badir Khan Bey. The Baghdad governors failed to diminish his power, leading him to move into Qajar territory. When the Qajars appealed to Russia for help, Mir Muhammad, realizing that a possible two-front war lay ahead, tried unsuccessfully to play off the Persians and the Ottomans. Although his own army defeated the Ottomans in 1836, the Ottomans convinced his troops in the name of Muslim fraternity to cease fighting. Ottoman agents assassinated him in 1837. Badir Khan, who had refused to join Mir Muhammad, established independent Kurdish rule in the 1840s. His Christian population supported him until Ottoman and missionary pressures turned them against him. The frontiers in eastern Anatolia remained fluid until after World War I. Kurdish chiefs continued to seek an independent Kurdish polity.

Bureaucracy and Education

Mahmud II also curtailed the power of formal religion, personified by the ulama, by placing religious officials within the framework of a government bureaucracy and dividing among several departments functions that previously had been under the authority of one religious hierarchy. A new ministry of education was authorized to handle the schools, while a special ministry of *awqaf* was created to administer income from waqf endowments. Having observed the successes of European and Egyptian armies, Mahmud II employed foreign military instructors and adopted foreign military drill and uniforms. As support systems to parallel creations of Muhammad Ali, Mahmud founded medical and military science schools and expanded engineering education. A music school as in Egypt was established, too. Turkish officers studied at Woolwich in England. In order to bridge the gap between traditional Quranic education and the new advanced schools, Mahmud II set up preparatory schools. Mahmud II had also hoped to make primary education compulsory, but his 1824 decree to that effect could not create the infrastructure needed to carry it out because of the lack of sufficient numbers of trained personnel.

After the Greeks of the empire began agitating for independence, Mahmud II turned again to training Muslim Turks as interpreters and translators. The sultan's plans for renovating society required up-to-date textbooks, especially in science and technology. Book printing under Mahmud II expanded. He also attached a translation bureau to the ministry of foreign affairs to improve the empire's diplomatic corps and international communications. This emphasis on language skills was to create a new Turkish elite versed in foreign as well as Ottoman and Turkish culture.

Mahmud II and Europe

The new Turkish elite also came into close personal contact with Europe by virtue of Mahmud II's continuation of the practice, initiated by Selim III, of stationing permanent diplomatic missions in European capitals. In the 1830s, foreign travelers also began to visit the Ottoman Empire in greater numbers than before, traveling on the new steamships in the Mediterranean. Mahmud II decided that government officials should wear European dress—suits and leather boots plus a headgear known to us as the fez or tarbush, banned in the twentieth-century Turkish Republic as being emblematic of the old Ottoman order. Ottoman elites who studied Europeans designed programs of their own to aid in the consolidation of the empire favored by Mahmud II and his successors. By the time of Mahmud II's death in 1839, he had succeeded to a great extent in shoring up the empire's defenses but had also yielded territory to Europe.

When Egypt's army moved into Anatolia in 1832, the presence of Russian troops near Istanbul brought about Anglo-French intervention. Mahmud II still signed the Treaty of Hunkiar Skelesi with Russia in 1833, secretly committing the Ottomans to close the straits to foreign ships of nations with whom Russia might go to war. British suspicions about the possible terms of this treaty led to agreement on an international convention dealing with the straits early in the 1840s, thereby internationalizing the straits ques-

tion and all future questions arising from passage through controversial but vital waterways. The Hunkiar Skelesi treaty was overturned in favor of an agreement closing the straits to warships when the Ottoman Empire was at peace and opening them to commercial passage in peacetime, though the sultan could use his discretion about commercial ships in time of war.

With the agreements which ended Muhammad Ali's threat to the Ottomans, Britain's stake there increased. By 1850, the Ottomans were supplying foodstuffs and raw goods to Britain in large quantities, receiving in exchange British manufactured goods. As in the case of Egypt, however, the Ottomans often faced war or revolts on several fronts and were consequently even more vulnerable to pressure than the Egyptians. The Anglo-Ottoman commercial agreement of 1838, extended to other Europeans in the 1840s, was probably of greater consequence than all of the treaties signed between Muhammad Ali and the Ottoman sultans.

Iran under the Early Qajars

Agha Muhammad Khan, a eunuch descended from the original kizilbash Turkomans, reunited most of Persia under his rule between 1779 and 1797, re-establishing the capital at Tehran and setting up the Qajar dynasty. After his murder, rule passed to his nephew Fath Ali Shah (1797–1834). Like his contemporary in Egypt, Fath Ali Shah had a large family and tried to expand the amount of territory under his rule. His son, Abbas Mirza (d. 1833) who as Crown Prince governed the rich and strategic province of Azerbayjan, started a nizam al-jadid army with soldiers trained in Iran and abroad. Although achieving limited military success, the Iranian forces after his death remained inept and disorganized because vested tribal and urban elites preferred a weak central government. In contrast to

Muhammad Ali, Fath Ali Shah made no effort at all to organize the resources of the state to provide systematic support for the military. He played off France, Britain, and Russia in hopes of holding his state together. There was no new order instituted in Iran by Fath Ali Shah.

European Intervention

European interference during the Napoleonic wars began when Russia invaded Qajar-controlled Georgia in 1800; after its loss, Fath Ali Shah received both British and French missions offering help. The French enticed Iran with an offer to sponsor the Iranian reconquest of the Caucasus and expansion into India based on Nadir Shah's example. By the Treaty of Finken-

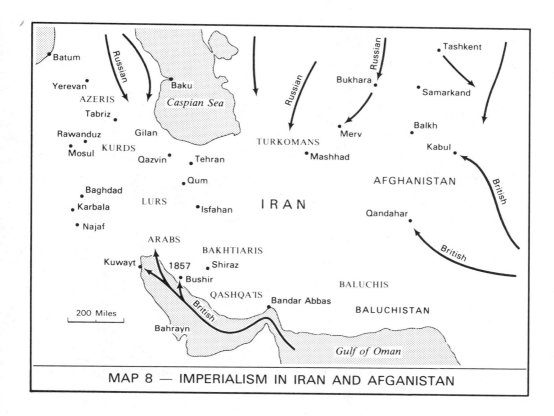

MAP 8 — IMPERIALISM IN IRAN AND AFGANISTAN

stein in 1807, France was to provide military assistance to the Qajar forces, and a French military mission arrived immediately after. When Russia and France temporarily made peace at Tilsit a few months later, Iran turned to Britain. But the British could not prevent further Russian incursions. From 1804–13, Iran and Russia continued to fight over Georgia. Russia won. In 1826, based on rumors of Russian oppression of Muslims, Fath Ali Shah launched a new Caucasus campaign that backfired. The Russians captured Yerevan in Armenia and even Tabriz in Azerbayjan.

By the Treaty of Turkomanchay in February 1828, the Iranians were forced to accept the loss of Yerevan and the Nakichevan districts. They also had to confirm the loss of places ceded earlier, including Georgia, Karabagh, and Shirvan with its principal city of Baku. Iran also had to pay an indemnity to Russia and concluded an economic agreement whereby Russian traders gained preference in Iran. The losses in the Caucasus showed Fath Ali Shah that he could not count on the British to uphold their treaty obligations and that he would have to accommodate Russia. The Turkomanchay treaty reserved the Caspian Sea for Russian ships, thereby making it a Russian lake. In 1833, Abbas Mirza challenged British interests by leading an army toward Herat, a former Safavid possession in western Afghanistan with a large Persian-speaking population, but he died before a conflict with Britain could arise. Map 8 shows nineteenth-century imperialism in Iran and Afghanistan.

Economy and Society

Old Qajar Iran under Fath Ali Shah represented rule by a Turkish tribal military aristocracy with Persian culture. Peasants provided the economic base although tax collection was irregular and often excessive. Iran's aridity kept the population dispersed. Bazaars in the towns remained the centers for traditional trade, commerce, and industry, but Iran's cities retained their isolation and individualism.

Qajar Iran did not fully control pastoral tribal areas, most of whose people were Sunni Muslim and non-Persian speaking. These semiautonomous peoples constituted an estimated one half of nineteenth-century Iran's population, with the most contentious among them the Turkomans, Baluchis, and Kurds. Lacking an organized standing army, the Qajars had to depend on rallying these various tribes for the defense of the state.

Religious leaders, especially Shi'i mujtahids, exercised great influence in town and country. Since the Qajars did not nationalize waqf, the mujtahids retained independent sources of wealth. There were government-appointed ulama serving as Friday prayer leaders and judges, but they were far outnumbered and outweighed in influence by independent mujtahids, rich and poor alike. Certainly, they were much closer to the population than were the Qajar rulers. Ulama administered most social welfare and collected funds to support hospitals, courts, and schools. A variety of state-appointed officials administered customary law in criminal cases.

Fath Ali Shah was succeeded by his grandson Muhammad Mirza (1834–48). British-Russian rivalry persisted during his reign; it resulted from a general extension of their interests in Afghanistan and India. In his internal policies, Muhammad Shah attempted to strengthen his society by banning torture and importation of slaves. But corruption was rife, with frequent selling of government offices. Muhammad Shah also faced disruption from the followers of the Bab, a representative of the hidden Imam who it was thought would restore social justice.

The Shaykhi Movement and Babism

Late in the eighteenth century, Iranian philosophy had been influenced by the *shaykhi* movement, intended to reform and strengthen Islam along the lines advocated by the Wahhabis in Arabia. Combined with Shi'i beliefs, the movement led many Iranians to expect the appearance of the Bab. In the 1840s, Ali Muhammad of Shiraz (1819–50) claimed to be the Bab. He rallied many Persians to his new ideology, introduced a new *Shari'a* called *Bayan*, and accused the ulama of corruption. The vigor of the Bab's followers produced a reaction from the Shi'i clergy and then from the Qajar government. The Qajars felt threatened by the social protest evidenced in the movement. It was fully suppressed by Muhammad Shah's son and successor Nasir al-Din Shah (1848–96).

Conclusion

During the era of European economic and political resurgence, Middle Eastern rulers and individuals addressed their internal and external problems by turning to military modernization and centralization. They also sought to upgird their religious heritage against foreign and secular influences. The new pressures created discontinuities and new challenges for rulers and subjects alike. Why did Muhammad Ali succeed more than Mahmud II in modifying the institutions of the state?

Mahmud II had to deal with a multi-ethnic state, vast in territory and under foreign military attack. Moreover, the long-standing nature of Ottoman institutions, each with its own constituency, and the circumstances of his accession hindered rapid adoption of new structures and methodologies. Yet, foreign pressures on the Ottoman Empire were so much more persistent and diverse than those on Egypt that necessary military modernization was far more urgent.

Iran under Fath Ali Shah had neither the will nor the means to restore centralization following the deliberate decentralization that had occurred in post-Afshar Iran under Karim Kham Zand. The general absence of military modernization in Iran, except for that of Abbas Mirza, retarded in a substantial way the development of state power and control over the provinces. The Qajars could not protect even what territory they already had from their more powerful neighbors.

The assault on Middle Eastern territory was only beginning. It was to result in European occupation of all of North Africa (see Chapter 9) and increasing formal outside interference in Ottoman and Iranian affairs. Within the Ottoman Empire, centralization brought on a new oligarchy against whom decentralizers, both Christians and Muslims, reacted. But individual non-Muslim subject peoples also moved toward demanding independence as ethnically distinct nations. Perhaps the Turks were the last large group in the Middle East to seek liberation.

CHAPTER SEVEN

The Middle East in Reorganization: Ottoman Heartlands, Egypt, and Iran

In the middle of the nineteenth century, Egyptian and Ottoman leaders came under internal and external pressures to reorganize previous centralizing measures. Egypt's rulers won greater autonomy from the Ottoman Empire while new orders of Muhammad Ali and Mahmud II continued to be emulated. Iran, under a single ruler for nearly fifty years and lacking military centralization experienced foreign interference and market-penetration analogous to that in Ottoman lands.

The Ottoman Tanzimat: An Overview

The Ottoman Tanzimat (reorganization) aimed at implementing measures to hold the empire together, in order to harness for the good of the state changes impacting on ethnic and religious groups increasingly oriented toward the outside world. In place of extraterritorial privileges acquired through affiliation with foreigners, the Ottoman Empire introduced new written guarantees of rights for all groups. Ottoman leaders assumed that, with new laws and structures safeguarding and protecting all subjects, foreign powers would relax pressures on the Empire. They expected abuses of the capitulations by both Ottoman subjects and foreigners to decline. Implemented through a localized government bureaucracy, the Tanzimat tried to mitigate the harsher aspects of Mahmud II's centralization program. The measures lasted from 1839 to about 1878.

Support for the Tanzimat was not broadly based. It concentrated power in the few hands of the new Turkish elite trained in the institutions according to the centralizing policies of Mahmud II. Though representing different socioeconomic backgrounds, these men had acquired knowledge of European languages, culture, and political practices. Mustafa Rashid (d. 1858)—ambassador, foreign minister, and grand vizir—was the son of a waqf official. Amin Ali Pasha (d. 1871), known as Ali Pasha, came from a shopkeeper's home. The father of Kechejizade Mehmed Fu'ad (d. 1869) or Fu'ad Pasha was an aristocrat. Kibrilsi Mehmed Pasha, frequently grand vizir in the 1850s and 1860s, came from the old palace school and had become a general under Mahmud II. Through their oligarchical tendencies, these leaders provoked a reaction from a new generation committed to the idea of citizenship in the Ottoman homeland in place of loyalty to a dynasty, with human rights constitutionally guaranteed. Midhat Pasha (d. 1883), coming late in the Tanzimat administration, sympathized more with these democratizing elements.

Hatt-i Sharif of Gulhane

Two imperial decrees, the Hatt-i Sharif of Gulhane (Honorable Rescript of the Rose Chamber) proclaimed in 1839 some four months after Mahmud II's death, and the Hatt-i Humayun (Imperial Rescript) issued in February 1856 after the Crimean War, contained general principles regarding human rights, justice, tax collection, military recruitment, education, and financial and economic policies. The first edict, issued on the advice of Mustafa Rashid who had recently visited England to enlist British help against Egypt, proclaimed guarantees of justice, admitting for the first time testimony of Christians

against Muslims in court cases and requiring trials for capital crimes. Tax farming as well as arbitrary conscription and taxation were to end. Mahmud II's advisory legal council formed to recommend laws to the grand vizir and his ministers was encouraged to function effectively. Because all measures were not implemented immediately, some scholars have called this rescript mere window dressing for Europeans debating the empire's fate following the war with Muhammad Ali. But there was no way in which instantaneous change could have been achieved.

The Crimean War and the Hatt-i Humayun

The Crimean War (1854–56) ensued from a dispute between France and Russia over control of holy places in Palestine, especially those in Jerusalem and Bethlehem. From the 1830s, both countries had stepped up their Holy-Land activities on the basis of capitulatory rights gained earlier. In the 1850s, the new French ruler Louis Napoleon demanded further privileges for French clerical interests. Both countries won concessions from Sultan Abdulmejid (1839–61). For example, France placed a coat of arms in the Church of the Holy Nativity in Bethlehem. When Russia in 1853 made new demands, the British Ambassador in Istanbul, Stratford de Redcliffe Canning, fearing a new Franco-Russian war, advised the sultan to refuse.

When Russia persisted in claiming historic rights and advanced into present-day Rumania as a prelude to full-scale war, the British concluded that the real issue was Russian expansion into the Ottoman Empire. Abdulmejid tried unsuccessfully to force a Russian withdrawal from occupied territory, resulting in destruction of the Ottoman fleet at Sinop in November 1853. At this point, the British fleet entered the Black Sea, but war against Russia began only in March 1854. Although Russia withdrew when Austria and Prussia joined France and Britain in the battle, the war endured for three years.

Though it gave us Florence Nightingale, founder of modern nursing, and Alfred Lord Tennyson's poem "The Charge of the Light Brigade," the Crimean War altered very little territorially. The Treaty of Paris (30 March 1856) gave greater autonomy to Rumania. More importantly, England, France and Austria promised to maintain the Ottoman Empire's territorial integrity and independence. Sultan Abdulmejid was invited to join the "concert of Europe," an ironic development since the same countries called the empire "the sick man of Europe."

Instead of being perceived as an alien enemy, the Ottoman Empire was now a European partner. With the promises of Austria and France, Britain could begin abdicating its self-appointed role as guardian of the Ottoman Empire and focus more on autonomous Egypt (which the Suez Canal was soon to make vital for the security of communications with British India). Though the Black Sea was formally neutralized by the Treaty of Paris, and the Danube was internationalized,

within fifteen years Russia remilitarized the Black Sea. A new Balkan crisis lay ahead.

Though the Hatt-i Humayun affirmed principles to which the Ottoman ruling elites were committed, its timing tended to reinforce the views of opponents of all persuasions—either that the elites were sincere but out of touch with the population, or that they were insincere, trying only to satisfy Europeans. The Hatt-i Humayun mentioned rights and privileges that supposedly already accrued to Muslims and Christians—freedom of worship, equal taxation, and military service. It also promised a greater degree of autonomy for non-Muslim communities. Foreigners' privileges expanded with permission to own and control property. Through extending education, Ottoman subjects would advance socially and economically. For Muslim Ottoman subjects, though, the reform decrees of both 1839 and 1856 seemed to create favoritism for non-Muslims without imposing on them duties of citizenship.

Socioeconomic Change under the Tanzimat

Refugee Policy

The contraction of the empire that occurred during the nineteenth century brought a stream of Muslim immigrants, mostly from lands taken by Russia, and of non-Muslim immigrants fleeing political repression after the 1848 revolutions in Europe. The Crimean War in particular led Tatars to enter the Ottoman Empire in large numbers. Nearly 1.5 million came from the Crimea alone between 1854 and 1876. The Refugee Code of 1857 addressed pressing social needs by providing land grants for Muslim and Christian immigrants, and exempting them from military conscription during a settling-in period. The arrival of Muslims fleeing the Balkans after 1876, though, contributed to a breakdown in communal relations

among new immigrants in Anatolia. From that time on, immigration into Anatolia accounted for a dramatic increase in both Muslim and Christian populations. The Refugee Code, introduced to benefit both groups, achieved mixed results.

The Economic Factor in Communal Relations

The same was true of the Tanzimat in the more distant provinces and among minorities. In Syria, the Ottomans did away with Ibrahim's administrative system, restoring former small *pashaliks* (*eyalets*) based in Aleppo, Damascus, and Beirut. The Beirut-centered eyalet of Saida encompassed most of the Lebanese mountains and Palestine, thereby contributing to the growth of Beirut as the region's leading city next to Damascus. Ottoman mixed courts replaced the locally staffed units set up by Ibrahim.

Foreign penetration continued. Textiles made abroad, often from Syrian raw materials, destroyed long-established Syrian industries. Even silk, without the intensive competition facing wool and cotton industries, suffered a long-term setback. Only soap, oil, and tobacco maintained their local markets. Muslim middle classes—artisans and traders— lost their positions to Christian and Jewish enterprises that had European connections, though these latter paid higher taxes. As the Muslim middle classes grew poorer, the gap between them and wealthier Muslims and minorities widened. The Ottomans emphasized public works—buildings, residences, and military facilities—to support extension of their own authority. In greater Syria, friction among various communities arose.

The Crisis in Syria and Creation of Mount Lebanon Autonomy

In Lebanon, the main parties were Druze and Maronites. Local administrators of different religions began to overtax villagers. In the 1840s, the sultan settled a local Maronite-Druze war, but disturbances increased in the 1850s, exacerbated by missionary expansion. Missionaries generally backed efforts of local Christians to exercise rights arising from the reform decrees. In 1856, anti-European and anti-Christian risings took place in Nablus, Gaza, and Marash, all elsewhere in greater Syria. After 1858, individual communities began stocking up on weapons.

Between 1858 and 1860, Ottoman authorities intervened on several occasions to forestall Muslim attacks against Christians in Syria, but when riots broke out in Damascus in July 1860, the weak Ottoman governor could not protect the Christians. Only the intervention of Algerian resistance leader Abd al-Qadir (see Chapter 9),

who had settled there in 1855, and other Muslim leaders helped save the lives of 12,000 Christians trapped in their own quarter. In recognition, the French gave Abd al-Qadir the Grand Cross of the Legion of Honor. At about the same time, Druze forces attacked Christians in Lebanon, bringing about a French landing and immigration of Syrian Christians to the coast and to Europe, Egypt, and Ottoman Anatolia. Those Syrian Christians who stayed began seeking new bases for relating to Muslims.

To settle the Syrian crisis, the Ottomans gave Mount Lebanon autonomy under the Charter of 1861. It was given a Christian governor, beginning with Da'ud Pasha, an Armenian Catholic who restored tranquillity. The charter was altered somewhat in the wake of the 1864 Vilayet Law but remained the law of Mount Lebanon until the imposition of the French mandate in 1920. With the charter, the presumption of a Christian identity for Lebanon was accepted. The Druze, backed by the British, found themselves subordinated, though geographical fragmentation allowed them a semi-independent status. Regions with predominantly Sunni and Shi'i Muslim populations were appended to Mount Lebanon by French administrators only after 1920.

Ottoman Millet Policy: The Armenian Example

Although foreigners viewed events in Lebanon as evidence of Ottoman neglect of minority rights, historians can easily draw the opposite conclusion from Ottoman millet policies of the 1860s. The Ottomans at that time were striving to promote millet identification with the empire, and they responded to demands for democratization of the millets to free them from their upper-class Ottoman elites. The Armenians, for example, wanted a constitution to protect them from arbitrary acts by their patriarchs, notables, and high officials (*amira*). The first draft approved by the Armenian General Council in April 1857 met with Ottoman objections because it created a "state within a state." After further objections and negotiations, Sultan Abdulaziz (1861–76) handed down the new document on 30 March 1863.

The Armenian constitution of 1863 provided for universal suffrage to elect a General Council that would then select the Armenian Orthodox partriarch. General councils corresponding to government departments superintended tax collection, education through the secondary level, civil and social litigation among Armenians, and parish councils to handle local affairs with membership from all classes. What disappointed many Armenians was that the sultan gave the new constitution to a patriarchal rather than a secular representative. Still, the document curtailed patriarchal and upper-class hegemony. When Abdulaziz had continued to reject the constitution after 1862 because of references to the Holy See of Etchmiadzin in Russian Armenia, Armenians demonstrated not against him but against their patriarch for having caused the delay. The constitution remained in force, in theory though not always in practice, until the demise of the empire in 1923.

Reorganization of Education

The Ottoman commitment to improved communal relations was also evident in the Tanzimat's new schools that accepted subjects of all religious persuasions. Evolution of government-sponsored education paralleled its development in Egypt at the same time. In 1866, a full-fledged Ottoman Ministry of Public Education was given responsibility for supervising the institution of secular schools. Elementary Quranic education was to be supplanted by secular elementary education. Above this level were the *rushdiye* (four years), *idadi* (three years), and *sultani* schools. Because non-Muslims as well as Muslims attended them, they learned Turkish (if they did not already know it) and could be hired as bureaucrats if the need arose. The most famous sultani lycee was located in Galata Palace in Istanbul. Students there studied foreign languages, physical sciences, and social sciences. Courses were taught primarily in French by a European-dominated staff that included Turks, Armenians, and Greeks. French Catholic and American Protestant missionaries developed popular education in Anatolia at the same time. Millet schools educated one quarter of the girls in elementary school and three quarters of all female rushdiye students. In 1895, more non-Muslims than Muslims received an idadi education. Even with the Ottoman promotion of general education, then, more Christians became better equipped for civil service positions.

Higher education expanded, too, with the establishment of teachers' colleges for both men and women, as well as professional and technical schools. After a false start in 1846 and scattered university offerings in the 1860s, Dar al-Funun University opened briefly in 1870–71, and finally in 1900. Americans founded Robert College (now Bosporus or Bogazici University) in 1863 and Syrian Protestant College (now the American University of Beirut) in 1866. French Jesuits who had started the still functioning Imprimerie Catholique in 1853 in Lebanon also established the Université de St. Joseph in 1875. While the Syrian Protestant College attracted Muslims as well as Christians and in the twentieth century became the Middle East's premier university, St. Joseph served the Maronites. These schools in the nineteenth century promoted cultural and literary renaissance in Anatolia and the Levant, as was evidenced by proliferation of books, journals, and newspapers.

Legal and Judicial Reform

In the area of legal and judicial reform during the Tanzimat, new law codes and courts were constituted, including the Penal Code, Commercial Code, and Maritime Commerce Code. Courts created to enforce the new codes included the mixed commercial courts and the mixed civil and criminal courts. In 1869, the Ottoman minister of justice set up secular courts that cut back the jurisdiction of Shari'a courts. Ulama did not object too strongly to the new system because the new civil code—the Mejelle—rewrote and codified Hanafi Shari'a. Developed between 1866 and 1888, the Mejelle formed the basis for laws operating in the Arab world after World War I. The Constitution of 1876 was also part of the redefinition process.

Socioeconomic Change in the Provinces: Vilayets and Land Tenure

Vilayet Law of 1864

Provincial developments in the Middle East were especially influenced by two measures, the Land Law of 1858 and the Vilayet Law of 1864. The Vilayet Law created provinces of about equal size, each with a formalized hierarchy of divisions and subdivisions, each headed by an official (named in parenthesis).

Vilayet/province	(vali)
Sanjak/county	(mutasarrif)
Qaza/district	(qaimaqam)
Nahiya/town	(mudir)
Qariya/village,quarter	(mukhtar)

In Syria, for example, two large provinces of Damascus and Aleppo were created (excluding autonomous Lebanon). Both valis and mutasarrifs were appointed directly by the sultan, but except for military matters, they and not the Istanbul government controlled local departments. Each divisional official had deputies. Consultative government was instituted through the setting up of local assemblies. Villagers chose their own mukhtars who were then confirmed by the qaimaqam of their local qaza.

Opportunities provided by the reorganization attracted better educated non-Muslims, especially at the qaza- and

sanjak-levels in finance and city administration. But non-Muslims found themselves generally excluded from judicial and administrative councils and police forces. While many educated non-Muslims began to identify more closely with the state, others felt frustrated because of limitations on their participation. Turkish and Kurdish Muslims in Anatolia resented them, moreover, because of their disproportionate roles. The well-intentioned restructuring, then, helped the new middle classes but heightened tensions in mixed areas among the lower classes. These erupted into full-scale hostility in the 1890s, paralleling the earlier problems in Syria. Ottoman concern for devising an effective system is shown by the fact that the reorganization took place only after grand vizir Kibrilsi Mehmed toured the provinces in 1860 to collect complaints. Ali, Fu'ad, and Midhat helped with its formulation.

The Vilayet Law did not affect all Ottoman lands uniformly. Ottoman rule in Iraq, for example, remained relaxed. At mid-century, both British and Ottoman firms operated river steamers on the Tigris and Euphrates. The Ottomans also sponsored construction of a telegraph line by British interests, connecting Istanbul to Baghdad and later to Iran. Until the appointment of Midhat as governor (1869–72)—who served ably in Bulgaria and Macedonia, too—the Tanzimat had little impact in Iraq. Midhat was the first to make the Vilayet Law and the Land Law operational, subdividing the large province of Baghdad.

Like his predecessors, Midhat faced resistance from rural, tribal-dominated areas. A revolt in the south convinced him to try to settle the tribes and establish their respect for central authority. He turned to the Ottoman Land Law, designed to secure titles and therefore security for landholders. Hoping that individuals would come forth to register their land, Midhat lowered taxes. After his removal before he had fully implemented his program, Ottoman governors ignored the spirit of the law.

The Land Law of 1858

The Ottoman Land Law of 1858 altered landholding relationships in Iraq and Palestine, among other places, with serious consequences. Application of the law in Iraq was hindered by the fact that tribal confederations, not individuals, held most land. Confederations contested with each other frequently for their control. Because the government had not given them the land, they viewed it as having no right to interfere. Instead of accepting deeds that would give them clear formal land titles, cultivators allowed their own tribal leaders and others to purchase their titles. The Ottomans co-opted these official owners into their administration.

The Musha System   In Palestine, the predominant form of holding before 1858 was village ownership under the cooperative (*musha*) system. Remaining state property, church lands and waqf also constituted substantial holdings. Church and waqf estates tended to protect peasants from excessive taxation, but other cultivators were more vulnerable. The 1858 law led peasants to avoid registration for fear of taxes or because they could not pay registration fees. Often, they did not know about the law. Both peasant cultivators and beduin lost their lands as wealthy compatriots, residing perhaps in Beirut or Damascus, registered the land in their own names. Rural indebtedness further eroded musha holdings. Profitable agriculture in Palestine required heavy investment. Neither village peasants nor landless share croppers and wage laborers could afford it.

Colonial purchasers, however, not only paid high prices but also drove them up. Foreign churches, followed by German and later by Jewish colonists, fueled land speculation in nineteenth-century Palestine. Confronted with a capital influx that offered the opportunity for big profits, large landowners began to sell. Small holders more often gave up their land because of indebtedness they incurred when they borrowed to fund capital investments. Much land that had been held and owned by Palestinians thus passed to state or foreign control. In the end, the Land Law of 1858 failed to protect those for whom it was intended.

Indigenous Reappraisal of the Tanzimat: The New Ottomans

The Ideology of Osmanlilik and Its Purveyors

These reorganization measures, as distinguished from principles contained in the reform edicts, addressed social and economic problems that the Ottoman government viewed as requiring urgent attention. From the mid-1860s to the mid-1870s, a counter elite challenged this centralizing thrust. Initially a literary movement, the *New Ottomans* (also known as Young Ottomans) opposed Ali and Fu'ad for having ignored the individual human-rights aspects of the 1839 and 1856 reform edicts.

In place of millet identity and rights, they proposed *osmanlilik* (Ottoman nationality) to encompass all segments of society, with rights guaranteed by constitutional and parliamentary government. Love of freedom and of fatherland (*vatan*) would unite all citizens. Since osmanlilik would define citizens of the state, religious hierarchies for civil purposes would no longer be needed. After their demise, the ideas of the Young Ottomans remained—especially their advocacy of human rights, despite European influences, in the name of Islam—to inspire an Ottoman political movement based in Europe.

Among the most important Young Ottomans were Ziya Pasha, Namik Kemal, and Ibrahim Sinasi. To publicize their ideas, especially the right to criticize the government, they utilized journalism. In 1865, the Ottoman government responded by introducing the first Ottoman censorship law; it shut down most of their newspapers. The New Ottomans, however, were not without influential allies. Mustafa Fazil, younger brother of Egypt's ruler Khedive Isma'il, patronized them, publicly calling on Sultan Abdulaziz to halt degeneration of the empire and to implement constitutional government. Although they eventually succeeded in securing a constitution in December 1876—the third noteworthy Tanzimat decree—it was abrogated in February 1878 and was not revived for over thirty years.

Protest and Uprisings in Ottoman Europe

Why was their success ephemeral? The New Ottomans propounded their ideas at the worst of times for the empire and then gained power in a coup d'etat that replaced Abdulaziz with an unstable son of Abdulmejid, Murad V, from May until August 1876. Just what misfortunes were plaguing the Ottomans at this time? Debt, revolt, and European intervention were three serious and interrelated problems. After the Crimean War, the Ottoman Empire fell into the same debt syndrome that inflicted other Asian and North African lands. The Tanzimat had aimed at regularizing tax collection not only to eliminate abuses of peasants but also to insure the state of incoming revenues while it was at war. But the Tanzimat's growing bureaucracy required additional funds at a time when government-controlled territory was shrinking. To meet expenses, the Ottoman government began to borrow money. At first, loans were small and contracted at interest rates of 3–4 percent.

But war and the expensive tastes of Abdulaziz led to large borrowings at much higher rates in the 1860s and 1870s. By 1875, the debt to bondholders—largely foreigners—was estimated at about £200 million. On 6 October 1875, the Ottoman government announced that it could pay in cash only half of the amount coming due. It would issue short-term treasury bonds for future redemption to cover the balance.

With an uprising on Crete in 1866–68 and a new Balkan war on the horizon, the announcement came at a most inopportune time. Excessive taxation to meet expenditures had provoked provincial disturbances in the first place. Revolts, which began in Bosnia and Herzegovina and were exacerbated by bad harvests in 1874, spread widely through the Balkans in 1875, reaching Bulgaria in 1876. Whereas the initial thrust of Bulgarian anger in the 1860s had been directed against the Greeks, by the 1870s the Bulgarians hoped to cast off Ottoman Turkish rule. Just as the Ottomans were finishing off the Bulgarian revolutionaries (killing an estimated 10–20,000) and the revolt further north, Serbia and Montenegro declared war on the empire.

Deposition of Abdulaziz

Into this unsettled milieu came the New Ottomans led by Midhat Pasha, who promoted osmanlilik and a constitution. Despite having retired to private life, he helped bring the New Ottomans to power in hopes of quelling the Balkan uprisings and preventing further European financial intervention. After demonstrations in May 1876, Abdulaziz appointed New Ottoman supporters in his government, including Midhat as minister without portfolio. But the new appointees dethroned him, first in favor of Murad V and then for Abdulhamid II.

In April 1877, Russia entered the Balkan fray. As the main proponent of pan-Slavic and pan-Orthodox ideologies in the Balkans, Russia hoped to extricate these groups from firm Ottoman rule. In March

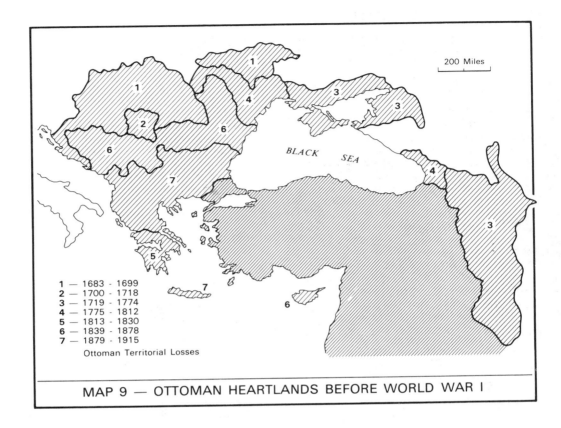

200 Miles

BLACK   SEA

1 — 1683 - 1699
2 — 1700 - 1718
3 — 1719 - 1774
4 — 1775 - 1812
5 — 1813 - 1830
6 — 1839 - 1878
7 — 1879 - 1915

Ottoman Territorial Losses

MAP 9 — OTTOMAN HEARTLANDS BEFORE WORLD WAR I

1878, after the Russian armies had reached within ten miles of Istanbul, the New Ottoman government agreed to the Treaty of San Stefano, temporarily creating a large Bulgaria and giving the Black Sea port of Batum and the stategic Anatolian towns of Kars and Ardahan to Russia. Objecting to the treaty, the concert of Europe convened the Congress of Berlin, opening in June 1878, to modify it.

The Congress of Berlin

Secret diplomacy preceded the congress. Ottoman leaders promised to place Cyprus under British administration if the Russians retained the eastern Anatolian territories, but Britain and Russia had already agreed on their retention. By the terms of the Berlin treaty, Bosnia and Herzegovina came under Austrian admin-

istration; Serbia, Montenegro, and Rumania became fully independent, and Bulgaria was restricted to a small area as an autonomous province still under Ottoman rule. In exchange for its full independence, Rumania gave Bessarabia to Russia. But Russia's Bolsheviks returned Kars and Ardahan to the Ottomans after the October Revolution of 1917. Maps 9 and 10 show the contraction of the Ottoman Empire.

Besides these territorial questions, the Congress of Berlin addressed for the first time in an international forum the Armenian issue. Armenians, at this time demanding increased autonomy in order to protect themselves from Turkish and Kurdish marauders and from arbitrary acts of Turkish officials, won European recognition of their grievances. Although the Ottomans had earlier made concessions in the San Stefano Treaty (1878), the Arme-

MAP 10 — THE OTTOMAN BALKANS

99

nians feared that these would be disregarded. Participants at the Congress of Berlin, though, could hardly give more than verbal support for Armenian autonomy when Armenians were scattered mainly in remote areas of Anatolia.

The cumulative effects of the uprisings, war, and foreign interference in Ottoman business on Abdulhamid II was considerable. From his vantage point, his nineteenth-century predecessors had brought the empire to the brink of disaster. Democratization appeared inappropriate. He did not intend to become a constitutional monarch. Moreover, concessions to non-Muslims in the empire were viewed as having failed to promote loyalty to the Ottoman state, especially in the Balkans. Militarily, the positive effects of changes made earlier in the century had not become fully evident because of the frequency of war during the Tanzimat.

The Ottoman Debt Question

After the Congress of Berlin, the Ottoman debt question remained. In 1881, Abdulhamid II set up a Council of Administration of the Ottoman Public Debt.

French, German, Austrian, Italian, and English (for English and Dutch) members represented bondholders in each country. The European-controlled Ottoman Bank and Ottoman bondholders also sat on the council. To pay the debt, the council would have control of selected revenues. It planned to improve the functioning of industries (such as the silk industry) under its authority. Bondholders agreed to accept amounts closer to what the Ottomans had actually received instead of the face values of the loan. Efficient operation of the council soon restored Ottoman credit in Europe and permitted continued investment in Ottoman economic life. But the allocation of large chunks of money for debt service restricted government finances. Turkish personnel working with the debt administration gained experience that the post-World War I Turkish state could utilize, but most of the Ottoman debt bureaucracy was composed of non-Muslim minorities, a factor that exacerbated communal tensions. The council itself was abolished with the birth of the Turkish republic, but other former Ottoman lands, such as Egypt, found themselves burdened with the debt because their revenues had been used to guarantee it.

Egypt in the Age of High Finance

Domestic developments in Egypt during the Ottoman Tanzimat continued to parallel those of the empire as a whole. Yet Egypt confronted a unique set of problems ensuing directly from its decision to permit a former French diplomat Ferdinand de Lesseps to cut a canal through the Isthmus of Suez, a dream de Lesseps had formed while serving five years as France's vice-consul and consul-general at Alexandria from 1832. While his father Mathieu had occupied the same post years earlier, Ferdinand had made friends with one of Muhammad Ali's eighty-four children, Muhammad Sa'id (known as Sa'id). This friendship was renewed when Fer-

dinand returned to Egypt, but because Mahmud II had not yet given Muhammad Ali hereditary rights to Egypt, de Lesseps could not have known that Sa'id would one day rule Egypt. As soon as that transpired in 1854, de Lesseps rushed to Egypt. There Sa'id showered him with preferential treatment as an honored friend and granted him the canal concession.

The Suez Canal Concession

By the terms of the twelve articles of the concession, the *Compagnie Universelle du Canal Maritime de Suez* (Canal Company) and Egypt made a ninety-year agreement to begin when the canal opened. The Paris-based company received two especially valuable provisions: 1) Egypt would supply the labor for building the canal; and 2) Egypt granted the company a two kilometer-wide stretch on each side of the canal and on each side of a freshwater canal that ran from the Nile to the canal site (to provide water for the laborers and other personnel). Egypt would collect no taxes on this land, and the company would reap the profits of any produce grown there. In exchange, Egypt received a preferred allotment of company shares providing 15 percent of the net profits. Other founding shareholders would gain 10 percent. The remaining 75 percent of the profits would go to ordinary shareholders.

The project was launched during the Crimean War—an inopportune moment for obtaining international cooperation. Because of the influence of Britain's ambassador with Abdulmejid, de Lesseps viewed British support for the project as necessary for securing the essential Ottoman approval. But potential backers in Britain were suspicious. When de Lesseps formed his company in 1858, neither Britons, Russians, Americans, Austrians nor Ottomans took up the shares reserved for them. Since Sa'id had agreed to buy any shares which were not subscribed, Egypt's ruler ended up with 44 percent of the ordinary shares, besides the founding shares. Construction of the canal began in 1859. Sa'id died in 1863, six years before its opening. Although Egypt had exchanged much for very little, Sa'id to his death remained a confirmed supporter of the project. Abdulmejid never approved the concession, but Abdulaziz did so in exchange for increased Egyptian payments and for support in suppressing the 1866–68 revolt in Crete.

What else can be noted about Sa'id's policies? He promoted indigenous Egyptians into the military officer ranks, giving them hopes for future advancement. However, he neglected education at al-Azhar and ignored a new public education project that would have helped the lower classes. Turko-Circassians and foreigners maintained their predominant political, social, and economic role. Sa'id assisted foreign schools catering to Christian and Jewish Egyptians. Foreign businessmen, though, soon outnumbered foreign educators. Attracted by opportunities for quick profits after the United States blockade cut off cotton shipments from the South during the American Civil War (1861–65), foreign hustlers poured into Egypt. Sa'id's nephew and successor, son of Muhammad Ali's son Ibrahim—Isma'il Pasha (1863–79)—had to deal with the consequences.

Isma'il and His Modernization Program

Historians have observed how ironic it is that Sa'id, a profligate spender, left Egypt with a debt of some £3–4 million while Isma'il, who had a reputation for shrewd management, stepped down in 1879 with a staggering debt of nearly £100 million of which he actually received £65 million. In the 1860s, European bankers granted Isma'il more and more credit in anticipation of reaping huge profits. He was a man of vision and initiative who came to power during an economic boom. The Egypt of the 1860s was not one of overpopulation and doomsaying. Rather, it contained hopes and dreams of prosperity for all Egyptians.

Isma'il planned to make Egypt a showpiece of modernization and efficiency, starting with the beautification of Cairo to rival Europe's great cities. Cairo and Alexandria were supplied with gas and running water. Under Isma'il, Egypt's railway system was extended south to the Sudan, and he constructed nearly 5,000 miles of telegraph lines. The privately owned postal service was nationalized. With the new demand for cotton, Isma'il invested heavily in some 8,000 miles of waterworks and improved Alexandria's port facilities. Moreover, he took over and expanded the merchant marine so that Egypt could carry its expanding trade. Egypt's prosperity led Isma'il to mortgage its future for these projects.

Renegotiation of the Canal Concession: Isma'il's Miscalculation

From the outset, the Suez Canal constituted a major, largely unproductive drain on Egypt's resources. In 1863, Isma'il saw that Sa'id had compromised Egypt's sovereignty by granting the company ownership of the land surrounding the freshwater canal. Moreover, Isma'il wanted to abolish the corvée (forced labor) provision. The British advised him to repudiate objectionable articles of the concession, but he felt honor-bound to negotiate them with the company. Then, failing to reach agreement, he allowed the dispute to be adjudicated by an all-French panel headed by Emperor Louis Napoleon! In exchange for paying canal workers and relinquishing land donated by Sa'id, the company won a generous indemnity.

Isma'il's lobbying efforts in Istanbul secured approval for the concession. Then, in 1866 and 1867, the sultan granted him a more prestigious title—*khidiw* (khedive)—and the right of his son rather than Muhammad Ali's eldest male heir to succeed him. Isma'il also obtained Abdulaziz's permission to proclaim decrees independently, except in foreign affairs. To prove to European leaders that Egypt had joined Europe, Isma'il invited them at Egypt's expense to attend the Suez Canal opening festivities in 1869. For Empress Eugenie of France he built a huge palace, now the Cairo Marriott Hotel, on the Nile's Gezira Island. He then commissioned Italian composer Giuseppe Verdi to write the opera *Aïda*. Although Isma'il spent at least two-thirds as much for the canal opening as for the concession revisions, canal-related expenditures brought him neither glory nor respect in the long run.

Educational and Legal Changes

Egyptians and historians have viewed Isma'il's educational and legal measures more favorably. Reconstituting the education department and adopting the lapsed plans for a national school system, he supported creative administrators such as Ali Mubarak. The ruler saw education as necessary for Egypt's socioeconomic progress, and not just as an arm of the military as in the days of Muhammad Ali. Only the medical and military schools remained from the latter's higher schools. Isma'il founded the School of Administration and Languages (later the School of Law) and the Muhandiskhana (Engineering School). A School of Egyptology opened along with specialized lower schools such as the School for the Blind (later Blind and Deaf) and the Technical School. But the new school with deepest roots among indigenous Egyptian Muslims was the teacher-training college for Arabic teachers, Dar al-Ulum, founded in 1872.

Through the Public School Law of 1868, Egypt established a national school system that eventually held control over *kuttabs*, too. Higher level primary and secondary schools would receive funds through an annual government education budget separate from awqaf. Boys' schools as well as the first girls' school—al-Siyufiyya in 1873—opened. Ali Mubarak felt that average al-Azhar shaykhs teaching in kuttabs were not sufficiently well-trained to teach in the national primary schools. Dar al-Ulum would admit the best of these and retrain them as modern teachers.

In the end, though for fifty years it was usually Egypt's second largest (after the medical school) higher school, Dar al-Ulum was too small and selective. Most of its graduates ended up as educational administrators or as teachers at the secondary or university level. Like the National Library (Dar al-Kutub) founded in 1871, Dar al-Ulum (now part of Cairo University) is among the most enduring of Isma'il's achievements. Plans for a national school system in Egypt, however, were not fully realized on a mass level until the 1950s. As in Europe, post-elementary mass education was not a characteristic of nineteenth- or early twentieth-century Egypt.

What legal reforms benefited Egyptians? The Armenian Nubar Pasha successfully negotiated with foreign representatives to set up mixed courts like those in the Ottoman heartlands to mitigate abuses of Egyptians by foreigners. They lasted from 1875 to 1949. Foreigners could no longer escape to their own consuls after having committed a crime. Such high standards were demanded of lawyers practicing in these courts that even by 1930 only half of them were Egyptians. Creation of the mixed courts lent impetus to a movement to fix the rule of law more firmly in Egypt by curtailing the ruler's autocratic power. Although Isma'il in 1866 created a consultative assembly, he did so more to gain approval for new taxes than to lay foundations for constitutional government.

Taxes left few areas of Egyptian life untouched. Faced with sharing the blame for hardships imposed on Egyptians, the assembly began to demand greater responsibility. Forced loans further aroused landowners. In 1871, desperately in need of hard cash, Isma'il tried to raise money by promising landowners that if they paid several years' taxes in advance, their tax obligation thereafter would be reduced by half. Made obligatory in 1874, the *muqabala* (future) loans failed to stave off bankruptcy. The assembly became a forum for expression of national discontent and demand for a constitution.

Meanwhile, Egypt gained legal autonomy. In 1873, Abdulaziz gave Isma'il the right to absorb the Sudan, to enlarge his army, and to arrange loans or commercial agreements with Europeans without the sultan's approval. Isma'il employed Englishmen Samuel Baker and Charles Gordon, along with veterans from the American Civil War, in his quest to solidify Egypt's hold over the Sudan. He aimed to halt the slave trade. Despite initial success in controlling the territory, Isma'il's officials collaborated with slavers.

In the mid-1870s, a decision to move into Ethiopia brought on a severe defeat in which Egypt's army sustained heavy casualties. While Isma'il could dismiss the Americans held responsible for the failure, he could not placate Egyptian officers and soldiers. Native Egyptian officers, dating from Sa'id's day, objected to having been passed over for promotion in favor of the Turko-Circassians who still constituted the bulk of the Egyptian elite. Their discontent was to form the basis of an emerging national movement.

Islamic Reformers and the Call for a Constitution

The spread of education and the creation of new elites contributed to another development with consequences for Egyptian nationalism—the spread of the printed word in Egypt. Early in his reign, Isma'il revived the journal *al-Waqa'i al-Misriyya*, placing it under Muhammad Abduh (who was soon famous at Dar al-Ulum, in Muslim reform, as an advocate of improving the status of women and as mufti of Egypt). Abduh used the journal to educate the public, calling into question the government's blind pursuit of Europeanization. As Isma'il's financial problems grew and as Syrian emigrés escaping Abdulhamid II's censorship policies arrived, more publications exposing the ills of Egypt began to appear. By the time Isma'il abdicated in 1879, ten Arabic newspapers, including today's *al-Ahram*, were being published.

Both the consultative assembly and the country's papers often reflected the ideas of Muslim propagandist Jamal al-Din, who called himself "al-Afghani" although he was Persian. Afghani, in Egypt in 1869 and from 1871 to 1879, toured the Muslim world then rapidly coming under European control. He was the pioneer of what became known as the Islamic reform movement. He inspired his listeners to have confidence in their own heritage and institutions and to fight for political equality and independence. In Egypt, his message lent support to al-Hizb al-Watani (the National Party) which hoped to speak for Muslims, Christians, and Jews alike. Like Abduh and Egyptian alim Husayn al-Marsafi, Afghani spoke out against those who would blindly adopt

European institutions and practices. He advocated representative and responsible government. In 1879, a constitution was readied for approval. As in the Ottoman heartland, it remained dormant because of Isma'il's deposition and the subequent British occupation.

Egypt's Financial Woes and the Dual Control

By 1875, Isma'il was so desperate for funds that he placed on the market his 44 percent of ordinary shares in the Suez Canal. Benjamin Disraeli purchased the shares for the British government. Isma'il gained £4 million from the sale of shares; these were to generate an annual income of several hundred thousand pounds. The sale left Isma'il with only his 15 percent share of annual profits. Controllers sold them at discount later. In 1876, the Khedive admitted that he could no longer meet his payrolls. An international debt commission was appointed. Thus dual control began, with British and French controllers operating on the principle that debtors should sacrifice on behalf of creditors. Some two-thirds of Egypt's annual revenue was to be spent for debt service.

The new administration was too demanding on Egypt's resources. By November 1877, even the British consul-general Vivian noticed that Egyptians could not sustain these sacrifices. Low Nile waters by 1878 caused disease, starvation, and widespread oppression of peasants by landlords. A cotton blight exacerbated the hardship. The English commissioner Major Evelyn Baring (Lord Cromer after 1892) finally consented to a modification of the debt arrangement early in 1878 on condition that Isma'il appoint a cabinet and distinguish between his own private income and revenues of the Egyptian state. Isma'il agreed, making Nubar the first prime minister. His cabinet included a French minister of public works and an English minister of finance. Resenting the imposition of Europeans in the government, Isma'il set about undermining their position in the consultative assembly and the army. When civil servants and military officers were placed on half-pay, with 2,500 army officers forcibly retired, a small protest occurred. Isma'il used it as a pretext for dismissing Nubar. He then secured from religious leaders of all persuasions, army officers, and notables a petition demanding removal of the European ministers. He proposed reinstituting European controllers but making his cabinet all-Egyptian. This effort at redefinition failed, despite assurances that Egypt would pay its debts. The European powers pressured Abdulhamid II to depose Isma'il (d. 1895). On 30 June 1879, he sailed to Europe on his yacht *Mahroussa* (which would also carry away King Faruq after the revolution in 1952).

Egypt under Isma'il embarked on a massive and rapid national expansion program that touched virtually every facet of Egyptian life. Ambitious in scope and often alien in nature, his various schemes brought forth internal and external forces beyond his control. In the short term, debts brought about foreign intervention, but in the long term, it may have been the Suez Canal that sealed Egypt's fate, especially when Britain, its principal user, became a major shareholder. The canal in the end cost an estimated £16 million instead of the original estimated construction cost of £3 million. Of this, Egypt paid about £11.5 million and foreigners only £4.5 million. The 1880 Law of Liquidation left Egypt without profits from the canal for the next fifty-six years.

Isma'il's Forced Abdication and the Urabi Movement

Isma'il's son and successor Tawfiq (d. 1892) chose a cautious policy, asking Europeans to compromise on the cabinet issue but also indicating that the new constitution ready for promulgation was unacceptable. No longer cabinet ministers, the Europeans' controller status was restored but with advisory powers in the cabinet and under their own governments' authority. Baring returned to Egypt in this role late in 1879. Despite these setbacks, nationalist forces did not give up. Afghani's exile did not hamper the new Muslim elites. Native army officers led by Ahmad Urabi continued to press for promotion. Constitutionalists pressed their demands for a constitution while journalists lent support to the popular movement. Although peasants remained aloof, Egyptian officers of peasant origin decried the plight of agriculturalists.

In February 1881, army officers pressured Tawfiq to appoint the Egyptian nationalist poet Mahmud Sami al-Barudi as war minister. Following up their success, nationalists instituted a new cabinet, reviving the idea of a constitution and an assembly. A year later, Britain and France sent a threatening note to the Egyptian government; they feared that the nationalists would diminish Tawfiq's questionable power and refuse to meet Egypt's financial obligations. In reply, the Egyptians raised al-Barudi to prime minister and Urabi to minister of war. By mid-1882, the new government appeared for a variety of reasons to have secured wide-ranging support among Egyptians united against European intervention.

British Forces Occupy Egypt

Still motivated by financial matters, Britain and France decided to intervene by sending a joint fleet to Alexandria. Abdulhamid II sent his own representatives to negotiate with both Tawfiq and the nationalists. Within four days, demonstrations in Alexandria prompted reports of deaths and injuries to Europeans. Urabi acted quickly to restore order and began to fortify Alexandria to protect the port. After further negotiations, the British admiral Seymour decided to attack. With a ten-hour bombardment following the evacuation of most British residents, Alexandria was soon in flames and most fortifications destroyed. The British tried to blame Urabi for the fire and by 13 July landed troops in the city. When Tawfiq finally declared Urabi a rebel on 24 July, he implied that it was because Urabi had mounted an inadequate defense against the British! Abdulhamid II refused to approve this rebel designation, but Urabi was still in danger.

Believing de Lesseps' assurance that Britain would be denied use of the Suez Canal, Urabi refused to block it as advised by British sympathizer Wilfrid Blunt. But in August a British force entered the canal, landing at Isma'iliyya. Egypt's troops fought valiantly, but in September 1882, British forces were able to march into Cairo, insisting that they would withdraw soon. The imperial imperative, however, resulted in British troops remaining in Egypt until 1956.

Iran to World War I

Suppression of the Baha'is

After Muhammad Shah died in 1848, followers of the Bab used the interregnum to foment revolt in Iran. The teenager Nasir al-Din Shah (1848–96) executed Ali Muhammad in 1850. When in 1852 a Babi group tried to assassinate the shah, he responded with a more brutal repression in which a prominent female Babi, Qurrat al-Ayn, was killed. Babism resurfaced led by Baha'ullah (1817–92) who in 1863 announced that he was the new prophet whose appearance the Bab had predicted. His followers, Baha'is, continued Babism's social reformist tendencies, promoting interests of the commercial classes and supporting women's rights. Baha'ullah made Babism more pacifist and universal. Baha'is modernized more rapidly than other Iranian groups and associated more closely with Europeans and Americans. As purveyor of a new international order, Baha'ullah was expelled by the Qajars. The Ottomans settled him in Akka where he continued his preaching. His son carried on his work, winning disciples by his pacifism and broad outlook, especially in Europe and the United States. Baha'ism remains an international spiritual movement that has a strong moral content and a proselytizing zeal, with its headquarters in Haifa. Iranians never officially accepted either Baha'is or Azalis (followers of Baha'ullah's brother) as protected by Islam because conversion from Islam—apostasy—is a capital offense. From time to time, Baha'is have undergone persecution in Iran, most recently in the aftermath of the Iranian revolution of 1977–79.

Nasir al-Din's Modernization Program: European Influences

Nasir al-Din embarked on a modernization program. He used English and Russian models initially guided by his able minister Mirza Taqi Khan (Amir Kabir). Printing developed apace after 1851 when an official newspaper was founded. Amir Kabir opened Dar al-Funun to provide higher military and civilian education based on European models. He nevertheless kept it small to curtail power of its new elites. Nasir al-Din continued establishing lower schools as begun by Muhammad Shah. Graduates of his schools were educated in western liberal traditions; many favored making Iran a constitutional monarchy. As in the days of Abbas Mirza, however, Iran's traditional elites preferred seeing Iran's government weak and decentralized. Despite the preponderance of Russian and British pressures before World War I, the most popular western language in Iran, as in international diplomacy, was French.

Nasir al-Din ruled Iran for almost fifty years, during an era of aggressive European imperialism. His own expansionist program conflicted with British and Russian plans. In 1856, Persian forces briefly succeeded in taking Herat, much to the chagrin of the British who had fought in Afghanistan between 1839 and 1841. By landing troops from India to the Gulf region, Britain forced the Persians to withdraw from Herat and to recognize Afghan independence. The Treaty of Paris in 1857 also gave Britain trading privileges already enjoyed by Russians in Iran. British-Russian rivalry shifted to the commercial arena. By 1900, at least thirteen other countries secured equal preference.

On Nasir al-Din's three long trips to Europe taken between 1873 and 1889 (diaries of which he published in Persian), he paid special attention to military matters and hoped to introduce western military technology and industries into his domains. Like early Ottoman modernizers, Nasir al-Din thought that adoption of western methods would protect Iran's independence.

Expansion of an Export Economy and the World Market

Historians have acknowledged that as is true of other Middle Eastern countries, Iran's further integration into the world market through expanding commercial and military ties brought mixed blessings. Iranians cultivated tastes for imported luxuries like tea and tobacco without building economic power to make them affordable. Export crops—such as cotton and opium—replaced food crops.

As elsewhere in the Middle East, the Civil War in the United States led to a cotton boom, but Iran suffered during the aftermath. Late in the 1860s, when Iran experienced famine, people starved because of contracting food crops. Military expenditures and wars led to costly arms imports and military consultants. Tariff protection allowed cheap European manufacturers to put indigenous producers out of business, especially in long-established industries such as textiles. Only a few Iranian crafts, including carpet-weaving, prospered although new aniline dyes reduced quality. Without an administrative overhaul, only the upper classes benefited to any great extent from Iranian-European rapprochement. Peasant classes paid higher taxes to subsidize modernization. Urban dwellers could more easily protest oppressive assessments while tribes often lay outside the state's authority and therefore suffered less.

European Concessions and Economic Development

Nasir al-Din felt secure enough to grant generous concessions to Europeans for road-building, railroad construction, telegraph communications, and schools, including those founded by missionaries. One of his broadest concessions was granted to British interests through Baron Julius de Reuter but arranged by Prime Minister Mirza Husayn Khan (d. 1881). Although the concession gave rights in oil and mineral exploitation, irrigation systems, railway and streetcar line construction, and in founding a national bank, Nasir al-Din cancelled it only one year later because Russia objected. De Reuter's son established the Imperial Bank of Persia after another sixteen years. Russians opened the Discount Bank of Persia in 1891 and won special fishing rights in the Caspian Sea. Meanwhile, Mirza Husayn Khan set up a postal system, a government cabinet organization, and a more centralized judiciary. His modernizing thrust was carried on after his death by Amin al-Dawla and the Armenian Mirza Malkum Khan.

The Cossack Brigade

The main new-order reform of Nasir al-Din involved modernizing Iran's military with the creation of a small Russian-advised unit, a brigade of Persian Cossacks based on a Russian model. This is ironic because it was Russia that expanded in the nineteenth century into Central Asian territory once governed by Iran (including the great cities of Bukhara and Smarkand). In 1882, Iran had to cede Merv as well. The Cossack brigade was based in Iran's northern cities, becoming

an instrument of repression for the shah's successors. Eventually, its Iranian officers overturned the Qajar dynasty.

Although Nasir al-Din's concessions subsidized foreign trips and carried out public-works projects, they did not meet with universal approval within Iran. Mirza Malkum, for example, lost his job because of protests against his arranging of a British-sponsored lottery; the lottery would have violated Islam's prohibition against gambling. Late in the 1880s, Nasir al-Din invited Jamal al-Din al-Afghani to return home. Arriving with the shah in 1889, Jamal al-Din soon turned against his patron, seeing in Qajar Iran the same ills he had observed elsewhere. Foreign economic penetration would pave the way for political intervention.

Afghani and the Tobacco Concession Protest

Jamal al-Din, hopeful that Iran's independent mujtahids would follow his lead in the name of democracy and the rule of law embodied in Shari'a, embarked on a campaign against a new concession that the shah proposed to grant to a British company. This was the tobacco monopoly of 1890. Afghani convinced local traders that the monopoly would harm small indigenous traders and compromise Iran's independence. Although Afghani was expelled to Iraq in 1891, he appealed to Mirza Hasan Shirazi, the Shi'i leader based there. This mujtahid declared a prohibition on smoking tobacco, of which the Iranians were heavy users, until the concession was withdrawn. They obeyed him, forcing the government to reconsider.

The alliance of religious authorities, small traders, and even modernizing intellectuals would re-emerge in the future. Nasir al-Din was obliged to pay the tobacco monopoly an indemnity, but he could do it only by borrowing £500,000 from de Reuter's bank, pledging the southern customs duties as security. Foreign encroachment increased and, in 1896, a disciple of Afghani assassinated the shah. Afghani, continuing his pan-Islamic program in the service of Abdulhamid II in Istanbul, was not extradited; he died of cancer in 1897. Iranians suspected the sultan of having done away with him for his democratizing, antiforeign views.

Nasir al-Din's son and successor, Mudhaffar al-Din (1897–1907), came to power under pressure from the new social alliance to roll back foreign influence. After having placed the administration of the remaining customs duties under Belgian personnel, Mudhaffar al-Din pledged the northern customs receipts as security on a Russian loan he obtained in 1900. Using this money to fund the first of three costly trips to Europe and to pay other Iranian debts, Mudhaffar al-Din contracted another huge loan from Russia. An agreement in 1901 gave Russia preferential tariffs for Russian goods entering Qajar domains.

The Oil Concession

During Mudhaffar al-Din's reign, concessions for oil exploration in Iran were granted for the first time. A British firm (later the Anglo-Persian Oil Company, then Anglo-Iranian, and finally British Petroleum or B.P.) commenced its search for oil in 1901. About to abandon the concession in 1908, it discovered oil in commercial quantities in southern Iran. By 1912, oil shipments from Abadan had begun and an oil refinery was built the same year. The British government acquired majority interest in the company after the onset of World War I, spurred on by the conversion of British naval ships from coal to oil. Iran was the first Middle Eastern country in which commercial amounts of oil were discovered and exploited.

The Constitutional Movement and its Suppression

The sociopolitical protest which arose in Iran between 1901 and 1906 was aided by internal and international developments. Government opponents criticized the government through books and underground newspapers published in Persian. At the turn of the century, Britain was bogged down in the Boer War in South Africa, and was thereby distracted from blocking extension of Russian influence. Then the Russians in 1904–5 embarked on a disastrous war with Japan that destroyed the Russian fleet. Iranians saw that European Russia was vulnerable and that an Asian nation could become a world power without compromising its cultural heritage. In Russia, a constitutional revolt challenged autocracy in 1905. Considering their own autocrat's weakness, Persian constitutionalists late in 1905 began rallying forces to pressure him into becoming a constitutional monarch.

The catalyst for the constitutional movement came with the government's intended punishment for price fixing of sugar merchants in Tehran. Merchants resorted to the Persian custom of taking refuge (*bast*) in a mosque to escape the flogging to which they had been sentenced. The shah forced their expulsion; this rallied many ulama. They organized a larger Tehran bast. Intellectuals also supported this protest in hopes of using it to achieve constitutional reform. Popular support for the protesters grew to such an extent that Mudhaffar al-Din agreed to convene a chamber of justice to consider grievances. Then he was felled by a stroke. This gave his minister an opportunity for greater suppression. Ulama gathered in Qum. Inspired by their example, groups around the country in July 1906—in Tabriz, Rasht, Shiraz, Isfahan, and in Tehran at the British embassy—staged what amounted to a national bast that virtually imposed a general strike. Guilds and political clubs assured distribution of food and maintenance of order.

By August, the shah capitulated to the bastis' demands: dismissal of the minister, establishment of a constitution and national assembly, and creation of law codes and courts to curtail abuses of Qajar princes who served as governors throughout Iran. Using a Belgian model, a commission wrote a constitution providing for a national assembly (*majlis*) which, though based on limited suffrage, would provide for election of representatives of all social and ethnic groups. By October 1906, the majlis held its first meeting, and by December, the constitution was approved and signed by both Mudhaffar al-Din and his son and heir Muhammad Ali. Democratic forces in the majlis, led by Tabriz deputies, recommended establishment of municipal councils and urged the adoption of equal legal status for all subjects. Newspapers again flourished.

The very ill Mudhaffar al-Din died in January 1907. Muhammad Ali, who had developed a reputation for ruthlessness while governor of Tabriz (which had fueled the constitutionalist movement in Azerbayjan), had no intention of allowing an assembly to control national spending or to encroach on his previous prerogatives of ruling by decree. He encouraged opponents of the constitution's secular thrust. Although the majlis tried to raise money for a national bank that would replace foreign banks in lending to the government, it could not secure sufficient capital for the success of the project. In August 1907, the government debated whether to accept a Russian loan after arrangements for a less threatening German loan had been obstructed. The government minister advocating the Russian loan was assassinated.

On the same day in 1907, Britain and Russia concluded the Treaty of St. Petersburg. This divided Iran into three spheres of influence. British supremacy in southeastern Iran, bounded by Kirman and Bandar Abbas in the west, was accepted by Russia. In return, Britain acknowledged special Russian interests in the Qajars' northern domains—Azerbayjan, Khurasan, and northcentral Iran encompassing both Tehran and Isfahan. A neutral zone in fact also became a British-dominated sphere. Although the agreement was justified as guarding against German penetration and protecting Iran's independence, Iranians who had no say in the matter felt that they had been abandoned to the Russians by the British. Britain and Russia also agreed to maintain the status quo of slight British predominance

in Afghanistan. In Iran, the agreement strengthened the resolve of democratic forces to uphold the new constitution and majlis.

In the end, the constitutional forces failed. In June 1908, the Cossack brigade with its Russian commander attacked the majlis' building and dissolved parliament. One committed constitutionalist shot himself rather than face returning home without having fought. Like the deputies, the shah still had no standing army other than the tribal forces upon whom he occasionally called. In this case, the Bakhtiaris in the west chose to support the constitutionalist side against the shah. Tabriz also rallied behind pro-majlis forces and was subdued only by a Russian occupation army. During the civil war, European interests were judiciously guarded in hopes that Europeans might intervene to support the constitutionalists. Women demonstrated in favor of democracy. In July 1909, the Bakhtiaris and northerners defeated the cossacks and entered Tehran. Muhammad Ali Shah fled to Russia while the majlis placed his eleven-year-old son Ahmad Shah on the throne, under guidance of regent Nasir al-Mulk.

Constitutional forces faced several handicaps. First, they had to work with old administrators because few new officers or bureaucrats could be found. Secondly, socioeconomic change was not a major thrust of their program. Thirdly, the American W. Morgan Shuster who came to Iran in 1911 to put its finances in order quickly offended old ruling elites by refusing them exemptions. He also irritated the Europeans by taking his duties as an Iranian civil servant seriously. Shuster met with Russian opposition, too. After failing in an attempt to restore the former shah, Russia invaded in 1911, killing constitutionalists at Tabriz and assaulting the holy shrine of Shi'i Imam Reza at Mashhad. Russia's demand for Shuster's ouster and the invasion did not break the resolve of the majlis to uphold the American minister, but Nasir al-Mulk's cabinet agreed to dismiss him and his American colleagues.

Despite popular support for the majlis, the cabinet dispensed with consultative government and the constitution. Nevertheless, the document of 1906 and the popular movement which it generated remained vivid memories in the hearts and minds of the Iranian people. The coalition of mujtahids, workers, and educated elites that achieved the Iranian revolution of 1978–79 looked back for inspiration to the democratic interlude of 1906–1909.

Conclusion

Constitutional movements in the nineteenth-century Ottoman heartlands, in British-occupied Egypt, and in early twentieth-century Iran achieved ephem-eral successes, only to be replaced by authoritarian regimes of one sort or another. In the former two areas, new movements surfaced even as the Iranian constitutionalists struggled to retain their recently won representative government. New nationalisms in the Ottoman Empire challenged ongoing Ottoman efforts at accommodation, thereby bringing on repression and reaction of ethnic and religious minorities. The strengthening of the Turkish element in Anatolia fueled Turkish nationalism, too. Social and economic changes of the nineteenth century had aroused deep hostilities that soon erupted in Ottoman Europe and Asia. Yet the Ottoman Empire could still count on most of its subjects for loyalty and support if only it could meet their aspirations for decentralization and autonomy.

CHAPTER EIGHT

Nationalism in the Ottoman Empire Before World War I

The late nineteenth and early twentieth centuries witnessed increased manifestations of nationalism in Ottoman lands. Most activities focused on redefining group identities in response to economic, social, political, and international pressures. Demands for autonomy from vocal minorities still did not necessarily imply desire for secession or separate nationhood. For Christian minorities, foreign conferences became sounding boards for airing internal grievances that had once been channeled through representative institutions in the empire. Foreign intervention probably exacerbated rather than resolved tensions. Two groups seeking autonomy, the Kurds and the Armenians, were concentrated in Anatolia. Although many Greeks lived there, too, they had their independent state already. The Balkans were separating from the empire under Russian-influenced pan-Slavism.

Although Ottoman decentralizers of all ethnic groups cooperated in search of a new national formula, most Ottoman leaders reacted defensively. Alongside separatist nationalisms arose a Turkish nationalism. If subject peoples insisted on their own identity, so too would Turks. Turkism and Turkification brought on more vigorous Kurdish and Arab Muslim self-assertion. By World War I, Kurds and Arabs of the Ottoman Empire were seeking autonomy and possibly independence, showing the extent to which the nation-state based on language, ethnicity, territory, and religion had won acceptance.

Ottoman Recentralization

Abdulhamid II renewed government-centralization, and expanded communications through telegraph lines and railroads. In 1888, the Orient Express connecting Istanbul with Paris and later Vienna was inaugurated. Telegraphic lines extended as far as New Delhi and London. Book-printing and newspaper publication spread, bringing both Ottoman Turkish and non-Turkish subjects into contact with the printed word. During Abdulhamid II's reign, education and learning received government attention as primary and secondary as well as teacher-training courses were expanded. The sultan refounded Dar al-Funun in 1900 but developed it very little. Greater focus was placed on professional training—law, commerce, medicine, and military. Expansion of military education and communications contributed to the rise to power of the Committee of Union and Progress (C.U.P.) after the turn of the century.

With the European debt commission operating, Abdulhamid II cooperated instead of trying to do away with foreign influence. As Britain focused more on Egypt, the Ottomans turned for developmental assistance and diplomatic support to the German state which, with the accession of Kaiser Wilhelm II in 1888, inaugurated an active Middle Eastern and North African policy. Coming as it did in the wake of France's occupation of Tunisia in 1881 and Britain's occupation of Egypt in 1882, the new German alliance was most welcome. Prussian General von Moltke had supervised Ottoman military training earlier in the century. German financiers had invested in the empire, gaining new concessions for Anatolian railway-building from the 1880s, and were involved in the debt settlement. The Ottomans admired the quality and reasonable cost of German manufacturing. To ce-ment the new friendship, Kaiser Wilhelm II made two visits to Istanbul in 1889 and 1898. During the second trip, he visited Palestine and the holy places.

Abdulhamid II's Exploitation of Pan-Islamism

In both foreign and domestic policy, Abdulhamid II turned to an instrument that had implications far beyond the primarily Muslim populations still firmly settled in the Asian and African parts of the empire. That instrument was the caliphate. Sultans before Abdulaziz usually had ignored this title, but when Muslims fell under non-Muslim rule in the eighteenth century, the Ottoman government began to claim the same protection over Muslims outside the empire that Europeans claimed over Christians within the empire. Europeans began to regard the caliph-sultan as a figure who could speak on matters of dogma and whose authority paralleled that of the Pope.

Abdulhamid II recognized the potential of this belief and made certain that the constitution of 1876 contained an article stating that the "Sultan, as Caliph, is protector of the Muslim religion." Abdulhamid II became the official symbol of pan-Islamism, a movement that aimed to reunify the Muslim world under a caliph. Jamal al-Din al-Afghani propagated the idea far and wide. Abdulhamid II used pan-Islamism not only to help sustain his own power in what was left of the empire, but also to extend it. Construction of the Hijaz Railway to facilitate the pilgrimage to Makka and Madina and the sending of emissaries to distant Muslim lands represented two aspects of this thrust. Even though the sultan was not of Quraysh descent, many Muslims accepted his claims. Why, then, did forces arise that addressed feelings and aspirations of Ottoman Turks? What led to the end of the multireligious, multiethnic empire and the beginning of a national Turkish identity?

Ottoman and Turkish Nationalism

New Ottoman Influence

Abdulhamid II, despite his success in arousing Muslims outside the empire, created internal opposition from the outset of his rule by betraying the New Ottomans and their constitutional and parliamentary aspirations. Moreover, his new schools, the erosion of empire, and the encroachment of foreigners who had financial control all contributed to the search for new solutions to the empire's problems. Students and teachers alike in the new schools continued to read works of the New Ottomans, some of them smuggled in from abroad where exiles continued publishing.

The *Young Turk* movement began among those who were neither young nor ethnically Turkish. The name seems to have originated with *La Jeune Turquie*, founded and published in France by a Lebanese Maronite Christian Khalil Ghanim. In 1889, a secret society was established in the Imperial Military School to overthrow Abdulhamid II, but it lasted only two years. Its founding members included Kurds and Albanians. The revolutionary movement gained ground when Armenian massacres raised fears of European intervention.

Armenian and Kurdish Nationalism

The Armenian nationalism in the 1890s that led to massacres and later genocide ensued from misfortunes of time and place. Like the Kurds, Armenians shared Anatolia with Turks who viewed the area increasingly as their exclusive homeland. While Turks could concede Balkan autonomy, Armenian and Kurdish territorial demands could not be countenanced. Preoccupied early in the nineteenth century

with communal differences, as Roman Catholics and Protestants challenged Armenian Orthodox predominance through providing education, Armenians in a literary revival were reminded of their distinctive linguistic, religious, and national heritage. The Russian advance into the Caucasus led Russia to support Armenian separatism. The Ottomans co-opted the Kurds through educational opportunities, political appointments, and land grants. In 1890, Abdulhamid II created a special cavalry, the Hamidiyya, to control Armenians in the east.

The Armenian national movement of the late nineteenth century involved varying ideologies and small numbers. Societies aiming not at independence but at achieving more autonomy perhaps on the model of Mount Lebanon included the Hunchak (Socialist Democratic), Dashnag/Tashnak (Armenian Revolutionary Federation), and Armenagan (Union of Salvation) parties. The first two groups operated in both Russian and Ottoman Armenia as well as in Europe. The Black Cross Society in Van was founded in 1878 specifically to protect Armenians from Kurdish and Turkish marauders. Ottoman Armenians, however, generally shunned the national movement for fear of exacerbating tensions. Many lived outside areas of Armenian concentration— the vilayets of Erzurum, Van, Bitlis, Diyarbakir, Sivas, Kharpert, and the area of Cilicia. Even there, Armenians did not constitute a majority, according to mid-century population estimates (see Map 11).

In 1890, political societies became more vocal in trying to enlist European support for Ottoman reform, but European nations, including the British who after 1879 helped to arm Kurdish leader Ubayd Allah, paid little attention. The first Armenian crisis began in 1894 with local inflammatory acts, brigandage, and Ottoman official provocation precipitating anti-Armenian actions by Turks and Kurds. In 1894 and 1895, scores of Armenians in Sassun (Bitlis province), Trabzon, Van, and elsewhere were massacred, bringing on revolts in Zaytun (1895–96)

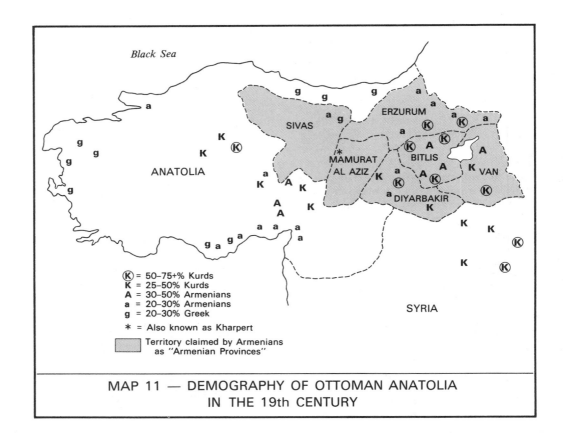

MAP 11 — DEMOGRAPHY OF OTTOMAN ANATOLIA
IN THE 19th CENTURY

and in Van in 1896 (brutally suppressed by the Hamidiyya). On 24 August 1896, an Armenian group in Istanbul reacted by occupying the Ottoman Bank and presenting demands hoping to compel European intervention by striking at the heart of European financial investment in the empire. Ottoman soldiers responded by leading mobs in Istanbul, killing an estimated 6,000 Armenians. Between 100,000 and 200,000 Armenians died in 1894–96, leading many to immigrate to the United States and Europe. Feeble protests from Europe ensued, taking the form of further insistence on reform. The English were the most vocal. Armenian revolutionary activity existed, but the intensity and brutality of the official reaction against peasants and townspeople could hardly be justified.

A plot by the military Union and Progress Society to overthrow Abdulhamid II, prompted by the Armenian episode in 1896, was discovered and its leaders exiled. Dissent spread despite Abdulhamid II's efforts to reconcile the protestors. Union and Progress, which gave its name to the C.U.P. (Ittihad ve Terakki) founded soon after, had taken its title from the idea of order and progress found in works of the positivist Comte. Discontent continued to grow after 1897 because of the empire's ongoing problems. Kurds in 1898 founded *Kurdistan* to propound Kurdish patriotism. During this period, Union and Progress was an Ottoman-oriented successor to the New Ottomans.

Decentralization Versus Centralization

In 1902, a congress in Paris illustrated two major strains of thought within the dissident ranks. The Ottoman nationalist faction, led by Prince Sabah al-Din, son of Abdulhamid II's sister Saniha Sultan and nationalist Prince Damad Mahmud Jalal al-Din, advocated a decentralized federal state under a constitutional monarch. This would satisfy aspirations of all minorities, especially of Armenians who still hoped to stay within the empire. The faction of Sabah al-Din believed that individual initiative would provide the basis for a strong society. The other faction coalesced around ideas of Ahmad Reza, whose mother was Austrian and whose wealthy parents had educated him in France. He and Ghanim had joined forces in 1895 to publish the newspaper *Mechveret* (*Consultation*) in both Turkish and French. In particular, Reza favored a firm central government, and resented the preponderance of non-Muslim Ottomans at the 1902 meeting. The congress collapsed in disunity, but all forces continued their activities.

Reza united his faction with a movement of army officers known first as *Vatan* (Fatherland), then as *Vatan ve Hurriyet* (Fatherland and Liberty), and finally as *Osmanli Hurriyet* (Ottoman Freedom). This military group originated among graduates of the War Academy in Istanbul and included Mustafa Kemal (later Atatürk). Based first in Damascus, the movement spread quickly after its organization in 1905. Mustafa Kemal decided that his home city of Salonika might provide fertile ground for revolutionary activ-

ity because of its diverse community and the presence of the disgruntled Third Army of Macedonia. There he found a future C.U.P. leader, Talat Bey, working at the post office. Kemal was transferred to Salonika in 1907. The merger with Reza's group to form the C.U.P. occurred thereafter.

In December 1907, nationalists convened a second Paris congress. Reza and Sabah al-Din chaired the meeting jointly with the Dashnag leader Maloumian. The Armenians influenced the conference to work if necessary for armed resistance to achieve constitutional and representative government. Although the Armenians sought to reconcile factions, Reza reconstituted his own group. Historians have not decided just why the revolution occurred early in the summer of 1908. Smaller uprisings had broken out because of the 1907 drought that followed a bad harvest in Anatolia. It led to higher prices, a decline in revenues reaching the government, and, therefore, inability to pay officials, including army officers and soldiers. In Macedonia the situation was particularly grave because of an upsurge in terrorism among Greek Christians that the Third Army had been unable to control. Local C.U.P. leaders concluded that Macedonian insurgents might join them in a fight for a constitution if they publicly announced to the European powers their program for a new system.

The Young Turk Revolution: The C.U.P. in Power

When Abdulhamid II learned of the movement, he investigated. C.U.P. leaders, including the future triumvir Enver Bey, fled to the hills where they collected taxes due the government. When Abdulhamid II's special commander was killed in Macedonia while trying to restore order, the sultan sent for troops from Anatolia. These joined the rebels instead

of supporting the sultan. Between 20 and 23 July 1908, the sultan received many telegrams urging him to restore the constitution. Immediately, he agreed to recall the Ottoman parliament.

Restoration of parliament had the effect of taking the wind out of the revolutionaries' sails. Aside from having hoped for a return of the constitution, they had no united program of action. Both Jamal and Talat, who with Enver dominated the later C.U.P. government, were among the leaders who traveled to Istanbul to assist with organizing a new government. Throughout 1908, the Ottoman government remained in the hands of previous politicians although new guarantees of individual freedom and legal protection were instituted in August 1908. Economic problems could not be resolved immediately, as the government tried to pare down its financial commitments by cutting down the bureaucracy. Political freedom allowed for public debating of diverse views. It also brought on public protest in the form of strikes by workers, especially unskilled workers, who still suffered economically. While elites grappled with problems of government, popular discontent increased. In November–December 1908, elections for parliament were held with an overwhelmingly majority for the still ethnically and religiously diverse C.U.P.

By this time, however, both the perceived collapse of Abdulhamid II's rule and the perception of Ottoman resurgence under the C.U.P. government led to revolt in Bulgaria, Bosnia, and Herzegovina as well as the announcement in Crete of union with Greece. These withdrawals strengthened the hands of anti-Christian forces in parliament and eroded support for decentralizers. Early in 1909, the C.U.P. consolidated its power and continued the secularizing thrust of the revolution. In April, forces of discontent including workers, supporters of the sultan-caliph, and proponents of an Islamic state, aided by First Army troops in Istanbul, brought down the C.U.P. government. Only the Armenians of Adana arose to speak up for the C.U.P., thereby provoking a massacre of some 20,000 Armenians by local troops and civilians. Turkish arson also destroyed account books kept by Armenian merchants and moneylenders, thereby illustrating an economic motive for the killing. The government also deported Armenians. These people were allowed to return later. That is why most did not resist "relocation" in

1915. After the C.U.P. defeated the counterrevolutionaries in 1909, they held a memorial service for Armenians and Turks who had died. Enver delivered the eulogy. The Dashnags continued to give the C.U.P. vigorous support. Third Army troops brought about the restoration of the C.U.P. government, deposing Abdulhamid II to signify that they opposed the counterrevolution. Mehmed Rashad came to power on 27 April 1909. Abdulhamid II died nine years later at his palace on the Bosporus.

C.U.P. Reforms

The new C.U.P. government introduced programs in the old Tanzimat spirit. Education at the intermediate and higher levels was to be conducted in Turkish. Secular education was expanded at all levels, with women in higher education though segregated. Two prominent women's liberationists were Ziya Gökalp and Halide Edip (Adivar). Educated first by Turkish shaykhs and English governesses, Edip (1883–1964) completed secondary school at the American College. Her popularity as a novelist and women's emancipationist was already established by 1909. Divorced from her first husband, Edip joined the Turkish Hearth organization to which Gökalp belonged and remained a C.U.P. supporter throughout World War I. Gökalp supported women's rights in the name of Islam and ancient Turkish society, opposing polygamy as degrading. He emerged as the most important idealogue of Turkish nationalism.

The opening of the government lycée in 1911 and the appearance of women in public without veils soon promoted demands for female equality. A new law in 1916 gave women the right of divorce in cases of adultery, violation of the marriage contract, or the husband's desire for other wives. Reforms benefited urban women. Rural women were neither aware of changes nor in a position to challenge male relatives.

The Young Turks introduced municipal transportation and utilities. Conscription of non-Muslims began, and the government worked to eliminate ethnic distinctions. Martial law was retained in Istanbul. Military modernization continued. But despite ambitious plans, nothing was done to alter basic economic relationships within the empire. A new Kurdish revolt broke out in 1910. And the national consensus, which included forces hoping for greater autonomy, disintegrated with the resurgence of local agitation.

War in the Balkans and in Libya

In 1911–12, Albanians revolted. Italy declared war in September 1911 on the Ottoman Empire because of ambitions in Ottoman Libya (see Chapter 9). This war lasted into 1912. Further trouble ensued when Bulgaria and Serbia launched an attack overrunning most of what remained of Ottoman Europe. In Istanbul, individual economic and personal suffering led to demonstrations which spread to other parts of the empire. Rival parties criticized each other for the government's failures. The empire had to make peace with invading Bulgars, Serbs, and Greeks. The C.U.P., though, had been excluded from power late in 1912; its members feared that the new government would concede too much in peace negotiations being conducted in London in December and January 1912–13.

On 23 January 1913, the C.U.P. led its army into the main government building in support of retaining Edirne. When the London conference could not reach agreement, the Bulgarians resumed bombardment of Edirne. Because the C.U.P. could not continue the war, it agreed to cede Edirne, all rights in Crete, and Thrace. What brought about its dictatorship and its intensive Turkification program was the attempt by rivals to overturn its rule. A prominent C.U.P. leader was assassinated. In a subsequent roundup of the opposition, the main rivals of the C.U.P. were largely eliminated. A second Balkan war broke out between Bulgaria and its former allies Greece and Serbia, after Albania declared its independence in 1912. In the ensuing struggle, the C.U.P. reoccupied Edirne because Rumania and Montenegro supported Serbia and Greece. The Treaty of Bucharest acknowledged Greek gains in Macedonia and the C.U.P. reconquest of eastern Thrace. Separate agreements ratified boundaries in 1913 and 1914.

The C.U.P. consolidated its hold by this recovery of lost territory. The new leaders were Talat, Enver, and Jamal. With the state limited to Anatolia and Arab lands except for eastern Thrace, the C.U.P. inaugurated new policies based on Turkish nationalism. Drawing their inspiration from Ziya Gökalp's writings, the C.U.P. began building a Turkish state, precipitating resumption of local Arab, Armenian, and to a lesser extent, Kurdish national sentiment. Gökalp emphasized Turkism as a basis for loyalty; this was taken up by Mustafa Kemal in the new Turkey after the collapse of the empire.

The Arabic Cultural Revival and Arab Nationalism

Intellectuals and Ideology

The writers who promoted Arab consciousness during the early years of the Arabic cultural revival beginning in the mid-nineteenth century were the Christians Nasif al-Yaziji, Butros al-Bustani, and Faris al-Shidyaq, all based in Lebanon. Communal problems contributed to the search for a new basis of identity. Even though Shidyaq converted to Islam, taking the name Ahmad, his primary interest remained in expanding the influence of Arabic. Both Yaziji and Bustani wanted to develop a modern literary Arabic. Al-Bustani also felt great affinity for Syria, and a few admiring students founded in 1875 a secret society advocating the autonomy of Syria and Lebanon within the empire. The society, though of brief duration, influenced later Lebanese separatists as well as advocates of an independent greater Syria. Protestant American missionaries played an important role in the careers of both Bustani and Shidyaq.

Jurji Zaydan (1861–1914), who studied briefly at the Syrian Protestant College, was another important transmitter of the Arab heritage. Besides founding the journal of *al-Hilal* (*Crescent*) in Egypt, he authored historical novels. These undoubtedly reached many more readers than his literary or historical studies. But Zaydan's cultural promotion of Arabism was not translated into political activity.

Among Muslim writers, Abd al-Rahman al-Kawakibi (1849–1903) was a forerunner of Arab nationalism because he promoted the reconstitution of an Arab, as opposed to an Ottoman Turkish, caliphate. Although his own family was Kurdish, Kawakibi seems to have felt that only Arabs could revive Islam. For Kawakibi, the central issue was the strength of the umma, but by distinguishing between Turks and Arabs, his line of argument encouraged other Arab Muslims to emphasize their Arab identity. He himself fled the domains of Abdulhamid II to seek refuge in Egypt and therefore made a special point of speaking out against tyranny as well as against Turkish domination.

Also significant in the evolution of an Arab national idea were the Christian Lebanese secularists, Shibli Shumayyil (1860–1917) and Farah Antun (1874–1922), both of whom also worked in Egypt. These men advocated establishment of a rational, just society in which religion and state would be separated. Shumayyil also promoted socialism (*ishtirakiyya*) which he defined as the state's taking an active role in furthering social welfare and eliminating divisive forces in society. Because he favored the rule of law, Shumayyil was an early Young Turk supporter but opposed the sort of exclusive nationalism to which the C.U.P. eventually turned.

Najib Azouri, another Lebanese Maronite, supported Kawakibi's idea of restoring an Arab caliphate. He was among the first publicly to advocate independence for the Arabs as a unit. His book, published in Paris in 1905, was called *Le Reveil de la Nation Arabe dans l'Asie Turque* (*The Awakening of the Arab Nation in Asiatic Turkey*). As a consequence of his experience in Europe and while working for the Ottoman government in Palestine, Azouri had noticed a developing confrontation between the Arab and Jewish national movements, a clash which he expected to continue "until one prevails over the other."[1] Azouri accurately predicted the prominence of this conflict in world affairs.

From the perspective of today, it is difficult to believe that Azouri's book was ignored in Palestine, but its publication in Paris and the sultan's censorship policies limited its circulation. Palestinians, with their own attachment to Filasteen (Arabic for Palestine) as a distinct region, were already alerted to Jewish immigration. Their consciousness did not mean either the desire for a specifically Palestinian political identity or denial of participation in a larger Arab entity. After the 1908 revolution, Azouri returned to Palestine to spread pan-Arabism. Although Azouri pioneered Arab ideas of statehood, such separatist notions in pre-1908 Ottoman Arab lands were rarely expressed.

Organizational Activity

After 1908, Arab Christians like Ghanim supported the C.U.P. in hopes that the end to autocracy would lead to Arab-

---

[1] Najib Azoury (Azouri), *Le Réveil de la Nation Arabe*. Quoted in Albert Hourani, *Arabic Thought in the Liberal Age* (London, New York, and Toronto: Oxford University Press, 1962), p. 279.

Ottoman fraternity. They supported creation of societies to promote this goal in major cities of the empire. Syrian emigrés in Egypt and elsewhere began to consider returning home to what they hoped would be a more open society. The counterrevolution and subsequent events began to alter this confidence. State unification through Turkish as the main educational medium alienated Arabs. Secret societies cropped up such as al-Qahtaniyya (1909), favoring a dual Arab-Ottoman monarchy and patronized by Arab Ottoman army officers like Egyptian Aziz Ali al-Masri. These were formed especially after suppression of Ottoman-Arab fraternities. Al-Masri continued to uphold the state, leading Ottoman forces against Italian invaders of Ottoman Libya, but eventually he looked to Arab ethnic separation.

Acceleration of support for Arab nationalism occurred between 1912 and 1914 when the Ottomans were incurring their final Balkan and North African losses. As the C.U.P. worked to consolidate its hold over its Arab Asiatic territories, Arab resistance increased. In 1912, Ottoman decentralizers tried to keep alive the multiethnic idea by advocating provincial autonomy and maintenance of both Turkish and local languages for official and educational purposes. Their Ottoman Decentralization Party had branches in Syria and Iraq. A reform committed based in Beirut also supported decentralization but was suppressed in 1913. Although the C.U.P. pretended to make concessions after protests spread, no action was taken to relax Turkification.

Two groups then emerged as leaders of the Arab anti-Turkish movement. The civilian organization al-Fatat (the Youth), organized in Paris, pressed for a multinational Ottoman state with equality for all citizens regardless of religion or ethnicity. Delegates to a 1913 convention organized by al-Fatat noticed that Turkification was rapidly alienating the empire's non-Turks. The second important group, al-Ahd (the Covenant), followed al-Qahtaniyya. Although al-Masri's association with secret groups brought about his trial for treason and his subsequent condemnation, he persisted in supporting the C.U.P. once World War I had broken out; he did so because he feared European intervention even more than Turkification. As al-Fatat promoted ties among the Arab intelligentsia so too did al-Ahd establish a bond between Arab army officers. This formed a basis for postwar nationalist activities.

Arabia Before World War I

After the Egyptians left central Arabia early in the 1820s, the Sa'udi forces began to regroup in the Najd under their new leader, Turki ibn Abd Allah (1823–34). Their principal rivals in Arabia included the Rashid family established at Riyadh and Ha'il in the Jabal Shammar of northern Arabia, the Hashimite guardians of the holy cities, the Zaydi imams of Yemen, and the British who arranged treaties with rulers in the coastal areas of eastern and southern Arabia, an area of British activity since the sixteenth century. By the end of the nineteenth century, Aden, Muscat and Oman, Bahrayn, Kuwayt, and seven small shaykhdoms which now constitute the United Arab Emirates (but were then the Trucial States) were all under direct or indirect British control. In all of Arabia, only the Hashimites, Rashidis, and Zaydis ruled territories under Ottoman scrutiny.

During the last half of the century, the Sa'udis expanded into northern Arabia. In 1902, from a base in Kuwayt and led by Abd al-Aziz ibn Sa'ud (1880–1953), the

Sa'udis crossed into Najd and took the Rashidi capital of Riyadh, making it their own capital instead. That the Sa'udis were the most dynamic state in the peninsula by World War I should not be a surprise, as they were inspired by religious fervor to reinstitute a strong Muslim society based on Quranic injunction. Rivals, by contrast, were under the thumb of some external power.

Yemen, for example, with the peninsula's largest population, was occupied by Egyptian troops acting on behalf of the sultan until 1840. Zaydi imams concen-trated their power in the interior because coastal areas were Sunni (Shafi'i mad-hhab). During the Tanzimat, a new army was sent to Yemen. Ottoman governors continued to be posted there, too. An uneasy relationship between the Otto-mans and Zaydis persisted until 1911, when Zaydi Imam Yahya revolted against Ottoman rule. Despite a settlement in which Yahya and the Ottomans would rule jointly, he strengthened his position in the interior, leaving the coast to the Ottomans.

Egypt and the Egyptians: 1882–1914

Historians writing about Egypt between 1882 and 1914 have usually focused only on the policies of Evelyn Baring (Lord Cromer), His Majesty's Agent and Consul-General at Cairo from 1883 to 1907. Although the khedive remained Egypt's legal ruler, Cromer and his successors acted as if in charge. Though not an economist, Cromer acquired a reputation for shrewd financial management. From the outset, he set about restoring Egypt to solvency, though the country was restricted by the 1880 Law of Liquidation allotting half of Egypt's revenue to the debt and the other half to state expenses, with any additional revenue over the estimated amount of £ 8.5 million going to the debt. Adjustment of the settlement required international agreement. Cromer obtained modifications from time to time.

Mahdism in the Sudan and the Anglo-Egyptian Conquest

The Mahdist movement in Sudan, usually blamed on Turko-Egyptian oppression, coincided with the lapse of leadership in both Egypt and Sudan in the wake of Isma'il's deposition. It began in Kordofan and spread very slowly to other parts of Sudan. The Mahdi, Muhammad Ahmad ibn Abd Allah, genuinely believed (like the Wahhabis in Arabia before and after him) that his mission was to establish the just rule of Islam as found in the Prophet Muhammad's day. Although he appeared to strike a blow for Sudanese independence, the theological component in his mission was paramount, especially since he claimed to be khalifa and imam, too.

The Mahdi's supporters included both the pious who believed in his message and the disgruntled slave traders and nomads who disliked the notion of government. Not surprisingly, the Egyptians received with trepidation the self-proclamation of this Mahdi in June 1881. Combined with his irregular forces, the Mahdi's organized army defeated Egypt's small garrisons who were handicapped by governmental turmoil in Egypt.

How did the Mahdi govern Sudan? He gave selected companions—khalifas broad authority over community affairs, maintaining a treasury and a court of law.

Coins of such high quality were issued in his name that they quickly passed out of usage. After the British occupation of Egypt, the British sent an Egyptian force south at Egyptian expense but commanded by British officer William Hicks. The Mahdists destroyed it on 5 November 1883. Former governor-general General Charles Gordon, who arrived in 1884, decided to reinstitute strong government in Khartum, and refused to take out his forces. In January 1885, Mahdist troops entered the city and killed Gordon. A relief expedition arrived two days later. By June, the Mahdi himself died and was succeeded by his closest khalifa Abd Allahi.

The loss and war cost led to the lone Anglo-Ottoman agreement for evacuation of Egypt. This was negotiated by Sir Henry Drummond-Wolff and Abdulhamid II. An interim agreement of October 1885 determined that Britain would continue to acknowledge Ottoman sovereignty and maintain payment of tribute. Representatives of both the Ottomans and British would supervise the Egyptian government. Britain would announce its departure schedule later. By terms of a final agreement proposed in 1887, the British were to leave in 1890. But Abdulhamid II concluded that the status quo was preferable to assuming the financial burden of Egypt and giving Britain the right of future intervention. The Ottoman government retained and extended its influence among Egypt's Turko-Circassian and native elites, who often traveled to Istanbul for study and leisure.

In Sudan, Abd Allahi's successor state tried to extend its territories. In April 1887, Abd Allahi called on Khedive Tawfiq to submit, but two years later, his armies lost to an Anglo-Egyptian force at Tushki. He also conducted an indecisive campaign in Ethiopia. With an end to the Mahdist state's northern expansion and onset of famine, Abd Allahi moved his unruly tribesmen to Khartum. Facing opposition, he began to withdraw from his people. Because of diplomatic exigencies,

the British government in 1896 decided to move an Egyptian force back into the Sudan. In March 1896, Ethiopian ruler Menelik II defeated Italian invaders.

Hoping to safeguard his Italian allies from a Mahdist attack and to preserve good relations with Germany, Cromer reluctantly launched the costly campaign led by Herbert Kitchener, later British governor-general in Egypt. By fall 1896, Dongola province was retaken and an east-west railway constructed between Dongola and Abu Hamad to avoid the longer Nile route. In July 1897, Abu Hamad fell to the Anglo-Egyptians. Gradually, the invaders reached Berber. In a battle near the Atbara river on 8 April 1898, the technologically superior Anglo-Egyptian forces inflicted a crushing defeat on the Mahdists and then proceeded to Omdurman across from Khartum. At Karari, six miles north of the city, the Mahdists made their last stand, sustaining some 27,000 casualties as opposed to a few hundred for the British and Egyptians. Abdullahi escaped south but was killed in a battle at Umm Diwaykarat in November 1899. British forces sought him out to destroy any possibility that the movement might regroup (see Map 7, p. 74).

An international crisis arose during the campaign against the Mahdists. In July 1898, a French force advanced from the Congo River to the upper Nile Valley. At the Sudanese village of Fashoda, they raised their flag to claim the territory for France. Kitchener responded by leading a much larger British force to the area. Heightened diplomatic activity forestalled an open clash. After the French withdrew, they surrendered their Sudan claims to Britain by treaty in March 1899. This agreement helps to explain Britain's imperialist mentality that characterized the later Sudan condominium. Essentially, Britain did not regard Egypt as an equal partner in deciding Sudan's fate, despite the joint conquest. The partition of Africa was a European prerogative.

The Anglo-Egyptian Conventions of 1899 set forth terms of the Sudan condominium, insuring avoidance of the

European competition present in Egypt. The khedive would rule nominally but Britain would choose the governor. Flags of both nations would fly, but other provisions of the agreement excluded Egyptians. The Sudan would make its own laws unless permitted to do otherwise by the British governor-general. Egypt's mixed courts were to have no jurisdiction in Sudan, and the legal apparatus resembled that of India. Britain acted as though Egypt had played no role at all in the reconquest. The British never even pretended to acknowledge Ottoman authority, which by extension should have applied to any territory conquered by Egypt. Europeans occupied the top posts while district officers, Egyptian at first, were gradually replaced by Sudanese. Lebanese were also employed. Egyptian lives had been sacrificed to Britain's imperial interest with no gain for Egypt. After less than a year as governor in Sudan, Kitchener was replaced by Sir Reginald Wingate who had led reconquest forces. From 1899–1916, he laid foundations for the Sudan government. In 1902, he opened Gordon Memorial College, but it served only a limited number of Sudanese. Isma'il's cotton cultivation program was continued and expanded while slave traders were eliminated once and for all. Although Britain viewed the condominium as a fiction, Egyptians kept trying to make it a reality.

Impact of British Occupation Policy on Egypt

How did Britain's occupation affect policies and developments in Egypt during the same period? Financial control meant that Britain supervised the government's military, agricultural, commercial, financial, administrative, and foreign-policy dealings. It gave the British power over health, education, communications, and taxation. Duties on tobacco, railways, and freight imports as well as new land taxes and improved collection contributed to increased revenues. Cromer intended to eliminate abuses of power by rural landlords and to better the lot of Egyptian peasants. He cited the abolition of the whip and of forced labor as two of his chief accomplishments.

Under Cromer, cotton cultivation expanded to provide more raw material for British mills and to bring cash into Egypt. Completion of the Aswan Dam (1902) made more land available for cultivation under perennial irrigation. As the British had intended, Cromer organized Egypt's finances efficiently enough to reduce the national debt and achieve budget surpluses. Healthcare delivery was greatly improved and the population increased. Besides the dam, the British built barrages and other public works. Railway mileage was doubled during the occupation. British policies encouraged the breakup of large landed estates. Historians cite these as among the occupation's "accomplishments."

Economic Consequences

These developments may have reflected British policies, but they did not necessarily represent progress or promote Egyptian welfare. Landlords continued to exercise great power over cultivators, and the breakup of a few large estates turned over the best lands to the upper classes rather than to poor peasants. By increasing the amount of land under cotton cultivation, Egypt had to import food for the first time. Expansion of perennial irrigation enabled the spread of the bilharzia snail that causes schistosomiasis, a debilitating disease. The doubling of railway mileage was accompanied by erosion of river commerce and road traffic—not by accident but by design to further British business interests. Moreover, the railways did not connect Egypt with other countries. Transit trade which had passed overland from Sudan to Egypt was diverted from Alexandria to newly constructed Port Sudan. This harmed Egyptian traders. British policies obstructed development of industrialization, to prevent the growth of competition for raw materials going to English factories.

Neglect of Education

What, then, were Britain's "sins of omission"? During the occupation, deliberate policies curtailed educational programs begun by Isma'il. The British preferred kuttab and specialized education to fulfill basic needs of the bureaucracy but that would not produce a nationalist opposition like that which had arisen in India. Small numbers of trained teachers were sent to England on the assumption that they would return as admirers of British civilization. However, such programs affected few people and failed to achieve the result desired.

British neglect of education backfired. Egyptians began at their own expense to send students not to England but to France (a country that encouraged Egyptian nationalists until the Anglo-French rapprochement of 1904). Neglect of secondary and higher education by government also increased private education. Cromer and his associates ignored the fact that government-sponsored education offered poor Muslims their only hope for upward mobility because foreign and private schools still catered mainly to Christians and Jews. Without a national secondary and higher education program, expansion of kuttab education would not advance the careers of poor, indigenous, rural Muslims. These people could study at al-Azhar if fortunate and perhaps could secure upward mobility through graduation from Dar al-Ulum, but Cromer kept Dar al-Ulum small because of the few national schools at which graduates could teach.

Later, Cromer claimed that international financial arrangements had restricted his freedom to spend more than the 1½–3 percent the educational budget had taken during the occupation. Evidence suggests, however, that it was his own decision not to do more. Copts and other Christians taking advantage of private education dominated government clerical positions and promoted communal tensions. Cromer also antagonized Egyptians by packing the bureaucracy with greater numbers of highly paid but poorly qualified British advisors who drained Egypt's administrative budgets. Highly qualified Egyptians, including those with foreign degrees, were kept in low-level posts while Englishmen with lesser qualifications supervised their work.

Cromer left Egypt under a cloud. In a controversial, well-publicized incident in the Delta village of Dinshaway in June 1906, British officers went pigeon-hunting. They soon encountered opposition from villagers who did not want to lose their pigeons. A peasant woman was wounded. Armed officers then killed a man who came to the aid of an officer who had collapsed of sunstroke. Other villagers then attacked the officers. Though on leave and ignorant of the details, Cromer decided to make an example of the villagers by trying them before a military court. Four villagers found guilty of murder were hanged; others received long prison terms or flogging.

Egyptian Nationalism: Political, Social, and Cultural Manifestations

The storm of protest generated in the British parliament and elsewhere in Europe forced Cromer's resignation. In Egypt the verdict left people in a state of shock. Nationalism was fueled. The decision and the haste with which it was implemented cast opprobrium on prosecutor Fathi Zaghlul and presiding Egyptian Coptic judge Butros Ghali. Ghali, signer of the Sudan condominium agreement, was later assassinated in 1910 when as prime minister he unsuccessfully urged Egypt's parliament to approve extension of the Suez Canal concession. Dinshaway was immortalized by poets Ahmad Shawqi and Hafiz Ibrahim in poems appearing mainly in *al-Muayyad* (founded in 1889 by Ali Yusuf) and *al-Liwa* (the Watan Party organ set up by Mustafa Kamil and later edited by Egyptian educator Abd al-Aziz Jawish). Dinshaway became the watershed of the occupation.

The Indigenous View of Egypt: The Khedive as a Focus of Nationalism

From the perspective of indigenous development, Egypt remained part of the Ottoman Empire under khedivial rule. Tawfiq preferred to cooperate with the British, but his seventeen-year-old son and successor Abbas Hilmi II (1892–1914) wanted to exercise his prerogatives as ruler. Abbas became the catalyst for activities of the Watan Party led after 1895 by Mustafa Kamil. Before his death in 1908 at age 34, Kamil had strongly advocated implementation of constitutional government. Apparently, Abbas toned down his support of the nationalists after the 1904 entente cut off his hope of French assistance in ending the British occupation.

Expansion of the Press and the British Reaction

The British allowed the printed word to become a vehicle for the spread of nationalism until Ghali's assassination brought about reimposition of the 1881 Press Law. This meant that continuously before 1910 Egypt's press was an important medium for educational social, political, literary, religious, and cultural material. Syrians, restricted by Abdulhamid II's censorship, published in Egypt. Besides *al-Muayyad* and *al-Liwa,* the most important were *al-Jarida* (edited by Ahmad Lutfi al-Sayyid and supporter of the Umma Party), *al-Watan al-Dustur* (published by Egyptians), and *al-Muqattam* and *al-Ahram* (published by emigrés).

The Salafiyya in Education and Social Change

Newspapers also spread views of Muslim modernists (*Salafiyya*). *Al-Manar,* for example, was published by a Syrian disciple of Abduh named Rashid Rida. Because the occupation disparaged Islam and Mus-lims, viewing them as inferior and responsible for their subjugation, Muslim modernists were significant in upholding Egypt's Islamic and Arabic heritage and identity. Advocating adoption of modern technology and ideas but within an Islamic framework, the Salafiyya movement was more educational and cultural than political, although some of its proponents were pan-Islamists. It backed firmly establishing Arabic as Egypt's national language despite continued usage of English and French in government documents. When the occupation authorities neglected education, Muslims founded private primary and secondary schools through new Muslim benevolent societies. In 1908, Egyptians led by Minister of Education and later nationalist leader Sa'd Zaghlul, Ahmad Lutfi al-Sayyid, Qasim Amin and Muhammad Hifni Nasif—who were also prominent activists in promoting women's rights—set up their own privately sponsored university. Not until 1925 did the government assume responsibility for it.

Intellectual debates in occupied Egypt addressed not only political and social questions but also economic and religious issues such as the establishment of a national bank in relation to Islamic prohibition of usury. Education and the role of women in society were discussed publicly with women such as Malak Hifni Nasif (d. 1918) who wrote under the pseudonym Bahithat al-Badiya. Selected Muslims and Christians sought a national consensus which pan-Islamism could not offer. Divisive forces isolated Egypt's Copts as occupation collaborators.

Productivity and Labor

Social changes became more evident under Cromer's successors Eldon Gorst and Herbert Kitchener. Ongoing population growth was but one factor in rural-urban migration. After a long period of prosperity, Egyptians were severely affected by economic crisis in 1907–1909. Overexploitation of Egypt's soil had finally brought about a decline in productivity of the cotton upon which the economy had been made to depend so heavily. Although Kitchener's government intervened after 1911 to prevent dispossession of landholders who could not pay their debts, the government's general attitude of minimum interference left many peasant households in desperate circumstances. The depression undoubtedly fueled peasant discontent and receptivity to nationalism.

Although native Egyptians with rural roots made inroads into domination by Turko-Circassion elites, most of Egypt's nationalists paid little attention to the circumstances of rural and urban workers. Guilds disappeared to be replaced by non-unionized industrial workers. In 1914, some 20,000 female wage laborers comprised 5 percent of the work force, though these workers often lasted only a few years because of the strenuous pace and the absence of maternity benefits. Egypt's population was still heavily rural, and local authorities had the greatest influence with rural villagers. As self-interested bourgeoisie, Egyptian nationalists prior to World War I never advocated fundamental social change in relationships between peasants (*fellahin*), village shaykhs (*umdas*), and landlords. In fact, long after 1922, government in the countryside continued to be regarded with suspicion and for good reason.

The Jewish Nationalist (Zionist) Movement and the Colonization of Palestine

Zionism began as a multifaceted movement to establish a Jewish religious or national homeland. Behind it was the belief that Jews constituted a separate people entitled to their own territory. It later focused on making Palestine a Jewish state. Today, the term Zionist generally means a supporter of Israel as a Jewish state, but it can also apply to promoters of worldwide Jewish immigration to Israel. Non-Zionists tend to be those who regard Zionism as a pre-state phenomenon. They recognize that the goal of a Jewish state has been achieved, and prefer to emphasize a local Israeli rather than an international Jewish identity. Anti-Zionists object to the creation of Israel and to the transformation of Palestine into a Jewish state against the wishes of its inhabitants. Zionism focuses on the Jews as a nation, not as adherents of Judaism. Both Jews and non-Jews can be found among Zionists, non-Zionists, and anti-Zionists.

European Jewry

The Jewish nationalist movement arose in Europe in the context of the eighteenth-century Enlightenment and nineteenth-century nationalism, but it was also related to past Jewish experience in Europe. Although Jews had flourished in Europe before the Crusades, many were murdered during them and fled to Muslim lands or to recently Christianized Poland. The thirteenth through fifteenth-centuries brought about the expulsion of Jews from England, most of France, Spain, and Portugal. A small percentage of Eastern European Jews may have descended from a Turkic Khazar, though Jewish, state in southern Russia. Polish Jews soon gained recognition as an autonomous people organized politically, religiously, and culturally, whose main interactions with Christians occurred in the framework of banking and commerce in which a few wealthy Jews predominated. Anti-Semitism usually affected the nonbanking majority. When Russia, Austria, and Prussia partitioned Poland in 1772, the Polish Jews of Russia lost their former status. Nicholas I (1824–55) tried to pressure them into conversion or assimilation. He also restricted them to former Polish territories (the *Pale*) and, within this area, to ghettos in which their employment opportunities were limited. Nicholas opened government schools that soon created a division between progressive Jews (forerunners of the Socialist Bund and Zionists) and Orthodox Jews. After his death, Alexander II relaxed restrictions and permitted freer movement and professional advancement for Jews. Discrimination continued, though, with the insecurity of the Russian population arising from changes in economy and society—the liberation of serfs and the integration of Russia into the world market.

In Western Europe, Jews faced not repression but gradual emancipation. Moses Mendelssohn, the composer's grandfather, in late eighteenth-century Germany sought both to raise the quality of Jewish life and to bring about civil equality for Jews. Jewish authorities banned his translation of the Hebrew scriptures into German, fearing that Jewish children would use it to improve their German to read nonreligious texts. Though religious opposition fueled the assimilationist movement, Mendelssohn's efforts helped bring about gradual emancipation for Jews in Austria and full citizenship in revolutionary France in 1791 following their recognition as a religious community in 1789. All legal limitations against Jews were removed in Belgium in the 1830s, in Denmark and the Netherlands in the 1840s, in Austria-Hungary in the 1860s, in Italy, Sweden, the German Empire, and Switzerland in the 1870s, and Great Britain in the 1890s. Greece at its

inception gave Jews equal legal status. Except in Rumania, toleration was the rule in southeastern Europe. While emancipation moved forward, racial anti-Semitism, exemplified by the works of the French Count de Gobineau and the Englishman Houston Stewart Chamberlain, was laying its foundations.

Among Jews, the *haskala* (enlightenment) pushed to its furthest extreme meant leaving Judaism altogether and adopting Christianity. Prominent Jews including Heinrich Heine, Benjamin Disraeli, and Karl Marx became Christians. All but one of Mendelssohn's children converted, too. Looking at the stagnation of Jewish masses in ghettos, assimilationists assumed that Judaism would eventually die out. Reform Jews revived Judaism by incorporating aspects of Christian practice into its worship and observances, especially in Germany and the United States. Orthodox Jews regarded Reform Judaism with hostility.

Early Zionist Ideology and the First Aliya

The surfacing of racial definitions of nationality challenged the identity of assimilated Jews who were citizens of their respective countries. The chronological development of Zionism in both Eastern and Western Europe, then, related first to the outright oppression of Jews in the East and secondly, to disillusion with assimilation in the West.

The idea of Jews as a nation is inherent in the Hebrew scriptures, particularly in the biblical covenants of Abraham and Moses with God. Genesis 12:1–2 states "Now the Lord said to Abram, 'Go from your country and your kindred and your father's house to the land that I will show you. And I will make of you a great nation.'" Orthodox Jews believed that a return to Palestine would be initiated by God after the coming of a messenger (See Malachi 3) and was inextricably linked with the covenant obligation to Moses summarized in Nehemiah 1:8–9 ("'If you are unfaithful, I will scatter you among the peoples; but if you return to me and keep my commandments and do them, though your dispersed be under the farthest skies, I will gather them thence and bring them to the place which I have chosen, to make my name dwell there.'"). "Next year in Jerusalem" is an important formula in Jewish prayers. Elderly Jews still went to Palestine to die; Jews elsewhere contributed to the upkeep of Palestine's small Jewish communities. For religious Jews, however, the idea of a Jewish nation-state as a focus for loyalty violated the covenant demanding supreme allegiance to God. Most late eighteenth- and early nineteenth-century projects for Jewish settlement in Palestine lapsed with the supposed success of assimilation.

A forerunner of socialist Zionism was the German Jew Moses Hess (b. 1812). His book *Rome and Jerusalem* (1862), identified anti-Semitism as a major and growing problem. He believed that even in Germany, Jews would never be viewed as fully German. Reform Jews had turned their backs on Judaism's national character while they watered down religious belief and practice. To Hess, both modernizers and Jews who rejected modern life were wrong. A bright future lay in building a socialist Jewish state in Palestine. Although Hess did not expect Western Jews to settle there, he saw great potential in Eastern European Jewry, where the great majority of Jews lived. Already aroused by the force of Hassidism, an important spiritual awakening in Russia and Poland, Eastern Jews would respond to the spiritual component of going to Palestine. In their cooperative state, the nation would own resources of the land. Hess' contemporary, Rabbi Hirsch Kalischer from northeastern Germany, also wrote in 1862 to advocate a political solution (but he spoke in the name of the Hebrew scriptures and commentaries). Kalischer's efforts resulted in the setting up of a Jewish agricultural school near Jaffa, nevertheless ignored by Palestinian Jews. The writings of Hess and Kalischer were noted only after more famous works by Leo Pinsker (*Auto-Emancipation,* 1882) and Theodor Herzl (*Der Judenstaat,* 1896) had received broad recognition.

In European Russia, especially the southwest, the years 1881–84 brought on the worst of early pogroms against Jews and their properties. Although Russian Jews dominated the sugar, textile, grain, and timber industries and were active in leather, tobacco, brewing, milling, and banking, only some 200,000 of the estimated five million were allowed to live in major cities outside the Pale. In response to outbreaks against them, Russian Jews began immigrating. By the 1890s, their immigration to the United States had reached such proportions that the American government sent to Europe two investigators to discover why so many Jews were leaving. Their report confirmed the abysmal circumstances of the vast majority of Russian Jews. Conditions led former assimilationists like poet Yehuda Lieb Gordon, Eliezer Perlman (better known as Ben-Yehuda, reviver of Hebrew), and Hebrew poet Chaim Nachman Bialik to join nonassimilationists like Peretz Smolenskin. The pogroms of 1881, followed by restricted laws of May 1882, lent support to an Odessa-based Zionist movement that spread to Jewish communities throughout Russia and was inspired by Leo Pinsker's book. Pinsker argued that because no amount of rationalization would remove prejudice against Jews, they required a country of their own, based on self-respect and dignity. He came to be associated with *Hibbat Zion* (Love of Zion) and its followers *Hovevei Zion* (Lovers of Zion) founded in 1887 from several Jewish associations. Basically philanthropic in their outlook, Hovevei Zion regarded settlement in Palestine as a means to improve the conditions of the 20,000 Jewish Palestinians and to pave the way for new immigrants. Despite its independent origin, the youth movement B.I.L.U. (acronym from Isaiah 2:5—"O house of Jacob, come, let us go") later drew upon Hibbat Zion for support. B.I.L.U. organized the immigration movement known as the first *aliya* (going up). Thereafter, those going to Palestine were called *olim* (ascenders).

Colonizers of Gedera, Petah Tikvah, Rosh Pinah, and Rishon le-Zion, founded by the first aliya (1881–1903) quickly discovered that they lacked resources to purchase equipment and build houses. They also knew little about agriculture. Baron Edmond de Rothschild founded new settlements and bailed out the agricultural communities, though he initially opposed political Zionism. Historians agree that his colonies functioned as paternalistic establishments controlled by his agents. He tried to introduce wheat cultivation, vineyards, and even silkworms, but only the planting of citrus groves, already found among Arab cultivators, allowed the colonies to reach self-sufficiency. Rothschild's financial backing eventually led colonists to forget their original work ethic, turning labor over to Arab workers, some of whom were the lands' original tenants.[2]

Early in the 1890s, Hibbat Zion sent one of its Odessa members Asher Ginzberg (Ahad Ha'am, 1858–1927) to investigate the colonial enterprise. His indictment *This is Not the Way* criticized Jews in Palestine for having focused on political and economic issues. Ginzberg's idea (cultural Zionism) was that Palestine should constitute a spiritual center for world Jewry analogous to the hub of a wheel. Unable to accommodate all of the world's Jews, it should inspire them. Moreover, it was already inhabited by Arabs who intended to remain the majority.

The first aliya represented the first concerted effort of Jews to settle in the holy land in modern times. From 60–90 percent of those who came to Palestine left. The Arabs of Palestine did not ignore the first aliya. Demonstrations in Nablus in 1891 led Abdulhamid II to ban immigration and purchase of land by Jews. Significantly, Jews circumvented these prohibitions thereby giving them the impression that legal barriers would prevent no real obstacle to achieving their goals. The first aliya's Zionists by 1914 bought about one quarter of all Palestinian land owned in 1948 by Jews. Lacking intensity, though, the first aliya could not have brought about creation of a Jewish state.

Theodor Herzl and the Second Aliya

Historians agree that the second aliya (1904–14) advanced Theodor Herzl's dream of establishing a Jewish state in Palestine. He reached many more western Jews than Pinsker and other predecessors. Why did he succeed where others had failed? From Budapest, Herzl by 1896 had completed a doctorate in law in Vienna, written several mediocre plays, and established himself as a journalist based in Paris after 1891. Early in the 1890s, he began to explore the problems of Jews.

During his years as a journalist in France, Herzl covered the Dreyfus case in which a French Jewish officer of Alsatian origin, Captain Alfred Dreyfus, was courtmartialed hastily and condemned for treason in 1894 on the basis of what later emerged as forged evidence. Only after some twelve years, during which prominent European intellectuals like Emile Zola (author of *J'accuse*) protested the nature of Dreyfus' military trials, did a civilian court acquit him. Historians now agree that the Dreyfus case has been overplayed as a source of Herzl's Zionist ideology, especially since democratic elements in France were able to obtain justice for Captain Dreyfus in the end. Anti-Semitism in that instance was overcome. Nevertheless, the case did influence Herzl in formulating the idea of a Jewish state.

---

[2] Walter Z. Laqueur, *A History of Zionism,* (New York: Holt Rinehart, and Winston, 1972), pp. 78–79; and Howard M. Sachar, "The Rise of Zionism," in *The Zionist Movement in Palestine and World Politics, 1880–1918,* N. Gordon Levin, Jr. (ed.) (Lexington, Mass., Toronto, London: D.C. Heath and Company, 1974), pp. 7–25.

In 1895, he approached philanthropist Baron von Hirsch, supporter of Jewish colonization in Argentina, with a plan for a loan fund for Jewish settlement in Palestine. Though critical of the baron for having perpetuated Jewish dependency, Herzl felt that the financial support of wealthy Jews was a prerequisite for launching a Jewish national fund. Philanthropy was not what he had in mind. Herzl wanted a commitment to a Jewish national state.[3]

His obsession with the Jewish question led Herzl to set down in 1895 views published in February 1896 as *Der Judenstaat* (The Jewish State). His vision involved the gradual building up of the state by Jews in need of work. Funded by Jewish capital, pioneers would create the infrastructure needed by the state: communications and farms, to be followed by banks, an army, and other enterprises, all under auspices of the state or a Jewish-owned joint-stock company. While ignoring the Arabs in *Der Judenstaat*, perhaps because he had not yet settled on Palestine as the site for the state, Herzl in his second Zionist work *Altneuland* (Old-New Land) portrayed them as eager to join the new society due to material benefits which would supposedly accrue to them.

Herzl's Plan: Search for a Charter

How did Herzl propose to establish his state? Disliking infiltration, Herzl sought a charter from a recognized government for a specific territory. That would prevent land speculation which raised prices or so he hoped. Undecided about Palestine or Argentina, Herzl nevertheless looked to Abdulhamid II for a Palestine charter. By August 1897, he also rallied enough Jews to convene a conference in Basle,

Switzerland, to formulate plans for carrying out his statehood proposal. The 197 delegates established a World Zionist Organization (W.Z.O.) and devised a Zionist program, stating as its goal the establishment of a publicly recognized, legally secured home in Palestine for the Jewish people. The congress listed four measures to reach the goal:

1. Promotion on suitable lines of colonization in Palestine by Jewish agricultural workers, industrial workers, and tradesmen.
2. Organization and binding of all Jews using local and international institutions in accordance with the laws of each country.
3. Strengthening of Jewish national consciousness and awareness.
4. Securing consent of governments whose approval would be necessary for realization of the Zionist goal.[4]

Although Herzl claimed that a Jewish state would be a reality within fifty years, an almost precisely accurate prediction, in 1897 his state was still a long way off.

Persisting in his plan to obtain a charter, Herzl met with Kaiser Wilhelm II in Jerusalem in November 1898 to seek his approval and intervention with Abdulhamid II. The Kaiser's lukewarm commitment to Jewish agricultural improvement in Palestine led Herzl to seek British help. Herzl did not care which power was willing to sponsor his project as long as it was sufficiently strong to help in the realization of the Zionist goal. Although Herzl won an audience with Abdulhamid II in 1901 and 1902, his proposal for Jewish

---

[3] Laqueur, p. 89; and Alex Bein, "Herzl on Dreyfus and Zionism," in Levin, (ed.), *Zionist Movement,* pp. 54–61.

[4] Israel Cohen, *The Zionist Movement,* (London: Frederick Muller, 1945), p. 73 is the source generally quoted. We adapted the version of J. C. Hurewitz (comp., ed., and trans.), *The Middle East and North Africa in World Politics: A Documentary Record,* 2nd ed., vol. 1: *European Expansion, 1535–1914* (New Haven and London: Yale University Press, 1975), p. 466.

company takeover of Ottoman state lands in Palestine became contingent on his alleviating, as promised, the sultan's debt problem. With no evidence of backing from Herzl, Abdulhamid II offered a Jewish homeland in Iraq. Herzl concluded that even a colony in Africa would be better than that.

His efforts in Britain were more successful. Colonial secretary Joseph Chamberlain offered a colony near al-Arish in Sinai. Lord Cromer in Egypt rejected the plan, as it required diversion of too much Nile water. Then Chamberlain suggested Uganda, although the territory he had in mind was in Kenya. The Kenya offer was an early indication of the close collaboration which would develop between Zionist leaders and British imperial interests. A pogrom in Kishinev in April 1903, in which fifty Jews were killed, gave Herzl the idea that Russian leaders might also encourage Jewish emigration. Indeed, they responded with assurances that Zionism would be assisted to the extent that emigration would contribute to the reduction of Russia's Jews.

The Sixth Zionist Congress equivocated on the East Africa proposal, although Herzl pleaded for it as an interim solution. When the 1905 Congress abandoned it entirely, Herzl was already dead. His political Zionism, which focused on winning international acceptance and legal sanction for a Jewish state, began more fully to incorporate practical Zionism. The practical strain called for implementation of the institutional infrastructure in Palestine. It did not wait for political approval. After 1905, Zionist Israel Zangwill left the movement because the Zionists refused to admit that Palestine, contrary to their slogan, was not "a land without a people for a people without a land."[5] His own solution for a "great trek" of Palestine's Arabs to some other part of the Arabic-speaking world remains influential in Israel today.

---

[5] Peter Buch in the introduction to Maxime Rodinson, *Israel: A Colonial-Settler State?* (trans. David Thorstad), (New York: Monad Press, 1973), p. 12.

Jewish Immigrants and the Palestinians

How much did Zionist leaders or early Jewish immigrants know about Palestine? Certainly, the leadership knew that it was the homeland of another people who intended to stay there, but early immigrants came with their own hopes and aspirations. Although displaced Arab cultivators occasionally protested the sale of land by attacking Jewish settlements, the early settlers comprised a numerically insignificant group who employed Arab labor. To the embarrassment of later socialist Zionists, the early settlers established a relationship, albeit a colonial one, with the indigenous population. As was true of colonists elsewhere in the Middle East, the first aliya did not consciously set out to expatriate the people of Palestine by taking over the whole country.

The Jewish National Fund and Avoda Ivrit

Colonies funded by Rothschild were turned over in 1900 to the Jewish Colonization Association set up by Baron de Hirsch for American colonization. Its Palestinian branch (P.I.C.A.) perpetuated Rothschild's ideas of colonization until its merger in 1957 with the crucial Jewish National Fund (J.N.F.) founded by the 1901 Zionist Congress. Rules of the Jewish National Fund altered the relationship of second-aliya settlers to Palestinians. Land purchases were centralized and placed under the Jewish Colonial Trust as inalienable from the Jewish people. Settlers would pay rent in exchange for an hereditary lease. No further land speculation would occur because that land would never again be sold.

The holders had to cultivate the land themselves. The rules were interpreted to mean that Jewish, not Arab, labor could be employed. Jewish national lands could be given only to groups of workers who had no money of their own. Prohibition of Arab labor, then, occurred not so much for moral reasons (prevention of exploitation of Arabs) but because new Jewish immigrants could not compete as laborers with local Arabs without protection. This *avoda ivrit* (Hebrew labor) policy, though fully applied only after the 1936–39 Arab protests, eventually set up a separate Jewish society in Palestine. The new Zionist order both excluded and undermined traditional Palestinian relationships.

Socialists of the Second Aliya

Jews in the second aliya, executors of the new policies, were mostly political Zionists from Russia who were inspired by populism and socialism. Many were disillusioned by the pogroms of 1903 and the failure of the 1905 revolution. Poalei Zion (Workers of Zion) and Hapoel Hatzair (Young Worker), inspired by Ber Borochov (d. 1917) and Nachman Syrkin (d. 1924), were the two most influential labor Zionist movements. Syrkin believed that international socialism would resolve anti-Semitism eventually but that in the meantime, Jews ought to have their own socialist state. Borochov focused more on reconciling Marxism with Zionism. Although his Poalei Zion affiliated with the Socialist International in 1907, the Russian-based branch gradually disassociated itself from Zionism. The Palestine section, led by David Ben Gurion (Green) and Yitzhak (Isaac) Ben Zvi remained Zionist, and gradually watered down its Marxism.

Neither Syrkin or Borochov ever settled in Palestine. A. D. Gordon (d. 1922), advocate of Jewish agricultural labor, did. He helped inspire the socialists to pursue avoda ivrit and establishment of cooperative agriculture. As *halutzim* or pioneers, they became the vanguard of a new social order. Hapoel Hatzair was relatively pacifist, but Poalei Zion's members were active in *Hashomer* (Guard), set up in 1907 to defend Jewish settlements.

Cooperative and Collective Agriculture

The most distinctive social experiment of the second aliya was cooperative and collective agriculture, supported by the Jewish National Fund. In 1908, the first *moshavim* appeared. In this system, individuals were allotted plots, as in the Arab *musha* system, but they predominated only after the 1930s. A communal farm (*kvutza*) set up near the Sea of Galilee in 1910 became the model for larger collective farms called *kibbutzim*. On the kibbutzim, all property belonged to the community, tasks were carried out collectively, and decisions were made democratically. Kibbutzim later provided much of the military and political leadership in both the Zionist movement and the state of Israel founded in May 1948. Yet few Jewish settlers out of the total population belonged.

The second aliya brought the founders of Israel to Palestine. These men and women determined that Palestine was their homeland. These settlers founded in 1909 the first Jewish city, Tel Aviv, and other new towns, They spoke Hebrew instead of the predominant Yiddish. Though outnumbered by first-aliya settlers and precolonization Jews, these olim laid the bases for Israel.

Palestinian Reaction to Zionism

Just as the first aliya provoked a reaction from Palestinian Arabs, so too did the second aliya. Under the Committee of Union and Progress (C.U.P.) Palestinians met with sympathy over their objections to Jewish colonization and what they perceived as state-building plans. The Ottoman parliament became a forum for complaints against Zionist immigration. Najib Nassar published in 1911 the first anti-Zionist pamphlet. The Patriotic Ottoman Party was founded the same year, partly to combat colonization. In Palestine, Arabs also communicated to Zionists their concern about the meaning of political Zionism for Palestine's inhabitants. Zionist leaders, though, shunted aside the few Jewish Zionists who objected to Jewish separatism and who tried to organize Arab as well as Jewish labor. Politically, economically, and socially, the Zionists had set the course for a new type of colonization that proposed to replace the present inhabitants of the land. Combining the nineteenth-century themes of colonialism and nationalism, Zionism was destined to clash with Arab national aspirations in Palestine.

CHAPTER NINE

Northwest Africa and Libya to World War I

Despite reimposition of direct Ottoman rule in Tripolitania and institution of new orders elsewhere, North African rulers in the nineteenth century could not halt further European penetration and direct control. Even by World War I, though, North Africa was not fully under European control, as there were strong local resistance forces in Libya and Morocco. Imperialism in North Africa contributed to national formation but largely through negative rather than positive policies.

Algeria and French Colonialism

In the early nineteenth century, Algiers was still a military oligarchy from which the native population derived little benefit. Algeria remained rural, heavily influenced by Sufi orders that offered social services and spirtual support not provided by the government in Algiers. The French occupation of Algiers ensued indirectly from financial entanglements, but in this case, the French were the debtors. In the 1790s, the French army had purchased wheat through two Jewish merchants in Algiers but had never paid for it. The ruler Husayn Dey (1818–30) kept hoping to collect the money. Meanwhile, French merchants in Bone and La Calle had armed their factories in violation of business agreements with Algiers. France's consul Pierre Deval refused to consider Husayn's legitimate grievance regarding the debt whereupon the dey struck him with a flyswatter. This insult of 29 April

1827 supposedly provoked the crisis and subsequent French occupation.

Why then did France wait over three years to invade Algiers? French politics appear to have been the deciding factor. Initially, the French called on the dey to initiate a gun salute to France's flag in Algiers. When he refused, they blockaded Algerian ports, an action that harmed French merchants in Marseilles more than the Algerians. Then, French officials approached Muhammad Ali in Egypt, asking him to take over the Ottoman principalities in the Maghrib. Although he allegedly agreed in October 1829, the French changed the terms; they exempted Algeria. At that point, the Egyptian ruler recognized the scheme as a French plot to serve France and compromise his own leadership in the Muslim world. France's leaders required a new tactic.

In June 1830, Charles X of France decided that if he struck against Algiers, he would insure victory for his party in the July French elections and forestall a revolution. A military expedition quickly forced the dey's surrender and looted his treasury. Although Husayn Dey agreed to give France official sovereignty over the whole of Ottoman Algeria, the party of Charles X lost the elections. He abdicated on 2 August 1830; Husayn Dey had already departed for Naples. The new French government insisted that the expeditionary forces would depart soon after suppressing piracy. They stayed for over 130 years.

French policy developed haphazardly and with little guidance from the home country. After the conquest of Algiers, the French spent years establishing their authority in the entire country (See Map 12). Their policies brought on protests and revolts. In the end, they consolidated their hold over the native population only through suppression and intensive colonization. In the 1830s and 1840s, France's military commanders and not civilian personnel administered policy. Shortly after Charles X's abdication, expedition leader Bourmont was replaced by Clauzel, who decided on aggressive colonization. This led to an influx of European settlers on the Mitidja plain and in the Algiers hinterlands. Although he gave the French foreign affairs minister a plan to place Constantine and Oran under Tunisian rule, the ministry regarded this as outside the military's jurisdiction. Yet French politicians turned a blind eye to the impact of the colonization program on ordinary Algerians. Any thoughts of carrying out a limited occupation of Algeria soon fell victim to unlimited ambitions of settlers who desecrated Muslim mosques and cemeteries. Hostility of Muslims to French rule after such acts in 1832 followed.

Algerian Resistance: Ahmad Bey and Amir Abd al-Qadir

Algerian Muslims had few effective weapons at their disposal for resisting the French. Initially, leaders in Tlemcen sought Moroccan help, but Morocco's forces were pushed back early in 1832. In the east at Constantine Ahmad Bey defied the French in the name of Mahmud II. After Clauzel's costly expedition against Constantine in 1836 during which the French lost over a thousand men, they prepared a second expedition while continuing to negotiate with Ahmad. When in 1837 the French fleet blocked the Ottoman squadron coming to relieve the defenders, Ahmad Bey had to surrender. However, he still refused to acknowledge French authority in Constantine, as he assumed that France planned to leave a local ruler in charge.

The most widespread and popular resistance of the 1830s and 1840s was led by Amir Abd al-Qadir, son of the leader of the influential, dominate Qadiriyya Sufi order. Beginning in 1832, the Qadiriyya leader proclaimed a holy war against the French, but Abd al-Qadir actually led the armies. Various tribes recognized Abd al-Qadir as their sultan; this shifted the resistance from the urban centers to the rural tribal areas. Because the amir had studied French policy and problems

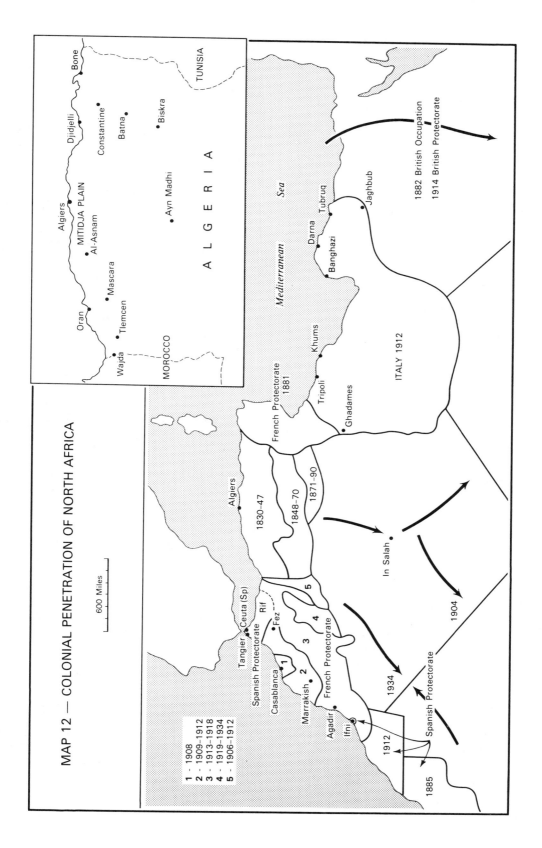

MAP 12 — COLONIAL PENETRATION OF NORTH AFRICA

600 Miles

1 - 1908
2 - 1909–1912
3 - 1913–1918
4 - 1919–1934
5 - 1906–1912

Tangier
Ceuta (Sp)
Spanish Protectorate
Rif
Fez
Casablanca
Marrakish
Agadir
Ifni
French Protectorate
Spanish Protectorate
1912
1885
1934
1904
In Salah

Algiers
1830–47
1848–70
1871–90
French Protectorate 1881
Tripoli
Ghadames
Khums
Banghazi
Darna
Tubruq
Jaghbub
ITALY 1912

Mediterranean Sea

1882 British Occupation
1914 British Protectorate

Inset (ALGERIA):

Bone
Djidjelli
TUNISIA
Constantine
Batna
Biskra
Algiers
MITIDJA PLAIN
Al-Asnam
Ayn Madhi
Mascara
Oran
Tlemcen
Wajda
MOROCCO
A L G E R I A

through newspapers and consultants, he thought that the French would recognize his authority in Oran, too. An agreement of 1834 concluded between Abd al-Qadir and the French general Desmichels gave the amir authority over Oran province, excepting French-controlled towns. The amir could assign consuls to these places. France would give him weapons and ammunition to firmly establish his authority in the countryside. Desmichels concealed from his own government the rights accorded to Abd al-Qadir by the agreement.

When Clauzel returned to Algeria in 1835 as governor general, a post combining civilian and military authority after 1834, he began to violate the Desmichels agreements as well as the limited occupation policy. When Abd al-Qadir chose to exercise his right to control trade with European countries without acting through the French at Oran, Clauzel attacked his capital, Mascara. Then, Clauzel occupied Tlemcen. After Clauzel left Algeria in February 1837, Abd al-Qadir and French officials signed the Treaty of Tafna (20 May 1837). It conceded to Abd al-Qadir territory extending from east of Wajda in the west to Ayn Madhi in the south and the Kabylia in the east, but not in Biskra, Batna, Bone, Bougie, Djidjelli, and Constantine. The French kept Oran, Algiers, and their environs. After the French capture of Constantine from Ahmad Bey, Abd al-Qadir tried to expand his influence there, too.

Despite popular support, Abd al-Qadir faced opposition. His Qadiriyya had quarreled with leaders of the rival Tijaniyya based at Ayn Madhi. These rivals decided to ally with France and called on other Muslims to do the same. The state which Abd al-Qadir set up in the 1830s represented a sort of new order with its own standing army, its own coinage, a tribal government, and (after the burning of Mascara by Clauzel) a mobile capital. Besides his personal army, Abd al-Qadir could rally local tribal auxiliaries if necessary, thus giving him a highly mobile force. In relating to France, he acted like a sovereign ruler and stable ally, viewed as

competent by knowledgeable politicians in France. Based on his understanding of the Treaty of Tafna, he began to extend his control to eastern Algeria. In reply, French forces in 1839 crossed into his territory, renewing the state of war. He quickly rallied his forces, invading the Mitidja plain and threatening Algiers. Faced with withdrawal or full-scale occupation, the French opted for the latter under a new governor general, General Thomas Robert Bugeaud, from February 1841 to June 1847.

Bugeaud arrived in Algeria authorized to occupy it entirely. Immediately, he intensified two pre-existing problems: 1) conflict between Muslims and French settlers over land; 2) French settlers' demands that Algeria be incorporated into France. During its conquest of Algeria, Bugeaud's army ruthlessly devastated the Algerian countryside and its inhabitants. Crops and animals were destroyed. In at least four proven cases, Algerians who surrendered were burned in caves. Abd al-Qadir could not effectively resist the methodical French campaign. From his base at al-Asnam (site of a 1980 earthquake), Bugeaud curtailed Abd al-Qadir's moves. The amir retreated to Morocco, winning initial support from the Alawis. The French, though, defeated a Moroccan force at Isly near Wajda and attacked Moroccan ports by sea. In August 1844, the Alawis signed a treaty with France at Tangier, promising to curtail Abd al-Qadir's resistance.

When Abd al-Qadir continued his activities in the Rif, the French began suspecting that he planned to set up a new state there. Eventually, he lost to the French and surrendered in December 1847. At first reneging on their agreement to let him go to Egypt or Palestine, the French in 1852 finally released him from prison. No Muslim leader with broad appeal emerged to take his place. Bugeaud, meanwhile, burned and looted his way into the Kabylia against the will of the French Chamber of Deputies. Forced to resign, Bugeaud was succeeded by Napolean III's son.

French Consolidation: the Evolution of Two Societies

Theoretically, Algeria was subdued in the 1850s since no widespread fighting subsequently occurred. French-conquered territory was administered by individual *bureaux arabes* with French and Muslim functionaries including soldiers. Since these teams tended to defend Muslim interests, settlers disliked them. But in 1848 Bugeaud's campaign had achieved its goal to incorporate Algeria into France. Settlers won the right to elect representatives to the French Chamber of Deputies. The laws of 1848 divided Algeria into two main communities: a privileged European community and an oppressed and supressed Algerian Muslim community. Algerian Jews, who shared Muslim culture, and non-French Europeans, did not receive the same privileges as the French. At that time, Algeria contained about 110,000 Europeans, about 85 percent of whom lived in big towns and favored extension of colonization. Though Bugeaud had advocated giving land to ex-servicemen, the established settlers agitated for their own land.

After 1851, the French began confiscating the most fertile tribal lands, even encroaching on inalienable habus properties. Napolean III prefered distributing lands not to settlers, who tended to be republicans, but to large companies. By encouraging colonization, Governor General Randon advanced European immigration so that by 1857, Algeria's European population had increased to 181,000 (107,000 French). Although large landowning companies employed French, they also rented land or hired Muslim laborers. Instead of developing new crops, Europeans focused on growing wheat and, to a lesser extent, grapes. French administrators in Algeria tended to apply laws in ways that would suit settler interests rather than those of indigenous Algerians despite efforts of the *bureaux arabes* to help cultivators erect dams, dig wells, and introduce crops.

Napoleon III tried after 1860 to formulate a "Muslim policy", calling Algeria an Arab kingdom and extending protection to tribal lands. But his officials laid foundations for further protests. In 1864, a brief rebellion broke out in central and western Algeria after French officers beat in public an assistant of the local tribal leader. In July 1865, based on his experiences during two visits to Algeria, Napoleon III issued a new document announcing that Algerian Muslims and Jews were French subjects who could enter military and civil service. Only if they agreed to abandon the jurisdiction of their religious laws, though, could they become French citizens. Few took advantage of this "opportunity."

For Muslims, the law remained in effect virtually until World War II, but Jews were decreed citizens in 1870. Instead of providing Muslims with equal opportunities and rights, the 1865 document had made them choose between equal status and their religious heritage. France's archbishop in Algiers after 1867, Lavigerie, looked to conversion as the basis for assimilation of Muslim Algerians. His arrival in Algiers coincided with the advent of calamities brought by locusts, cholera, and drought. Lavigerie worsened communal tensions by placing Muslim children in Christian orphanages instead of in the care of their relatives. By the time of Napoleon III's deposition after the Franco-Prussian War of 1870–71, Algeria had become polarized.

Settler Predominance and the Kabyle Revolt

Settlers approved the return of republicanism to France, because it restored election rights abrogated in 1864 and confirmed the French annexation of Algeria. The French army's loss to Prussia disgraced military in the *bureaux arabes* who had provided at times a mitigating force in the occupation. Algerian Muslims in

Kabylia, ruined economically and seeing their status eroded by settlers, launched a rebellion they hoped would spread. Perhaps one third of Algeria's Muslims eventually participated.

By June 1872, the revolt was over, but most indigenes were impoverished. In Kabylia, France imposed a huge indemnity and tribal lands were expropriated. Individuals could buy back their land, but those who could had to spend their available capital. Many became sharecroppers. The government used the indemnity to further colonization instead of to compensate European settlers victimized by the uprising. By 1898, about 200,000 French citizens were living in the countryside. A new generation of French Algerians, educationally and socially segregated, arose with their own identity and prejudices against Jews and Muslims. With French Algerians serving as the main administrators, Muslims were kept "in their place."

France's Muslim Policy and Muslim Modernizers

From 1871–1919, Muslims paid special taxes which supported colonization. Travel for Muslims was restricted to prevent contacts between them and Muslims elsewhere. To prevent uprisings, the French coopted ulama by making them government officials. While the Tijaniyya won rewards for their early collaboration, Muslims generally felt that their society was being undermined. Not only did the French restrict entry into European schools but they also curtailed formal Muslim education. Besides high taxes and cultural oppression, a special law code governed Algeria's Muslims. French justices took over cases previously handled by qadis. Colonial administrators could harass and restrict Muslims without right of appeal. At the turn of the century, Algeria acquired financial autonomy, with settlers deriving the main benefit. Although Muslims gained a majority on an advisory council set up for the whole territory, this body remained unimportant.

In the 1890s, a movement of modernist Muslims concerned with social and economic issues arose in Tlemcen, Algeria's "Muslim capital" and in Bone. The group surfaced in 1900 when it sent a memorandum to the government requesting the right to vote and to elect representatives. Initially labeled *Young Turks*, these men came to be knows as the *Jeunes Algériens* (Young Algerians). They focused on bridging French and Muslim culture, particularly through Franco-Muslim *medersas* (schools). French liberal opinion looked with favor upon both these Algerians and the similar Young Tunisians. Despite the more visibly European orientation of these North African Muslims, they shared with Muslim modernizers in the Arab East the search for a means of accommodation to and liberation from European political, economic, and cultural imperialism.

Husaynid Tunisia and its New Order

When the Ottomans embarked on centralization early in the nineteenth century, the Husaynids tried to resist since they had been virtually autonomous following the Algerian evacuation in 1756. Connections with the empire had not required regular tribute, although the Husaynids still allowed the Ottomans to invest them as beys. Tunisians themselves regarded the Husaynids as their real rulers. At the turn of the century, Tunisia was ruled by Hammuda Bey, who promoted security and prosperity. He assisted local merchants by giving them state loans, as his father before him had done. Like Muhammad Ali, Hammuda lived simply. To develop responsibility and competence in his successor, he delegated his heir-apparent as tax collector in the countryside. Apparently, he encouraged criticism from his advisors and consulted frequently with rural leaders over state affairs. Although he tried to instill military discipline among his Ottoman troops, their rebellion led him to rely on tribal forces for his regular army. The disappearance of resolute leadership after his death in 1813, though, led to increased European economic penetration.

In the 1820s, French olive oil merchants were angered by the policies of Husayn Bey (1824–35) that required advance payment. When the harvest of 1829 failed to bring in the purchased oil, the government had no funds with which to repay the merchants. French consul Mathieu de Lesseps pressured Husayn Bey to sign a treaty in August 1830 to end state monopolies on the sale of produce. As in Egypt, the French wanted a free market and forced Husayn to promise to observe Ottoman capitulations.

After the Algerian invasion, Husayn Bey cooperated with France instead of backing Ottoman efforts; he was apparently lulled by French promises of Husaynid rule in Oran and Constantine. Early in 1831, he instituted a new-order military force to be trained by French officers. To placate Ottoman anger, Husayn claimed that his cooperation had saved Tunisia from a French invasion. As a gesture of loyalty, he asked Mahmud II for permission to adopt new Ottoman uniforms for his army. Mahmud II saw through this ploy, and told the Tunisians to pay regular tribute and to assist in imposing direct Ottoman rule in Tripolitania.

Ahmad Bey's Policies and External Pressures

Once the French began settling down in Algeria and the Ottomans re-established their rule in Tripolitania, Tunisia drew closer to the empire. Ahmad Bey (1837–55), who had influenced his father not to recognize Ottoman sovereignty, was willing to send gifts to the sultan but would

recognize only his religious authority. Ahmad basically played off the French against the Ottomans and vice versa. He also emulated Muhammad Ali's new order, establishing in 1840 a military officer's school and increasing his army's size. Like Muhammad Ali, he retained monopolies other than the compromised agricultural produce monopoly. Besides contributing to costly military modernization, Ahmad funded religious institutions, thereby winning the loyalty of ulama.

Since his resources were much smaller than those of Egypt's ruler, Ahmad's policies resulted in oppression of peasants who could not support his level of expenditure. Without the wealth to sustain military reforms, palaces, and lavish gifts to the sultan, he severely undermined Tunisia's economy. When his resources were slim, Ahmad Bey did not admit that he could not afford the expense, but sold his household jewelry to pay for troops to fight for Abdulmejid in the Crimean War.

Eventually, Ahmad Bey sent his modernizing vizir Khayr al-Din (of Circassian Mamluk origin) to France to borrow money. Buy Khayr al-Din opposed the loan and delayed in arranging it. Ahmad Bey died without having incurred a foreign debt. Yet he left his successors with a modernizing economy that resulted in debt problems like those in Egypt, Iran, and the Ottoman administration. Humanitarian measures instituted by Ahmad Bey—manumission of slaves and an end to slave trading at Tunis—were dismantled by his successor Muhammad Bey (1855–59).

Muhammad Bey's administration reversed the decline of Tunisian agriculture through reduction of taxes. This measure, however, decreased revenues to support the government without sufficiently alleviating Tunisia's trade imbalance with Europe that had been inaugurated by Ahmad's extravagance. By the end of his reign, Muhammad Bey obtained his first loan. Although he borrowed from Tunisians, many sold their treasury bills to foreign merchants at discount because they doubted the ruler's redemption promises. Foreign interference in Tunisia increased, with Britain encouraging Tunisia's Ottoman ties and France trying to keep the bey uncommitted. Both consuls, after an incident involving a Jew in 1857, pressured Muhammad into promulgating a basic law guaranteeing his subjects equality before the law and security of person and property. It also gave foreigners the right to own property. A committee was formed to draw up a constitution. Issued in 1860, it was the first such document in Muslim Southwest Asia and North Africa.

Khaznadar and Khayr al-Din: Frustration of Reform

Under the constitution, Tunisia became a limited monarchy with the bey as head of state and an appointed council to which ministers were responsible. Khayr al-Din Pasha influenced the constitution's structure and became the council's first president. To his dismay, he discovered that Mustafa Khaznadar, chief minister for some twenty-five years, could ignore the provision requiring him to be responsible to the council. Khayr al-Din consequently resigned as president. Tunisia's financial situation worsened as Khaznadar used his office to make large profits on state-funded projects and contracted foreign loans in which Tunisia received 57 percent of the amount to be repaid. As in Egypt, debt problems soon engulfed the country. Imposition of a special tax to pay for the loans produced a rebellion in town and country alike, leading to abolition of the construction. Despite their earlier pressures for reform, Europeans did not try to resusicitate the constitution because its implementation had hindered their bribing of officials to obtain favors. They also objected to its application to foreigners who owned property. Other Europeans' cases remained under consular jurisdiction.

As in Algeria, Tunisia late in the 1860s experienced drought and cholera. Khaznadar kept borrowing. Finally, the creditors forced on Tunisia an international debt commission with French, British, and Italian members to straighten out the government's finances. Khaznadar appointed Khayr al-Din as president of the supervisory committee overseeing the work of the executive committee to assure proper management, and yet he himself kept profiting at state expense. French and Italians began struggling for paramount influence in Tunisia.

Fearful of European political intervention, Tunisians tried to formalize OttomanTunisian relations. At first blocked by French diplomats in Istanbul, Muhammad al-Sadiq Bey (1859–1882) in 1871 won Abdulaziz's recognition as governor of Tunisia in exchange for sending troops when called upon, payment of annual tribute, and issuance of coins in the sultan's name. The British consul had favored the new official Ottoman-Tunisian ties; he anticipated securing longlasting benefits for British companies in Tunisia. Allying with Khaznadar, he arranged for concessions to establish a bank, build a railway, and provide Tunis with gas. But Khaznadar's days in the government were numbered. Late in 1873, he was dismised for having abused his office. Khayr al-Din succeeded him.

Khayr al-Din's assumption of the vizirate brought about great expectations. By this time, however, he had grown disillusioned with the viability of western institutions in Tunisia. Although he tried to re-establish the government's respectability and efficiency, he did not request restoration of the constitution of 1860. Abuses of tax collectors were curtailed, and state lands were distrubted to peasants. Khayr al-Din instituted a modest educational reform by founding Sadiqiyya College to train civil servants; it offered a western-style curriculum of Italian, French, science, and mathematics. However, his attempt to set up a mixed courts system failed because of Italian and French opposition. Only a provisional tribunal with limited authority came into being.

During his first three years as prime minister, Khayr al-Din benefited from a prosperous economy, and he managed to meet Tunisia's financial obligations. He could not manipulate, however, the squabbles of European diplomats. The English concessions proved unprofitable and were closed down. When Khayr al-Din rejected the request of the French consul Roustan to connect Tunisia's railways to those of Algeria, knowing that the French might use them to invade his country, Roustan pressed for his dismissal. To aggravate problems created by a poor harvest in 1876, Roustan spread rumors about Tunisia's financial position. In July 1877, Khayr al-Din was dismissed and entered the service of Abdulhamid II in Istanbul, acting briefly as grand vizir. The new administration under Roustan's protege Mustafa ibn Isma'il returned to earlier self-aggrandizement practices.

Europe Acquiesces to the French Occupation

Meanwhile, the diplomatic wrangling continued. When at the Congress of Berlin in 1878 Germany and Britain agreed to concede Tunisia to the French, Italy (whose citizens constituted the largest foreign community there) objected, refusing even to be mollified by promises of Tripolitania. Faced with a public opposed to further colonization in North Africa as well, the French government proceeded cautiously at first. When the bey refused to agree to a protectorate in 1879, the French began to seek a pretext for intervention. Muhammad al-Sadiq Bey, however, was always willing to cooperate with them regarding their complaints.

The French nevertheless proceeded with their occupation. On 12 May 1881, Muhammad al-Sadiq accepted the Treaty of Bardo. It stated that the occupation was temporary and would end following the "restoration of order," a familiar occupation formula. France took control of Tunisia's foreign relations, including the holding of veto power over international agreements arranged by the bey. Soon the French realized that they lacked a formal protectorate, and that the treaty restricted freedom of action. Their resident-minister Paul Cambon secured British, Italian, and then Tunisian approval to end international control over Tunisia's

finances. Muhammad al-Sadiq died shortly thereafter. The new bey, Ali, agreed to the al-Marsa Convention that set up the French protectorate. Concluded in June 1883, it was approved by France's Chamber of Deputies in April 1884. Tunisia after that resembled Egypt during the British occupation. Officially, the bey and his ministers ruled, but ultimate power resided with the French resident-general.

During the nineteenth century, despite a dramatic increase in the number of French citizens in Tunisia, Italians outnumbered them until the early 1930s. Whereas in Algeria settlers were often given land, in Tunisia they had to purchase it. For this reason, the French population in Tunisia prior to the twentieth century consisted of administrators, traders, professionals, and some farmers. Many more Italians belonged to the working classes. In Tunisia, the French avoided the worst abuses that characterized their rule in Algeria. The presence of so many Italians restricted narrow French self-interest. Although tribal populations in southern Tunisia resisted the protectorate, Tunisians elsewhere cooperated with it because it did not seem to jeopardize severely their personal and economic status. Reformers saw it as an opportunity to modernize without compromising Islam.

In 1896, the Khalduniyya School was founded for graduates of the traditional Zaytuna mosque-university. Like Dar al-Ulum, it gave shaykhs a secular education, but the institution did not endure. Sadiqiyya College, on the other hand, prospered and provided Tunisia with an educated Muslim elite. This elite became the nucleus for the *Young Tunisians* who aimed at achieving cooperation with the French to innovate and improve Tunisian society. But two incidents in 1911 and 1912 involving Muslim rights led the French to impose martial law, promoting an atmosphere of confrontation rather than harmony. Tunisians already regarded themselves as a nation. What they desired was restoration of their independence.

Towards National Formation in Libya

When the French invaded Algiers, Yusuf Qaramanli in Tripolitania, like Husayn Bey in Tunisia, signed a treaty with France promising to suppress piracy and avoid intervening in Algeria. But Yusuf, even with a revival of trans-Saharan trade, could not pay his debts. As he lost the ability to uphold his position, he began to face internal opposition. First, the Sayf al-Nasr tribe rebelled in 1831, establishing its authority over Fazzan. Then, tribes in Tripolitania opposed Yusuf when British pressure to pay his debts led him to impose special taxes. The rebels advocated deposing Yusuf in favor of his nephew Muhammad, but he abdicated in favor of his son Ali. The French and British intervened, supporting the rival candidates.

Fearing imposition of European military intervention but claiming to be investigating Albanian claims against Tripoli, the Ottomans sent an emissary in mid-1832 in hopes of settling the dispute. When the Husaynids in Tunisia also began making claims on Tripolitania, Mahmud II decided to take resolute action. In May 1835, an Ottoman fleet arrived, deposed the Qaramanli dynasty, and announced that henceforth Tripoli would be ruled directly by Istanbul. By this action, Mahmud II blocked expansion from the west and began laying the foundations for a modern Libya consisting of Tripolitania, Cyrenaica, and the Fazzan. He reconquered areas taken by the Qaramanlis' opponents, leaving the tribes a measure of autonomy though they still paid taxes.

Ottoman Libya's economy continued to depend on trans-Saharan trade. At mid-century, despite ongoing European pressure to stop it, the slave trade constituted the major part of commodity-trading as Ottoman demand remained high. Through trans-Saharan trade, the Ottomans in Libya came into conflict with the French who began entertaining thoughts of occupying Ghat in the southwest. But in 1875, the Ottomans took control of it. After France's occupation of Tunisia and the Congress of Berlin, European and especially Italian economic penetration into Libya increased. In Cyrenaica, the Sanussi order protected the trade route that passed through its territories.

The Sanussis' establishment in Cyrenaica, appealing to not fully Islamized beduin there, dated from the time of Abd al-Qadir in Algeria. The Algerian founder, Muhammad ibn Ali al-Sanussi (d. 1857) won the nomads' respect by giving them Muslim instruction in zawiyyas established along trade routes. Although the Sanussiyya were lukewarm about Ottoman control, they regarded the French, who were extending their influence throughout the western Sahara, with even greater apprehension. By charter, Sultan Abdulmejid exempted the Sanussiyya from paying taxes but authorized them to collect Shari'a taxes. Sanussi-Ottoman cooperation characterized the administration of Cyrenaica.

Italy Secures a Foothold

The Italians still felt slighted by their exclusion from North African rule. Even when some Italians pointed out that Libya would be an economic liability, influential forces kept suggesting Libya as a rich land that would become Italy's "fourth shore," helping to solve Italy's problems of overpopulation. By 1902, all of Europe's major powers—France, Britain, Germany, and Austria-Hungary—had agreed to Libya's annexation by Italy. Gradually, the Italians established their presence with a post office, flour mill, medical care, and mill for esparto grass.

With the victory of the Young Turk revolution in 1908, the Italians began to fear a more vigorous Ottoman reassertion of sovereignty. The Germans aggravated these suspicions by setting up competitive enterprises in Libya. Since Italy could not point to financial problems as a pretext for intervention, it claimed that its citizens were endangered by C.U.P. activities. Although the Ottomans were willing to grant economic concessions desired by the Italians, the occupation-decision had already been taken. The Italians asserted that the sending of an Ottoman ship and weapons to Tripoli in September 1911 jeopardized the safety of Italians there. The Ottomans continued to negotiate, not fully comprehending Italy's determination to declare war.

But Italy expected a short war, and mistakenly assumed that the Libyans would support it against the C.U.P. They were wrong. In the year of fighting between October 1911 and October 1912, the Italians could not break out of Tubruq, Banghazi, Tripoli, Darna, and Khums, towns they occupied in the war's first month. The Sanussis rallied to the Ottoman defense. Egypt's Aziz al-Masri commanded a training section for volunteers in the Ottoman army. Mustafa Kemal served as an aide to Enver Pasha. Although the Italians were not prepared for the heavy casualties they sustained, the Ottomans could not afford a prolonged conflict either, because of the Balkan War.

When the Ottomans agreed to recognize Italian sovereignty and withdraw, Libyan forces continued to resist with the Sanussis hoping to achieve popular recognition of their leadership. To support their claim, they asserted that Enver had actually given Libya its independence under Sanussi protection and authority. Tripolitanian authorities, however, discounted Sanussi hegemony, with counterclaims of their own. They in 1915 set up a republic in Misurata. By the onset of World War I Italy had taken the coastal areas and the main towns of Fazzan but had to retreat from their southern positions by late 1914. Sanussis continued to fight long after that.

Morocco and its Incorporation into the European System

The Alawi rulers of the nineteenth century confronted circumstances similar to those faced by their eighteenth-century predecessors. Mawlay Sulayman (1792–1822) and his nephew Mawlay Abd al-Rahman (1822–59) both had to reconquer the country. Regional qa'ids (leaders) imported arms from Europe and maintained private armies that were generally better equipped than those of the rulers. To retain a measure of authority, the Alawi rulers tried unsuccessfully to restrict the access of their subjects to European consuls.

When France began to occupy Algiers, Morocco like the rest of North Africa was drawn into the conflict. After early efforts to assist the Algerians failed, the Moroccans' territorial integrity was secured by a British pledge. Britain aimed at expanding the already dominant interests of its businessmen and at safeguarding from European threats its position at Gibraltar. When Bugeaud's army defeated the Moroccan force at Isly, the Moroccans discovered the worthlessness of the British pledge. Mawlay Abd al-Rahman's prestige in the countryside was severely eroded by this defeat.

Expansion of European Economic and Political Activity

The French soon expanded their economic interests in Morocco, especially in mining and the wool trade. Some Moroccans grew rich, and the sultan instituted government monopolies usually handled by Jewish merchants. As elsewhere, monopolies provoked a reaction from free-trade oriented Europeans. During the Crimean War, increased demand for Moroccan products and the consequent higher government revenues from duties made Abd al-Rahman more willing to reduce monopolies. A Moroccan-British agreement in December 1856 retained only tobacco, ammunition, and arms import monopolies, with 10 percent duties to be assessed on all imports. Export duties were higher. Long independent and having no capitulations agreements, Morocco now accepted British consular jurisdiction over cases involving British subjects. Britons were also allowed to own property. Other European nations could adhere to the treaty. Most of them did, with the exception of Morocco's neighbors across the sea, Spain and France.

French and Spanish objections ensued from their respective interests in North Africa. France wanted to divert trade to Algeria. Spain, planning expansion into the Rif, felt that the British treaty excluded further Spanish penetration. Aiming to consolidate their northern Moroccan holdings, the Spaniards built new fortifications in Ceuta. Shortly thereafter, local tribesmen demolished these defenses, providing Spain with a pretext for invasion. In February 1860, Spanish forces occupied Tetuan. Abd al-Rahman's successor, his son Muhammad (1859–73) thereby suffered further erosion of support.

Though he quelled a local revolt in the north by 1862, terms of the Spanish-Moroccan treaty of May 1860 weighed

heavily. Besides commercial privileges like those granted Britain, the Spaniards forced on Muhammad an indemnity in exchange for evacuating Tetuan. Spain also gained new port facilities. A separate agreement of November 1861 contained additional commercial terms. It gave Spain permission to send Christian missionaries and a consul to Fez, the sultan's capital. Spanish customs officials now administered a segment of Morocco's customs duties. After the sultan unsuccessfully sought a British loan to help resolve his financial difficulties, the British pressured Spain to reduce the indemnity (October 1861) and to evacuate by May 1862. The sultan still had to borrow money, but with the indemnity's reduction, the British obliged him with a loan.

Events of the early 1860s compromised Muhammad's ability to rule Morocco and accelerated European interference. Spain's tax commissioners and European agents contributed to the sultan's declining prestige, especially in Morocco's ports. Besides instituting a sanitation system, individual European consulates launched their own postal systems. As in the Ottoman Empire earlier, significant numbers of indigenes, including local leaders, came under European protection.

Mawlay Hasan's New Order

Mawlay Hasan (1873–94) tried to reverse this trend by introducing a new order. Having observed that the Moroccans had lost their battle with Spain because of the Spaniards' superior artillery, he imported updated weaponry and European military instructors. Instead of viewing his army only as a personal one for keeping internal order, Mawlay Hasan created a national army for confronting external enemies, levying troops from major cities and regions. These new-order forces owed loyalty to him rather than to qa'ids. Not surprisingly, both local leaders and Europeans within Morocco preferred the old system that allowed them maximum interference because it kept the central government weak. Although Mawlay Hasan used his new troops to reassert his authority, his successors were unable to contain Morocco's divisive influences.

Like earlier modernizers, Mawlay Hasan thought that he could protect his country by superimposing European forms on his own society. He sent students abroad for technological training. To pay for his military program, he instituted efficient and equitable tax collection. He aroused opposition from groups previously exempt from taxation, however, without providing sufficient income to pay for his projects. Mawlay Hasan's bureaucratic reorganization consisted of dividing Morocco into smaller administrative units and then, to cement ties, visiting remote areas. The strong currency introduced as part of his stabilization program actually undermined the economy because foreigners took it out illegally. Although the ruler hoped to rally his subjects behind him by making Morocco strong, his programs increased the European domination he was trying to avoid. As elsewhere, his modernization program threatened old elites and institutions without creating viable new ones (except perhaps for the army). When at the Madrid Conference of 1880 Hasan tried to check European interference and extension of consular protection to Moroccans, Europeans thwarted his goal, although they agreed that their nationals should pay taxes. The rapidity of technological advances in Europe, especially in the military realm, hindered Mawlay Hasan's chances of succeeding with his new order. By his death in 1894, Morocco's traditional elites were still resisting centralization. His fourteen-year old son lacked strength to counteract internal and external threats. In the short term, Mawlay Hasan's new order failed to construct a modern-based nation-state but it laid foundations for the future.

Toward the French Protectorate

Mawlay Abd al-Aziz (1894–1908) and his successor and brother Mawlay Abd al-Hafidh (1908–13) fell prey to the same combination of European pressures and local insurgency that had challenged Mawlay Hasan and his predecessors. In 1901, after failing to agree with France on the Moroccan-Algerian boundary in the south, Abd al-Aziz accepted French military intervention in Morocco should the sultan be threatened. Both nations would maintain border posts in the disputed area. This intervention clause later gave France the pretext for establishing the Moroccan protectorate.

In 1904, the Anglo-French Entente Cordiale brought about British acquiescence to an eventual French takeover in Morocco. Special allowances were provided for a Spanish zone. France and Spain signed separate agreements demarcating spheres of influence. The young Abd al-Aziz apparently did not comprehend the nature of these agreements, and the Europeans avoided explaining their implications. Mawlay Abd al-Aziz was further handicapped by his youth and by controversy. His accession had not been accompanied by prior consultation with and approval of the country's religious leaders. This approval was signified by the oath of loyalty. Mawlay Abd al-Aziz alienated his subjects by spending extravagantly on European material possessions of no national value. Like his predecessor, he employed foreign military advisors. When efficient tax collection lapsed, partly because of his spending habits, Mawlay Abd al-Aziz turned again to foreign loans. Morocco received, as elsewhere, considerably less than the sum to be repaid.

Toward the end of his reign, Mawlay Abd al-Aziz faced in the northeast rebellion by a pretender Jilali ibn Idris, while in the northwest, Ahmad al-Raysuni harassed Europeans by kidnappings that required the sultan to pay ransoms. In the southwest, Berber confederacies of the Glawa, Gundafa, and Mtuga opposed the centralizing authority of a sultan who refused them preferential treatment. The sultan's brother Abd al-Hafidh, hoping to check the influence of the Rahamna Arabs around Marrakish where he governed, first warned Abd al-Aziz and then in 1907

CHAPTER TEN

World War I and Its Consequences in the Middle East

As a result of imperialism, mostly economic and political, most of the Middle East and North Africa had by 1914 entered the European sphere of influence. Yet the Ottoman Empire was not occupied by foreign troops. It remained the strongest indigenous independent state in Africa and Asia. Whereas France, Britain, and Russia had long been engaged in competition for the Middle East, newly unified Germany represented an additional factor in the late nineteenth and early twentieth century. Middle Easterners from Iran to Morocco welcomed German merchants, goods, and political support. Although the three large imperial powers resented German economic and political penetration into "their" sphere of interest, they had accommodated Germany's imperial interests until the time of World War I. With the onset of war, the Middle East assumed new strategic significance. All participants viewed control of the Middle East as a key to victory and postwar ascendancy.

Although World War I was principally a European war, it profoundly affected Middle Eastern history. Southwest Asia's two dynastic polities—the Ottomans and Qajars—met their demise soon after war's end but not until Europe's powers had first sought to control their respective destinies through secret agreements. Postwar Turkey's war of independence and Egypt's revolution forced a reconsideration of the division of spoils the Europeans had in mind. Yet, the mandate system allowed for the retention, though veiled, of colonialism in Arab parts of Southwest Asia freed from Ottoman rule. Northwest African and Libyan political status remained hardly changed.

148

Alliances and Objectives

World War I ensued from entangling prewar alliances contracted by European nations. On 28 June 1914, Serbian nationalists assassinated the heir to the throne of Austria-Hungary, Archduke Franz Ferdinand, in Sarajevo, capital of Bosnia. As guardian of Balkan Orthodox Christians, Russia moved to protect Serbia from the Austrians after the latter's harsh ultimatum of 23 July. Though Serbia agreed to virtually all Austrian demands, diplomacy failed to resolve the crisis. Germany and Austria attacked Belgrade, and on 1 August 1914, Germany formally declared war on Russia. France's treaty obligations to Russia brought France into the war, while Britain's pledge to defend Belgian neutrality forced British entry after Germany had invaded France through Belgium. World War I in Europe was characterized by trench warfare after German forces (which had rapidly overrun northern France) were halted at the Marne River. In the east, German troops inflicted heavy losses on the Russians who held on until 1917 when the Bolshevik government signed an armistice, leading to the humiliating treaty of Brest-Litovsk in 1918.

War Aims in the Middle East

Middle Easterners and North Africans were involved in this war. Despite the close association that Germany and the Ottomans had established before the war, there is evidence that the Young Turks might have preferred a wartime alliance with France. Serbia, however, was former Ottoman territory, and Russia still sought to control Constantinople's straits and parts of eastern Anatolia. When France and Russia became allies, the Ottomans turned to Germany. On 2 August 1914, the day German forces marched into Luxembourg and Belgium, Germany and the Ottoman Empire concluded a secret alliance. Thus when German ships passed through the Dardanelles on 11 August, the Ottomans purchased them as Russia and western Europeans protested the violation of neutrality. After the "Ottoman" ships attacked Russia in October, Russia and its allies replied by declaring war on 5 November. The Ottoman sultan then proclaimed a jihad against the Triple Entente (Britain, France, and Russia).

This declaration probably had a greater but still minimal effect in non-Ottoman, foreign-occupied areas with substantial Muslim populations such as India, than it did on Ottoman subjects. British policy makers, however, feared that Muslims, in response to the jihad call, would take the side of the Ottomans and that Britain's communications with India and Africa, of which the Suez Canal constituted a key element, would be broken. To counter this perceived threat, the British allied with Makka's ruler, Sharif Husayn ibn Ali, thereby profoundly influencing modern Arab history.

What Middle East goals did Germany formulate? In a war with France, Britain, and Russia, it was desirable for the Germans to have an ally on Russia's Caucasian border. The Ottomans were also in control of the Dardanelles and Bosporus (where they could bottle up Russia's fleet), and they presented a threat to British and French interest in the Middle East (including to communications). The kaiser had worked to persuade Muslims that Germany would champion their cause against the colonial occupation of North Africa and foreign attempts to occupy areas still under Muslim control. The presence of German officers in Anatolia throughout the war suggests that the Germans believed more strongly in their own leadership than in that of the Ottoman army officers and that they intended to increase their regional influence after war's end.

War aims of the Entente were contained in secret agreements negotiated soon after the outbreak of war. New allies joined in pursuit of territorial gain. Most agreements were only temporary, but some had far-reaching impact. The Constantinople Agreement (March 1915) between France, Britain, and Russia, gave Russia support for annexing the straits on condition of free navigation and a free port at Istanbul. Russia also agreed to stay in northern Iran while the British would keep both their southern zone and the neutral zone. The parties agreed on Arab independence in Arabia but planned to partition Ottoman Asia later. France hoped to gain control of Cilicia, an area of Christian concentration, and Syria.

Italy entered the war because of the Secret Treaty of London (April 1915). Promises of southwestern Anatolia including Antalya conflicted with France's designs on Cilicia. Italy's allies approved Italy's occupation in 1912 of the Dodecanese Islands and future annexation of Austria's Tyrol (still resented by today's Tyroleans). Later, Italian-French rivalry over Cilicia led to further promises in the St. Jean de Maurienne Agreement (April 1917). Italy agreed to give up Cilicia for Smyrna (Izmir), previously promised to Greece in exchange for a Greek declaration of war on which King Constantine reneged. The Greeks revived their claim when the Entente was winning the war. Neither Italy nor Greece contributed much to the defeat of Germany, Austria-Hungary, and the Ottoman Empire.

Britain and the Hashimite Alliance

During the war, Britain was also a party to three other agreements, two of them vague and all controversial. Before the war, British representatives in Cairo were in contact with Abd Allah, son of Hashimite Sharif Husayn ibn Ali of Hijaz who governed Makka and Madina. Abd Allah approached Lord Kitchener to find out what aid the Arabians might receive if they revolted against the Ottoman Empire. When the war began, Kitchener, newly appointed Secretary of State for war, contacted the sharif as a potential ally. In the early stages of the war, the sharif, an Ottoman appointee, refused to aid his Ottoman sovereign. To exert pressure on him, the Young Turk government cut off pilgrimages and trade to Hijaz, important sources of the sharif's income. This disruption forced Husayn to depend on the British in India for food.

Arab Nationalists and the Hashimites

Early in 1915, representatives of al-Ahd and al-Fatat in northern Syria looked to the Hashimites as Arab nationalist allies. Husayn's son Faysal provided the link. When, between June 1915 and May 1916, over one hundred Arab leaders were executed in Syria, Faysal witnessed some of the killings in Damascus. Although Jemal Pasha of the C.U.P. aimed to curtail Arab nationalist contacts with foreigners, he further alienated Ottoman Arabs. Husayn's ties with the nationalists led to the Damascus Protocol. Issued in July 1915, it contained preconditions for Anglo-Arab cooperation. Husayn forwarded it to the new British High Commissioner in Egypt, Sir Henry McMahon.

The Husayn-McMahon Correspondence

The ensuing exchange of letters between July 1915 and March 1916 is known as the Husayn-McMahon correspondence; the materials contain the first of Britain's wartime commitments referring to Palestine. Because of the correspondence, Husayn launched his revolt in support of Britain's war effort in 1916. Although the letters became one "legal" basis for asserting Arab sovereignty and for contesting postwar decisions, the correspondence was not a treaty and was inconclusive as to territorial definitions. Moreover, it has never been established that Britain had the right to decide the future of either its wartime allies or of territory detached from the Ottoman Empire.

Eight letters constituted the correspondence. In the Damascus Protocol, Arab leaders called on the British to recognize an independent nation uniting all Arabs from southern Turkey to southern Arabia, and from the Mediterranean Sea to the borders of Iran. Husayn agreed to exclude Britain's protectorate in Aden. When McMahon equivocated on the question of boundaries, Husayn replied that such an agreement was a critical prerequisite to the alliance. Three more letters exchanged between July and September 1915 failed to resolve the differences.

New factors, however, came into play, leading the British to settle the question. Disturbances had arisen in British-occupied Sudan. The Libyan Sanussiyya campaigned against Britain's Italian allies. In Mesopotamia, the British encountered military difficulties, while in India the population grew restive. The British intelligence network finally confirmed the importance of a greater Syrian nationalist movement. Underlying Britain's fears remained concern about the Sultan's power to mobilize Muslims against the allies.

Britain Supports Arab Independence

On 24 October 1915, McMahon wrote a letter that convinced the sharif to ally with Britain. The British agreed to "support the independence of the Arabs in all the regions within the limits demanded by the Sharif of Makka." Britain excluded "portions of Syria lying to the west of the districts of Damascus, Homs, Hama, and Aleppo." This reserved area is present-day Lebanon. McMahon's letter referred to the above as areas that could not be described as "purely Arab." This suggests that "Arab" was being used synonymously with "Muslim" since these areas were inhabited by Arabs, both Muslim and Christian.

Britain's promise applied only to areas in which Britain was "free to act without detriment to the interests of her ally, France." The districts of Mersina and Alexandretta in Cilicia were specifically omitted because of France's interest in Christians there (France was also concerned about the Maronite Christians of Mount Lebanon). Nothing in the correspondence suggested either a clear-cut French claim elsewhere or the exclusion of Palestine from areas promised to Husayn. Indeed, the correspondence did not even mention the region of Palestine nor did it employ any political or geographical terms then in use for referring to it.

Commitments to Arabian and Gulf Rulers

The letter did mention commitments to Arab chiefs in Arabia and the Gulf. The shaykh of Kuwayt, for example, had aided Britain's Mesopotamia campaign because he was promised support in obtaining independence from the Ottomans following the war. The British in India were also in the process of signing a treaty of friendship with another Arabian chief, Abd al-Aziz Ibn Sa'ud of the Najd, a rival of Husayn's Hashimite clan. Although he did not actually fight against the Ottomans, Ibn Sa'ud attacked the Rashidi Emirate, an Ottoman ally, and refused to fight for the Ottoman sultan. In exchange, the government of India gave him a yearly allowance and recognized his independence. Qatar's ruler also signed an agreement with the British (November 1916) but the document curtailed rather than confirmed his independent status. British promises to both Husayn and Abd al-Aziz reflected the different interests of the British Foreign Office and the Government of India as well as the British effort to line up allies among the Ottomans' Arab subjects. To Britain, the Husayn-McMahon exchange represented a statement of intentions rather than a treaty commitment or firm agreement.

McMahon's responsibilities as British representative in Egypt entailed supervision over the Arab Bureau in Cairo, to which officials like T. E. Lawrence were attached. Based on contacts with Kitchener, Husayn had every reason to believe that McMahon was speaking for the British government. There is no indication that Husayn was aware of Britain's negotiations with Abd al-Aziz in the Najd or that he would have gone along with the British had he known about them. Possibly the two arms of the British were negotiating independently of each other. The Foreign Office's main interest was in the Levant and the Hijaz while the Indian government dealt with Iraq, Iran, the Najd, and the Gulf. The obvious lack of coordination among the various British agencies was surely fueling a future conflict in Arabia as well as elsewhere in the Middle East.

What did Husayn really want? It appears that despite his Syrian connection he was a dynastic nationalist rather than an Arab nationalist. As guardian of the holy cities, he already possessed prestige in the Arab and Muslim worlds. Whether he sought to be a king, a caliph (an intention he formally disavowed in the correspondence), or just an autonomous ruler, Husayn—like his rival Ibn Sa'ud—aimed to establish a dynasty. Although he lost the struggle in Arabia to the Saudis, Abd Allah and Faysal emerged as rulers of Transjordan (later the Hashimite Kingdom of Jordan) and Iraq (until 1958). Saudi-Hashimite rivalry soon provided a central theme in inter-Arab politics.

The Sykes–Picot Agreement: Secret Diplomacy

Three weeks before Husayn thought he had fulfilled his commitment by starting the Arab revolt, the British reneged on their promises to him by arranging the Sykes-Picot agreement (16 May 1916), confining the proposed independent Arab state to present-day Saudi Arabia and Yemen. Sir Mark Sykes of the British Foreign Office and Francois Georges-Picot, France's official in Cairo in charge of Syrian affairs, worked it out in a series of exchanged notes. The agreement granted the straits and northeastern Anatolia to Russia, and Cilicia to France.

Alexandretta would be a free port. The best that the Arabs of Syria could hope for was autonomy under French protection while the Iraqis faced the same alternative under the British. As for the Arabs of Palestine, their homeland from Gaza to Tyre was to be given over to international control except for a British enclave around Akka. After coming to power in Russia in November 1917, the Bolsheviks published the documents; knowledgeable Arabs were enraged.

The Balfour Declaration: A Public Letter

The third and equally vague promise regarding Palestine was made in a letter known today as the Balfour Declaration. Issued publicly on 2 November 1917, it was addressed by Britain's foreign secretary, Arthur James Balfour, to Lord Rothschild, a prominent English Zionist. It read as follows:

> His Majesty's Government view with favour the establishment in Palestine of a national home for the Jewish people, and will use their best endeavours to facilitate the achievement of this object, it being clearly understood that nothing shall be done which may prejudice the civil and religious rights of existing non-Jewish communities in Palestine, or the rights and political status enjoyed by Jews in any other country.[1]

Why the Balfour Letter?: Some Hypotheses Why did the British War Cabinet declare its sympathy for Zionist aspirations? Before 1917, the British government ignored Zionist lobbying for a public commitment to support Zionism in Pales-

---

[1] See Hurewitz, *Middle East and North Africa in World Politics*, vol. 2: *British-French Supremacy, 1914–1945* (New Haven and London: Yale University Press, 1979), pp. 101–106. A photocopy of the document can be seen in John Norton Moore, ed., *The Arab-Israeli Conflict: Readings and Documents*. Abridged and revised edition (Princeton: Princeton University Press, 1977), p. 885.

tine. When the March revolution in Russia began to weaken the allied effort, though, Britain's leaders were more receptive. The British wanted not only to keep Russia in the war but also hoped to arouse American enthusiasm for the war. Because of the high proportion of Jews in the Russian revolutionary movement and the presumed power of Jews in the United States, Britain believed that a pro-Zionist statement would achieve these two goals. Similarly, its leaders assumed that leaflets explaining the declaration and dropped over enemy territory would lead influential Jews to weaken the war effort in Germany and Austria-Hungary. In short, a declaration of sympathy with Zionism was supposed to help Britain win the war.

What other motives have been suggested? Lord Balfour may have wanted to compensate for having influenced as prime minister the passage of the Aliens Act of 1905: the Act curtailed Jewish immigration into England. Perhaps Balfour wanted to discourage Jews from coming to Britain by giving them a homeland elsewhere. There is also speculation that Britain wished to reward Russian-born Chaim Weizmann, chemistry lecturer at Manchester University and president of the English Zionist Federation for his war contribution in the field of explosives. There is no question that Weizmann used his connections and influence to further Zionism.

Historians have also suggested that the British wanted to keep the French out of Palestine, but the Zionists had already won French and Italian acquiescence to the plan for a homeland. In addition, the British may have been convinced by Zionist suggestions that a Jewish Palestine would give Britain a friend in the Palestine corridor, the approach to the Suez Canal and to Egypt. Like the pharoahs and other Egyptian rulers over the centuries, the British realized the strategic import of Palestine to the security of Egypt. Ottoman attacks on Sinai early in the war heightened this awareness. This last factor might indeed have been the most important reason for the issuance of the Balfour declaration.

There remains one other crucial motive, one which acquired paramount significance with the unfolding of the Holocaust in Europe and the development of the Palestine Mandate. Usually called the humanitarian motive, it embraced Christians who believed that the return to Zion was a religious imperative, an essential element in the course of history. These were known as Christian Zionists. However, it also involved the non-Jewish secular liberals concerned for the plight of Jews. The deeply felt humanitarian motive was to become a preeminent factor in the virtually unquestioning support by the West for Israel.

Did Britain expect the Zionists to forget about the Balfour letter? This seems hardly likely considering the prewar Zionist campaign. In 1914, Zionist headquarters were located in Berlin. The most probable ally in the Zionist campaign was Germany, and Germany's wartime ally was the Ottoman Empire that controlled Palestine. Germany was also fighting Russia, a country universally detested by Jews for past pogroms and persecutions.

Zionist Pressures in Europe and the United States   As Zionist leaders disputed the question as to which world powers would win, they agreed that the war required their taking a neutral position. To maintain their network, they moved their headquarters to Copenhagen but remained active in both London and Berlin. The movement's center of gravity soon moved from the European continent to Britain and the United States, with the growing acceptance of the British Zionist view that the Entente and its allies would win. Chaim Weizmann and Justice Louis Brandeis of the United States Supreme Court won over leaders of their respective governments. By mid-1917, Weizmann intercepted a special mission sent by President Wilson to convince the Ottomans to sign a separate peace. The mission, led by Henry Morganthau, was dissuaded from leaving Gibraltar. The Zionists wanted the Ottomans to stay in the war so that British (and Jewish) forces would be able to conquer Palestine. The connection between the mission and American oil interests has been suggested but is not clear.

Despite the official neutrality of the international Zionist organization, the convictions of the English Zionists had led to the formation early in the war of a mule corps composed of 900 men. Eventually, three battalions or about 5,000 men joined Allenby's British army and helped the Arabs take Palestine. Participation of Zionists in the war led the British government to grant them special communications and travel privileges, including the use of codes and diplomatic pouches.

Opposition to the Balfour Letter Although the Zionists had won support from British officials like Balfour and Sir Mark Sykes, not all prominent British Jews agreed with the Zionist goal. Sir Edwin Montagu, secretary of state for India, objected to the idea that Jews were a nation and not a religious group—he believed that Zionism jeopardized his English identity. British Jews in prominent positions also felt threatened by a large influx of eastern European Jews. Montagu tried to convince the War Cabinet that the Zionists in Britain represented a bare rather than an overwhelming majority. He influenced the terminology of the Declaration by insisting on guarantees for rights of Jews outside Palestine.

The other qualifying clause represented a demographic outrage to Palestinians, who though constituting some 92 percent of the population, were referred to as "non-Jewish communities." The basic assumption was that this majority was the *other*, not the main group in Palestine. Palestinian life was disrupted by the transformation of the country into a battleground. Palestinians hoped for the return of stability under an Arab government based in Syria. Some disruption was expected from the fact that the Ottomans had absconded with maps and tax registers. The Balfour letter came as a shock to the Arabs of Palestine.

After the Declaration, the small Jewish community organized an administrative structure both in Jerusalem and in outlying areas. Jews selected representatives whom they hoped the British would accept as a national assembly. In March 1918, the British allowed a Zionist commission to visit Palestine. These foreign Jews advised the British on affairs relating to both Palestinian and international Jewish communities. Chaim Weizmann took pains to assure Arabs in Egypt and Palestine that Jews wanted to work *with* the people of Palestine, not against them. The Balfour letter did not promise Palestine as a Jewish state but referred to a "national home" to be constituted "in Palestine." The language was carefully chosen, as the British assiduously avoided giving all of Palestine to Jews or to supporting creation of a Jewish state. Like other European victors, the British did not plan to stick to the letter and spirit of every wartime agreement. Yet they gave the Zionists the basis for achieving the Zionist goal of controlling Palestine as a Jewish state.

Theaters of War

During World War I in North Africa, only Egypt and Libya hosted large foreign armies. To assist the Ottoman war effort, the Sanussis attacked the British in Egypt in November 1915. They were, however, defeated. Italian forces stayed near the coast. Ongoing opposition to the French protectorate in Morocco did not keep Lyautey from sending thirty-seven battalions to France in exchange for sixteen composed of older soldiers and territorials. Like Iran, Morocco's interior was not immune from foreign, especially German, intrigues, but Lyautey with his paternalistic outlook felt secure enough to initiate trade fairs in Casablanca and enlist

Moroccan cooperation. Between December 1916 and March 1917, Lyautey served as France's minister of war. He found his estate in France destroyed by Germans and grew disgusted with French military strategy. In Morocco, resistance to the protectorate revived east of Fez, but other Moroccans, like many fellow North Africans, fought for France. In Tunisia, for example, about 100,000 Tunisians assisted France's war effort, with 63,000 of these in the army. Over 10,000 died fighting for France. Algerian Muslims, encouraged by the small educated elite, also enlisted in the army. Nearly 175,000 Algerian Muslims fought and 25,000 died in World War I. Another 119,000 Algerians worked in France's industries.

In Egypt, the British declared the protectorate and dispensed with the legal fiction of Ottoman sovereignty over the Nile Valley. Without the Protectorate Egyptians in England were being treated as Ottoman subjects—enemy aliens! Egypt was transformed into Britain's principal Middle Eastern defensive and offensive base. Peasants were impressed into serving this large force, officially for six months but usually with no freedom to leave after that time. Some 150,000 Egyptians in all aided Britain. The Young Turks knew that the British would go to great lengths to safeguard their eastern empire by attacking the Ottomans' Asiatic possessions, Syria and Iraq in particular. The Young Turks therefore tried to forestall the anticipated British attack on Syria by advancing to Sinai and attempting to reach the Suez Canal. The defense held, and the Egyptians sustained heavy casualties. With the failure of the assault, the Ottomans lost psychological or military advantages thereby inspiring the British to pursue new strategies early in 1915. These broadened the theaters of war. Postwar territorial objectives began to be formulated.

The main theaters of war were northwestern and eastern Anatolia, the Dardanelles area (principally the Gallipoli Peninsula in Europe), the Levant, Iraq, and Iran (see Map 13). As soon as war between Russia and the Ottomans had been declared, the Russian army invaded northern Iran. Ottoman forces attacked Russia in December 1914 to cut Russia's Caucasus communications and to aid separatist Muslims. In January–February 1915, though, aided by Russian Armenian volunteers, Russia took Erzurum in Ottoman Armenia, defeating its Turkish garrison. By April, they had occupied both Bitlis and Trabzon and backed formation of an Armenian government in Van. The October revolution of 1917, however, effectively took Russia out of the war.

While the Russians attacked in the east, the British and French amassed their best and most powerful ships in the Aegean Sea. They did so to attack Turkish positions along the Dardanelles, 42 miles long and guarding the entrance to the Sea of Marmora. The Ottomans had already placed mines there, but in February 1915 the fleet quickly eliminated the defenses with long-range artillery. They also sent minesweepers ahead to clear the 1–4 mile-wide channel.

When the British entered the straits, however, they faced renewed attack from positions they thought they had silenced. The largest French battleship, the *Bouvet*, sank after hitting a mine, and two British ships suffered the same fate. When the allied fleet failed to take the concealed fortifications, the ships moved outside the range of Turkish fire while an expedition of 50,000 British and French troops gathered in Egypt for a land assault. After a disastrous land attack on a mined beach at Gallipoli, they were joined by another 50,000 Australians and New Zealanders whose nations still commemorate their heroic attack. Although these forces established a foothold on the beach, within a few months they had sustained such heavy losses that the offensive had to be aborted. By then over 200,000 allied troops had disembarked on the peninsula. Thousands of casualties, over half of them deaths, were taken by Europeans by December 1915. The Ottomans suffered equally heavy losses but defeated their attackers. The Entente aim of destroying the Turkish war effort and taking Istanbul failed due to the Ottomans' spirited and well-

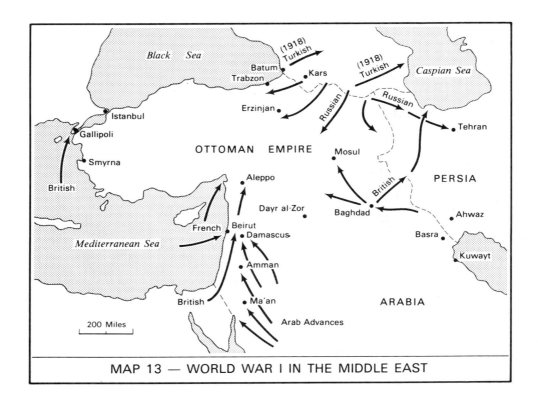

MAP 13 — WORLD WAR I IN THE MIDDLE EAST

planned defense. But the Ottomans and their German advisors passed up the opportunity to cripple the Anglo-French allies. The large force was evacuated by January 1916.

The Gallipoli campaign brought to the fore Mustafa Kemal. After his emergence as a prominent military commander, he conducted a brilliant rearguard defense in Arabia and Arab lands south of Anatolia, keeping British general Allenby and his allies well-occupied. At Gallipoli, Turkish officers and soldiers gained pride that later inspired them to join Mustafa Kemal in his postwar struggle for Turkish independence.

Besides these efforts, the British in mid-1915 sent troops to southern Iraq, to secure oil fields, and north to Baghdad. However, the Ottomans forced the British to surrender in April 1916 after defeating them at the ancient city of Ctesiphon, near

Baghdad. A new British expedition captured Baghdad in March 1917; they were thus able more firmly to control Mesopotamia. These expeditions were intended to protect British, not Arab, interests, and were under the direction of the British India Office. British forces also from Iraq established themselves in Transcaucasia after the Russian Revolution. They launched attacks from their base in Baku.

On 5 June 1916, the Arabians entered the war against the Ottoman Empire. Led by Faysal, the campaign began in Arabia and extended northward to the borders of Anatolia. After taking Madina and laying siege to Makka, the Arabians accompanied by T. E. Lawrence moved up the eastern flank of the Jordan River Valley while General Allenby's troops advanced in the west. The Arabian army, joined by local Arabs, harassed the Turks in greater Syria along the Hijaz railway and provoked anti-Turkish uprisings. They made the triumphal entry into Damascus on 1 October 1918, though an Australian contingent arrived first. In Damascus, Faysal set up an Arab government administering, with British approval and aid, Occupied Enemy Territory Administration East (O.E.T.A. East). The Arab military effort of over two years ended when the Ottomans asked for peace on 30 October 1918.

Not surprisingly, Arab participants in the Middle East and North Africa anticipated European respect for their contribution and self-determination following the war. Yet secret treaties and agreements among Europeans took precedence over any made between them and Arabs. No appreciable attitudinal or policy-change took place.

The Armenian Demise

The last chapters of the Armenian question in Anatolia occurred during and after World War I. In pursuit of its war aims, the C.U.P. government made further moves against the Armenians, justifying them by perceived needs to secure lines of communication with the Arab provinces and to tighten security in the east against Russia. Certainly many Armenians openly opposed the Ottoman war cause. C.U.P leaders regarded them as a potential fifth column. The first directives from Talat against Armenians were issued in February and March 1915. In eastern Anatolia, Russian Armenians encouraged fighting between Armenians and Turks. It culminated in the establishment of the Van government.

The Young Turk government's perception of the Armenian danger far exceeded the actual threat from this group. On the evening of 24 April 1915, commemorated by Armenians today as the anniversary of Armenian genocide, two hundred prominent Armenians in Istanbul were rounded up. They were soon deported and later executed. The Armenian communities in Anatolia were then told on very short notice, usually about twenty-four hours, that they were being moved temporarily. In nearly every case, their leadership advised them to cooperate. Officially, the forced deportation,

confirmed by a May order, removed Armenians from sensitive areas in southern and eastern Anatolia. In fact, Armenians throughout Anatolia began marching southward or eastward into the Syrian desert wastes. Turkish and Kurdish forces denied them rest, food, and water. Thousands died on the way. Those who did not were often killed when they reached Dayr al-Zor on the Euphrates. Most Armenians caught in the east were killed outright.

Historians have not determined how many Armenians died. Few family or church records survived, thus creating a documentary void on the Armenian side. Armenians often had failed to register births with the government due to fears of persecution and taxation. At the war's outset, the Ottoman government imprisoned and later killed most of the Armenian educated elite—writers, teachers, businessmen, and prominent clergy who might have written about the event. The rare survivors of deportations and massacres tended to be young orphans or adults who encountered odd circumstances they wished to conceal. Estimates of the number who died vary. It is an incontrovertible fact that Greek, Kurdish, and Turkish noncombatants in Anatolia died during the war due to hunger and disease, but these were not singled out for death in an organized campaign. Including perhaps 200,000 executed by the government, historians generally accept that as many as 1.5 million Armenians may have died. Contrary to recent arguments, properties of deportees were not protected but were confiscated along with those of the few Armenians who forestalled or avoided deportation. Turks moved into the vacant houses.

Missionaries and Syrian Armenians saved many orphans. Other children were taken into Turkish homes as servants. Some Muslim Turks helped their Armenian neighbors prior to deportation or rescued orphans afterward. Turkish administrators in a few districts ignored the deportation orders, thereby accounting for the survival of significant numbers of Armenians. Occasionally, missionaries influenced officials to disobey orders. Some Armenians converted to Islam. A few avoided deportation through bribery or when German Protestant officers influenced Turkish officers to exempt Protestants from the order. Even then, the male heads of households were killed. In Syria, Armenians were also saved by Arabs.

Still, Armenians in cities, towns, and villages faced deportation not by whim or requirements of military security but apparently as a result of a deliberate, coordinated policy by certain Ottoman leaders. As in the later Jewish genocide, survivors often punished themselves for having been spared. Most historians have described this campaign as a genocide that wiped out the bulk of western Armenian speakers and that met conditions specified in the United Nations Genocide Convention of December 1948. Much of Armenian Adana, Bitlis, Diyabakir, Erzurum, Kharpert, Sivas, Trabzon, and Van ceased to exist.

There is a postscript to the Armenian tragedy of World War I. Those who had survived returned to their homes in allied-occupied Anatolia at war's end. Jenanian College of Dr. Haigazian, the man after whom Haigazian College in Beirut is named, reopened in Konya. Teams, especially those of the American Near East Relief, roamed Anatolia in search of Armenian orphans. The French in Cilicia encouraged Armenians to come back. To the east, Armenians in May 1918 created an independent republic, determined to recover the "lost provinces" according to recommendations made by President Woodrow Wilson and sanctioned by the 1920 Treaty of Sèvres.

On 15 May 1919, the Greek government invaded western Anatolia. The forces of Mustafa Kemal resisted these campaigns, driving back the Greeks while former allies maintained a hands-off policy. Kemal's reconquest of Anatolia delivered the coup de grace to Armenians who had fled from western Anatolia and then returned. In Marash, for example, half of the Armenians left when the French evacuated in February 1920 died. Haigazian saved his teachers but died in Turkish custody. Armenians therefore fell victim to a double tragedy ensuing from two wars: World War I and the Turkish war of independence. Many survivors found refuge in Lebanon, especially in Beirut where they recently constituted about 20–25 percent of the population. Others made their way to Greece, Western Europe, or the United States. In eastern Anatolia, the fledgling Armenian republic was caught in a squeeze between the new Bolshevik government in Russia and the Turkish independence forces. Its brief independence ended with its absorption by the Soviet Union, confirmed by the Treaty of Gümrü in December 1920. Though an eastern Soviet Socialist Republic of Armenia was born, western Armenians became refugees. The Treaty of Lausanne (1923) confirmed Turkish sovereignty over Anatolia.

In southwest Asia, this was not the last time that a people would suffer. One might argue that the Palestinians, like the Kurds who were not allowed national status, and the Armenians who were eliminated while pursuing it, could become the third of the roving Middle Easterners who by circumstances of history are now a people without a nation.

Postwar Positions and the Paris Peace Conference

At war's end, the European allies established an Allied Control Commission in Istanbul and immediately inaugurated competition for various parts of southwestern Anatolia, with British, Italian, and French troops taking the initiative. Before the opening of the conference at Versailles (January 1919), the British, French, and Americans took pains to assure their Arab allies of support for the "establishment of national governments and administrations deriving their authority from the initiative and free choice of indigenous populations."[2]

Woodrow Wilson's fourteen points, especially the two affirming self-determination and commitment to open covenants, were taken seriously by Arabs. The Damascus government, for example, assumed that the allies' statements represented official positions to be upheld at the peace conference. Chaim Weizmann, on the other hand, supported by the allied Zionist Commission and the Balfour promise, had already in March 1918 laid the cornerstone of Hebrew University on Mount Scopus in Jerusalem. He fully expected the eventual emergence of a Jewish state in Palestine.

What happened at Versailles? Of the areas liberated from Ottoman rule—Arabia, Cilicia, Armenia, Iraq, Palestine, Kurdistan, and Syria—only Arabia gained its independence. Instead of obtaining liberation, Arabs were presented

with semi-independence (supposedly independence with development aid from their allies). Soon, it transpired into European occupation. In eastern Anatolia, the decimated Armenian minority won support for its new state. Kurdish autonomy in southeastern Anatolia with the aim of eventual independence from Turkey also won approval. With their premeditated plans, the British and French refused to participate in the peace conference's one effort to discover the wishes of Southwest Asia's inhabitants. They ignored the commission led by Americans Charles Crane and Henry King.

The King-Crane Commission

Woodrow Wilson proposed the King-Crane Commission as a way of finding out if the French were really desired in Syria, the British in Iraq, and the Zionists in Palestine. It also questioned whether the proposed Armenian and Kurdish states were feasible. Since the commission carried out its work between May and August 1919, a special Arab National Congress convened in Damascus in July to present the visitors with concrete evidence of support for their program. It reaffirmed the goal to maintain the unity of Syria including Lebanon and Palestine, but with autonomy for Lebanon and rights for Jews in Palestine. Based in Damascus, the independent state was to be headed by Faysal, the preferred choice of Muslims, Greek Orthodox, and Druze. The Syrians objected to the mandate system of semi-independence but if it proved necessary, the congress favored American tutelage. Only Lebanese Maronites advocated a French mandate. In Palestine, the com-

---

[2] Hurewitz, vol. 2 pp. 110–112. Other British and French statements are also cited there. Taken from the Anglo-French Declaration of 7 November 1918. Earlier Woodrow Wilson had influenced the British to make a strong commitment to this ideal. It is evidenced by their modification in July of earlier reassurances to Arab leaders.

missioners found total objection to Zionism except among segments of the small Jewish population. Armenians and Kurds in Anatolia expressed their desires for independence.

Based on their investigations, King and Crane recommended to the conference a limited mandate for Syria. Faysal was to be head of state. Iraq was also to be mandated. They concluded that the 2,000-year-old Jewish claim to Palestine was inappropriate. Implementation of the Balfour Declaration would require at least 50,000 soldiers due to adamant opposition of the population. Since the Europeans had opposed the study, they disregarded its conclusions. Even President Wilson, who left the conference due to illness, probably never saw the report. With the American retreat from the world arena and British, French, and Zionist opposition, the King-Crane report was suppressed and remained unpublished until 1922, by which time the mandate system had been set into place.

The Ottoman Demise and the Turkish War of Independence

European Occupation of Anatolia

The Ottoman government agreed to the Mudros armistice on 30 October 1918, thus ending the war in Southwest Asia. By its terms, the straits from the Aegean to the Black Sea came under allied occupation (See Map 14). Telegraph and railroad lines were taken over. Having formally disbanded the Ottoman army, the allies retained the right to occupy any area formerly under Ottoman control. Ottoman army officers regarded their nation as undefeated and the terms as inappropriate, although terms for Bulgaria, an Ottoman ally, were even harsher.

In the wake of the armistice, Greek, Kurdish, and Armenian nationalists in most of Anatolia except the central plateau received encouragement. With Anatolia partitioned among Italy, France, Britain, the Kurds, the Armenians, and the Russians, few areas were left for the Turks and their national goals although they too received assurances that their security would be safeguarded. Turkish nationalists in Anatolia, however, perceived that the defeated Ottoman state lacked the will to defend Turks against encroachment by the diverse territorial rivals.

Mustafa Kemal Organizes Turkish Resistance to the Occupation

Among the army officers who felt that the government had given up the fight prematurely was Mustafa Kemal. The name *Kemal* (meaning perfection) was awarded to him at school for his excellence in mathematics and military science. Regarded as a loner, Mustafa met C.U.P. members prior to the 1908 coup but was not accepted by them. He disappeared from the public eye in 1909 because of his disapproval of the C.U.P.'s failure to carry out radical reform. Yet Mustafa distinguished himself in both the Tripolitanian and Balkan wars (1911–13).

When World War I began, Mustafa opposed the Ottoman entry into the war on the German side because he expected Germany to lose. He preferred neutrality. At first posted to Sofia as military attache, he sought a command. While Enver feared Mustafa's power, he needed tal-

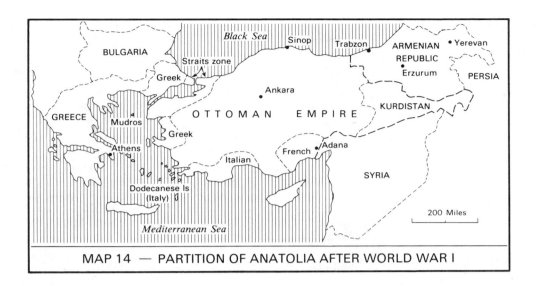

MAP 14 — PARTITION OF ANATOLIA AFTER WORLD WAR I

ented military officers to defend the Dardanelles. Mustafa's success at Gallipoli led him to ask for the war portfolio, but the C.U.P. sent him to fight the Russian invaders in the east. After his success there, they recalled him to the west where he inflicted losses on Allenby's forces. His rejection of the Mudros armistice is not surprising.

The Greek Invasion of Anatolia

The Turkish national struggle, then, began with the Ottoman leadership's failure to defend the Anatolian heartland while its army commanders were still willing to fight. When Mustafa was told to disband the Anatolian army in May 1919, he refused because of the Greek invasion that had begun on the 15th of the month. Instead, he vowed to fight the foreign occupation and issued the Amasya Protocol on 22 June to that effect. Convening nationalist congresses in Erzurum (July) and Sivas (September), Mustafa rallied the disparate resistance groups throughout Anatolia who accepted his Amasya statement as the National Pact. Did those who joined Mustafa Kemal understand that he opposed not only foreigners and the central government as stated in the pact but also the sultan? The evidence indicates that freedom-fighters thought they were striving for restoration of Islam and the Ottoman sultan in Asia Minor, not for a secular state that would depose their ruler. Nevertheless, the Greek invasion and atrocities committed by Greeks in western Anatolia united Turks in their opposition to foreign incursions.

With this growing movement in Anatolia, the government in Istanbul could not remain aloof. The leadership strove to cooperate with Kemal's forces. Many Ottoman parliament members sympathized with Kemal and hoped to avoid further allied intervention by proposing a compromise. Their plan, issued in January 1920, advocated unity and independence for Anatolia while agreeing to self-determination for Arabs and for the populations of western Thrace and parts of eastern Anatolia. These leaders even agreed to grant international protection for minorities and internationalization of the straits, contingent on allied agreement to continued presence of the sultan in Istanbul.

The British, with the revolution in Egypt and discontent in Iraq, perceived the Turkish national movement as a further threat to stability in Southwest Asia and security of the straits. Although Mustafa Kemal had been branded as a rebel by the central government and had been endangered by several assassination attempts, he was growing stronger. Between the opening of parliament on 20 January 1920 and mid-March, the British concluded that the time had come to nip the movement. Nationalists, whom Kemal had warned to stay away from Istanbul, were rounded up and deported to Malta, as the British in March occupied the city and dissolved parliament. The British action, aided by the French, catalyzed support for Kemal's forces.

A Grand National Assembly convened in Ankara in April and elected Kemal as its president. Deputies who still hoped for a government favorable to the sultan opposed the formation of a new Turkish government, but Kemal's viewpoint prevailed. A rival government to that of the sultan in Istanbul was constituted, but its members proclaimed their loyalty to the sultan. With the assembly assuming all executive and legal authority for a new Turkey, the sultan's place in the new order was still unclear.

Treaty of Sèvres: The Partition of Anatolia

Meanwhile, the allies at Sèvres proceeded with the partition of the empire, ignoring the Ottoman parliament's plan. They gave to Greece not only western but also eastern Thrace including Edirne. Armenian independence and Kurdish autonomy were confirmed. The Greeks received Smyrna but only on condition that a plebiscite be held after five years to resolve its status. The allies gave control of the straits to an international commission. Instead of abolishing the hated capitulations, British, French, and Italians administering the Ottoman debt gained new authority over Turkey's finances. From the partition of Southwest Asia, the Turks could see that the victors were less interested in self-determination than in territorial aggrandizement. By limiting Turkey's armed forces to 50,000 men and by controlling Turkey's armaments, the Europeans expected to prevent any attempt by the Turks to disrupt the settlement.

The Turkish Victory in Anatolia

They were wrong. Mustafa Kemal's army confronted forces that remained fragmented with no unifying strategies or policies. Kemal easily overcame the Armenians in the east in 1920, securing Russian cooperation against the western allies in the process. The Kurds and the sultan's army also lost to the highly motivated, well-organized Turkish forces. An agreement with Italy ended the Italian occupation in southwestern Anatolia. While the Turks focused on these enemies, Greek armies advanced in both Anatolia and Thrace. During the advance, the only Greek losses took place in two battles fought in January and March 1920 at Inönü, from which Turkish leader and second president Ismet gained his surname.

In September 1921, the Greeks and Turks fought a decisive battle on the Sakarya River. The tide was turned against the Greeks. The Greek appeal to the British for aid came to naught. For nearly a year, the Greeks neither advanced not retreated from the Sakarya. Kemal's forces prepared the final onslaught while overextended Greek forces lost the initiative. From August to September 1922, the Turkish armies drove the Greeks out of Anatolia. During this bitter retreat, the Greek armies overran many Turkish villages and killed their inhabitants. The Turkish armies took revenge against Greeks and any Armenians remaining in western Anatolia. Smyrna was occupied on 11 September. Since many Greeks and Armenians had fled there, the city was filled with refugees in addition to the predominantly non-Turkish population. A fire broke out shortly after the occupation, destroying much of the city and its people. Allied ships watched from the harbor.

With the completion of the Turkish victory in Anatolia (see Map 15), the

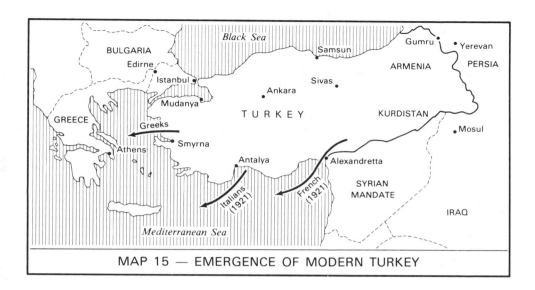

MAP 15 — EMERGENCE OF MODERN TURKEY

French and Italians guarding the Asiatic side of the straits moved to the European side. France had already signed a secret agreement with the nationalists in October 1921. The British were left to negotiate the end to the occupation by the Mudanya armistice on 11 October 1922. Turkey won back eastern Thrace but the final settlement was left to the international conference convened in November at Lausanne. At that point, the Ottoman sultanate was abolished. Mehmed VI was sent into exile and Abdulmejid II was elected as caliph.

Treaty of Lausanne: Recognition of the New Turkey

The Treaty of Lausanne was signed on 24 July 1923 by Bulgaria, England, France, Greece, Italy, Japan, Rumania, the Soviet Union, Turkey, and Yugoslavia. Despite its earlier interest in the area, the United States already withdrawing from world affairs, sent only observers to Lausanne. In the deliberations, Turkey's Ismet refused to be bullied by the British Lord Curzon and other allied delegates.

In the final settlement, Turkey, Greece, and Italy divided the contested Aegean islands. Russia agreed that Tur-

key could reassert full sovereignty over the straits. The Mudanya agreement regarding Thrace was confirmed. A compulsory exchange of Greeks and Turks did not apply to Istanbul or to Turks in western Thrace, and Greeks and Armenians remain in Istanbul to this day. From Anatolia, though, 1.5 million Greeks (*Greek Orthodox Turks*) moved to Greece, while 500,000 Turks (*Muslim Greeks*) left Greek territory for Turkey. Questions left outstanding were the demilitarization of the straits and the Mosul border. The British were to negotiate those issues on behalf of Iraq.

There were important economic provisions in the Lausanne treaty. Turkey secured the abolition of the capitulations and the debt administration. Foreign-occupied states arising from the empire's partition agreed to take on proportionate shares of the debt. The allies cancelled prewar economic agreements and concessions while Turkey agreed to maintain present tariff levels. Turkey thereby gained the freedom to establish a new framework for future concessions, soon utilized in an agreement with Americans interested in oil and communications. Americans secured for the first time a stake in western Asia's oil. In that process,

Turkey sustained her hard-won independence in a key area.

The now more homogeneous state that had been born in Anatolia moved its capital to Ankara. Turkey became a republic on 29 October 1923. By March 1924, led by president Mustafa Kemal, Turkey had decided that the caliphate no longer served a clear purpose in a republic that had powers of its own. Abulmejid II and his family were sent into exile. The government took over functions formerly administered by religious authorities. The Ottoman Empire had passed on, but a new Turkish state in Anatolia and western Thrace had taken its place. The abandonment of the imperial capital at Istanbul, the attack on the caliphate, and the displacement of religious institutions were clear harbingers of the revolutionary direction in which the new Turkish leadership would move.

Establishment of the Mandate System: Semi-independence in the Arab East

In Arabic-speaking parts of the Ottoman Empire, the participation of several hundred thousand Arabs, especially Egyptians, in the war effort failed to insure fulfillment of allied self-determination promises. The equal status as victors that Arabs assumed they had won proved to be ephemeral. They did not take this breach of pledges lightly. In every region, Arabs resisted implementation of the new form of colonization that set into place a native ruling elite under foreign supervision. Only in Arabia, thought to be a wasteland, was an indigenous group allowed to establish a truly independent state (see Map 16).

Syrian Resistance

Fearing disregard for their desires, the Damascus Congress nationalists in March 1920 proclaimed the independence of Syria under King Faysal, with the Congress as national legislature. But at San Remo in April 1920, the allies agreed to a French mandate over Syria, a decision confirmed by the League of Nations in 1922. French general Gouraud, already ensconced on the coast, ordered Faysal in July to recognize the mandate. When the affirmative reply was delayed, Gouraud attacked Damascus, forcing Faysal to leave. French forces soon occupied the whole country.

Before the mandate had received official confirmation, the French proceeded to pursue a divide-and-rule policy, cutting off Lebanon in 1920 and dividing Syria into four ethnically and religiously determined states: Aleppo, Damascus, Jabal Druze, and Latakia. Instead of trying to create a homogeneous Lebanon, the French attached to it predominantly Muslim areas, both along the coast and in the interior. Today, Syria and Lebanon are still reaping the bitter harvest of this decision.

Like Iraq and Transjordan, Syria fell into the category of *Class A Mandate*, a territory nearly ready for independence but still requiring supervision of a great power. Yet Iraq avoided official mandate status. Initially, the British placed it under the India Office. Unlike the Foreign Office, administrators of India had avoided associating with traditional tribal rulers. They began to treat Iraq as a colony, maintaining firm control over government and administration under Sir Arnold Wilson.

The Iraqi Revolt of 1920

Wilson's Iraq, which lasted from 1918 to 1920, resembled British India and Egypt in the days of Lord Cromer in that it was characterized by increasing centralization

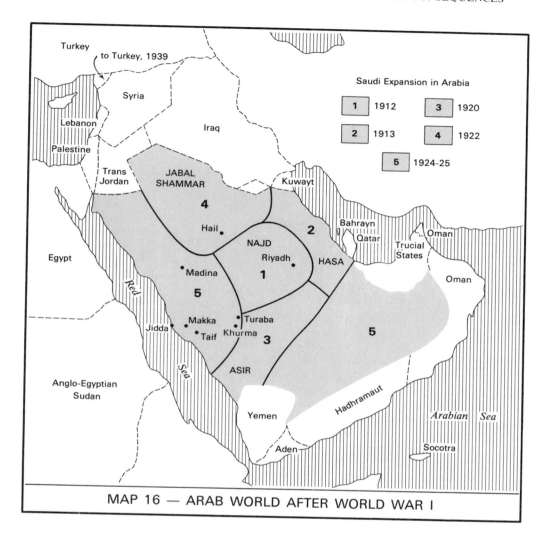

MAP 16 — ARAB WORLD AFTER WORLD WAR I

under foreign administrators. To insure support for his policies, Wilson rigged a plebiscite designed to gauge the population's feelings. Nationalists who objected to the British stranglehold were either expelled from Iraq or were ignored as unrepresentative. Where opposition was strong and vocal, Wilson either suppressed the results or held no plebiscite at all. He succeeded by such means in guaranteeing his preferred and predetermined results, calling for a British-controlled Iraq under the direction of pro-British Arab officials. By disregarding the feel-ings of the people, Wilson precipitated a revolt.

Both Sunni and Shi'i Iraqis, inspired by resistance of their neighbors in Syria to the French, joined together in revolt soon after the San Remo Conference had awarded Britain a Class A Mandate for Iraq. Class interests played some role in the opposition, but people of all classes, rural and urban alike, joined it. Although the British defeated the Iraqi coalition, they paid a high price financially and in casualties. Following the exhaustive and expensive effort in World War I, the British could not afford the cost of continuing their high-handed policies. With Faysal's expulsion from Syria (though the Syrian Congress had indicated preference for his brother Abd Allah as Iraq's future ruler), the British placed Faysal on the throne and sought an alternative solution to Abd Allah's expectations. To give the appearance of self-determination, the British allowed Iraqis to vote in a plebiscite that gave them no real choice. The Cairo Conference of March 1921 confirmed Faysal as ruler; his coronation took place in August. Despite its formal state of independence, the conditions were almost identical to the Class A Mandate terms initially proposed. They were contained in a treaty signed with Britain in 1922. Iraq waited many more years before successfully terminating British control over some aspects of Iraqi affairs.

Britain, France, and Iraqi Oil

Questions relating to Iraqi oil also came up after the war. In mid-1914, the Turkish Petroleum Company (T.P.C.) had held the rights to exploit Mosul oil. The owners of T.P.C. were the Deutsche Bank (25 percent), Anglo-Saxon Petroleum Company (Royal Dutch, 22½ percent), D'Arcy Exploration Company (Anglo-Persian, 47½ percent), and Calouste Sarkis Gulbenkian, an Armenian businessman who had organized the company's formation (5 percent). The Sykes-Picot Agreement, though, awarded Mosul to France. As the war wound down in 1918, the British began to agitate for addition of Mosul to their Mesopotamian claims.

At the Paris Peace Conference, the two contestants reached the Long-Berenger agreement. It equally divided between Britain and France oil rights in Galicia, Rumania, and Russia. They agreed to allow each other options to buy 34 percent of the available oil in their respective colonies. The French would gain the Deutsche Bank's 25 percent share in the company in exchange for which Britain would build two pipelines across French-controlled territories, from Mesopotamia to the Mediterranean Sea. In another agreement in 1920, France won the right to purchase 25 percent of Mesopotamian crude oil and also 25 percent of any oil produced by the Anglo-Persian Company using the pipelines. The American government later insisted on participation of United States companies in the Iraq concessions, but it was at San Remo that Britain and France resolved their own economic differences in the Middle East.

Establishment of the Hashimites in Transjordan

The San Remo Conference, in addition to confirming allied plans for Iraq and Syria, granted Britain a mandate that combined Palestine and Transjordan (the area across or east of the Jordan River). Prior to partition, Palestine had been part of greater Syria, while present-day Jordan was viewed as part of both Syria and Arabia. Ottoman administrative divisions had not included the terms *Palestine* and *Jordan*. When Britain obtained the mandate for Palestine at San Remo, the intention was that a national home for Jews should be set up in Palestine, but it was stated explicitly that not all conditions of the mandate would necessarily apply to the entire area.

Until the demise of independent Syria, Faysal and his forces administered the east bank of the Jordan. Between April, when the mandate was assigned, and July, when the Syrians were defeated at Maysalun Pass, British High Commissioner Sir Herbert Samuel (who was sent to set up the combined mandate) established four small republics in Transjordan, each of which governed under a council and was advised by a British official. These divisions exacerbated intergroup rivalries and quarrels over boundaries. The Arab republics died out in the aftermath of France's victory over the Syrian nationalists.

Meanwhile, many exiles from Damascus fled to Transjordan. They used the area as a base for guerrilla attacks into Syria and for heightening tensions between British and French administrators on both sides of the border. Faysal's brother Abd Allah moved into Transjordan with his forces, ostensibly to aid the effort against the French in Syria but possibly to protect his claim to a throne. Since Abd Allah had fought on the allied side during the war, the British acknowledged some obligation to him. Samuel accepted Abd Allah's informal takeover of areas in Transjordan. Abd Allah, however, proved to take seriously his own commitment to drive the French out of Syria. The British were faced with a potential French offensive unless they were willing to fight Abd Allah themselves.

In the end, the British decided that circumstances in the barren area east of the Jordan did not warrant further military activity. Abd Allah's move, coinciding as it did with the Cairo Conference of March 1921, allowed the policymakers led by Winston Churchill, the British colonial secretary, with Samuel and Lawrence as advisors, to offer him Transjordan in exchange for giving up his claim to the Iraqi throne and his fight against the French. Transjordan would still become part of the Palestine mandate approved by the League of Nations in 1923, but its territories were specifically excluded from provisions relating to a Jewish national home. Although the Zionist Executive accepted this stipulation in 1922, Zionists claimed later that this action partitioned territory promised to the Jewish state, even though Jews had been promised neither a state nor all of Palestine.

The Faysal–Weizmann Talks and the Palestine Mandate

The fact that the British appointed Samuel, a Jewish Zionist, as the first high commissioner for Palestine indicates that they took their commitment to the Jewish homeland seriously. The San Remo decision to award a mandate for Palestine to Britain was greeted with violent Arab and Jewish demonstrations in Jerusalem and Jaffa.

Having earlier recognized Faysal in Syria as a popular Arab leader, the Zionist leadership selected Weizmann to approach him to achieve Jewish-Arab cooperation in Palestine. In 1918 and 1919, the two men held talks in both Palestine and England to clarify their aspirations. Weizmann and his fellow Russian Jew Nahum Sokolow had been chosen by Jews in Palestine to represent their interests at the Paris Peace Conference. They were the official negotiators of the Palestinian Jewish community. Faysal, too, was to appear at the conference.

The culmination of their conversations came with the so-called Faysal-Weizmann agreement of January 1919. Faysal recognized the Balfour declaration and approved Jewish immigration into Palestine on condition that Arab Palestinian rights be preserved. In exchange, Weizmann committed Jews to further the economic development of the Arab community. The British would arbitrate disputes between the two communities. The crucial qualifications inserted by Faysal into the agreement stated that he would not "be bound by a single word of the present Agreement which shall be deemed void and of no account or validity" if the independence aspirations of the Arabs were not fully realized.[3] Faysal's statement left no doubt that he would not take responsibility for the agreement except under these circumstances. Statements suggesting that Faysal authorized the creation of a Jewish state in Palestine distort the letter and spirit of the agreement. When he made this limited concession to Zionism, Faysal most likely had in mind the enlarging of the Jewish millet in Palestine. Certainly, he neither

---

[3] George Antonius, *The Arab Awakening*. (Philadelphia, New York: J.B. Lippincott, 1939), p. 439.

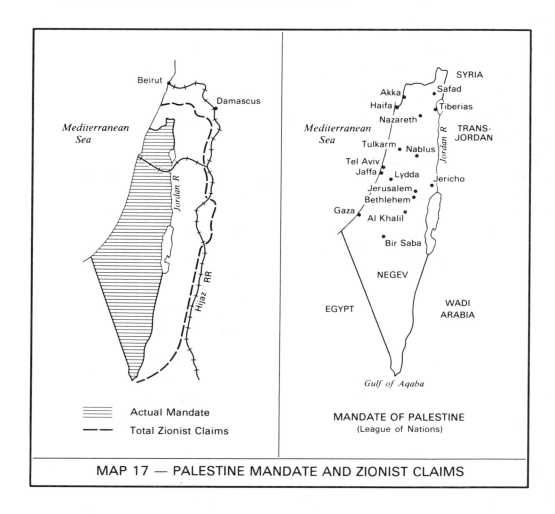

MAP 17 — PALESTINE MANDATE AND ZIONIST CLAIMS

advocated nor approved the establishment of a Jewish Palestine.

Having been informed of the Faysal-Weizmann agreement, the Syrians at the Paris Peace Conference unequivocally affirmed Syria's claim to Palestine but stated a willingness to permit Jews to settle there. Despite their negotiations with Faysal, the Zionists insisted that Palestine ought to be groomed for eventual status as a Jewish commonwealth.

The Palestine mandate approved by the League of Nations in 1923 (see Map 17) was inherently unworkable, then, because the Zionists wanted not a homeland in Palestine but all of Palestine to be a Jewish state. Arab Palestinians expected to rule their country themselves. There was no way for the British to satisfy the Zionists without compromising the right of the Palestinian Arab majority. The British were to spend nearly thirty years trying to referee the conflicting claims. Denied their right of self-determination, the Arabs of Palestine refused full cooperation even with British officials sympathetic to their plight. But it probably would have made no difference because of international pressures of the 1930s and 1940s.

Egypt: The 1919 Revolution and Its Aftermath

Declaration of the Protectorate: British Wartime Policy

When World War I began in the Ottoman Empire, Abbas Hilmi II was away from Egypt. The British deposed him and replaced him with the more pliant Husayn Kamil, upon whom they bestowed the title of sultan. Along with the protectorate declared on 18 December 1914, the accession represented two significant departures from practices and procedures established by Ottoman firmans in the days of Isma'il. First of all, Husayn Kamil was Abbas' uncle, not his son. Secondly, the British replaced the Ottoman title of khedive with one connoting supreme rule—sultan.

During the war, the British took over many public buildings, particularly schools, for housing their troops or for use as hospitals. Educational institutions suffered under this regime. Though the wealthy profited, providing goods and services for the British, most urban dwellers underwent hardship. The 10 percent of the population, who owned 75 percent of the land, gained from inflation. Prices doubled during the war. With the nationalist movement's wings clipped by the protectorate declaration, by censorship, and by martial law, the educated and landed elites played a waiting game, hoping that the war's end would bring them the right to send a delegation (*wafd*) to the peace conference. They believed this would happen because of Egypt's war contribution and Wilson's fourteen points.

The leadership of Kamil's old Watan Party spent the war in Germany and Switzerland, where they worked for the defeat of Egypt's occupiers. Muhammad Farid and Abd al-Aziz Jawish became advisors

of Egyptian students in Germany, too. British intelligence officers in Europe focused on these leaders outside Egypt, thereby missing the genuine resentment growing among Egyptians in Egypt. The British in Egypt, too, viewed the nationalists as a selfish, isolated elite.

Egyptians Demand Restoration of Their Independence

When the war in Europe ended, Sa'd Zaghlul, whom Lord Cromer had praised as an industrious, intelligent, and capable leader in 1906, gave the British high commissioner a statement tantamount to a demand for independence. By this time, Husayn Kamil had died and had been succeeded by his brother Ahmad Fu'ad (Fuad) in 1917. The high commissioner Reginald Wingate recommended to his superiors in the British Foreign Office that Zaghlul and his wafd be allowed to go to London to negotiate, but the feeling there was that Zaghlul had no official status.

With the failure of these modest attempts to gain recognition for Egypt's national rights, Zaghlul proceeded to utilize widespread frustration to organize a national resistance movement. Egypt's government was brought down by British refusals, with Zaghlul pressuring the sultan not to cooperate with the occupation authorities by appointing successors. With the peace conference already in session in Paris, Zaghlul, along with Isma'il Sidqi, Muhammad Mahmud, and Hamad al-Basil (all prominent wafdists), was arrested on 8 March 1919 by British military (not civilian) authorities. He was deported to Malta.

The Egyptian Revolution

Within a few days, Egypt—town and country alike—was in revolt against British. The national nature of the reaction illustrated the fact that Egyptians, for many different reasons, wanted independence and respect from British. Contrary to British assertions, what seemed dearest to most British officials despite exceptions like Wingate was the honor of the British Empire. Although the British rapidly squelched the uprising, its magnitude and nature was not entirely lost on officials in Cairo and London. Allenby was brought in as high commissioner while a delegation led by Lord Milner was dispatched to Egypt to discover the causes underlying the disturbances.

Zaghlul and his companions were freed to attend the peace conference and present their demands. American recognition of Britain's protectorate, however, came as a blow to their hope for the United States to back Egyptian independence. Milner's commission realized that the Egyptians who had suffered from wartime inflation, family separation, hardship, indenture, and death had not received their due reward. With the acknowledgment of Zaghlul as the man with whom British would have to negotiate Egypt's future, he was brought into talks with Allenby.

A Nominal Independence: Four Reserved Points

In April 1920, as a followup to these conversations, a proposal for an independent constitutional monarchy was drawn up. Britain, however, would still control Egypt militarily. Besides Britain's special diplomatic rights, British citizens would continue to advise key Egyptian ministries, and these citizens had some veto power over Egyptian legal change. Zaghlul could hardly view the agreement with enthusiasm. Independence looked suspiciously like a modified version of the protectorate. When Zaghlul tried to alter or clarify points, Milner refused to discuss the treaty further. Adli Yakan, Egypt's prime minister, could do no better because while the protectorate continued Egypt was not really free to choose a future course.

Due to Zaghlul's continued agitation against Britain's ongoing presence in Egypt, Allenby finally lost patience and deported him again, this time to the Seychelles Islands in the Indian Ocean. The failure and resignation of Adli brought in yet another prime minister, Tharwat (Sarwat) Pasha. He, too, failed to negotiate successfully for independence. Egypt's leaders had painstakingly tried to accommodate the British with whom they probably shared more in common than with Egypt's masses. Yet British leaders denied them the respect due to representatives of a sovereign state.

In the end, Egypt won a nominal independence not by negotiation but by a unilateral declaration of the British high commissioner on 28 February 1922. The terms of independence drew upon the treaty about which Zaghlul had equivocated. Britain reserved to its own government four points: the defense of Egypt, protection of communications, protection of foreign and minority interests, and the administration of the Sudan. The British action made Fuad king. The parliamentary system established by the constitution issued on 21 April 1923 created two legislative bodies, a senate and a chamber of deputies, the former with three fifths and the latter with all of its members elected. Power to appoint the other senators and all of the cabinet ministers was given to the king. But Egypt remained under the thumb of the British for over thirty years. Fuad's acceptance of the reservations made him a British collaborator and created a genuine rivalry with the nationalist forces. Egypt's politics came to be characterized by a three-way struggle between the king with the minority parties, British officialdom, and Egypt's Wafdist (as the Wafd became a political party) leaders who had refused to compromise on independence. The alienation of all of these from the Egyptian masses was to create a popular base for the religious and paramilitary movements of the interwar period and after.

The Qajar Demise and the Emergence of Pahlavi Iran

Wartime Foreign Intrigue and Occupation

Not only in the Ottoman Empire did a new order take hold in Southwest Asia. After the Anglo-Russian agreement of 1907 divided Iran into rival spheres of influence and a neutral zone, the Qajar boy-shah Ahmad (1909–24) fell under the domination of Bakhtiari chiefs. He began to repress nationalists whose leadership soon fled the country or were executed. Foreign intrigue, mainly among Germans, Russians, and the British, resulted in a secret treaty between Germany and the Qajar government. The Germans promised support for Persian independence if the Persians would assist Germany in the war. The government in Kirmanshah, under Ottoman-German protection, exerted loose authority over the population at large.

When the war began, both Britain and Russia moved to consolidate their positions. Whereas the British strove to secure control of the oil reserves necessary for maintaining their fleet, and tightened their hold over Mesopotamia and southern Iran, the Russians moved more firmly into the north. Germany's Ottoman ally began fighting the Russians in the northwest. When the Bakhtiaris and Qashqa'is (Qashqais)—responding to efforts instigated by Germany's "Lawrence", the consul Wassmuss—began to threaten Britain's southern Iranian interests, the British organized a new force to cope with the tribesmen. Toward the end of the war, Russian and British troops extended their occupations. The Russian revolution allowed the reoccupation of Azerbayjan by Germans and Turks, although the end of the war brought a Russian attempt to detach Iran's northern provinces as Soviet republics.

With the cessation of hostilities, the Iranians, like their neighbors to the west, wanted to attend the peace conference. Chief among their demands was an end to the British occupation. Britain apparently aimed to bring Iran firmly into its orbit. The opposition of Persia's leadership to a major victor in the war, however, prevented Iranians from airing their goals in Paris.

British–Soviet Rivalry

More accommodating Persian leaders succumbed to British pressures and signed a treaty on 9 August 1919. This gave Britain rights similar to those enjoyed in Egypt and Iraq—rights objectionable to populations in all places. In the treaty, Britain gained control over the administration, economy, communications, and defense of Iran. In exchange for lending money to Iran at a favorable interest rate, Britain took control of Persian tariffs and customs. With its independence so totally compromised by the treaty, the Iranian majlis refused to consent to the agreement. Because of the pressure exerted by the United States and assurance of control of the Anglo-Persian Oil Company's concessions, the British opted not to fight the Persians for control of the country.

The decision left Iran still facing a Soviet threat. Although the Bolshevik government had denounced all Russian-Persian treaties as imperialist, it used their abrogation as an excuse to pursue into Iran the opposition forces of General Denikin during the Russian Civil War. It was in this context that the Bolsheviks tried to affirm the independence of a Soviet republic set up in northern Persia. After the League of Nations (which Iran joined) failed to take action, the Persians opened negotiations with the Soviet Union. On 29 February 1921, the Bolsheviks renounced former czarist treaties and policies, except those relating to fisheries in the Caspian Sea. Iran's debts were cancelled, but the Soviet Union retained the right to send troops in case of a threat to Iranian independence. Iran agreed to retain concessions given up by the Russians, thereby assuring the Soviet government that Iran intended to remain sovereign.

Reza Khan's Coup D'Etat

Ironically, as the Persian negotiators were concluding these negotiations in Moscow, a Russian-trained Persian cossack, Reza Khan, carried out a successful coup d'etat intended to abolish the Qajar monarchy and replace it with a republic. Reza Khan appointed the influential Sayyid Ziya al-Din Tabataba'i his prime minister, but eventually he himself took this position. At that point in 1923, he sent the Qajar shah Ahmad on a long vacation to Europe. Reza's plans for the republic were proceeding well until the Turkish parliament took the radical step of abolishing the caliphate. The Persian ulama reacted by insisting on the unacceptability of republican government. Still determined to rid Iran of the Qajars, Reza agreed to the change of plans only on condition that he himself be recognized as shah. In 1925, the Persian majlis voted out the Qajar dynasty and replaced it with that of the Pahlavis, in whose male line the succession would reside. The fifty-four-year history of Pahlavi Iran began.

The Aftermath in Arabia: Saudi Triumph Over the Hashimites

With official British backing for both the Hashimites of the Hijaz and the Saudis of the Najd during the war, it was no surprise that the two rivals fought each other for control of Arabia once the war was over. By leading the Arab revolt, Husayn thought he had won the promise of an independent, united Arab state. In October 1916, he publicly proclaimed himself king, thereby further enraging the Saudis. Fully confident of the allied commitment, Husayn received a rude shock when Britain, France, and their allies proceeded with the partition of the Middle East, including lands promised to him. Taking seriously Britain's award of the Khurma oasis, though it was held by Abd al-Aziz ibn Sa'ud, Husayn sent Abd Allah with an army to seize it. But Abd al-Aziz so thoroughly defeated the Hashimite force at Turaba that Abd Allah was fortunate to escape. The two cities in the Utayba Highlands of eastern Hijaz controlled the caravan routes from Najd to Makka. This incident in 1919 was but a preview of the struggle ahead.

With the installation of Abd Allah in Transjordan in 1920 and that of Faysal in Iraq in 1921, and with the continued presence of the Hashimites in the Hijaz, the Saudis began to feel surrounded. First, they sent a force into southwest Arabia to defend the interests of the Idris family in Asir. In November 1921, Abd Al-Aziz also defeated the Rashidi amirate at Ha'il in the Jabal Shammar area of northern Arabia. He assured their future quiescence by bringing their key leaders to his own court in Riyadh.

After these successes, Ibn Sa'ud negotiated two neutral zones with the British in north Arabia, one on the frontier of Iraq and the other on the border with Kuwayt. These zones would allow for mutual grazing or water rights. The Shaykhdom of Kuwayt lost some two thirds of its previous sphere of authority, but Shaykh Ahmad of Kuwayt nevertheless agreed. The agreement of November 1922 establishing the protocol of Uqayr, signified recognition by the British of growing Saudi influence in Arabia. Their former ally Husayn, because of his anger and humiliation, had refused in 1921 the offer of a kingdom in Hijaz as well as an apparently permanent subsidy. The British handout represented a pittance compared to the dream of a united Arab Kingdom. Left without the subsidy, despite British attempts to renegotiate in 1923 and 1924, Husayn and his oldest son Ali could not hold their position in western Arabia indefinitely, especially after a dramatic step taken by Husayn in 1924.

After the Turkish Republic abolished the caliphate, Husayn offered himself as a rightful claimant to the title. This action came on the heels of the British statement that payments to all Arabian rulers would end on 31 March 1924 and British insistence that Husayn and not the Saudis should control Khurma and Turaba. Ibn Saud was shocked by the audacity of his rival, whom he regarded as an inappropriate candidate for the revered caliphal role. Many tribesmen regarded Husayn as more European than Arab; he was urbane and condescending. Egyptians, too, had been alienated by Husayn's failure to safeguard pilgrims to Madina and Makka. Husayn's claims on the caliphate provided Ibn Saud with the pretext for launching his drive to unify Arabia under the Saudi umbrella.

Abd al-Aziz ibn Sa'ud in 1924 had few sources of income. In the previous year, his difficulties had led him to grant an oil concession to the Eastern General Syndicate, a concession abandoned after the payment of only two years' rent when experts concluded that the area would produce no oil. From Ibn Sa'ud's perspective, control of the Hijaz would bring both wealth and prestige.

In August 1924, Abd al-Aziz began a military campaign against his Hashimite rivals. He defeated them and occupied the holy city of Makka on 16 October. Although Husayn had abdicated on 3 October in favor of Ali, the latter had no resources with which to continue the fight. Ali gave up in 1925, moving to Faysal's capital at Baghdad. Husayn, meanwhile, had suffered a blow from which he never recovered. Eventually, he joined Abd Allah in Transjordan, and died in 1930. Acknowledged by the people of Hizaz as king, Abd al-Aziz emerged from the aftermath of the war as head of a united Arabian state. The British, however, annexed to Transjordan the northern province of Hijaz, including Aqaba. The Saudis acquiesced to the annexation only in 1965.

North Africa West of Egypt

After Tunisia's unsuccessful effort to send a delegation to the Paris Peace Conference, the North African areas of contention after the war were mainly Libya and Morocco. With the British defeat of the Sanussis in Libya, Sanussi leader Sayyid Ahmad al-Sharif left the country. His cousin Sayyid Muhammad Idris decided to stay out of international conflicts, and opened negotiations in 1916 with Britain and Italy. Meanwhile, the Tripolitanian republic based in Misurata continued through the war, and was formally proclaimed in 1918. Its leader Ramadan al-Suwaylhi hoped to rally other Libyan leaders. Urban Tripolitanians viewed the Sanussi, Sayyid Muhammad Idris, as too traditional. In 1920, Suwaylhi was killed in battle. New attempts for joint TripolitanianCyrenaican cooperation failed to overcome plans of the Italian governor of Tripolitania, Giuseppi Volpi. Italy consolidated its hold over Tripolitania.

Because of the Sanussi withdrawal during the war, Britain tried to mediate the Sanussi-Italian dispute. Sayyid Muhammad Idris negotiated an agreement with Italy in October 1920 that acknowledged him as hereditary amir in Cyrenaica and extended his authority to oasis inland. He soon realized that the Italians did not intend to honor the agreement, especially in light of the rise to power in Italy of Benito Mussolini in October 1922. The Sayf al-Nasr leadership in Fazzan, which opposed the Sanussis, refused to fight the Italians on behalf of their rivals. Sayyid Muhammad Idris would not fight, but moved to Egypt, leaving another Sanussi, Sayyid Safi al-Din, in charge. Military matters were left to a devoted Sanussi supporter, Umar al-Mukhtar. These leaders decided to pursue the war against Italy. They resisted successfully between 1923 and 1931.

In the remainder of North Africa west of Egypt, Maghribis who had fought for France in the war gained no concessions for their contributions. This added fuel to the nascent nationalist movements of Algeria, Morocco, and Tunisia. Despite the formal legal distinctions between the protectorates and Algeria, French officials continued to favor settlers over natives in economic, educational, and political matters. Although Lyautey in Morocco issued a circular in 1920 alerting his countrymen to trends in the Muslim world and to the expectations of Moroccans who had defended France, his warning was ignored. Soon Lyautey faced the independent republic set up by Abd al-Karim (Krim) in the Rif. With Lyautey's dismissal in 1925, French governors-general turned away from his evenhandedness toward preference of settlers. France did not control all of Morocco until 1934.

Conclusion

Although the Arabs of the east had fought for independence and had lost while those of the west had struggled for their colonial masters in the hope of an improved status that did not come about, the developments of World War I represented the emergence of a new framework in Southwest Asia and North Africa. The old Ottoman and Qajar empires had disappeared. Arabs who had aided the enemy against their Ottoman sovereign had fallen under colonial domination. The Turks of Anatolia, who had provided the bulk of the defeated forces in the Middle East, won an independent Turkish national state. Thus in one of the ironies of history, the vanquished emerged politically free while the victorious found themselves still foreign chains.

CHAPTER ELEVEN

The Struggle for Statehood in Turkey, Iran, and Northeast Africa

Between about 1918 and the late 1940s the struggle for independence absorbed the attentions of countries under European occupation. Turkey, Iran, and Egypt emerged as the region's largest and most important countries. In Turkey and Iran, new regimes sought to introduce secularism in order to further erode the power of religious elites. Loyalty to the state was to replace religious or more localized loyalties. Egyptians focused on removing British constraints on political freedom. At the same time, intellectuals debated questions relating to Egypt's Arab and Islamic identities. By the end of World War II, Egypt had not yet achieved full independence. Sudan remained a point of contention between Britain and Egypt. Libya was still being colonized by Italy.

Atatürk's Turkey: The Secular Experiment

In many ways, Mustafa Kemal was a successor to Ottoman and Young Turk modernizers. Historians still debate the short-term and long-term results of his secularization program. Unlike his predecessors, Kemal faced only one internal minority problem: that of the Kurds in eastern Anatolia. Neither westernization nor efforts at secularization were in themselves progressive developments, but Kemal seems to have viewed them as essential components in the modernization of Turkey. In this respect, he differed from others in the area who sought to evolve an Islamic modernization program or at least one that would not deliberately aim to undermine the influence of religious beliefs or institutions.

Legal Change as a Vehicle for Turkish National Consolidation

Early changes implemented by Kemal included separation of religion and state, abolition of waqf control by religious bodies, termination of the Shari'a courts' authority, an end to religious schools, and introduction of coeducation. Wearing of clothing associated with religion was banned. The previously modern headgear, the fez, was to be replaced after 1925 by hats that had visors—a protrusion that would interfere with the act of prayer. This particular law has attracted much commentary because the Turkish government took it seriously and punished severely leaders who counseled against its observation. With abolition of Shari'a came also an end to the millet system. Armenians, Greeks, and Jews renounced their right to be judged according to their own religious laws and placed themselves under the rule of Turkish law.

What, then, was Turkish law? To replace the old personal status laws (including the Mejelle), the Turkish government in 1926 resorted to adapting the Swiss legal code. Under the new law, polygamy and the practice of repudiation allowed to men in marriage were supposed to disappear. The law gave women equal rights in marriage and divorce. Theoretically, only civil marriage existed after 1926, but the government could not easily enforce the ban on religious observances accompanying weddings. Introduction of European penal and commercial codes did not meet with equal resistance because of nineteenth-century reforms incorporating western legal provisions. In this area, secularization was effective only to the extent that it did not interfere with strong religious beliefs and social customs, and to the extent that it could be enforced.

In other efforts to cut off the population from the Islamic Ottoman past, the republicans substituted a European calendar for the Islamic one and abandoned the practice of beginning the new day with sunset. Because Atatürk objected to the complete covering of women associated with Islam, he made several attempts to forbid them from wearing the veil that covered not only the head but also the face. But no laws were passed requiring women to unveil. With so many areas out of the immediate reach of government authorities, any such regulation would have been unenforceable, and women themselves were slow to accept the idea.

Atatürk introduced changes in Turkey's voting sysem to increase participation of women in public life. In 1924, nontaxpaying men could vote. Six years later, women voted in local elections for the first time. In 1934, not only were women allowed to vote in national elections but they also had the opportunity to run for office. Nearly 5 percent of the parliament in 1935 was composed of women. As in the West, legal emancipation and increased opportunities for education did not necessarily alter views of men and women toward their customary roles. The government, however, seems to have taken the legal changes far more seriously than did Western governments whose women were also in the early stages of emancipation.

Theoretically, the removal of Islam from the Turkish constitution in 1928 separated enforcement of the law from the practice of Islam. However, full freedom to choose a religion did not come about until 1934. This freedom proved ineffective because of pressures families and communites could exercise on members who tried to change their religion. Through the 1970s, one still read reports of individuals killed by their families after they announced conversion to another faith. Moreover, non-Muslims and non-Turks were not full and equal partners in the state.

Kurdish Revolts

Although the Kurds constituted an ethnolinguistic rather than a religious minority, frustration of their nationalist movement and fixing of regional boundaries left them divided and unhappy. Atatürk's regime, by trying to impose secularism among Kurds heavily influenced by the Bektashi order, added fuel to the fire. The 1925 Kurdish revolt, despite its religious overtones and leadership (Shaykh Sa'id) represented a protest by Kurds against the government's abolition in 1924 of all Kurdish societies, schools, publications, and institutions, including the religious. The Kurds had expected to be given special treatment for having aided suppression of the Armenians in the east. The revolt of 1925 was quelled quickly. Over fifty Kurdish leaders were executed in Diyarbakir and another four hundred were killed in Kharpert (Elazig). The Turkish government convinced the foreign press that the revolt represented religious reaction, not a move toward independence.

The government followed up the revolt by deporting Kurds to other areas; many fled to Iran or Iraq. In Lebanon, Kurdish leaders did a turnabout and established ties with Armenian revolutionaries who still hoped to liberate both Turkish and Soviet Armenia. Although the Turkish government allowed the return of exiled Kurdish leaders (seeking to ward off a joint Kurdish-Armenian action), a new Kurdish revolt in 1929, aided by Iran, provoked further military intervention. The Kurds lost when Iran withdrew its aid. Turkish forces surrounded the rebels from Iranian territory. Then Turkey and Iran agreed on boundary adjustments in the Van-Ararat area.

The Turkish government approved the killing of thousands of Kurdish civilians in the name of quelling the rebellion. Turkey's prime minister and later president, Ismet Inönü, announced that only Turks could fully enjoy national and ethnic rights in Turkey. Further deportations of Kurds ensued. From 1935 to the end of 1938, residents of the remote area of Dersim fought the Turkish army rather than acquiesce to deportation. The Kurds lost when their ammunition ran out. But as a large minority variously estimated at 10–20 percent of the population, the Kurds in Turkey still sustained their independent identity.

Language Reform and Creation of a New Turkish Past

To promote Turkish identity more peacefully, Atatürk strove to eliminate Arabic influences by decreeing that the call to prayer should be made in Turkish. Persian and Arabic words were targeted for replacement, too. In 1928, the Turkish government replaced the old Arabic script with a new Latin script, following a model adopted earlier in the Soviet Union which used the Cyrillic alphabet more readily to accommodate Turkish sounds not found in Arabic. What was the impact of this change? First of all, the new Latin Turkish alphabet was simpler than the Arabic. Atatürk regarded it as a vehicle for the expansion of literacy. More significantly, it facilitated creation of a new past and a new future for Turkey. Young people in the state schools would be cut off from all past writings except those the government chose to print in the new alphabet. The Quran had to be rendered in the new script. Ottoman history became the target of a Turkish revisionism often highly chauvinistic in outlook and content. Multiethnic ideas of the past were no longer available to the reading public; Turkish identity was made paramount. Atatürk's reform disassociated newly strong and independent Turks from the former image of the "sick man of Europe."

Changing the language involved far more than the unilateral step of altering the writing system. As with the new language academies of Egypt and Syria, the Turkish government set up the Turkish Linguistic Society in 1932 to recommend Turkish forms to replace Arabic and Persian vocabulary. The elites commissioned to perform the task were not the people most likely to support applying Turkish roots. Since Arabic and Persian words had been absorbed centuries earlier, the committee propounded the *Sun Theory* which stated that Turkish was the original human language. Therefore, the alleged derivation of words from Arabic and Persian was irrelevant.

Turkish Literature

Turkish literature during the period had to adjust to new social and linguistic realities. Halide Edip Adivar continued to write, drawing on her experiences from the war of independence and inspired by writings about peasants by French authors Zola and Balzac. Because of her support for the Progressive Republican Party, a short-lived effort of a few intellectuals to set up an opposition based on disapproval of Atatürk's secularism, Edip (along with her husband Adnan) was exiled from Turkey from 1926 to 1939. After Atatürk's death, she returned and became until her death in 1964 professor of English literature at Istanbul University.

Another writer who stressed peasantry and Anatolian heritage was Mehmet Emin Yurdukal. Yakup Kadri Karaosmanoglu drew upon the topics of Anatolian patriotism, heroism, and nationalism. In his fictional work *The Stranger,* he addressed the plight of an officer who tried during the Turkish war of independence to assimilate with villagers who in the end decided to support the Greeks. Like others examining peasant life in Anatolia, Karaosmanoglu as an urban author wrote with detachment. These works, however, paved the way for the social realism of the 1940s and 1950s. Another important writer was the poet Nazim Hikmet, who was persecuted for Communist activities.

As part of their revival of an ancient Turkish past, the Turkish government adopted the Hittites as their ancestors. The much later migrations of Turks into the Anatolian region were discounted. For many years the Turkish government continued to emphasize Hittite culture, but in the 1980s they began reviving Islamic heritage.

Introduction of Surnames

To further set a new course, Mustafa Kemal assured in 1934 passage of a law requiring every man to choose a surname in place of being known as *so-and-so-son-of-so-and-so.* Honorific titles were abolished in favor of uniform labels for men and women. For his own name, Kemal received from the Turkish National Assembly the distinctively Turkish Atatürk, meaning *father of the Turks.* He dropped the Islamic Mustafa but retained Kemal as his first name. Ismet adopted Inönü in remembrance of the Turkish war of independence. Women generally assumed their husband's surname upon marriage.

Political and Economic Life

The Grand National Assembly did not necessarily provide a forum for serious debate. Atatürk ruled largely as an autocrat who increasingly tolerated little if any opposition. The Republican People's Party (R.P.P.), Atatürk's own creation, supported Atatürk's programs and ideas by dominating the assembly. Control over the vilayets was maintained under the Vilayet Law of 1929. Governors of the vilayets won their posts not through local elections but by appointment through the central government. Municipalities in 1930 were also given a separate corporate legal identity. Only in 1950 was the Grand National Assembly elected by direct vote.

Foreigners and minority groups, particularly Jews and Christians, had regulated the Turkish economy and debt to a great extent under the Ottoman Empire. Although a few Greeks and Armenians remained in and around Istanbul after the postwar victory, the initiative in Anatolia passed to Turks, who had been formerly more involved in agriculture than in business. Atatürk worked to achieve national self-sufficiency in place of dependency. In this, he was not alone as the Soviet Union, Japan, Germany, Italy, and the United States, among others, were also trying to protect domestic industries from outside influence. Tariff restrictions imposed by the Lausanne Treaty ended in 1929, the year of the stock market crashes and the onset of world economic depression.

Government Agricultural Policy

What specific actions did Atatürk take? Five-year plans on Soviet models were introduced from 1934 on. With the idea of more centralized planning came the encouragement of national monopolies in agriculture, commerce, and industry. Although it has been argued recently that the Turkish industrialization program proved to be a long-term failure for lack of agricultural investment, the Kemalist government—especially in the 1920s—introduced new laws and programs designed to help peasants.

The Ministry of Agriculture began providing loans as well as advice on new methods and machines for both small and large farmers. When credit offered proved insufficient, cooperatives were set up around the country to help meet the demand. Agricultural taxes were reduced as an incentive to increase production. Seeds were supplied by state organizations to introduce new crops such as tea, potatoes, lemons, and hazelnuts. Government-owned experimental stations tested new varieties and gave advice to farmers. In order to help farmers take their crops to market, the rural road networks steadily expanded. Turkey in the 1920s was self-sufficient in agriculture and was able to export agricultural products.

Despite increases in acreage and production to World War II, many peasants remained landless and the low agricultural taxes left the country dependent on the small urban population for the bulk of the government's income. Without major tax reform, agriculture could not sustain industrial expansion.

State Planning in Industry

Turkey's industrialization program has won mixed reviews. It set up industries that substituted Turkish products for previously imported consumer and industrial goods such as textiles, glass, paper, cement, sulphur, anthracite, iron, steel, synthetics, and phosphates. State banks managed and established these industries. State corporations regulated monopolies of staples including salt, tea, and matches. To introduce properly the five-year plan and to take over communications, Turkey received small loans, first from the United States and later from the Soviet Union, France, Britain, and Germany. Critics of industrialization called the new products substandard and management inefficient. Nevertheless, the industries survived, supplying the domestic market. In an era of cheap energy, the government did not need to concern itself with export income to pay for energy supplies.

Only with the benefit of hindsight can one ascertain that Turkey's investment in industry was endangered in the long term by the failure to alter the tax system so that agriculture could provide for industry. Most of today's successful industrial models, especially in South and East Asia, focused on agriculture before turning to industry, with encouragement of private enterprise and capital investment. In Turkey, where much of the bourgeosie had been expelled or killed during World War I and its aftermath, private investors, whether Turkish or Kurdish Muslims, Jews, or Christians, were likely to be cautious. Perhaps the only real alternative open to the government was to embark on industrialization itself.

The industrial proletariat that grew during the program was theoretically protected by a labor code designed to improve working conditions and increase output, but the code was introduced only in 1936. Pregnancy and postnatal leaves for women were provided at half-pay, but we cannot ascertain the extent to which provisions were enforced. One regulation that was fairly effective, though, was the ban on organizing and striking!

Atatürk's Six Principles

As a framework for his programs, Atatürk announced six principles in a manifesto in 1931. Incorporated in 1937 into the constitution were republicanism, nationalism, revolutionism, secularism, etatism and populism. Republicanism confirmed the idea that the old Ottoman Empire, with its framework of rulers and ruled, had now given way to a republic in which each citizen had a stake and from which each received security and well-being. Nationalism supported the idea of Turkification and declared Anatolia as the homeland of the Turks. Revolutionism symbolized the regime's commitment to rapid rather than evolutionary change, with the rejection of tradition when it proved detrimental to the national interest. Secularism meant separating religion from the governing apparatus, establishing new educational and legal systems and eroding the authority of both religion and religious functionaries. Etatism worked toward economic self-sufficiency through a mixed economy dominated by state-controlled or state-operated industry. Finally, populism was to reinforce republicanism by emphasizing political and legal equality as well as participation in governing the country through representative government.

Turkey's Foreign Policy: Neutrality and Regional Security

In his foreign policy, Atatürk focused on keeping Turkey at peace and on good terms with neighbors. The Mosul settlement from the Treaty of Lausanne still required negotiations with the British in Iraq. Turkey agreed to give up Mosul in exchange for receiving 10 percent of the production from the latter's oil fields. Britain promised to end its previous support for Kurdish and Armenian aspirations. To consolidate and protect its boundaries further, Turkey negotiated treaties with Greece and other Balkan neighbors. In July 1932, Turkey entered the League of Nations. Bilateral treaties were followed up by participation in the Balkan Entente Treaty of 1934 and the Saadabad Pact (with Iran, Iraq, and Afghanistan), the Middle East's first regional friendship treaty in 1937. A treaty

with Syria was also signed in 1926 but fell apart during the Alexandretta crisis.

Syria Loses Alexandretta to Turkey

The League of Nations mandate for Syria prevented altering its boundaries. But Atatürk wanted Alexandretta annexed to Turkey. The League of Nations heard Turkey's complaint against French intentions to include Alexandretta in provisions for Syrian independence. Turkey agreed to an autonomy plan that would leave foreign affairs under the control of Syria, but the Syrians objected to any moves that might pave the way for a future Turkish takeover. For its part, Turkey was less pleased when the results of elections in November 1937 assured minority status for Turks there.

As the clouds of war gathered, France agreed to allow Turkish troops to occupy Alexandretta. The French presence gave Turks an advantage in securing a majority in the subsequent elections of 1938. Alexandretta was renamed Hatay, and was set up as an independent entity. It immediately called for union with Turkey. In July 1939, France acceded to Turkey's annexation of Alexandretta in exchange for a nonagression pact that would assure Turkey's neutrality during World War II. The British signed a similar agreement with Turkey. The Syrians, however, never accepted the detachment of Alexandretta from Syria. Although the area was predominantly Arab and Turkish, its annexation precipitated a new exodus of Armenians who had found refuge there. In a final question of importance to Atatürk, Turkey by the Montreux Convention in 1936 obtained the right to remilitarize the Bosporus and the Dardanelles. All of the parties to the Lausanne Treaty eventually agreed.

Inönü's Wartime Policy

When Atatürk died in November 1938, Ismet Inönü succeeded him. Inönü was soon faced with World War II and pressures from the major combatants. Since the Soviet Union had just allied with Germany, it objected to Turkey contracting open alliances with France and Britain. Turkey's agreements represented a positive neutrality that excluded the possibility of fighting the Soviet Union. When Turkey's allies in the Balkans were invaded by Germany and Italy in 1940, Turkey remained detached. Though pressured by Germany to close the straits to all ships, Turkey refused the further step of allowing Germany transit for its troops to Arab countries. In 1941, with Germany at war with its former Soviet ally, many Turks were inclined to throw their support behind the likely victor, Germany, but Inönü decided to steer a straight course. Turkey's nonagression pact with Germany did not preclude honoring other obligations. Inönü preserved Turkey's neutrality throughout the war, but he also took extra steps to deter an invasion.

During the war, Inönü kept an army of one million men mobilized. Both industrial and agricultural production dropped despite the implementation of forced labor laws in key industries. With few sources of revenue, the government imposed the capital levy to raise revenues through assessment of capital goods. Those who could not pay were subject to property confiscations. Assessment committees used the tax to discriminate against Jews, Greeks, and Armenians who had stayed in Turkey but who were viewed as not fully Turkish. Many old and infirm men were imprisoned and died in jail because of inability to raise the full amount. Minorities, representing about 5 percent of the population, paid about 53 percent of the total collected. Muslims paid only 37 percent. Foreigners paid the balance. The capital levy provided a major impetus in the postwar period for minority emigration and transfer of capital abroad.

In the middle of the war, Turkey benefited from the allied lend-lease program on the grounds that the country needed arms before it could enter the fighting. Although Inönü accepted advisors and weapons thus supplied, he refrained from breaking his agreements with Germany until early 1944. He declared war only in February 1945. Turkey's cooperation with Germany was resented by the Soviet Union. In March 1945, the Soviets broke the Turkish-Soviet treaty of 1925. The Soviet Union then proceeded to claim territories given up in earlier wars. Its leader Joseph Stalin also pressed for a revision of the Montreux Convention to permit passage of Soviet ships through the straits in both wartime and peacetime as well as the construction of bases there. Fearing that the Soviet Union would further encourage Communists in Turkey and Greece, the Turkish leadership turned to the United States. President Harry Truman in March 1947 proclaimed what became known as the Truman Doctrine: the offer of economic and military aid to countries threatened by the Soviet Union (in this case Greece and Turkey). The American alliance became a cornerstone of Turkish foreign policy throughout most of the postwar period.

Pahlavi Iran under Reza Shah

There are many parallels between Iran and Turkey during the interwar period. One difference, though, is that Iran's ulama rejected the republican form of government. The Persian majlis voted out the Qajar dynasty in 1925. In the following year, Reza Khan was crowned the first Pahlavi Shah. In calling his dynasty Pahlavi, the shah was looking back to the Sassanians. To emphasize his point, he asked that foreigners use the more ancient Iran instead of the Greek Persia. Like Turkey, Iran was focusing on its pre-Islamic national heritage. Nationalism in both countries provided governments with a powerful unifying force to combat foreign influences. Moreover, Iran did have a glorious past.

One of the weaknesses of the Qajar dynasty had been military decentralization. Reza Shah assured that the majlis passed a conscription law and unified the army. To help insure its loyalty, he provided its men with modern weapons. The army helped the shah to extend his control throughout Iran. An important aspect of the government's establishment of greater control was its policy of bringing Iran's disparate ethnolinguistic groups under state authority. While recentralization of this type had already taken place in the Ottoman Empire during the nineteenth century, Iran shared with Morocco and Arabia the enactment of this process during the twentieth century.

Socioeconomic Policy: Centralization and Self-sufficiency

Like Atatürk, Reza Shah believed that the best way to modernize Iran was to avoid dependence on foreigners, to discourage foreign intervention, to industrialize, to modernize education, and to build a new society in which women would play a more prominent role. Only a strong central government could bring about profound change within a short time, and Reza was willing to work to achieve his goals. He hoped other Iranians would emulate his work ethic.

Although Reza employed an American financial advisor from 1922 to 1927, his economic program focused on making Iran less dependent on outsiders. As with the Turkish efforts, he looked to local industry and commerce as a means of creating national self-sufficiency. The shah invested in textile factories (silk, wool, cotton), sugar refineries, and cement plants. To help promote internal commerce, the Trans-Iranian railway connecting Bandar Shahpur on the Gulf to Bandar Shah on the Caspian Sea was built

between 1927 and 1938. Special levies on sugar and tea, both items of heavy consumption in Iran, paid for the railway. The network of roads was also expanded.

As in Turkey, state monopolies were set up to market exports and to establish controls over imports. Through these institutions, Iran developed a largely favorable trade balance. Monopolies were required because the Soviet Union, with about one third of Iran's total foreign trade, maintained them too. Abolition of capitulations in 1928 helped Iran establish a stronger local economy. Moreover, Reza Shah founded the Bank Melli as an Iranian national bank that maintained the sole right to issue currency.

Reza Shah wanted to earn the foreign exchange required for industrial purchases abroad by developing export markets for its raw materials, especially for petroleum. Since the oil industry developed by Anglo-Persian brought profits mainly to itself and not to Iran, the shah requested an increase in Iran's royalties. In 1932, after the company refused, the shah abrogated the concession. The British took the case to the League of Nations on behalf of the company, but Iran won increased payments. The renegotiated contract remained in force until the nationalization of 1951. Although petroleum revenues helped compensate for the lack of growth in agriculture, the emphasis on industrialization in Iran may have harmed agriculture in the long run.

Like Atatürk, Reza Shah looked to secularism as a way of modernizing Iran and of eroding the power of mujtahids, but he did not aim to undermine completely the influence of religion in society. New penal and civil codes were introduced, and Shari'a courts lost many of their previous functions after the introduction of civil marriage and divorce. The shah founded government schools for both boys and girls in an effort to make state education compulsory. Evening classes for adults were scheduled in urban and rural areas. To help provide teachers for the new schools, teacher-training colleges began operating in the mid-1930s, and Tehran University was opened in 1935.

Like Atatürk, the shah sent students to Europe for further training.

As in Turkey, surnames were to be adopted by all subjects. The shah abolished traditional titles, too. Instead of their native dress, Iran's diverse peoples were ordered to wear European clothing. This regulation applied to both men and women but as in Turkey the government could hardly force people to abandon their clothing and customs.

Reza also undermined the power of religious groups by depriving them of complete control over waqf. As in Turkey, only qualified religious functionaries could wear religious dress. Plays (called *ta'ziya*) depicting the martyrdom of Husayn at Karbala, so important to community religious observances, became targets of suppression. Reza Shah restored Zoroastrianism to the status of an approved religion, but as was true of his effort to purge Persian of foreign words, the act was associated more with nationalism than with religion. Along with promoting language reform, Reza Shah emphasized instruction in Persian, just as Atatürk focused on Turkish. However, at least 40 percent of the population viewed itself as non-Persian. The Persianization program did not necessarily meet with approval among these groups.

Literary Developments

Iran between the wars witnessed a literary renaissance of sorts with the appearance of novels and short stories as well as the established genres of poetry and drama. The most influential of the new writers was Sadiq Hedayet. Influenced by Franz Kafka and French social writers, Hedayet, though of aristocratic background, empathized with the poor and dispossessed. His novel *The Blind Owl* was autobiographical and was characterized by pessimism and despair. Hedayet wrote many more introspective and individualistic short stories.

Muhammad Ali Jamalzadeh is usually credited with having introduced naturalism into Persian literature. In *Preface* (1919), he criticized authors who ignored the masses and wrote an elitist literature that emphasized form over content. Other important prose writers were Ali Dashti and Muhammad Hejazi. The most important prominent poet, Nima Yushij, instituted a new style that departed from classical rhymes and imagery. He influenced postwar poets who took up free verse. Political themes expressing support for freedom and social change also became more common in Iranian poetry.

Reza Shah and Atatürk: Similarities and Differences

In the political arena, Reza Shah maintained the majlis without encouraging an atmosphere conducive to debate. Late in the 1920s, a handful of political parties existed, but the shah desired a party to parallel Atatürk's R.P.P. It was to be a bastion of the state, promoting national unity and ongoing reform throughout the country. Deputies were slow to accept the idea, but in January 1939, the Society to Guide Public Opinion finally arose to mobilize people behind the shah. It stressed loyalty to the nation in a manner characteristic of Fascist Italy and Nazi Germany. As in Turkey, then, Iran's regime meant exercise of power by an autocrat. The shah visited Turkey in 1934 and was very impressed by the results of Atatürk's measures. The two men established a strong rapport.

How did Iran and Turkey differ during this period? Reza Shah did not possess the charisma or national background of Atatürk. He lacked a largely homogenous population with which to work. Prior to Atatürk's regime, the Ottomans unlike the Qajars had been modernizing steadily since the eighteenth century. Possibly the greater emotional involvement found in Shi'i practices made religious observances in Iran less subject to externally imposed change. Moreover, religious leaders in Iran had served as protectors and defenders of the poor and oppressed, especially against unjust rulers. Efforts to erode their power were unlikely to meet with popular approval. Although like Atatürk Reza did not change the basis of land tenure in Iran and pursued a harsh ethnic policy, he did confiscate estates of the rich for his own use. His ethnic policies provoked more than one revolt by the Kurds in northwestern Iran.

Foreign Policy of Reza Shah

In developments that paralleled those in Turkey, Iran worked to improve relations with its neighbors. Like Turkey it signed the Saadabad Non-Aggression Pact. Reza concluded treaties with the Soviet Union to promote trade and guarantee national security, but at the same time suppressed suspected Communists, most of them intellectuals and labor leaders. With Germany and Russia as major trading partners on the eve of World War II, Iran could not easily maintain its neutrality.

Iran's Wartime Dilemma

Two main problems faced Reza Shah. Iran had ordered manufactured goods from Germany. The British announced that even neutral countries should not receive shipments from there. Iran regarded the supplies as vital to continued development and turned to the Soviet Union, which was still on stable terms with Germany, as a possible route. But as German-Soviet relations worsened, Iran's government faced heightened pressures to curtail ties with Germany. This was not easy because German citizens were employed in government ministries and in business in Iran. Reza's first problem, then, was that his relations with Germany were both endangered and threatening to his own nation's security.

The second problem related to the first. After Germany invaded the Soviet Union in June 1941, the British looked to Iran as a route for sending supplies to their Soviet allies. Moreover, the British wanted to assure that strategic British-controlled oil fields would not be sabotaged by German agents. Both Brit-

ain and the Soviet Union, then, had good reasons for wanting the Germans out of Iran. The Turks, who could not fulfill the role intended for Iran, were allowed to remain neutral in the war. Iran was not.

Not long after the shah refused to expel the Germans and allow for the resupply of Russian forces through Iran, the two countries embarked on a joint occupation not unlike that of World War I. With Soviet troops in the north and the British in the south, Reza Shah abdicated rather than acquiesce to foreign occupation. Britain forced him into exile, first in Mauritius and later in South Africa where he died in 1944.

Accession of Muhammad Reza Shah

The new shah was his twenty-year-old son Shahpur Muhammad who came to power as Muhammad Reza Shah. Educated in Switzerland and Iran, Muhammad Reza had acquired both military training and practical experience through travels with his father. During the war, he could hardly rule Iran freely, especially after he signed a formal treaty of alliance with its occupiers in January 1942. These latter promised Iran political freedom, independence, and sovereignty, and they claimed to be utilizing the country only temporarily. They would evacuate their troops within six months after hostilities ended. Iran agreed to provide facilities for the allied war effort. From that time on, the country became the key route for supplying the Soviet Union. American troops entered Iran to help coordinate transport. Iran broke relations with Italy, Germany, and Japan, and in September 1943 made an official declaration of war on Germany.

The joint occupation and proclamation of political freedom brought about the unanticipated consequence of encouraging activities on the part of both mujtahids and Tudeh Party communists. Support for the Tudeh group came mostly from new middle classes whom Reza Shah had encouraged. The wartime economic conditions of high prices, inflation, and scarcity hampered the ability of the Iranian government to function in this new democratic atmosphere. Although a new majlis was elected in 1943, each cabinet found that the various foreign and domestic pressures were beyond its control.

Foreign Pressures in Iran and the Northern Republics

The year 1944 brought demands for new petroleum concessions from British, Soviet, and American interests. The majlis decided to avoid controversy by barring conclusion of concessional arrangements with foreigners until the end of the war. The Soviets encouraged demonstrations by Tudeh-related groups, especially in northern minority-dominated regions. In December 1945, Kurdish and Azeri autonomous republics came into being in areas cut off by Soviet troops.

With the war over, Iran objected in 1946 to what was perceived as continued interference by the Soviet Union, and lodged a protest with the United Nations. Only when the Iranians agreed to the formation of a Soviet-Iranian petroleum company to exploit northern Iran and to a negotiated peace with the autonomous republics did the Soviets agree to withdraw. Tudeh was brought into the government in 1946 but only briefly because southerners protested against its inclusion. Leaders in Azerbayjan then reneged on an agreement to permit supervised elections. The Azeri government fell to an Iranian attack in December 1946, and the Kurdish Mahabad state collapsed not long after.

Kurdish patriots have argued that Mahabad represented a genuine effort of Kurds to set up an independent state in territory no foreign troops had occupied during the war. Two movements, the Komala movement and the Kurdish Democratic Party, took the lead in political organization. Provisions for the state included implementation of Kurdish as the national language. Prominent Iraqi Kurds such as Mustafa Barzani were attracted to the new state. Since Tudeh participated in both the Mahabad and Azeri governments, the British and Americans viewed them as Soviet puppets although other groups were well represented. During the suppression, the Iranians tried and executed Kurdish president Qazi Muhammad and members of his family; massacres of Azeris took place in Azerbayjan.

There is merit, then, in the argument that the Tehran regime feared encouraging minority independence and moved against the republics to assure quiescence among other groups that might have made similar demands. In the short term, the new shah's decision to continue his father's Persianization thrust may have succeeded, but in the long term it also backfired. One needs only to look at minority activity during the Iranian revolution of 1977–79 and its aftermath to see the evidence that minority feelings in Iran are still very much alive.

Semi-independent Egypt

The establishment of the Egyptian kingdom, with its parliamentary system and restricted independence, meant that Egypt's political life came to be dominated by bourgeois politics characterized by squabbles between rivals for power. The constitutional setup permitted and encouraged the standoff because it allowed the king to appoint prime ministers who were not of the majority party. Issues left to the British by the unilateral declaration of independence remained paramount to politicians. They expended their greatest efforts in trying to remove the conditions, but their own internal divisions often obstructed their ability to negotiate with the British. Lacking confidence in the voting public and engaged in their own rivalries, parties often distributed money to secure votes for their candidates.

Egypt's Political Parties

Government had for centuries been regarded with suspicion. A largely wealthy and indigenous Egyptian oligarchy could establish itself as the main participant in politics. The Wafd, the only mass party, was led by Sa'd Zaghlul until his death in 1927, and later by Mustafa al-Nahhas. Prominent Wafdists included Zaghlul's nephew Fath Allah Barakat, Makram Ubayd, Ahmad Mahir, Mahmud Fahmi Nuqrashi, Wasif Ghali (son of Butros Ghali), and Wisa Wasif. In 1937, Mahir and Nuqrashi were expelled because of internal disputes; they proceeded to form the Sa'dist Party. When Ubayd found himself out of the party, too, he not only formed a new group, the Wafdist Bloc in 1942, but also published *The Black Book* discrediting Nahhas. Each of the Wafd's offshoots viewed itself as more truly nationalist than the Wafd.

Distinguished more by its membership than by its popularity, which was limited, the Liberal Constitutionalist Party (al-Ahrar al-Dusturiyyun) was largely a successor to the old Umma Party. Its most well-known members included Ahmad Lutfi al-Sayyid, Adli Yakan, Muhammad Mahmud, Abd al-Aziz Fahmi, Isma'il Sidqi, Muhammad Husayn Haykal, Hafiz Afifi, and Abd al-Khaliq Tharwat, nearly all of whom were also prominent intellectuals with whom Zaghlul could not get along. While the Wafd during the interwar period aimed at removing all of the conditions on Egypt's independence at once, the Ahrar tended to support a step-by-step approach of limited but steady gains. As members of a minority party, the Ahrar—Yakan, Mahmud, and Tharwat —were periodically called upon by the king to form cabinets whereupon they proved to be no more tolerant of other parties and no better at governing then the Wafd.

In 1930, Sidqi left the party upon becoming prime minister. In moves designed to assist the king in crushing the Wafd's power, Sidqi exacerbated the pre-existing constitutional crisis first by locking the gates of parliament, then by disbanding parliament, and finally, by introducing a new constitution to replace that of 1923. Sidqi formed his own party, the Hizb al-Sha'b (People's Party) to contest the 1931 elections. Although it formulated a primarily economic platform, this party never attracted constituents. Like the king's Ittihad (Union) Party it served a limited, special-interest group. The Watan Party also survived during this period; its most noteworthy member was Abd al-Rahman al-Rafi'i, who wrote a series of books tracing Egypt's contemporary history and political life.

The Stack Assassination Crisis

The first big crisis in semi-independent Egypt occurred in November 1924 when a secret society connected to a former Wafdist lawyer assassinated Sir Lee Stack, the British commander of Egypt's army. British High Commissioner Allenby responded unilaterally and independently of his own government by issuing a set of demands designed to punish the Egyptians. These included the following: 1) punishment of the assassins; 2) an official apology; 3) withdrawal of Egyptian units stationed in the Sudan; 4) Egyptian consent for unlimited irrigation of the Sudanese gezira that would reduce water available for Egyptian irrigation; 5) payment of a £500,000 indemnity; 6) prohibition of political demonstrations; 7) appointment of British advisors in finance and justice. Obviously, the assassination harmed Zaghlul because though he had no knowledge of the affair, Allenby held him responsible. While Zaghlul went along with payment of the indemnity, he could hardly accept the measures regarding the Sudan, especially in the wake of his failure that summer to negotiate a treaty based on demands for British withdrawal from Sudan. After he had resigned, a minority-led cabinet accepted the British ultimatum although the irrigation provision was later modified. Disapproving of Allenby's high-handedness, the British government replaced him, too. Thereafter, the most controversial and sensitive questions for politicians remained the status of Sudan and the presence of the British army. Zaghlul never again served as prime minister in Egypt.

Egypt's Uneasy Democracy: The Wafd and Its Rivals

Parliamentary life enjoyed a rocky existence at best. Although the Wafd would win the elections, the king usually appointed the prime minister from among minority party politicians. On occasions when a Wafdist served as premier, he was soon dismissed due to some conflict with the king and/or the British. Minority governments could not sustain themselves for long because of lack of popular support. Throughout the interwar period, the denial of power to the Wafd enhanced its popularity, but it also made the Wafd impede resolution of differences between Britain and Egypt.

The Wafdists did not act without justification. In 1928, the Ahrar government led by Muhammad Mahmud dissolved parliament and then instituted direct monarchical rule, aided by the cabinet. This began the constitutional crisis that culminated in the Sidqi dictatorship of 1930–33. When Mahmud in early May 1929 reached an agreement with the British over the division of the Nile waters between Egypt and Sudan, the Wafd condemned it as creating a new obstacle to reunification. In late May, after the Labour Party won power in England, Mahmud accepted the opportunity to negotiate the long-desired treaty. Although he secured British agreement to withdrawal of British troops to the Canal Zone and the placing of responsibility for minorities and foreigners in Egyptian government hands, the British leaked out its terms to the Wafdists who assured its demise and that of the man who negotiated it. Adli became premier long enough to

organize new elections and was soon succeeded by the victorious Nahhas in January 1930.

The British apparently expected Nahhas to agree to terms they had offered Mahmud, but he insisted on removal of restrictions regarding the Sudan. The result was that Nahhas had to go home empty-handed. His failure was heightened by the economic problems of the worldwide depression. Nahhas could offer no solution. The only mitigating legislation the Wafdists introduced and passed was a protectionist bill to safeguard Egypt's few industrial enterprises. When Nahhas could not secure the king's approval of a pet project, he resigned, assuming that Fu'ad would recall him. Instead the king turned to Sidqi.

The Sidqi regime lasted for three years. It too failed to resolve Egypt's economic and political crises. As the effects of the depresssion worsened in the predominantly agricultural economy, Sidqi created two credit banks to aid farmers, one to prevent foreclosures on land for unpaid debts and the other to buy back lands for farmers who had lost them because of indebtedness. Because the government continued its policy of strict tax collection, these measures did little to alleviate rural hardship. Sidqi also suppressed activities of labor unions, and then called for improved social welfare and political representation. Sidqi's generally hostile policies provoked strikes and protests by laborers and students. The political parties took advantage of the situation by subsidizing student demonstrations. Press censorship curtailed open criticism.

New Ideologies and Movements: Young Egypt and the Muslim Brothers

Young Egypt Most historians agree that the Sidqi period exercised a profound influence on subsequent political developments. Restraints on political behavior were dropped in favor of greater activism and violence, especially on the part of students. A young law student, Ahmud Hasayn, who in late 1931 organized the Piastre Plan to collect money from private citizens for industrial development, founded in 1933 the Young Egypt Society (Green Shirts), Egypt's first paramilitary organization. Both Husayn and his colleague Fathi Radwan had previously been involved in the Ahrar's youth group. In the early years of the society, it was most closely linked with the Ahrar and the Watan Party. That the Wafd regarded this group as a serious challenge is indicated by the Wafd's founding of its own paramilitary group called the Blue Shirts. The Wafd, after coming to power in May 1936, also tried to suppress Young Egypt.

Generally speaking, Young Egypt began as part of the youth-oriented movements of the 1920s. Groups that were set up were the Boy Scouts, the Y.M.C.A. (Young Men's Christian Association), the Y.M.M.A. (Young Men's Muslim Association), and the Society of Muslim Brothers. Ideologically, Young Egypt resembled the latter two at the outset, as it called for Egyptian leadership in the Arab and Muslim worlds, patriotism, expansion of industry and agriculture, improvement in the quality of life, curtailment of non-Egyptians' privileges, an end to immorality in Egypt, and a "martial spirit."[1] Other youth movements arose elsewhere in the Middle East during the same period, notably in Syria (the Silver Shirts), Lebanon (the *Kata'ib* or Phalange), and in Palestine (*Najjada*). Like Young Egypt, they sought an alternative to European-style parliamentary government, one which would address social problems and contribute to national pride. To some extent, they looked to the model, then current in Europe, of National Socialist (Nazi) and Fascist organizations.

Although it was the only youth-led youth movement when first established, Young Egypt during the mid-1930s branched out to reach industrial and rural workers. After having declared itself a

political party in 1936, it became more closely associated with Ali Mahir, one of the king's supporters. Late in the 1930s, its leaders were attracted to German Fascism as a strongly nationalistic ideology. Although they objected to German expansionism in Europe, they viewed Germany as a vehicle for their own liberation from Britain. In 1938 and 1939, the group addressed the Palestine question, an issue that previously had been of greater interest to the Muslim Brothers. In fact, Ali Mahir and Aziz Ali al-Misri pushed Young Egypt toward a merger with the Brothers. Exigencies of the war, however, removed the benefits to be derived from a union. The Muslim Brothers went on to lead the urban and rural Muslim middle and lower classes, while Young Egypt, after 1940 under the banner of the Islamic Nationalist Party, tried unsuccessfully to compete.

By the end of World War II, Young Egypt was focusing more on anti-imperialism and social reform. Although proclaiming itself as the Socialist Party of Egypt, it advocated the right to own private property. It concentrated on restricting the sizes of agricultural holdings so that more peasants could be property owners. In foreign policy, it became pro-Soviet in the expression of solidarity with the Koreans and Chinese. Many of Young Egypt's ideas later turned up in Gamal Abd al-Nasir's Egypt after having been adopted by the Egyptian mainstream of the early 1950s. Abd al-Nasir himself belonged to Young Egypt.

The Muslim Brothers The Muslim Brothers (al-Ikhwan al-Muslimun), founded by Dar al-Ulum-graduate Hasan al-Banna, won a much larger popular following than Young Egypt. They were able to do so by stressing from the outset disparities between rich and poor, particularly the foreign-oriented rich and the Muslim poor. Instead of focusing on political goals such as complete independence and withdrawal of British troops, the Ikhwan set about establishing institutions to serve the lower middle classes: schools, factories, mosques. During the mid-1930s

---

[1] James Jankowski, *Egypt's Young Rebels.* (Stanford: Hoover Institution, 1975), p. 14.

when other groups avoided action about Palestine, the Muslim Brothers sent food, supplies, and organizers there. Like the Wafd and Young Egypt, the Ikhwan established paramilitary groups called the Rovers and Battalions.

The heart and core of Muslim Brethren ideology, though, was in their affirmation of Islam as a comprehensive system appropriate to all times and places, and based firmly on the Quran and traditions. The Brothers viewed themselves as the heirs of the Salafiyya movement of the late nineteenth and early twentieth centuries—they were Islamic modernizers who drew their inspiration from their own heritage. Because of their belief in the universal applicability of Islam, the Brothers openly proclaimed that theirs was not only a religious, social, or political organization but also one involved in culture, education, business, and athletics. The political component, however, emerged on the eve of World War II as Ali Mahir and other palace politicians sought to use the Brothers as a weapon against the Wafd and later against the Left. Indeed the Ikhwan were to become the primary mass-based rival of the Wafd. The Ikhwan reached its apogee of influence right after the war; its ideas have remained part of the Egyptian political fabric.

The Accession of Faruq and the Anglo-Egyptian Treaty of 1936

While these movements were partial legacies of the Sidqi period, there were other reasons for their growth during the 1930s and 1940s. King Fu'ad had tried to rule rather than reign in Egypt, but in 1934 his health was failing fast. His son Faruq was still a teenager. Apparently, Fu'ad had concluded that his son ought to seek popular support rather than rely, as he himself had done, on a palace clique. The British were not anxious to restore a vigorous parliament; they preferred that the old group represented by Ali Mahir remain in power. Faced with apparent British resolve against restoring and consitution, the political parties formed a united front and demanded that the king reinstate it. After the king had agreed, the front indicated its willingness to reach a treaty agreement and requested a British commitment to negotiate in good faith. In April 1936, Fu'ad died and was succeeded by Faruq who excited the imagination of hopeful subjects.

The Wafd won the 1936 elections and embarked on securing the elusive treaty. The time was ripe because the Italian invasion of Ethiopia and expansionist ambitions in the Red Sea alarmed both Egyptian and British security concerns. In August 1936, agreement was reached on what could only be characterized as a treaty of alliance in which Egypt was definitely the junior partner. Militarily, British troops would be withdrawn to the Canal Zone. Within twenty years, the question of these troops would be decided upon by both parties. British forces were not to exceed 10,000 land-based and 400 air-based troops. Egypt would pay expenses for building roads and barracks for these troops, but Britain would pay rent for civilian accommodations and would subsidize construction of the others. As the British would be allowed to occupy the entire country, impose censorship, and establish martial law in wartime, these other provisions were designed as aids for the British, not the Egyptians. The treaty skirted the Sudan question although it restored unrestricted Egyptian immigration into Sudan and allowed Egyptian troops to enter Sudan if called upon by the British governor general.

What, then, did Egypt gain? Article 3 recognized Egypt as an independent, sovereign state to be sponsored for admission into the League of Nations by Britain; Articles 12 and 13 restored to Egypt control over foreigners and promised removal of the hated capitulations, to be accomplished through negotiations with other capitulatory powers. Although the Montreux Convention in 1937 brought about the international agreement, the old mixed courts were phased out gradually.

Foreigners were finally subject to Egyptian laws administered by Egyptians (Egypt promised them equal protection). Egypt also acquired full responsibility for safeguarding minorities. Of the four reservations of 1922, this last point is the only one the treaty altered in any substantial way.

Egypt agreed to the articles basically because they represented a change, however modest, in the status quo. Intellectuals like the Ahrar regarded the treaty as only a very small step in the continuing struggle for Egypt's independence. Even Nahhas, who headed the negotiating team, admitted that the treaty was not ideal but viewed it as the best that could be obtained. The British were willing to give up the outmoded idea of capitulations in exchange for facilities in case of what appeared to be an approaching war.

Restoration of Egypt's independence had constituted the primary goal of Egypt's politicians. Its alleged achievement meant that they had to address more fully the country's economic and social ills.

Economy and Society: Domination of the Upper Classes

Agriculture

Egypt was in fact fairly prosperous despite the onset of depressions in 1921, 1926, and 1930. Still overwhelmingly agricultural, it was increasingly vulnerable to changes on the world market because of dependence on cotton as a cash crop. Successive Egyptian governments were unable to develop policies to cushion the country against international fluctuations, mainly because they did not control the terms of trade. High cotton prices benefited the rich because, though they fueled inflation, these people could afford to pay. Poor people suffered because profits accrued to the landowners.

While large landowners were in the cash economy, Egyptian *fellahin* operated within a subsistence economy, and they

had little hope of escape. Even when depression threatened smaller landowners with foreclosures on loans and mortgages, the government stepped in to help out. But the poor in the countryside experienced little amelioration of their plight, perhaps because most politicians were landowners themselves. Poor people came to view Egyptian governments of this interwar period as no better than British colonial rule. This attitude is expressed intensely in Abd al-Rahman al-Sharqawi's novel about the period, *al-Ard* (*The Land*). Looking back, historians now see that overpopulation in the countryside, not obvious at the time to all but a few observers, began during this period.

Although diseases associated with perennial irrigation and lack of hygiene were rampant among the agricultural population of Egypt, these tended to debilitate rather than kill adults. Although infant mortality remained high, the birth rate more than compensated as children were valued as economic and social assets. Since the amount of land available for cultivation could not provide work for a growing population, the rural surplus began to seek employment in the cities. This movement in turn made the government more aware of the need for jobs. Industrial development seemed to hold out the best hope of making productive use of migrants from rural areas.

Industrial Expansion

Industry and business in general remained the province of foreigners and minorities. They owned the bulk of Egypt's debt and the Muslim oligarchy's external trade. The British continued to own the railroads, while French and British interests controlled the Suez Canal company. Jews in Egypt owned most of the large department stores and participated heavily in the stock market. The Greek and Italian communities, based mainly in Alexandria, were equally active. These urban elements have been immortalized by Lawrence Durrell whose *Alexandria Quartet* hardly mentions ethnic Egyptians except in very subservient roles.

Ethnic Egyptians, however, did begin to participate more fully in business and industry. By the end of World War II, their share in the country's economy was far greater than before. Tal'at Harb was the most important of the new capitalists. In 1920, he founded the Bank Misr (Bank of Egypt) which expanded into a group of industries involved in spinning, weaving, mining, petroleum, steamships, pharmaceuticals, cement, fisheries, river transport, and cinematography, among other things—all before World War II. Harb obtained some capital for his projects from Egyptian landowners, but tensions remained between indigenous business and agricultural elites. Ethnic Egyptians also entered the military academy to train as officers. The junior officers who launched the 1952 revolution were its graduates.

Labor Discontent

Just as landowners cared little about safeguarding the agricultural majority, so too did the industrialists devote scant attention to improving the lot of workers. The appeal of labor unionism grew as conditions worsened, especially during the depression of the 1930s. Although the government responded by granting worker's compensation for accidents and by passing protective measures for women, children, and those employed in dangerous industries, it rarely made any effort to enforce the law. Organizations such as the Muslim Brothers used the general discontent to arouse support for their own goals. The government did not actually recognize the numerous unions until World War II when strikes by transport and textile workers, among others, threatened to disrupt the wartime economy, already characterized by high inflation. Labor unrest was difficult to ignore because most factories were located in and around Cairo and Alexandria. In 1944, new labor legislation was passed recognizing that employers had obligations to workers in regard to working conditions, health and safety, and payment of wages.

Four years later, following the outbreak of labor demonstrations arising from postwar unemployment, the government took responsibility for arbitrating industrial disputes. Although industry was still largely under foreign or minority ownership, many ethnic Egyptians—men and women, as well as minorities or foreigners—were employed in factories, especially in areas that had a tradition of industrial work dating back to Muhammad Ali's textile factories. These Egyptians could identify more with Egyptian than with foreign capitalists, but when their own interests were at stake, they did not hesitate to strike.

Intellectual Trends: The Era of Liberalism

Occasionally, intellectuals like the Coptic Fabian socialist Salama Musa involved themselves with the problems of rural and urban workers. Not only interested in social justice, Musa thought that western culture would provide the key to social reform. In particular, he advocated the spread of secular education and the types of clothing changes being introduced in Iran and Turkey. Musa favored a Latinized alphabet and the replacement of literary Arabic by the vernacular. He was not alone in supporting these language proposals; they were vigorously debated in the Arabic Language Academy, an elite group of twenty scholars of all nationalities founded in the early 1930s and modeled after the Academie Francaise.

Language, however, did not arouse nearly as much controversy as did questions relating to nationality, religion, and culture. Authors such as Taha Husayn and Ali Abd al-Raziq created an uproar when they suggested that religious texts could be challenged as to their veracity or that the caliphate might not be essential to the practice of Islam. Although their books were banned, their ideas reached the intended audience, forcing believers to go back to the sources for a fresh look. Teacher and writer Tantawi Jawhari wrote a pioneering commentary on the Quran in which he addressed questions raised by modern science. These authors tried to show Muslims that application of critical thought was in tune with Islam.

Egyptian feminists, especially Huda al-Sha'rawi and Ceza Nabarawi, pressed for legal and social equality, especially for equality of education and employment opportunities. Through the Egyptian Feminist Union, Wafdist Women's Committee, and the *Egyptienne* (1925–40; a feminist magazine), they focused both on women's rights, health care, and on political demands shared with urban males, including prison reform, homes for the old and disabled, and controls over polygamy and divorce. The movement was not broadly based and it achieved only limited political success. But women activists of the 1940s were among the first to respond to a serious cholera epidemic.

The liberal mainstream among intellectuals was largely sympathetic to women's rights. They also embraced the issues of secularism, Egyptian nationalism, and individual freedom. It sought an intellectually free society liberated from the tyranny of rulers when most people were concerned about coping with daily life free from upper-class oppression. Lutfi al-Sayyid attended the opening ceremonies of Hebrew University in Jerusalem and praised it as an achievement because he was an educator imbued with liberal values. Not suprisingly, when the Palestine revolt broke out in 1936, it was not the intellectuals but the Muslim Brothers led by an Arabic teacher who raised funds for its support. By looking to needs of their Arabic-speaking neighbors, the Ikhwan helped raise the consciousness of their more inward-looking compatriots of Egypt. At the same time, they renewed the association of Islam with social justice.

Wartime Occupation: Social Protest

World War II in Egypt brought ferment and change in many areas of life. In accordance with treaty obligations, Egypt was placed under martial law and censorship. Perhaps half a million British and American troops passed through Egypt during the war. Relations with Germany and Italy were broken. Early German victories in the war, however, created discontent, especially early in 1942 when Germans were approaching Egypt's population centers. Many Egyptians looked upon a German victory as a key to Egypt's liberation from Britain. After pro-Rommel demonstrations in early February 1942, the British government told Faruq that he must appoint a popular Wafdist government. When the king hesitated, the British surrounded the palace with tanks and forced his acquiescence. In the long run, both Wafdist leader Nahhas and King Faruq suffered. The Wafd had allowed itself to be used as a weapon to demoralize the young king. Soon, the British would undermine the Wafdists, too. In 1944, the Sa'dists formed a new government. The tide in the war had turned by that time in favor of Britain.

Wartime and growing involvement of the entire Arab world in the Palestine question inspired leaders to begin discussing postwar plans. Old Arab nationalists such as Nuri al-Sa'id of Iraq still thought in terms of large Arab state embracing the former greater Syria and Iraq. Saudi Arabia, Egypt, and Yemen emerged as supporters of an association of sovereign states. In 1944, a document called the Alexandria Protocol set up the framework for the League of Arab States (Arab League) that came into being the following year. From its foundation, the group's attention was focused on Palestine.

In general, the British used their powers during the war to crack down on dissidents in Egypt, especially on Axis sympathizers. They also encouraged industrial expansion to help the war effort. Anwar al-Sadat, a young army officer at the time, was among those imprisoned for anti-British activities.

An industry that expanded during the war was the Egyptian cinema. In contrast to the critically acclaimed social dramas produced after the revolution, the wartime and early postwar films were comedies, farces, musicals, and melodramas, designed to help people cope with daily frustrations. Between 1945 and 1948, an average of fifty-five films per year emerged from Egyptian studios.

The wartime occupation also fueled inflation, urban prostitution, and social disruption (poignantly described in Nagib Mahfuz's *Midaq Alley*).[2] Obviously, the war brought wealth to profiteers, but disparities between rich and poor kept increasing. The Muslim Brothers and others decried the spread of immorality and corruption. The unpopularity of the war was further illustrated by the assassination of Prime Minister Ahmad Mahir on 24 February 1945. The killing took place as he was reading to parliament Egypt's declaration of war on the Axis. Although a young man in the Watan Party was apprehended, the crime epitomized an increasingly widespread expectation of future turmoil in Egypt.

Sudan Between Britain and Egypt

The interwar period in Sudan marked the rise of Sudanese nationalism. An indigenous administration incorporated tribal chiefs, and Sudan expanded its agricultural potential in the Gezira region. The British even before 1924 were determined to remain the condominium's senior partners. While Egypt insisted that there was no difference between its people and those in Sudan, the British went out of their way to accentuate not only Egyptian-Sudanese differences but also those dividing northern from southern Sudanese. In the south, British authorities permitted Christian missions to operate at will, hoping to dilute Arabic and Islamic influences. Administration of the south was kept separate and retained tribal divisions. During the period, *al-Hadara* (*Civilization*) functioned as the country's only Arabic newspaper and as a mouthpiece for the government's programs and policies. The newspaper emphasized Sudan's uniqueness and benefits of the British administration.

Despite the suppression of Mahdism in the late nineteenth century, traditional religious elites remained strong. The country's two main religious leaders were Sayyid Ali al-Mirghani, head of the Khatmiyya religious order, the Sayyid Abd al-Rahman al-Mahdi, posthumous son of the Mahdi. These men tended to uphold the British position throughout most of the period, avoiding discussions between Egypt and Britain about Sudan's future. The Khatmiyya, however, remained more favorable to retaining Egyptian ties. The Mahdists, after all, had initially sought independence from Egypt and its Turko-Circassian ruling classes.

Sudan's New Elites and Pro-Egyptian Sentiment

New elites who had graduated from Gordon College or the Military School, both of which had Egyptian teachers, were far more attracted to Egyptian culture and viewpoints. Since the administration needed their skills, their careers were not obstructed by Egyptians. Moreover, they did not recall hardships of Egyptian rule during the nineteenth century.

They established in Omdurman the first postwar political group. Called the Sudanese Union Society, it attracted many future leaders of Sudan and organized a propaganda campaign to support Nile Valley unity and to oppose *al-Hadara's* views. In 1923 some of its members, including leader Ubayd Haj al-Amin, left the organization to join the recently established White Flag League. The founder of the group, a second lieu-

---

[2] Naguib Mahfouz, *Midaq Alley* (trans. Trevor Le Gassick), (London: Heinemann, 1975).

aid to insure peace within Sudan. By war's end, they acknowledged that Sayyid Abd al-Rahman had become a political leader. His Ansar were to find expression in his Umma Party, founded in 1945. The Umma Party backed gradualist measures recommended by the Sudan government. Sayyid Ali emerged as a supporter of al-Azhari's party, the Ashiqqa (Brothers), that had opted for a program of cooperation with Egypt.

Call for Self-determination

Prior to the political split, the Congress in 1942 sent a memorandum (after consultations with the two religious leaders) to the Sudan government calling for self-determination as soon as the war was over, unification of education in northern and southern Sudan, cessation of immigration except under the Anglo-Egyptian Treaty of 1936, promulgation of legislation defining Sudanese nationality, allowance of free movement for Sudanese within Sudan, creation of a judiciary separated from the executive, Sudanese control over the economy and administration, formation of a Sudanese legislature, and

imposition of restriction on companies' hiring so that Sudanese would receive a far share of jobs. The memorandum also asked the government to halt subsidies for missionary schools. The government rejected the proposal and the authority of those who issued it. As in the case of other war allies, the Sudanese nationalists tried to reason with the government but to no avail. British hostility encouraged the split between supporters of ongoing dialogue with the government and advocates of militant action in favor of self-determination.

For the most part, then, Sudanese elites during the interwar period focused on organizing efforts to build confidence among the population and the administration. Suffering from feelings of inferiority backed by British attitudes and policies, and by Egypt's often patronizing stance, Sudanese strove to provide the educational and intellectual basis on which they could achieve both respect and a greater role in the government. Both traditional elites and the new elites focused on negotiation and cooperation rather than on confrontation as a means to these ends.

Colonization in Libya

Sanussi Resistance

Intensive Italian colonization characterized the interwar period in Libya. Sanussi forces fought the occupation until 1932. In Tripolitania, the battle lasted only a few years because other groups, notably the Sayf al-Nasr chiefs who felt that Sanussis had usurped their authority in Fazzan, did not back them. Cyrenaica proved to be a different story. Although most Sanussi leaders either arranged deals with the Italians or left the country, the troops fought on in their name. The banner of the Sanussiyya was raised as a symbol of freedom by individuals fighting to preserve their homes and way of life.

How did they hold out for so long? First of all, they could elude the Italians because their tribal organization often concealed those actually involved in the fighting. Secondly, they taxed themselves to pay for the war. Thirdly, they received supplies from Egypt. The only way Italy defeated them was by mounting an offensive on the entire population of Cyrenaica. Libyans were rounded up and placed in concentration. Umar al-Mukhtar, the resistance leader, was caught and hanged in September 1931, and by 1932 the war was over.

While the war raged on in Cyrenaica, the Italians under Count Volpi began developing their colonization program in

Tripolitania. Volpi was an early supporter of Italian dictator Benito Mussolini. A financier, he set up a modest program designed to increase Italian investment in the local economy. He expropriated lands held collectively by tribal groups, and sold them under concessional arrangements to Italian businessmen. Whereas previous settlers had been obliged to possess substantial capital, Volpi's program created a public domain to which Italians with more modest resources could gain access.

Italy's "Fourth Shore"

From 1925 to 1929, Libya's governor was General De Bono, who had reservations about encouraging colonization involving large landowners. Mussolini visited Libya in 1926. He decided to approve De Bono's decision to dispossess Libyans of the best lands and give them to colonists. Expropriated lands could be sold only to Italians. The indigenes lacked legal knowledge and could not easily defend against seizures. Because the Italians decided cases in advance, even educated Libyans could rarely retain their property. Individuals or groups obtained inadequate payments in compensation. After the loss of land, Libyans could only lease it or hire themselves out as wage laborers. Lost in dreams of the Roman North Africa of antiquity—Italy's fourth shore—the Italians somehow expected to reconstitute the area as part of a new Italian empire.

Despite the offering of incentives to Italian colonists from 1928 on, the main push for colonization still lay in the future. General Badoglio (1929–34) tried to eliminate unprofitable concessions granted in previous years. He then moved in the direction of social reform, perhaps because Libyan resistance had ended. Libya's primary empire builder was his successor Italo Balbo, governor from 1934 until his death in a plane crash in 1940. Balbo viewed Italian colonization in Libya as providing the best solution for Italy's population crisis. He assumed that in the long run, Italy's peasant farmers would

prosper in Libya and promote its full integration into Italy. In order to achieve his goal of bringing 100,000 colonists to Libya, Balbo mounted a propaganda campaign. It achieved only limited results, though, because it was inaugurated on the eve of war in 1938.

With his aggressive push for colonization, Balbo built up Libya's infrastructure. He constructed an east-west highway to facilitate both expansion and population control. His efforts resulted in building modern Tripoli and many new villages. Italian archeologists began excavation in Leptis Magna on the Libyan coast. Despite the focus on Italians, Balbo did not ignore Libyans. Unlike the French in Algeria, Balbo upheld Muslim law and institutions. He even encouraged and facilitated participation in the *hajj*. New mosques and schools were built. Although the schools were Italian, students took Islamic courses taught in Arabic. The governor also for the first time offered lands to Libyans. But Balbo assumed that he was creating Muslims who would admire and respect Italian civilization.

World War II in Libya: Consequences of Italy's Defeat

There is no denying that Balbo's policies allowed the new Italian colonists to prosper. In 1939, Italy and Libya were formally united. But Italy's colonial enterprise in Libya was destined for failure because of the Italian defeat in World War II. In 1940, Sayyid Idris in Egypt decided that the British were going to win the war and should receive as much Sanussi help as he could rally. In 1941, the British conquered Banghazi but were pushed back by Rommel's Africa campaign. After the turnaround at al-Alamayn, the British regained eastern Libya. By January 1943, they were also able to take Tripoli and eventually join forces with Anglo-American troops in Tunisia. Meanwhile a Free French force had taken up positions in the south and along the Tunisian frontier at Ghadamis. Separate administrations for Tripoli and

Cyrenaica were established by the British, while the French encouraged Sayf al-Nasr separatism in Fazzan.

Having seen the opportunity provided by the Italian defeat, Libyan leaders began to plan for independence. But Libya lacked both a well-organized nationalist movement and any traditional rule other than that of the Sanussis and the Tripolitanian elites. The postwar National Front focused on creating an independent Cyrenaica under Muhammad Idris, while the Umar al-Mukhtar Society aimed at uniting Tripolitania and Cyrenaica. More cautious supporters of Idris feared that the urban proponents of unity would overwhelm them if the two groups joined forces, especially because the Tripolitanians were more involved in inter-Arab nationalism. In fact, Tripolitanians had begun agitating on their own because of Italian efforts to retain the territory. In their view, a united Libya was to be formed. Although they still lacked enthusiasm for Sanussi overrule, they recognized that only through accepting Sayyid Muhammad Idris as their ruler would they have a good chance of thwarting Italian designs.

For their own part, many Cyrenaicans regarded these Tripolitanians as opportunists. Despite having obtained the support of key western nations for retaining Tripolitania, the Italians saw their partition plan—with Britain receiving Cyrenaica; France, Fazzan; and Italy, Tripolitania—defeated by the United Nations General Assembly, which rejected the idea of trusteeship for Libya. The vote in May 1949 paved the way for Libyan independence.

Conclusion

The struggle for statehood in Iran and Turkey meant forging a strong independent nation in a new international context. Egypt achieved only modest success in eliminating British control, while in Sudan the separation from Egypt helped to promote Sudanese nationalism but with a strong cultural affinity with Egypt. Libya, with its tiny population compared to the others, was still in the throes of colonization but nevertheless achieved independence early in the postwar period. In all cases, the course of international affairs limited the ability of nationalist elites to direct internal developments. In Turkey and Iran, military leaders had inspired national resurgence. Postwar Egypt, Sudan, and Libya were to be characterized ultimately by the same development.

CHAPTER TWELVE

The Struggle for Statehood in the Arab East

Between the wars, much of the Arab east was placed under British and French tutelage. While Syria and Lebanon were ruled under a French mandate, Iraq like Egypt found itself semi-independent. Transjordan, poor and mainly homogenous, functioned as a mandate under British supervision. (Palestine is treated in Chapter 13.) Although much of Arabia was united under the Saudis, the Gulf remained divided into shaykhdoms ruled by traditional authorities under British protection. In southern Arabia, the British base at Aden was viewed as a threat by neighboring independent Yemen. The British, however, never seriously challenged Yemeni independence during this period. Oman also had a treaty relationship with Britain.

Syria and Lebanon: France's Divide–and–Rule Policies

The interwar period under the mandate in Syria and Lebanon was one of general well-being for elites, of nationalist frustration and division, and of popular discontent. Shortly after defeating the nationalist government, France set about organizing its divide and rule administration of Syria. Nearly one half of Syria's population consisted of religious and ethnic minorities: Shi'a, Druze, Kurds, Alawis, Maronites, and Armenians. The mandate authorized France to render "advice and assistance to the population" and "to further enact measures to facilitate the progressive development of Syria and the Lebanon as independent states."[1] France was obliged to see "that no part of the territory of Syria and the Lebanon is ceded or leased or in any way placed under the control of a foreign Power." To safeguard Syria's cultural heritage, France was charged with drawing up and enforcing an antiquities law to regulate archeological expeditions and disposition of their finds. Religious missions functioned with few constraints. The territory was to be governed by an organic law to be written within three years.

Administrative and Political Divisions in Syria

The early division of Syria, however, created an initial obstacle for the smooth functioning of political life. Sunni Muslims opposed the division at the outset, campaigning for unity, independence, and Arab unity. They viewed all Syrians as Arabs. After an initial separation lasting until 1925, the main areas of Syria, including Damascus and Aleppo, were joined together to form the state of Syria.

The principal political party of the period in Syria was the National Bloc, an amorphous group of bourgeois elements and landowners. Their main platform demanded complete independence and support for Arab nationalism. One of the Bloc's more autonomous parties was the Istiqlal (Independence) Party that maintained branches in other countries. Early in the 1930s, an ideologically oriented party emerged for the first time: the Parti Populaire Syrien (P.P.S.) Active in both Syria and Lebanon, the P.P.S. (founded and led by a Greek Orthodox Lebanese born in Brazil—Antun Sa'ada)—advo-

cated union of greater Syria, strict separation of church and state, abolition of oppressive land tenure, and unity of the people, regardless of religion, ethnicity, language, and nationality. Neither in Syria nor in Lebanon did the party win much support except among the Greek Orthodox, but its activities appealed to Lebanese communities overseas.

In creating separate administrations for Jabal Druze, Latakia, Jazira, and Alexandretta, and by cutting off Lebanon entirely, France claimed to protect minority rights. Latakia State, for example, contained the bulk of the Alawis whose beliefs combined Shi'ism with Christian and Persian practices and holidays. Based in the mountains around Latakia, the Alawis had managed over the centuries to preserve their customs and beliefs. Coastal cities such as Latakia port were populated by Sunni Muslims who were wealthier and who employed Alawis in subservient positions. Although their separation delayed their integration into the Syrian mainstream, the Alawis benefited from France's policy of encouraging education, communications, improved health care, and agricultural assistance. Many joined the army as a vehicle for upward mobility. Syria's most durable president of the post-World War II period—Hafiz al-Asad (1970–)—is an Alawi army officer.

In the Jabal Druze, a member of the prominent al-Atrash family took up the governorship early in the mandate. But upon his death, the Druze turned to a French army officer. By 1925, his administration had become so high-handed that the Druze arose in revolt. In the initial stages, the Druze led by Sultan al-Atrash defeated French forces in the area. General discontent in southern Syria and Lebanon fueled protests elsewhere. After the French suppressed the rebellion in Damascus by bombings that killed over one thousand people, and the revolt by 1927 had petered out, the authority of traditional leaders in Jabal Druze was restored. France ceased to interfere in Druze society.

In the Jazira (eastern Syria), an auton-

---

[1] *Mandate for Syria and Lebanon* (Geneva: League of Nations, 1922) and *Mandate for Palestine* (Geneva: League of Nations, 1922) are referred to here and in Chapter 13. The text of the former is found in most histories of Syria listed in the bibliography. Hurewitz, *Middle East and North Africa,* vol. 2, pp. 305–310, contains the text of the Palestine mandate.

omous administration arose from the existence of an assortment of ethnic and religious minorities—principally Kurds, Assyrians, Armenians, Syrian Catholics, and Syrian Jacobites (Monophysites). Like Kurds elsewhere, those in Syria desired an independent Kurdistan. At the very least, since the French were promoting ethnicity, the Kurds wanted official recognition of their language in predominantly Kurdish areas. The Christian groups, largely refugees from persecution, tended to maintain a low profile and create new lives for themselves. Alexandretta received special status because of its large Turkish population. Turkish was among its three official languages.

Enlargement of Lebanon and Introduction of the Confessional System

In the Lebanon, the French hoped to secure their position by appending predominantly Muslim areas—now north and south Lebanon, the Biqa Valley, and Beirut—to the former area protected by Ottoman charter after 1861. Together, these areas were twice the size of the old region. Not surprisingly, their populations wanted to join Syria. By attaching these territories to Lebanon, France assured that the Maronites who had dominated the old Mount Lebanon would remain dependent on the French for protection against inclusion in a greater Syria where they would be overwhelmed.

In 1926, a constitution was adopted, establishing the Republic of Lebanon and incorporating the system of proportional and confessional representation. The unwritten National Pact of 1943 made this system part of the political setup after independence. In the bicameral legislature, seats were apportioned according to religious affiliation, not by party membership or ideology. This arrangement was based on the assumption that it was religious identity that would exercise the strongest influence on political behavior. The legislature elected the president.

With power to appoint cabinets and dismiss parliament, the president would also choose the prime minister. Based on accepted proportions of the various religious divisions within the population, the presidency would go to a Maronite, the premiership to a Sunni Muslim, the speakership of the Chamber of Deputies to a Shi'i Muslim, and other positions to members of smaller communities such as the Greek Orthodox and the Druze.

The confessional system did not preclude formation of blocs that crossed confessional lines. Leaders (*zu'ama*) representing the principal families among the landed aristocracy in different regions of the country formed political lists to contest the elections. They tried to win to their side members of minorities within their geographical areas, promising delivery of services in exchange for their support. In any one district, rival leaders bid for and secured the support of smaller groups, thereby promoting rivalries within small areas. In 1932, two large blocs were constituted, both led by Maronites but comprising other religious groups.

The National Bloc, despite its name, was not associated with the one in Syria. In fact, it propounded Lebanese rather then Arab nationalist goals. Its leader Emile Eddé typified those Maronites who felt more at home with the French than with their fellow Arab neighbors. The Constitutional Bloc under the leadership of Bishara al-Khuri, later independent Lebanon's first president, pursued a course more like that of the National Bloc in Syria, aiming toward eventual reunification and the diminution of French influence. Both groups, however, depended on loyalty to their zu'ama and secondary leaders, not to particular ideologies or platforms.

Expansion of French Influence in Syria and Lebanon

The French administered both Syria and Lebanon from Beirut. They were represented by a high commissioner who held absolute power and his own cabinet, independent of the indigenous governments. As in the Maghrib, special officers circulated in the countryside to keep the high commissioner in touch with local opinion and the indigenes in touch with the administration. The French centralized services including customs, currency, utilities, and communications.

Economic and cultural development in Syria and Lebanon under the mandate favored extension of ties with France. French diplomatic services were at the disposal of Syrians and Lebanese. Education became an important vehicle for spreading French culture. Particularly in Lebanon, and among Maronites, obtaining higher education in France or at the Université de St. Joseph was preferred. The pre-mandate American institutions continued to attract members of different religious groups because of policies that encouraged Arab culture. The fact that education in Syria and Lebanon remained largely sectarian, however, promoted separate development of minorities and impeded both national unity and eventual reunification of Syria and Lebanon.

In the economic sphere, the French deliberately furthered Syrian and Lebanese dependency. At a time when independent countries in the region were trying to free themselves of foreign control over utilities, communications, and finance, the French in Syria and Lebanon established themselves in these areas. Extension of the communications networks facilitated both economic penetration and population control. Roads were built to the previously more remote parts of the territory. Beirut port, modernized in 1937, expanded the city's commercial role. Buses going from Syria to Iraq began operating. French-owned concerns dominated principal sectors of the economy. With the influx of manufactured goods from France, local cottage industries again suffered.

The French brought in experts to assist in developing the country's infrastructure. Agronomists advised on crops and produce, especially on varieties of cotton. Land surveys were carried out to recommend modes of land utilization and alloca-

tion of water resources. The antiquities service came into being but did not always protect Syrian interests. A French Institute in Damascus promoted French scholarship.

Did the mandate fulfill its goals? Agitation for independence continued both in Syria and in Lebanon. The French in Syria held elections in 1927 that were won by the National Bloc. Although Lebanon had already been declared a republic with a constitution, the Syrians did not obtain such recognition until the high commissioner decreed it in 1930. People in Syria and Lebanon viewed these documents as inadequate because France's administrators still ran the country. In 1932, the high commissioner suspended Lebanon's constitution because of demonstrations. Two years later, a new document dispensed with proportional representation in the chamber of deputies and eroded the legislature's already limited powers.

Renegotiation of the Mandate: Failure and Frustration

The Socialists who came to power in France in 1936 were more willing to revise the terms of government in Syria and Lebanon. Neither of the subsequent treaties negotiated satisfied nationalists in either Syria and Lebanon or in France. The draft treaty with Syria (1936), intended to last for twenty-five years, reunited Syria. French troops would remain in Latakia and Jabal Druze. Although France retained control over defense and foreign affairs, Syria was to be sponsored for admission into the League of Nations. Syria agreed to honor any obligations France undertook on its behalf. The treaty met with Syrian approval and ratification because, although it still left Syria in a state of semi-independence, it rejoined the various parts of the country (including Alexandretta but not Lebanon or areas under the British) and gave Syria an international forum for airing future disputes. Nationalists disapproved of the continued presence of French troops; French colonialists complained of insufficient guarantees for minorities. The Franco-Syrian treaty resulted in the conclusion of a similar separate agreement with Lebanon.

After Syria had ratified the draft treaty, a new French government came to power but was opposed to the concessions granted by the Socialists. Syrians, led by Shukri al-Quwatli, refused new demands presented by the French who then abandoned the treaty. The French also turned down the treaty with Lebanon. For a short time, however, the provisions of the treaty were put into effect, placing previously autonomous regions of Syria under Syrian rule. Appointment of Syrian officials from outside the region provoked revolts in Kurdish and Druze areas in 1937, and among the Druze and Alawis in 1939. Arab nationalists of the Syrian government blamed French administrators for having promoted separate development in these regions. The rejection of the draft treaty in France eventually provided the French with an excuse for detaching Alexandretta from Syria and for reconstituting the various subdivisions in Syria. In Lebanon, despite restoration of the 1926 constitution, direct administration was also reimposed.

Instead of preparing Syria and Lebanon for independence, then, France in many ways perpetuated the old Ottoman administration's negative characteristics without introducing or even preserving measures of responsible government. Education, communications, health, and even agriculture to some extent had all received attention from the Ottomans. What they Syrians desired after World War I was complete independence. What they ended up with instead was a regime that aimed to consolidate its hold over the territory in contravention of the mandate authorizing its presence.

Could an independent Arab government have won the loyalty of local leaders in the autonomous areas? Perhaps if an independent government had included all elements in the population on an equal basis at the outset, then a united Syria might have emerged in the mandate period. The French would still have won the respect for French culture but they would have also achieved gratitude for having fulfilled their obligations. Instead they received opprobrium for having suppressed emergence of a strong, united Syria.

Though the French administration was often repressive, arbitrary, and high-handed, both Damascus and Beirut maintained universities that provided forums for limited debate. Early in the 1920s, the Syrians set up a language academy in contact with linguists elsewhere in the Arabic-speaking world. Their concern was to adapt Arabic to contemporary realities. Although Egypt, Iraq, and Syria were separated politically, they continually interacted as they had in earlier historical periods. One of the most prominent early writers on Arab nationalism was Abu Khaldun Sati al-Husri, born in Aleppo, whose early career had been spent as an Ottoman and Turkish educational official. During World War I he supported the efforts of Faysal to form an Arab state in Syria. When the French crushed it, he followed Faysal to Iraq, serving as head of education. But Syria remained a center of Arab nationalism.

Syria's Role in Inter-Arab Affairs

In 1937, following the promulgation of the Peel Commission's partition plan for Palestine (See Chapter 13), the Arab National Congress met in Bludan, Syria to discuss its consequences. When the Arab Higher Committee of Palestine was suppressed, it was to Damascus that its leaders fled. The British in Palestine were so worried about what they termed "infiltration" from Syria that they built a wall along the Syrian border. In 1945, when the Arab League had begun to play an active role in organizing Palestinians whose leadership had been dispersed, it was the Syrian Jamil Mardam who was most influential in reconstituting the Palestine leadership into a consultative body. This active role in Palestinian and inter-Arab affairs underscores the affinities and relationships shared by Arabic speakers during the mandate period. Although the imperialist divisions of World War I survived despite political independence, individuals sustained and perpetuated their cultural and intellectual ties. Moreover, many Levantine Arabs continued to feel that Syria, Lebanon, Palestine, and Transjordan were components of a Syria that Europeans had partitioned against their will.

The Syrian and Lebanese Independence Struggles

During World War II, Syria and Lebanon found themselves caught in the struggles between the British, the Vichy French, and the Free French, especially after France fell in 1940. In 1941, fearing that a pro-German movement might jeopardize regimes in Egypt, Palestine, and Iraq, the British joined with Free French troops in a successful invasion of Syria and Lebanon. Charles de Gaulle, leader of the Free French, proclaimed that the new armies were liberators who would allow the populations to become independent, either as a single unit or as two states.

Instead de Gaulle allowed the local French commander Catroux to perpetuate the largely colonial role that had characterized the previous regime. In 1943, the French were pressured by Britain into permitting free elections in both Syria and Lebanon. When anti-French pro-independence forces swept to victory, they insisted that the French hand over the administration and put an end to French-owned monopolies. France continued to insist that only the League of Nations could end its mandate and that the new governments grant preferential rights to French interests in any final settlement.

On 11 November 1943, Catroux responded to the Lebanese parliament's removal of all constitutional restrictions on

sovereignty by jailing President Bishara al-Khuri, Prime Minister Riyad al-Sulh, and most cabinet members. Emile Eddé accepted appointment as head of state, thereby discrediting himself with the nationalist body politic. A combination of demonstrations and Anglo-American pressure forced the French to release the detainees on 23 November. This date is now celebrated as Lebanon's Independence Day.

Political leaders in Lebanon then agreed to the National Pact that had two dimensions: the Muslims acquiesced to a theoretical Christian majority in Lebanon; and in exchange the Christians recognized Lebanon's integration into the Arab rather than French sphere. France in 1943 also attempted to suppress the independent parliament in Syria that had elected Shukri al-Quwatli as its president. By late 1944, Syrians and Lebanese had assumed control of much of the administrative apparatus, but de Gaulle was not yet ready to depart from Syria and Lebanon (he feared increasing pressure on France's North African colonies). On 27 February 1945, both Syria and Lebanon declared war on Germany and Japan, thereby prompting an invitation to attend the founding conference of the United Nations. Both countries also joined the Arab League inaugurated in March 1945. In May, though, de Gaulle landed new French troops in Lebanon.

It is still unclear why de Gaulle attempted to perpetuate French rule in Syria and Lebanon when French allies had voiced such strong support for their independence. Even Francophile nationalists were antagonized by de Gaulle's demands for French economic and political supremacy. By landing forces, France provoked an uprising. When France bombed Damascus, about four hundred civilians were killed. Britain, with the support of the United States, obliged France to desist only by threatening to fight on behalf of Syria and Lebanon. Despite recognition of their independence by most countries by mid-1946, Syria and Lebanon remained occupied until late in the year.

Iraq and Transjordan under Anglo–Hashimite Rule

Most people in the entities that became Transjordan and Iraq would have preferred inclusion in some larger entity—the Arabs in an independent Arab state and the Kurds in a Kurdish state. Still, local leaders in these regions accepted the installation of two Hashimite rulers. The demise of the independent Arab government in Damascus brought about the return to Iraq of Arab nationalists including Nuri al-Sa'id and Sati al-Husri. The Amir Faysal was chosen King of Iraq by the Iraqi Council of State that met in July 1921. The Iraqi mandated territory consisted of a population comprised of Kurds in the north, rural Shi'i and Sunni Arabs in the south (though mainly Shi'i), urban Sunni and Shi'i, and minorities such as the remnants of the ancient Jewish communities. Arab nationalist sentiment was found mainly among urban Sunnis.

Many Shi'is favored setting up an Islamic theocracy. Leaders of local groups preferred whatever regime would preserve the greatest measure of independence for them. The wartime British administration and its successor, however, fostered a kind of national unity that allowed for a temporary shelving of differences and an agreement on the new Arab kingdom. The task before Faysal and his government was to forge a nation in which Iraqi national aspirations could be reconciled with local interests.

State Structure Under the Anglo-Iraqi Treaty of 1922

The Anglo-Iraqi Treaty of 1922 differed from the mandates for Syria and Lebanon in that the Iraqis were allowed some control over foreign affairs and a much more localized internal administration. The most powerful official in the state was the British high commissioner and consul general, who held responsibility for financial, foreign, judicial, and military matters. Iraq agreed to accept only British advisors if foreigners were to be brought in. Until the country had a parliament, the treaty could not be approved.

A Constitutioned Monarchy

In 1923, an Iraqi assembly met to discuss a constitution and to consider the treaty. Despite strong opposition by nationalists, the treaty won approval because many members abstained or remained absent. Iraq became a constitutional monarchy. The constitution gave the king broad powers—the right to issue laws, to appoint members of the upper chamber (senate) of the bicameral legislature, to decide when the legislature should meet, to approve all government appointments, and to act as commander-in-chief of the armed forces.

The legislature, the lower house of which was elected, voted on laws. The state's official language was to be Arabic and its official religion Islam, but Christians and Jews as in the millet system retained the right to be judged in certain matters by their own religious courts. Only male taxpayers could vote for representatives in the legislature. Through this requirement, only urban Sunnis, urban Shi'a, and tribal shaykhs could vote. Because they would have been overwhelmed by the predominantly Muslim electorate, Christians and Jews gained special representatives, but the Kurds, who were an ethnic rather than a religious minority, received no special status.

The New Intelligentsia and the Old Oligarchy

Iraq's early leaders represented the first generation of Arab nationalists—men who had fought with Faysal during World War I and its aftermath. By allying with former Hashimite supporters and army officers, Faysal institutionalized nationalism. Army officers constituted a sizable part of the country's new intelligentsia because the most available form of higher education within the Ottoman system had been military education. While less than seventy men had graduated from nonmilitary colleges in Istanbul and Beirut between 1900 and 1917, over 1,200 had completed education at the military college in Istanbul between 1872 and 1912. Since Iraq's population was only about 2.5 million after the war, these military men formed a thin elite layer drawn mostly from the Sunni middle classes. Shi'is had not attended these schools because they regarded the Ottomans as infidels. The military education of this elite predisposed its members to military solutions to society's problems. Faysal gave these supporters land grants early in the postwar period, thereby co-opting them into the old landed classes. For reasons of stability, the British supported this old order.

Yet the new government could not be described as particularly stable. In the administration, British officials received higher salaries than their Iraqi supervisors; this led to resentment. Because the well-to-do parliament represented only a narrow segment of society, Iraq like Egypt was actually governed by an oligarchy that had vested interests in the system. The king functioned as a check on its power only because he was popular and dedicated to national unity. The system did not effectively embrace either the Kurds in the north or the Shi'i Arab majority in the south. Iraqi elites, like their neighbors, preoccupied themselves with achieving a complete and genuine independence.

British Policy in Iraq

During the 1920s, the British won control over the former Turkish Petroleum Company, aiming to exploit its oil concession in Mosul. To do so, however, they needed to assure that it would be joined to Iraq, not Turkey. In the arguments over Mosul, neither Britain nor Iraq nor Turkey admitted that the region's inhabitants were Kurds who had sought their own independent state. The League of Nations supported the British-Iraqi claims. Historians agree that Britain's influence assured that Mosul would be incorporated into Iraq. Into the League of Nations' agreements Britain wrote guarantees for Kurdish rights, including recognition of the Kurdish language and employment of Kurds in the region's administration and schools. The assumption was that these rights would insure stability for British oil interests. The Iraqi government proceeded to grant the T.P.C. a concession. The British could now afford to consider Iraqi demands for a new treaty that would grant the country full independence.

Under the terms of the Treaty of 1930, Iraq and Britain signed a twenty-five-year alliance. Britain would support Iraq's admission to the League of Nations. Iraq would grant Britain use of air bases near Baghdad and Basra, all services and facilities in case of war, diplomatic precedence, and the right to move and supply troops in peacetime. Britain promised Iraq military assistance in exchange. The treaty followed the pattern established by Britain in relations with Egypt and Transjordan. As in the other cases, Iraq was not an equal partner in the arrangement, but parliament ratified it notwithstanding. Within two years, Iraq's independence was achieved, but as in Egypt, Britain retained considerable control over foreign affairs and military policy.

During the mandate, the new intelligentsia expanded because of increased civilian education. Between 1921 and 1940, equal numbers graduated from military and nonmilitary institutions. Shi'a entered the ranks of this intelligentsia for the first time, but the officer corps of the army remained almost devoid of them. During the 1930s, worldwide depression produced unemployment among educated Iraqis, especially among lawyers. Government layoffs occurred because Iraq's exports had declined and taxes could not be collected. The dividends reaped by these years were the military coups and counter-coups that took place between 1936 and 1941.

Politics and Power in Iraq

What was the nature of Iraqi political life in the 1920s and early 1930s? The Nationalist Party formed in 1922 represented localized Iraqi nationalism and served as the training ground for future political leaders. Many artisans and shopkeepers were led by prosperous merchants to join this party. The first party to pay attention to the lower classes, the group was characterized by relentless opposition to British interests. Among its leaders were Mawlud Mukhlis (associated with the prewar al-Ahd), Ja'far Abu al-Timman (later leader of the People's Reform founded in 1937 and the National Democratic Party of 1946), Muhammad Mahdi al-Kubba (who founded the Independence Party in 1946), Abd al-Qadir Isma'il (writer for *al-Ahali* newspaper and prominent in the Communist Party during the 1940s–60s), and Yusuf Salman Yusuf (secretary of the Iraqi Communist Party during the 1940s).

Early in the 1920s, Iraqis also participated in the clandestine pan-Arab Party of the Peninsula; it attempted to combat French, British, and Jewish interests. On the marginal side was the Association of Liberals that was active in the late 1920s. Opposed to domination of religious leaders, this group supported secular pan-Arabism, linking religion with poverty and deceit. Poet Jamil al-Zahawi, who

had served in the 1908 Young Turk parliament, indicated in his poem "Revolution in Hell" (1929) that the "other world" is also unjust. The main pan-Arabist tendency, however, associated pan-Arabism with Islam. In his memoirs, General Salah al-Din Sabbagh, a leader in the *Golden Square* coup of 1941, derived objectives for the pan-Arab movement from Quranic verses and the traditions of the Prophet—he stressed high moral standards, equality, consultation with the public on community matters, Arabism, and use of force.

On the local level, politics was tied to local shaykhs whose power was built up by the British as a counterweight to the urban politicians. These leaders owned and ruled their districts as tribal laws gave way to arbitrary rule. They enforced their authority through coercive troops that constituted about 10 percent of the total population. The troops were divided into groups that performed different tasks, including the guarding of crops or the carrying out of corporal punishment. Peasants, the backbone of Iraqi agriculture, were very poor, especially in the south where their share in the crop averaged about 25 percent minus dues. Women suffered most in the system because they could be pledged as wives while still babies or could be given in marriage to a rural shaykh or exchanged as part of a settlement of tribal disputes.

The Assyrian Question

Among the early communal problems in Iraq was the Assyrian question. Originating in territory incorporated into modern Turkey, the Assyrians early in World War I supported Russian advances into Anatolia. After a failed effort to set up a buffer Assyrian state, these refugees settled among an older but smaller Assyrian population located in what became northern Iraq.

From the outset, Britain favored the Assyrians, both because they were good fighters and because they were perceived as a tiny Christain minority in need of a protector. Assyrians, especially the recent immigrants, tended not to identify with other Iraqis; they regarded themselves as a foreign elite. Their religious leader, the Mar Sham'un, had become patriarch as an eleven-year-old and had studied in England. He failed to take up Iraqi citizenship. In the early 1930s, he was in his early twenties, and viewed himself as the Assyrians' spokesperson in Iraq.

The British promoted Assyrian separatism by using special troops to suppress Kurdish and Turkish dissidence in northern Iraq. In 1924, after a dispute with shopkeepers in Kirkuk, two companies of these troops assaulted the commercial district, killing about fifty people.

Historians have asked whether British concern for the Assyrians plus the Assyrians' self-conscious assertiveness did not harm the community in the long run. Both elements regarded the conclusion of the 1930 treaty as a potential source of minority oppression because it would give Iraq's government more responsibility for safeguarding their rights. Between 1931 and 1933, the Assyrians tried to pressure both the British and the League of Nations into granting them special status as a national group entitled to a homeland. Meanwhile, Faysal tried to placate them but without success. Many Assyrians left the levies, taking their arms with them under a self-defense agreement with the government. In June 1933, with British approval, Iraq's government sent reinforcements to the northern troops commanded by Bakr Sidqi.

What happened after that has been subject to debate. After having refused a British suggestion that they simply accept Iraqi citizenship and join in building the nation, armed Assyrians crossed into Syria in July 1933. The Iraqis asked the French authorities there to disarm them and keep them away from the border. In August, however, an Assyrian force crossed back into Iraq and deliberately attacked an army post. With the discovery of mutilated bodies left by the Assyrians,

the Iraqi forces launched reprisals, joined by local Kurds and Arabs. In recent years, historians have concluded that the Assyrians chose to provoke an armed conflict. Although many Assyrians left Iraq after these events, others remained. In September 1933, King Faysal died and was succeeded by his twenty-one-year-old son Ghazi. The new king rewarded Sidqi and his troops for their successes against the Assyrians.

The Reform–Military Alliance: The New Intelligentsia in Power

Ghazi's rule was marked by increased political turmoil. Whereas Iraq between 1921 and 1933 had seen fifteen governments, over twenty-one governments were formed between 1933 and 1936, with an increase in authoritarian cabinets. At this point, the new intelligentsia came to the fore. Early in the 1930s, the newspaper *al-Ahali* began to speak for those who advocated social reform under the label of *populism*. The group formed around *al-Ahali* became a specifically political organization in the mid-1930s. In 1946 it evolved into the National Democratic Party. *Al-Ahali* supporters promoted patriotism rather than chauvinism, reform but not revolutionary change, and liberal democracy rather than the prevailing oligarchy. When the group began to achieve some success in organizing youth and other reform-minded individuals, the government clamped down, imposing censorship. In reply, the reformers joined forces with another segment of the intelligentsia, the military. They chose as their prospective leader General Bakr Sidqi.

The military had grown increasingly discontented because of the politicians' inability to achieve national consensus. They admired military leaders in neighboring Iran and Turkey who had taken charge and begun to forge strong nations. By late 1936, Sidqi had been placed in temporary charge of the army's general staff and allied himself with the Ahali reformers in the National Reform Movement. The man who helped bring the two groups together was Hikmet Sulayman (his elder brother had been instrumental in the Young Turk takeover of 1908). With his authority in the army, Sidqi on 28–29 October 1936 sent King Ghazi a letter demanding formation of a new ministry headed by Sulayman. When an immediate reply was not forthcoming, Sidqi launched bombing raids on Baghdad. Some civilians died. The new cabinet, including three Ahali members, was accepted. The former ministers, mainly first generation nationalists such as Rashid Ali al-Gaylani and Nuri al-Sa'id went into exile rather than face possible assassination by the Sidqi forces.

Although the National Reform Movement claimed to advocate increased personal freedom and social reform, its Ahali members were soon dicharged as Sidqi imposed a military dictatorship. Sulayman survived by abandoning the liberals, but he too found himself pushed into the background by Sidqi. Sidqi's own men assassinated him in August 1937, thus bringing to an end the first military coup in the twentieth-century Arab world.

Iraqi Foreign Policy

Iraqi's foreign relations during the interwar period focused on resolving disputes with neighbors and establishing harmony along its borders. This policy derived almost from necessity because of internal dissension. Iraq established diplomatic relations with Iran and Turkey late in the 1920s despite problems along the formerly disputed frontiers. The boundary with Syria was finalized early in the 1930s with League of Nations mediation. On the border with Najd, the Iraqis and Saudi leaders could not control activities of Arabian beduin who periodically raided and killed settled Iraqis, both in Iraq and in neighboring Kuwayt. In 1929, the Saudis finally defeated the Ikhwan dissidents. In the following year, Ibn Saud met with King

Faysal. In 1931, the Iraqis, represented by Nuri al-Sa'id, signed a friendship treaty with Ibn Saud. Similar arrangements were made with Egypt, Transjordan, and Yemen. Contacts with western European nations and the United States expanded.

Iraq's leadership also became increasingly involved in the Palestine question during the 1930s. During the 1936 general strike in Palestine (See Chapter 13) expressions of support for Arab Palestinians became more visible. Besides sending money, some Iraqis influenced the Palestinians to end the strike and to cooperate with British commissions of inquiry. By displaying solidarity with the Palestinians, successive Iraqi governments grew in popularity and fueled support for Arab nationalism. Iraqis attended the Bludan meeting in 1937, the Cairo Conference of 1938, and the London Conference of 1939.

One dispute resolved—temporarily as it turned out—concerned the Shatt al-Arab between Iraq and Iran. By the Treaty of Erzurum (1847) and a boundary agreement in 1914, Iraq owned the whole waterway rather than the western half because unlike Iran it had no long coastline. The League of Nations tried to settle differences raised by Iran's new claims. In July 1937, after further negotiations, the frontier was reaffirmed but as a concession Iraq granted Iran an anchorage area opposite Abadan. Iraq and Iran joined Turkey and Afghanistan in the Saadabad Treaty. In the 1970s, however, Iran revived its old claims regarding the Shatt al-Arab, resulting in 1975 in a boundary revision. The change was a factor precipitating the Gulf War of 1980.

Nuri al–Said and the Regency During World War II

Despite ups and downs of Iraqi political life, Nuri al-Sa'id served regularly as prime minister or foreign minister of Iraq. An early supporter of the British alliance and an old nationalist, he was in power for the fifth time when World War II began. In accordance with the Anglo-Iraqi treaty, he broke diplomatic relations with Germany. As in other countries occupied by Britain and France, this move was unpopular among those who assumed that a German victory would end imperialism in the area. In April 1939 King Ghazi, the weak, popular, and flamboyant young man, died as a result of injuries sustained in a car crash near his palace in Baghdad. Some nationalists blamed the British; Britain's consul in Mosul was murdered.

Because Ghazi's son Faysal II was only a small child, a regency was constituted. The regent, Ghazi's cousin Amir Abd al-Ilah, was the same age as the former king and brother of Ghazi's wife. Unlike Ghazi, Abd al-Ilah had acquired a reputation as an intelligent, serious, and charming man. He could be expected to work closely with old Hashimite supporters such as Nuri al-Sa'id. Nuri, however, fell from power in February 1940 after his respected Shi'i finance minister and a close ally was murdered. Briefly restored when Rashid Ali al-Gaylani, head of the Royal Diwan, declined the appointment as premier, Nuri resigned again in March. This time Rashid Ali accepted his own appointment and made Nuri Iraq's foreign minister. This national government seemed destined for longevity since it brought together different political factions. It worked at carrying on economic development, especially irrigation and other agricultural projects. Petroleum and agriculture provided the major part of its income. Archeological excavations also continued.

The *Golden-Square* Coup in Iraq

As elsewhere, the German victories early in the war made many Iraqis feel that they had allied with the wrong side. Iraq's army leaders in particular were anxious to renege on obligations to Britain, especially as the war had curtailed British military supplies to Iraqi forces. Although Nuri kept voicing support for Britain,

others expanded contacts with German leaders. Rashid Ali sympathized with the Axis, and drew closer to four pro-German generals—the *Golden Square*. To promote cabinet harmony, Nuri resigned as foreign minister in January 1941. But Abd al-Ilah did not want to work with Gaylani. When Gaylani was forced out, the generals pressed for his restoration. In April 1941 after one of their members received a transfer notice, the Golden Square staged a coup. The regent took refuge with his uncle in Transjordan. Gaylani became the government's leader.

Immediately, the government deposed the Regent and appointed an elderly Hashimite in his place. Abd al-Ilah's supporters, among them Nuri, left to join him. The generals, however, soon discovered that their internal and external backing was slim. Neither the members of parliament nor the tribes were enthusiastic. In terms of subsequent Iraqi history, though, it is now recognized that the coup aimed at continuing what the 1920 uprising had begun: elimination of British influence in Iraq. Moreover, it divided a new generation of pan-Arab nationalists from old Sharifians like Nuri. The generals and their backers established close ties with other Arab leaders in touch with the Axis, including the Palestinian exile Haj Amin al-Husayni, displaced mufti of Jerusalem. The British feared that this nationalistic government would renege on its treaty obligations.

Within a few weeks, Gaylani accepted and then rejected the landing of additional British troops sent from India. The British landed the troops anyway and occupied Basra. Historians agree that Gaylani himself did not seek a crisis with Britain although he disliked the British. Unlike the Golden Square generals, he did not advocate an alliance with Germany. However, he went along with the generals who were more determined to fulfill neither the letter nor the spirit of the 1930 treaty. Iraqi troops surrounded the Habbaniyya military complex on 29–30 April to force Britain to stop using its air base. Historians agree that the Iraqis could have overrun the base because relief troops from Jordan's Arab Legion had only just begun their march east. Britain refused the demand and began to bomb Iraq's troops and planes. The Iraqis held their ground, shelling the base but not moving in to take it. With the aid of the Arab Legion, British forces eventually chased Gaylani, his generals, Amin al-Husayni, and the new regent out of Baghdad.

Britain Restores the Old Order

Having brought down the nationalist government, the British turned to strengthen the country's defense and to send troops against the Vichy French in neighboring Syria. British forces in Iraq included Indians, Poles, and others. These occupiers established good relations with the local population by providing employment and securing delivery of food and supplies. As elsewhere, though, the war brought inflation and profiteering. In 1941, coup officials and generals were captured in Iran and returned for trial and subsequent execution or imprisonment. Nuri al-Sa'id, as prime minister, could not easily maintain his cabinets because of economic and political pressures. The government's declaration of war on the Axis, however, created no particular reaction in Iraq. As Britain and its allies began winning the war, the British supported the reopening of Iraqi schools and the establishment of new institutes to promote education and health.

In 1943, Kurdish leader Mustafa al-Barzani raised the banner of revolt in Barzan (in Iraq's northeast corner). The Iraqi army could not contain the Kurdish forces. Only in 1945 did the British Royal Air Force suppress this rebellion. The Kurds retreated into neighboring Iran where the Mahabad government happily received them. When this Kurdish republic too was crushed, Barzani and his men found asylum in the Soviet Union. They returned only after the 1958 Iraqi revolution.

Toward the end of World War II, economic conditions in Iraq worsened. An elderly politician, Hamdi Pachachi, replaced Nuri as prime minister. Like his predecessor, Pachachi was committed to an external policy of support for Palestine and Arab unity. Both men represented Iraq at the meeting in 1944 that led to the foundation of the Arab League. At home, though, Pachachi faced renewed social pressures. An Iraqi Communist movement had arisen, supportive of the British war effort following the Nazi invasion of the Soviet Union. It was encouraged to counter fascism. The Communists' reformist thrust appealed especially to minorities—Kurds, Jews, Armenians, and Assyrians. Like others in the new intelligentsia, these Communists opposed the old oligarchy that as in Egypt and Syria had failed to promote social change. Although the Communists were forced underground after the war, the restoration of democracy in April 1946 brought about other political parties, some of them socialist.

To summarize, Iraq's nationalist leadership, heavily military in its outlook, achieved only modest success in attracting support from a broad constituency. Representing mainly an old Sunni elite, the oligarchy failed to incorporate sufficient numbers of the new elites into the government to forestall pressures for revolutionary change. Although the constitution itself did not suffer autocratic manipulation as in Egypt and Syria, the leadership stifled the formation of truly democratic institutions among a population long accustomed to repressive governments.

Even when allowed to function, parliamentary government in Iraq enjoyed a rocky existence. Nuri became more and more detached from new elites who brought about his demise, and that of the monarchy, in 1958.

Abd Allah and the British: Anglo-Hashimite Collaboration

In contrast to Iraq, Transjordan was a poor country, consisting of small towns and villages, a preponderance of desert, and no large rivers. Amir Abd Allah perceived the fragility of his position without British support and wholeheartedly embraced the British alliance. Transjordan under Abd Allah evolved as a British-Hashimite autocracy in which Arab nationalists, some from neighboring Syria, tried to introduce more democratic and representative government.

Under the new administration, land surveys were undertaken, collection of taxes was regularized, and an Arab bureaucracy was trained to assume an administrative role although many of its members came from the neighboring Palestine mandate territory. Englishmen filled the chief administrative posts. Abd Allah, constantly pressured to reform, found it difficult to maintain close contact with the initially receptive population.

In 1928, Britain and Transjordan agreed on an Organic Law and a treaty. The treaty reserved to Britain control over foreign affairs, finance, foreign communities, and defense. Under the Organic Law drafted by British officials, Abd Allah was to govern with the aid of a legislative and executive council. Appointed by the amir, the executive council recommended legislation. The legislative council could only discuss laws and could be dismissed at will by the ruler. Although nationalists disliked the constitution, Abd Allah suppressed them by imposing martial law. Elections for the legislature promoted rule by oligarchy, drawn from Muslim religious leaders, the small Circassian population, and landowners.

Abd Allah never eroded Britain's reserved powers except in very small ways. He supported them in developing loyal armed forces that helped to maintain him and his successors in power. Under the guidance of two British officers, F. G. Peake and John Glubb (Glubb Pasha later), an Arab force was recruited, first from among villagers and later more successfully among desert nomads. The co-opting of what had been disruptive elements along the frontiers into the state army helped bring about relative tranquility in the mid-1930s. To encourage the nomads to cease their local squabbles, the govern-

ment created a suervisory body for administering tribal justice and gave land grants to each group. Through these funds, many beduin became settled farmers or seminomads. The Arab Legion fought both in Iraq and against Vichy forces in Syria during World War II. Most observers regarded the Arab Legion as the region's best Arab fighting force.

Perhaps Transjordan's greatest interwar problem was how to escape dependency on the British when its population was doubling and economic resources were few. Only limited inroads had been achieved in expanding education, and the country employed large numbers of Arabs from elsewhere. Britain realized that Abd Allah's considerable wartime assistance merited a reward. In 1946, a still conditional independence was granted. Abd Allah became king of the Kingdom of Transjordan. Ongoing dependence prevented the country's admission to the United Nations until 1955. Cold-war relations between the Soviet Union and Western powers were a factor in the delay.

In the newly independent kingdom, Abd Allah retained most of his former powers. Nationalist protests brought about modification of British controls in 1948, with British officers still present in the Arab Legion. During the 1947–49 Palestine War, Abd Allah received British encouragement to enlarge his kingdom. In hopes of avoiding the fighting, he negotiated in secret with Jewish leader Golda Meyerson (later Golda Meir). Arab League pressures, though, obliged him to fight in the war. Abd Allah's interest lay not in protecting or securing independence for a Palestinian Arab state but in incorporating its territories into his own. When Jordan and Israel reached their armistice agreement in April 1949, only Egyptian-controlled Gaza proclaimed an independent Arab state. By 1950, Abd Allah had won parliamentary approval for a new united state: the Hashimite Kingdom of Jordan. In the new state, Palestinians constituted the majority of the population, prompting an Israeli argument that the Arab Palestinian state had been achieved and that it was called Jordan. Abd Allah's assassination by a Palestinian in 1951 demonstrated that Palestinians found this conclusion unacceptable.

The Arabian Peninsula

Building of the Saudi State

The independent state of Saudi Arabia was inspired by the purifying zeal of Wahhabism and accomplished through the charismatic leadership of Abd al-Aziz and his tribal forces. Through Abd al-Aziz, a large territory roughly the size of India and populated by independent but interconnected clan groups was united in 1932 as the Kingdom of Saudi Arabia.

Officially, the law was the Quran and Shari'a, but because of urbanization and contact with the outside world through trade and the hajj, the Hijaz was administered under its own set of regulations. Local councils with advisory functions only were established in the Hijaz to assist the ruler's representatives. From 1930 on, the national government worked to build up the country's infrastructure of communications (roads, railroads, post, telegraph), health, and education as well as foreign affairs and finance. The main interwar focus was on developing services as pressures arose. Change occurred in conjunction with petroleum-exploration concessions granted to American interests in 1933 and with the discovery of commercial quantities of oil in 1938.

Before the influx of foreign workers and petroleum royalties during the 1930s and 1940s, the Saudis could not maintain a very sophisticated governmental structure. They lacked economic development and were experiencing a decline in the traditional economy based on animal husbandry, cultivation of dates and other crops, and pearl diving. Control over clan groups was maintained by loyal troops who respected the ruler, including the Ikhwan fighters. The Ikhwan eventually were disbanded for both raids across the frontiers and for resisting minor innovations, such as radio.

Abd al-Aziz consolidated his alliances through intermarriage (achieved by his marrying and divorcing a large number of women whose families thereby achieved greater influence and prosperity). In all, Abd al-Aziz's marriages produced forty-three sons, twenty-eight of whom were still alive in 1983, and over twenty daughters. The house of al-Sa'ud continued to grow astronomically in subsequent generations. Abd al-Aziz's son Sa'ud (later King) alone had over fifty sons. All members of the royal family received stipends from the state—initially poor but later phenomenally wealthy.

With the bulk of the population remaining within a patriarchal social structure and a largely self-sufficient economic structure, the fact that the government could not at first invest heavily in the economy did not seriously affect loyalty to the ruler. What mattered was the establishment of relations based on mutual respect between individual leaders, from the most local chiefs to the head of state. Individuals could approach the king personally with grievances, usually at open sessions held in his palace or in villages. The extension of Hanbali law throughout the kingdom helped bring about increased security and a reduction in crime.

In pre-petroleum Saudi Arabia, people valued most their relative influence and autonomy. They did not place as much emphasis on acquisition of material possessions, although there was greater class differentiation in the towns. The idea of manual and wage labor was largely irrelevant in this precapitalist environment. Slavery existed in Saudi Arabia but in a form common to earlier Islamic societies in which slaves could reach positions of wealth and/or power. The personal slaves of Abd al-Aziz's sons, for example, were their companions who sat at table with the al-Sa'ud during meals and accompanied them on journeys.

An era of social change began with the advent of the oil industry and the incorporation of Saudi Arabia into the world market. The industry's demand for workers was modest during the prewar and World War II periods, but even then, Saudis were not easily attracted to jobs that required them to alter their lifestyles and accept the authority of foreigners. The American enclave at Dhahran brought increasing numbers of Saudis into contact with materialism and a lifestyle that increased dependence on the outside world because it demanded importation of consumer goods. More importantly, with the new industry came, for the first time, large numbers of foreigners from the Middle East and Southern Asia, all of them needed to build up the infrastructure of goods and services upon which the oil industry depended. Saudi Arabia was transformed after the war from a self-sufficient though very poor country into a wealthy but dependent nation.

Resolution of Saudi–Yemeni Differences

In foreign relations, Saudi Arabia settled its squabbles with the Hashimites but waged war with Yemen in 1934 over Asir. After Saudi forces led by then Prince Faysal had defeated the Yemenis, the two countries agreed on a new frontier and established friendly relations. The Yemeni leader Imam Yahya (1903–48) kept his country relatively secluded under his personal and absolute authority, strengthened by his acceptance as both the Zaydi Imam and the political ruler. Like Abd al-Aziz, Imam Yahya solidified his authority through marriage alliances and control over appointments, but the fact that his dynasty had been in Yemen since the ninth century also brought forth few

challenges. Those which did arise were serious and fatal for the imam.

A reformist opposition gathered, mainly outside the country in Cairo and in the British colony at Aden. In 1948, the imam was assassinated and replaced by adherents of reform. In a countercoup supported by Saudi Arabia, the Yemeni crown prince Ahmad defeated the revolutionaries and re-established a modified version of the previous regime. Saudi Arabia in the postwar period continued to regard developments in Yemen as highly significant to its own security, and it was to intervene in Yemeni affairs when it judged necessary.

Foundations of U.S.-Saudi Cooperation

The entry of American companies into Saudi Arabia and the increasing recognition by American State Department officials of the significance of Saudi oil brought the two countries into a close relationship during World War II. When the war curtailed both petroleum output and the conduct of the pilgrimage, King Abd al-Aziz turned to the United States for a loan that was provided indirectly. In exchange, the Saudi King cooperated with American requests to construct an air base at Dhahran.

In 1945, in a now famous shipboard meeting, Abd al-Aziz and President Franklin Roosevelt discussed Middle Eastern affairs, most notably the crisis in Palestine. The Saudi monarch tried to impress on the president his failure to understand why Western democracies were pressuring the British administration in Palestine to admit more Jews instead of settling them on American or European soil. His viewpoint that Middle Eastern Arabs should not be obliged to pay for the sins of Europeans represented widespread Arab sentiment at the time. Although Roosevelt promised Abd al-Aziz to take no action without consulting with both parties, he died shortly thereafter and was succeeded by his vice-president, Harry Truman, who proved more vulnerable to Zionist pressures.

Protectorates in Arabia

The rest of the Arabian peninsula during the interwar period was as in the nineteenth century under some form of British protection. In southern Yemen, the British set up separate administrations for the Crown Colony at Aden (from 1937) and for the eastern and western portions of the protectorate. To defend these territories, the British raised local levies. Included within the area were at least twenty-three separate units ruled by different individuals who had traditional titles (amir, shaykh, sultan). Although Imam Yahya in Yemen was wary of British expansion, he signed a treaty of friendship with Britain in 1934, and the British respected his independent status. Britain's main interest in southern Arabia was to preserve Aden, a protectorate that employed workers from Yemen and other Indian Ocean countries like Somalia and India. Southern Yemen's neighbor Oman also had a treaty-relationship with Britain, although the agreement of 1891 applied only to coastal areas. Similar relationships were set up with rulers along the Gulf.

Interwar petroleum exploration in Kuwayt and Bahrayn strengthened their ties with western oil interests. Development of the oil industry not only added to Bahrayn's significance but also brought an improvement in living standards at a time when its coastal neighbors were poverty-stricken (though perhaps freer of foreign control). Unlike Bahrayn, Kuwayt did not begin to profit from oil until after World War II when the ruling Sabah family found itself with a huge surplus of funds. Before that time, Kuwayt, like its Gulf neighbors, had been very poor, sustained by marine-related activities such as pearl diving, fishing, and maritime trade.

Rise of the Oil Industry in Southwest Asia

The idea of granting foreigners or foreign companies special rights or concessions was well-established in Southwest Asia by the twentieth century. Companies began as private enterprises designed to generate profits. Agreements often allowed foreign governments to interfere in local politics. In the twentieth century, the primary arena for profitable investment in the area became the oil industry and its offshoots.

Iran and Iraq: Expansion of Production

Oil exploration in the Middle East began before World War I in Iran and Iraq. Indebted countries with low energy demands willingly granted concessions because they themselves lacked the capital, technology, and expertise required to discover and exploit their own oil. An important characteristic of early and subsequent oil concessions was that they brought individual American and European companies together in a single entity that then reached agreements with the appropriate Middle Eastern rulers. These consortia generally acquired more partners when their capital requirements and political pressures for increased participation expanded. They, not the Middle Eastern rulers, controlled the oil industry.

Prior to World War II, the principal oil producer in the Middle East was Iran. Under early concessions, Anglo-Persian prospered and was able to expand operations. Reza Shah became the first Middle Eastern leader to secure a better agreement by revoking the initial concession (1932). By 1938, Iran's oil production had reached some 215,000 barrels per day—over 9 million tons per year. The second largest producing country was Iraq. Although the British and French had settled their differences there, American companies were dissatisfied. Negotiations during the early 1920s produced agreement in 1923 between American interests and the T.P.C. The entrepreneur Gulbenkian, however, voiced some objections. While negotiations were continuing, the Iraqi government in March 1925 granted the company a concession. In 1928 shares in the company were allocated as follows according to the final T.P.C.-American agreement:

D'Arcy Exploration Company
   (Anglo-Persian)   23 ¾%
Anglo-Saxon Petroleum Company
   (Royal Dutch/Shell)   23 ¾%
Compagnie Française des
   Pétroles (CFP)   23 ¾%
Near East Development
   Corporation   23 ¾%
Participations and Explorations
   Company (Gulbenkian)   5%

American partners holding equal shares in the Near East Development Corporation included the Standard Oil Company of New Jersey (now Exxon), the Standard Oil Company of New York (now Mobil Oil), the Gulf Oil Corporation, the Atlantic Refining Company, and the Pan American Petroleum and Transport Company. The last three companies later sold their shares to the firms that became Exxon and Mobil, thereby giving them 50 percent each of the Near East Development Corporation's share.

According to what after 1927 became known as the Red Line Agreement, the partners in T.P.C. promised not to act individually in regard to further oil concessions within a large part of the former Ottoman Empire. In 1929, the company adopted the name Iraq Petroleum Company (I.P.C.). Its partners went on to form the Mosul Petroleum Company (M.P.C.) (with concessions from 1932 in northernmost Iraq), and the Basra Petroleum Company (with its concession from 1938 in southern Iraq).

The first large oil field discovered by I.P.C. was in 1927 in Kirkuk, a predominantly Kurdish region. Oil from the M.P.C. though located in 1939, was not piped from the area until 1952. Throughout the years, the Kirkuk field has continued to provide the greatest amount of Iraqi oil. Only after the war, however, did pipelines connect the field with Mediterranean ports.

Discovery of Oil in Bahrayn, Saudi Arabia, and Kuwayt

The Saudi and Bahrayni concessions originated with Major Frank Holmes, a New Zealander interested in developing Gulf oil production. Holmes initially went to Bahrayn Island as a water-development specialist, but he made use of his position to approach Abd al-Aziz to grant an oil concession in eastern Arabia near Bahrayn. The agreement soon lapsed from lack of interest. In Bahrayn itself, however, Holmes won a concession in 1925. When he acquired an extension period, he turned to American companies. Standard Oil of California was alerted by Gulf Oil (which had been forced to abandon an initial concession because of the Red Line Agreement), to the opportunity presented by the Holmes concession. Although the British government at first advised the ruler of Bahrayn to agree only to a concession for a British-run operation, in 1930 the Bahrayn Petroleum Company, owned by Standard Oil of California, was assigned one.

Through these activities in Bahrayn, Standard Oil of California decided to search for oil in Arabia, only twenty-five miles away. The company delayed approaching Abd al-Aziz because Holmes was negotiating with Kuwayt on behalf of Gulf Oil. When oil was struck in Bahrayn early in 1932, Standard Oil approached the king directly. Under the terms of the concession, signed in May and ratified by Saudi royal decree in July 1933, the California Arabian Standard Oil Company (C.A.S.O.C.) would make an annual payment to the Saudi government of 30,000 gold sovereigns. Renegotiations because of the gold embargo declared by the United States during the depression allowed payment in dollars or sterling. In 1936, C.A.S.O.C. acquired a joint owner in the Texas Company (later Texaco). Once Saudi petroleum resources had been confirmed with greatly increased demands on capital and marketing facilities, the company was open to taking on further partners. Having adopted in 1944 the name Arabian-American Oil Company (A.R.A.M.C.O.), the American firm in 1946 added two partners, the future Exxon and Mobil Oil corporations. Since the two were also partners in I.P.C., their participation required revisions of the Red Line Agreement; these were not completed until late in 1948. Mobil became owner of 10 percent of the shares while the other firms owned 30 percent each.

Although oil exploration in eastern Arabia began in 1933, the first well yielded no oil in commercial quantities. Only when the company decided to drill a deep well of over 4,500 feet did it make a productive strike in March 1938 near the coastal village of Dammam. The company soon expanded the town of Dhahran and constructed a pipeline to the coast. Eventually, Ras Tanura, north of Dammam, was chosen as the permanent marine terminal. King Abd al-Aziz paid a visit to the company's installations to inaugurate the tanker loading services at Ras Tanura in May 1939.

During World War II, oil production in Saudi Arabia declined. A.R.A.M.C.O. was forced to curtail production in Arabia after an initial bombing raid on Dhahran by Italian planes, danger in shipping lanes, reduced Indian Ocean demands, and inaccessibility of other markets. The huge Abqaiq field discovered late in 1941 could not be developed under these wartime conditions. Drought further hampered company operations. The company turned to camels for transport.

Until 1943, Saudi oil had been transported to Bahrayn for refining. In that year, however, the American government decided that war requirements created a severe drain on U.S.-produced oil. To create a new source of refined oil, the United States gave A.R.A.M.C.O. mate-

rials for building a refinery and other facilities at Ras Tanura. Completed in 1945, despite construction difficulties, the refinery could accommodate Saudi production. Within five years, daily production amounted to ten times the refinery's capacity.

Meanwhile Gulf Oil succeeded in winning the Kuwayt oil concession in partnership with Anglo-Iranian. Although oil was first discovered in 1938 (the concession began in 1934), the war delayed its exploitation until 1945. From that time on, Kuwayt's oil production soared under the Kuwayt Oil Company (K.O.C.). The I.P.C. partners also won concessions for onshore production in both Qatar and Abu Dhabi during the 1930s, while the oil of Oman passed to a concession owned 85 percent by Shell, 10 percent by Compagnie Française des Pétroles, and 5 percent by Gulbenkian interests.

Control of Oil: The "Seven Sisters"

A comprehensive look at these concessions reveals the basis for the generally acknowledged assertion that oil through the 1980s has been under the control of the so-called *Seven Sisters*—Exxon, Shell, British Petroleum, Gulf, Texaco, Mobil, and Standard Oil of California—with Compagnie Française des Pétroles having the next largest holdings. The involvement of these companies in the pre-World War II exploration and exploitation of Middle Eastern oil helped them to establish the basis for domination of the worldwide oil industry. Moreover, because most concessionary agreements stipulated a period of at least seventy-five years, any country wishing to renegotiate was placed in the position of having to appeal to the concessionaire for reconsideration, with the new agreement certain to diminish company post-royalty profits. The weakness of Middle Eastern countries generally prevented them from winning more than minimal concessions from the oil companies until well after World War II.

CHAPTER THIRTEEN

Palestine During the Mandate

The history of Palestine during the mandate has influenced subsequent Middle Eastern history profoundly, culminating as it did in the territory's partition and the emergence of Israel. What internal and external developments characterized the two communities who struggled for control in Palestine: the principally indigenous Christian and Muslim Arabs and the predominantly Eastern European immigrant Jews? How did economy and society evolve? What was the nature and imact of British policy from the 1918 occupation to the withdrawal of British forces in May 1948?

The Palestine Mandate: An Overview

Exactly how many people lived in Palestine after World War I is not known. Population estimates for 1918 have varied between 640,000 and 670,000. Since many Jews left Palestine during the war, their numbers had declined from about 85,000 to between 50,000 and 66,000. Following the Balfour Declaration and the allied victory, the Jewish population within three or four years grew to its former level. Christians, comprising about 10 percent of the population, included not only Arabs but also Greeks, Russians, Armenians, and assorted Europeans, many of whom were connected with the various holy places. About 75–80 percent of the population was both Arab and Muslim, including Druze. The Arab population owned or worked some 98 percent of both cultivable and noncultivable land. Although these statistics should be accepted with some reservations, historians generally accept the fact that in 1920 about 90 percent of Palestine's population consisted of Arabic-speaking Palestinians. It is quite remarkable in light of this fact that the Palestine mandate awarded by the European allies to Britain at San Remo in April 1920, confirmed by the League of Nations in 1922, and brought into operation in 1923, contained virtually no reference to Arabs except in relation to the official languages: English, Arabic, and Hebrew.

During the mandate, British administrators tried to govern the country while fulfilling the stipulations of the mandate. British imperial interests and domestic policies influenced decision-making of mandate administrators, but the mandate's structure created special problems. Palestine could not be treated like the "Class A" mandates of Iraq and Syria that required any organic law to "take into account the rights, interests, and wishes of all the population inhabiting the said territory."[1] The bulk of Palestine's indigenous population opposed the mandate, specifically because of its major provision that required Britain to "secure the establishment of the Jewish national home." If Britain developed the self-governing institutions called for in Article 2 of the mandate too rapidly and with consideration for the population composition, the majority Arabs might obstruct plans for creating a Jewish national home, especially since the mandate gave rights to a "Jewish Agency" without reference to an equally privileged "Arab Agency."

On 15 June 1969, Israeli prime minister Golda Meir told *The Times* (London) that there was no such thing as "Palestinians." Regardless of how they may have identified themselves, the majority of Arabs in Palestine thought that they were entitled to self-determination instead of occupation against their will. This denial of human rights became the basis for Palestinian protest throughout the mandate period. We cannot speak, therefore, of two analogous groups struggling for possession of the same land. What were the fundamental differences inherent in the Arab and Jewish communities?

The Arabic-speaking population had constituted the majority in the area for hundreds of years. They took their status for granted. As with Indians in North America, the indigenes, with their own long-established culture, tried to combat foreign penetration but had no large or significant external group to which they could appeal for support, financial aid, or additional numbers. Because Palestinians were fighting what they perceived to be a foreign invasion aided and abetted by a powerful foreign power, the main, though not the only, thrust of their movement was defensive, directed at expelling rather than cooperating extensively with the British occupiers.

The class structure of Palestinian society merits attention in explaining why Palestinians failed to safeguard their rights. Under the millet system, Palestinian Muslims and Christians of different sects had remained relatively isolated. The British policy of treating the Arabs only as "Muslims" and "Christians" obstructed efforts at presenting a united Arab front. At least three-quarters of the Christian population in 1931 was urban, while nearly the same proportion of the much larger Muslim community was rural. Urban elites, including those who controlled peasant lands, established rivalries in the nineteenth century. These persisted throughout the mandate period. But the groups also interacted and shared far more in common with each other than with their less influential coreligionists who made up the bulk of the population. Though these elites constituted the primary participants in the Palestinian national movement, it was also they who served as a primary target of the widespread disturbances that began among Palestinian Arab masses in 1936. The masses resented not only the immigrant Jewish community but also a leadership that had failed to safeguard lands and jobs. As the landed elite participated in dispossessing many Palestinian peasants through

---

[1] All quotations from mandate documents cited above appear in Chapter 12.

land-sales and transfers, many entered the wage-labor market and were "proletarianized" without necessarily acquiring new skills. This essentially peasant group was to suffer the greatest hardship in the wake of the 1947 partition.

Although Palestine's leadership transcended—in family ties, land ownership, and the like—the boundaries of mandated Palestine, other Arab territories were also under either French or British occupation. The mandates created divisions unrelated to historical ties of greater Syria's people, but the indigenes were expected to adjust to their new circumstances. With their fellow Arabs also under the thumbs of foreign occupiers, even the Palestinian leaders could not do much more than commiserate with their neighbors.

In this present age of oil power, we must not forget that in the past the Arab world possessed no vast economic resources or overseas communities with which to influence politicians or public opinion. In fact, not only the Arab world but most of the Muslim world as well was under European occupation. The British were in India and in eastern, western and northeastern Africa; the French were in north and west Africa; the Italians in Libya; the Dutch in Indonesia; and the Russians in central Asia. Among large non-Arab Muslim nations, only Iran and Turkey were truly independent.

The *yishuv* (Jewish community in Palestine) began the post-World War I period by continuing preparations for a Jewish national state, not just for the "home" mentioned in the Balfour Declaration. Their population established a government, lower schools, utilities, social services, and labor unions, in addition to much publicized agricultural settlements, higher educational institutions, and military organizations. Their concepts of political and social relations gave them a greater degree of community solidarity. Despite ideological differences among Jews in Palestine, they created a structure whereby they could debate their views, transcend differences, and formulate policy. They cooperated with Jewish groups

abroad who, along with immigrants, provided some 86 percent of Jewish national and institutional funds in Palestine during the period of the mandate. Besides capital, the new settlers often possessed European technologies unavailable in Palestine.

Despite these differences, there was a crucial dimension that tilted the balance in favor of the Zionist movement. Scholars agree that without the persecution of German Jews in the 1930s and the destruction of an estimated six million Jews under German control in World War II (five million or so non-Jewish Europeans were also singled out and killed), the Jewish state would probably have remained a dead letter. These ghastly events produced the sudden and huge immigration of Jews to Palestine. The result was partition by the United Nations in 1947.

Before 1925, Jews had gone from Europe to the United States or to Africa and Latin America. They had also left Eastern Europe for Western Europe. Early in the 1920s, about 8,000 Jews entered Palestine each year. Introduction of anti-Jewish legislation in Poland and restrictive U.S. immigration laws led nearly 50,000 Jews to immigrate in 1925–26. However, the worsening economic situation in Palestine in 1927 led more Jews to emigrate (some 5,000) than to immigrate (about 3,000). The following year, about 2,100 Jews entered and left Palestine, and until the persecutions in Germany began, only about 4,000 Jews entered Palestine annually. Hence it appears certain that without the added impetus of persecution the Jewish community in Palestine would have grown too slowly to have permitted implementation of a Jewish state.

It is emotionally difficult to discuss Palestinian rights in the face of the inhuman treatment to which European Jews were subjected in the 1930s and 1940s, but it remains true that the implanting of a large Jewish population in Palestine took place at the expense of the native Palestinian majority that bore no responsibility for European persecution of Jews. It should not be surprising that Palestinian

Arabs consistently worked to curtail Jewish immigration and land purchase, and to secure recognition and implementation of Arab political and economic rights ignored by the mandate.

British Administration in Palestine: Search for Balance

The mandate text of 24 July 1922 instructed Britain to work toward the establishment of a "national home for the Jewish people in Palestine" while "safeguarding the civil and religious rights of all the inhabitants of Palestine, irrespective of race and religion." As the text implied, the mandate focused on Britain's commitment to Jews and gave the Arab majority the status of *other*, as in the Balfour Declaration. The evidence of the actual administration, however, suggests that the British did try to act as referees. Whatever the private biases and personal interests of the Palestine administration, and whatever the shifts in policy of the London governments, personnel involved in the implementation of the mandate by and large hoped to reconcile the apparently irreconcilable goals.

A few historians have suggested that with British honor at stake, more Arab compromise and cooperation might have strengthened the hand of administrators determined to protect Arab rights. While some British in Palestine may have been anti-Zionist or anti-Jewish, others certainly felt a moral obligation to safeguard the Palestinian Arab community because His Majesty's Government had undertaken to do so. On the other hand, it may be more accurate to say that Arab-Jewish relations in Palestine from the inception of the mandate were tinged with mutual suspicion and even mutual contempt. The real British failure in Palestine may have been the unwillingness to admit that their dual obligations in Palestine could not be carried out and were inherently unfair.

Samuel and the Problem of Self-government

During the mandate, the London government tended to favor the Zionists while administrators in Palestine recognized the existence of conflict and promoted British-Arab Muslim ties. The Palestine administration was certainly a challenge to human ingenuity. Sir Herbert Samuel, the first high commissioner who headed the administration, was a proclaimed Zionist, but he sought in his own way to satisfy all parties. He arrived in Palestine in July 1920 and left in June 1925. From the beginning, Samuel confronted at least four foci of power. First of all, he was charged with directing the British administration and the various departments of government with their British directors. Secondly, Samuel had to deal with the yishuv, including its governing bodies and institutions. Thirdly, the international Zionist organization with its headquarters in London kept in close touch with the Zionist Executive in Palestine. London Zionists often exerted pressure on British governments to pursue policies to their own liking. Finally, the British High Commissioner needed to interact with Arab Palestinians.

One of Samuel's first actions in Palestine was to establish a civilian government in place of O.E.T.A. South. The Arabs had begun to organize in 1918 following the Zionist Commission's anniversary parade commemorating the Balfour Declaration. Leading Arab families of Palestine cooperated to found the

Muslim-Christian Associations in Jaffa and Jerusalem (notables included the Husaynis, the Nashashibis, and the Dajanis). Other associations that began as "greater Syria" proponents included elements of the Palestinian leadership. After the collapse of Faysal's regime in Syria, these groups reoriented their activities. Samuel sought the cooperation of these Palestinian elites from the beginning.

Palestinian Organizations: The Arab Executive and the Supreme Muslim Council

In December 1920, the third Palestinian Congress meeting in Haifa called on the British to set up self-governing institutions. Thirty-seven delegates represented the membership of Palestine's Muslim-Christian Associations who attempted to present a united Christian-Muslim front. The concept of a mandate was not entirely opposed but the Balfour Declaration was rejected unequivocally. The executive committee of the Congress, elected by the membership, was inaugurated at this meeting, with Musa Kadhim al-Husayni as president and Arif al-Dajani as vice-president. Already in his seventies, former Jerusalem mayor Musa Kadhim won widespread respect as head of the Arab Executive (A.E.).

Although the A.E. began by claiming to represent the whole Palestinian population (it consisted of a select group of Husayni-led urban notables) it promoted Muslim-Christian (especially Arab Greek Orthodox) consensus on the need to protect Palestine's Arabs. With the death of Musa Kadhim in March 1934, the A.E. provided a new arena for displaying factionalism among rival Palestinian elites. Both the Husayni and Nashashibi factions as well as non-Jerusalem elites eventually abandoned the A.E. By the end of 1935, the committee had virtually disappeared.

Another important Palestinian association existed as well, with Samuel bearing personal responsibility for its leadership. In May 1921, Samuel appointed as mufti of Jerusalem Amin al-Husayni, who had been implicated in but later pardoned for

disturbances of April 1920. When the British arrived in Jerusalem, the mufti had been his older half-brother, Kamil al-Husayni. Traditionally, qadis had been responsible for handing down judgments in Shari'a courts. Because of Kamil's accommodation to British rule, his scope was broadened to include the functions of qadis. The Husaynis had served as muftis of Jerusalem off and on since early in the seventeenth century, but Samuel circumvented the law in making al-Hajj Amin—fourth in the elections—mufti. He hoped that al-Hajj Amin would moderate his conduct, but the appointment paved the way for him to emerge as the most prominent, though not the most highly respected Arab Palestinian leader of the pre-World War II period. His main power base was the Supreme Muslim Council (S.M.C.), founded in January 1922. He served as its president from 1922 until his removal by the British on 1 October 1937 during the Palestinian revolt.

Despite his appointment, al-Hajj Amin apparently helped to incite anti-Jewish riots in Jaffa in May 1921. These were provoked in response to the Hebrew Socialist Workers Party's (M.O.P.S.I., founded 1920) anti-Arab outbursts. Both Arab and Jewish atrocities were reported. Both the A.E. and the Muslim-Christian Association in Jaffa disavowed a connection with the disturbances and called on supporters to keep the peace. As these events occurred before the League of Nations mandate, the A.E. still hoped to influence Britain to modify the commitment to the Jewish national home. In August 1921, the A.E. met with Colonial Office officials to present proposals again requesting representative institutions, an end to Jewish immigration and the national home, and the right of Palestine to associate with its Arab neighbors.

Churchill's White Paper of 1922 and the Mandate Administration

Negotiations between the A.E. and the Colonial Office led to the first *white paper* (statement of British policy)—Winston Churchill's memorandum of June 1922. In this paper, Churchill, in a manner characteristic of British policy to 1939, both gave to and took from both sides, specifically repudiating Jewish claims to statehood and Arab insistence on self-determination. Chaim Weizmann's assertion that Palestine would become "as Jewish as England is English" was false; Arab fears of being subsumed in a Jewish state were unfounded.

Although Churchill's memorandum was a response to concerns of the A.E., the mandate administration never officially recognized the A.E. as representing the Palestinian community, allegedly because it had not been elected by a broad constituency. In fact, the reason was because the Arab leadership consistently refused to support Balfour Declaration principles. Only in times of crisis did the British government take seriously representations of the A.E. Britain preferred to encourage opposition groups. Limited efforts to set up joint consultative bodies in the early 1920s failed because the Arabs could not overcome their built-in inferior status.

When Samuel first arrived in Palestine, his administration resembled that of a British crown colony, with two main consultative bodies: his own British Executive council and an advisory council with twenty-two members, ten of whom represented Palestine's population. The advisory council perpetuated the millet mentality with three Jews, four Muslims, and three Christians. Muslims were greatly underrepresented. British officials, among whom were some British Jews, could outvote the locals.

Palestinian Resistance to the Mandate Administration

After the Churchill memorandum, the British tried to form a consultative legislative council for the government of Palestine, in accordance with the fundamental law issued on 10 August 1922. The new council would consist of the high commissioner, ten government officials, eight Muslims, two Christians, and two Jews. Arabs felt that this composition would allow the Jews and government officials to prevent passage of resolutions opposed to the Jewish national home. The new council was restricted from the start because it could not consider anything contradicting the mandate: proposals to end Jewish immigration and land sales, for example. In retrospect, the Arabs may have erred in assuming that British officials favored Zionism, especially because Zionists were not enthusiastic about having only two Jewish members. Apparently, the Zionists did not believe that the British would give them full support.

After the Arabs organized a successful boycott of council elections, the mandate administration was forced to forego the idea of an elected body. In 1923 they attempted to form another advisory council. Ten Arabs, including Jerusalem's mayor Raghib al-Nashashibi, accepted at first. They withdrew once they realized that the British had not accepted their precondition: that participation not be construed to acknowledge the Jewish national home. Belatedly in July 1923, Britain tried to form an Arab Agency to parallel the Jewish Agency sanctioned by the mandate's terms.

Palestinians did not see much point to an Arab Agency. They did not view their position as comparable to that of the Jews. While the Jewish Agency cooperated with Zionists abroad to further Jewish immigration and development of Jewish institutions in Palestine, Arabs already were the majority who owned or held most of the land. Palestine was an Arab country. To accept an Arab Agency would imply a diminution in their national status. Although Palestinians rejected collaboration with these various schemes, they failed to change the inherently pro-Zionist mandate. At the same time, they promoted greater hostility among British officials in London.

Arab–Zionist Collaboration: Kalvarisky's Projects

While anti-Zionism formed the main reason for refusal to cooperate with the mandate administrators, individual Arab leaders and families dealt with both the government and Zionists. Some of the same leaders who objected to the mandate did not see any contradiction in working in the mandate administration. Nonrecognition of the mandate was rather ineffective opposition so long as individual Arabs served as government officials, even if some used their positions to oppose Zionist programs. Secondly, individual Arab leaders participated in various Zionist schemes to exploit inter-Arab rivalries. During the early and mid-1920s, the main Jewish liaison with Palestinian Arabs and head of the Zionists' Arab Agency, Chaim M. Kalvarisky, had many contacts with Arab leaders. Arab heads, even the highly respected Musa Kadhim, accepted bribes or otherwise collaborated. Kalvarisky set up and funded the National Muslim Association (N.M.A.) that divided Muslim and Christian Palestinians. The group won its greatest number of adherents in northern Palestine, probably because of local resentment of the Jerusalem elites' control over Palestinian affairs and because of greater Muslim-Christian discord there.

In the end, the N.M.A. failed to take over the Arab movement because A.E. leaders knew that the Zionists had organized and funded it. Moreover, when funds began to dry up, the leaders lost interest. Even Kalvarisky had to admit that the N.M.A. could not gather all opponents of the Husayni-controlled A.E. In 1924, the Zionists tried another tactic, founding agricultural parties among rural village shaykhs to take advantage of resentment of the urban elites. Like their predecessors, these parties faded away when subsidies dried up. Israeli efforts of the 1980s to create collaborationist bodies in the occupied territories are reminiscent of these earlier efforts.

The Zionists' problems in the 1920s led to greater Arab-Jewish cooperation. Kalvarisky and A.E. secretary Jamal al-Husayni reached a compromise on a new plan for a legislative body in Palestine. But when Samuel insisted on an advisory body only, the initiative died out, to be revived in 1926 with broader participation.

Plumer, Chancellor, and the Revival of Palestinian Politics

Six men succeeded Samuel as high commissioner in Palestine: Field Marshal Lord Herbert Plumer (1925), Sir John Chancellor (1928), Sir Arthur Wauchope (1931), Sir Harold MacMichael (1937), Field Marshal Lord Gort (1945), and Sir Allan Cunningham (1945–48). Only the tenure of Lord Plumer can be considered a period of quietude. He came to Palestine in August 1925 with a reputation for high principles and sensitivity to human concerns. The appearance of administrative goodwill and the dissipation of the Zionist threat led Palestinian Arabs again to consider their boycott of legislative institutions and to entertain compromise on representation.

After negotiations with Lord Plumer on the question of a constitution and representation, the election of the Supreme Muslim Council in 1926 and municipal elections in 1927 resulted in heightened competition among the varied Arab leadership. Most Arabs with whom Plumer spoke supported Jamal al-Husayni's proposals for a parliament. The new structure would have resembled that of the Iraq mandate. With the Zionist movement apparently on the wane, Palestinians did not object to excluding from discussion questions relating to the Jewish national home.

Plumer, however, not entirely convinced that Arab negotiators had the support of the Arab population at large, made the municipal councils testing grounds for self-government. While he voided the results of the S.M.C. elections and appointed two Husaynis and two Nashashibis to fill the vacancies, the second set of elections brought about significant gains for the Nashashibis. Prior contacts of the Nashashibis with Jews in Haifa, Safad, Tiberias, and Jerusalem undoubtedly helped them gain the Jewish vote that won the victory. No further development took place in creating representative government for Palestine.

In general, Plumer kept the peace. Britain effected a substantial troop reduction during his tenure of office. Perhaps in retrospect the Plumer period was only the calm before the storm. As Palestine's economy evidenced an upswing and as Jewish immigration again exceeded emigration, the Palestinian political elites buried their differences to convene after five years their seventh National Congress (1928). Forty-eight leaders, thirty-six of them Muslims, were elected to represent Palestinian Arabs in calling on the mandate authorities to implement parliamentary government.

This Congress of June–July 1928 revitalized the dormant A.E. by broadening its composition, but debate also showed that a Pan-Arab younger generation had emerged that was not willing to compromise Palestinian national rights. These new voices were to become much more prominent in years ahead. Efforts of the movement were compromised by Plumer's departure. His successor, Sir John Chancellor, proved to be sympathetic to Palestinian demands. Chancellor felt that he could not resist Arab requests when Britain was implementing plans for representative government in much less sophisticated Transjordan.

A change of government in Britain helped Chancellor. The Labour Party under Ramsay MacDonald, with socialist Sydney Webb (later Lord Passfield) as Colonial Secretary, came to power in June 1929. With a sympathetic London government, Chancellor's proposals had every possibility of achieving the success that had eluded previous proposals. What Chancellor offered and Arabs accepted in 1929 was much less than the offers of 1922–23. Arab leaders were prepared to participate in a government-appointed legislative council consisting of ten Muslims, two Christians, and three Jews, plus fourteen British officials including the high commissioner. Since negotiations for the new body were kept secret, the facts of both inter-Arab and Arab-British agreement were not widely known. The course of discussion pointed to a realignment of Arab forces, too, with al-Hajj Amin leading the new more radical voices and Musa Kadhim and Raghib al-Nashashibi representing the A.E. and more traditional forces. By 1936, when the A.E. disappeared, al-Hajj Amin had a ready power base for assuming leadership of the Palestinian movement. Even the emergence of other parties failed to curtail his preeminence. The main event that promoted radicalization of Palestinians was the *Western Wall* conflict of August 1929. After that, ten years of crisis beset the Palestine administration before World War II. British investigative commissions were sent to study the disturbances.

The Arabs of Palestine: Frustration in Nation-Building

Between the mandate's inception and 1939, the Palestinian Arab majority was reduced from a proportion of about nine to one to that of two to one. Palestinians did not constitute a monolithic population united in opposition to Zionism. While publicly claiming to oppose Zionism, a number of Arab leaders took advantage of high prices offered by the Jewish National Fund (J.N.F.) to sell their agricultural land. Since J.N.F.-purchased land could be worked only by Jews, such land sales, if land was already cultivated, expelled Arab peasants from the land. In Palestine, cultivators still lived in villages surrounded by their fields, not on individual or even collectively held farms. When land was sold, villagers usually chose either to remain unemployed or they sought work elsewhere in towns or as hired laborers. The village provided few or no opportunities for agricultural workers who had lost their fields. Theoretically, Arabs who worked the land were protected by the mandatory power from 1920 on, but the failure of the law to function properly led Lord Plumer to encourage new legislation. Even the new laws did not protect tenants, and from 1928 on, land sales to Jews increased.

Economy and Society

There were about 850 villages in Palestine populated by Arabs. Low income, high rents, and indebtedness kept most farmers in poverty. As land prices skyrocketed due to Zionist colonization, landlords who did not sell increased rents. It has been suggested that the 70 percent of the Arab population in agricultural areas derived some benefit from an increased market provided by the influx of Jewish immigrants into Palestine's cities. However, although peasants who retained their fields continued to produce, only from 20–25 percent of production, excluding citrus, ever went to market because cereals emphasized in peasant agriculture tended to be consumed locally. Those who profited from the growth in the urban Jewish population were land-owning *effendis*, notables who lived in the towns and cities and who collected rents. Besides rents, taxes (though a small proportion of state revenues) also overburdened the Arab peasantry. Peasants suffered from indirect government taxes levied on necessities. Comparison of the relative tax burden on Arab cultivators to that of Jewish agricultural workers reveals that Arabs suffered much more taxation because deductible production costs in the Jewish sector were much higher. The government subsidized the more productive, capital-intensive Jewish sector at the expense of the Arab small-holder or tenant who in 1936 earned only one fifth of the personal income enjoyed by his Jewish counterpart.

What, then, was the extent of land alienation in Palestine? Where was most land purchased? Who bought and sold land? Before 1928, much land purchased by or for Jews was uncultivated and sold by Arab landlords residing in Beirut or Damascus. When the economic depression occurred, many Arabs bought back some of this land at reduced prices. However, after 1928, land purchased tended to be already cultivated and owned by resident Palestinians. It was at this time that the land question acquired pre-eminence in discussions among Palestinian nationalists. Throughout the 1930s and until partition, the issue grew in importance. The Arabic press began to agitate for an end to land sales to Jews.

The A.E. organized land purchases to prevent land from falling into Zionist hands. The S.M.C. also took an active role in discouraging land sales to Jews. For example, when cooperatively-worked *musha* land was put up for sale, the S.M.C. would try to buy it. These purchases created difficulties for villagers who wanted to sell to the Zionists because purchasers would then have to cultivate the land in partnership with the S.M.C. By this method, the S.M.C. prevented the sales of some musha lands, though occasionally village smallholders sold to Jews first. In such cases, the S.M.C. could not intervene, and in the 1930s, it began an extensive propaganda campaign to discourage Palestinians from succumbing to the temptation of attractive offers from Jews. The S.M.C. argued that Muslims who sold land to Jews were committing both a treasonous and a sinful act. The S.M.C. asked Christians to support the campaign in the name of Christianity, but only laymen agreed to cooperate by issuing public statements. The success or failure of these attempts cannot be fully determined because after the campaign wound down in 1935, land transfers proceeded.

In terms of the proportion of land acquired by Jews, land alienation by 1945 still was not widespread. But in certain subdistricts of Palestine, significant and sizable land tracts passed to Jewish control, especially in the fertile coastal plans near Haifa and Jaffa where profitable citrus growing was highly developed. Substantial portions of land were also acquired around Tiberias Lake (also called the Sea of Galilee and Lake Kinneret) and the Beisan and Nazareth subdistricts to the south and west. In no subdistrict, however, did the Jews own more land than the Arabs. Indeed, in the Bir Saba and al-Khalil subdistricts, Jews owned less than 1 percent of the land. Estimates of Jewish land ownership by partition in 1947 vary from no less than 6 percent to no more than 20 percent, depending on whether one counts cultivated land, cultivable land, state lands, or lands in areas claimed by Jews for a prospective state.

Finally, it cannot be stated conclusively how many peasants were caused irreparable harm by Jewish land purchases. In the early 1930s, British surveys concluded that only 664 cases of compensation requests were valid under the law, although over 2500 had been presented. The law, however, disallowed several categories of Arab farmers who had lost their lands. An Arab whose land had been taken first by non-Jews though the new owners transfered it to Zionists could not be compensated. Agricultural laborers or former landowners who continued to work on land that had been theirs were likewise ineligible. Peasants who bought new land after losing their own, even if the land was not suitable for agriculture, could not make a legitimate complaint. Moreover, any peasant established in a new occupation was excluded. Britain later guessed that the actual number of evicted peasants was far greater than their survey had suggested. Also, the high rural population growth rate created further problems for unemployed or poorly employed Palestinians.

An important factor to be considered along with the land question is the transformation of the Palestinian economy. The influx of capital and technology that came with Jewish immigrants gradually brought about the replacement of the non-capitalist local economy by a capitalist one in which Jews were the major participants. The few large industrial enterprises set up by Jews eroded the economic well-being of the Arab craft sector. European immigrants who had capital could be absorbed by the growing Jewish economy. Even

though the Arab agricultural sector also grew in productivity because of increased investment in citrus, vegetables, and animal husbandry, it lacked the capital to provide for increasing numbers of unemployed Arabs and to be eligible for tax breaks. Moreover, the Arab industrial sector that appeared late in the mandate was still quite small and restricted to food and clothing-related enterprises. Although government regulations required some Jewish businesses to hire Arab workers, Arabs generally found jobs in the public sector or in construction. Arab workers earned only a fraction of salaries earned by Jewish workers in the same field. Even the government used different wage scales.

A main reason for the discrepancy lay in the fact that most Arabs as well as Middle Eastern Jews were not organized. The internationally minded railway workers union was among the only mixed unions, but the Histadrut (General Federation of Jewish Workers, founded in 1920 with 4,500 workers) was not at all supportive of the idea of a joint workers' union. In 1934, the Histadrut set up an affiliate for Arabs. This insured the separation of Jewish and Arab workers. As a Zionist organization, the Histadrut was not interested in advancing Arab workers to the point of securing equal wages for them. The Histadrut's own public works firm, Solel Boneh (now Israel's largest construction firm) paid Arabs lower wages.

Until World War II, the other main Arab union was the Palestine Arab Worker's Society founded in 1925. Its membership, including railway workers, tobacco workers, and a few others, was small. During the war, demand for Arab labor increased because of the British war effort. In 1942, the Communist-led Federation of Arab Trade Unions and Labour Societies began to develop. By the end of the year, over 100,000 Arab laborers were employed, of whom some 20 percent joined unions by mid-1945. During the war, Jews and Arabs sometimes cooperated in strike activities, but generally speaking, Jewish-Arab harmony even among workers was limited.

In the social structure of Arab Palestine what emerges is the domination of the economy and society by a small group of urban land-owning notables. Peasants had little political or economic clout. Besides these, there were various craftsmen, shopkeepers, and professionals constituting a small middle class, as well as numerous unskilled workers, other craftsmen, and the unemployed poor. Clan group identification was still the crucial social factor governing individual relationships, and society was predominantly patriarchal. Palestinian women generally did not work outside the family structure and did not participate in political organizations.

Political Structure

The Palestinian political elites of the 1920s owed their leadership to the Ottoman period when individual clan groups had established themselves in positions of power. Of these, the Husaynis achieved the greatest influence during the mandate through the A.E. and S.M.C. In the 1930s, after the death of Musa Kadhim, any semblance of consensus disappeared as the Palestinian movement split into some half-dozen political parties.

Rivalry between the Husaynis and Nashashibis had heightened when the British in 1920 removed Musa Kadhim as mayor of Jerusalem because of his opposition to making Hebrew an official language in the city (although Britain alleged that a speech made before the Nabi Musa outbreaks had caused the dismissal). Jerusalem governor Ronald Storrs had already secured a commitment from Raghib al-Nashashibi to serve in Kadhim's place. Nashashibi retained this post until 1934. The party he organized in the 1930s was the National Defense Party (N.D.P.). In 1935, the Husaynis founded the Palestine Arab Party (P.A.P.) that won support from the Husayni-backed Palestine Arab Worker's Society in Haifa and Jerusalem (though not in Jaffa).

The N.D.P. leadership adopted a moderate, if not collaborationist, platform that included support for Amir Abd

Allah's plan to unite Palestine and Transjordan with special rights for Jews. This alliance continued after the partition of Palestine. The Nashashibis also kept up good relations with mandate authorities.

In contrast, the P.A.P.'s National Pact kept calling for an end to the mandate and termination of the Zionist program. The Husayni efforts to discourage land transfers were incorporated into the party platform, with encouragement for the Arab National Fund to assist in purchasing Arab lands. Officially, Jamal al-Husayni led the P.A.P., but al-Hajj Amin also was instrumental in implementing the party's programs. The P.A.P. sponsored the Futuwwa, a paramilitary youth group.

Other parties included the Islah (Reform) party led by Dr. Husayn Fakhri al-Khalidi (who defeated Nashashibi in 1934 to become Jerusalem's mayor), the National Bloc Party of notables from Nablus, the Congress Party of Arab Youth, and the Istiqlal (Independence) Party led by the Abd al-Hadis and affiliated with pan-Arab parties elsewhere in the Arab world. Palestine's largest landowners, the Abd al-Hadis sold huge tracts to Zionists. In 1935–36, only the Istiqlal refused to participate in renewed efforts to pressure the mandate government to establish legislative bodies in Palestine.

When the general strike began in 1936, the parties coalesced to form the Arab Higher Committee (A.H.C.). The A.H.C. rejected the Peel Commission's partition proposal in 1937. Al-Hajj Amin escaped arrest and fled the country while other A.H.C. leaders were either deported to Seychelles or were simply expelled. During the rebellion that reached its height early in 1938 and its aftermath, the Palestinian resistance lost much of its leadership to death or deportation. During World War II, the Nashashibis collaborated with Britain's war effort while al-Hajj Amin propounded anti-British and anti-Semitic propaganda from his base in Germany. Since political activity within Palestine had been forbidden, the remnant of the Palestinian leadership operated abroad, with limited resources.

In the years immediately preceding

partition, then, Arab Palestinians were relatively leaderless, isolated, and unarmed. Musa al-Alami attended the founding meeting of the Arab League in 1944 and then attempted to construct a network for dissemination of pro-Palestinian publicity. Syrian leader Jamil Mardam helped reconstitute a consultative body of Palestinian leaders in the fall of 1945. When both Jamal and al-Hajj Amin al-Husayni returned from exile in 1946, the Arab League pressured Palestinians to accept their leadership in a Higher Arab Executive which soon resumed the name A.H.C. But al-Hajj Amin remained in Cairo because he was denied entry into Palestine. Britain finally recognized the A.H.C. as representative of Arab Palestinians. After the United Nations voted for partition, the A.H.C. waited over four months before suggesting that Arab officials plan to take over their departments once the British had left. Coordination of the disparate Arab military groups after the British evacuation on 14 May 1948 was completely inadequate to the task at hand. The final attempt of the Husaynis to set up a Palestinian government based in Gaza failed. By 1949, there was no Palestinian state at all.

The Yishuv in Palestine: Establishment of a Nation

Because Britain treated the Jews as a unity, it was much easier for them to set up national institutions under a nominally religious framework. Arabs, by contrast, were categorized as Muslims and Christians. The language of the Balfour Declaration, the wording of the League of Nations mandate, and the internal and external structure of Jewish communities in and out of Palestine were also advantageous to Jewish nation-building in Palestine. By the time the mandate was fully acknowledged (post-Treaty of Lausanne in 1923), the Jews already had established a democratic state structure, a Zionist labor organization, educational systems, medical services, a military group, and several colonization organizations. The Jewish National Fund, the Keren Hayesod (Reconstruction Fund), the Anglo-Palestine Bank, and the Palestine Land Development Company were all created by the Zionist organization to promote the Jewish national home. The P.I.C.A. also kept functioning and was absorbed by the J.N.F. only in 1957; it retained its preference for and support of the Rothschild model of agricultural colonies.

Herzl's World Zionist Organization (W.Z.O.) was the oldest Zionist organization. Its arm, the Zionist Executive (Z.E.), carried out Zionism's program in Palestine until the founding of the Jewish Agency (J.A.) sanctioned by the mandate (1929). The Jewish Agency as organized in 1929 was supported by a significant number of non-Zionist Jews. Besides securing their philanthropic support and capital investment, the Zionist leadership hoped to gain their political favor. The World Zionist Organization and the Jewish Agency worked in tandem to further Zionist aims.

In 1920, the yishuv elected a national assembly of some three hundred representatives who then chose the Vaad Leumi (National Council). The national community (Knesset Israel) won the right to vote for the National Assembly by paying a small tax. From its inception, the Vaad Leumi coordinated community life, including defense, and eventually assumed some responsibility for education and social welfare.

Of the main Jewish organizations existing in the 1920s, only the extreme Orthodox Agudat Israel (Union of Israel), which had been founded in 1912, opposed to Zionism, and refused to participate in yishuv activities including National Assembly elections. Agudat Israel began to share in the community's political life only after the establishment of Israel in 1948.

Through efforts of foreign Jews, Palestine's Jewish population became the healthiest in the Middle East. In August 1918 Hadassah, the Women's Zionist Organization in the United States led by Henrietta Szold, sent a medical unit to Palestine. It formed the core of the Hadassah Medical Organization charged with providing health care to the yishuv. Hadassah set up a hospital on Mount Scopus in Jerusalem, and another in Safad for treating tubercular diseases. The Histadrut's Sick Benefit Fund also offered health care.

Mandate authorities introduced various regulations and health services to combat major diseases. Drainage and medical treatment to curb malaria was undertaken. Despite the new Jewish services, most health care continued to be delivered by Christian missionary and indigenous groups.

The yishuv's educational structure predated the mandate. In 1914, a Hebrew school system responsible to the World Zionist Organization had been founded. The Jewish Agency took it over in 1929, but in 1932, its administration was transferred to the Vaad Leumi. Three main trends of education existed during the mandate: general, religious, and labor. General schools taught Zionist-nationalist ideology. Religious training had a nationalist orientation, and secular subjects predominated in the curriculum. Religious schools, connected to the Mizrachi movement founded by European Jews in 1902, focused on training pious rather than nationalistic Jews to give the "national home" a solid spiritual basis. The Histadrut's labor schools emphasized practical training and the social sciences. These schools were far more dedicated to teaching such values as egalitarianism, associated with the labor movement, than they were with religious training. A fourth branch of education existed outside the mainstream in the Agudat Israel schools. Zionists also invested in higher education. The beginnings of the Israel Institute of Technology in Haifa (the Technion) that emphasizes science and technology dated back to 1912, and the foundation stone for Hebrew University of Jerusalem in July 1918 led to the opening of the school in 1925.

Economic Structure and the All-Embracing Histadrut

Both Jewish and Arab economies in pre-mandate Palestine were mainly agricultural. With capital and western technology, the Jewish agricultural sector modernized rapidly. Like Arab industry, Jewish industry experienced its fullest development during World War II. In 1943, Jewish capital investment and value of production accounted for about 85 percent of Palestine's industry, while the Jewish industrial sector handled about 95 percent of production for the British armed forces in Palestine. As in the Arab economy, the role of handicrafts in capital input and output declined precipitously. Hand-in-hand with Jewish economic development came rapid urbanization. By 1945, Haifa had aquired a Jewish majority although Jews had formed only a tiny segment of the population in the 1920s. By 1945, some 62 percent of Palestine's Jews were urban. Many initially agricultural settlements among the pre-1948 agricultural villages had become towns. Industrial development occurred not only in urban areas but also in these agricultural villages, especially in the kibbutzim.

Of all the institutions in mandated Palestine, probably the most significant for Jewish community development was the Histadrut. Though not the first Jewish workers organization in Palestine, it grew rapidly after 1920. It began as both a Zionist and a labor organization—a settlers' trade union committed to encouraging Jewish labor. By 1936, over 85,000 Jews belonged. Activities besides health and education embraced general welfare funds, an agricultural marketing company (Tnuva), a sales cooperative, a construction and industrial firm (Solel Boneh), an insurance company, a banking system, a worker's colonization venture, and housing cooperatives.

During the mandate, the Histadrut acquired a virtually monopolistic status in the yishuv; after the mandate government it was its largest employer. By 1945, some three quarters of Jewish workers were members, and they included not only physical laborers, but also clerks, office workers, agricultural workers, and professionals such as teachers, doctors, and lawyers. Enterprises of the Histadrut affected virtually every Jew in Palestine. Moreover, as a Zionist organization, it inherently supported the twin ideas of Jewish labor (to the exclusion of Arab labor) and Jewish produce (with a boycott of Arab goods), with dues collected specifically to implement them. Despite its Arab affiliates, the Histadrut built up Jewish labor to the detriment of the Arabs. It also controlled the yishuv's underground defense organization, Hagana (Self-Defense). The Histadrut was thus not merely a labor organization but also a monopoly of cooperative enterprises that influenced almost every facet of life in the yishuv.

The Political–Agricultural–Military–Labor Complex

The interrelationships of land settlement federations, political parties, and defense organizations involved with the Histadrut, as well as those outside it, merit special attention. Labor Zionist settlements or villages belonged to the Histadrut from its inception. At that time the two workers' parties—Ahdut Ha'avoda (Labor Unity, a merger of Poalei Zion with several parties in 1919) and Hapoel Hatzair—maintained separate settlement organizations. By 1930, Ahdut-Ha'avoda-Poalei Zion and Hapoel Hatzair had merged into a single political party, *Mapai*, but their settlement organizations remained separate. During the 1940s, the

leftist settlement organization within Mapai set up a new wing, again called Ahdut Ha'avoda; it had its own slate in the mid-1940s. In 1948, shortly before Israeli independence, Ahdut Ha'avoda joined with the most Marxist of the Zionist Labor factions in the Histadrut, Hashomer Hatzair, to form the United Workers Party (*Mapam*). Although these groups realigned again after independence, their actions illustrate the important connection between political-party formation and land-settlement organization.

Integration of Military and Labor Organizations

Agricultural settlements, despite their small numbers, lay at the heart of Zionism. The Jewish National Fund paid for all land used for post-World War I settlements. Besides the agricultural and industrial foci, some settlements began as defense outposts intended to establish a Jewish foothold in new fertile areas including western and northern Galilee and the Jordan Valley. Hagana's thirty-six "stockade and watchtower" settlements built between 1936 and 1938 during the Arab revolt were of this nonagricultural type. With settlements used to expand the practical claims of the future Jewish state, it is not surprising that defense organizations so prominent in founding Israel were closely associated with both the settlements and the labor Zionist ideology they represented.

When World War I had ended and the 5,000-strong Jewish Legion had been disbanded, Vladimir (Ze'ev) Jabotinsky founded a new defense force that provided the nucleus of Hagana. He felt that four Jewish settlements in northern Galilee, set up near war's end with a view to future colonization, required protection. During the Nabi Musa demonstrations in 1920, mandate authorities imposed a fifteen-year prison term on Jabotinsky for activities of his defense force in Jerusalem's Jewish quarter. Soon pardoned, he became leader of Zionism's revisionist wing. In the meantime, a Histadrut committee began organizing

Hagana, soon to be funded and directed by the Vaad Leumi and the Jewish Agency.

From its inception, the activities of Hagana were wide-ranging. As later in the mandate, Hagana members used Jewish settlements to smuggle in illegal immigrants. It also formed a Labor and Defense Battalion that trained as a military reserve while engaging in useful activities like road-building for the mandate government. Arms for Hagana were obtained abroad and smuggled into Palestine, but the yishuv also constructed an underground armory in northern Galilee.

During the 1936–39 uprising, Hagana formally advocated self-restraint (*havlaga*) to avoid giving the impression that a civil war was going on in Palestine and to deter the British from curtailing Jewish immigration. The Jewish Agency influenced the government to approve Jewish settlement police. Virtually all of these Jews who legally were bearing arms by 1937 were also Hagana members. They paved the way for eventual legalization of the Jewish underground army.

Labor Zionists called on Hagana to adopt a more aggressive stance, as signified by a 1936 resolution of the national council of Hakibbutz Hameuchad, one of three settlement federations. Under the leadership of Yitzhaq Sadeh, mobile units began conducting night ambushes on Arab villages. These units became the basis for more fully operational field companies (F.O.S.H.) also under Sadeh. The yishuv financed them through its monthly arms levy, but settlement police also contributed part of their salaries. Sadeh introduced an intelligence service with Arabic-speaking members and an educational branch. Even Orthodox volunteers were brought into the organization.

In 1938, some members of the revisionist Irgun Zvei Leumi (I.Z.L., Etzel), or the National Military Organization founded in 1931 and commanded by Jabotinsky, rejoined Hagana. I.Z.L. had initiated anti-Arab terrorist raids as early as November 1937. Known early in its history as Hagana B, I.Z.L.

offered an alternative for Jews disgruntled with Hagana's labor orientation. Despite cooperation of the I.Z.L. with F.O.S.H., the I.Z.L. retained its independent character, making random attacks on Arabs. In 1939, F.O.S.H. was dissolved but its members had already participated in Special Night Squads, Jewish-British units formed by British officer Orde Wingate. By World War II, the Hagana leadership had replaced F.O.S.H. with H.I.S.H., a territorial home guard. This force and others represented a sound nucleus for the Jewish national army, ideologically oriented toward labor Zionism.

While labor Zionism emphasized a secular socialism, there were also more religiously oriented Jewish supporters of labor ideas. In 1922, the Mizrachi movement formed its own party, Hapoel Hamizrachi. Because of its combined labor-religious orientation, Hapoel Hamizrachi attracted more support than did strictly religious parties—though not nearly as much as the secular Zionists who eventually formed Mapai. Though lacking a separate trade union, Hapoel Hamizrachi maintained a kibbutz federation of the same name.

The Labor-Zionist Leadership

Generally speaking, individuals closely associated with labor Zionism can be credited with building the Jewish state in Palestine. Yitzhak Ben Zvi was Israel's second president. Berl Katzenelson (editor of the Histadrut newspaper *Davar*) was among the spiritual labor Zionists, and he had also fought in the Jewish Legion of World War I. In setting up and maintaining the Jewish state, David Ben Gurion was the principal leader; he played a prominent role in the Histadrut. During World War II, he headed the Jewish Agency. It was he who read Israel's proclamation of independence on 14 May 1948. Serving as prime minister from 1948–53 and again from 1955–63, Ben Gurion proved instrumental in establishing Israeli militancy. His successors as prime minister, Moshe Sharett (Shertok), 1953–55, and Levi

Eshkol (1963–69) also had come to Palestine in the second aliya. The third aliya of the early 1920s brought Golda Meyerson (Meir), Israel's fourth prime minister (1969–74) and other Russian Jews trained by Zionist youth movements in Europe.

The Yishuv and Nazi Germany: The Politics of Rescue

The fact that the yishuv was dominated by Jews of Russian and Polish origin was a factor in Jewish immigration of the 1930s. When German persecutions were beginning, the bulk of new Jews continued to come from Slavic countries. Why did only one fifth to one eighth of Jews entering Palestine between 1932 and 1935 come from Germany? During the 1930s, Zionist leaders arranged with the Nazi government for the transfer of Jewish assets to Palestine. This was possible because Nazis favored ridding Germany of its Jews. But German Jews tended to have assimilated and preferred to stay in the hope that they could somehow adapt to the Nazi's repressive policies exemplified by the 1935 Nuremburg Laws. Those who left preferred refuge in the West to new homes in Palestine. Critics of yishuv policies favoring Eastern Europeans tend to forget that most Jews wiped out by Hitler came from lands, such as Poland, that were occupied by Germany during World War II.

In May 1938, President Roosevelt called together representatives of thirty-two countries to discuss the problem of refugees from Nazi rule. Meeting at Evian-les-Bains in France, conferees agreed that Palestine should be excluded from the agenda since Palestinians were not represented at the conference except by occupier Britain. Of countries present, only the Dominican Republic expressed a willingness to take in Jewish refugees. The United States, which had organized the conference, had in 1935 admitted only some 6,250 Jews while Palestine was being forced to accept over 60,000! The United States was reluctant to welcome more Jews even with the crisis of 1938.

Some Zionist historians have concluded that it was wrong to omit Palestine from the Evian talks. Yet, why should a tiny country the size of Palestine have been forced to absorb refugees when the world's richest and most powerful countries refused? Most Jewish refugees at this time sought only a place of refuge, not necessarily homes in Palestine. Had the gates of the United States or Australia or Latin American countries been fully opened, surely more Jewish refugees would have gone there.

Ironically, the greatest number of Jewish refugees from Nazism between 1935 and 1943—nearly two million of them— were saved not by the Jewish Agency or western nations, but by the Soviet Union, which had occupied eastern Poland early in the war. However, Stalin has also been blamed for deaths of Jews killed when Germany first invaded eastern Poland and Russia, mainly because he suppressed news of atrocities against Jews prior to that time. Moreover, in Ukraine and White Russia, few Jews were saved by their neighbors. Thus while the Soviet Union helped many Jews escape death at Nazi hands, other Jews died *because* of Soviet policies. This factor made Palestine seem more attractive to survivors. Ben Gurion, who on the eve of war had expressed the fear that if too many Jews found refuge in the West then Zionism would lose its momentum, no longer had to worry.

Revisionism, Communism, and Binationalism in the Yishuv

Certainly the most influential of the non-labor Zionist organizations in mandated Palestine was Jabotinsky's revisionist movement. Although he belonged to the Z.E. that in 1922 approved excluding Transjordan from any Jewish home, his movement wanted a Jewish state on both sides of the Jordan River, in the whole of southern Lebanon to the Litani River, and in much of present-day southwestern Syria. Basically, these were the demands the Zionists presented in Paris in 1919. During the 1930s, revisionists formed their own trade union, Histadrut Haleumit (National Trade Union), mainly in order to break strikes organized by the Histadrut. They also maintained a youth movement, Betar, which resembled paramilitary youth groups in Europe. Jabotinsky made contact with Italian Fascists at an early date, and his I.Z.L. operated as an anti-Arab group during the 1936–39 revolt. Jabotinsky died in 1940 and was succeeded as I.Z.L. leader by David Raziel. In order to obtain his release from prison, Raziel agreed to collaborate with Britain's war effort, but he died in 1941 while helping suppress the coup d'etat in Iraq.

The Irgun resumed its anti-British activities late in the war under recent arrival Menachem Begin (prime minister of Israel from 1977–83). About 1,500 Jews belonged to I.Z.L., and it was financed both by American and by Palestinian Jews. More will be said about its terrorism that helped convince the British to leave Palestine. The post-independence settlement and political group Herut, and the later Likud Bloc, were direct heirs of the pre-state revisionists.

On the other side of the ideological spectrum was the Palestine Communist Party and its two predecessors. M.O.P.S. (the Socialist Workers Party, founded in 1919) and M.O.P.S.I. Despite its role as a Zionist party that fomented the Jaffa riots of 1921, in 1923 M.O.P.S.I. did an about-face on Zionism. Its members were expelled from Histadrut in 1924. Apart from its role variously as anti-Zionist and defender of Arab and Middle Eastern (Oriental) Jewish rights, and its development of unions during World War II, the Palestine Communist Party never achieved much recognition in either the Jewish or Arab communities. Its importance lay in the fact that it constituted one organization that Jews and Arabs could join together.

The binational trend was advocated also by two other main labor-oriented groups, the League for Jewish-Arab Rapprochement and the Ihud (Unity). Both wanted to see some sort of Jewish entity realized in Palestine. They differed from mainline Zionists primarily in the area of tactics. Chaim Kalvarisky led the League. When it decided to oppose the Biltmore Program of 1942 (which advocated Palestine as a Jewish state), it was joined by Hashomer Hatzair. Ihud came about after and because of the Biltmore Program. Although its leader was Hebrew University president Judah Magnes and it attracted support from Henrietta Szold, it failed to alter Zionist plans.

Protest in Palestine and Commissions of Inquiry

Most historians agree that the summer of 1929 provided a turning point in the Palestine conflict. A decade of unrest followed it, along with attempts by British commissions to ascertain causes and offer solutions. Before 1929, only one important commission had been convened: the Sir Thomas Haycraft (Chief Justice of Palestine) Commission to investigate the Jaffa violence of May 1921. Before it could present its report, Samuel broke off Jewish immigration and made a special point of blaming M.O.P.S.I. rather than the Arabs. His response influenced the Zion-ist decision to focus on self-defense so that the British would have no reason to blame Jews for violent outbreaks and thereby halt immigration.

The 16th Zionist Congress and the Haram al-Sharif/Western Wall Dispute

In summer 1929, Chancellor was negotiating with Arab Executive representatives to form a Palestine legislative assembly. At the same time, the World Zionist Organization convened its sixteenth congress that set up the Jewish Agency. The congress provided the occasion for a widely reported speech by Jabotinsky in which he called upon Britain to open greater Palestine to the "great colonizing masses." The Zurich Accord of this congress and Jabotinsky's speech gave the Arab leadership in Palestine the idea that Jews were about to mount a mass attack or a colonial inundation. That is probably why the changing of the status quo at the Western Wall in Jerusalem provided the spark for renewed Jewish-Arab conflict.

The Haram al-Sharif (holy sanctuary) in Jerusalem is the home of the Dome of the Rock (or Mosque of Umar)—one of Islam's oldest structures—and of al-Aqsa Mosque. This area, as starting point for the prophet Muhammad's night journey, made Jerusalem Islam's third holiest city. The sanctuary's western wall represented for Jews the remains of the ancient Jewish temple built by Solomon and rebuilt by Herod the Great. As waqf, the whole Haram al-Sharif was under Muslim jurisdiction. In the nineteenth and twentieth centuries, Jews could worship at the wall, but without benches, screens or scrolls of the Torah. In 1920, the Jewish leadership in Jerusalem asked the government to give the Jewish community control of the wall. During the 1920s, Jews despite restrictions brought benches and scrolls to the wall. In 1925, Leonard Stein, secretary of the W.Z.O. executive, agreed that Muslims both legally and politically were justified in resisting official change in the status of the wall. Repeated Jewish pressures, however, led the S.M.C. to publicize throughout the Muslim world the presumed campaign of Jews to take over Jerusalem's Muslim holy places.

When on Yom Kippur in September 1928 Jews brought partitions to the wall, the S.M.C. protested to British authorities who agreed that such innovations were prohibited. On 15 August 1929, Betar demonstrated at the wall, thereby provoking an unofficial, non-S.M.C. Muslim demonstration the next day. About a week later, massacres of Jews took place in Safad and Khalil (Hebron), Muslim towns that had old Jewish communities. Some Jews retaliated by desecrating mosques. In all, about one hundred Jews and one hundred Arabs died.

The Shaw Commission, White Paper, and Black Letter

This violence brought two commissions to Palestine. The Shaw Commission under Sir Walter Shaw began its work in September 1929. Its report recognized the conflicting nationalisms present in Palestine and the creation of a "landless and disoriented class" of Arab peasants resulting from land transfers. As a remedy, the report suggested the following: 1) redefinition of the mandate's interpretation of "safeguarding of Jewish communities," that is, the writing of Arabs into the mandate; 2) restriction of Jewish immigration; 3) protection of Arab farmers; 4) reaffirmation that the Jewish Agency was not Palestine's government.

The Shaw report resulted in the sending of the second commission in May 1930, headed by Sir John Hope-Simpson, a man involved in the Greek-Turkish transfer of the early 1920s. His recommendations were contained in the Passfield White Paper of 1930. They emphasized the dual nature of Britain's commitment in Palestine and recommended limiting Jewish immigration to a total of about 50,000. This was based on the assumption of a limited "absorptive capacity," a term that would come under discussion frequently. British efforts to free state lands for Arab purchase were soon lost with the massive Jewish immigration of the mid-1930s. Moreover, Chaim Weizmann resigned from the presidency of the J.A. and W.Z.O. in protest. He was especially annoyed that the British proposed to restrict transfers and immigration just when he had obtained more money from U.S. Jews and when immigration was rising. Pressured by Winston Churchill and by other Zionists, Ramsay MacDonald issued on 21 February 1931 a refutation of the White Paper in a letter to Weizmann, known to Arabs as the *Black Letter*. Weizmann later credited this letter with having made possible Jewish gains of the 1930s and 1940s in Palestine.

Sir Arthur Wauchope tried to minimize the damage done by the White Paper-Black Letter. From 1933–35, over 135,000 Jews entered Palestine legally, thereby doubling its Jewish population in only six years. Between 1932 and 1938, some 218,000 Jews in all came into the country so that by the beginning of World War II, Jews constituted about 28 percent of the population of 1.5 million. At that rate of increase, Arabs perceived that they would become a minority in their own country by 1952. They could not sympathize with Jews fleeing Europe, especially since so many German Jews arrived with capital. When Wauchope tried to institute the promised self-government, Jewish leaders opposed it while the Arabs hesitated. The 1935 Zionist congress called for Jews to encourage resettlement of Palestine's Arabs while the Arab Congress of the same year demanded democratic government, an end to land transfers, and an end to Jewish immigration. Wauchope's parliamentary proposal gave Jews a disproportionate number of appointed though not elected representatives, but Britain's houses of parliament objected, demonstrating to the Arabs that their position was at a disadvantage in Britain.

The Arab Revolt of 1936–39

In April 1936, before implementation could begin, the Arab revolt began. An Arab bus robbery resulted in the killing of two Jewish passengers. The next day, Jews killed two Arabs in the neighborhood. Mutual atrocities began. A Jewish funeral procession erupted into anti-Muslim violence and then into a riot in which some twenty Jews died. The A.H.C., led by al-Hajj Amin, declared a general strike to last for six months or until the British agreed to end Jewish immigration. What happened in April 1936 amounted to both organized and unorganized Arab protest by a community

which had concluded it lacked constitutional means to bring about an end to a movement calculated to result in its own removal. Disturbances that lasted until 1939 have been characterized as mostly a peasant revolt, involving inter-Arab violence as well as Arab-Jewish, Jewish-Arab, Arab-British, and British-Arab killings.

What did the general strike of April–October 1936 accomplish? Historians generally agree that the strike that implemented an anti-Jewish boycott succeeded. Arab produce that helped feed Jews in the cities was cut off. However, the strike encouraged Jewish self-sufficiency in agriculture. Once the Arab leadership realized that the strike had been counterproductive, they called it off. In the meantime, violence had spread among the unemployed and frustrated. Britain used the revolt to detain suspects without trial and to penalize entire villages. Arab government officials stayed in their jobs so that Jews would not be hired in their place, but they assisted strikers by giving 10 percent of their salaries to a special fund. In August 1936, a new element was injected into the Palestine equation—the arrival of a band of Iraqis and Syrians led by Syrian guerrilla Fawzi al-Qawuqji. From this time, the Arab world became much more involved in the Palestine question. The Muslim Brothers of Egypt sent their first missionaries and aid to Palestine. When the strike ended, the British were about to send out a new royal commission. Over 1,000 nonfatal casualties as well as some 187 Muslim Arab, 10 Christian Arab, 80 Jewish, and 28 British dead had been counted. The British, who should have understood the situation in Palestine by that time, wanted to know why this violence had occurred.

The Peel Commission and its Aftermath

At first, Arab leaders in Palestine boycotted the Peel Commission, mainly because Britain had just issued new immigration quotas. Only intervention by neighboring rulers convinced the Palestinians to talk to the commission. By then, over fifty of the total of sixty-six meetings had been held, and prominent Zionists were in close touch. The Peel recommendations that were announced in July 1937 provoked the second phase of Arab protest. Of all royal commission reports, that of Peel's group is considered to have been most favorable to Zionists. For the first time, partition was proposed as a solution to the conflicting nationalisms of Palestine (see Map 18). Jews would receive the best lands, including those of Safad where Jews formed only 4 percent of the population and the Akka district where .001 percent of the population was Jewish. The proposed Jewish state would have almost as many Arabs as Jews, not counting beduin.

Neither Jewish nor Arab leaders were pleased with the plan. Arabs objected in principle, just as they objected to the entire mandate: Palestine was their country and could not be divided. The Jewish Agency and Zionist Congress were pleased finally to have a Jewish state, but they were dissatisfied with the boundaries. Ben Gurion stated that "No Zionist can forego the smallest portion of Eretz Israel." Weizmann, too, disliked the boundaries, but he suggested that the Zionists would eventually obtain southern Palestine: he stated that "It will not run away."

Zionists felt that it was better to keep open negotiations in order to secure the best parts of Palestine for the Jewish state. Nevertheless, the Zionist congress of 1937 rejected the Peel plan. Members were irritated that because the Jewish state would possess the most fertile lands, it would have to pay a subsidy to the Arab portion to be attached to Transjordan. Although a minority of Palestine's Jews led by Magnes felt that partition would lead to Jewish-Arab warfare, the Jewish Agency refused to consider his appeals for new Jewish-Arab negotiations.

The Arab National Congress meeting at Bludan in Syria in September 1937 denounced partition, too. When the pro-partition district commissioner of Galilee,

Lewis Andrews, was murdered in October 1937, the A.H.C. was dissolved and its leaders arrested and deported. Al-Hajj Amin, already deprived of his organization, had fled abroad in July. Mutual terrorism began again, especially as Jewish defense forces abandoned *havlaga*. While the total number of rebels probably amounted to no more than 5,000, many people in both communities sympathized. In 1938, nearly 1,700 people were killed— 486 Arab civilians and 1,138 Arabs defined as rebels.

Apparently, the expulsion of Arab leaders removed most individuals with influence over Palestine's Arabs. This left the Palestinians without the political leadership that they would so desperately need later. The A.H.C. continued its activities based in Damascus but could exercise little control over military bands that were constituted into regional groups in Palestine. During summer 1938, public services in major Arab towns—Bethlehem, Nablus, and Ramallah—stopped functioning. To curtail infiltration from neighboring countries, the British with Jewish aid built a wall on the Syrian border. Only the publication of a new report by the Woodhead partition Commission succeeded in reducing the momentum of the rebellion.

The Woodhead Commission issued its report in November 1938. In each of three alternative partition plans, significant amounts of territory would remain as mandates, but two plans still allotted much of predominantly Arab Galilee to the proposed Jewish state. In all cases, Jerusalem, Nazareth, and Bethlehem would be kept under mandate administration. Jaffa would be an island of the Arab state surrounded by Jewish or mandated territory, except in plan C (see Map 18). However, the Woodhead report also concluded that any partition would be problematic. Britain therefore convened a joint conference in London during February and March of 1939 so that Jews, Arabs, and British could express their opinions. It failed due to inter-Arab rivalry and Jewish-Arab disagreement. Arabs were represented not only by the

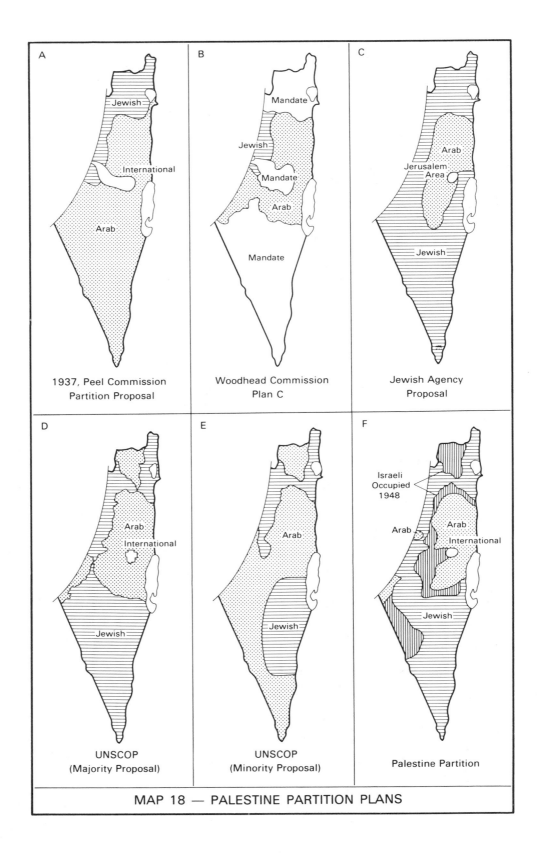

A — 1937, Peel Commission Partition Proposal
- Jewish
- International
- Arab

B — Woodhead Commission Plan C
- Mandate
- Jewish
- Mandate
- Arab
- Mandate

C — Jewish Agency Proposal
- Arab
- Jerusalem Area
- Jewish

D — UNSCOP (Majority Proposal)
- Arab
- International
- Jewish

E — UNSCOP (Minority Proposal)
- Arab
- Jewish

F — Palestine Partition
- Israeli Occupied 1948
- Arab
- Arab
- International
- Jewish

MAP 18 — PALESTINE PARTITION PLANS

Palestinian leadership but also by delegates from Saudi Arabia, Iraq, Transjordan, Egypt, and Yemen. By inviting Arab leaders, the British finally admitted that Palestine was an Arab national question.

For the first time, British authorities released the official documents bearing on the Palestine question. They did so out of a genuine effort to see what had been promised Husayn in 1915. In March 1939, the conference broke up after both Jews and Arabs had not only rejected a final set of proposals but also had refused to meet face-to-face. Britain, faced with the increasing possibility of a European war, decided to issue a prewar policy statement that it hoped would secure order among Palestine's Arab and among Arabs elsewhere in the Middle East. Despite the inflammatory actions of Jewish revisionists, the British assumed that the yishuv would not oppose the anti-Nazi war effort.

The 1939 White Paper and Its Political Consequences: The Biltmore Program

Britain's White Paper issued in May 1939 brought about widespread condemnation, especially by Zionists and the British Labour Party. According to this document, Palestine would be given independence within ten years, conditions permitting, and the country was divided into three main areas, with unqualified Jewish land-purchase restricted to the coast. In order to safe-guard the Arab majority, Jewish immigration would be limited to a total of 75,000 during the next five years. The White Paper repeated that "it was not part of the Government Policy that Palestine should become a Jewish state, regarding it as contrary to their obligations to the Arabs under Mandate."

The Zionist leadership condemned the White Paper as "monstrous," in the context of the unfolding tragedy in Europe. When it came out, Ben Gurion announced the Jews would "fight with Great Britain in this war as if there was no White Paper, and ... fight the White Paper as if there was no war." This dual commitment was

carried out by the yishuv. Wartime Zionist policy was under the leadership of Weizmann (still World Zionist Organization president), Ben Gurion (head of the Jerusalem Jewish Agency office), and Moshe Sharett (head of the J.A.'s political department). Weizmann and Ben Gurion were often at odds. Ben Gurion favored extension of Zionist contacts with American leaders and expansion of support among U.S. Jews, including non-Zionists. He wanted a state soon, as he thought in terms of a Palestine with hundreds of thousands of Jews immigrating within a short period. With leaders raising money—mainly for immigration, agricultural settlement, and propaganda—the budget of the Jewish Agency between 1939 and 1946 increased by nearly ten times to £P 6,500,000.

Ben Gurion's plans came to fruition at a conference with American Jewish leaders held in May 1942 at the Biltmore Hotel in New York. About 600 Jews attended. The delegates' statement praised the results of Jewish colonization in Palestine. The 1939 White Paper was rejected as cruel and illegal. In the statement American Jews asked that Palestine's Jews be allowed to fight under a Jewish flag. Finally, the Biltmore program urged that "the gates of Palestine be opened" and that "Palestine be established as a Jewish Commonwealth."

What did the Biltmore Program mean? Ben Gurion apparently viewed it as a defeat for Weizmann although the latter agreed with its thrust to give new impetus to Zionism. The Zionist leadership in Palestine, whether they took the program seriously, as utopian, or as a mere slogan, accepted the idea of pressing for Palestine as a Jewish state. Except for members of Hashomer Hatzair, the Zionist Action Committee in Palestine adopted the Biltmore Program. In the United States, the program encouraged both Jewish and Christian Zionists to accelerate their activities. American Jews gave in increasing amounts to the United Jewish Appeal, with contributions for Palestine Jewry reaching $50 million in 1947 alone. Combined with horror at Hitler's extermination plan, news of which began to circulate in 1942, the Biltmore Program aroused American Jewry to join in the Zionist effort. Between 1939 and 1945, over 150,000 Jews joined the Zionist Organization of America (Z.O.A.).

Perhaps if some of the energy focused on immigration to Palestine had instead been directed toward opening the United States to Europe's persecuted Jews, more Jews might have been saved.

From Military Support to Terrorism

Over 135,000 Jews of Palestine volunteered to fight against the Nazis in World War II, but only about 32,000 actually served in Britain's army, some of them undertaking dangerous missions in Europe. Although the yishuv wanted to see Germany defeated, it also wanted to fight as an independent Jewish force. The British in Palestine perceived dangers inherent in allowing this to happen, and they did not even want Jewish volunteers in the British Army. Since members of Hagana had cooperated in suppressing the Arab revolt, the British knew that the yishuv already possessed a well-trained military force loyal to Zionism first and foremost. By incorporating Jews into the British Army, the British would be giving them access to military knowledge. Britain was aware that it might incur "obligations" in return. Such a force would contain the potential for fighting against Britain once the war was over. At first, the British allowed Jews into the army only if an equal number of Arabs volunteered. Since few Arabs wanted to fight for colonial Britain, the idea of parity was abandoned. Yet the British tried to restrict Jews to noncombatant roles.

The Jewish Agency kept requesting a more active and visible presence in the fight against Germany. Sharett had to agitate constantly within the yishuv against setting up an underground army to resist the Germans should they reach Palestine. He felt that Jewish interests lay in helping the British even in 1941 when the future looked bleak. Hagana's High Command believed otherwise and decided to create the elite Palmach striking force in May

1941. It would defend the yishuv against a possible Nazi invasion and against random attacks on Jewish settlements. Training under Yitzhak Sadeh emphasized guerrilla warfare.

Between 1939 and 1941, the British remained ambivalent about Jewish participation in the war. Periodically they encouraged or withheld official sanction. Nevertheless, the Zionists persisted. Jews served with Britain in special missions in Syria and Lebanon and assisted in planning for the defense of Palestine. Many of Israel's postwar leaders, including Moshe Dayan, used these operations to acquire information vital to a future Jewish state. When the battle for Palestine began later, Palmach had trained not only an army but also a navy and air force, joined by thousands of Jewish veterans.

Besides this assistance in the war, the yishuv also engaged in violations of mandate policy. Arms factories that had been in operation since the early 1930s began turning out more sophisticated weaponry, all coordinated by a home weapons industry. Mortars, mortar shells, bullets, Sten guns, and grenades came out of these illicit operations. Illegal immigration also continued, beginning with the training of cadres to help bring Jews to Palestine from Europe. The Jewish Agency tried to capitalize on several incidents involving ships. When they mistakenly blew up the ship *Patria* in Haifa harbor in November 1940, killing some 250 immigrants on board, the Zionists concocted a story of mass suicide to score a propaganda victory. Nearly 1,000 more Jewish refugees died in 1941 on ships that sank, one in the Sea of

Marmora and the other by torpedo fire in the Black Sea.[2] Mossad (the intelligence organization) took over illegal immigration in 1942 under Hagana's High Command, but most of its plans were put into operation after the war had ended. Arms procurement, also under Hagana, was carried out by a group called Rekhesh, which raided British bases for ammunition and robbed military transports. After the war, Rekhesh also purchased diverse arms in Europe, especially surplus war material and scrap metal from sunken ships.

The I.Z.L. and Hagana decided toward the beginning of the war not to fight Britain. A dissident group led by Abraham Stern split off from I.Z.L. in protest as early as 1940 (the group after 1942 was called Freedom Fighters for Israel—L.H.I. or Lehi). British authorities called this terrorist organization the Stern Gang because it resorted to robberies to raise money. Initially revisionist, Lehi murdered some Histadrut officials in 1942. After Stern's death that year, the organization suffered somewhat but revived under its new name. Because of Lehi terrorism, the British began to blame the Jewish Agency for all violence. Ben Gurion replied by branding as anti-Semitic anyone who opposed Zionism.

In November 1944, two Lehi members went to Cairo and murdered Lord Moyne, Britain's Minister of State, presumably because he had met with Arab leaders during the Alexandria conference that October. Besides setting up the framework for the Arab League, this meeting provided an occasion for Arab leaders to call upon Britain to implement the White Paper of 1939. The two men were executed but not without winning the sympathy of some Egyptians who had suffered from their own anti-British activities. The two Sternists claimed to favor a joint Arab-Jewish effort to expel the British from Palestine. Available evidence suggests that Lehi's lean toward socialism, anti-imperialism, and even a measure of anti-Zionism was a major element in its differences with I.Z.L.

Since I.Z.L. had already announced its resumption of anti-British terrorism, the Jewish leadership used the Moyne slaying to round up I.Z.L. and Lehi members. Officially, the Jewish Agency disassociated itself from the two groups. Yet Hagana (including Palmach), I.Z.L., and Lehi remained in close touch and often worked together once the war had ended. At the least, the three bodies maintained a tacit alliance in the effort to set up the Jewish state. As soon as the independence struggle had succeeded, the two terrorist groups were absorbed into Israel's mainstream, the I.Z.L. members going to Herut and the Lehi to both rightist and leftist parties.

Anti-British Pressures and International Intervention

As World War II was ending and the extent of the Jewish tragedy in Europe

[2] These incidents are discussed in many sources, among them Christopher Sykes, *Cross Roads to Israel* (Bloomington, Indiana: Indiana University Press, 1967), pp. 234–238; Yigal Allon, *Shield of David: The Story of Israel's Armed Forces* (London: Weidenfeld and Nicolson, 1970), pp. 156–157, 159–160, 162, 165–166, 178, 187, 212–213 (on arms procurement in general); Nathan Weinstock, *Zionism: False Messiah* (trans. and ed. by Alan Adler). (London: Ink Links, 1979), p. 205.

began to be revealed, Zionist organizations especially in the United States heightened lobbying efforts to make Palestine the only available refuge for displaced Jewish survivors. President Roosevelt tried to accommodate Zionist wishes as stated in the Biltmore Program, but he was also aware of the plight of Palestinians. While meeting with Abd al-Aziz ibn Saud in February 1945, the Saudi king told Roosevelt that Palestinians were in no way responsible for what had happened to Jews in Europe. Roosevelt later promised him that no changes in United States-Palestine policy would occur without full and advance consultation with both Arabs and Jews.

The U.S. president died not long after that and was succeeded by Harry S. Truman, who chose to pressure Britain immediately to admit 100,000 Jews into Palestine. The new president, who was clearly concerned with the Jewish tragedy, later justified his policy by stating that although there were many Zionists in America, he did not see multitudes of Arabs in the electorate. Considering the new international leadership role of the United States, Truman's actions and statements bolstered hopes and aims of Zionists while eroding the positive feelings of newly independent Arab countries toward the United States. Despite U.S. pressures, the British Labour Party government which took power under Clement Atlee in July 1945 on a pro-Zionist platform refused to modify restrictions on Jewish immigration into Palestine. Jewish refugees caught trying to enter found themselves either deported or detained in camps within Palestine.

The Anglo-Jewish Conflict in Palestine

The Jews and British in Palestine entered into a conflict in which Arab Palestinians played no great role. The well-armed and well-coordinated yishuv could afford to ignore the relatively disorganized and poorly armed Palestinians at this stage. Even though Musa al-Alami perceived that Arabs outside Palestine had achieved a greater degree of consensus on the Palestine question than those within, he still could not prevent factionalism among his compatriots. While the Palestinians were fragmented, Jews in Palestine and outside inaugurated the militant phase of the struggle. The detention issue supplied the spark.

In October 1945, Hagana, with the help of local Jewish settlement police, broke into a detention camp and freed the Jewish detainees. Since the refugees insisted on taking their soon abandoned belongings with them, their trail was easy to follow. Hagana rallied Jews from neighboring communities to join the refugees so that the British would not be able to sort out the new arrivals. The tactic succeeded. Hagana showed that not only would the yishuv be able to back up its actions but also that it could carry out operations efficiently. This event was quickly followed by a concerted series of attacks by I.Z.L., Palmach, and Lehi on 31 October and 1 November 1945. Because of this acceleration of terrorism, the Labour government decided to send yet another commission of inquiry. In view of American pressure, the British insisted that the United States accept responsibility for consequences of decisions being urged by the American government.

The Anglo–American Inquiry

In November 1945, an Anglo-American Commission of Inquiry was charged with exploring possibilities in Palestine for Jewish immigration and with checking out Jewish victims of persecution in Europe. This twelve-member group did not focus on Arabs. The commission's main work began late in 1945, not long after the U.S. Congress approved a resolution calling for the transformation of Palestine into the Jewish national home. In 1946, the commission surveyed the situation in Europe and then moved to Cairo to consult with Arab League leaders. Arab opinion continued to point out that Palestine was still an Arab land in which Jews could claim only minority status. Abd al-Rahman Azzam, the League's main administrator, explained that Arabs in Palestine did not wish to be dominated and "civilized" by European Jews. After all, colonizers nearly always claimed to be acting in the best interests of the indigenous population in the prospective colony. By March, the commission had left for Palestine.

Just before the commissioners arrived, Jews carried out several sabotage operations. During the interviews, Ben Gurion refused to provide any information about Hagana. Arab representatives such as scholar Albert Hourani gave impressive testimony on behalf of Palestinian interests, but the commissioners still remained hopeful that they could persuade Arabs to approve admission of another 100,000 European Jews. Judah Magnes spoke in favor of immigration only if the Arabs were granted self-government in Palestine. He felt that immigration and not statehood should be the main Jewish interest. After hearing these and other witnesses, the commission made trips to Saudi Arabia, Syria, Lebanon, and Iraq.

The commission's report of April 30, 1946 tried to reach a compromise. The ideas of partition or of making all of Palestine either a Jewish or Arab state were rejected in favor of binationalism. However, 100,000 Jews should be granted immigration, Jewish land-purchase options should be restored, and the territory should be administered as a trusteeship. As a concession to Arabs, the committee ordered the abolition of *avoda ivrit* for J.N.F. enterprises.

Neither the British nor American governments approved the report, the British because it was too pro-Zionist and the Americans because it was not pro-Zionist enough. Before its publication, Lehi launched a terrorist attack on a British military car park, killing seven of the eight British guards. Other British soldiers replied by raiding a Jewish village near Tel Aviv. Because Americans continued to insist on immediate admission of 100,000 Jews, even in the face of terrorism, the British were especially resentful. Britain possessed concrete evidence of Hagana, Lehi, and I.Z.L. collusion by this time.

How, then, could the British acquiesce to the admission of Jews who might join the ranks of Jewish military forces and provoke Arab terrorism, too? In exchange for considering the new immigrants, Britain demanded the disbanding of all illegal armies, Jewish and Arab, in Palestine. Included of course was Hagana. Perhaps British colonial secretary Ernest Bevin miscalculated. The Jewish Agency and the United States had spent so much

time focusing on the 100,000 that the British could have won international support just by accepting this number.

In the end, this chance to outflank the Jewish Agency was lost and Bevin in June added to the antagonism by saying that Americans supported Jewish immigration to Palestine only because they did not "want them in New York."[3] Palmach responded by attacking communications in Palestine. In reply, the British arrested the J.A. leadership as well as Palmach members. The Zionist press sensationalized accounts of the arrests in order to discredit Britain's antiterrorist campaign. On 22 July 1946, the Irgun blew up one wing of the King David Hotel in Jerusalem, wounding forty-five and killing ninety-one Arabs, British, and Jews. Although only the I.Z.L. actually carried out this terrorism and the J.A. appeared shocked, Hagana had conceived a similar plan. As violence accelerated in 1946, more plans for partitioning Palestine were suggested, including one proposed by the Jewish Agency.

Ships loaded with illegal immigrants continued to arrive at Palestine's shores. As British authorities responded with further detentions, investigations of suspected arms caches, and general measures to curtail illegal immigration, Hagana went deeper underground. Leaders obtained false identity cards, and new factories and arms caches were established. When immigrants could not be brought by sea, they were smuggled in overland. In the atmoshere of Jewish-British hostility, British civil servants and military began to take security precautions.

U.N.S.C.O.P. and the Partition of Palestine

Early in 1947, frustrated and exhausted from wars and subsequent withdrawal from India and elsewhere, the British government announced that it could no

---

[3] Sykes, p. 313; and Weinstock, p. 226.

longer deal with the Palestine question and would turn it over to the United Nations. U.N.S.C.O.P. (United Nations Special Committee on Palestine) embarked on yet another fact-finding mission, this time on behalf of an international body determined to resolve the crisis. Most of Africa and Asia, of course, was still under colonial domination so the composition of both U.N.S.C.O.P. and the United Nations as a whole did not represent the world's nations.

When U.N.S.C.O.P. reached Palestine in summer 1947, only Jewish and British leaders would talk with its members. Most Palestinian Arabs boycotted the commission, although leaders of other Arab countries did not. In order to impress the commissioners, the yishuv made certain that another ship would arrive to coincide with the visit. The *Exodus,* carrying some 4,500 passengers from Germany in July, became the focus of intense bargaining. U.N.S.C.O.P. members observed that Hagana seemed to constitute a competent, well-organized body and interviewed its leaders. Hagana informed them that the yishuv would be able to defend any Jewish state that might be established in Palestine.

When the commission finally deliberated its alternatives, eight representatives (from Canada, Australia, Europe, and Latin America) agreed on a majority plan (see Map 18) that would partition Palestine into a Jewish state, an Arab state, and an international zone, with the two states joined in an economic union. The three members from India, Iran, and Yugoslavia supported the idea of a federated state (see Map 18). By 1 September, U.N.S.C.O.P. proposals were ready for debate by the U.N. General Assembly.

Neither plan met with approbation of Arab states. The Palestinian Arab majority concurred with Arab opinion elsewhere. In the yishuv, the proposals were welcomed because a Jewish state would finally emerge, albeit in a territory smaller than that which the Zionists had in mind. Both the United States and the Soviet Union backed partition, but Britain would cooperate only if both Jews and Arabs in Palestine accepted the plan. As amended (see Map 18), the plan was accepted by the necessary two-thirds majority of U.N. members. Ten countries abstained (including Britain), while thirteen countries, including the five independent Arab states, voted against the plan.

The approved plan consisted of six segments plus a Jerusalem enclave. Boundaries were drawn so that virtually all Jewish settlements would fall within the Jewish state occupying some 56 percent of the mandate. However, a large majority of land in this state was under Arab ownership, and counting beduin, over 50 percent of the Jewish state's population would be Arab. By contrast, the Arab state would contain few Jews and virtually no Jewish-owned land. Jaffa would be an Arab island, surrounded by Jewish territory on three sides but leaving the Arabs with a port. Created in a hostile environment, the plan was destined for failure from the outset. The idea of economic union was hardly appropriate for two peoples whose economic intercourse had diminished over the years. Neither Palestinian Arabs nor Jews were enthusiastic about their trisegmented states whose boundaries would be almost indefensible at points of contact.

The First Palestine War

The partition vote took place on 29 November 1947. It touched off the scramble for Palestine and the first Palestine war of 1947–49. Arabs vowed to fight partition while Jews accepted international recognition of Jewish statehood. Early in the battle, each side sought to control key roads and to take over coveted territories allotted to the other state. For Jews in particular, it was deemed crucial to occupy the towns in which few Jews lived or owned land because the vast Arab majorities in those places intended to fight their inclusion in the Jewish state. Jews also set out to occupy or "create facts" in areas not allocated to their state. Neither the northern nor southern segments of the Jewish area had many Jews. The yishuv feared for the safety of the Jews of Jerusalem, particularly in the Old City. One Jewish offensive focused on cutting a swath through Arab territory to reach the city. While the yishuv had long planned for these hard days, Palestinian Arabs, their leaders still dispersed, had no comprehensive infrastructure that could promote a coordinated effort for them to retain what they had been given. In December 1947, Hagana terrorists entered the northern Arab village of Khissas and with hand grenades and machine guns, and killed ten Arabs. In January 1948, irregular Arab troops from neighboring countries began to enter Palestine, led by Fawzi al-Qawuqji. They attacked the Kafr Etzion block south of Bethlehem, killing all of its Palmach defenders.

As the fight intensified, atrocities took place on both sides. Perhaps the most famous and critical instance of brutality occurred at the small village of Dayr Yassin west of and on the road to Jerusalem. The I.Z.L., aided by Palmach and Lehi, massacred some 254 men, women and children although the village had deliberately refused to allow Arab troops to occupy it for fear of such an attack. In *The Revolt: The Story of the Irgun*, I.Z.L. leader Begin justified the massacre on military grounds and claimed that without it, the Jewish state would have been stillborn.[4] Occurring as it did in early April 1948, the onslaught encouraged the exodus of Arabs. Villagers expected to face another Dayr Yassin if they refused to evacuate their villages when pressured by

Jewish forces. Even in Akka, an overwhelmingly Arab city allotted to the Arab state, Arabs were frightened into leaving. Based on preplanned movements, Jewish forces began moving into western Galilee, part of the proposed Arab entity. Entire populations had no choice but to leave so that even before the British had evacuated and the Jewish state had been proclaimed, some 300,000 Arabs had fled from their homes. On the Arab side, Dayr Yassin was followed by an Arab attack on a medical convoy that was on its way to the Hadassah medical complex in Jerusalem. Although over seventy-five men and women professionals died in the ambush (also justified by the perpetrators on military grounds), the killing remained an isolated incident rather than a symbol of a concerted effort taking place all over Palestine. Nevertheless, it rightly raised an alarm within the yishuv of the need for increased security of transport.

During the violence, the British remained aloof, retreating to security zones without giving any direction for the future government of areas being vacated. With no formal handing over of official functions, Jews and Arabs fought for control. The United Nations finally had to admit that the partition commission it had appointed to enact an orderly transfer could not carry out its duties. Under American prodding and for reasons related to the "cold war" between the United States and the Soviet Union, the U.N. General Assembly began debating a new American plan that proposed a ten-year trusteeship instead of partition. While the U.S. State Department embarked on this plan, President Truman began pursuing his private diplomacy. From this point on, the U.S. presidency became the focus of U.S. policy-making in the region.

Palestinians accepted the trusteeship idea because it put off the hated partition, but the Zionists threatened to oppose it with force if necessary. Armed with the promise of U.S. President Harry Truman to recognize the Jewish state, the Jewish Agency prepared to declare the independence of the new state to be named Israel (Zion was also suggested). Despite the

---

[4] Menachem Begin, *The Revolt: The Story of the Irgun*, rev. edition (New York: Nash Publishing, 1977), pp. 163–165; and Weinstock, p. 235.

fact that the British had announced a departure date of 15 May, High Commissioner Allan Cunningham led his forces out of Palestine by sea one day early.

Israeli Declaration of Independence

On 14 May, Ben Gurion read the proclamation of independence of the Jewish state. It emphasized the ancient connection of Jews with Palestine, their efforts to establish foundations for a state, the suffering of Jews in Europe during World War II, the Jewish contribution to the war effort, and their "natural right to be masters of their own fate." The "ingathering of the exiles" was to be a major goal of the state. The thirty-eight signatories promised that Israel would cooperate with the United Nations in implementing partition and called on Arabs in Israel to "participate in the upbuilding of the state on the basis of full and equal citizenship and due representation in all its provisional and permanent institutions." Neighboring Arab countries were told that the new state wanted to help advance all Middle Eastern countries. Finally, Jews around the world were asked to support the new state in promoting Jewish immigration and a strong Israel.

Such promises in the wake of the preceding six months' campaign did not convince either Palestine's Arabs or those outside. There was no Arab declaration of independence. King Abd Allah of Transjordan wanted to incorporate the proposed Palestinian state into his own kingdom. Indeed, early in May, he sent the Arab Legion to Jerusalem to help in fighting there. Various Arab bands carrying out guerrilla operations lacked consolidated leadership, and the old leaders had been displaced and were still regrouping. Since Arabs within Palestine could not by themselves resist Israeli forces, five Arab League countries on 15 May 1948 followed through with their commitment to the Palestinians by sending in portions of their armies. The U.N.-appointed mediator, Swedish Count Folke Berna-

dotte, was expected to convince the various parties to stop fighting. Yet what ensued was the second phase of the first Palestine war. The first stage after November 1947 had involved Jews and Arabs in Palestine. The second phase began the *Arab-Israeli conflict*, still ongoing but under different circumstances.

Second Phase of the Palestine War: Arab Armies in Palestine

The Israelis call the events of 1947–49 their *war of independence*, but to the Arabic-speaking peoples of the Middle East, it came to be known as "the disaster." As Jewish forces coalesced into the I.D.F. (Israel Defense Forces), they carried out preconceived plans. Historians have often speculated as to why the more numerous and supposedly better-equipped Arab armies did not win the war. The answer is much simpler than one might expect.

Nearly all Arab countries that sent forces to Palestine were still under some measure of foreign occupation and only recently independent. Faced with security problems at home, they did not commit substantial numbers of men or equipment to the battle. Of the promised troops, only some 25,000 actually entered Palestine along with an undetermined number of irregular Arab volunteers. Egypt contributed the largest force, but Jordan, Syria, Iraq, and Lebanon also sent at least 2,000–3,000 men each. Saudi Arabia promised to be a major participant but ended up with less than 1,000. These outsiders lacked the leadership, cooperative spirit, and high motivation that characterized Jewish forces at the outset of the war.

Palestine's Arabs were promised arms by the Arab countries on the assumption that they themselves would supply the bulk of the defensive forces. However, while they possessed the will, they lacked the basic expertise, advance planning, and united leadership necessary to combat the highly organized Jewish troops. The promised arms did not arrive. Well-documented Jewish plans to take over most or all of Palestine had no Arab counterpart.[5] Each Arab state had its own aims, some of them selfish and contrary to independent Palestinian aspirations. The 6,000 Arab Palestinian veterans of World War II could not begin to compare with the 32,000 Jewish veterans and much more numerous Hagana and other military forces available to Israel. Since Jewish armies had begun implementing their plans long before 15 May, the battle was well underway before Arab national armies entered Palestine. All things considered, the motley assortment of Palestinians, Arab irregulars, and Arab regular armies acquitted themselves better than could have been expected under the circumstances. Israelis, still shocked by the Holocaust, felt that they were engaged in a life-or-death struggle. Annihilation was perceived as the only alternative to victory.

In the early fighting after the establishment of Israel, the Egyptian army met with some success in the south although its drive north was delayed for six days by the spirited defense of Jewish kibbutzniks at Yad Mordechai. Apparently, the Egyptians had gathered accurate intelligence about Hagana strength but had acquired insufficient data about the preparedness of kibbutz defenders. The delay proved costly to Egypt's war effort because it gave Israeli forces further north a chance to regroup. During late May and early June 1948, I.D.F. troops moved to complete the occupation of western Galilee. An attempt to conquer old Jerusalem failed although Arab quarters in the new part of the city were occupied. When the first ceasefire negotiated by Count Bernadotte began on 11 June, the military situation was as follows:

The Arab Liberation Army (A.L.A.) of Qawuqji held central Galilee. Al-though western Galilee villagers had held back the Jewish regulars, they agreed to let the A.L.A. take over. But the A.L.A. lost western Galilee, and the I.D.F. destroyed Arab villages there. Eastern Galilee was under Jewish control. West of the Jordan river and just south of Tiberias Lake, Syrians had established a position. Jordan's Arab Legion remained in east Jerusalem and guarded the valley to the west where Lydda and Ramle were located. The Egyptian armies had cut off the Negev from the northern parts of Palestine. The Iraqis were entrenched in the triangle area north and west of Nablus.

During the ceasefire, Israeli forces received a big boost to their war effort—the shipment of over one hundred tons of military cargo airlifted from Czechoslovakia. The ceasefire was also used to plan takeover of key communications installations such as railroads and the Lydda airport, as well as for the seizing of main towns east of Tel Aviv, notably Ramle and Lydda. Another objective was the crossroads at Latrun that could be used to cut off Ramallah and Jerusalem. The plan aimed to demoralize the Arabs and give the Israelis the initiative.

When fighting resumed on 9 July, Israeli forces took Lydda airport. Because of vicious house-to-house fighting that accompanied the conquest of Lydda town, Ramle's inhabitants surrendered. At Latrun, however, a small Arab Legion contingent defended the town against more numerous Palmach I.D.F. troops. The Syrians remained entrenched in southeastern Galilee, but the A.L.A. forces lost the Arab town of Nazareth. Despite Israeli efforts, Jerusalem's Old City remained in Arab hands when the second ceasefire began on 18 July.

U.N. Efforts for a Negotiated Settlement: The Second Ceasefire

During these two stages of the struggle, Count Bernadotte kept seeking a peaceful solution. He finally presented a plan the Israelis could not accept at all. It resem-

---

[5] Allon, pp. 185–227; Nafez Abdullah Nazzal, "The Zionist Occupation of Western Galilee, 1948" *Journal of Palestine Studies 3* (Spring 1974):58–76; and Lt. Col. Netanel Lorch, *Israel's War of Independence, 1947–49* (Hartford, Conn.: Hartmore House, Inc., 1966), p. 89.

bled the original Peel Commission proposal. Western Galilee would go to the Jewish state, but except for an internationalized Jerusalem, the rest of Palestine would be in Arab hands. The Negev would be given to Transjordan. Between Haifa and Akka, a neutral zone would be constituted. Bernadotte also tried to win Israeli acceptance for admission of Arab refugees who had fled during the fighting, but the Israelis wanted all matters left open for negotiations with Arab countries. Already in camps, the refugees were viewed by the Israelis not as Palestinians attached to their homes but as Arabs who could easily be absorbed by the poor Arab countries. Arabs were generally pleased with Bernadotte's efforts, but in mid-September 1948, Lehi assassinated him. An American, Dr. Ralph Bunche, replaced him.

Although the ceasefire contained provisions for supplying Jewish settlements cut off by the Egyptian Army, the Egyptians were not anxious to see them assisted, mainly because arms supplies were sure to reach the kibbutzniks. The I.D.F. leadership was worried that unless the status quo were changed, the Israeli state would lose its southern allotment. On 15 October 1948, the war for the Negev began. Newly arrived aircraft helped the Israelis cut the Egyptians' supply lines, lift the state of siege, and take Arab Bir Saba. Egyptians trapped at Faluja, led by a Sudanese brigadier, included a young Egyptian major named Gamal Abd al-Nasir. They resisted appeals to surrender. Not until early 1949 was a negotiated withdrawal achieved. The October campaign, however, did not end the war with Egypt. That happened only between 22 December 1948 and 7 January 1949, with the I.D.F. using an old Roman road to move into the Negev and northern Sinai. When Britain tried to intervene, the I.D.F. shot down its planes although the British used the justification of their 1936 treaty obligations to Egypt. Israel finally agreed to withdraw from areas south of Rafa (southern Gaza) and to accept an armistice instead of a peace treaty that might have proved more durable.

In the north, the I.D.F. pushed the newly equipped A.L.A. back into Lebanon and consolidated its hold over Galilee. Although the Israelis reached the Litani river, they withdrew to the frontiers of mandated Palestine. The Syrians, who had stayed at their base in eastern Galilee, returned home following their defeat. Theoretically, the second truce never ended, but it was in this last bit of fighting that the initial boundaries of Israel were established. Over 500,000 Arab Palestinians had fled from their homes in Israeli-occupied areas. In November 1948, the United Nations set up its relief operation superseded in 1949 by U.N.R.W.A. (United Nations Relief and Works Agency.)

The Rhodes Proximity Talks

Peace negotiations organized by the United Nations finally took place on Rhodes beginning in January 1949. No Arab state recognized Israel. Instead of meeting face-to-face, the parties held "proximity talks" in which Bunche shuttled between the delegations. The Egyptians and Israelis concluded their armistice on 24 February. The Lebanese signed in early March. Then, the Israelis, engaged in negotiations with the Jordanians, began a new operation to secure a foothold on the Gulf of Aqaba. The town of Umm Rash Rash became the port of Eilat, and the Israelis won in the process the western coast of the Dead Sea with its rich potash deposits. There is some evidence that Abd Allah agreed in advance to the Israeli gains. The Jordanian armistice was reached on 3 April. Last to sign were the Syrians. The Syrian role in the Arab defeat and the armistice of 20 July contributed to the first of several coups that were to rock postwar Syria. Iraq never concluded any kind of peace with Israel.

Conclusion

Efforts to make peace in the Middle East continued after the armistices. The

U.N.C.C.P. (United Nations Conciliation Committee for Palestine) was set up by the U.N. General Assembly on 11 December 1948 to take over the mediation role, to help the disputants' governments reach a final settlement, to protect the holy places in Palestine, to present proposals for an international regime in Jerusalem, and to help with the repatriation or resettlement of the war's refugees in accordance with their own wishes. Initial contacts in Beirut with individual Arab states illustrated that they would not discuss a comprehensive settlement with Israel until repatriation. Israel said at first that it would consider repatriation as part of an overall agreement, but later insisted that resettlement in Arab countries was the only solution. Unlike Israel, Arab countries eventually agreed to the internationalization of Jerusalem (the Arabs felt this arrangement would deprive Israel of control over the much larger new areas of the city).

At the Lausanne conference of spring 1949, Israel, Egypt, Lebanon, Jordan, and Syria agreed to protocols for which the 1947 partition would provide the basis for further discussion. Belatedly, the Arab states realized that they could possibly have avoided losses by backing partition, odious as it was. Despite Israel's signature, the Israeli government proved unwilling to consider more than minor boundary adjustments. On the refugee question, Israel offered only a limited "family plan" and a proposal for settling the refugees in selected areas such as crowded Gaza if Egypt would give the area up.

After the war, Egypt remained in control of Gaza while Transjordan occupied and later absorbed the West Bank, the only other portion of the Palestinian Arab territory. Arab hopes that they could pressure Israel for concessions in exchange for admission to the United Nations failed when Israel was admitted in mid-May 1949. American pressure on Israel also failed to yield results on repatriation. The issues of frontiers and repatriation became paramount in years following and contributed to mutual suspicion and hostility. The Zionist goal of a Jewish state had reached fruition but at a cost both to Jews and Arabs throughout the Middle East. The unresolved, long-standing Palestine question has been the fulcrum of inter-Arab and Arab-Israeli relations ever since.

CHAPTER FOURTEEN

The Struggle for Statehood in the Maghrib

Of the Middle Eastern subregions, the Maghrib alone during the interwar period was under occupation by a single European power—France. Morocco, however, was not yet fully under French control after World War I, and Tunisia closely resembled the French mandates of the Arab East. Integrated into France, Algeria's settler-dominated administration pursued a steady course of colonial supremacy. Nationalist movements arose in all areas to challenge the French. We should also note that Mauritania, an Arabic-speaking country bordering Morocco, was resisting French rule in the postwar period, too, but it was administered as part of French West Africa rather than the Maghrib. Like Somalia, Mauritania only began to be reintegrated into the Arab world after independence in 1960.

Cosovereignty in Tunisia

The early stages of Tunisian nationalist activity involved cultural and political reform exemplified by the *Young Tunisians*. Because France treated the protectorate like a colony, nationalists led by Shaykh Abd al-Aziz al-Ta'albi were ready by 1919 to call for independence. Ta'albi, who was also involved in the modernist Islamic reform movement, attended the Paris Peace Conference after World War I in hopes of rallying international support for independence. Disillusioned by his failure, he and a colleague, Ahmad Saqqa, published *La tunisie Martyre: ses revendications* in

1920.[1] The essence of the book was that French occupation had interrupted Tunisia's nineteenth-century development as a modernizing Muslim country. Indigenous institutions had been replaced with alien ones. The authors called for the restoration of Arabic as the medium of instruction in schools, development of social services, reorientation of the economy to the indigenous population, reestablishment of the supremacy of Shari'a, and the readoption of the 1860 constitution. To popularize the book and reach a wider audience, Ta'albi and his colleagues formed the Destour (Dustur or Constitution) Party. They demanded independence, formation of a national army, transferring of settlers' property to Tunisians, and admission of greater numbers of Tunisians into the administration of the country.

Socioeconomic Change and the Development of Tunisian Nationalism

The early Tunisian nationalists came from the upper classes, both religious and secular. Their constitutional focus appealed to few Tunisians. By stressing change through legal action, the nationalists tended to lose sight of their professed social program. During the 1920s, the Destour's political impact waned as it failed to attract the new intelligentsia who were products of the Franco-Arab school system and who tended to come from the lower and middle classes.

In regard to education, Tunisians were caught in the same dilemma as were many other colonized or occupied peoples. In order to achieve equality with the settlers,

Tunisians desired an education comparable to theirs. However, if they could secure such an opportunity, they risked alienating their children from their own cultural heritage. In the Young Tunisians' early days, French education was preferred, but a more popular trend developed combining the French and Arabic systems. French was introduced in *kuttabs,* but Arabic was not neglected. When the government provided only a few such schools, Tunisians set them up on their own, especially along the east coast or Sahil. Fortunate graduates gained admission to the higher division of Sadiqiyya College. Those who graduated from Sadiqiyya could achieve upward mobility without losing touch with their roots.

Although French settlers objected to giving Tunisians French education, they did not obstruct Tunisians' efforts to modernize their indigenous system. Unlike Algeria, Tunisia was never viewed as part of France, intended only for the benefit of the French. Even though the colonials took the best land in Tunisia, their numbers never reached 10 percent of the population; of these, only 10 percent were in agriculture. The urban environment provided the main arena of interaction between French and Tunisians. In the cities, the Tunisians could live in much the same way as Arabs in Beirut or Damascus during the mandate. They worked in the professions, taught in schools, edited newspapers and magazines, and moved around freely. But the French did not view them as equal.

The concept of cosovereignty practiced by the French in Tunisia illustrated this attitude. Although they ruled officially in the bey's name, the French more or less disregarded his authority. French settlers acquainted the government with their own views through a consultative body that met every two years. In 1922, the French instituted the Grand Council that had separate French and Tunisian sections. Tunisian representatives, representing slightly more than a third of the total membership, won their positions not by election but by government selection. In local government too,

---

[1] Abd al-Aziz al-Ta'albi and Ahmad Saqqa, *La Tunisie Martyre: Ses Revendications,* Paris, 1921 is discussed in Howard Nelson, ed., *Tunisia: A Country Study,* 2nd ed., Foreign Area Studies, The American University (Washington, D.C.: U.S. Government Printing Office, 1979), p. 40; Henri Grimal, *Decolonisation: The British, French, Dutch, and Belgian Empires, 1919–1963,* trans. Stephan DeVos (Boulder, Colorado: Westview Press, 1978).

French representatives always outnumbered Tunisians. Thus, over 80 percent of the population was subordinated to the wishes of a 7 percent minority. This situation persisted until after World War II.

Because the French in Tunisia were engaged mainly in mechanized agriculture and industry—capitalist economic activity—Tunisian-French interactions often occurred in the framework of employee-employer. With few Tunisians operating businesses, most labor disputes involved Tunisian workers and French employers. Nationalist overtones hence pervaded Tunisian labor protests. Although Tunisian laborers in the early 1920s could join the French Confédération Générale des Travailleurs (C.G.T.) whose French leadership spoke out against social inequities, the union could hardly fully accommodate Tunisian anticolonial grievances. Muhammad Ali, a German-educated Tunisian, tried to raise the consciousness of Tunisian workers by organizing strikes and establishing in 1924 a strictly Tunisian labor union, the Confédération Générale des Travailleurs Tunisiens (C.G.T.T.). More attuned to the idea of class struggle and liberation of the oppressed (including women), Muhammad Ali wanted Tunisians to stand up for themselves in pressing for social and economic restructuring in a Tunisia where half of the budget supported French officialdom. Although he was arrested and both his union and the C.G.T. were suppressed, the idea that trade unionism and nationalism went hand-in-hand persisted in Tunisia.

Bourguiba and the Creation of the Neo-Destour

The most important development of the period was the rise of the Neo-Destour, a political party led by a Sadiqiyya and French-educated lawyer, Habib Bourguiba (Abu Ruqaiba). When he returned to Tunisia in 1927 laden with academic honors, he could find no regular employment. In 1930, the French in Algeria celebrated the hundredth anniversary of their conquest of Algiers. Not to be outdone,

the French in Morocco and Tunisia held their own special celebrations. In May 1930, a Eucharistic Congress opened in Carthage organized by its archbishop, Msgr. Lemaitre. Because both the bey and the shaykh al-Islam representing the Muslim community attended its opening session, the conference may not have been intended to provoke confrontation. For Bourguiba, though, the congress struck a sour chord echoed in many segments of Tunisia's population. From that time on, he devoted himself to a reformist Islamic nationalism first expressed in journalistic activity through a nationalist newspaper.

In 1932, Bourguiba joined with three colleagues to publish the paper *L'Action Tunisienne*. The Destour party took on concrete political, economic, and social goals in addition to constitutional reform. The group stressed the importance of building up a Tunisia in which all religions and ethnic groups would flourish, but it tried to appeal to the Muslim masses through support of Islam. Ironically, Bourguiba, who later implemented legal reforms that changed the status of women in Tunisia, gave public support to the idea of veiling women. Between 1932 and 1934, *L'Action* supported an interpretation of Muslim law holding that Tunisians who had taken advantage of an opportunity presented by a 1923 law to become French citizens were no longer Muslims and were not entitled to burial in Muslim cemeteries. Destour leaders held that these people had not abandoned their religion, though they were no longer subject to the Shari'a.

When the party censured Bourguiba for having opposed the burial of a child whose family was naturalized, he left and formed the Neo-Destour. This event in March 1934 marked the beginning of the growth of nationalist agitation instigated by the new party (although the movement soon went underground). Officially banned for the next twenty years, the Neo-Destour emerged in the 1950s to lead Tunisia to independence. During the 1930s, though, the Neo-Destour was to be a mass party, appealing not only to the educated elites. The clandestine party's administrative structure was based on elective and representative local and national party members.

Bourguiba's Neo-Destour initially carried on an intense rivalry with the Destour and its leaders. Between 1934 and 1936, Bourguiba was imprisoned because of his role in disturbances between the two groups. Then in 1937 he was involved in undermining the efforts of Ta'albi, who had recently been allowed back into Tunisia, to shore up the declining following of the Destour.

In 1938, Bourguiba was implicated in disturbances arising from a labor dispute in which both the reorganized C.G.T.T. and Neo-Destour were involved. Because of rising tensions in Europe, the French suppressed the nationalists by imprisoning in France many of the leaders, including Bourguiba. The war served to quiet the opposition because even after the French defeat, the Vichy government was able to control Tunisia.

World War II: Its Impact on Tunisian National Development

November 1942 marked the beginning of the allied landing in North Africa, and the arrival of German forces in Tunisia. The new Husaynid Bey Munsif (Moncef), who had come to power that June, began to play an active role in the nationalist movement. Both the bey and the nationalists viewed the war as giving them a chance to win a greater measure of independence for Tunisia. American agents operating in the country encouraged the nationalists. Munsif Bey further demonstrated his commitment to the nationalists by appointing a new government under the Neo-Destour supporter Muhammad Shaniq (Chenik).

While the Germans occupied Tunisia, they released Bourguiba from prison in Marseilles. They did not know that he had secretly told his followers to side with France. Reaching Tunisia in April 1943, Bourguiba gave a public address in May affirming that the future lay with France, not Italy or Germany. He fully anticipated that his unexpected support would lead the French to reciprocate once the war ended. When the Free French took Tunis in May, however, General Juin denounced Munsif Bey as a Nazi supporter and deported him to Laghwat in violation of the La Marsa Agreement. As for Bourguiba, the efforts of French settlers to brand him as anti-French, anti-Jewish, and anti-Ally failed, along with plans of the military to arrest him for treason. The U.S. consul backed Bourguiba. As the war came to a close, Bourguiba left Tunisia, unbeknownst to the authorities, to rally support for Tunisia abroad, first from the Arab League in Egypt and then from a variety of countries around the world. Subsequently, Tunisian leaders continued their gradualist but steady approach to securing independence from France.

Algeria Between the Wars

Roots of Nationalism: The Evolués

The development of an Algerian nationalist movement after World War I had its roots in the Jeunes Algériens. These Algerians presented themselves as French Muslims rather than as Muslim modernizers like those in the Arab East. Campaigning for educational development, political rights, and progress, the group won a modest amount of support among the educated and urban population, but they alienated devout Muslims. Despite the moderation of their goals, Europeans presented them abroad as revolutionaries advocating an Arab Algeria. In the postwar period, these Young Algerians continued to agitate for equal rights rather than for independence. Among the early nationalists who favored assimilation was Farhat Abbas. In his writings between 1921 and the late 1930s, he expressed the hope that France would apply to Algerians the values taught in French schools. The French used the label evolué (evolved) to describe those who advocated assimilation.

Algerians, especially the nearly 300,000 who had helped the war effort as workers and soldiers, expected some reward once the war had ended. In 1919, the French government made one feeble attempt to give Muslim Algerians a greater though still rather minimal role in local government affairs. When French settlers objected, the government relented and even granted extra funds for development of the French sector. As soon as governor Maurice Viollette (1925–27) tried to accommodate and understand the Young Algerians, French settlers obtained his recall. Neither the new Algerian elites nor the masses who had aided France in the war made any substantial gains in the early postwar period.

Messali al-Hajj: Separatist Nationalism

Not all Algerians who worked in France during the war returned home. Wages in France were much higher than those in Algeria, although conditions were often difficult and not unlike those facing Middle Eastern workers in Europe in the 1970s and 1980s. It was there that a true nationalist movement arose, one which advocated a future for Algeria without France. Led first by Ali Abd al-Qadir and then by Messali al-Hajj, *Étoile Nord-Africaine* (North African Star) started as a social-action, Marxist-oriented group during the mid-1920s. Between 1933 and 1935, Messali was in prison. After his release, he sought refuge in Switzerland where he met Shakib Arslan, an exiled

Druze leader. Arslan lived mainly in Switzerland between 1918 and his death in 1946, serving Arab nationalism through his periodical *La Nation arabe* and through sustaining North African nationalists like Messali. Apparently through discussions with Arslan, Messali decided that his main efforts ought to be directed toward nationalism rather than toward a more international Marxism. But he appealed most to urban workers.

Kabyles and Algerian Nationalism

A disproportionately high number of workers, both in France and in Algeria, came from Berber Kabylia. French repression in the 1870s had promoted rural-urban migration. The subsequent combination of dispossession and higher birth rates when stability had returned created a surplus population that could not be supported at home. When the French discovered that the Kabyles worked well as teachers, bureaucrats, shopkeepers, and other petite bourgeoisie in the towns, they began to regard them as more industrious than other Algerian Muslims. During World War I France recruited most heavily in Kabylia for overseas workers. The assumption that Kabyles would prove more sympathetic to French colonial rule proved erroneous because as they became more proletarianized, they grew more nationalistic, too. Borrowing from French culture without losing their individuality, Kabyles were to play an important role in the Algerian struggle for independence. They were especially attracted to Messali's movement.

Messali and Ben Badis: Islam in Algerian Nationalism

When the Popular Front government in France allowed Messali to return to Algeria, he attended the Islamic conference organized in June 1936 by Algerian Muslims close to the Young Algerian movement, the Algerian Communist Party, and the ulama. The congress drafted a charter demanding equality with Frenchmen and the abolition of a separate administration for Algeria. When Messali objected to perpetuating the existing links between France and Algeria, he won the delegates' opprobrium. Yet his pessimism about the French willingness to share Algeria was justified when the Blum-Viollette Bill of December 1936, which would have granted full citizenship rights to some 20,000 Algerian Muslims, failed to pass the committee charged with examining it prior to its presentation to the French Chamber of Deputies. Messali in 1937 replaced Étoile with the Parti Populaire Algérien (P.P.A.) that called for an independence to be reached in collaboration with France. This modified nationalism brought him new supporters, especially in urban areas. Although he spent the war in prison, Messali's stance came to be the one accepted by most Algerians.

Messali's movement was not the only one to reject the evolué emphasis on assimilation. Influenced by Muhammad Abduh's thought and the activities of Shakib Arslan, Abd al-Hamid Ben Badis advocated an Islamic revival to increase national pride and to emancipate the country. Through his periodical *al-Muntaqid* (*The Critic*), founded in 1925, he stressed the importance of Arabic and decried the seizure of habus (waqf) lands by the French. At the same time, he preached against Sufi orders, whom he regarded as collaborators and corruptors of Islam.

In 1931, Ben Badis joined with other shaykhs to set up the Association of Ulama. This group focused on establishing independent Arabic schools including even adult education to promote an Islamic social system and community between Arabs and Berbers. The ulama's message and slogan was clear: "Algeria our country, Islam our religion, Arabic our language." Christian French were clearly excluded.

Whereas Messali al-Hajj's movement derived its strength from the working classes, the Badisiyya (followers of Ben Badis) came from old Islamic towns such as Tlemcen and Constantine (Messali's home town). Besides appealing to the urban petite bourgeoisie, the Badisiyya won a rural following among independent peasant smallholders. Unlike the French whose land was heavily planted in vineyards, these Algerian Muslims devoted almost all of their cultivated land to wheat. Only more prosperous peasants who could afford workers could plant the vines that required far more labor. Landless agriculturalists tended to dislike the Badisiyya mainly for their anti-Sufi posture. Many of them left the land for urban jobs, and eventually drifted toward the nationalists of Messali.

At the Islamic Congress in 1936, the Badisiyya supported the assimilationist position rather than the confrontationist stance of Messali. Ben Badis regarded the victory of the Popular Front in France as a sign that the times were changing in favor of greater recognition for Algerian Muslim rights. He believed that by showing solidarity with the new French government, Algeria's Muslims would be identified with progressive and positive forces. However, when efforts to improve Algerian Muslims' status failed and the government fell from power, even Farhat Abbas began to regard the drive for assimilation as futile. In 1938, he founded a new party called Union Populaire Algerienne (U.P.A.) that renounced assimilation in favor of an association acknowledging Algeria's cultural separation. All of Algeria's Muslim leaders continued to hope for peaceful change, but the hardening of France's position on Algeria after the demise of the Popular Front fueled a more militant nationalism, embracing all of the movement's divergent strands. The stage was set for confrontation.

World War II: Impact of the French Defeat in Algeria

As in other French-controlled territories, France's defeat early in World War II created an atmosphere of uncertainty in Algeria. The nationalists tended to favor Abbas' position of continuing to support France despite the revelation of French weakness arising from the German defeat. The rise of Vichy France, with its fascist leanings, allowed Algerian French fascists to run amok against Muslims and Jews with little fear of restraint on the part of the government. Then in 1942 American forces landed in Algeria, creating an environment in which nationalists could speak up in public. With so many Algerians again serving in the French armed forces, pressures for equality were bound to increase.

Abbas and DeGaulle: The Call for Self-Determination

Abbas became the most vocal nationalist. He established close ties with the Americans. But the Americans were not running Algeria. The Free French leader, General deGaulle, had appointed a governor of his own; at best, the Free French were heirs of French liberals willing to concede very modest measures to Algeria's Muslims. While Messali was in prison until April 1943 and under house arrest until 1946, Abbas joined with other Algerian Muslims who leaned toward assimilation to draw up the Manifesto of the Algerian People, issued in February 1943. Demanding self-determination, recognition of Arabic as Algeria's language, agrarian reform, and free compulsory education, the group hoped for cooperation from France's Committee of National Liberation. The Free French governor in Al-

geria, Georges Catroux, turned instead to the old Blum-Viollette proposals that offered concessions only to a small elite. When Abbas insisted on a new basis for cooperation, Catroux jailed him.

Although Abbas was soon released, the French response to him indicated how detached they were from Muslim Algerian aspirations. Abbas represented not the Algerian mainstream but a tiny segment of Algerians who were still willing to look to a future of Franco-Algerian federation. The French settlers regarded him as an American-backed radical. Like the British in Egypt after World War I, the French in Algeria targeted the wrong group for attack, and thereby misunderstood entirely the substantive feelings and aspirations of the bulk of concerned Algerians. This majority was still inspired by Messali who in conversations with Abbas kept insisting that only through struggle was France likely to accept the idea of an Algerian Algeria.

In December 1943, de Gaulle promised educated Algerians the right of full citizenship, a commitment he fulfilled in March 1944. Although the new decree did not change the status of the vast majority, the French assumed that it would dilute Algerian demands for self-determination. Abbas, though, created a new organization, the Amis du Manifeste de la Liberté (A.M.L.), committed to Algerian independence but only in federation with France. He even began publishing *Egalité* (*Equality*) to appeal to the French public. Allowed to function in Algeria, the A.M.L. attracted many Algerians who were far more sympathetic to Messali's desire for a separate Algeria. With Messali still under house arrest, delegates to an A.M.L. congress in March 1945 called for his release and for Algerian independence without affiliation with France.

Social Protest at Sétif

The further extent of the popularity of Messali's program was illustrated in events at Sétif, southwest of Constantine, early in May 1945 (preceded by sporadic demonstrations of pro-Muslim and anti-French sentiment). Historians have suggested several hypotheses about the protests. The poor wartime harvests had created extreme poverty among the Muslim masses. With the victories in Europe, the official occasion for the May demonstrations, Algerians expected the French to institute changes for the betterment of all. Farhat Abbas stated in his memoirs *La nuit coloniale*[2] that the French used the demonstrations as a pretext for suppressing the A.M.L.

The several thousand demonstrators who gathered in Sétif for the victory celebrations carried placards calling for Messali's release and Muslim-Christian equality. They bore, in addition, the green and white banner of nineteenth-century resistance leader Amir Abd al-Qadir. Shots were fired by the police, provoking widespread anti-French rioting, not only in Sétif but also elsewhere. By the time the rioting had ended, over one hundred Europeans had been killed, an infinitesimal number compared to those massacred in the subsequent French reprisals.

For over a week in May 1945, the French struck at Algerian Muslims in regions affected by the demonstrations. Official French sources claimed to have killed only 1,165 Muslims. Algerian nationalists gave estimates ranging from 45,000 to 80,000. Historians have suggested that the truth lies somewhere in between the underreported French figures and the lowest Algerian estimate. Numbers aside, the repression, coming as it did on the heels of a victory to which Algerians had contributed in no small measure, proved to be a turning point and a lasting symbol for the Algerian nationalists. The presumed leaders of the riots were executed or imprisoned, and the A.M.L. was banned. From that time on, the reliance of Algerians on legal, evolutionary change gave way to a conviction that, left to themselves, the French in both France and Algeria would never grant full equality and respect to Muslim Algerians. The old leadership, including Messali, was ultimately superseded by new elites of lower or middle-class origins who were unwilling to wait any longer.

Morocco and Resistance to Franco-Spanish Rule

The administrations established in the French and Spanish protectorates prior to and during World War I were characterized in the early postwar period by continuity and consolidation. Moroccan nationalism developed largely as a response to French and Spanish policies. In the Spanish-controlled Rif, local leaders counted on Spain to continue the policy of ruling through them. Ahmad al-Raysuni had proved sufficiently troublesome to the Spaniards that they agreed in 1915 to recognize him as governor of the Jbala region. Once the war had ended they forced his retreat through a military campaign. Though undefeated by the Spaniards, Raysuni lost his stronghold at Tazirut to Abd al-Krim in 1925.

Abd al-Krim's Republic

The efforts of Abd al-Krim to set up an Islamic republic in the Rif, based on preservation of traditional leadership, marked

---

[2] Farhat Abbas, *La Nuit coloniale* (Paris: R. Julliard, 1962).

a turning point in the history of protectorate rule in Morocco. Events affected both the French and Spanish administrations. In contrast to Raysuni and his history of brigandage, Abd al-Krim and his father Muhammad (who was qadi and tribal leader) stood for indirect rule and for upholding of the sultan's authority; they supported an autonomous republic under the Alawi umbrella. As Europeans hoped to gain mining concessions in the region, they supplied foreign instructors and weapons. Attacking Spanish garrisons with tribal troops who supported his goals, Abd al-Krim in February 1922 announced formation of his republic and began to organize the structure. Although Abd al-Krim created a government-apparatus of individual ministries, he relied on his religious authority and charisma to maintain the loyalty of those in his state. With no concrete territorial concept, the boundaries of the republic would be those he could secure. Unfortunately for him, failure to restrict his territorial ambitions led him from victory over the Spaniards in 1924 and 1925 to defeat at the hands of combined Franco-Spanish forces in 1926.

The consequences of the fall of Abd al-Krim's state were much greater than he might have anticipated. Had Abd al-Krim stayed out of French-administered territory, he might have achieved more support for indirect rule. Instead, his campaign south of Spanish Morocco undermined Lyautey's efforts to minimize French pressures for immigration and land expropriation. Because Lyautey had allowed Abd al-Krim's forces to threaten French rule, the French removed him as commander of French forces in Morocco. With Lyautey's departure in 1925, French administrators turned the protectorate into a colony, characterized by direct rule and the replacement of Moroccan officials by French civil servants. Abd al-Krim, despite his failure, inspired traditionalist Muslim reformers to cast political protest within a religious framework. Muslim leaders based in Fez provided the nucleus of a Moroccan nationalist movement.

French Land and Industrial Policy in Morocco

The most important new law that favored colonialist expansion was the 1919 *dahir;* it allowed for the division of and transfer to the protectorate of lands held collectively for distribution to French colonists. These lands encompassed those classified as inalienable by an earlier dahir of 1914. French authorities selected tribal lands for seizure, operating on the assumption that French farmers required more land than rural Moroccans. Moreover and not by coincidence, the French always chose the best lands for allocation to their settlers.

These land policies produced two major consequences. First of all, the European settler population in Morocco quadrupled during the interwar and World War II period, reaching 300,000. As in Tunisia and Algeria, many of these were not French but rather other Mediterranean peoples. Settlers acquired more and better lands as numbers increased. As the second consequence, Moroccan (like other North African) farmers were gradually proletarianized. Having lost much land and being unable to benefit from governmental modernization schemes because of lack of capital, large tracts, and the relevant skills, they hired themselves out as agricultural laborers or moved to such cities as Casablanca in search of work. Many remained unemployed, and relied on occasional unskilled work. Unable to pay for urban housing, they built tin shacks on the outskirts of towns (giving rise to the term *bidonville* or city of tin). As in Algeria, economic destitution fueled anticolonial protest.

Settlers as elsewhere focused on building up European agriculture, banking, and industry. The protectorate Council of Government combined elected representatives from these sectors. The few Moroccans who gained access to the council did so only by appointment. That the council's organization arose from economic divisions in society is indicative of the protectorate's orientation toward the European economy. Each sector had its own chamber and acted as a pressure group for its own interests. Collectively, and by consensus, council representatives dominated economic decision-making in Morocco.

Under laws instituted by Sultan Abd al-Aziz around the turn of the century, farmers were supposed to pay a land tax, but in 1923 French farmers succeeded in obtaining a rebate for those who utilized European methods. Because most Moroccans did not operate capital-intensive operations, they ended up paying most of the taxes while European farmers reaped the benefit of the rebate. On occasions when their desires were not adequately met, Europeans organized demonstrations and publicity campaigns to attract attention in France.

Government policy also had an impact in mining and industrial development. Because of the importance of phosphates, the government set up a monopoly. Other natural resources—cobalt, lead, and manganese—were developed by French banking interests. For the most part, mining focused on extracting for export rather than on setting up local processing industries. To facilitate transport of raw materials, the French constructed roads throughout the country and completed a railway system begun before the war. An electrification program also benefited European, rather than Moroccan, industry and homes. France's decision to make Casablanca the country's main port contributed to rural-urban migration. World War II was to bring prosperity to Moroccan traders living there. Many of these merchants came from Berber areas in the south, especially from the Sus Valley.

France's Berber Policy

The Sus Valley was an area which came under French control only in the 1930s. Lyautey had encouraged indirect rule there, as he respected local Berber customs. But Berbers themselves did not con-

stitute a single concretely defined group. The most isolated Berbers lived in remote areas such as the Tafilelt oasis. Though Islamized, they spoke only Berber and employed customary rather than Islamic law. Berbers in the High Atlas region were slightly Arabized; their upper classes spoke Arabic and applied aspects of Islamic law. A third group lived close to predominantly Arab areas, where men, though not necessarily women, knew Arabic. In legal matters, Shari'a exerted considerable influence. Finally, there were fully bilingual Berbers, both men and women, who subscribed to Arab customs—women were secluded and the population adhered to Shari'a.

France's idea of a Berber embraced all of these people, perhaps 40 percent of the population. Under the mistaken belief that the Berbers' loyalty could be preserved by substituting a French identity for Arabic influences, Lyautey founded several Franco-Berber schools in the 1920s. His successors set up a teacher-training college for Berbers employed in these French-oriented schools. Arabic education, though discouraged by the French, continued.

The French in 1930 introduced the Berber dahir to solidify the authority of the indigenous Berber courts and place them within the French system. Appeals of decisions would be referred to higher French courts. The unit of justice that existed under the authority of the sultan applied to Muslims. By distinguishing between Muslims and Berbers, who were also Muslims, the French provoked a reaction both religious and nationalistic in orientation.

Those who opposed the dahir most vigorously were the Muslim modernists based in Fez. During the early postwar period, local merchants and craftspeople in the city had begun to experience harm from the accelerated imposition of a capitalist economy that continued to bring manufactured imports into the country at lower prices than those charged for handicrafts. Moneylenders suffered a decline in business as transactions shifted to the import-export center at Casablanca. Traditionally the center of authority as capital of the Alawi state, Fez also found its hinterlands being detached through the policies of the French Affaires Indigenes officials. Added to this was the fact that Berbers were closely associated with Sufi orders. Fez Muslims had already been trying to use their independent schools to provide a more firmly Muslim education.

The dahir of 1930 symbolized to the Arab Muslim elites French efforts designed to eliminate Berbers' religious, cultural, and political identities. In fact, individual French administrators occasionally used the Affairs Indigenes officers to convert Muslim Berbers to Christianity. For their part, many Berbers preferred being governed by their traditional laws but objected to French efforts to cultivate racist attitudes toward Arab Moroccans.

Consolidation of French Power

How did the French "pacify" outlying districts that restricted their rule? The core of the army consisted of regular soldiers who could be used either in Morocco or overseas. In 1933, Moroccans fought against their own people. Many officers were Moroccans. With their high positions in the French army, they tended to back the state. In 1938, there were over 30,000 soldiers in the regular army.

Another group used in Morocco was the Arab-Berber (but mainly Berber) *goum*, each with 160 men who functioned as both infantry and cavalry. A volunteer force, its members served for one year at a time. Goum soldiers lived at home, but their children could attend special schools. The French, some of whose noncommissioned officers served with them, gave them training in modern arms. As a local gendarmerie, they kept order in their localities. The goums served the French, too, as a vehicle for transmitting French ideas to the population. This force was about one-quarter the size of the regular army.

The third group, the *makhzanis*, was so-called because its members were paid from the state budget. Of equal size to the goums, the makhzanis were often young men from influential families. They were not subject to military discipline, and the French paid them more than the goum soldiers.

Finally, France employed tribesmen under the authority of local qa'ids. At first, these troops tended to be Arabs, but later Berbers joined in greater numbers.

The French thus imposed direct rule through use of mostly Moroccan troops. The French helped maintain military loyalty through provision of pensions (though low) and preference in employment. Whereas Moroccans had helped the French fight Syrians in World War I, during World War II they were sent to Tunisia to ward off the American invasion. When they arrived, they discovered that the Americans had already succeeded; they were used against the Germans instead. Though the French had not instigated military modernization in Morocco, they maintained and built up the Moroccan fighting forces and utilized them to achieve French goals.

Moroccan Nationalism: The Role of Modernist Muslims

With the Berber dahir of 1930 and subsequent pacification of the country, the Muslim-led elites began to become more visible politically. Two organizations that had functioned as discussion groups during the mid-1920s in Fez and Rabat joined together in 1930 to protest the dahir. They called themselves the National Group (*al-Jama'a al-Wataniyya*) but remained underground. The top leadership—the Zawiyya—stayed aloof from the members. Within two years, they had adopted a new name, the National Action Bloc, but kept their members down rather than expand their base of support.

Efforts of the Zawiyya during the 1930s were focused on restoring the position of the Alawi ruler. Mawlay Muhammad had been named sultan in 1927—not by Moroccans, but by the French. When he appeared receptive to new initiatives, an alliance of sorts was forged. Through their relationship with Mawlay Muhammad, Zawiyya members hoped to promote introduction of a more enlightened administration in Morocco. Their modernist Muslim program included both the strengthening of Islam and the implementation of social reforms in government and industry based on French practices in France. Those who laid out the reform plan in 1934 were not the Muslims in Fez but those in Rabat who had acquired education in France. They tended to be more cognizant of the need for social change. Led by Umar Abd al-Jalil, Muhammad Lyazidi, Ahmad Balafrej, and others, they managed to attract more traditional Muslim Fez elites, such as Allal al-Fasi, to their point of view. Despite occasional misunderstandings and resentments caused by their different orientations, the two groups that had formed the National Action Bloc remained united.

A more activist posture was assumed in 1936 when the Bloc decided to exploit the resentment of workers for having been excluded from permission to form labor unions granted to non-Muslims. Opening its membership to urban workers, the Bloc attracted support because the workers' leadership viewed the movement as one of national liberation through which they could achieve their own reformist aims. The bloc also appealed to the rural population through al-Fasi's appeal as a Muslim reformist leader. In 1937, the success of the movement was illustrated by the government's decision to ban it without suppression of its leadership. Its members soon regrouped as the National Party.

The atmosphere of toleration did not last long. In autumn 1937, when French administrators were predicting a possible famine in the coming year, French settlers insisted on using so much water that the population in and around the city of Meknes experienced a severe water shortage. Muslims demonstrating against the administration's misuse of scarce water resources engaged in a police confrontation in which many civilians died. The National Party replied by staging new protests. By late October 1937, the French had clamped down on the National Party leadership. Al-Fasi was deported to the African colony of Gabon and was not released until after World War II. His memoirs, *The Independence Movements in Arab North Africa,* were published later.[3] Despite the suppression of the new party, the French on the eve of war tried to introduce measures to alleviate some grievances of Moroccan Muslims. They provided new waterworks and increased political representation. With the leadership at a distance, political activity abated for awhile.

World War II and the Expansion of Nationalism

World War II, as elsewhere, gave nationalists new opportunities to revive their activities. Early in the war, some exiled nationalists returned. The country's occupation by the United States and public pronouncements by U.S. officials helped to create an atmosphere in which nationalist sentiment could grow. When Ahmad Balafrej returned too, following the U.S. entry into Morocco, he revived the Nationalist Party and then reframed its program under the banner of *Istiqlal* (Independence) Party. A public statement in January 1944 announced the party's revised goal. Because Balafrej had used his exile to strengthen contacts with Moroccans in the poor and largely uncolonized Spanish protectorate, the party retained the potential for functioning as a national organization committed to independence. As in Tunisia, nationalists continued in the postwar period to press for a peaceful transition. In both cases, though, a terrorist campaign proved decisive.

---

[3] 'Allal al-Fasi, *The Independence Movements in North Africa,* trans. H. Z. Nuseibeh (Washington, D.C.: Middle East Institute, 1954).

Conclusion

The struggle for statehood in Southwest Asia and North Africa involved a rocky course of frustration, repression, disappointment, and mistrust. The focus on political independence often obscured the much greater need for social and economic reform. Nationalist activities usually began with elites drawn from the traditional ruling and generally prosperous classes, but their leadership was soon challenged by the new intelligentsia and other more radical elements. By the end of World War II, much of the Middle East had secured political independence, but in North Africa and in the smaller countries of Arabia, the struggle still lay in the future. For those who had achieved the goal of independence, an era began in which the liberal idea of bourgeois democracy was judged unsatisfactory in addressing social and economic needs. Classes and interest groups emerged that did not share the viewpoints of the ruling elites. Yet authoritarianism did not necessarily offer appropriate solutions either.

Afterword: An Overview of the Postwar Middle East and North Africa

Most of the Southwest Asian and North African countries spent World War II under some form of foreign occupation, either as mandates, protectorates, colonies, or military bases. Ruling elites in the area emerged from the war under pressure either to win their countries' political independence or to secure it on a sound footing. In some cases, the leadership felt constrained to rely on postwar collaboration with one of the big powers, often against the wishes of emerging new elites, particularly young military officers. The various nations, whether democratic, revolutionary, or authoritarian, used similar methods to mobilize their peoples in support of their regimes. Overall, active participation in international affairs was viewed as natural and appropriate. Membership in the United Nations signified international acceptance of a country as independent. Countries and peoples, both those independent and those striving for independence, looked to the international body for assistance in resolving conflicts and in safeguarding their territorial and national integrity.

The first decades of international relations in the postwar Middle East were characterized by expansion of cold war politics into the area. The United Nations was effective in addressing regional concerns only when individual interests of the major powers coalesced. The United States and the Soviet Union, allies during World War II, rapidly developed an adversary relationship exemplified by the cold war, so-called because the two countries avoided direct military confrontation. They, along with the principal colonial powers France and Britain, devoted themselves to manipulating the Southwest Asians and North Africans. In particular, the United States' emergence from World War II as the dominant world power profoundly affected the newly independent as well as the still colonized countries of the area.

The U.S. establishment of postwar domination may be attributed to several factors. During the war and the preceding years, the colonial and noncolonial powers of Europe had exhausted themselves trying to preserve and/or extend their territorial possessions. Most suffered devastation during the war. The domestic demands on national resources as well as pressures from protectorates, colonies, and noncolonial powers forced the Europeans to plan, in most cases reluctantly, their formal withdrawal from areas under their control, including those in Southwest Asia and North Africa.

The Soviet Union, too, had suffered from a substantial population loss during and after the war, some of it self-inflicted. In the Western parts of the country, especially the Ukraine, Byelorussia, and the Baltic states, the joint trauma of wartime occupation and political oppression by a government determined to protect its western frontier from future invasion at all costs weighed heavily on the people. Faced with such potential internal problems, the Soviet Union could not easily afford foreign adventures too far afield. It focused its main energies on securing its borders against hostile neighbors. The Soviets used allied acquiescence to their plan of assuring the presence of "friendly" states on their boundaries, pressed at the wartime Yalta Conference, to support the installation of Communist governments in eastern Europe. The Soviet Union also shared a border with Middle Eastern countries with which it had maintained varying degrees of involvement over the years, and it sought immediately after the war to secure that frontier by involvement in the Greek civil war to put pressure on the borders of Turkey and Iran.

Of the major countries involved in World War II, only the United States emerged with its huge industrial, territorial, and demographic resources largely intact, and with its economy in a state of growth rather than decay. Despite a brief recession that followed the war, the strength of the U.S. economy was unparalleled by European and East Asian countries in the early postwar years. American firms dominated the international economy. Because of sophisticated weapons development, especially nuclear technology, the United States during the late 1940s and throughout most of the 1950s and 1960s also enjoyed military superiority over its main rival, the Soviet Union. This combination of economic and military might enabled the United States to intervene successfully in the affairs of

Asian, African, and Latin American countries, at least until the Vietnam War. The Middle East, strategic hub and reservoir of huge oil deposits, was certainly a prime area of U.S. interest and intervention, especially as the process of decolonization unfolded after the war opening up the prospect of local unstability that the Soviets might exploit.

Syria and Lebanon had assumed an end to the French mandate following the early Nazi victory in France, but it required the assistance of foreign pressure to end the Free French occupation and secure independence. In Palestine, the United States gave immediate recognition to the Jewish state of Israel. The former Palestinian majority found itself in a new diaspora, especially under Jordanian control. These Palestinians assumed their exile would be temporary, and United Nations relief, heavily supported by the United States, expected an early resolution to the Palestinian refugee crisis. The British-dominated monarchies in Egypt and Iraq faced postwar discontent that toppled them in 1952 and 1958 respectively. When the Sudanese were given a choice about independence, they chose separation from Egypt, but because of north-south economic, ethnic, and religious differences the task of working for national consolidation led to a civil war resolved only in the 1970s. Saudi Arabia emerged from the war with a well-established monarchy that did not yet face serious challenges, though it fought a proxy war with Egypt in North Yemen in the 1960s. Kuwayt, despite territorial claims of neighbors, began building a bright future based on oil wealth under its ruling Sabah family. For over twenty years after the war ended, the Arab Gulf principalities and South Yemen (Aden) remained British-dominated states. Iran, occupied during the war by the allies and the site of an important wartime conference, had to negotiate foreign troop withdrawal and the end to Soviet-sponsored "independent" republics set up in northern areas. Turkey, only commercially and politically touched by the war, nevertheless began to feel serious economic and ideological tensions related to its secular and statist policies. The Turkish Republic confirmed its political independence but like Greece joined the North Atlantic Treaty Organization (NATO), organized by the United States and European allies as a regional defense pact. Cyprus, occupied by Britain since 1878, won its independence only to see continued warfare between the Greek-speaking majority and Turkish-speaking minority.

In North Africa, decolonization was an equally prominent postwar issue. Libya, the least developed country politically, was the first to win its independence (1951) largely because its colonizer Italy had been defeated in the war. Morocco and Tunisia, after a prolonged period of protest, secured independence by negotiation in 1955–56. In Algeria, however, only a vicious and bitter war of liberation, combined with international pressure, succeeded in freeing the country from over 130 years of French colonization. Mauritania, also decolonized in the postwar period, found itself in joint occupation, with Morocco, of Western Sahara following the withdrawal of Spain. It also faced a war of national liberation with a group of Sahrawis.

The militarization of the Middle East is not unrelated to the process of political decolonization. Faced with both internal and external challenges to their authority, Middle Eastern governments began arming in the postwar period to the extent that the area became the most heavily armed in the world, next to the major powers. Middle Eastern countries in the 1970s and 1980s also ranked near the top in per capita military expenditure as a percentage of gross national product. Because of the high social and economic costs, especially for the region's poorer countries, militarization became a prominent postwar issue. Furthermore, arms sales and grants were among the means whereby great powers continued to exercise influence in the politically decolonized countries.

Both military and economic realities provide evidence that, despite political decolonization, relationships between Southwest Asian and North African countries on the one hand and the developed countries on the other could often be characterized as neocolonial because of continued dependence. Without changes in the international economic structure, most countries have been unable to alter the nature of their relationships with the outside world. Even in the case of those countries which, by virtue of small populations and proportionately huge oil revnues, have achieved new economic status, we find foreigners playing a substantial and even essential economic role.

The larger trends in international relations, clear in hindsight, were signaled by specific realities during the war, not the least of which was the presence on a large scale of Allied troops and service units. Iran became a major allied conduit for lend-lease supplies to the Soviet Union. Allied troops operated militarily in the Levant and especially in North Africa (which became the allied gateway for the invasion of Europe from the south). Cairo was the headquarters of the Middle East Supply Center, which in one way or another became the central feature of the allied military and political operations in North Africa and the Middle East.

The concern with actual and potential Axis subversion in North Africa, the Levant, Egypt and Iran added urgency to wartime contingency planning for this crucial area. While some leaders and movements in the area had established connections, or hoped to, with the Germans or the Italians as a matter of ongoing ideological affinity, most of the people in the area saw the Axis powers as a force for liberation from the continued or thinly disguised imperial control of the Western democracies. Indeed, the Western allies were trapped by the irony of their own widespread propaganda against Axis tyranny and dictatorship aimed at a people who knew through experience the loss of political freedom at the hands of the Western democracies. The new presence of the United States, with its relatively untarnished and widely admired image as a noncolonial power, helped relations with the allies, but the extensive effort to make the Soviet communist presence in the democratic alliance against fascism acceptable was to muddy the ideological waters of the area. In short, the pursuit of the war effort required the allies to raise the levels of expectations in their former or existing colonies, and, at the same time, to minimize the actual dilution of imperial control. The resulting frustration contributed to a heightened ideological debate about the means to and ends of national liberation in both North Africa and the Middle East.

The struggle against colonialism and neocolonialism was sharpened and made more violent by what to many in the Arab World at least was a new and not-so-subtle kind of neocolonialsm—Western support for the aspirations of the Jewish people in Palestine. Suffice it to note here that the issue of a Jewish state in the Middle East was to become then—and remains to this day—a central issue in the continuing drama of national cohesion and liberation and progress into modernity. In the post-World War II period, the question of Palestine was to inflame domestic passions and conflict, and lead, after the creation of the state of Israel, to the breakdown of the social and political order erected after World War I, and the emergence of a Middle East state system dominated by military elites.

While nationalism as a doctrine of political liberation was being tested, it was also being transformed. Most importantly it was being honed more sharply to accommodate new ideas about social justice. While Marxist/Communist doctrine developed among small sectors in various countries of the area, the more pervasive concept of a European-refined Socialism began to enter the political lexicon of the area. Arab Socialism was to become a key concept in the politically and socially more advanced Arab states.

In addition, the post-World War II era saw the first major appearance in the colonial period of a phenomenon now called the Islamic movement. Although we have

underscored in the modern history of the area the progressive weakening of the inherited Islamic tradition of social organization in the face of an aggressive, expanding, and colonial West, there remained alive (if somewhat dormant) the memory of a past filled with power and glory and inspired by a meaningful revelation. Throughout Islamic history, reformers have surfaced to recall Muslims to the meaning of that revelation, when society seemed particularly corrupt and unjust. The Wahhabi uprising of the late eighteenth and early nineteenth centuries affected Muslim thinkers throughout the Muslim world. The Wahhabi call to theological purification, not itself a response to the West, but rather in line with Muslim traditions of reform, came to be an important political call for Muslims to seek political salvation through spiritual regeneration. The later thinkers already discussed, Afghani and Abduh, not themselves Wahhabi in spirit (i.e. puritanical), preached the same doctrine as did numerous others since. All faced a new Muslim world altered in the eighteenth through twentieth centuries by the concepts of secularism and nationalism, the institutions which supported those ideas, and the incorporation of the region into an international capitalist economic system. The direct colonization of the area was to add a visible presence and an enemy. And both world wars, especially World War II, with large numbers of allied troops spending and socializing in the area, underscored the enormity and the poignancy of the clash of cultures.

In Iran and in Egypt especially the toll was high. In both countries Islamic movements or Islamic tensions grew as they did in Palestine, Jordan, Syria, and Sudan. Such tensions and movements challenged the widely accepted view of the secular nationalists that salvation—political, economic, and social—lay in the rejection of the past and in the adoption of western ideas about organizing societies, polities, and mobilizing nations. These movements and men articulated the general sense of unease that, having tried and failed through the western models, the Islamic option deserved the opportunity of dealing with ongoing problems of political impotence, economic backwardness, social chaos, and psychological trauma. The relative certainty which animated the nationalist thinkers in the twenties and thirties was to begin breaking down in the forties and fifties. It was to give way in the sixties and seventies to a gnawing doubt, that for all the movement of these peoples toward a modern society, the largely Muslim societies of Western Asia and North Africa were relatively impotent vis-à-vis the West.

CHAPTER FIFTEEN

Turkey and Iran After World War II

After World War II, Turkey and Iran faced new and different challenges. In Turkey, politicians pressed for democratization of political life, but it was the military that came to view itself as the guarantor of Turkish democracy. Militarily and economically, Turkey's leaders in the 1950s and 1960s tied the country to the West, particularly to the United States. The 1970s, however, brought on an era of labor disputes and political unrest in which opposition groups attacked the western alliance, especially after some countries imposed sanctions on Turkey following the Turkish invasion of Cyprus in 1974. Postwar Turkey continued its modernization thrust, but without the insistence on secularism that had characterized Atatürk's program. Turkish workers flocked to Europe as the indigenous economy slowed down. Their remittances in the late 1970s helped to mitigate Turkey's foreign exchange problem. In the field of literature, Turkish poets and novelists continued to focus on Anatolian themes.

Iran's postwar regime, in contrast to that of Turkey, represented strong continuity with the prewar period. The young shah Muhammad Reza tried to shake off the humiliations of British and Russian dictates that had been imposed during the war. As petroleum production rose, Iran's requests for foreign aid met with rejection. Pressures for nationalization increased and came to a head early in the 1950s. Although Iran's efforts to nationalize oil in 1951 did not fully succeed, the country gradually gained more favorable terms for royalties and then for participation in this vital industry.

The nationalist crisis allowed the shah to assert himself as the dominant ruling force in Iran. Relying on the support of the military, he introduced land tenure as well as administrative and educational changes. Iran enjoyed a startlingly high growth rate, but the heavy investment in military equipment coupled with the influx of foreign experts, mainly from the West, aroused social protest. Religious leaders in particular viewed the importation of secular culture as threatening to society. The shah's land policies undermined their position in rural areas, but urban mujtahids were aware of stresses created by the new realities. Political repression, particularly of leftists (socialists and Marxists), brought together secular and religious-oriented Iranians in a movement that in 1977–79 overturned the shah's regime and instituted an Islamic republic.

With this goal achieved, religious and secular nationalists became engaged in their own power struggle while various ethnic minorities within Iran grew restless. The U.S. hostage crisis from November 1979 to January 1981 gave the regime an external target but it nevertheless faced continuing upheavals. In a vigorous campaign, prominent writers and intellectuals, as well as many young people, died under condemnation by revolutionary courts. Historians, sociologists, political scientists, and religious scholars will spend years trying to sort out how the revolution was produced and sustained.

The Rise of a Political Opposition in Turkey

As World War II was winding down, a new leadership arose to reorient the direction of Atatürk's revolution. Adnan Menderes, one of these men, belonged to an influential, large landowning family in western Turkey. He studied at the American College of Izmir and later completed legal studies at the College of Law in Ankara. As a member of the government commission on land reform, Menderes advocated relaxing state economic controls and introducing modern agricultural technology. During the debate in the Grand National Assembly (G.N.A.) over the United Nations Charter in 1945, Menderes insisted that by signing the charter, Turkey had committed itself to implement a genuine democracy, presumably based on a western model. With three other members, Celal (pronounced *Jelal*) Bayar, Fuad Köprülü, and Refik Koraltan, Menderes presented a motion calling for modification of all dictatorial or constitutional laws. In the aftermath of its failure, all four either resigned or were expelled from the ruling R.P.P.

Soon after their departure, the four men founded and registered the Democrat Party (D.P.) in January 1946. The party during its formative stages focused on upholding the constitution. It represented the beginning of opposition in G.N.A. Celal Bayar headed it from 1946–50 prior to the Democrat triumph. A banker, Bayar had served twice as minister of national economy, once before 1924 and the second time from 1932 to 1937 when he served briefly as prime minister. When Ismet Inönü became president, Bayar stepped down from his new post. Like Menderes, Bayar favored liberalized economic policies. Of the other two party leaders, Köprülü was a distinguished historian; Koraltan was a politician from Konya.

The first elections contested by the Democrats were held in July 1946. Despite their still small organization, they won about 15 percent of the G.N.A. seats and a majority of seats from Istanbul. The new R.P.P. government instituted some economic measures called for by the Democrats, but the country still experienced inflationary pressures arising from postwar currency adjustments and from the use of reserves from wartime chrome sales to Germany in order to import consumer and capital goods. When the Democrats criticized the government's economic difficulties, repression of all oppositionist elements, including Communists, ensued.

Inönü, however, did not want to jeopardize the new relationship being forged with the United States. Turkey had been granted economic aid under the inspiration of the Truman Doctrine of 1947. Between 1947 and 1949, Turkish leaders implemented democratic reforms that upheld the constitution. In this more liberalized atmosphere, the Nation Party emerged, rejecting etatism in favor of strong individualistic capitalism. All parties began to move in this direction. In 1949, a Faculty of Divinity opened at Istanbul University, and the R.P.P. authorized the reopening of religious schools and the teaching of Islam as an optional subject based on parental request.

On 15 February 1950, a new electoral law passed the G.N.A. It stipulated free elections to be conducted by secret ballot.

In May, the Democrats swept to victory. Economic issues predominated during the campaign. The Democrat Party seemed to offer voters a change from R.P.P. rule. The peaceful transfer of power seemed to confirm the viability of democratic institutions in Turkey.

The Democrats remained in power from May 1950 to May 1960. Celal Bayar was elected president. Adnan Menderes, the new prime minister, also took over the party leadership. In later years Bayar was blamed for the ruthlessness of certain government policies and for Menderes' failure to form a bipartisan coalition cabinet. Although Köprülü was appointed as foreign minister and Koraltan served as assembly president, Bayar and Menderes dominated Democrat rule and shouldered most of the responsibility for its failures in the trials that followed the May 1960 revolution.

The Democrat Years (1950–60)

With the assembly fully behind them, the Democrat leaders embarked on implementation of measures designed to fulfill their economic, religious, and political promises. The magnetic Menderes faced the same problems that had always confronted Turkish leaders: economic development and rural versus urban interests. Apparently, Menderes honestly intended to work through the parliamentary system, but the pace of his program awakened opposition and made him choose between modifying his plans or forcing them on the country by suppressing the opposition. In choosing the latter course, Menderes reverted to methods he had criticized when the R.P.P. had employed them.

At the outset, the Democrats attempted to modify press restrictions. In accordance with the party's economic platform, the government encouraged private capital and private enterprise, hoping to liberate production from bureaucratic intervention. By spending only minimal amounts for industry, the Democrats hoped to transform the country's deficits into surpluses. An economic plan would provide appropriate guidelines.

Economy and Society: Modification of Etatism and Secularism

Menderes had so firmly committed himself to free enterprise and to the acquisition of foreign capital that he placed these considerations above the need for careful planning to avoid further deficits. Turning away from Atatürk's self-sufficiency, he assumed that the United States and other foreign countries would foot the bill for

Turkey's development. By 1958, however, the government had not yet published a plan or even outlined an orderly, balanced program to utilize Turkey's resources.

What projects did the Democrat government favor? It devoted special attention to rural reform, assisted by the U.S.A.I.D. (U.S. Agency for International Development). The government built a rural road network, introduced electricity into remote areas, increased cultivation of wheat, and imported huge amounts of farm machinery in hopes of mechanizing Turkey's agriculture. To change the initial emphasis on private enterprise, the government expanded industrial development, particularly in industries that would provide substitutes for imported consumer goods—textiles and processed food, and, later, durable goods. It also invested in new schools and expanded health care into rural areas.

The programs succeeded only at the cost of runaway inflation and huge spending deficits. With the goal of encouraging the population to vote for them, the Democrats often constructed factories in inaccessible provincial locations, far from sources of raw materials. Successes of the first three years increased consumer demand so that when recession set in during the mid-1950s, the government could not counter either inflation or the unavailability of goods. The farm mechanization program bogged down with the government's inability to supply spare parts. Often the machinery itself was not well-suited to the terrain in which it was employed. Wheat production, however, did increase early in the postwar period. The United States promoted Turkish dependency, though, through farm machinery purchases funded by A.I.D. Spare parts had to be obtained from U.S. firms, but deliveries were often slow because the U.S. was a distant supplier.

The government's investment in the economy kept increasing because private enterprise, though active, could not carry the burden alone. Turkey's strong trade unions and working classes objected to the government's focus on agriculture and its

reliance on manufactured imports. In many ways, the failure of agriculture to sustain economic growth through the 1950s promoted the import-substitution industries as a solution to Turkey's inability to keep up the pace of consumer imports. Because rising costs affected both rural and urban populations, Menderes could not rely on the peasantry to keep his party in power indefinitely.

In the religious sphere, the Democrats tried to meet a genuine demand for relaxation of imposed secularism by lifting the bans on religious radio broadcasts and the use of Arabic for the call to prayer. Immediately, Muslims reverted to Arabic, thereby indicating that people had objected to praying in Turkish. Government funds for constructing village mosques were made available, and the annual pilgrimage to Makka received subsidies. In an appeal to Turkey's Ottoman past, the government allowed the public to visit the tombs of the sultans and invited surviving members of the Ottoman dynasty to return. Instead of making religious instruction optional, as under the R.P.P., the Democrats made exemption from religious instruction the option. The Democrats' religious measures did not so much change the religious outlook of the population as it allowed for free expression after nearly three decades of suppression. Rural Turks had been less subject to government dictates to begin with, but secularism had produced a new generation of urban Turks who regarded religion and religious observation as a private matter. The government thought that a freer expression of religious feeling would not threaten national stability.

Political Protest and Censorship

The Democrats' commitment to political freedom did not last long. In 1953, the government turned against the Nation Party, holding it responsible for an assassination attempt in 1952 against journalist Ahmet Amin Yalman, an early Democrat supporter. By 1954, the Nation Party was banned altogether. Peasant support in the 1954 elections kept the party in power, but the Democrats had by that time imposed press censorship laws of their own. From 1955, the R.P.P. organized boycotts of municipal and provincial elections to protest the government's curtailing of democracy introduced by the R.P.P. The government replied by prosecuting journalists and by continuing purges begun in 1954 of university and civil service intellectuals who opposed it. Dissatisfaction with the government's handling of the Cyprus dispute and concern for minority Turkish Cypriots provoked anti-Greek rioting in Istanbul in September 1955.

Not all Democrats agreed with their government's policies. The application of press laws led to the resignation of nineteen Democrat deputies in 1955. Some of them formed the Freedom Party the same year. A new censorship law of 7 June 1956 and a subsequent electoral law of 27 June brought on new protests. Under the electoral provisions, opposition parties that previously could have united to present a single electoral list were prevented from doing so. In any single province, the party that secured the largest number of votes, even if there were no majority, would gain all of that province's assembly seats. The two regulations militated against the success of any opposition, but in October 1957 elections (which historians seem to agree were rigged), the Democrats won less than 50 percent of the total vote. The new laws still gave them a two-thirds majority in the assembly. In 1958, the by-now defensive government jailed Yalman for having published in the United States an article critical of the regime. Köprülü had also left the party by this time.

Menderes continued to appeal to peasants, especially because he escaped "miraculously" from a plane crash in England that killed fifteen others. His disregard for Turkish intellectuals and the ongoing economic crisis, however, helped to bring about his downfall. A fundamental failing was his inability to tolerate even constructive criticism of government policies, especially those pertaining to the economy. Menderes' legal background prompted him to use legal methods to achieve undemocratic ends. Those who had placed confidence in Turkey's democracy responded with frustration and anger to his curtailment of intellectual freedom, especially in universities and in the press. Charismatic and opportunistic, Menderes might have sustained his position and that of his party through compromise, but instead he became increasingly dogmatic and autocratic.

Foreign Policy

Turkey's foreign policy under the Democrats continued the R.P.P.'s alliance with the West. Turkey sent troops to fight in Korea in 1950 and joined NATO in 1952. The following year, treaties were signed with Greece and Yugoslavia. In April 1954, Turkey and Pakistan agreed to a mutual defense pact that led in November 1955 to participation in the U.S.-sponsored Baghdad Pact. During the Suez War of 1956 (see Chapter 16), Turkey supported the U.S.-backed withdrawal of British and French forces from Egypt. One year later, Turkey joined with other Baghdad Pact members in forming the Central Treaty Organization (C.E.N.T.O.). During the 1957 crisis in Jordan, Turkey massed troops along the Syrian border. In all of these actions, the country pursued an anti-Soviet policy in support of U.S. objectives.

Turkey's major foreign policy concern, however, was Cyprus. The Cypriot national struggle heightened when the British released from detention in the Seychelles nationalist leader and primate of the Greek Orthodox church in Cyprus, Makarios III (Mikhail Khristodolou Mouskos). On 19 February 1959, Britain, Greece, and Turkey, as well as Greek and Turkish Cypriots, agreed on a formula for a new Cypriot constitution that would take the country to independence in August 1960. Makarios became the first president of Cyprus. The agreement stipulated that while the president would be Greek Cypriot, the vice-president would be Turkish Cypriot, and the Muslim Turkish population would hold one third of the seats in parliament. Turkey supported the agreement, but the government continued to view itself as the protector of Turkish Cypriots, ready to intervene if and when Cypriot independence might be threatened.

Despite ongoing political problems, the economy of Cyprus grew considerably throughout the postwar period. There were two particularly rapid expansion periods: 1950–57 and 1965–present. In the earlier period, the Cypriots benefited from increases in the British military forces and stimulation of the copper industry. The economy slowed down, however, during the independence struggle.

The Turkish Revolution of 1960 and Its Aftermath

In May 1960, the military intervened to bring down the Menderes-Bayar government because of economic and political dissatisfaction, demonstrated by public protest. General Gürsel led the coup. Alparslan Türkes (pronounced *Türkesh*), later leader of the National Action Party (N.A.P.) participated. The coup was preceded by R.P.P. appeals to the populace. The people's enthusiastic response to Inönü's trips into Anatolia's interior in May 1959 and April 1960 appeared to prove his charisma. The government responded to R.P.P. actions by suppressing opposition in the G.N.A. and by announcing a three-month suspension of political activity. In April 1960, five students were killed and forty injured in antigovernment protests in Istanbul, thereby prompting a government declaration of martial law. On 27 May 1960, the army arrested Bayar, Menderes, and most of the D.P. leadership. The first Turkish Republic had come to an end.

Although the coup was bloodless and successful, former D.P. leaders were put on trial at Yassiada Island in the Bosporus from October 1960 to August 1961, mostly on charges of having violated the constitution. Turkey's national leaders agreed not to make an issue in the coming elections of death sentences, eight of which were received by Menderes alone. The government on 15 September 1961 executed him along with his foreign minister Fatin

Rüstü Zorlu and his finance minister Hasan Polatkan. Bayar's four death sentences were commuted to life imprisonment because of ill health. He lived for a long time thereafter. Menderes remained popular in the memories of Turks. Within five years after the coup, virtually all imprisonend Democrats had been released. The coup did not destroy the D.P. but allowed for its resurrection as the Justice Party (J.P.) led by Ragip Gümüspala (*Gumushpala*) until his death in 1964. It was subsequently led by Sulayman Demirel. The J.P. adopted old D.P. symbols in order to reach the voters.

While trials continued in May 1961, a new constitution was approved providing for a bicameral legislature with an assembly and a senate. The document mentioned social justice as a goal of the state. True to its promises, the military restored civilian government. In the October 1961 elections, the R.P.P. won 173 seats to 153 for the J.P. in the assembly, but in the Senate, the J.P. secured 70 seats to only 36 for the R.P.P. General Gürsel was elected president. The man called upon to form the first cabinet in Turkey's second republic was Ismet Inönü. The J.P. agreed to cooperate with the new government.

The first few years under the new system brought on two attempted army coups protesting government cooperation with the J.P. The military and civilians were now enaged in a potentially confrontational relationship. If the government failed to perform to the military's satisfac-

tion, there was always the possibility of a coup.

The Second Turkish Republic: Search for Consensus

The second Turkish republic (1961–80) experienced considerable political upheaval. Frequent national elections, including by-elections, took place. Government by coalition arose as a solution to the usual inability of any party to secure a majority. Inönü remained prime minister from 1963 to 1965, though the J.P. made impressive gains in the senate during the period. Later, R.P.P. leader and poet Bulent Ecevit (*Ejevit*) served as minister of labor between 1961 and 1965.

In 1962, the R.P.P. government revealed a new five-year plan, followed in 1963 by an agreement with the European Economic Community (E.E.C.) that would grant Turkey membership by stages. In the first stage, Turkey would receive economic aid and preferential treatment for some exports. During the second stage, the E.E.C. would reduce tariffs gradually. Turkey hoped to gain full membership by 1995.

In October 1965, the J.P. finally won a majority of parliamentary seats and took over the government under Demirel's leadership. President Gürsel stayed on until 1966 when Cevdet (Jevdet) Sunay replaced him. Demirel favored encouraging industrialization and opposing Communism. Turkey's political climate for the next few years was characterized by a revival of conservatism, continued support for the J.P., respect for the memory of Menderes, desire for modifying Atatürk's changes, and a leftist lean by the R.P.P. R.P.P. opposition included people who did not favor Turkey's participation in NATO and the growth of U.S. bases. The R.P.P. began to support social reform and socialism.

The Demirel government backed both the five-year plan and eventual participa-

tion in the E.E.C. Like earlier governments, the effort of the J.P. focused on import substitution in industry. New industries, though, often replaced not foreign concerns but smaller local factories. With industrialization pushed into the fore again, the number of Turkey's industrial workers rose. Although under Ecevit's programs from 1963 on workers won the right to bargain and to strike, their wage-increases fell below rising productivity and inflation. Turkey's only official union confederation was Türk-Is (Trade Unions Confederation of Turkey) founded in 1952 on the model of the American Federation of Labor (AFL).

In 1961, in the wake of constitutional changes, some trade unionists joined with intellectuals in setting up the Worker's Party of Turkey (W.P.T.). It won a few seats in the 1965 elections, and attracted sufficient attention to help cause the leftist shift in the R.P.P. In 1967, the self-description of the R.P.P. as the leftist opposition caused a new group to break off to form the Reliance Party. In that same year, dissident unionists led by Kemal Türkler, general secretary of the Metal Workers Union, formed a new generally leftist union federation (D.I.S.K.) which attracted well-paid industrial workers, including many W.P.T. members and perhaps a third of Türk-Is' membership.

The J.P. reacted to D.I.S.K.'s success by introducing in June 1970 a new union law designed to erode the union's membership. Meanwhile, student and labor unrest brought about reimposition of political controls. The Turkish People's Liberation Army (T.P.L.A.) arose in response to assassinations of leftists in the universities and elsewhere by Colonel Türkes' N.A.P. fighters. Kurdish separatists, many of them in the workers' movement, agitated for recognition of their national rights. By December 1970, Demirel had only a one-vote majority in the assembly. With the continuation of disturbances, the military in March 1971 intervened a second time. The W.P.T. and various student, worker, and teacher organizations were banned. Kurdish dissidents faced mass arrests and trials in Diyarbakir.

Under the new political and social strictures, including martial law in selected provinces, Turkey's government tried to restrict terrorism and encourage large industrialists at the expense of workers. It approved the formation in August 1971 of the Association of Turkish Industrialists and Businessmen (T.U.S.I.A.D.). While this organization promoted business interests, the R.P.P. kept moving left with Ecevit's election as party leader in 1972. Subsequently, following the 1973 elections until the military takeover of 12 September 1980, either Demirel's J.P. or Ecevit's R.P.P. directed the government, hoping to form stable coalitions but with little success.

The elections of October 1973 indicated the increasing polarization of Turkish politics. The NATO question had persisted, especially after the murder of two NATO technicians in March 1972 by the T.P.L.A. Protests also occurred against continued agreement with the United States to ban cultivation of poppies (source of opium) despite U.S. subsidies to the government to compensate farmers. The money had rarely reached the recipients. Although Ecevit's R.P.P. secured the largest number of votes, the rightist parties combined won over 60 percent. Demirel still could not form a government because the minority parties, notably the Party of National Salvation

(P.N.S.), led by Necmettin (Nejmettin) Erbakan and the Democratic Party (another J.P. splinter group), refused to join him. The P.N.S. reflected more religiously-oriented Turks who resisted the ongoing secularism of Atatürk's successors. The party remained influential as an ideological party. As the politicians sought to resolve their governmental crisis, the 1973 oil embargo (see Chapter 21) had already begun to affect Turkey's workers in Europe because of shutdowns and layoffs. Remittances of Turkish overseas workers early in the 1970s exceeded $1 billion per year, more than 150 percent as much as export earnings.

The parliamentary impasse temporarily resolved itself when the P.N.S. joined Ecevit in January 1974 to form a new government. Ironically, the P.N.S. specifically opposed secularism (a key part of the R.P.P. heritage) and favored reintroducing Arabic script and veiling of women. Turkey could ill afford economic adversity at this time because of rising unemployment at home as well as abroad, but the new Ecevit government had no choice but to increase prices of basic commodities, especially of petroleum. Private industry adopted a wait-and-see attitude while the economy floundered.

During this time, the W.P.T. reconstituted itself, but it was no longer the only socialist party. The more openminded and somewhat leftist attitude of Ecevit's government encouraged the founding of the Socialist Party, the Turkish Socialist Worker's Party, and the Turkish Labor Party, all in 1974. None of these achieved a wide following, although S.P. leader Mehmet Ali Aybar was well-known from the 1940s as an advocate of democracy. The T.L.P. was the main Maoist party; it indulged in as many struggles with the left as with the right.

The Cyprus Invasion

The Cyprus question resurfaced to provide an opportunity for the Ecevit government to rally enthusiasm for its weak coalition. After Cyprus became independent, Turkey had watched with apprehension the development of the *enosis* movement that favored union of Cyprus with Greece. Turkey suggested partition to ward off perpetual conflict. In 1964, the United Nations intervened by sending an emergency force to maintain peace. When incidents involved Greece and Turkey as parties to the fighting, the United States warned Prime Minister İnönü that it could not tolerate Turkish military support for Turkish Cypriots.

The U.S. policy helped promote a period of anti-Americanism, anti-NATO feeling in Turkey, and the effort of Turkish governments, whether under the R.P.P. or the J.P. to expand contacts with the Soviet Union. Relations between Greek and Turkish Cypriots smoldered. President Makarios tried to minimize the influence of the enosis forces, but he allowed Greeks to serve in the Cypriot National Guard. In 1974, the National Guard overthrew Makarios. The new government under Nikos Sampson announced plans for enosis. Turkish Cypriots were the objects of massacres. Rather than continue to stand by and hope

for a diplomatic solution, Ecevit sent Turkish forces into northern Cyprus in July 1974.

The move was popular in Turkey because it preserved the minority on Cyprus, but it hardly maintained the status quo there. Greek Cypriots fled from their homes in the north. Turkish-occupied parts of Cyprus began experiencing economic stagnation. Greece returned to civilian government under Constantine Karamanlis, but the Greek and Turkish governments could not agree on Turkish withdrawal arrangements. Even after a new Greek coalition led by left-leaning, U.S. educated Andreas Papandreou won power in Greece, the impasse dragged on. Periodic attempts by Turkish Cypriot leader Rauf Denktash to resolve differences proved unsuccessful. The Greek Cypriot area maintained its vitality. Ecevit perceived that his enhanced prestige would enable him to prompt new elections through his resignation in September 1974. The R.P.P. would be given a big victory. Realizing this, the minority parties refused to cooperate. Again Turkey remained without a government.

The J.P.-R.P.P. Impasse: Political and Economic Upheaval

In March 1975, Demirel brought together the P.N.S., the Republican Reliance Party, and the extreme-rightist N.A.P. in a Nationalist Front. The new coalition embarked on suppressing the left, especialy through use of N.A.P. thugs, the League of Idealist Youth. This rightist violence of the mid-1970s from both secular and religious groups led to enhanced backing for a leftist resistance, often supported by external elements such as Palestinians. Turkey continued to move toward bankruptcy because of high-cost energy imports and industrial funding. The Cyprus invasion had led to a U.S. arms embargo. Ecevit, now in opposition, turned

to the two large trade unions to rally support against the rightist coalition.

In 1977, many Turks looked forward to June elections in hopes of bringing in a new government. D.I.S.K. decided to hold a large rally on Istanbul's Taksim Square on May Day, an internationally celebrated labor holiday. Despite efforts to avoid disturbances, random shots and police sirens frightened the crowd. As police blocked the main exits from the square, people sought escape through alleys and smaller streets. Over thirty people were trampled to death in the process; many more were wounded. The May events helped Ecevit's cause, but his party still failed to win a majority. Briefly forming the country's first minority cabinet, Ecevit soon had to give way to Demirel in July 1977. By January 1978, Ecevit was back in power, this time with a few, mainly independent coalition partners.

Ecevit's government lasted nearly two years, until October 1979. Increased factional fighting in Turkey, often with ethnic or religious overtones in Kurdish and predominantly Shi'i areas, obliged the government to impose martial law in selected provinces. With Turkey's mounting energy bills, Ecevit resorted to asking trade unions to moderate their demands. Türk-Is accepted the measures. D.I.S.K. did not, thereby causing the R.P.P. to lose much of its support in Turkey's industrialized west. Ecevit also met with declining confidence of T.U.S.I.A.D., whose members had long favored a J.P.-R.P.P. coalition that would promote business. They objected most to his refusal to force enough concessions from labor to promote industry according to a plan proposed by the I.M.F. This plan would help Turkey obtain further loans despite its estimated $17 billion foreign debt. Obviously, Ecevit could not easily have satisfied all of his constituents or won over his opponents. Unlike Demirel, Ecevit did not view Turkey as an integral though developing part of Europe; he regarded it rather as a developing nation that should not tie itself too firmly to any one bloc. Yet he sustained the NATO and E.E.C. alliances.

In October 1979, Ecevit's government fell because the number of R.P.P. supporters in the assembly and senate had dropped appreciably during fall elections. In November, Demirel formed another minority government because he too did not command a majority. His ten months in office failed to resolve the ongoing po-

litical and social violence in Turkey, fueled by armed leftist and rightist groups, ongoing high (15 percent) unemployment, and triple digit inflation. An additional factor was the influence of the Iranian revolution of 1977–79 among religious activists, both Shi'i and Sunni. The Demirel government did commit itself, however, to an economic policy from January 1980 under the guidance of former World Bank economist and P.N.S. supporter Turgut Ozal (who resigned in July 1982). His program aimed at controlling inflation, reducing Turkey's balance-of-payments deficit, and increasing domestic savings, all via a redirection of Turkey's economy according to the I.M.F. model. Encouraged by these moves, the I.M.F. granted Turkey a $1.6 billion loan in June 1980.

Although workers initially resisted the austerity program, military suppression quelled the workers' violent protests. Strikes, however, continued through summer, inspired mostly by D.I.S.K. which feared losing its constituents if it supported the government. D.I.S.K.'s Türkler was assassinated in July 1980. With ongoing labor unrest, the government's plans were disrupted. Added to this was political factional fighting that by August 1980 killed an estimated 2,000 to 4,000 people and over which the government had obviously no control. Dissidents obtained arms from abroad. University students were polarized. A retired air force general stated in August that another military takeover was not the solution because people needed to acquire faith in democracy. What the government should focus on, he said, were the social and economic roots of discontent—urbanization, high unemployment, and crowded educational facilities.

Demise of the Second Turkish Republic

On the night of 11–12 September 1980, however, the military did take over, placing the country's main political leaders,

including Ecevit, Demirel, Erbakan, and Türkes, under detention. Many Turks welcomed the coup, led by armed forces chief of staff, 62-year-old Kenan Evren, who placed the country under a National Security Council (N.S.C.). With parliament dissolved, the constitution abrogated, D.I.S.K. and its more recent fascist rival M.I.S.K. shut down, the N.S.C. embarked on rounding up suspected terrorists and their numerous arms caches. The N.S.C. arranged for a constitutional assembly to draw up a new constitution and by 1985 return the country to civilian rule.

The new constitution was approved overwhelmingly by referendum in November 1982; Evren began serving a seven-year term as president. The orientation of the regime included a mixture of Demirel's austerity and *Kemalism,* newly defined as a sort of nationalism, westernization, and secularism but without the etatism so characteristic of Atatürk's economic program. Instead, economic plans stressed capitalism, encouragement of export industries, and foreign investment (more akin to Menderes' programs than to those of Atatürk). Terrorism was curtailed drastically through detention and imprisonment of an estimated 25,000 people. Though Turkey's government provoked criticism because of ongoing torture of suspected terrorists by political police, it defended its policies by pointing to the daily pre-1980 terror.

The government clamped down on leftists with particular decisiveness perhaps because they were connected more closely to Kurdish dissidents in the southeast. It was still a crime in Turkey to claim to be a Kurd—the government interpreted such language as a threat to national unity. Confronted with the example of their fellow Kurds in Iran to establish autonomy within the state, Turkey's Kurds in 1983 continued to hope for recognition as Kurds rather than "mountain Turks."

The combination of the antiterrorism, labor moderation, and economic recovery programs succeeded from 1980 to 1982 in drastically curtailing inflation in Turkey. With savings up and industrial exports outweighing in value those of agriculture for the first time, Ozal hoped Turkish industries would be able to keep expanding their export markets, especially in the Arab world. The government also implemented tax reform to encourage personal saving. To promote exports and remittance of money by overseas Turkish workers, the government devalued the Turkish lira.

Turkey's government faced decisions regarding its longstanding relations with Israel. At the third Islamic Summit Conference held in Saudi Arabia in January 1981, delegates debated proposals to impose sanctions on Israel. As the only Organization of the Islamic Conference (O.I.C.) member maintaining relations with Israel, Turkey agreed to downgrade the level of its diplomats in Tel Aviv. Heavily dependent on Arab oil and hoping for increasing exports to the Arabic-speaking countries, Turkey continued to hope to trade with all Middle Eastern states.

Society and Culture in Postwar Turkey

As Turkey in the postwar period became increasingly urbanized and proletarianized, writers continued to seek inspiration from the Anatolian peasant past. Turkey's most prominent novelist has been Yashar Kemal. Born in southern Anatolia's mountains in 1922, Kemal cultivated an early interest in Turkish folklore.

Although a school dropout, he eventually studied on his own and began to write about his people. His first novel *Memed My Hawk* is part of a trilogy describing the life of a young man who tries to establish social justice through life as a brigand.[1] In *The Legend of a Thousand Bulls* and *The Saga of the Seagull,* he addresses the topic of change in Anatolian society. A master storyteller, Kemal has produced works translated into European and Middle Eastern languages. He is often touted as a future Nobel Prizewinner.

Like many of his contemporaries in Turkey, Kemal has discussed relations between landowners and farmers, factory owners and workers, and various social classes. He has dealt as well with oppression, injustice, illiteracy, and lack of schools, but others have been imprisoned for expressing the same views. Orhan Kemal, author of *Cemile,* and Mahmut Makal who wrote *Village in Anatolia,* are two well-known writers who suffered such imprisonment. Among Turkey's most prominent postwar poets are Mehmet Basharan, Necati Cumali (Jumali), Fazil Husnu Daglarca (Dalarja), and Orhan Veli Kanik (d. 1950). The memoirs of Aziz Nesin, *Istanbul Boy,* have been translated into English.

The Turkey of today has in many ways realized Atatürk's goal of a modern and secular state, with its consumerism, materialism, and industrial development. If Atatürk hoped to cut Turkey off entirely from its Islamic past, he failed, but if he aimed at lessening the influence of religious institutions in Turkish national life, he most certainly succeeded. The overwhelming majority of Turks today are Muslims who value their religious heritage. Many continue to question the secular thrust of modern Turkey. They are also Turks who look to a national past with pre-Islamic roots as defined by the Atatürkian order.

Yet not all of Turkey's citizens have benefited from the changes. The material improvement in the lives of the Kurds, for example, has not fully compensated for the lack of recognition of their culture, language, and heritage. Turkey's rulers of the future will have to decide how best to preserve national unity in the context of increased personal freedom and pluralism. Modernization in twentieth-century Turkey has finally brought about improved health care, education, and communications that reach far into the interior. With over twenty-five universities, as well as more specialized colleges and institutes, Turkey is emphasizing higher education to provide for Turkey's future needs. Whether these new elites will accept the Euro-centered vision or turn toward Ecevit's idea of Turkey as leader of developing nations, they will certainly influence internal developments in the coming years. As the Middle East's most populous country, equipped with mineral, agricultural, and human resources, Turkey holds the potential for future prosperity and tranquility even as it continues to debate its regional and international destiny.

Postwar Pahlavi Iran and the Revolutionary Regime

World War II in Iran represented a period of national humiliation. Democratization of Iranian political life threatened to undermine the autocratic rule established by the young shah's father. Having recognized that future development would rest on petroleum revenues, and being angered by Britain's wartime occupation, Iranians increasingly called for renegotiating the agreement with the A.I.O.C. so that Iran could obtain higher profits. Dr.

---

[1] Yashar Kemal, *Memed My Hawk,* trans. Edward Roditi (London: Collins and Harvil Press, 1961) see also his *The Wind from the Plain,* trans. Thilda Kemal (London: Collins and Harvil Press, 1963).

Muhammad Musaddiq rallied these oil-control proponents into his National Front (N.F.), but the best-organized party was Tudeh. Directing its appeal to workers and the intelligentsia, Tudeh secured widespread influence both through its Central United Council of Trade Unions (C.U.C.T.U.) and periodicals. When in 1949 its members were accused of having plotted the shah's assassination, Tudeh was officially banned.

Musaddiq and the Nationalization Crisis

Pressures for nationalizing petroleum kept building especially in the *majlis*. Prime Minister Razmara was assassinated for being regarded as too "soft" on the oil issue. The new prime minister, lawyer Musaddiq, was well-equipped to propose terms. His honesty and straightforwardness won him respect among not only the new middle classes, intellectuals, and students but also landowners, labor leaders, and mujtahids. In March 1951, the government nationalized Iranian oil.

Historians consider this nationalization as a turning point in twentieth-century Iranian history. As was true of the 1906–11 revolution, the act attracted widespread favor in Iran but was subverted partly through external intervention. Ultimately, it too inspired a future generation of nationalists.

The A.I.O.C. symbolized foreign influence and interference. Yet when the nationalists drew up the takeover plan, they proposed compensating the company and retaining foreign workers. The government's main problem was that the British were not willing to concede the industry to Iran. Presumably, if the foreign workers had remained to maintain output and if Britain had not organized among its allies a boycott of Iranian oil, Iran might well have ended up with a republican government. Moreover, because oil was plentiful at the time, Kuwait and Saudi Arabia compensated for the decline in Iranian exports.

Instead, Iran's economy suffered a disastrous setback because of a precipitous decline in oil revenues. With less national income, leadership could not press ahead with economic programs. Musaddiq's coalition began to disintegrate. Although Musaddiq himself took Iran's case to the International Court of Justice, no agreement was reached. In August 1953, when the shah tried to force his resignation, Musaddiq stayed anyway. Bolstered by demonstrations in Tehran, the prime minister seemed to be strengthening his hold. The shah made a hasty though brief exit from Iran.

Why didn't Musaddiq's government survive? The army under General Zahedi remained loyal to Muhammad Reza Shah. But had Musaddiq intended to quarrel with the shah at the outset? There seems to be no substantial evidence to prove so. Hoping to solve the nationalization crisis, Musaddiq approached the United States for assistance. Particularly after Dwight Eisenhower's election as president late in 1952, however, the United States did not trust the reliability of the Iranian government.

Although Tudeh had only just begun supporting Musaddiq, the United States portrayed him as a Communist sympathizer. The cold-war climate of the times was not suited to a nationalist leader trying to liberate his country's main economic resource from foreign hands. In the context of a disintegrating N.F., the American C.I.A. assisted Zahedi in turning out Musaddiq's government and bringing back the shah. Indeed, the United States was already advising the Iranians in organizing police and armed forces. These events were to have profound implications for the United States in the aftermath of the Iranian Revolution of 1977–79.

What the shah seems to have abandoned in the wake of the Musaddiq interlude was the neutrality Iran had maintained under his father. The shah embraced a new role in the western alliance. Moreover, he emerged from his skirmish with the nationalists as a stronger national force, determined to take the reins of government himself. Historians admit that Musaddiq did not initiate any genuine social reform, but whether this was because of his preoccupation with the oil nationalization, lack of funds because of the drop in oil revenues, or because of lack of interest is not clear. The shah waited several years before embarking on any serious reforms himself.

The nationalization crisis resulted in a modification of arrangements regarding Iranian oil. In a settlement negotiated in 1954, British Petroleum (B.P.) agreed to share production with an international consortium consisting of Royal Dutch/ Shell, Gulf Oil, Mobil Oil, S.O.C.A.L.; the future EXXON, C.F.P. and Iricon Agency, representing seven smaller U.S. firms. The Iranian government won a share in the industry for the National Iranian Oil Company (N.I.O.C.) which had been created by the nationalization decree of 1951. N.I.O.C. secured sole distribution rights of oil within Iran and could make exploration arrangements, especially offshore, with other small companies outside the old B.P. concessional area. Nevertheless, the consortium retained control over some 95 percent of Iranian production and marketing. This agreement was not modified again until 1973.

In the aftermath of the crisis the shah moved to strengthen his authority, initially through use of purges. With U.S. help in 1957, he set up S.A.V.A.K. (National Security and Information Organization), famous in the 1960s and 1970s as an agent of domestic repression. In parliament, the shah created also in 1957 two political parties: the Nation Party to support the government and the People's Party to serve as an official opposition. Iranians referred to these as the *yes* party and the *of course* party since they merely divided up parliament's traditional ruling elites, especially landowners, rural leaders, and government officials—the shah's allies. When the N.F. early in the 1960s tried to provide a genuine alternative to these artificial parties, the shah assured that its members could not serve in parliament. Moreover, the Front's individual parties could rarely agree on concrete goals among themselves. After rigging elections in 1960 and 1961, the shah appointed a "reform" government to counter criticism and student discontent.

Under new prime minister Dr. Ali Amini the shah dismissed parliament in order to enact decrees that its members might not approve. What influenced the shah to rule without parliament even after he had packed it with his own supporters? Apparently, the new U.S. administration of President John F. Kennedy refused to grant new loans to the shah unless he instituted a reform program like that which the United States had hoped would change the social structure of Latin America—the Alliance for Progress. The United States believed that without reforms in the countryside, the government would undermine itself from within, thereby making itself more vulnerable to Communism. Although the shah switched from relying on his supporters to adopting ideas of his opponents, Amini was ousted in late 1962 for being too independent and popular. From 1954 until his escape in 1979, the shah allowed no potential rivals to retain positions of great authority.

The White Revolution: Inadequate Solution to Socioeconomic Problems

The shah's reform program was known variously as the *White Revolution* or *The Shah and the People Revolution,* as the shah circumvented elites to make a direct appeal to peasants. Reform focused on three general areas: land reform, education, and expansion of social services into villages. Before land reform, large landowners owned the bulk of Iran's agricultural properties. These owners tended to be religious institutions, the royal family, and the landed upper classes. Announced in January 1962, the program broke up these estates, allowing their owners to choose the best lands for their own retention. Because the few mechanized farms were exempted along with orchards, tea plantations, and pastures, the most prosperous enterprises did not change hands. Distributions thus excluded the best and some of the biggest holdings.

Historians disagree about the results of land reform on the lives of peasants. Prior to redistribution, peasants had often worked either as sharecroppers for absentee landlords or had cultivated small holdings of their own. But some of the former had been hired not by the owner but by a tenant or a sharecropper who had an agreement with the owner. Such landless indirect hires received no allocation at all.

The old system left the peasant within the subsistence economy while the landowner or prosperous tenant functioned within the market economy. While peasants were largely self-sufficient, they did not prosper from any surplus they generated. In addition to crop payments, they often had to work for the landlord or hired themselves out as casual laborers to help make ends meet. Land reform brought many more peasants within the scope of the market economy, but historians disagree about the number or percentage of peasants involved.

What does seem clear is that peasants who received land rarely received enough to benefit fully from redistribution. Less than one quarter could fully subsist on their allotment alone. Those whose holdings were insufficient gradually became more impoverished because they had no means of investing in equipment or other technological improvements that might have increased their harvest. Many had to borrow money at high interest rates to make ends meet. Rural cooperatives set up as part of the land reform program also failed to meet borrowing needs. Therefore those peasants who could not retain what they had been given because of inability to pay their debts were added to the estimated 50 percent of the peasantry who had received no lands at the outset. Others kept their lands only through extra work. Instead of making the peasantry independent, then, reform perpetuated dependency and fueled rural-urban migration of landless and poor peasants.

Moreover, because the government charged the peasants for land allotments and paid compensation to landowners, old landed classes remained prosperous. Not only had they held onto half their lands, but they also continued to gain from their former holdings and began investing in industry, too. What changed for these wealthy rural Iranians, religious and secular, was their relationship with the government. It became the guarantor of their status in the countryside, instead of the reverse. State officials replaced landlords as primary authorities in rural areas.

In conjunction with the White Revolution, the state initiated a literacy corps designed to co-opt Iran's young people into a massive campaign to end rural illiteracy. Members assumed much of the responsibility for government-provided education of peasants. Improved health care and agricultural education were also promoted. Historians credit these rural programs with having won loyalty for the shah because peasants expected their lot to improve. Discontent began to set in when the programs failed to deliver what the shah had promised.

Two major failures in agriculture besides the early peasant redistribution program were the government's agricultural corporations and large transnational agribusinesses of the 1970s. From 1967 on, Iran's government established some ninety-four corporations in which peasants supplied land in exchange for shares proportionate to the value of their holdings. The idea was that well-trained government agronomists would make better managers than the peasants could be. Instead of being in charge, then, the peasants had to hire on with the corporations as laborers to work their former lands. Productivity in the corporations did not reach the anticipated yields partly because peasants did not feel they had a genuine stake in the system.

Agribusiness proved even less successful despite the fact that land seized for use was well-watered, located below dams, and was leased at favorable prices. Transnationals, as elsewhere, sought high returns in the short-term and an expansion of their own investment opportunities.

They sent to Iran foreigners with little or no knowledge of local customs and conditions. As so often happens in the developing world, the corporations did not embark on sufficient studies before inaugurating their projects. They often introduced machines and technology not well-suited to conditions in Iran. Machinery operators were not sufficiently well-trained in advance. Like the agricultural corporations, transnationals operated farms that were unwieldy in size. After some transnational enterprises had failed, the government stepped in to rescue them and transformed them into the nearly as unsuccessful farm corporations.

At the end of the shah's reign, Iranian peasants still lived in conditions not unlike those at the outset. Agricultural investment had remained low as the remaining large landlords and big concerns tried to maximize profits. The poor could not afford to invest at all. Iran's production of staples such as grains in no way compensated for the population-increase during the period. Instead of being self-sufficient, Iran became a major food importer. Government food-price subsidies undermined local agricultural interests because they, too, were obliged to keep their prices low. Not surprisingly, many Iranians migrated to the oil-enriched cities. This weakened the rural social and economic fabric even more. Departees tended to be young men who would have been more productive agricultural laborers than those they left behind. With insufficient labor available, some farmers restricted land under cultivation to that which they could maintain. They sold the rest or kept it fallow. Those who purchased land often converted it to produce nonfood export crops such as cotton, or they made it suitable for industrial use.

Achievements of the literacy and health corps were also modest at best. Between 65–75 percent of the population remained illiterate. Educational programs benefited mainly those in cities where investment and development was concentrated. Many of the new educated elites acquired a stake in the system. Others, however, especially students in the United States and Europe, reacted against the authoritarianism and repression that increasingly characterized the shah's regime. Rather than return home to participate in the country's development, they took well-paying jobs outside while calling for revolutionary change at home. Having paid for their education, the government did not look kindly upon overseas Iranian protesters who were regarded as subversive elements. S.A.V.A.K.'s operations extended to the United States in an effort to identify dissidents. Ironically, many of these intelligentsia who returned after the 1977–79 revolution eager to build up the republic, died at the hands of the new revolutionary courts. Though the White Revolution decrees gave women the right to vote, this meant little in a country in which the ruler did not respect democratic institutions.

Muhammad Reza's Efforts to Quell Dissent

In its immediate aftermath, the White Revolution failed to end antigovernment protests by workers, religious leaders, and the intelligentsia. Workers objected to high inflation. Intellectuals protested the futility of education when the government seemed to have established no concrete objectives. Religious leaders decried the imprisonment of leaders such as Ayatollah Ruhollah Khumayni (later exiled in Iraq and France), who was influential among traditional bazaar merchants and the urban poor.

These groups lacked confidence in the government's commitment to genuine social reform despite anticorruption trials in the late 1950s and early 1960s. Moreover, it appeared to them that the shah's regime had attached itself too closely to the United States. The N.F. continued to demand open and free elections, especially after Amini's dismissal. In June 1963, thousands of Iranians demonstrated against the regime in the streets of Tehran and other major cities. In Tehran, Qum, and Mashhad, an estimated 3,000–6,000

Iranians were killed when the army intervened to halt the protests.

Within two years, the N.F. faded away. The shah's two parties, independent in name only, remained in existence until 1975. Worker and student protests continued during the interim, and new organizations opposing the government appeared, notably the Iranian People's Fidayin Guerillas (O.P.P.F.G.). When in October 1971 the shah organized costly celebrations for Iran's 2,500th anniversary, few Iranians shared his joy. Announcements of arms purchases from the United States aroused further protests. Muhammad Reza decided to restrict political and literary freedoms even further.

In 1975, he created a single mass party, the National Resurgence Party (N.R.P.). All Iranians were called upon to join. As a prop of the regime, the party provided the shah with a pretext for determining which Iranians were loyal to him. All Iranians who refused to sign up were classified as opponents to be expelled or imprisoned. Public servants in particular felt obliged to join in order to keep their jobs. The shah followed up this political "reform" by shutting down most newspapers and periodicals, allegedly because of low circulation. Those who could still publish books, newspapers, or magazines did so only with extreme caution.

Literary protests

Why did the shah decide to clamp down further on the country's already restricted political life and on public expression? Changes in Iran between the protests of the early 1960s and the oil boom of 1973–74 had encouraged the emergence of writers willing to criticize the regime. Tabriz-born Samad Behrangi (1939–68) was among those addressing problems faced by poor villagers, inequities between rich and poor, and the tribulations of rural migrants to the cities. A trained teacher, Behrangi composed books drawn from local folklore and village life. He believed that education could be used to improve society. Caring deeply for his students, he translated well-known Persian authors'

works into their native Azeri and composed a grammar that would have simplified teaching if the government had agreed to print it. In the allegorical story "The Little Black Fish," Behrangi describes how a small fish confined to its locality sought a wider world against the advice of fellow fish, finally sacrificing its life so that other fish could live in peace. Both a writer and a revolutionary, Behrangi did not fear the authorities. Although he died in a suspicious drowning accident in 1968 and all of his stories except "The Little Black Fish" were banned in 1973, he emerged as one of Iran's most highly respected twentieth-century writers.

Female poet Furugh Farrukhzad (1935–67), better known as a social rather than a political rebel, wrote a daring poem commemorating the death of Dr. Musaddiq (which occurred shortly before her own). As one of Iran's outstanding twentieth-century poets, Farrukhzad referred to some future time in which ruling families could be eliminated without being missed. Comprised of short lyrics, most of her poetry focused on love themes. Like Behrangi, she died in an accident.

Ghulam Husayn Sa'edi, Jalal Al-i Ahmad, and Firidun Tunkabuni also criticized developments in Iran. Sa'edi suffered arrest many times during the shah's regime and was tortured in prison. A close friend of Behrangi's, he spoke at his funeral. His most well-known work, *The Mourners of Bayial*, deals with the deterioration of life in the countryside. One of Iran's most acclaimed films, *The Cow*, was an adaptation of this work. Al-i Ahmad, an early critic of the shah's regime, wrote in praise of another opponent of the regime, deceased poet Nima Yushij, in his story "The Old Man Was Our Eyes." In particular, Ahmad protested against social injustice. In 1974, at age 46, he too died under conditions made more suspect by the fact that S.A.V.A.K. refused to allow his family to arrange the burial. Tunkabuni has been both a writer and critic of Iranian revolutionary literature.

Among the Shah's more well known

critics were Reza Baraheni and Sa'id Soltanpur. Baraheni, who like Behrangi is of Azeri origin, gave special attention in his Persian language writings to oppression of minorities. His *The Crowned Cannibals,* published in 1977, deals more fully with repression of intellectuals under the shah. Poet and dramatist Sultanpur came to the fore again in summer 1981. The former victim of torture under the shah was arrested at his home by Iran's revolutionary regime. At his trial, Sultanpur decried the course of the revolution, proclaiming it reactionary and corrupt. Like many other leftists and liberals, Sultanpur met his death not by the hands of the shah but at those of his fellow revolutionaries. It was a sad fate that many other intellectuals who somehow survived the shah's repression were to share.

Roots of Revolution: Quest for Social Justice

What were the roots of social and intellectual protests? Iran's oil boom even before 1973 attracted foreign businessmen and speculators. With them came inflation and hardship, especially in cities. Industry, often funded by landed elites, grew rapidly, employing displaced rural migrants. Iran increased production of consumer goods such as electronic equipment and automobiles. Heavy industry, like steel, began to expand as the government shifted its focus away from the import-substitution light industries of the 1960s. Iran also developed industries in petrochemicals associated with oil and natural gas. Iran was the leader in raising petroleum prices when Arab producers cut production in 1973. By 1974, revenues reached $18 billion from $2.5 billion three years earlier. The government had sound hopes of ample funds to develop not only agriculture and industry but also discoveries of coal, copper, and iron.

Inevitably, rising expectations and mismanagement caught up with the shah. Throwing money at problems did not solve them. Aware of the government's vast wealth, workers began striking for

higher wages and benefits which they often received because of Iran's shortage of trained manpower. But the government had committed itself to more ambitious expenditures than it could afford. An oil recession followed the boom of the early 1970s.

Iran's ethnic and linguistic minorities also desired a greater share of national leadership and more autonomy at home, mainly to express their cultural heritages. Like their counterparts in Iraq, Syria, and Turkey, Iran's Kurds focused on winning recognition of their own separate identity. The Sunni Baluchis in the southeast and the Arabs in the oil-rich southwest, as well as the Azeris in the north, sought autonomy. Recognizing that Persians are merely the largest minority in Iran, the government resisted all of these independent-minded national groups. The Pahlavis never encouraged a highly decentralized state organization. Their successors began by pursuing the same policy. Faced with non-Persian nomads and settled minorities, the government is bound to face continual challenges to centralization.

However, there was a religious dimension to the shah's opposition. The shah's agricultural reforms struck at Iran's mullas and mujtahids by making the state and its officials the main rural power. In cities too, the shah encouraged foreign institutions and structures, for example, banks, at the expense of traditional merchant interests. His spending priorities, both personal and public, invoked the wrath of religious as well as more secular-minded opponents. With such great disparities between rich and poor, the vast amounts expended on weaponry, airports, and the like seemed inappropriate and wrong to those in contact with the majority of Iranians. Widespread corruption accompanied the influx of foreign contractors and experts, all wanting a share of Iran's wealth and willing to pay to get it.

It was not merely a case of overly rapid change. Devout Muslim Iranians objected to the types of changes being imposed on the society by the apparent desire of the government to imitate the United States.

Increasing personal freedom for women, which had led them into higher education and the professions, aroused objection, especially as many young Iranians abandoned the traditional *chador* (body and head covering) for less modest dress and often behavior. Movies seemed to encourage social immorality. Social change also undermined traditional family relationships as sons and even daughters began enjoying higher incomes than their parents. Government repression of those who had the temerity to criticize in public involved many more Iranians in the struggle. Who could ignore the disappearance, torture, and often murder of children, parents, and neighbors? The omnipresent S.A.V.A.K. struck at all segments of society, but most often at intellectuals and the urban poor.

The religious opposition did not lack an ideologue. Ali Shari'ati came from the N.F.'s "clerical" wing composed of devout Muslim technocrats led by Mehdi Bazargan (revolutionary Iran's first prime minister). The Sorbonne-educated Shari'ati viewed Islam as a liberation ideology that could overthrow the monarchy in Iran and replace it with a committed religious elite who would then implement Islamic revolution in society. This elite, or a charismatic leader, would rally Iran's Imami masses already embued with the ideas of martyrdom against unjust rulers. Because he opened a school in Iran in which he taught his views, Shari'ati was imprisoned and went into exile after his release in 1976. The following year, he died of a heart attack. Many Iranians believed that S.A.V.A.K. agents had instigated it. His ideas, circulated clandestinely by his followers, reached both intellectuals and local religious leaders. Iran's revolution in 1977–79 wholeheartedly took up his ideas.

One aspect of Shari'ati's thought had particular implications for the later course of developments in Iran. Shari'ati viewed Marxism as a particularly dangerous ideology that rivaled his own. In this, he agreed fully with later revolutionary leader Khumayni. In public pronouncements at the outset of the revolution, Khu-mayni left no doubt that he would not permit leftists into the new government. He expected them to try to take control without popular support—they would thereby become traitors.

Marxists came under fire partly because of their key role in the revolutionary struggle of the 1970s. During that time, two main groups of fighters emerged as active: the Fidayi and the Mujahidin. The former emphasized class struggle and elitist leadership, while the latter focused on a Maoist Marxism. An Islamic-oriented Mujahidin faction that adhered to Shari'ati's ideals acquired greater prominence later. The shah's government tried unsuccessfully to suppress all of these groups through arrests, imprisonment, torture, and execution. Khumayni was willing to cooperate with these fighters during the struggle to achieve his own goal, but their only hope of success lay in winning a larger following than his among Iran's people. Since the clergy in sermons and actions had led Iranians to fight the shah as an oppressor, the Marxists' hopes of controlling the revolution were slim indeed. Moreover, disaffected urban merchants had long tended to be allies of the ulama.

Five main tendencies existed within the opposition during the upheavals of 1977–79.[2] *Religious conservatives* favored a political revolution to turn out the shah. They did not necessarily advocate a social revolution to change the country's social structure. Ayatollah Shari'atmadari, who later criticized the excesses of the revolution, represented this trend. Shari'ati's followers were found mainly among the *religious radicals* who advocated vague social reform after overthrowing the shah. *Religious traditionalists* constituted the third group. Opposing everything western and favoring the strict reimposition of Muslim law and custom, these traditionalists were to gain the upper hand in the early aftermath of the revolution. Specifi-

---

[2] Ervand Abrahamian, "Iran in Revolution: the Opposition, Forces," *MERIP REPORTS No. 75/76* (March–April 1979), pp. 6–8.

cally disavowing the radical social change espoused by secular radicals, they immediately turned against their allies in the revolution.

Two secular-oriented groups also opposed the shah. The intelligentsia, many of them involved with the N.F., supported restoration of democratic, constitutional government. More radical secularists, including Tudeh, Fidayi, and other Marxist associations objected to a religious state, favoring a secular one in which workers would play an important role. They would have preferred almost any regime other than the one that emerged under the religious traditionalists. A rapprochement between the religious and N.F. segments ensued after February 1978 when a prominent newspaper published an article attacking Khumayni.

Although these groups represented the opposition's leadership, many Iranians rose up spontaneously against the shah because of social and economic problems. Each group tried to win the amorphous public. In the end, the religious elements gained the upper hand because they outmaneuvered their allies in the revolution and because they won the support of the masses. Islam seemed to provide the solution to Iran's growing pains, and Islamic leadership of protest movements was most familiar to Iranians, already in daily contact with their religious leaders.

Iran's Foreign Policy Under Muhammad Reza Shah: The U.S. Alliance and Gulf Domination

Taking a look at Iran's foreign policy under the shah, we must recognize that the shah's early struggle for recognition of his authority influenced his conduct of foreign affairs as well as his domestic policies. After requiring U.S. and British help to establish himself as Iran's ruler, the shah planned to make his country the dominant power in Western Asia. In this, he could count on U.S. support.

Why did the U.S. give such strong backing to the shah and then seem to withdraw it in his hour of greatest need? In the early postwar years, the United States wanted to preserve Iran as a bulwark against Communism and Soviet expansion. The United States backed the shah because he seemed to offer the greatest hope for maintaining the status quo in Iran. Whether the shah was autocratic or democratic mattered little to U.S. policymakers. Iran joined the Baghdad Pact that became C.E.N.T.O. In exchange, the United States supplied the shah with arms. Although President Kennedy showed concern for the use of U.S. funds in Iran and prompted declaration of the White Revolution, fewer U.S. efforts were directed toward revival of democratic institutions.

Iran's strategic location in relation to the Soviet Union was but one factor in American support. Petroleum also played a part, especially during the 1970s. As Britain withdrew from the Gulf states, the United States helped to establish the shah as the regional protector. As the Vietnam War was winding down, Iran purchased from the declining U.S. defense industries arms which over a ten-year period amounted to an estimated $20 billion. By the 1970s, Iran had already undertaken military missions in the area, helping the royalists in the Yemen civil war of the 1960s. In 1971, Iran showed its power by seizing from Gulf shaykhdoms Sharjah and Ras al-Khayma three small islands—Abu Musa, Greater Tunb, and Lesser Tunb—on the eve of their joining with Abu Dhabi, Ajman, Dubai, Fujayra, and Umm al-Qawayn to form the United Arab Emirates. Not long after, the shah sent Iranian forces to fight against insurgents in Dhufar in western Oman. From 1973 to late 1976, the shah's troops helped Sultan Qabus (1970–) win a victory in Dhufar. Iran, with its own large Baluchi population, sent economic and military aid to Pakistan when Baluchis in the latter country were organizing guerrilla actions early in the 1970s.

At the same time, the shah began to

assist Iraqi Kurds in their longstanding battle with the Iraqi government. In 1975, the aid ended when Iran won concessions from Iraq to share sovereignty over the Shatt al-Arab waterway. The Kurdish struggle collapsed in the immediate aftermath. It could be argued that the shah's Gulf policies were just as likely to threaten petroleum channels as they were to protect them through provoking conflict with neighbors. The shah could not always hope to be victorious or to maintain unpopular regimes in power. He made no secret of his intentions to make Iran one of five great international powers.

U.S. Policy and the Collapse of Pahlavi Iran

The United States undoubtedly realized the shah's intentions—he stated the goal publicly and repeatedly. Especially under the "southern strategy" of national security advisor and U.S. Secretary of State Henry Kissinger during the Nixon presidency, the United States hoped that Iran would be satisfied with functioning as one of four American partners in the region. Along with Egypt, Israel, and Saudi Arabia, Iran would help the United States carry out its own regional goals. The shah in the 1970s was clearly the United States best paying arms customer. Israel provided military and intelligence training to Iranian army officers and S.A.V.A.K. members. When the United States obtained Israeli cooperation in withdrawing from Sinai after the 1973 war, Iran supplied Israel's petroleum needs. Iran and Israel were also trading partners, albeit on a modest scale. After the 1973 war, the shah extended economic aid to Egypt, the latter open to giving Iran a greater role in Arab affairs. In return, Egyptian president Sadat offered refuge to the shah following his expulsion from Iran and his unsuccessful attempt to find a haven in the United States and elsewhere. The shah was to die of cancer in Egypt on 27 July 1980. He was buried in Cairo's al-Rifa'i

Mosque. It had been his father's burial place for several years after he too had died in exile.

The U.S. abandonment of the shah reflects the perception of the Carter administration that the shah did not represent Iran's future. Carter, however, proclaimed in public not long before the shah's fall that the Iranian leader was a great man who enjoyed the full backing of the United States. With substantial economic and military interests in Iran, the United States under Carter failed to establish a firm position for or against the regime, especially on the question of human rights. The shah had every reason to believe that the United States, which had upheld him for so long, would not abandon him. The United States, however, finally recognized the breadth of the anti-shah forces and hoped that he could ease himself out gracefully.

In the last days of the shah's Iran, oil strikes shut down much of the petroleum industry, especially the oil-rich Arab Khuzistan province. But these came at the end of nearly two years of persistent strikes and demonstrations against the shah. They intensified in the fall of 1978 when workers began their strike. In November 1978 the government announced the imposition of martial law. Each new demonstration created new martyrs. Forty days later, commemorative services for the dead would provoke repression and further martyrdom. Women participated actively in the protests.

The United States decided at this eleventh hour that perhaps a constitutional government could be instituted to stave off the religious and secular radicals. Shahpur Bakhtiar set up a civilian government supposedly to preserve the monarchy while making moves toward democracy. The shah made his exit on 16 January 1979, never to return. Bakhtiar did not last much longer. Long-time government opponent and spiritual revolutionary Ayatollah Ruhollah Khumayni returned triumphant from exile in France, and a new government led by N.F. leader Mehdi Bazargan took over.

The Early Years of the Iranian Revolution

At the departure of the shah, many Iranians were engulfed by a euphoria that hardly prepared them for the power struggle that emerged among the revolutionaries. In the early stages, Khumayni elevated the Muslim technocrats who had supported him during his years in exile—men such as engineer Bazargan and economists Abu al-Hasan Bani Sadr and Ali Reza Nobari. While these technocrats were focusing on restoring order in the Iranian economy, revolutionary courts began executing prominent officials and military personnel of the old regime who had remained in the country. Bani Sadr was among those who justified the rapid "justice" by pointing to the history of the French revolution that was born in violence but which eventually inspired the rise of democracies. By November, nearly seven hundred Iranians had died at the hands of revolutionary firing squads. Iranians did not protest. Those executed were viewed as having perpetrated great crimes against the people while they were in power.

The Hostage Crisis

In November 1979, the regime faced its first great international crisis. The United States, under President Carter's leadership, had judiciously avoided the appearance of continuing to support the shah. In October 1979, Carter came under pressure from prominent U.S. businessmen and former shah friends to allow the former ruler into the United States for emergency surgery. Iran warned that any actions by the United States that seemed to indicate a pro-shah policy would be followed by retribution against American interests in Iran. The shah left Mexico for New York, and on 4 November 1979, Iranian student revolutionaries mobbed the U.S. embassy compound in Tehran and took its occupants hostage, demanding that the United States return the shah

to Iran to face trial. Ironically, the students were armed with some of the 300,000 weapons—U.S.-made—looted from army stores.

In the long run, the entire hostage episode was to contribute to the downfall of two presidents, President Carter of the United States and Bani Sadr, elected as Iran's first president in January 1980. Although during the initial stages of the crisis, the revolutionaries released blacks and women (with the exception of two female diplomats), they held onto fifty-three others, only one of whom gained an early release because of illness.

The most disturbing aspect of the episode at its outset was the support given to the hostage-takers by Iran's government. On previous occasions when embassies—internationally recognized as safe havens—had been violated, the government of the foreign country had intervened to protect the embassy. Who would send diplomats abroad were it not for international agreements regarding conduct toward them? On this occasion, though, the Iranian government declared that the invaders were acting on behalf of the country.

For nearly fifteen months, the United States expended its energies on trying to secure the hostages' release. The United States sent a rescue mission that failed not because of Iranian opposition but because it was aborted in the desert during its early stages. The hostage episode proved far more traumatic for the United States than for Iran, and historians of the future will probably agree that it was a tangential episode in Iranian history. Its major impact in Iran was its contribution to the fall of President Bani Sadr.

Consolidation of a New Political and Social Order

In November 1978, early in the revolution's political life, Khumayni established an Islamic Revolutionary Council (I.R.C.) to supervise the transfer of power to a new revolutionary government. After the appointment of Bazargan as prime minister in February 1979, the council began functioning as a rival government, giving orders and directing the revolutionary tribunals. With the hostage crisis, the council assumed full executive authority, and Bazargan was forced to step down. Khumayni declared that until the approval of a theocratic constitution and the election of a president and assembly, the I.R.C. would govern the country. For the first time, membership became public. Among the most influential members were Bani Sadr, Hojat al-Islam Muhammad Javad Bahonar, Ayatollah Muhammad Beheshti, and Sadiq Qutbzadeh, all of whom were out of the picture by mid-1982. In November 1979, Bani Sadr was Iran's finance minister and acting foreign minister. With Khumayni's blessing, he became revolutionary Iran's first president in January 1980.

The assembly, however, was dominated by ulama from the outset. Bani Sadr served at the will of Khumayni. Under the banner of the Islamic Republican Party (I.R.P.), traditionalists began purging the revolutionary left. What then happened to workers who had demonstrated in the streets in support of Khumayni inspired not by the traditionalists but by radical secularists?

In the immediate aftermath of the revolution, many factory owners and landlords fled the country. Workers' councils were set up to manage some factories. Landless peasants often seized farms abandoned by absentee landlords while the government's new officials went into the countryside from time to time to redistribute land. Iranian industry suffered in particular during the consolidation phase. Worker unrest continued because of unemployment resulting from the economic slowdown. Iran's oil workers staged strikes to protest the withdrawal of concessions won after the strikes of 1978.

Petroleum exports, the mainstay of foreign exchange, fell as production declined from a prerevolution level of 5 to 6 million barrels per day to 1.5 million barrels. Inflation and profiteering continued because of shortages in commodities. The Iranian government's technocrats saw their decisions overridden with increasing frequency by the I.R.P. members of the I.R.C. Urban Iranians reacted to the regime's failure to deal effectively with the economic and social ills that fueled revolutionary fervor.

The Gulf War

The situation was not at all helped by the Iraqi attack of September 1980 that launched the Gulf war. Iraq's leaders finally tired of Khumayni's unwillingness to renegotiate the 1975 Shatt al-Arab agreement and to withdraw Iran's forces from the United Arab Emirate islands. Moreover, Khumayni had insisted on calling on Iraq's Shi'i majority to revolt against their government. Iraq in earlier years had sheltered Khumayni after his expulsion from Iran.

The Gulf war dragged on through 1983 as the Iraq offensive found itself bogged down not far from the frontier. Observers at the time assumed that the army had been so debilitated by the killing of its generals and lack of sufficient spare parts that Iran would soon give in. But Iran raised a people's army (*pasdaran*) to assist in the fighting. The pasdaran maintained their own general staff and political organization. Although the pasdaran and regular army forces were not well-coordinated, Iran managed to keep Iraq from achieving victory. Mediation efforts by the United Nations and the Organization of the Islamic Conference proved fruitless. Then, between April and June 1982, Iranian forces recovered the initiative and retook Khoramshahr. Iraqi President Saddam Husayn announced the withdrawal of Iraq's troops from Iran; yet, the war went on.

Although President Bani Sadr initially won support for his close attention to the war effort and his frequent presence at the front, eventually his position was compromised both by failure to drive out the Iraqi invaders and by reactions within Iran against the agreement that finally freed the U.S. diplomatic hostages in January 1981. Oddly, however, Bani Sadr played no role in the last month of negotiations over the hostages. In fact, his newspaper

Islamic Revolution claimed that I.R.P. leaders were fussing over having received U.S. assets that had belonged to Iran in the first place. A key role in the negotiating process was carried out by Algeria's foreign minister Ben Yahya (killed in 1982 while mediating the Gulf conflict), but neither the United States nor Iran displayed long-range gratitude. In June 1981, Bani Sadr went into hiding as Iranians called for his removal after Khumayni forced him to step down as military commander-in-chief. Counterdemonstrations were held in his favor, principally by members of the Mujahidin led by Mas'ud Rajavi.

Dissent at Home

During this time, Mujahidin were engaged in full-scale warfare with the regime. To replace Bani Sadr, Khumayni chose prime minister Muhammad Ali Raja'i, a mathematics teacher and former Mujahidin member. Like many others in Iran, he experienced arrest and torture under the shah. Before elections could be held, over seventy members of the ruling I.R.P., including Ayatollah Beheshti, were killed in a bomb attack at a secret meeting. Among the dead were four cabinet ministers, six deputy ministers, and twenty-seven members of parliament. Raja'i worked with assembly speaker Akbar Rafsanjani to retain control over the government and arrange an orderly succession. The bombing accelerated the government's campaign to wipe out the Mujahidin.

In July 1981, Raja'i won 88 percent of votes cast to become Iran's president-elect. A few days later, Bani Sadr and Rajavi fled to Paris with the aid of the Iranian pilot who had flown the shah into exile. No sooner had Raja'i and his new prime minister Bahonar been sworn in with their cabinets in August than both were assassinated on the 30th of the month in another bombing at a secret meeting. Clearly, the Mujahidin, with an estimated 100,000 fighters had penetrated every level of the regime. While Hojat al-Islam Sayyid Ali Khamine'i became Iran's new president, Rajavi announced plans to form a government-in-exile, and Bani Sadr continued to insist that he was Iran's true president. Meanwhile, in April 1982, Qutbzadeh was arrested, imprisoned, tried, by the regime for having plotted a coup; he was executed in the fall after having acknowledged his guilt. The leadership of revolutionary Iran was heavily decimated, but it stabilized.

As Iran's ethnic minorities, principally the Kurds led by Abd al-Rahman Qassemlu, sought self-determination, Khumayni barred any change in the status quo. Associated with the Mujahidin and espousing democratic government, Qassemlu felt that Bani Sadr had been more open to Kurdish autonomy. He insisted that morale among Kurds—who had lost an estimated 10,000 fighters since 1978—remained high and that they would fight until they achieved their goal. Past Kurdish history would lend support to the idea of ongoing struggle.

The nature of the Islamic Republic in the forseeable future could not be predicted. It was engaged in ongoing war at home and abroad. Khumayni, already in his eighties, seemed unlikely to live much longer. Despite the growing pains of the republic, the revolution and its apparatus continued to be functional.

Conclusion

Turkey and Iran, both neighbors of the Soviet Union, with similar interwar leaders, diverged considerably in the postwar period. Bolstered by a new confidence in democratic institutions, Turkey's new leaders repeatedly tried to make them work. Military coup leaders followed through on promises to restore civilian government, though not always to the satisfaction of critics. Never far removed from their people and always cognizant of the military's willingness to step in, Turkish politicians had to be responsive to domestic needs, regardless of foreign pressures.

Iran's shah represented continuity with the past, but he became increasingly isolated and authoritarian instead of open to internal criticism. What he spawned was a multifaceted opposition that with few legal means of expressing dissent turned to revolution and ousted him. All the arms in the world could not save his regime because it was so unpopular. Turkey's governments avoided radical political change by proving adaptable. By remaining rigid, the shah created the conditions that brought him down in the end.

International pressures certainly affected both countries in the postwar period. With the growth in petroleum production and revenues, Iran became increasingly vital to the western alliance (including Japan) in a way that Turkey, though also of strategic interest because of its location, was not. The combination of location and hydrocarbons made Iran far more vulnerable to western interference because of the greater involvement of foreigners in the indigenous economy and because of foreign exchange dependency on oil. Even with U.S. bases on Turkish soil, Turkey seemed far more able to set its own postwar course.

Both Turkey and Iran continued the modernization thrust. Although Turkey was far more advanced in this regard, Iran could use oil wealth to implement rapid change where desired or where possible. Yet in Turkey, the tradition of secularism or at least separation of religion and state, had a much longer history and was well-established. Modernization did not threaten religion in Turkey as it seemed to challenge Iran's religious elites and ordinary people. Foreigners did not cause in Turkey the kind of social disruption and corruption that became prevalent in Iran under the shah. Socioeconomic factors, then, highly influenced the differences that characterized postwar Iran and Turkey.

CHAPTER SIXTEEN

Palestinians and the Evolution of Israel: From New State to Regional Power

Israel's "baptism by fire" during the years 1947–49 greatly influenced its social and national evolution. Security and continued immigration were prestate priorities that carried over to the present day. Israelis could hardly have been expected to forget the Holocaust; they often used the slogans "never again" and "no alternative." The hostility of Israel's neighbors from the outset appeared to carry a further threat of annihilation that could only be taken seriously.

To these issues were added new social and political concerns. The socialist ethic of the founders gradually gave way to a more capitalistic economic structure and outlook. Israel from the 1948 Declaration to the present day, established no internationally recognized boundaries. The Is-raelis themselves have never achieved consensus on what those boundaries ought to be. Neither the Jewish Israelis, nor the Christian, Muslim, and Druze Arab Israelis, were monolithic groups—politically, economically, and socially—but Israel was not able to evolve a fully pluralistic society.

In one of the world's most vigorous multiparty systems, Jewish Israelis have enjoyed the greatest freedom to debate most issues in public without fear of suppression. For Arab Israelis, the main concern has been to devise ideologies and strategies for treating their national dilemma. Among both peoples, poetry, short stories, novels, and memoirs have emerged as expression of and responses to everyday realities.

The Law of Return and Israel's Population Growth

Zionism, in its original form, assumed that all Jews in the world were one nation. As soon as a Jewish state could be formed, the Jewish people would become synonymous with the population of that country. The raison d'etre of the state would be the "ingathering of the exiles." Zionists did not envision a Jewish state in which a large non-Jewish population would enjoy equal rights. Nor did they expect the vast majority of world Jewry to remain outside Israel.

When Israel was founded, however, the state found itself confronted by unanticipated realities. The relationship between the Israelis and world Jewry has been marked by great affinity but also by dissonance. World Jewry has come to view itself as Israel's backbone. While Jewish Israelis have appreciated financial and political support, they have also borne a measure of contempt for Jews who refuse to become Israelis. They have come to use Hebrew as an adjective referring to themselves, reserving Jewish for religion, outsiders, or newcomers.

Israeli schoolchildren learn that Israel is a Jewish state, created by and for Jews. The non-Jews who again constitute about 20 percent of the population (excluding occupied lands) are regarded by themselves and by Jewish Israelis as a marginal element who by definition are "in but not of" the state. The right of Jews to become Israelis was embodied in the Law of Return (1950). Between 1949 and 1952, the Jewish population of Israel doubled due to a massive program organized by David Ben Gurion. The program included mes-sianic appeals to Jewish Yemenis (who responded enthusiastically) and a Zionist campaign in Iraq which eventually led most Jewish Iraqis to leave.

Generally speaking, the creation of an Israel that claimed Jews as citizens also seemed to threaten the welfare of Jews in Arab countries. Many left rather than live in fear of discrimination. Others were enthusiastic about moving to a Jewish state. Jews in the Arab world, however, did not initially flock to Israel. Between 1955 and 1964, 200,000 Jews from Egypt and Algeria entered Israel strictly as a consequence of Israel's attack on Egypt in 1956 and Israeli support for France against the nationalists in Algeria's war of independence.

Before 1948, about 90 percent of Jewish immigrants to Palestine came from Europe and the United States. Between 1948 and 1954, with the arrival of Arab Jews as well as Jewish refugees, an appreciable demographic change took place in the Jewish population. Although immigration bursts took place again in the early 1960s and in the early 1970s when pressure was placed on the Soviet Union to permit Soviet Jews to emigrate, the population in Israel grew more by natural increase than by immigration after its first decade. Because of their much higher birth rate, Jews of Arab-world origin by the 1980s easily outnumbered the European founders who continued to dominate the government and military hierarchy. The even greater percentage growth among Arab Israelis promised to keep increasing their proportion in Israel's overall population.

Absorption of Immigrants and the Israeli Economy

How did Israel develop the capability to take in masses of immigrants within a short period of time? Israel received massive financial support from abroad including gifts from world Jewry, loans and private investment, U.S. government support, German reparations which from 1952 to 1966 added nearly $1 billion to the economy, and other aid. Although the large influx of unearned income produced inflation that caused devaluations of the Israeli pound (later called the *shekel*) steadily from 1962 to 1983, this capital and investment enabled Israel to undertake ambitious development projects. Israel has remained throughout its history the greatest per capita recipient of foreign aid in the world.

In conjunction with foreign aid, an extensive land-development program was among new projects that helped the absorption of new people. The Jewish National Fund took over some three million dunums of Arab land and property through the absentee laws. Businesses, citrus groves, fields, and homes were turned over to Jewish Israelis. Even lands of Arabs who were still in Israel were declared vacant because the owners had temporarily fled to some other part of the country. Still other Arab Christian and Muslim Israelis were expelled from their homes for security reasons, especially in regions such as Galilee where the Arab population was concentrated and from which it had not fled in large numbers. Dozens of Arab villages were destroyed and new Jewish settlements were constructed in their place. Moshe Dayan once said, "There is not one single place built in this country that did not have a former Arab population."[1]

The Israeli government also used modern machinery and technology to increase the productivity of the land. From 1948–49 to 1971–72, the crop area doubled, some half of which was irrigated. To provide for increased population and irrigation demand, Israel needed to exploit fully the waters of the Jordan River, particularly in building the National Water Carrier from Lake Tiberias to Rosh Hayyin near Tel Aviv. Israel's neighbors with claims on Jordan waters—Syria, Jordan, and Lebanon—disputed Israeli diversion projects. Expansion of the Israeli population whether by immigration or by natural increase was regarded by them as placing an excessive burden on scarce resources.

Industrial development, as well, helped Israel provide a livelihood for its rapidly growing population. Whereas agriculture accounted for less than 10 percent of the labor force, industry provided jobs for increasing numbers of Israelis, especially after economic revivals that followed the 1967 and 1973 wars. Employment in the public sector, commerce, tourism, and in financial and other services absorbed about 50 percent of the labor force.

Israel was one of the world's largest producers of polished diamonds. South Africa served as the main supplier and the United States was the principal market. Indeed, the United States was most often

---

[1] *Ha'aretz* (*The Land*), 4 April 1969; see also Uri Davis, "A Land Superimposed," *The Middle East* (April 1981) pp. 23–25.

Israel's largest trading partner both in imports and exports. Citriculture accounted for the bulk of Israel's agricultural exports. In addition, Israel developed a sizable electronics and weapons industry. Between 1978 and 1981, the value of Israel's arms exports quadrupled, with military sales accounting for some 40 percent of its total export earnings. South Africa and Argentina were the largest purchasers. Phosphates from the Dead Sea and tourism, especially after the absorption of many holy places after the 1967 war, also brought in substantial revenues. Hotel-investment represented a growth area for the construction industry encouraged by government incentives.

Yet the country's dependence on foreign inputs to sustain economic growth contributed to triple digit inflation late in the 1970s and early 1980s. Moreover, the country's heavy military spending fueled high taxation. Israel's per capita military expenditures in 1977 exceeded those of every country in the world except tiny oil-rich Qatar. Finally, the fact of Israel's growing demands on scarce water resources, including those of the occupied West Bank, remained an issue of concern to many Israelis as well as to neighboring countries. For petroleum, following the 1977–79 Iranian revolution, Israel was obliged to turn to Mexico. Israel's economic future seemed closely tied to foreign policy and internal political decisions.

Because of the European orientation of the Israeli government and society, European and American Jews among new immigrants tended to adapt more rapidly to and derive more benefit from the state. They were given preference in housing and employment. Middle Eastern Jews with capital, though, achieved some improvement in their status by the 1980s. The cultural gap in Israel remained a major social problem with political and economic overtones.

The Religious–Secular Dilemma

The Law of Return was but one of the laws that compromised the equality of all races, religions, national origins, and sexes proclaimed in the Israeli declaration of independence and in the Equal Rights for Women Law of 1951. The religious-secular dilemma emerged as an oft-debated question. As author Lesley Hazleton expressed it, "Israeli Jews are Israeli by citizenship but Jewish by nationality."[2] Like those in the Ottoman Empire, religious hierarchies in Israel were given full power by the Rabbinical Courts Jurisdiction Law of 1953. They could decide matters of personal status. With this triumph of Jewish orthodoxy, civil marriage and divorce became impossible, and Jews were forbidden marriage to non-Jews, including to those who viewed themselves as Jews but did not fall within the religious hierarchy's definition.

The influence of the Jewish religious establishment over the lives of Israelis has extended far beyond the realm of personal status laws. On Saturday—the Sabbath—public transportation stops. Air traffic and activity in Israel's ports has been halted from time to time. Military and government food services apply Kosher dietary laws. More recently, the religious establishment has pressured the government to bar women from military service. Although many of Israel's nonreligious Jews object to the extensive Orthodox in-

[2] Lesley Hazleton, *Israeli Women: The Reality Behind the Myths* (New York: Simon and Schuster, 1977), p. 38.

fluence in Israeli life, others defend it as necessary for the preservation of the Jewish character of the state even if they themselves are not observant. Religious law has always been allowed to override civil law where the two conflict, except in notable cases involving prominent personalities who defied it.

The crucial question "Who is a Jew?" has proved necessarily vital in determining who can share fully in national life. Only children of a Jewish mother or of one who has undergone ritual conversion are accepted as Jewish. Religious authorities generally refuse permission for ritual conversion solely to enable a non-Jewish woman to marry a Jewish man. Petitioners must demonstrate a sincere intention to follow the religion's precepts; indeed, they must show that they have observed Jewish prohibitions and laws in the past.

As a result, there are few ritual conversions in Israel. Lists of suspected non-Jews are maintained by a variety of Israeli agencies, particularly as Arab Israelis try to pass as oriental Jews in the cities in order to earn a better living.

The division of Israeli society according to religion, along with the ascendancy of religious rather than civil law, has effectively eliminated the ability of Jewish, Christian, and Muslim Israelis, as well as men and women, to interact with each other on all levels freely and equally. How have the religious parties in Israel, then, been able to maintain the establishment's hold over personal status and secular concerns despite the fact that most Israelis consider themselves Jewish by culture rather than by religion? It is because they have held the balance of power in Israeli politics ever since the state's creation.

Israeli Society and Culture

Jewish Israelis have had to build their society in an atmosphere of crisis. The memorial to Jewish victims of the Holocaust, Yad Vashem in Jerusalem, is both a commemoration and a research center dedicated to establishing a history for every individual who died. At Tel Aviv University, another museum features the history of Jews in the diaspora. Military deaths are recalled on a special memorial day.

Israelis, however, have also created a vibrant, diverse Jewish society whose culture is most closely tied to Europe but which also acknowledges aspects of the Middle Eastern heritage of the majority. Searching for the ancient Jewish past has absorbed the efforts of archeological teams from Israel and abroad. Excavations at the hilltop fortress of Masada where Jewish resisters committed suicide rather than submit to the Romans made it a national symbol of freedom. Excavations at the Western Wall in East Jerusalem aroused periodic protests (about desecration) from Orthodox Jews within and outside Israel even though knowledge illuminating ancient Jewish history may be revealed in the process.

National and Labor Organizations

Equally important to the national life of Israel are the labor and national organizations that have prestate roots. The Histadrut has remained Israel's largest labor organization. Not until the governments of Levi Eshkol (1963–69) were Arab Israeli workers allowed to become full members. The Histadrut still has a national membership that embraces members who hold different philosophies, although the majority support the labor parties. Other labor unions, including Hapoel Hamizrachi and Poalei Agudat Israel, participate in the Histadrut's insurance programs and trade union activities despite their independent status. The National Labor Federation belonging to the rightist movement has retained its own insurance and health programs, an active youth movement, and industries.

The Histadrut's operations are much more wide-ranging. Solel Boneh continues to be the largest firm, with extensive international operations in Africa, Asia, Latin America, and parts of the Middle East. Koor has functioned as an industrial holding company while Tnuva has been maintained as the agricultural marketing cooperative. Histadrut also keeps a section for kibbutz industries and a cooperative to supply agricultural settlements. Especially during the era of labor coalitions, Histadrut often participated in joint projects with the Israeli government and other private companies. Among these was Zim, the national shipping line. The Histadrut also has since 1960 operated the Afro-Asian Institute for Labour Studies and Cooperation. Several thousand students from developing countries have been trained there and by Israeli experts overseas.

The World Zionist Organization, Jewish Agency, Jewish National Fund, Youth Aliya, the United Jewish Appeal and Keren Hayesod are all pre-Israeli Jewish organizations that have maintained important roles. Despite the achievement of Zionism's goal of a state, W.Z.O. has kept up its activities among diaspora Jews: supporting immigration, preserving and encouraging Jewish and Hebrew education, strengthening the Israeli state, and protecting the rights of Jews in other countries. In 1971, the Jewish Agency incorporated the World Zionist Organization to become a large coordinating body for immigration and fund-raising activities around the world, including those of the United Jewish Appeal and Keren Hayesod. The Jewish National Fund has continued to be the trustee of land in Israel while Youth Aliya has sponsored programs in Israel for Jewish young people from other countries.

Education

Israelis have devoted special attention to education, especially to Jewish education. Children attend either state schools or religious schools, according to parental preference. The government maintains separate Jewish and Arab schools. Although Hebrew, Arabic, and English are all official languages in Israel, Arabic is an optional subject in Jewish schools. Arab Israelis, though, begin studying Hebrew in primary school. Because of these educational differences, Jewish Israelis are most likely to know English and/or French but not Arabic. This isolation, coupled with a good deal of physical isolation in Israeli society, has perpetuated mutual hostility, although some authors have argued that hostility between Jewish and Arab Israelis increases with extensive contact.

Throughout Israel's history the proportion of Arab Israelis in postsecondary institutions in Israel has been far lower than their percentage in the school-age population. It is not unusual for Arab Israelis who seek an education outside the country to be imprisoned or detained upon their return because of political activities, especially contact with Palestinian nationalist groups, engaged in while abroad. Although some young Arab Israelis do come home following study abroad, others choose to join the Palestinian diaspora.

Israel's most well-known institutions of higher learning are the Hebrew University of Jerusalem, the Technion, Tel Aviv University, the University of the Negev, and the Weizmann Institute of Science which specializes in postgraduate research. Since the early 1950s, Israel has been active in developing nuclear technologies and maintains its French-supplied reactor in Dimona (from 1962) in the Negev. The reactor has not been subject to international scrutiny because Israel is not a signatory to the Nuclear Non-Proliferation Treaty, but most analysts agree that Israel became the world's seventh nuclear power in 1967 and carried out tests in South Africa in 1979 and 1980. Generally speaking, the Israeli commitment to research and development has produced innovations and discoveries in science and technology that have won international plaudits.

Literature and the Arts

In arts and literature, Israelis have also been active. Israel's Philharmonic Orchestra, founded in 1936, is known around the world, but Israel has other orchestras, an opera company, a cinema organization, and groups specializing in theater and dance. Israelis have evolved a literary tradition most closely associated first with the Jewish experience in Europe, immigration to Palestine, the Holocaust and, more recently, with Israel's national and social development. Polish-born S. Y. Agnon, Israel's Nobel Laureate in Literature, focused on Jewish themes rooted in Eastern European Jewish (Yiddish) culture. Both a Zionist and a religious Jew in the Hassidic tradition, Agnon portrayed challenges to religious Jews of the twentieth century in stories rich with individual details and symbolism. Unlike most other observant Jewish writers, Agnon wrote in Hebrew rather than in Yiddish, the language of the Hassidim (the Hassidim are European-descended Jews who recognize rabbis' special ties with God).

Another Polish-born Israeli author, Aharon Megged, paid particular attention to the generation gap and to the effects of the Holocaust. Aharon Appelfeld, born in the Ukraine, has dealt with psychological problems of Holocaust victims. More recent writers in Hebrew have also treated Jewish and Israeli subjects but have been interested in individual experience as well. The war of independence in 1947–49 provided the setting for "The Prisoner" by S. Yizhar (Yizhar Smilansky) and "Seven of Them" by Nathan Shaham. In these stories, the writers address the question of individual responsibility for behavior, especially in regard to Arab Palestinians, and in matters of life and death.

A. B. Yehoshua and Amos Oz emerged as the two most prominent Israeli prose writers during the 1960s. Both are self-proclaimed Zionists who display an understanding and appreciation of Palestinian claims and aspirations. To these writers, the right of Jews in Palestine is the right of historical necessity based on a nonreligious definition of the Jewish people. They realize that the Arab-Israeli conflict has ensued from Zionist and Palestinian insistence on governing the whole of Palestine. Yehoshua's critically acclaimed story, "Facing the Forests" uses several levels of symbolism to address Israel's transformation of the Palestinian homeland. The dilemma of an ambivalent fire-watcher commissioned to guard a Jewish forest built over a Palestinian village is that of the individual who has only limited power to change a world he did not create. Charged with protecting the forest, the intellectual instead is exhilarated by its destruction that might then allow for a new beginning. Amos Oz has explored Jewish Israeli society in novels such as *My Michael*. Although Yehoshua has been one of the few Israeli writers of Middle Eastern origin, he has been joined in the 1970s by authors including Sami Mikhail, whose family came from Iraq. Mikhail is an author who has created plausible Arab characters in his books. Other new writers include Yitzhak Ben-Ner and Yakov Shabtai.

According to Ben-Ner, the Israeli reading public probably does not exceed 100,000 people. The fact that so many Israeli novels, short stories, and memoirs have been translated from Hebrew into English indicates their popular reception in other countries. One problem which Israeli writers in Hebrew faced in the past is the fact that Hebrew was for them a new language. The literary language has a much older history, of course, than the recently revived spoken tongue. As with Arabic authors, writers in Hebrew have struggled to create a literature accessible to the average person.

Arab Israelis

Scholars addressing Israeli history have achieved no consensus on how to approach the subject of Arab Israelis. Are citizens of Arab origin Israeli Arabs or

Arab Israelis? Should they be treated instead as Christian or Muslim Israelis? Or are they Palestinians living in Israel? We have preferred the term Arab Israeli, but in fact their historical experiences have given them few reasons to feel as though they can share equally with Jewish Israelis, either as individuals or as a group, in the Israeli national experience.

Restrictions on Personal Freedom

Despite the Israeli independence declaration in 1948, ongoing war at the time quickly eroded the positive effect of proclaimed equality of social and political rights, of full participation promised therein. Most of Israel's Arab citizens were living in villages that relied on agriculture. They found themselves placed under military rule, subjected to the Emergency Defense Regulations which the British had applied to Palestine in 1945. In itself, military rule meant that every Arab was required to carry a pass and could not move freely from place to place. Citizens could be searched or held by the military without charge or trial, and leaders were often deported or placed in administrative detention without trial under the authority of Regulation III. Since Arabs had to apply for Israeli citizenship after 1948, unlike Jews who received it more or less automatically regardless of national origin, Arabs who had opted to become Israelis were disappointed by such discrimination.

Arab Israelis did not accept their plight without protest. When the First Jewish International Congress of Lawyers and Jurists met in Jerusalem in July 1969, nine Arab Israeli lawyers (including Sabri Jiryis), one of the most outspoken Arab Israelis, submitted an appeal to the conferees to pressure the government to suspend the emergency regulations retained despite the abolition of military government in 1966. The memorandum quoted Israel's minister of justice, Y. Shapira, who had spoken against the regulations in 1946 when they were being applied against Jews:

The regime established in Palestine with the publication of the Emergency Regulations is quite unique for enlightened countries. Even Nazi Germany didn't have such laws . . . a regime of this type only fits a country having the status of an occupied territory. No government is entitled to enact legislation of this kind."[3]

The lawyers pointed out that they themselves had been subjected to detention and could not practice their profession freely. The Israeli High Court had refused to consider their petition to give cause as to why the regulations were being kept. In appealing to the conferees, the lawyers hoped that the congress would take initiatives in restoring freedom of movement, progress, and democracy. Their action was that of citizens trying to enhance their participation as Israelis; it was not an appeal hostile to the state.

Land and Labor

Besides restrictions on personal freedom imposed by Israel's preoccupation with security, Arab Israelis through losing their lands and homes became proletarianized. Besides expropriations through the Absentee Property Law of 1950 and the Land Acquisition Law, Israel's government also took over land for "emergency" reasons. In 1958, the Israelis instituted a new regulation that required Arab farmers to prove they had been cultivating their lands between 1928 and 1943. As a result, lands under Arab ownership were reduced by the mid-1970s to one-quarter of their size in 1949 after the War of Independence. Expropriations also took away inalienable properties (waqf) or musha land. Most state-owned lands passed into Jewish Israeli hands.

The Israeli government has argued that it originally offered to pay the inhabitants for their land. When these overtures were rejected, the government seized the property or demolished it for security reasons under Article 125 of the Emer-

---

[3] Shapira's memorandum is found in Sabri Jiryis, *The Arabs in Israel,* trans. Inea Bushnaq (New York and London: Monthly Review, 1976), p. 11.

gency Defence Regulations. Both Christian and Muslim villages, such as al-Birwa in Galilee, were demolished and replaced by newly constructed Jewish villages.

Israeli authorities have continued to the present day policies designed to de-Arabize and to Judaize predominantly Arab Galilee. In 1976, Israel Koenig, District Commissioner for the North, made in his Koenig Report a series of twenty-three recommendations intended to expel Arab Israelis from Galilee. Among the recommendations were the reduction by Jewish employers of non-Jewish employees, limitation of educational opportunities for non-Jews, withholding of family incentives from non-Jews, discrediting of Rakah (New Communist List) as a proponent of Palestinian rights, and creation of obstacles to the return of young people studying abroad. The Labor government of Yitzhak Rabin (1974–77) never repudiated the report or its proposals, and the Begin regime (1977–1983) advocated similar policies intended to reduce Israel's Arab population.

How have Israeli Arabs—about 70 percent Muslim, 20 percent Christian, and 10 percent Druze—managed to survive in this environment? Druzes have enjoyed a privileged status and have served in Israel's armed forces. Most have responded favorably to the government's policies. The Israeli government, however, further isolated Arabs by setting up special Arab offices in virtually every department of government, supposedly to give the Arabs special protection. Once rural Arabs began losing their local agricultural employment, they were bound to come into contact with Jewish Israelis who controlled the greater part of the cash economy. As wage earners, former peasants improved their economic status and welfare but became dependent on the Jewish Israeli sector. The proletarianization of the Arab peasantry in Israel created pressure for equal opportunity and equal pay.

The Histadrut excluded Arab Israelis at first as outside the Zionist framework, but it sponsored an Arab union. Even after the admission of Arabs as full members, the organization continued to maintain separate Arab departments and could not insure payment of equal wages to both Arabs and Jews as mandated by Israeli law in 1952.

Israeli Government and Politics

The founders of Israel decided that instead of writing a fixed constitution at the outset, they would let their constitution evolve through legal change. A written constitution would have required a statement about Orthodox Judaism unacceptable to secular Jews. The supreme authority was to be the Knesset, a legislative assembly with 120 members. The Knesset was charged with electing the president who would perform largely ceremonial functions and could serve a maximum of two five-year terms. Five of Israel's first six presidents, beginning with Chaim Weizmann, were senior politicians from eastern Europe. Yitzhak Navon (1978–1983) is of Middle Eastern origin. Although the president appoints the prime minister in consultation with the various political parties following elections, it is the prime minister and the cabinet who lead the country and determine day-to-day policies and actions.

Representatives for the Knesset are chosen through a system of elections characterized as general, national, equal, secret, and proportional. What this means in practice is that all Israelis except those under military rule can vote. Several areas with predominantly Arab populations were under military rule until the mid-1960s. The proportional system gives each party the number of seats in the Knesset proportional to its overall vote. Each party contesting the election meets in advance to rank-order its list of candidates, with the most important party members heading it. Candidates, then, run nationally on a party list rather than individually for a seat representing a particular district. The constituency is the nation. For example, the Mapai Party which dominated the ruling coalition between the first elections in 1949 and 1977 held forty seats in the third Knesset, having received 32.2 percent of the vote in the 1955 elections. The top forty names on its list were declared elected.

Political Parties in Israel

No party in Israel's history has ever succeeded in achieving an absolute majority. As a result, Israelis have been governed by coalitions in which the religious parties (usually polling about 12–15 percent of the vote) have held the balance of power. These include the National Religious Party, Agudat Israel, and Poalei Agudat Israel. The National Religious Party was formed by Hapoel Hamizrachi and Hamizrachi. Mapai, the main labor standard-bearer, often formed coalitions with the more left-wing Mapam and with Ahdut Ha'avoda (when it contested elections separately). One short-lived offshoot of Mapai was the Rafi party established in 1965 by former prime minister David Ben Gurion and military hero Moshe Dayan. Dayan later formed Telem which did not outlast his death in 1981. The Mapai leaders, all of Russian or Polish origin, who served as Israel's prime ministers from 1948–77 were David Ben Gurion (1948–53, 1955–63), Moshe Sharett (1953–55), Levi Eshkol (1963–69), Golda Meir (1969–74), and Yitzhak Rabin (1974–77). To the left of the labor parties were two Communist factions. The Israel Communist Party (Maki) has remained a Zionist party, while the New Communist List (Rakah) functions as an Arab nationalist party.

Various other groups have cropped up in response to issues of the day. A small leftist group, Haolam Hazeh (This World) or New Force, won two seats in the 1965 Knesset when it first ran on a peace platform. Led by Uri Avnery, the party lost its seats in the wake of the 1973 war but regained them later. In 1977, the Democratic Movement for Change (D.M.C.) led by Yigael Yadin polled the third highest vote (11.6 percent) mainly because of discontent with the Labor Alignment. Four years later, the Mapai-Mapam alliance regained most of its voters but not enough to replace Likud. In any one election, perhaps fifteen lists may have been presented which failed to win enough voters (1 percent is required) to hold a seat in the Knesset. Examples of these in recent years included the Women's Party, Kach led by U.S.-born rabbi Meir Kahane (founder of the Jewish Defense League: J.D.L.), the Arab Reform Movement, Hofesh (Black Panthers), Zionist and Socialist Renewal, and the Yemenite Beit Yisrael party. The national and proportional system of voting has resulted in severe underrepresentation in the Knesset for both Jews of Middle Eastern origin and Arab Israelis.

Finally, we must mention the rightist Herut led by former I.Z.L. leader Menachem Begin, which in the postwar era was often allied with the centrist Liberal Party to form Gahal. During the first twenty years of Israeli history, Herut and its partners polled between 21 and 29 percent of the vote. Herut's platform included a more capitalist approach to the economy and absorption of all of mandated Palestine and Transjordan. Although Gahal joined Mapai in a national unity government in 1969, it left in 1970 when the government accepted U.S. mediation efforts regarded as moving toward a return of lands occupied during the 1967 Israeli offensive. Gahal, by resigning from the government, was able to transform itself gradually into a vehicle whereby all who wanted to retain the territories, regardless of other ideologies, could unite. Among the groups calling for retention was the Land of Israel movement. Gush Emunim later emerged as an even more determined group insisting on the right to settle anywhere in the occupied territories, with or without permission. Herut differed from these others in that it advocated retention of the West Bank and expansion into the East Bank but not necessarily holding onto occupied Sinai or Golan.

These elements eventually joined together in the Likud bloc. Just as the annexationists won support from highly respected writers like Agnon (though he died in 1970), the Labor government moved toward further incorporation of occupied lands by expropriating agricultural and other West Bank areas for Israeli settlements. Labor's coalition partner, the National Religious Party, favored keeping the West Bank. Likud, though, remained the primary standard bearer of those who regarded the West Bank and Gaza as part of Israel's natural heritage, and in the 1977 elections it emerged on top with massive support from non-European Jews who constituted a majority of Jewish Israelis settled in these lands. Begin became prime minister. His bloc succeeded in holding onto power after the 1981 elections. While the economy and accusations of corruption against the Rabin government helped unseat the Labor coalitions, ideology proved crucial in the Likud's second victory. In particular, Begin's military assaults on neighboring countries and his commitment to the West Bank as Judea and Samaria (see also Chapter 19) proved sufficiently popular among the Israelis to win a narrow plurality for Likud, sustained and strengthened by the 1982 invasion of Lebanon.

Arab–Israeli Political Life

Arab Israeli politics were characterized both by relative quiescence and periodic attempts to create Arab political parties and organizations. They were inhibited by Israeli bans against "Arab nationalist" parties. The former wealthy Arab peasantry which initially tried to collaborate with the Israelis has judiciously avoided involvement in politics except when asked

to run for office by a Zionist party. Both the poorest peasants and those who have achieved upward mobility in Israeli Arab society are more likely to take an interest in politics. The most active Arab Israelis politically have been the urban, often Christian, Arabs who live in predominantly Jewish cities. Unlike the rural-based majority, these Arabs have experienced harassment and discrimination on a regular basis. It is they who have been barred most often from employment.

Fawzi Al-Asmar is a Christian poet and writer who became active politically because of discrimination witnessed and experienced early in life. Because of his mother's writings and family support for Mapam rather than Mapai, his family was singled out for expulsion. Only the intervention of Mapam prevented their deportation. As a teenager, al-Asmar worked on a Mapam-affiliated kibbutz. He was a student at the Greek Orthodox High School in Haifa when, on the eve of the 1956 war, nearly fifty Arab Israeli villagers were massacred by Israeli forces in the village of Kfar Qasim. Only the Communist party and a few Jewish Israelis protested the killing of these villagers who had been returning from their fields, perhaps because the incident was not well-publicized in the Hebrew press.[4]

Although many Arabs looked to the Communists for support, in the late 1950s Arab Israelis formed a new movement that came to be known, after its periodical, as *al-Ard* (the Land). Its platform advocated equal rights for Arab Israelis, repatriation of refugees, recognition of Arab nationalism as a "decisive factor" in the Arab world, neutrality toward the great powers, and integrating Israel into the Middle East as an assurance against future conflict. Al-Ard attracted a widespread following from Arab Israelis of varying ideologies because it represented an independent Arab political force.

Although al-Ard did not intend to re-

---

[4] Jiryis, pp. 96–115; Ian Lustick, *Arabs in the Jewish State*. (Austin and London: University of Texas Press), pp. 86–87.

main isolated from Zionist parties, its efforts to enlist their support failed. Al-Ard could not afford to publish its newspaper in Hebrew (through which it might have reached Jewish Israelis generally cut off from their Arab compatriots). Instead, Jewish Israelis read in their own newspapers that al-Ard was a subversive group bent on undermining Israeli society. The fact that al-Ard sought legal status and published its opinions openly was ignored, as was its nonviolent thrust. Leaders affirmed their belief in the right of Jews to their own state.

Israeli military authorities imprisoned or detained al-Ard's leaders under the Emergency Defence Regulations. Eventually, the movement was declared illegal. Efforts of Arab intellectuals to form cultural or literary associations were also hindered. When Fawzi al-Asmar, Christian poet and writer, tried to publish books like Gamal Abd al-Nasir's *Philosophy of the Revolution*[5] in Arabic (it was already available in Hebrew and English), he was accused of disseminating propaganda. So, Arab Israelis who tried to affirm their Arab cultural heritage were denied outlets for expression. The Arab Israeli public had few opportunities to read books in Arabic other than those approved by the government.

When the Israeli Communist Party split into two factions in 1965, Rakah became the voice of Arab nationalist sentiment. Various Zionist parties continued to construct separate Arab lists for elections. After the 1967 war, when Israel occupied the West Bank and Gaza, Arab Israelis still tended to identify more with Arab nationalism than with the specifically Palestinian nationalism found abroad. One obvious reason for this difference is the fact that Arab Israelis had not experienced life in Arab countries, a life that tended to fuel Palestinian nationalism.

The Israeli Military

The importance of the military in Israel is exemplified by the requirement that every Israeli except Arabs and Orthodox Jews serve (although many exemptions are given). Druze Arabs' special status allows them to join, too. An acknowledged source of Israel's military leaders has been the kibbutz which in preindependence days functioned as both an agricultural and a military settlement. Three principles have dominated Israeli military thinking: (1) Israel must be able to defeat any possible combination of Arab armies; (2) Israel must develop and obtain a regular arms supply; (3) Israel must have defensible boundaries. The militaristic aspect of Israeli society has led to the state's characterization by political scientist J. C. Hurewitz as a "garrison democracy."[6]

Israel was, in the past, the only country in the world that drafted women into the military. This has often been given as an illustration of equality of men and women, but the realities lead to a much different conclusion. Women in the Israeli army cannot occupy the great majority of positions. Tasks restricted to women include typing and parachute-folding, and women also dominate the lower bureaucracy and social services. Heavy work, combat positions, and jobs regarded as having unsuitable conditions are three categories completely closed to women even though

---

[5] *Egypt's Liberation: The Philosophy of the Revolution*, introd. Dorothy Thompson (Washington, D.C.: Public Affairs Press, 1955).

[6] J. C. Hurewitz, *Middle East Politics: The Military Dimension*, 2nd ed. (Boulder; Colorado: Westview, 1983).

they fought in Palestine during the mandate. Although married men serve in the reserves for years, married women, mothers, and expectant mothers do not. In fact, women married prior to the usual entry age of eighteen never enter the army at all. Other women are exempted for religious reasons.

Moreover, some one quarter of all women have been disqualified from military service because they lack basic skills and education. Most often these young women are of non-European origin. The end result has been that only half of young Israeli women actually do their military service. While the army may have aided non-European men in achieving upward mobility in Israeli society, it did not prove to be the same integrating force for Israeli women of different origins; nor did it give them new skills or leadership opportunities that might be of use to them in the future. However, the incorporation of women into the army bureaucracy freed men for combat.

During the early years of Israel's existence, the refugee problem led to instability along its borders. Israel's admission to the United Nations had been made contingent on resolving the question of displaced persons, but Israeli leaders could not agree on the number, if any, which the country would accept. Sharett's recommendation that 100,000 Palestinians be readmitted, a suggestion to which Arab countries agreed, was refused by other Israelis even though Israel was engaged in absorbing much greater numbers of foreign Jews. With leaders debating the political question, Palestinians often sneaked across the border, usually to try to reclaim property left behind or to return home. Isolated attacks also occurred.

The Israeli army replied to a grenade attack in October 1953, which killed a Jewish Israeli woman and two children, by attacking the Jordanian village of Qibya. Besides demolishing forty houses, the assault force killed over fifty men, women, and children. Moshe Dayan led Israel's retaliation forces, and Ariel Sharon, later agriculture (1977–81) and defense (1981–83) minister, carried out the attack. The Israeli policy of massive retaliation became a hallmark of the Israeli army. The targets of both Arab Palestinian and Israeli operations, however, were rarely those who had perpetrated attacks.

Met with an international outcry, the Qibya incident brought down Prime Minister David Ben Gurion. Before he left, Ben Gurion assured that the occupants of the offices of prime minister, minister of defense, and army chief of staff would not be able to get along with each other. Dayan, despite his responsibility for Qibya, was awarded the last post. Pinchas Lavon, a nonmilitary man with a dovish reputation, became defense minister and suddenly very hawkish. New prime minister Sharett tried to pursue a policy of conciliation and normalization with Israel's Arab neighbors.

Toward the Suez War: The Egyptian Factor in Israeli Foreign Policy

Some Israeli politicians feared both the Egyptian revolution of 1952 and the growing rapprochement between the United States and new Egyptian leader Gamal Abd al-Nasir. They advocated an attack on Egypt to assure that the Egyptians would present no future threat to Israel's security. Sharett, however, maintained that it would be dangerous for Israel to risk jeopardizing its relationship with the United States to strike at an Egypt quite preoccupied with internal concerns.

In summer 1954, Abd al-Nasir used a variety of informal contacts to try to reach an agreement with Sharett. Apparently, Sharett's political pressures and personal beliefs prevented him from making a serious response to the Egyptian overtures. What happened instead during that summer was a series of bomb attacks and fires in Cairo movie houses, the American Embassy in Cairo, Egyptian post offices, and various British interests. That July, it was revealed that Israeli agents, including a few Egyptian Jews, had been ordered to sabotage the United States-Egypt rapprochement and negotiations for British troop withdrawal from Egypt. In Israel, Lavon was forced to take the blame.

Years later, the discovery that Ben Gurion had engineered the operation discredited him and forced his second departure as prime minister. All along, Lavon had denied knowledge of the plan. In February 1955, two of the convicted men were hanged in Cairo, one committed suicide, and others involved in the conspiracy received prison terms. One spy was released in 1967 in exchange for Egyptians captured during the June war. Having been temporarily discredited, Lavon resigned. Ben Gurion replaced him. Before the month was over, he had authorized an Israeli attack on an Egyptian post in occupied Gaza. In the February 17, 1955 raid, nearly forty Egyptians were killed and Egypt's Gaza headquarters were destroyed. Despite his earlier peace feelers, Abd al-Nasir could hardly ignore an action that so clearly illustrated Egypt's vulnerability and Israeli hostility. This event began in earnest Egypt's emotional involvement in the Arab-Israeli conflict. It also instigated the Arab-Israeli arms race with the dramatic turn of Abd al-Nasir to the Soviet bloc for arms unavailable in the West. It culminated in the nationalization of the Suez Canal and the October 1956 attack on Egypt by Britain, France, and Israel aimed at unseating Abd al-Nasir.

During the course of these develop-ments, Abd al-Nasir declined to bring Egypt into the Baghdad Pact. American Secretary of State John Foster Dulles objected to the idea of a neutral, independent Egypt actively participating in nonaligned affairs like the Bandung Conference of April 1955 even though Egypt was cultivating no special relations with the Soviet Union at this time. Abd al-Nasir at Bandung emerged as a major nonaligned leader, forming friendships with China's Zhou En-lai, India's Jawaharlal Nehru, and Yugoslavia's Josip Broz Tito, and urging the Chinese to support independence for French-occupied North Africa. Soon, the Soviet Union offered to help Egypt obtain arms unavailable from the United States, Britain, and France because of an arms sales limitation agreement France had already broken by supplying Israel.

Jordan's King Husayn followed Abd al-Nasir's lead by staying out of the Baghdad Pact. Then in March 1956, the British-trained Husayn fired the Arab Legion's commander, Sir John Glubb. Blaming this act on Abd al-Nasir, Britain's Conservative prime minister, Sir Anthony Eden, withdrew all British officers from Jordan. Eden's experience as British foreign secretary before World War II, particularly his memory of the crisis over appeasement of Germany and Italy, led him to compare Abd al-Nasir to Hitler or Mussolini. He felt that only without Abd al-Nasir could Britain retain its primacy in Middle Eastern affairs. They became bitter rivals over regional defense. In May 1956, Egypt recognized the People's Republic of China (P.R.C.), leading Dulles to renege on a U.S. offer to finance a major portion of the Aswan High Dam regarded by Abd al-Nasir as a key to Egypt's food and energy needs. The U.S. had hoped by its offer to counter Soviet penetration of Egypt. When the United States withdrew its offer, Egypt lost matching World Bank and British funds.

Nationalization of the Suez Canal and the Tripartite Attack on Egypt

Egypt moved swiftly to make a direct challenge to the West based on withdrawal of the loan offers. On 26 July 1956, Gamal Abd al-Nasir announced in a dramatic speech in colloquial Egyptian Arabic that from that day on Egypt would own the

Anglo-French Suez Canal company as well as the canal Egyptians had funded and built. Company owners would be compensated in full.

The British and French response appears rather irrational in historical perspective, and historians still debate their motives. Abd al-Nasir had placed a national asset under Egyptian control without violating any precepts of international law. The action clearly had been precipitated by the need to come up with a means of financing the High Dam. A pragmatist, Abd al-Nasir quickly demonstrated to the world that Egypt was capable of operating the canal efficiently. Any hope on the part of Britain and France for a collapse like that which had followed the Iranian oil nationalization of 1951 faded.

What did Britain and France fear? Both countries objected to Gamal Abd al-Nasir's increasing regional prominence. Britain worried about loss of control partly because over 50 percent of its petroleum imports passed through Suez. France resented Egypt's support for the Algerian revolution. Israel's main weapons supplier at this time was France, but what were Israel's aims in collaborating with the other two in their October attack? The Israelis hoped to accomplish (1) an end to Egypt's blockade of the Gulf of Aqaba; (2) termination of Palestinian *fidayeen* (freedom fighters; *fidayun* in literary Arabic) incursions; (3) overthrow of Abd al-Nasir arising from concern over his emergence as a regional leader.

The overthrow of Abd al-Nasir was the key to British-French-Israeli collaboration. Yet since the United States had already thrown its weight on the side of a diplomatic solution to British and French discontent, the two had little reason to believe that U.S. President Eisenhower would condone their seizure of the canal which Egypt was running efficiently. Both Britain and France naïvely assumed that they could conceal their collusion with Israel, sealed by agreement on 24 October 1956. The consequences, in restrospect, hardly seem to have warranted taking such a risk.

The initial stages of the plan were carried out successfully. Israel attacked Egypt on 29 October, almost on the eve of the U.S. presidential elections. Israel moved into Sinai, and thereby cut off Egyptian-occupied Gaza. Under the pretext of trying to resolve the crisis, Britain and France issued an ultimatum to both countries calling on them to withdraw from the canal zone. Because Israel's troops had not yet reached the canal, and because the canal was part of Egypt, Abd al-Nasir refused. In the next stage, the two European countries wiped out Egypt's air power capabilities. Egypt was bombed and invaded. The Israelis' withdrawl was actually an advance, as they had not arrived at the place from which they were supposed to be withdrawing. French and British troops landed on 5 November. Egypt's radio station, Voice of the Arabs, was also put out of commission. Yet in its hour of triumph, the so-called tripartite aggression proved a dismal failure.

Abd al-Nasir did not fall from power and in fact emerged with enhanced prestige not only in Egypt but throughout the Arab and nonaligned countries. Egypt's response to the invasion was to block the canal, while Syria blew up pipelines to curtail the British and French oil supplies. Instead of insuring their energy needs, France and Britain had embarked on a policy that threatened Europeans' supplies in general. If Britain and France had hoped to safeguard their canal interests, their attack proved even more disastrous. Egypt canceled its agreement with Britain which had brought about the British troop removal by mid-1956 (see Chapter 17) and took over the British air base, supplies and all. French and British property in Egypt was nationalized. What the two countries had in fact accomplished was not the preservation but rather the destruction of their longstanding holdings in Egypt.

The Israelis fared somewhat better. The Soviet Union and the United States joined in condemning the attack. President Eisenhower renewed the U.S. commitment to Israel but not to Israeli expansionism. As the United States had objected to Soviet intervention in the

Hungarian revolution occurring at the same time, it could hardly back French-British-Israeli aggression in Egypt. The United States eventually pressured the Israelis to withdraw from Sinai in exchange for the opening up of the Gulf of Aqaba to Israeli shipping. United Nations troops stationed the entrance to the Gulf at the Straits of Tiran would monitor the agreement. Other U.N. forces took up positions on Egyptian territory along the Israeli-Egyptian border; Israel refused to allow these troops on Israeli soil. Between January 1957 and May 1967, these troops (United Nations Emergency Force or U.N.E.F.) helped to maintain peace between the two countries. Israeli withdrawal was not fully completed until June 1957. The U.N. role in establishing this peace exemplifies the principle that their intervention in the region could succeed only when the interests of the major powers coalesced.

The Aftermath of the Suez War

Although the United States was instrumental in arranging the Israeli withdrawal from Sinai, it was still viewed as Israel's ally. Consequently, the Soviet Union could still present itself in the region as a viable alternative to the Western countries as a friend and ally. The later Arab lean toward the Soviet Union, then, resulted less from a strong ideological affinity than from the rejection by U.S. leaders of the concept of neutrality and national pride represented by Abd al-Nasir and the ongoing and obvious U.S. sympathy with Israel.

The advent of what scholar Malcolm Kerr has called the "Arab cold war"[7]—the growing attraction of socialist-Arab nationalist doctrines such as Nasirism and Ba'thi socialism, the quest for Arab unity, and the growing radicalization of the Middle East—followed and were influenced by the Suez attack. These political events also had an effect on Egyptian trade. The United States, Britain, and France instigated a blockade of Egyptian goods. The United States barred Egypt's major product—cotton—from its markets after 1956. This action forced Egypt to seek new trading partners. As Egypt was departing from the sterling area, too, much of the new trade involved Eastern Bloc countries. Moreover, the delivery of weapons by Western countries to Israel and to Yemeni royalist forces resulted in the need for increased arms expenditure in Egypt. To pay for these arms, Egypt was pressured continually to expand commodity exports. Moreover, Egypt intensified support for Algeria's independence war and began using more anti-imperialist rhetoric. Significantly, previously isolationist Egypt emerged as the leader in the Arab unity movement.

The Palestinian Diaspora

Transjordan before the incorporation of the West Bank had been an unsophis-

ticated desert kingdom. The Palestine war transformed it into a state in which better educated, more urbanized, and politically frustrated Palestinians, including refugees from lands absorbed into Israel, constituted an estimated two-thirds majority.

---

[7] Malcolm Kerr, *The Arab Cold War: Gamal Abd al-Nasir and his Rivals, 1958–1970* (London and New York: Oxford University Press, 1971).

Moreover, half of the population of the new union lived on the West Bank. Since much of the Palestinian leadership had fled to Transjordan during the fighting that preceded partition, Palestinians in Jordan were also more urbanized than those left behind in Israel. Palestinians cut off from their lands worked to adapt to the new realities.

Unlike the Israelis who received a capital infusion from abroad, the Jordanian government lacked the funds to develop Palestinian areas during the union's early years. Rivalries among Palestinian factions caused the assassination of King Abd Allah in July 1951 by followers of former Palestinian leader Amin al-Husayni. Abd Allah's son Talal implemented changes designed to placate Palestinians. In 1953, however, he was replaced by his eighteen-year old son Husayn who by the early 1980s had survived coups and assassination attempts.

Much of the development in Jordan in the early years took place under the auspices of U.N.R.W.A. authorities. The 500,000 Palestinian refugees supported by U.N.R.W.A. received health care, education, food, and other social services, while the 400,000 West Bank Palestinians who were not refugees fended for themselves. Life in the refugee camps dehumanized many Palestinians who kept hoping for repatriation. Through education and training, younger refugees began to acquire skills that enabled them to leave the camps. After the tripartite assault on Egypt in 1956, the Jordanian government cut its ties with the British, who had been subsidizing the government. King Husayn then turned to the United States to help put down a plot by pro-Egyptian army officers and officials to overthrow him.

By the 1960s, American aid to Jordan had been invested in development of an infrastructure to promote economic and social progress. Jordan began to devote more attention to agriculture in the Jordan Valley and to tourism in the holy places, especially in Jerusalem and Bethlehem. The East Ghor Canal project was designed to expand agricultural output on the Jordan River's east bank. While new investments provided employment opportunities for Palestinians in Jordan, the Palestinian population also benefited from remittances sent by Palestinians outside the country to their families.

In Gaza, placed under Egyptian administration but theoretically represented by a Palestinian government, U.N.R.W.A. set up facilities like those in Jordan. As a result of U.N.R.W.A.'s schools, the literacy rate among Palestinians in Gaza was quite high. After the Egyptian revolution of 1952, the government of Egypt encouraged Gazans to enroll in Egyptian universities. Economically, though, the refugees in Gaza, like those in the West Bank, lived in poverty although they were probably better off than the bulk of the Egyptian population. Since the Egyptians did not aim to annex Gaza, more encouragement was given to Palestinians' national aspirations. Nevertheless, when the Israelis overran the area in 1956, the small groups of fidayeen who had individually or collectively staged sporadic operations into Israel following the 1955 Gaza raid were ill-equipped to fight the Israeli army. The U.N. forces that were placed on the Gaza boundaries after the invasion did not impede the development of Palestinian liberation forces in Gaza under the P.L.O. (Palestine Liberation Organization) after 1964.

The Water Question

With the high standard of living and rapidly growing population of Israel, increased demands on limited water supplies became an issue time and time again. Despite the mediation of American negotiator Eric Johnston early in the

1950s, the riparian states could not agree on a plan to divide Jordan River waters. Israel proceeded to construct the National Water Carrier. Because the Jordan's sources were in Lebanon, Syria, and Jordan, these states were concerned about the Israeli action although the Israelis claimed not to have exceeded what Johnston's plan would have given them. Gamal Abd al-Nasir viewed Syria as the most likely candidate to try to block Israel's completion of the project.

In December 1963, Abd al-Nasir invited Arab leaders to consider appropriate action at a meeting to be held in Cairo in January 1964. Even states not directly involved, such as Tunisia and Morocco, attended. The Cairo conference was significant for several reasons. Arab government heads decided to avoid direct military confrontation with Israel. Rather, they chose to begin projects that would divert the river's Syrian and Lebanese sources. As Arab leadership could provide no guarantees that diversion projects would be protected, both Syria and Jordan were hesitant about proceeding.

Establishment of the P.L.O.: A National Structure for Palestinians

At the conference, the leaders agreed that the time had come to set up an organization that would address Palestinian national aspirations. The organization was the P.L.O. Opposition of Jordan's King Husayn prevented the P.L.O. from constituting itself as a government-in-exile; he feared the detachment of the West Bank. Palestinians met in May 1964 and selected as chairman of the P.L.O. Ahmad Shuqayri, a lawyer. A Palestine National Council was constituted and soon adopted a charter, setting up some national institutions at a meeting in Jerusalem. The motley liberation army won volunteers from among Palestinians living under Egyptian and Jordanian rule as well as from those in refugee camps.

The first national charter called for a program that would have political, military, and popular aspects. Among the political goals was the establishment of a secular state in all of mandated Palestine based on self-determination of the population. It would include Jews. However, the focus was clearly on Palestinian Arabs who had not yet achieved national status in Palestine. The Jewish state as it existed would then have to be dismantled because of its inherent discrimination against non-Jews.

Although foreigners tended to misrepresent the national charter as advocating the destruction of Jews rather than of Israel, Holocaust survivors in particular could envision assurance of complete equality and security for themselves only in a Jewish or Zionist state. Ignoring identification of Arab Palestinians with their homeland, Jewish Israelis felt that there were so many Arabic-speaking countries that Palestinians ought to be willing to evacuate Palestine. To them, the national charter was a threat.

On the military side, Palestinian resistance groups never seriously threatened Israel. But the armed struggle commitment affirmed by every Palestine National Council meeting after 1964 represented a danger to individual Israelis and their interests. The widespread publicity given to statements by Shuqayri and Abd al-Nasir, in which Jews rather than Israelis were singled out as targets for destruction, certainly eroded confidence in P.L.O. statements about equality of Jews, Christians, and Muslims in a future state. Whatever they reflected about actual policies, they were widely quoted as indicative of Arab intentions. Statements by Israeli leaders that threatened Arabs or Arab countries tended to remain with Israel.

Shuqayri was never very popular within the P.L.O., and momentum shifted to a small movement led by Yasir Arafat called *al-Fatah* (The Triumph). Striking at Israeli projects judged detrimental to Palestinian interests, Fatah in its operations killed very few Israelis prior to the 1967 war. Another national group that achieved popularity among Palestinian refugees was the Arab National Movement (A.N.M.) associated with Nayyif Hawatmeh and George Habash. After the formation of the P.L.O., the A.N.M.'s Palestinian sections were gathered into the National Front for the Liberation of Palestine (N.F.L.P.).

The Israeli Response

The Syrians openly supported Palestinian groups in their guerrilla warfare against Israel. Israel decided to hold Syria responsible for any Palestinian raids. In the spring of 1966, Israeli forces also initiated attacks on the Yarmuk diversion project in Syria; the government publicly threatened Syria with invasion.

In November 1966, three Israeli soldiers were killed by a mine along the Jordanian border. Israel then decided to strike at Jordan rather than against Syria. The Israeli attack destroyed 125 houses in the Jordanian village of al-Samu. When the Jordanian army reached the village, fighting broke out in which 18 Jordanians were killed. Palestinians in Jordan protested against inadequate Jordanian protection. The U.N. Security Council unanimously condemned Israel.

What made the attack more significant was the fact that it followed by a few days the signing of a military alliance between Syria and Egypt. Although he was not a party to the agreement, King Husayn blamed Abd al-Nasir for standing by, especially when Egyptian troops were fighting fellow Arabs in Yemen (see Chapter 18). The question of inter-Arab loyalties heightened the tension among Israel's Arab neighbors. In 1967, Fatah began to carry out raids in the vicinity of Lake Tiberias, where Israeli settlers were cultivating the demilitarized zones that under the armistice agreements were supposed to be no man's lands. The Syrian-Israeli armistice commission met to consider the dispute, but Israel withdrew from the commission before the issue could be settled. In April 1967, Israeli and Syrian planes engaged in a battle during which Damascus was bombed.

The 1967 War: Causes and Conquest

In May 1967, the Levant states moved toward war. Syria's leadership, the radical Ba'thist government that had come to power in February 1966, told Abd al-Nasir that an Israeli attack was imminent. A few days later, Israeli spokesmen announced that the overthrow of the Syrian government was an objective of Israeli policy. This exacerbated Syrian fears. Soviet military intelligence confirmed that the Israelis were massing troops, and on 15 May, the Israelis celebrated their independence day with a military parade in Jerusalem. In retrospect, it can neither be affirmed or denied that an Israeli attack was planned. The small size of the country enabled rapid military mobilization with little forewarning.

Unlike Israel, Egypt—with open desert to the east of Suez—could not conceal troop concentrations. When Egypt responded to Syria's requests for support by transferring troops into Sinai in accordance with the Syrian-Egyptian alliance, the Syrians claimed that Egypt was hiding behind the U.N.E.F. troops stationed on the border. Gamal Abd al-Nasir asked U.N. Secretary-General U Thant to remove the U.N. troops there, but not those in Gaza or Sharm al-Shaykh. U Thant, however, challenged Abd al-Nasir's authority to make the request, thereby compelling him either to withdraw from his position or to take further, more decisive action.

On 18 May, Abd al-Nasir requested the removal of all U.N. troops on Egyptian territory. When Israel refused them permission to station themselves on the Israeli side of the boundary, they simply had to withdraw. Egypt, meanwhile, made it clear that its intention was to protect Syria, not to launch an attack on Israel. Evidence suggests that Abd al-Nasir had not planned to promote a conflict; his armed forces were largely in Yemen and he initiated no action to bring them home. However, after replacing U.N. troops at Sharm al-Shaykh with Egyptian troops on 21 May, he could hardly avoid closing the Straits of Tiran to Israeli shipping. Israel regarded the act as a *casus belli* even though shipping through that passage was at a low level.

What happened between 21 May and 5 June to lead Israel into its devastating surprise attack on Egypt, Jordan, and Syria? Why did Israel not start the war earlier? What occurred during the interim was a propaganda war to which was added the conclusion of a military alliance between Jordan and Egypt on 30 May. While Abd al-Nasir affirmed that Egypt would be ready for war if necessary, P.L.O. leader Shuqayri, whose forces were insignificant, threatened the Israelis with annihilation. But Shuqayri's statement came on 4 June, and the Israeli leadership had already made the decision to attack on the 3rd.

Between 21 May and 5 June, Israeli officials pressured Prime Minister Eshkol to allow the more hawkish David Ben Gurion and Moshe Dayan into the cabinet. Israeli leaders began to visit European capitals where they were assured that their military forces were far superior to any combination that could be put into the field against them. President Lyndon B. Johnson of the United States urged Abba Eban, the Israeli foreign minister, to desist from launching an attack. Europeans and the Americans seemed to accept the Israeli belief that international law had been violated by the closure of the straits, but the International Court of Justice had not ruled on the matter.

The diplomatic stalemate angered Arabs and Israelis alike. While the Soviet Union was pressuring Egypt to keep the peace, the United States was exercising influence on both Egyptians and Israelis. Charles Yost, later U.S. ambassador to the United Nations, promised Abd al-Nasir as late as 3 June that the Israelis would not attack as long as negotiations were continuing. Trusting in the U.S. promise, Egypt sent its top negotiator, Vice President Zakariyya Muhiyy al-Din, to Washington on 4 June for discussions while submitting the Tiran dispute to the International Court. Both Moscow and Tel Aviv were informed.

The government of Israel, however, had already decided to attack because the Israeli army could not remain mobilized indefinitely. Given the course of negotiations which seemed to portend an Egyptian-American rapprochement, Israel would have to give up something in a diplomatic settlement. The 1967 war brought a quick, lopsided victory to Israel. On 5 June, Israel's air force attacked Egyptian airfields, destroying the Egyptian air cover before the planes could get off the ground. Attacks on airfields in Jordan, Iraq, and Syria followed. Egyptian forces in Sinai were completely exposed, and several thousand soldiers died. Yet there was sufficient fighting that Israeli forces took almost five days to reach the Suez Canal. In a bitter three days of fighting, the Old City of Jerusalem and the West Bank were also occupied, thereby prompting Jordan to accept the U.N. proposed ceasefire on 8 June. Egypt agreed the following day, but Israel continued the war against Syria, the main target being the Julan heights which had been used for shelling Israeli settlements near Tiberias Lake.

Then, in an event played down by the United States at the time, the Israeli Air Force bombed the U.S.S. Liberty, an American intelligence ship flying U.S. colors off the Israeli coast. Over thirty Amer-

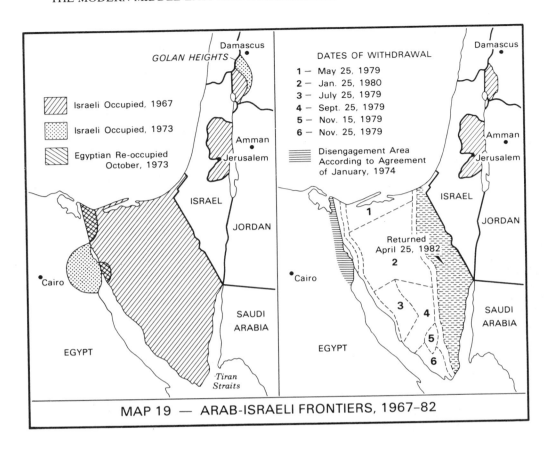

MAP 19 — ARAB-ISRAELI FRONTIERS, 1967–82

icans died in the deliberate attack. Israel later offered compensation, but the official silence has stimulated from survivors and others questions about the meaning of the event and its implications for American-Israeli relations.

On 10 June, the town of Qunaytra in Julan fell to Israeli troops. Syria, too, agreed to the ceasefire. In six days, Israel had tripled the land area under its occupation (see Map 19). Whatever the Israeli intentions regarding the territories, subsequent Israeli maps removed all suggestions of occupied territory and previous boundaries, referring only to a united area with its ceasefire lines. The apparent hope that the territories might be exchanged for peace soon gave way to an intensified debate over security borders and the historic frontiers of the land of Israel.

CHAPTER SEVENTEEN

The Assertion and Protection of National Independence in the Arab World

The indigenous political and cultural developments in the postwar Arabic-speaking world have been influenced by the following national and international circumstances:

1. The ongoing struggle for political independence, especially in North Africa.
2. The process of eliminating remnants of British, French, Italian, and Spanish colonial rule in nominally independent countries.
3. The efforts of superpowers to co-opt countries into their own alliance systems.
4. The quest for Arab unity as a means of strengthening individual regimes and regional power.
5. The replacement of old landed elites by the new intelligentsia, including technocrats and military officers.
6. The increasing importance and volume of Southwest Asian and North African petroleum and natural gas production.
7. The transfer of ownership of petroleum companies to producing countries.
8. The identification of regimes with *third-* and *fourth*-world countries, especially in Africa and Asia.
9. The Palestine question and the Arab-Israeli conflict.
10. Militant Islamic renewal.

With these overarching considerations, and the accompanying changes that occurred after World War II, countries in the region adopted new priorities and readjusted others. The dramatic redistribution of wealth brought to the fore new candidates for regional leadership. By the early 1980s, it was clear that while oil wealth carried with it a certain clout, influence arose from a combination of factors, many of them less tangible: individuals' personalities, geopolitics, history, ideology, and internal circumstances.

Who were the major postwar Arab leaders of not only national but also regional significance?

Egypt: Presidents Gamal Abd al-Nasir, Anwar al-Sadat, Husni Mubarak.
Sudan: President Ja'far al-Numayri.
Libya: President Mu'ammar al-Qadhdhafi.
Morocco: Kings Muhammad V and Hasan II.
Tunisia: President Habib Bourguiba.
Algeria: Presidents Ahmad Ben Bella, Houari Boumedienne, and Chadhli Ben Jadid.
Syria: Presidents Shukri al-Quwatli and Hafiz al-Asad; Colonel Adib al-Shishakli.

Jordan: King Husayn.
Iraq: Nuri al-Sa'id and King Faysal (pre-revolution); Abd al-Karim Qasim, Abd al-Salam Arif, Abd al-Rahman Arif, Ahmad Hasan al-Bakr, and Saddam Husayn.
Saudi Arabia: Kings Faysal, Khalid, and Fahd; oil minister Shaykh Ahmad Zaki Yamani.
Palestinians: Yasir Arafat.

Lebanese leaders, such as former presidents Charles Helou, Camille Sham'un, Sulayman Franjiyya, and Elias Sarkis, as well as Druze socialist Kemal Jumblat and President Amin Jumayyil may have been highly influential in Lebanon but have had less significance regionally. The same claim is true, in the eastern Arab world, for Iraqi Kurdish leader Mustafa al-Barzani, Syrian Communist leader Khalid Baqdash, and Syrian nationalist and later Communist leader Khalid al-Azm. Similar status exists for politicians Salah Ben Yusuf, Ahmad Ben Salah, and Ahmad Mestiri in Tunisia and Mehdi Ben Barka of Morocco.

New Postwar Ideologies

The most prominent postwar ideologues were Michel Aflaq (Christian) and Salah al-Din Bitar (Muslim) who in 1952 joined their Ba'th (Renaissance: Resurrection) Party with Akram Hurani's Arab Socialist Party to promote Arab socialism and unity. Anti-Communist during its formative years, Ba'thi ideology for many years agitated for unions between Arab countries, particularly Egypt, Syria, and Iraq, especially after the latter two came under Ba'thi regimes. Ba'thism acquired wide influence in the Arab world partly because of the idealism and eclecticism of Aflaq's thought. The main strains—nationalist, liberal, democratic, socialist, Islamic, and elitist—incorporated different and contradictory philosophical assumptions. Was it the individual, the nation, the mas-

ses, the party, or God which was to be exalted? Aflaq believed that the means and ends were spiritual and that the Ba'th's first goals should be moral and intellectual revitalization. Ba'thism specifically diverged from communism in its focus on the spirit, its stress on Islam as a factor in Arab unity, its avoidance of internationalism, and its view of socialism as an economic order rather than a comprehensive world view. In 1966, Aflaq and Bitar were expelled from Syria's Ba'th and took refuge in Beirut. Following a reconciliation, Aflaq resumed his activities in politics but moved abroad during later power struggles. After Hafiz al-Asad's new government signed an agreement with Egypt and Libya to form the Union of Arab Republics, Aflaq and Bitar were sentenced to death by Syria in absentia. Aflaq moved to Iraq. Bitar left politics and was pardoned in 1976. In 1981, he was assassinated.

Whereas Ba'thi ideology viewed elites as the vehicle for social change, a related strain of action and thought that came to be known as Nasirism (after Abd al-Nasir) sought to achieve its aims through mass mobilization. Six principles formulated toward the beginning of the revolution in Egypt, in 1952, laid the foundation for Nasirism. Anti-imperialism, democracy, and a strong military were to go hand in hand with socioeconomic change, especially implementation of social justice, elimination of capitalist domination, and an end to feudalistic agriculture. In practical terms, however, Nasirism focused on the persona of Gamal Abd al-Nasir as an anti-imperialist and third-world liberation advocate. The socialist component of Nasirism remained vague, and efforts to create mass parties met with limited success. Nasirism, though tainted by its association with repression and detention centers, outlived the man with whom it was associated, because like Ba'thi socialism it combined the ideas of national social revolution but upheld religion and nonexploiting or small-scale property ownership.

Libya's Muammar al-Qadhdhafi emerged as the Arab world's most innovative ideologue of the late 1970s and early 1980s. In his *Green Book,* he extolled the virtues of a democracy based on popular congresses, social justice, and Islam. Although he objected to liberal democracy, individualism, and capitalism, he also shunned the Soviet type of bureaucracy as exploitative. For Qadhdhafi, Islam provided the key to a just society, when its spirit was properly interpreted, but with time, his religious ideology grew more eclectic. Emphasizing the divine rather than individual prophets such as Jesus or Muhammad, Qadhdhafi saw his own guidebook rather than Hadith and Sunna supplementing the Qur'an as a guide to daily living.

Not surprisingly, Qadhdhafi backed the Iranian revolution for its puritanical thrust but regarded the Muslim Brothers as too sectarian and probably funded by the American C.I.A. While the *Green Book* stated that violent revolution may be the only way to overturn or correct a dictatorial regime, it also said that revolution is basically undemocratic. Qadhdhafi's commitment to Arab union followed in the footsteps of Ba'thi and Nasirite ideology, but all of his projected unions failed for one reason or another. Early in the 1980s, it was difficult to say how much of his ideology might be exportable. His socioeconomic program sustained by Libya's oil wealth and small population achieved social change in Libya. Aspects of his Islamic thrust, especially his populist philosophy centered on the idea of *Jamahiriyya* (people's republic), resonated in parts of the Muslim world. His ideas, however, aroused concern among some conservative Arab regimes. While not usually considered part of the mainstream Islamic movement Qadhdhafi's Islamic vision must be seen as a future option.

Background to the Egyptian Revolution

Developments in Egypt after World War II profoundly influenced the Middle East as a whole. The assassination of Mahir in 1945 began a new era of violence and protest. A look at interrelated issues of 1946–9 reveals the growth of anti-British sentiment that arose not only from the presence of British forces in Egypt but also from British policies in Palestine and the Sudan. The Muslim Brothers took the lead in anti-British and antiforeign protests, including attacks on Jewish interests in Egypt. Although many Egyptians had profited from the war, its end influenced workers adversely partly because wartime labor legislation was ignored. Workers continued to suffer from inflation and sporadic unemployment. Communists played an important role in organizing labor protests in the Nile Delta textile industries. The Muslim Brothers were also active among workers, although they counseled against strikes. At times, the Brothers seemed to be tacitly allied with King Faruq, who was still at odds with the Wafd.

Meanwhile, Egyptian businessmen gained increased control over the economy and now held the bulk of the Egyptian debt. Egyptianization of industry and utilities tended to maintain the old elites in power rather than lead to better options for workers. Although Egypt, like Iraq and India, emerged from the war as Britain's creditor, the British managed to whittle down the debt through protracted discussions and devaluation of the British pound—they judiciously avoided a debt settlement that would turn over the Suez Canal holdings as desired by the Egyptian government. Egypt derived little immediate benefit from the government's decision to 1947 to leave the sterling currency area, an action carried out over a ten-year period. With the wartime emphasis on growing more cotton, Egypt in the early postwar years, with its rapidly growing population, encountered food shortages.

Politicians' Attempts to Secure a British Evacuation and Nile Valley Union

These factors promoted and perpetuated an atmosphere of instability. Egypt's political leadership continued to be drawn from among the old politicians. Succeeding Mahir as prime minister in 1945 were Nuqrashi and Sidqi. Nuqrashi discredited himself quickly by putting down a worker-student demonstration on Abbas Bridge

in Cairo. Although he announced the twin goals of "evacuation" and "unity of the Nile Valley," themes taken up by his successors, he proved unable to achieve progress toward fulfilling them.

It was Sidqi who in autumn 1945 initiated overtures to the British for a resumption of negotiations over questions remaining from the 1936 treaty. In January 1946, the Labour government responded favorably, much to the surprise of the Wafdists who had wrongly assumed that the British would negotiate with them alone. The Wafd refused to cooperate in the Egyptian commission constituted for the occasion (the group included most of the well-known minority politicians). Discussion in the British parliament about evacuation arising from a speech made by Clement Atlee in the House of Commons on 7 May 1946 led opposition leader Winston Churchill to accuse him of "the liquidation of the fruit of sixty years of diplomacy and administration."[1] The only British evacuation that actually took place was that of the citadel's garrison in Cairo. British leaders kept pressing for military concessions in wartime, and also encouraged the Sudanese Advisory Council (S.A.C.) to advocate self-government for Sudan (see Map 20).

Sidqi finally extracted an agreement for the British to evacuate Egypt within three years and to unify the Nile Valley under the Egyptian crown. Sudan was to be allowed self-determination at some later date. When the project reached the public in December 1946, Sidqi was forced to resign because of the vague military provisions. He felt betrayed.

Nuqrashi returned to head the government that same month. He hoped that by taking the Anglo-Egyptian dispute to the United Nations, international opinion would support Egypt against British wavering on Sudan and other questions. While he was at the United Nations in

---

[1] Statement of 7 May 1946 quoted in Jacques Berque, *Egypt: Imperialism and Revolution.* trans. Jean Stewart. (London: Faber and Faber, 1972), p. 580.

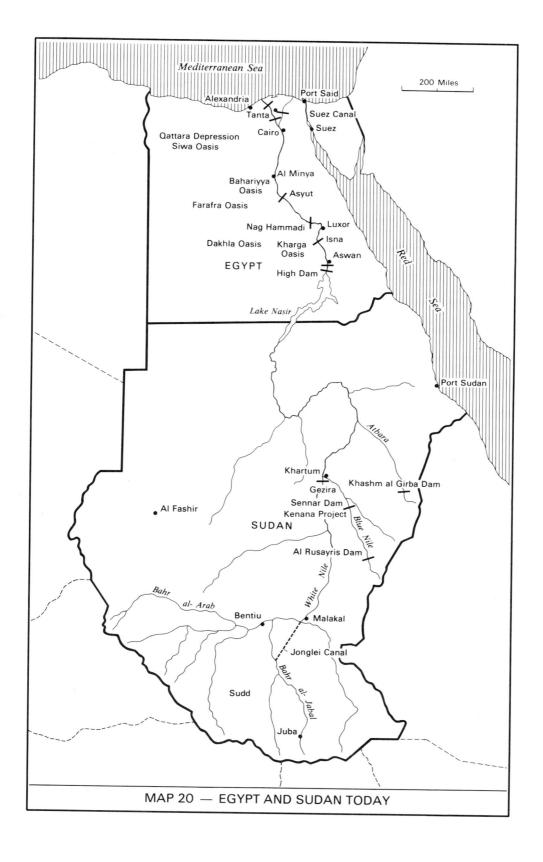

MAP 20 — EGYPT AND SUDAN TODAY

summer 1947, the Wafd tried to undermine his position by claiming that he did not fully represent Egypt. In September, the United Nations chose to refer the argument back to the disputants instead of reaching a solution. It was on 29 November 1947 that the United Nations passed the Palestine partition resolution, thereby exacerbating the crisis atmosphere in Egypt, a country committed to support any Arab initiative to prevent its implementation.

Collapse of the Old Order

During the next six months, the Nuqrashi government proved helpless against violence perpetrated by the Muslim Brothers. The main Jewish quarters and department stores in Cairo were wrecked or bombed, with an acceleration of outbreaks after the government's declaration of martial law on 15 May 1948 arising from the Palestine war. The Muslim Brothers, long active in the Palestine struggle, appeared more and more threatening to an Egyptian government regarded as corrupt and weak. Cairo's police chief, Salim Zaki, was murdered by a Brother, thereby prompting Nuqrashi to order the organization's dissolution and the confiscation of its funds and properties. Twenty days later, on 28 December, another Brother killed Nuqrashi. In the tension that followed, the palace engineered in February 1949, the assassination of Muslim Brotherhood leader Hasan al-Banna. For the next two years, the Muslim Brethren remained quiescent. The dissatisfaction evidenced by Muslim Brotherhood activity, though, was amplified in other quarters.

On 11 January 1949, Egypt signed an armistice with Israel. Young officers like Gamal Abd al-Nasir felt betrayed by the regime's lack of commitment to the war effort and by the widespread corruption that had prevented effective use of available resources. They began plotting the overthrow of the government. Among the conspirators with Abd al-Nasir were Anwar al-Sadat, Abd al-Hakim Amer, and Zakariyya Muhiyy al-Din, all of whom assumed prominent roles in the later revolutionary period.

After the war, dissatisfaction with the Palace and Sa'dist politicians swept the Wafd, still led by Nahas but now with the dissolved Muslim Brothers' backing, back into power. His tasks remained the same as those of previous governments, but he was hampered by the fact that Sudan had without Egyptian approval already been given its first legislature in December 1948. The British in 1950 and 1951 persisted in their assumption that any agreement would still allow them to keep their troops in Suez. In October 1951, however, Nahhas denounced and abrogated the treaty of 1936. The Egyptian parliament proclaimed King Faruq—already world-famous as profligate—monarch of a united Nile Valley one week later.

The British reacted to the initial abrogation by proposing with its allies—the United States, France, and Turkey—a joint Middle Eastern command to patrol the Suez Canal. After the parliamentary declaration, British troops in the Canal Zone were reinforced. Demonstrations broke out in the area as people suspected that the government would not defend its interests. When in January 1952 the British told the police chief of Isma'iliyya to order his men to lay down their arms, the government took up the challenge and ordered him to resist. Between fifty and sixty Egyptians died during the fighting.

On the 26th of the month, auxiliary troops announced a strike while the government continued to promise revenge. A fire that began in a Cairo cabaret spread to foreign enterprises, night clubs, department stores, the Shepheard's Hotel, and movie houses. It expressed Egyptian rage against British imperialism and the entire political, social and economic structure which it sustained. The fact that the politicians and king could not curtail the rampage that accompanied this "black Saturday" seemed to show how tangential they had become to leadership in Egypt.

The Egyptian Revolution of 1952 and Its Consolidation

On 23 July 1952, the young officers—most in their early thirties—overthrew the government in a virtually bloodless coup. As their figurehead, the officers settled on General Muhammad Nagib after their first choice, old nationalist Aziz Ali al-Masri, had declined. The presence of a senior military officer in his early fifties helped legitimize the young officers and allay the fears of outsiders that the revolution would threaten their own interests. On 26 July, King Faruq was deposed in favor of his infant son Ahmad Fuad II and was allowed to sail away with his riches on the *Mahroussa* that had taken Khedive Isma'il into exile. Politicians supported these early moves because they saw no danger to their vested interests. The officers stated their intentions to eliminate corruption and restore the spirit of the constitution. They turned to Ali Mahir as the new prime minister who would help lead the revolution, but they maintained their own executive, the Revolutionary Command Council (R.C.C.).

During the first year of the revolution, the officers dispensed with most of the civilians involved in government because they seemed unwilling to implement substantive social and economic change. Prior to the revolution, 160,000 individuals owned most of the land while one million farmers owned none. Landless peasants or those owning only small parcels entered the agricultural labor market either as year-round workers or as casual laborers on large estates. Such peasants, especially year-round workers, were usually given a plot of land to cultivate for their own use. During World War II, landlords began to rent out their land, often to prosperous peasants owning up to fifty feddans. These peasants collected rent

from the poorer farmers (as in Iran). When the Korean War began, demand for Egyptian cotton increased and rents rose.

The R.C.C. attempted to reduce the potential for class conflict and direct money to industry by passing a decree in September 1952 limiting land ownership to two hundred feddans. Although the poorest peasants remained poor, the redistribution of farmland broke up the largest estates. Nagib replaced Mahir as prime minister.

The main orientation of the officers at the beginning of the revolution was pragmatic and reformist, focusing on social justice, discipline, unity, and hard work. With no definite ideology, the officers were willing to experiment, especially in the reconstruction of Egypt's political life. The multiparty parliamentary system was declared a failure. As its replacement, the officers opted for guided democracy based on a grass-roots mass party, the Liberation Rally created in January 1953 with the promulgation of a new constitution. On 18 June, the R.C.C. abolished the monarchy and declared Egypt a republic with Nagib as president, prime minister, and R.C.C. chairman. Abd al-Nasir, acknowledged as the real leader, became deputy prime minister and minister of interior (security). Within six months, the government moved against the increasingly militant opposition, including the Wafd, the Communist Party and especially the Muslim Brothers, all regarded as potential rivals for power.

In that context, a struggle was underway between Nagib and Abd al-Nasir. The former took his positions seriously, although in the R.C.C. his was one of twelve voices. In February 1954, Nagib resigned, precipitating a split in the R.C.C. An uprising in the cavalry and popular demonstrations of support led to his reinstatement in March, but differences among R.C.C. members remained. On 25 March, Abd al-Nasir announced that the revolution had come to an end and that parliamentary rule and a free press would be restored. At the same time he organized demonstrations to support continuation of the revolution. By "popular demand," R.C.C. rule persisted.

While the revolution was consolidating itself internally, its leaders adopted a friendly posture toward the world at large. In February 1953, the British and Egyptians agreed that the Sudanese should choose their own future path. For the first time, the Sudan question was separated from the issue of British troops in the Suez area. These latter negotiations continued between April 1953 and October 1954. Although the discussion with the British was bogged down by technicalities, the two sides agreed to the following on 19 October 1954:

1. Withdrawal of 80,000 British troops within twenty months (18 June 1956).
2. Upholding of the 1888 canal convention.
3. Formal end to the 1936 treaty.
4. Egyptian permission for five years to reactivate the British bases in case of an attack on either an Arab state or Turkey.

What the civilian governments had failed to accomplish during several years, the revolution had promptly dispatched.

The government also hoped to stay out of the evolving cold war between the United States and the Soviet Union. The U.S. diplomats tended to regard the new Egyptian regime as dedicated and nationalistic, but efforts of Dulles to line up Egypt in a regional defense pact against the Soviet Union led to disenchantment on both sides. Abd al-Nasir avoided entanglements with other Arab countries, too, and tried to stabilize the border between Egyptian-occupied Gaza and Israel.

The foreign policy of the R.C.C. antagonized the Muslim Brothers who objected to Sudanese self-determination and the possibility of future British military activities in Egypt. The rivalry between Nagib and Abd al-Nasir was resolved when the former was implicated in a Muslim Brotherhood plot and assassination attempt on Abd al-Nasir's life on 26 October 1954. The leaders of the plot were hanged, but the Muslim Brothers went into eclipse until the 1970s. Thousands were imprisoned or chose exile including Sayyid Qutb. He emerged later as the major ideologue of not only the Muslim Brothers but of the Islamic movement worldwide. General Nagib was forced to resign his posts. These events of fall 1954 ended the R.C.C. period of consolidation. The R.C.C. then began increasing the regime's popularity as it turned to regional affairs.

Gamal Abd al-Nasir: An Overview

Who was Gamal Abd al-Nasir? First of all, he was a son of rural Egypt. His grandfather was a peasant, and his father worked mainly in villages as a postal employee, also serving briefly in Alexandria. Abd al-Nasir's secondary school years in Alexandria and Cairo coincided with the turbulent political years of 1928–35. He attended the Military College in the first year that it was open to nonaristocrats. Through his early experiences, he acquired a deep-seated distrust of politicians and a military view of social development. The events of 1942 led directly to the formation of the Free Officers Movement.

As Egypt's leader for sixteen years, Abd al-Nasir was also an enigma. His practical orientation led to his taking action first and philosophizing about it later. Attempts to rally the masses in a single movement involved several experiments. The Liberation Rally was succeeded by the National Union in January 1956 which elected him president on 23 June 1956. When elections in January 1957 led to an assembly that had critical tendencies, he targeted it for dissolution. The creation of the United Arab Republic (U.A.R.), uniting Egypt and Syria in 1958, led to the U.A.R. National Assembly that was not even convened until 1960, the year before its breakup. A new committee set up a Congress of Popular Forces to recommend future actions. Their suggestions were embodied in the National Charter of 30 June 1962, proposed by a congress of 750 men. From this new document arose the Arab Socialist Union (A.S.U.) based on representation by occupation with 50 percent worker-peasant membership. It survived well into the Sadat era.

Abd al-Nasir's social and economic programs arose in conjunction with but not necessarily because of international events and pressures related to Israel, British and French imperialism, American designs, Soviet availability, and the quest for Arab unity. Until the prelude to the Suez war, Abd-Nasir focused on domestic issues in hopes of addressing Egypt's burgeoning population and health problems. After the war, nationalizations of British and French financial interests began to affect Egyptian-owned businesses as the government turned to a policy of public-sector expansion. Egypt's private sector had proved inadequate in promoting Egyptian development. The transfer of the Suez Canal to Egyptian-government ownership gave the public sector its first important moneymaker.

The Arab East before the U.A.R. Era

The idea of Arab unity preceded the post-World War I division of the Arab East into French and British spheres of interest. The humiliation in Palestine convinced many Arabs that it was this fragmentation that had caused the debacle. Palestine remained the symbol of Arab frustration. Arab unity offered hopes of achieving regional power, but because it did not exist, it became the basis for a struggle over the heartlands of the Arab East—formerly greater Syria. Egypt and Iraq, as representatives of revolutionary and traditional conservative government respectively, vied for regional leadership that would bring Syria within their individual orbits.

As with the later movement for African unity, the Arab-unity idea involved achieving independence for countries, principally for those in North Africa still under colonial rule. Arab unity also provided an answer to the problem created by Western attempts to bring Middle Eastern countries into anti-Soviet alliance blocs. Protection and assertion of independence, then, were two important reasons for which Arab unity appeared attractive. Internal problems also fueled the Arab-unity movement.

Syria's Search for Consensus

Postwar Syria, for example, experienced some eighteen military coup d'etat attempts before 1971, a legacy of France's divide-and-rule mandate policy. Colonel Husni Za'im (Za-eem) inaugurated the era of coups in March 1949, expelling President Shukri al-Quwatli and abolishing parliamentary life. As with later coups, the new intelligentsia viewed Za'im as the prophet of social reform as well as of the revision of old political relationships. Before the year was out, however, fellow officer Sami al-Hinnawi killed Za'im and proceeded to initiate moves to bring Syria closer to the Hashimite regime in Iraq.

The forces that overthrew Hinnawi early in 1950 were led by reformers who objected to union with the conservative Iraqi monarchy. Although coup leader Colonel Adib al-Shishakli initially collaborated with Akram Hurani in introducing a new constitution embodying progressive ideas such as social justice, workers' rights, health care, education, land reform, and nationalization of natural resources, Syria's vested interests blocked their implementation. Because Shishakli made no attempt to lay groundwork before flooding the country with new laws, it was difficult for him to rally public support.

Within two years, Shishakli dispensed with the parliamentary order through a second coup. The disenchanted Hurani then joined his own party with the Ba'th. The new party opposed Shishakli's attempt to forge a single mass party, the Arab Liberation Movement (A.L.M.) that would lead progressive forces throughout the Arab world. The goals of the A.L.M. were associated with the old P.P.S., and politicians avoided it. Ba'th leaders felt that Shishakli had sold out to Western interests while dispensing with political freedom.

In summer 1953, Shishakli answered his critics by offering a new constitution and a presidential referendum, but they refused to be silenced because these measures only consolidated his position. Because the Syrian economy had enjoyed great prosperity, mainly because of Shishakli's measures to stabilize the cotton industry and the private investment of merchants, they could not criticize the regime on the pretext that the population was suffering. What brought down Shishakli was a combination of external and internal forces of which he was aware but which he could not control.

Based in the Druze countryside, in the city of Homs and in minority and merchant-dominated Aleppo, the opposition began to meet at the time when the new constitution was formed. Ba'this and Communists participated in the plotting. Demonstrations in Aleppo ensued in December 1953, sparked by an attempt to burn the American high school for having presented a supposedly anti-Arab play. Opposition leaders in Homs published reports of police brutality against students. The Druze also protested when their possession of Ba'th anti-Shishakli literature prompted the arrest of Druze leaders.

Iraq, which had been funding Syrian politicians in hopes of achieving a dominant role there, proposed to the Arab League in January 1954 a plan for Arab

union to begin with Jordan, Iraq, and Syria. Shishakli made no secret of his opposition. Apparently, the Iraqi regent Abd al-Ilah was hoping to procure a throne in Syria because Faysal II had reached his majority in summer 1953. The Iraqi moves inspired both Egypt and Saudi Arabia to reaffirm their support of the Shishakli government. Anwar al-Sadat was especially influential in this matter. The Lebanese tried to mediate the dispute, too.

Fall of Shishakli and Its Consequences

The Shishakli regime was overthrown in late February 1954 by army commanders based in Aleppo and Dayr al-Zor. These commanders were representative of opposition groups in Aleppo, Homs, and Hama. Soon the army in Jabal Druze joined the insurrection. Shishakli left for Beirut rather than involve the country in a drawn-out struggle that would prolong bloodshed. Fearing a Druze-Iraqi plot on his life, Lebanese authorities assured that Shishakli would not remain in Lebanon. He sought refuge in Saudi Arabia and later moved to Brazil where in 1964 he was shot to death by a Druze.

Shishakli had given Syria its first taste of extended military rule. Retrospectively, many Syrians continued to respect him for having consolidated Syrian nationality in the postwar period and for having held firmly against Western designs. The army, having been given a role in politics, never fully abandoned it. Both old and new political elites inaugurated a power struggle of their own in which the Ba'th and Communist parties emerged as the main contestants.

The Communists' leader was a Kurdish Syrian, Khalid Baqdash—a skilled orator, a disciplined thinker, and a masterful debater. He joined the Communists in 1930 at age eighteen and received training in Moscow after a brief period of imprisonment by the French in 1931 and 1932. Baqdash cooperated with the French Communist Party during the short-lived Popular Front government. During World War II, he announced a party platform that was essentially nationalist. In Syria, though, the association of the Communists with the Soviet Union led to the temporary dissolution of the party and its assumption of underground activities.

After the overthrow of Shishakli, the Syrians held parliamentary elections under the 1950 constitution. The custodial government of Sa'id al-Ghazzi, a Damascus lawyer, assured that the elections would be by secret ballot and would involve an electorate of both men and women, although only women with an elementary school certificate could vote. The People's Party, which along with the National Party represented the old politicians, gained 30 of the 142 seats. The National Party won 19. The Ba'th was to hold 22 seats. But the largest bloc of 64 seats was occupied by independents such as Khalid al-Azm. Baqdash was the only Communist deputy elected. Election analysts interpreted the decline in the People's Party as a rejection of Fertile-Crescent unity schemes of which it was the major proponent. The emergence of the Ba'th was attributed to the organizational successes of Aflaq (who did not run for parliament) and of Hurani and Bitar (who won seats in Hama and Damascus respectively). The first major challenge to the new government derived from the Western alliance idea that culminated in the Baghdad Pact.

Struggle Over Foreign Alliances: The Baghdad Pact and its Impact

The United States at first viewed the alliance as a southern encirclement of the Soviet Union in which Arab participation was desirable but not essential. The British looked upon it as a way of preserving their position in the region following troop withdrawals from Egypt. Abd al-Nasir apparently warned Dulles as early as 1953 that participation in such an alliance would undermine individual Arab governments and would prove counterproductive to the West.

The scuffles over the Baghdad Pact became a stage on which inter-Arab rivalries were played out. Nuri al-Sa'id in Iraq supported the proposed alliance as a pivot for Iraqi regional leadership. Abd al-Nasir reaffirmed his objection to outside intervention. In January 1954, he spoke out in favor of separate Arab and African blocs. When he realized that Iraq was determined to participate nevertheless, he launched a more pointed propaganda campaign against nonregional alliances. Because the Iraqis regarded a Soviet threat as more serious, they held firm. Egypt began to be viewed in the Arab world as the main proponent of independent Arab progressives. Iraq concluded that its own participation would be meaningful only if other Arab states joined.

The two states sought to negotiate their differences. During this process, the Egyptian representative mistakenly concluded an agreement that promised consultation with the United States and Britain over regional defense and that seemed to acquiesce to Nuri's plans for a united Syrian-Hashimite state. When disagreement on these points became evident, Nuri resorted to a new tactic of trying to make Turkey part of an Arab alliance in which the United States and Britain would be consulted. The Egyptians failed to see his objective and thought that the Iraqis were trying to draw Turkey away from Egypt. In January 1955, as the Iraqis and Turks announced their pact and called on Egypt to join, the Egyptians finally saw that the goal was to bring the Arab world into a larger Western-sponsored alliance. Egypt's continued neutrality rested on its ability to keep other Arab states out of the pact. As both Iraq and Egypt realized, Syria was the pivotal country.

Late in January, Arab prime ministers met in Cairo to consider Egypt's complaints against Iraq's plans to sign the treaty in February. Despite mediation efforts of representatives from Syria, Lebanon, and Jordan, Nuri al-Sa'id refused to reconsider. The Syrian government fell over the issue as neutralists gained the upper hand. Led by Khalid al-Azm, Akram al-Hurani, and some dissidents from the National Party, the neutralists brought Syrian foreign policy into line with that of Egypt. When the pact was signed by Turkey and Iraq on 24 February 1955, Radio Cairo accused Iraq of having allied with "friends of Zionism" and called on the Iraqi people to crush it. Egypt was engaged in trying to firm up its own leadership. Four days later, the Israelis attacked the Egyptians stationed in Gaza.

Israel's attack helped Egypt to rally other Arab countries to stay away from the Baghdad Pact. Egypt, Syria, and Saudi Arabia agreed on joint military and economic cooperation. Although this agreement never really took effect, it demonstrated the extent to which Egypt and Saudi Arabia were anxious to keep Syria out of Iraq's orbit. Even Hashimite Jordan abstained from participating in the Baghdad Pact. The Soviet Union promised to protect Syria after reports in March that Turkey and Iraq had sent troops to

their borders with Syria. Both Syria and Egypt turned to the Soviet Union for arms supplies with which to combat external threats. Contacts established at Bandung in April promoted the sales that nevertheless mortgaged future crops. Apparently neither the Americans nor the British took seriously Abd al-Nasir's statement that if they would not give him arms, he would obtain them from the Soviet Union.

By November 1955, Syria and Egypt had concluded a new defense pact to which Israel replied by attacking Syria's Julan positions. Its intention, as in the case of the Gaza raid, was to demoralize the opposition. But it actually strengthened Syria's rapprochement with Egypt. Jordan decided to cooperate more closely with the two countries in foreign policy. The Suez War further strengthened ideologically-motivated political movements—the Ba'th, the Nasirites, and the Communists. The decolonization of North Africa, still in progress at the time in Algeria, contributed to this development, too.

Libya under the Sanussis

Independence did not come easily to Libya, Morocco, Tunisia, and Algeria (see Map 21). When the U.N. refused to partition Libya, it became the first nation to achieve independence. In June 1949, Britain recognized Cyrenaican independence. After considerable great power scrambling which also involved the U.S.S.R., the United Nations in November approved independence for the whole of Libya. The French conducted elections in Fazzan in February 1950, setting up a sort of protectorate in conjunction with assembly leaders. The British and French actions in Cyrenaica and Fazzan strengthened the bargaining position of leaders there vis-à-vis the more urbanized and cosmopolitan Tripolitanians. With the final date for Libyan independence set

for 1 January 1952, U.N. advisors came to Libya to work out a plan that would satisfy Libyan aspirations.

Regional rivalry within Libya presented the major obstacle to an easy solution. Moreover, Egypt aspired to control of all of Libya and led the Arab League to oppose Libyan independence. Although the Tripolitanians, equal in number to the populations of Cyrenaica and Fazzan combined, preferred a unitary state, the independence plan approved by the United Nations set up a federated monarchy under Sayyid Idris. An appointed assembly would be constituted with an equal number of representatives from each region. Egypt failed in its effort to replace the idea of an appointed body with that of an elected one. Newly independent Libya,

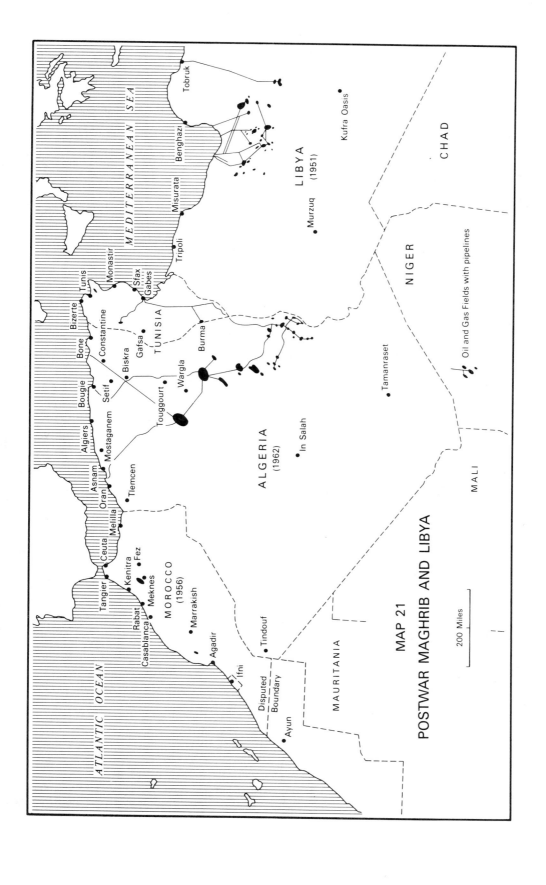

MAP 21

POSTWAR MAGHRIB AND LIBYA

ATLANTIC OCEAN

MEDITERRANEAN SEA

MOROCCO (1956)

ALGERIA (1962)

TUNISIA

LIBYA (1951)

MAURITANIA

MALI

NIGER

CHAD

Tobruk
Benghazi
Misurata
Tripoli
Gabes
Sfax
Monastir
Tunis
Bizerte
Bone
Constantine
Biskra
Gafsa
Burma
Wargla
Touggourt
Setif
Bougie
Algiers
Mostaganem
Asnam
Oran
Melilla
Tlemcen
Ceuta
Tangier
Kenitra
Fez
Meknes
Rabat
Casablanca
Marrakish
Agadir
Ifni
Ayun
Tindouf
In Salah
Tamanraset
Murzuq
Kufra Oasis

Disputed
Boundary

Oil and Gas Fields with pipelines

200 Miles

then, emerged late in 1951 as a state preserving the position of the old religious and tribal elites while conceding little to the more cosmopolitan elements in the population.

Under Sanussi leadership, Libya in the first fifteen years of independence saw the strengthening of the king's power and continued reliance on foreign powers for economic well-being. France evacuated Fazzan only in 1956. The United States and Britain leased military facilities and gave the government its main source of revenues. Between 1954 and 1971, the United States maintained the lease for Wheelus Air Base while Britain in 1953 contracted a twenty-year alliance with Libya. Italy contributed to Libyan development, too. Although Italian colonists were given ownership of land, many went back to Italy. Those who remained found their holdings expropriated in 1970 after the revolution. The Soviet Union recognized Libya in 1955 but played no important economic or political role. Despite the Arab League's initial opposition to Libyan independence, Libya became a member.

Idris took advantage of independence-arrangements to consolidate power in his own hands. Instead of co-opting the Arab nationalist elements into his regime, he based decisions for appointments on family and tribal considerations. Although the government theoretically included a cabinet, ministries, and legislatures, the royal diwan was the real center of power. Often ruling by decree, the king made sure that the key ministries—interior, defense, finance, and petroleum—remained under his personal control. Since he had no son, Idris named his brother's son as heir to the throne.

Changing economic realities and forces within the Arab world numbered the days of the Sanussi monarchy. With the advent of petroleum concessions (1955) and exports (1961), Libya no longer needed to rely on foreign aid or income from military bases. Outsiders wondered when the military, more in tune with Abd al-Nasir in Egypt than with Idris, would overthrow the increasingly isolated monarch. The coup came on 1 September 1969, led not by senior military officers but by eleven captains and one lieutenant who drew their inspiration from the Egyptian revolution. The military-technocrat alliance was to forge a new order for Libya.

The Moroccan Struggle for Independence

Morocco was the second North African country to achieve postwar independence. In both Morocco and Tunisia, the French planned to perpetuate the protectorate because they already controlled important sectors of the economy. They felt that they had furthered Moroccan and Tunisian development, and did not aspire to minority status as foreigners in independent countries. The well-established settlers intended to secure maintenance of their power by assuring themselves of parity in any governing bodies. Nationalists desired to move in the direction of full equality and restoration of the protectorate spirit.

The French governor in Morocco after March 1946, Erik Labonne, tried to introduce some liberalizing measures but met with opposition from all quarters. Settlers viewed the changes as a sellout, the Istiqlal forces as a means of perpetuating colonial rule, and the sultan as contributing to further erosion of his position. In a speech in April 1947, Sultan Muhammad Ben Yusuf emphasized his intention to restore his rule in Morocco by referring to the "unity of the Sharifian Empire" and praising the Arab League. Demonstrations followed in Tangier and Casablanca. French settlers insisted that Labonne's policies had prompted this assertion of control over both French and Spanish-occupied Morocco.

General Juin's appointment as resident-general in his place meant a return to authoritarianism. In Juin's view, Muhammad Ben Yusuf presented the main obstacle to continuation of French influence. If Juin could force the sultan to accept concessions as an alternative to abdication or dethroning, then the French could maintain their power. Meanwhile, the Istiqlal had begun cooperating with the Islah and Maghrib Unity parties in Spanish Morocco. The stage was set for a nationalist confrontation.

In fall 1950, French president Auriol refused Muhammad's requests for revisions in the protectorate treaty. Juin removed nationalists from the governing council. At the end of January 1951, Juin gave the sultan a choice: he could disavow the Istiqlal or agree to his own abdication. The French allowed Berber leaders—large landowners such as the Glawa—to intimidate the sultan. Formally he acceded to French demands, but the nationalists continued to regard him as their natural leader. Forming a nationalist front, the various parties in both the Spanish and French portions of Morocco intensified their campaign for independence, obtaining both U.N. and Arab League support. The sultan early in 1952 demanded only the establishment of his own government within the protectorate framework. Tensions increased as the nationalist-influenced trade unions began to play a greater role.

In December 1952, workers in Casablanca struck in protest against the assassination by French nationalists of Tunisian trade unionist Ferhat Hached. In the ensuing suppression, several hundred Moroccans died. The United States was among the countries to back the idea of putting the Moroccan question on the U.N. agenda for December. But the new resident-general Guillaume pursued a neutral course to avoid antagonizing the settlers.

Deposition and Restoration of Muhammad Ben Yusuf

A landmark in the Moroccan independence struggle was the deposition of Muhammad Ben Yusuf on 20 August 1953. The sultan was sent first to Corsica and later to Madagascar as Thami al-Glawi's candidate, Mawlay Ben Arafa, replaced him. A more docile sultan, Ben Arafa accepted French numerical parity with Moroccans. As nationalists rallied around the deposed sultan, Europeans, the Glawa, and Ben Arafa became targets of attack. A National Liberation Army was formed. European counter-terrorism began to meet the supposed nationalist threat. Some French leaders recognized that their situation was deteriorating because of the unpopularity of Guillaume and his Moroccan allies.

French Prime Minister Faure acknowledged the problem in spring 1955 and held a conference at Aix-les-Bains in August to search for a solution. In agreements made there, Ben Arafa was deposed but did not abdicate. The French promised to constitute a government of national union for purposes of negotiation and the establishment of a throne council. Nationalists persisted in trying to obtain a role for the ex-sultan in the new framework. In September 1955, the French contacted Muhammad Ben Yusuf, who agreed that a new government should negotiate full sovereignty for Morocco. Ben Arafa withdrew, and even Thami al-Glawi did an about-face and renewed his allegiance to Muhammad. In the Rif, the army revolted on his behalf. On 29 October 1955, the ex-sultan returned to occupy his role as Alawi monarch, taking the name Muhammad V. Both French and Spanish Morocco were brought to independence in February 1956. The Istiqlal constituted an important contingent in the cabinet of the new government. Muhammad V, though, assumed the predominant position in independent Morocco.

Independence brought about neither a social nor a political revolution in Morocco. Three quarters of the population was illiterate. With the domination of the king and a small ruling elite, no constitution was formulated during his lifetime. Although the political parties engaged in debates with each other, the press could not discuss political issues freely. Maghrib Agence-Presse, the independent press agency, became a government-controlled body. The nationalists themselves published two newspapers but were not always careful about the news they printed. Allal al-Fasi continued to lead the Istiqlal, although he had objected to the independence agreement because it had excluded Arab Mauritania. The party, linked with Islam, backed the king in any case. In 1959, the Istiqlal split into two factions. The new group was called the Union Nationale des Forces Populaires (U.N.F.P.). Among its supporters was Mehdi Ben Barka, one of Istiqlal's founders. Between 1956 and 1958, he served as president of the appointive Consultative Assembly but went into exile after the accession of Hasan II in February 1961.

During this early period of Moroccan independence, no substantive economic changes were introduced, although French holdings were gradually taken over. The United States gave Morocco grants and loans which between 1957 and 1963 amounted to about $400,000 worth of agricultural aid. Until 1963, the United States also maintained bases in Morocco. The closest economic relationship continued to be with France, partly because many French settlers remained.

The Early Years of Hasan II in Morocco

Moroccan politics since the accession of Hasan II have been characterized by power struggles between the king and the largely conservative opposition. Hasan II's authority in Morocco has to some extent depended on the Moroccan tradition of charismatic and sharifian leadership. As part of his installation as king in 1961, Hasan II accepted the oath of allegiance from the ulama. Yet he periodically sought to lend a democratic veneer to his rule through parliamentary structures. To counteract the opposition parties, the king also created his own from time to time.

It was Hasan II who introduced Morocco's first constitution in 1962 in order to minimize the influence of the opposition. The new document drafted by French lawyers under the king's direction gave him the caliphal title *amir al-mu'minin* and referred to his responsibilities as preserver of Islam. This traditional thrust won the support of the Istiqlal which urged its followers to vote in favor of the document. But the U.N.F.P., associated with Ben Barka, boycotted the voting. The overwhelming vote affirming the constitution weakened the political parties.

To further its own cause, the palace formed the Front for the Defense of Constitutional Institutions (F.D.I.C.). Supporters of the former king from among the landed bourgeoisie and towns, a few liberals, and many merchants joined. In the legislative elections of May 1963, the Istiqlal and U.N.F.P. outpolled the F.D.I.C. in popular votes but ended up with an equal number of seats. Local elections held the same year brought victory to many independents. From 1965 to 1970, parliamentary government in Morocco came to a halt after demonstrations in Casablanca, Fez, and Rabat were held to protest the limitation of access to higher education. Hasan II continued to face pressures for substantive change.

To Independence in Tunisia

In Tunisia, too, the French began the postwar period by trying to preserve the protectorate. French trustees adopted a method like that used in Morocco—further erosion in the power of the traditional ruler and of the French-Tunisian parity in the council. Bourguiba remained in Cairo, trying to promote a Maghribian action movement. The French rejected Tunisian proposals for a constitutional monarchy and internal autonomy, thereby prompting advocates of autonomy (for example, trade unions) to join forces with the Neo-Destour in calling for independence. In April 1950, Lamine Bey called on President Auriol of France to expand Tunisian-French cooperation. Not long thereafter, Bourguiba went to Paris with his seven-point autonomy plan, accepted by French Socialists. A new French resident-general, Périllier, was to guide Tunisia to internal autonomy.

As part of the reform package, the French restored protectorate government with a Tunisian cabinet under Shaniq. French settlers who saw their predominance threatened reacted negatively to the extension of suffrage. They gained the support of the army and the more conservative political parties, thereby forcing the government to suspend negotiations between the Tunisians and Périllier.

Having seen their fortunes suddenly reversed, Tunisians protested the new policies in demonstrations at Enfidaville on 25 November 1950. Although an administrative referendum in February 1951 was intended to end direct rule, Tunisians still had to contend with opposition from settlers. French government promises that the settlers could retain their right to participate in Tunisian politics and that links with France would be maintained were not convincing. Tunisians objected to cosovereignty in principle.

A new resident-general de Hautecloc-que decided to clamp down on the nationalists. Bourguiba, who had just returned from Egypt, was arrested along with Shaniq and others. A terrorist campaign ensued between the Tunisian Fellaghas and the European Red Hand. Again, the French had to retract their policy, especially since they could not afford to contend with nationalist movements in Morocco, Tunisia, and Algeria all at the same time.

When in July 1954 the French government acknowledged that Tunisia was entitled to at least full autonomy, it had to enlist the support of the suppressed nationalists. The Neo-Destour, led by Bourguiba, agreed to new conventions with France in June 1955, representing an evolutionary approach to the national question. Bourguiba returned to Tunisia as a hero, but more activitist nationalists led by Salah Ben Yusuf objected to anything less than full independence. The Neo-Destour, representing a more localized nationalism, backed Bourguiba instead of the more Arab-oriented Ben Yusuf. But Ben Yusuf's goal was achieved nevertheless once France promised full independence to Morocco. The French on 26 March 1956 announced that Tunisia was now fully independent. In a postscript to Ben Yusuf's role, the Neo-Destour expelled him because of his independent campaign. Forced to flee Tunisia, he was assassinated in exile in 1961. Bourguiba emerged as undisputed leader.

Tunisia in the 1950s and 1960s: Political Stability and Socioeconomic Policies

During the early years of Tunisia's independence, Bourguiba set up a one-party state governed by the Neo-Destour. In 1959 it changed its name to the Socialist

Destour. Bourguiba established his power by manipulating or eliminating his early rivals, such as Salah Ben Yusuf. He also proved adept at choosing suitable collaborators and avoiding doctrinaire positions. In inter-Arab relations, he often disagreed with other Arab leaders on questions of mutual interest. His suggestion in 1965 that Arab countries recognize Israel brought on condemnation, but two years later he sent a few troops to fight in the June war (although they arrived too late to participate). Tunisia received cultural and technical aid from France.

One of Bourguiba's earliest associates in building an independent Tunisia was Ahmad Ben Salah, who like Bourguiba had received his education at Sadiqiyya College and in France. After the assassination of trade union leader Ferhat Hached in 1954, Ben Salah took over as head of the U.G.T.T. associated with the Neo-Destour. Ben Salah during the 1950s advocated radical change, including nationalization of all resources and the utilization of trade unions to promote social and economic change. Ben Salah's attitude toward relations with France was confrontational and contrasted with Bourguiba's more cordial approach.

Although Ben Salah lost his trade union position shortly after independence, he became involved in social services after that time. Under his administration, health care improved. A campaign against trachoma was implemented. Ben Salah also created a social security system. Between 1961 and 1969, Bourguiba placed him at the head of Tunisia's economic planning apparatus. Although Ben Salah was not a Marxist, he was a socialist who supported collectivization in agriculture in the form of cooperatives composed of small peasant holdings. He also interpreted Destourian socialism as promoting cooperation between private and state-owned sectors of the economy.

Agriculture after independence declined with the departure of Italian and French settlers and because of poor weather that adversely affected harvests in 1955, 1957, 1959, and 1962. In 1964, the Tunisian government nationalized settlers' land and instituted government coops that Tunisian farmers disliked. Five years later, Tunisian private land was also taken. This, combined with floods in October 1969, provoked a revolt among small-property owners in the Sahil region. Good harvests followed, though Tunisia was forced to import wheat from time to time. Although Ben Salah had gathered a talented group of bureaucrats to promote his economic programs, the protests against the agricultural reforms as well as his success in winning a personal following created a falling-out with Bourguiba in 1969.

In contrast to Morocco, Tunisia's Husaynid dynasty was abolished with independence. Circumstances of Moroccan political life—the strength of the Alawis and the relative weakness of political parties—made Muhammad V the focus of aspirations to independence, whereas in Tunisia, Bourguiba and the Neo-Destour guided the country through negotiations with France. Yet in subsequent political life both Bourguiba and the Neo-Destour, on the one hand, and Muhammad V and Hasan II, on the other, grew increasingly authoritarian although Bourguiba proved more flexible in allowing political liberalization from time to time.

The Algerian Struggle for Independence

The struggle for independence in Algeria was the most bitter, the longest, and the one involving the greatest measure of Arab-world support. The special circumstances pertaining to Algeria's status as an integral part of France explain postwar developments. In postwar Algeria, the disparity between the French and the five sixths of the population that was Algerian widened. Muslims remained divided among the M.T.L.D. led by Messali al-Hajj, integrationists led by Dr. Ben Jallul, and federationists led by Ferhat Abbas.

Because the French pursued conflicting goals—improvement of the population's social and economic welfare, preservation of a French Algeria, and defense of the French minority—they were on a collision course from the outset. On 20 September 1947, a new Algerian law set down modified regulations that did little to meet the Algerians' desire for a separate political identity. Under the new law, French in Algeria would hold all rights of French citizens, but only those Algerians who renounced their Muslim status could be governed by French laws passed by the French National Assembly. A divided Algerian Assembly of 120 members would also be formed. The 52,000 Europeans and Muslims under European laws and the 1,400,000 Algerians who had opted for Quranic law were each represented by sixty individuals. The assembly was charged with handling budgetary matters, women's affairs, Arabic education, and communal relations. With only one quarter of the deputies' support, a two-thirds majority vote could be called for on any issue. That meant that Europeans could still control the assembly. What France was offering resembled the cosovereignty rejected in Morocco and Tunisia, without any real concessions to Algerian Muslim identity.

The European response, though, was to boycott implementation of the new law. The governor general, who governed with a six-member council under the terms of the law, arranged the electoral districts so that nationalist representation would be restricted. Over 80 percent of the first representatives were classified as independents. Positive features of the statute for Algerians were ignored or manipulated to their disadvantage. The government encouraged Europeans to continue modernizing the agricultural sector through mechanization that contributed to Algerian unemployment. With few opportunities for voicing their opposition, the

nationalists gained support. Even Muslims who had sought assimilation with the French had to admit that they would never be accepted as fully French.

The Algerian war of independence, proclaimed on 1 November 1954, lasted nearly seven and a half years. Beginning in the Auras and Namansha regions, the revolution was promoted by the Revolutionary Committee for Unity and Action (C.R.U.A.), a section of the M.T.L.D. that created the National Liberation Front (F.L.N.). The stated objectives of the insurrection were as follows:

1. A sovereign, democratic, and socialist Algeria.
2. Acknowledgment of an Algerian nationality.
3. Elimination of laws incorporating Algeria into France.
4. Release of political prisoners.
5. Negotiations based on Algerian sovereignty.

All Algerians were called upon to join the revolt, but both the militants and masses resisted fully committing themselves until the French had failed to crush the revolt in its early stages.

Muslim Algerian Proposals and the French Reaction

Early in 1955, three quarters of Algeria's national representatives in the Algerian college called for full equality between French citizens and Muslims. To quell opposition sentiments, the French sent reputed progressive Jacques Soustelle to initiate reform measures. However, both French and Algerians opposed him. In the course of the year, Oran and Constantine joined the revolt, too. The French had to admit that their attempt to curtail and suppress the rebellion was inadequate, but they were determined to stay in Algeria after the debacle at Dien Bien Phu in 1954. Soustelle gradually moved toward full support of the settlers' position.

On the Algerian side, some representatives spoke out in public for the liberation of Muslims. Other Algerian leaders decided that their role was to be played in the revolution's Cairo headquarters. Their presence in Cairo naturally increased their contacts with Arab leaders, Arab politics, and Arab intellectual and cultural life. The "Algerian question" in 1956 began to occupy the center stage in Arab decolonization as Morocco, Tunisia, and Sudan all achieved full independence.

Although Socialist Guy Mollet became France's new prime minister in February 1956 and was pledged to achieve peace in Algeria, he continued to insist that Algeria maintain strong links with France. Prior to carrying out negotiations with Algerian representatives, the country was to be pacified and the revolt to be ended. Mollet's policy ensued from the assumption that the rebels had little support inside Algeria and that Algeria's French would approve the idea of indigenous autonomy. He proved wrong on both counts. In order to enforce his policy, over 400,000 French soldiers were sent to Algeria to achieve "total victory."

The army employed tactics such as population deportation and resettlement to disrupt the revolt's internal organization. People were tortured to extract information. During the course of the war, publicity was given to men and women like Jamila Buhrayd, a young educated Algerian woman active in the resistance who was subjected to brutal torture but who refused to reveal the names of her associates. Egypt's cinema industry immortalized her in the film *Jamila* while her lawyer and later husband, a French citizen from Reunion Island in the Indian Ocean, publicized her case through a book published in France. Even if France could win a military victory, it was losing the propaganda war.

The French further antagonized world opinion by downing a civilian aircraft in flight from Morocco to Tunis in Algiers. They did so to kidnap a group of Algerian leaders, later president Ahmad Ben Bella among them. Not long after, France joined in the Suez attack against Algerian supporter Egypt. In the United Nations,

the Algerian question became just as important as it already was in the Arabic-speaking world.

As a symbol of a dying era, French Algeria managed to survive a few years beyond the debacles of 1956. After petroleum was found in Algeria in 1957, the government in France became more sympathetic to the settlers' demands that France retain Algeria. Settlers played an important role in supporting the demise of the French Fourth Republic, followed by the rise to power of General Charles de Gaulle. To strengthen their own case, the Algerian revolutionaries formed a government-in-exile.

De Gaulle's Search for a Solution: Toward Evian

De Gaulle's policy disappointed the settlers. On 4 June 1958, he visited Algiers after announcing that all Algerians should enjoy equal rights and that Algerian development would be speeded up. He felt that Algerians could not achieve a rapprochement until they could interact on the basis of equality. He promised Algerians full French citizenship within Muslim law and customs as well as a unitary electoral college. Although these measures aroused hope even among F.L.N. members, there were no long-lasting results. Consequently, an exile government was set up under Ferhat Abbas. By 1959, the Algerian independence movement had rallied the support of Asians and Africans who assured that it would not be forgotten.

Finally, on 16 September 1959, De Gaulle made a statement about the options he thought would be open to Algeria after the fighting had ceased. His personal belief was that though Algerians could choose independence, it would be a disaster. He did not expect Muslims to approve the alternative of full and direct union with France. He preferred an association with France involving a federal structure and communal rights in Algeria. Although he agreed to contact the revolutionaries, he refused to grant them political recognition in advance. However, the fact that he had embraced the principle of self-determination for the Muslim majority assured that Algeria would be able to choose complete independence.

Nearly three more years passed before the Algerian drama was fully played out. Settlers allied with certain army factions, determined to fight any separation from France. In the last week of January 1960, settlers rioted in Algiers. De Gaulle within six months publicly spoke of an Algerian Algeria. In September, an army opposition led by General Salan declared its total opposition. When De Gaulle visited Algiers in December 1960, Europeans in both Algiers and Oran staged violent demonstrations. Muslim Algerians replied by sending multitudes with F.L.N. banners into the streets. Boycotts of French products such as alcohol and tobacco were organized. De Gaulle was convinced that Algerians supported the F.L.N.

The year 1961 brought about the unsuccessful army uprising of April in Algiers, the opening of the Evian conference in May, deadlocked negotiations in June, and the (European) Secret Army Organization (O.A.S.) terror campaign that culminated in the assassination attempt on De Gaulle's life on 8 September. At the outset of the Evian negotiations, the French released Ben Bella and other F.L.N. leaders. De Gaulle and the nationalists became deadlocked on the issues of European minority status, establishment of a joint truce, and the future of the Sahara with its oil and minerals. He still hoped that Algerians might agree to a special canton for French or Algerians who wished to remain part of France. He also hoped for special privileges for French companies exploiting Algeria's resources.

The last of the Evian conferences took place in March 1962. Algerians and France agreed to end the military struggle immediately. A provisional government would be constituted under a high com-

missioner while the future of Algeria was being settled. Sovereignty and independence were promised to Algeria based on the principle of self-determination but cooperation with France would continue. In April 1962, French voters approved the settlement. The vote in Algeria of 1 July 1962 was overwhelmingly (99.7 percent) in favor of independence. Although the French in Algeria (known as *pieds noirs*, or *black feet*) regarded their rights as having been violated, they helped resolve their own problem by abandoning the country. Fully four fifths of the estimated one million Frenchmen decided that they did not want to be part of Algerian Algeria.

Aftermath to Independence: Political Rivalries

With the achievement of independence, the power struggle in Algeria began in earnest. Algerian leaders faced the problem of reviving the countryside; it had become impoverished during the war. They hoped to take over the most productive agricultural lands, which had been owned by French Algerians. The government's potential for solving these problems was enhanced by the rapid increase in petroleum revenues during the 1960s. But the power struggle delayed implementation of substantive economic and social change until the 1970s.

Algeria achieved its independence through a victory more political than military. Some 80,000 Algerians who had fought with France reassimilated, but others were murdered or moved to France. The nationalist movement was divided among those who had fought the war and political leaders who had spent the war in detention and/or abroad. The Algerian revolution, like the Iranian revolution of 1977–79 was to consume much of its early leadership.

In the early years of independence, the main contenders for power were Houari Boumedienne, the leading army commander, and Ahmad Ben Bella, the leading politician. Ferhat Abbas served as president but differed with the leadership over the question of party rule. He wanted a state in which parliamentary institutions would dominate. In 1963, he stepped down as president, was imprisoned in 1964–65, and left politics after his release.

Muhammad Khider was another early casualty. A colleague of Ben Bella in the F.L.N., he resigned when it appeared that Ben Bella would predominate. Transferring some $12 million in party funds to Switzerland from Lebanon, Khider used the money to finance an opposition to Ben Bella from Europe. Condemned to death in absentia, he was assassinated in 1967.

Kabyle leaders in the independence movement also contested for power in independent Algeria. Husayn Ait Ahmad, Muhand al-Hajj, and Krim Belkacem (known also as Belkacem Krim) objected to the one-party system of government. Having served the revolution in hopes of a democratic Algeria in which Kabyles could retain their individualism, they found the new government taking a course jeopardous to both their economic and cultural interests. By late 1964, they too were eliminated as serious contenders for power. Belkacem was assassinated in 1970.

Ben Bella and Boumedienne were left. In order to counter Boumedienne's control over the military, Ben Bella strengthened his relationship with Algeria's communists. On 19 June 1965, though, Boumedienne arrested Ben Bella and took over the government. Until his death in December 1978, he gave Algeria a stable government. Ben Bella remained in detention until November 1980.

Conclusion

The early postwar years in individual Arab countries were preoccupied with settling unresolved questions related to political independence. Only to the extent that these were addressed satisfactorily did governments then turn their attention to social or economic issues. The interwar period had seen the rise of Soviet communism and European socialism. Arab leaders viewing the rapid material progress of the Soviet Union could not exclude aspects of the system as development models; nor could they ignore the concepts of social and economic justice emphasized by socialism.

The new postwar ideologies exemplified efforts to alter interwar relationships. A period of experimentation ensued in which many Arab governments turned to state capitalism to solve the problem of low private capital investment. With oil revenues still restricted in the 1950s to a handful of Arab countries who received relatively low returns, petroleum was not yet a major factor in Arab economies. Except for the monarchies and emirates, most Arab governments came under military-based rule within twenty-five years after World War II ended, partly because of the military's penchant for quick solutions and impatience with the efforts at problem-solving of the bourgeois regimes. With the ongoing Arab-Israeli-Palestine conflict and perceptions of Arab weakness, Arab leaders increasingly looked to Egypt as a focus of Arab aspirations.

CHAPTER EIGHTEEN

The Pan-Arab Era:
The United Arab Republic
and Its Regional Impact

Despite Gamal Abd al-Nasir's involvement with the Arab unity movement, historians must approach with caution the idea that he was responsible for the hastily concluded agreement that on 1 February 1958 united Egypt with Syria. Egypt had spent most of the twentieth century trying to confirm the unity of the Nile Valley—Egypt and Sudan. Until the resolution of the dispute with Britain, especially regarding the Sudan, Egypt's leaders showed very little interest in the Arab world as a whole. The combination of the agreement with Britain, the consolidation of the revolution in Egypt, Egypt's move toward non-alignment, and the Gaza raid brought Egypt more fully into regional politics, including the Arab-Israeli conflict. They enabled Abd al-Nasir to reciprocate and to initiate overtures for closer relations with the eastern and western Arab worlds.

Resolution of the Nile Valley Question

The Sudanese in the postwar period grew disillusioned with Egypt's insistence that they were not entitled to self-determination. Egypt was willing to grant home rule. When the revolutionary government in Egypt agreed to separate the Sudan question from the troop-withdrawal issue, Egyptian and Sudanese leaders accepted self-determination and self-government for Sudan. In February 1953, provisions were made for the liquidation of the 1899 condominium, an electoral commission to schedule parliamentary elections, a Sudanization commission to assure that Sudanese would take over administrative posts, and a governor general's commission to supervise the transition. In March, the self-government agreement was attached to these earlier stipulations; together they formed the basic charter for Sudan during most of the years preceding the 1969 bloodless coup that brought Ja'far al-Numayri to power. The National Unionists (N.U.P.), consisting of Ashiqqa and others, won the parliamentary elections held in January 1954. Isma'il al-Azhari became prime minister.

Between 1954 and the subsequent independence, Umma Party leaders showed that they would obstruct plans to unite with Egypt. In August 1955, southern Sudanese troops revolted against the new government, especially against its unionist character that emphasized Arab-Islamic ties. The departure of the half-Sudanese General Nagib from the Egyptian revolutionary regime sealed the victory for advocates of independence. The Republic of Sudan came into being on 1 January 1956. It brought on an era of power struggles among the old and new elites.

Sudan's postindependence years witnessed three major problems: the economy with its dependence on cotton for export earnings, north-south relations, and the political structure. The civilian government from 1956–58 was surprisingly characterized by Khatmiyya (People's Democratic Party or P.D.M.)-Mahdist (Umma Party) cooperation, with leadership in the nonsectarian remains of the N.U.P. passing from Isma'il al-Azhari to Abd Allah Khalil. Yet these groups disagreed about foreign policy when former unionists advocated more support for Egypt during the Suez attack in 1956. When the economy deteriorated, the parties disagreed over the issue of American aid (which N.U.P. leaders favored).

The military government which overturned this regime quietly was backed by N.U.P. leader Khalil and by Mahdist and Khatmiyya leaders Ali al-Mirghhani and Sayyid Siddiq al-Mahdi. It soon won foreign aid from both superpowers and embarked on development projects such as the Khashm al-Girba and al-Rusayris dams. Accusations of corruption and the government's view of the southern Sudan as a military problem brought on the peaceful civilian coup of 1964. In the new government, communists and Muslim Brothers were given a role for the first time. Numayri considered himself an heir to the initially conciliatory approach of this government to north-south differences. New political alignments arose that pitted the Umma and N.U.P. against the communists and the P.D.P. Muslim Brotherhood leaders backed the more conservative Umma-N.U.P. group.

Sadiq al-Mahdi took over the presidency of the Umma Party, whose older, more conservative elements broke off. After Sadiq became prime minister in 1966, his government brought about, with World Bank and I.M.F. help, an economic recovery. Moreover, a constitution was readied for approval. Rivalry between N.U.P. and Umma leaders, however, disrupted an early settlement and Sadiq had to step down from his post. Under the N.U.P.-conservative wing Umma coalition, Sudan hosted the 1967 Khartum meeting, severed relations with the United States and Britain, and drew closer to the Soviet Union. Economic neglect again worsened the country's finances. When the P.D.P. merged with the N.U.P. to form the Democratic Unionist Party (D.U.P.), it emerged triumphant in the 1968 elections and formed a government in coalition with the conservative Umma. Further political differences, combined with ongoing economic and north-south disruptions, brought on the officers' coup of May 1969, led by Ja'far al-Numayri. His regime by 1982 had achieved the greatest longevity among Sudan's postindependence governments.

The Rise and Fall of the United Arab Republic

The Egyptian decision to stop insisting on its long-standing policy regarding the Sudan demonstrates that the revolutionary regime was not interested in foisting itself on unwilling partners. But because of Abd al-Nasir's enhanced prestige following Suez, he became the pivotal figure in inter-Arab relations, especially in the Arab east. In 1957, internal rivalries among Nasirite and Ba'thi factions, Communists, and others were sharpened by the announcement by the United States in January 1957 of the Eisenhower Doctrine. This offered economic and military aid to countries endangered by international Communism which was a euphemism for pan-Arab nationalism led by Abd al-Nasir. Only Jordanian King Husayn, Iraq's Nuri al-Sa'id and the Lebanese accepted. Elsewhere, the Eisenhower Doctrine was resented. When Britain withdrew its troops from Jordan and ended subsidies to Jordan's government, not only the United States but also Egypt, Saudi Arabia, and Syria stepped in to keep the regime afloat. A nationalist and socialist effort to usurp King Husayn's prerogatives in Jordan and to restore relations with the Soviet Union, however, brought about U.S. intervention though not troop landings in April 1957. Britain continued to hope for unity between Jordan, Iraq, and Syria, an irony considering Britain's role in preventing a united eastern Arab world following World War I.

In Syria, the neutralist government, which had begun to receive Soviet aid, feared that the United States would intervene in its affairs, too. American policy was counterproductive because the Ba'th, who regarded the Communists as ideological rivals, could not afford to alienate their own supporters by turning to the United States for help against the Com-

munists. When the Syrian government announced in August 1957 the discovery of a U.S. plot, and when Turkish troops appeared on the border with Syria, the Egyptians sent troops to Latakia.

The Communists and their sympathizers suggested that Syria merge with Egypt. The Ba'th was forced to follow the same line that appeared to present guarantees for preserving the shaky Syrian coalition. Apparently the Communists never expected Gamal Abd al-Nasir to respond positively to Syrian initiatives for a closer relationship. Once it became clear that the Ba'th and the Egyptians were prepared to merge Egypt and Syria, the Communists tried to achieve a reconciliation with the Ba'th. After all, Abd al-Nasir had not proved sympathetic to Communists in Egypt. But the Ba'thists pressed on, inspired by the fact that a first step was being taken to unite the Arab world. They assumed that in a united state, they would serve as the main ideologues and political organizers. Their opponents would lose out entirely.

They were wrong. Abd al-Nasir did not desire a shotgun marriage to be dominated by the minority Ba'th of Syria. He preferred a cautious approach that would allow the Ba'this to achieve internal unity in Syria before embarking on plans for union. When Abd al-Nasir nevertheless agreed to the union, he insisted that it be centralized, that the army stop interfering in politics, and that all political parties be dissolved. The union would give Syria and Egypt a common foreign policy with economic guidelines. Essentially Abd al-Nasir decided the form of the union after the Ba'th had requested it. That was the price paid by the Ba'thists. They were later to conclude that the price had been too high.

The United Arab Republic lasted from February 1958 to September 1961. Egypt's complex bureaucracy was transferred to Syria. Then Abd al-Nasir excluded the Ba'th from providing the ideological backbone of the new mass party—the National Union—and assured its representatives only a tiny fraction of seats in the National Union Assembly elected in July 1959. Many Ba'thi candidates withdrew rather than face the fact that their popularity had declined because of the Egyptianization of Syria caused by the union. Conflicts within the Ba'th divided Hurani from Aflaq and Bitar. Other party members left to promote Nasirism.

To consolidate his own position in Syria, Abd al-Nasir sent his trusted associate Abd al-Hakim Amer to govern with both legislative and executive powers, but the honeymoon was already over. Abd al-Hamid Sarraj, Syria's interior minister, enhanced his own position by collaborating with Amer, (the Ba'thi ministers in the government having resigned by 1960), to insure that the National Union would function as a mouthpiece for the regime. In September 1960, Sarraj acquired new posts: president of the Syrian Executive Council and minister of state. Not long after, he took over Amer's post as well. The Ba'th which had inspired and requested the union in expectation of a partnership thus found itself replaced by a military strongman.

Collapse of the U.A.R.: An Unequal Partnership

Why did the U.A.R. fail? One major reason was the inequality in the partnership that was reflected in military, political, and economic policy. Egyptians, though not necessarily Abd al-Nasir, viewed the union as providing an opportunity for Egyptian colonization of Syria. Egyptian financial institutions could operate in Syria, but Syrian concerns were denied reciprocity in Egypt. The government brought Egyptian products to Syria tax-free but charged special taxes on Syrian goods exported to Egypt. Egypt required Syria to import certain products only from or through Egypt, but the Egyptians could not always meet Syrian requests. The U.A.R. also altered Syria's trading relationships with other Arabic-speaking countries, mainly for political reasons. Trade with Iraq declined precipitously, especially in Syrian exports to its neighbor. Exports and imports to and from Jordan, Kuwayt, and Saudi Arabia declined too, although illegal trade grew. An economic organization created in March 1961 and controlled by the state led Syrian entrepreneurs to expect against their will Egyptianization and possible nationalization of their own concerns.

The reception of government agricultural and labor reforms was more mixed. Labor policy involved trying to take control of Syria's unions to incorporate them into the government structure as in Egypt and working to organize new groups among previously unorganized workers. The new efforts resulted in abrogation of the right to strike and expanded disciplinary measures of management over labor. The new legislation that passed in April 1959, however, was followed up by better enforcement so that social provisions such as health care, accident prevention measures, unemployment compensation, and the like were actually implemented. Nevertheless, Syrian workers on the whole resented government control and the decline in their economic status.

Agricultural reform measures that were announced in September 1958 followed the Iraqis' projections for such change in Iraq. The Syrian measures in agricultural relations had already been prepared by the Ba'th. They attempted to set forth mutual obligations between employers and laborers in agriculture. Workers were given the right to unionize, but this provision was never enforced because Abd al-Nasir objected to it. Enforcement of his law in general remained spotty. The land-reform measures derived not from Syrian experience but rather from that of Egypt where farming was intensive. Requirements about the amount of land that could be farmed or irrigated were based on Egyptian models. The more extensive

Syrian system required larger holdings than intensive farming would need. Moreover, the government tried to place independent farmers in its own cooperatives. Peasants resisted when the government took the crop without paying in full, but some cooperatives achieved their objectives and won the peasants' gratitude. Land distributed to peasants on an individual basis, though, was not always the best land. As in the case of such reform in Egypt, peasants could not always meet their payments and eventually lost the land.

The U.A.R. failure also involved a diminution of the role of Syria's military in running affairs of state. Although Abd al-Nasir had stated clearly his intention to remove the army from politics, Syrian officers had not anticipated their replacement by Egyptians or a reduction in their numbers. In the U.A.R., Syrians viewed the Egyptians as corrupt because of extensive dealings in contraband. There were no comparable numbers of Syrian troops employed in Egypt, although certain Ba'thi officers were moved there to reduce the possibility of opposition in Syria.

Abd al-Nasir's nationalization measures of July 1961 helped to seal the fate of the U.A.R. By nationalizing all banks, insurance companies, and a number of large firms (fully and partially), he created a huge public sector and a small mixed sector to exist side by side with the private sector. Critics have characterized the reform as having implemented state capitalism rather than socialism. In Egypt, the measures affected foreign-owned companies, but in Syria they struck against the interests of indigenous businesspeople. These latter adopted a more cautious policy toward projects that would have provided jobs for Syrian workers. Business and industry suffered from the relative inefficiency brought about by the introduction of unqualified managers. The initial impact of the reform measures was therefore highly negative in Syria, although time brought about a more positive governmental interest in national development.

In Egypt the measures—sharing prof-

its with workers, placing workers on company boards, introducing a progressive tax system, and limiting compensation for highly-placed managers—were of greater benefit to the urban middle classes than to workers, but they led workers to hope for better days. The reason that nationalization helped the middle classes was that numerous jobs were provided in the rapidly expanding government bureaucracy. The government guaranteed jobs to technical school and university graduates whose numbers were expanding rapidly because of the expansion of educational opportunities. In Egypt, then, the nationalizations achieved more substantive long-range restructuring of the economy than in Syria.

Civil War in Lebanon and U.S. Intervention

The U.A.R. prompted an early reaction from Iraq and Jordan, who set up their own federation. Nasirism as well as Muslim nationalism in Lebanon increased in influence as President Sham'un, who had accepted the Eisenhower Doctrine, sought to change the Lebanese constitution to perpetuate his administration. When in May 1958, an anti-Sham'un, pro-Nasirite newspaper editor was killed, civil war broke out. Historians generally agree that the conflict was focused on Lebanese identity and Lebanon's role in the Arab world. Sham'un had emphasized a Christian and pro-Western orientation in a state that had only a theoretical Christian majority. Trying to preserve his definition of Maronite hegemony by altering the constitution to serve a second term, Sham'un had alienated not only Muslims but also other Christian groups in Lebanon. With the increasing involvement of the U.A.R. with Sham'un's opponents, the Lebanese president called on U.S. troops to intervene. The United States refused at first, but on 14 July, the Americans entered Lebanon because of a more dramatic event which was taking place in Iraq. In Lebanon, the Americans insured the installation of a more neutral government under Fu'ad Shihab once Sham'un's term as president had expired. The British landed troops in Jordan.

Lebanon's postwar economy was built on the service sector: tourism, banking, and related functions. Lebanon's universities—especially the American University of Beirut, St. Joseph, the Lebanese University, and the Arab University—trained many of the elites of the Arab world. Agricultural production, especially fruits and vegetables grown on mountain terraces and in the Biqa Valley, contributed both domestic and export crops. The freewheeling nature of the service economy, in which few people paid taxes, relegated the Lebanese government to a minor role. The open economy and temperate climate attracted the Gulf and Saudi elites to invest money and spend vacations there. Beirut port was the conduit of goods from all parts of the world. With virtually no army, this "Switzerland of the Middle East" managed until the 1970s to remain outside the most turbulent events of regional and international politics after the 1958 events.

The Iraqi Revolution of 1958 and the Reaction in the Arab World

What precipitated the Iraqi revolution of 1958? In view of the events in Lebanon, two Iraqi army officers—Abd al-Karim Qasim and Abd al-Salam Arif— refused the orders of the Iraqi government to take advantage of the conflict by destabilizing Syria. Instead, they overthrew the regime, viewed in the West as the most stable, dependable Arab ally. A deeper reason for the coup was the involvement of the Iraqi oligarchy, symbolized by Nuri, in the western alliance. Ongoing ties with Britain had been cemented by the Treaty of Portsmouth (1948) that revised the 1930 Anglo-Iraqi Treaty. Young King Faysal II, Nuri al-Sa'id, and the former regent Abd al-Ilah were killed by the revolutionaries. Arif was a Ba'thist who favored uniting Iraq with the U.A.R. immediately, but Qasim preferred an independent revolu-

tionary regime. He imprisoned Arif and came increasingly into conflict with Egypt. Viewing now-revolutionary Iraq as a rival for power in Syria, the Egyptians moved to consolidate their hold in the U.A.R.'s junior partner.

The Communists of the U.A.R. were rounded up as Gamal Abd al-Nasir attempted to present Egypt at an anti-Communist bulwark. The arrests, taking place from 31 December 1958 on, set a pattern for dealing with future opposition. Shortly thereafter, Ba'thists in Syria and Iraq secured Abd al-Nasir's support for an attempt to overthrow the Iraqi regime. Sarraj, who had not yet moved fully into the Egyptian camp, viewed the prospective coup as one which would result in Iraq's incorporation into the U.A.R. Based in Mosul, the revolt that was launched in February 1959 failed because local soldiers, Kurds, and Arabs in Mosul refused to support it.

Qasim's own forces played a lesser role, but the result of the effort was to strengthen his own position and undermine that of U.A.R.-unity advocates. Qasim remained in power by manipulating the Arab nationalist and Communist forces. Because of this posture, Abd al-Nasir in the waning days of the U.A.R. moved closer to two Arab world conservative states, Saudi Arabia and Jordan. American food aid to Egypt was soon forthcoming. Though he claimed to support revolutionary regimes against wealthy oil shaykhdoms, Abd al-Nasir, basically because of Iraqi-Egyptian rivalry, backed Kuwayt during the Iraqi takeover attempt in 1961. Clearly, the U.A.R. had influenced events in Iraq but was also affected by subsequent Iraqi developments.

Final Demise of the U.A.R.

The U.A.R. was brought to an end by a Syrian army coup of 28 September 1961. Abd al-Nasir blamed the Saudis, reactionary and feudal forces, and Syria's upper classes for the failure of the union. He never accepted responsibility himself, and refused appeals of the Syrian coup leaders to allow for a U.A.R. in which each section would be autonomous. Apparently, he did not realize how strong opposition to Egyptian rule had become until his own troops refused to obey his orders to march on Damascus. Although he insisted that he would allow Syria to go its own way, he remained resentful. In particular, he felt betrayed by the Ba'thi leaders who with Khalid al-Azm signed the 2 October manifesto supporting Syria's secession. Bitar later repudiated his signature. Hurani, too, fell out with the new government after it rescinded most of the previous regime's social reform legislation. By 1963, he had forged a new alliance with al-Azm and Syria's Muslim Brethren, and had left the Ba'th party. The Ba'th remained committed to Arab unity, viewing the failure of the U.A.R. as a disgrace to be rectified by renewed effort.

Egypt After the Collapse of the United Arabic Republic

Egypt's bitterness after the union's failure is exemplified in its retention of the name U.A.R. throughout the Abd al-Nasir era. While keeping alive the idea of Arab union, Abd al-Nasir turned his attention toward more militant revolutionism at home and abroad in what he called a war against feudalists and reactionaries. Following up his nationalizations, he broke up the properties of Egypt's wealthiest landed families who had thus far not been affected by previous reform measures. The government limited land ownership to one hundred feddans, cut peasant payments by one half, and extended them to fifteen years. Abd al-Nasir encouraged cooperative projects which his government would assist through provision of seeds, fertilizers, pesticides, and advice about irrigation.

He also embarked on organizing a new political structure to be guided by a Charter of National Action. Presented to a representative congress which met in May 1962, the charter disparaged democracy that did not incorporate social justice and distribution of national wealth. To help marshal economic resources, the government would assume ownership of the communications networks, financial institutions, heavy industry, and various public services. Both international and domestic trade would come under government control but agricultural land would still be privately owned. The charter envisioned an Egyptian countryside that would reach the standard of living available in the cities.

Having long since dispensed with the idea of bourgeois parties, the Abd al-Nasir government proposed the creation of the Arab Socialist Union to bring together the masses who together would constitute half the membership in a National Assembly. Beginning at the village level, party representatives would join together in electing successively town, district, governorate, and national bodies, the highest of which would be the assembly. After October 1965, however, Abd al-Nasir isolated from the mass party a guiding elite to be trained at the newly founded Institute of Socialist Affairs.

In the social sphere, the charter referred to the need for family planning (birth control) in order to achieve the social goals of the revolution. Family planning was and has remained a sensitive issue, especially for Muslim Egyptians. Abd al-Nasir also envisaged equality between men and women. It is difficult to know just how he intended to implement this goal. Village women often controlled land and animals; these supported them even if their husbands died. Such a woman would not need to work for wages and might even be able to buy a shop. Often acting as managers as well as advisors to sons and daughters, women in the village could participate in village political life. In this respect, they tended to enjoy more freedom economically than urban women who were more likely to be employed as wage laborers, often on an occasional and temporary basis.

Even though the National Charter was approved without alterations, the provisions regarding women did not end discrimination in the workplace. Nearly twenty-five years later, Egypt's working women still found themselves subject to harassment, unhealthy working conditions, unpaid maternity leave, and low wages, but they still tended to regard themselves as better off than women in the countryside. Many more prosperous women secured secondary and higher education, though, and found good jobs in the government or in private enterprise.

Despite its new national action program, Egypt remained an active participant in inter-Arab affairs. Threatening in August 1962 to leave the Arab League, Abd al-Nasir told his fellow Arabs that he was aiming at "unity of purpose" without which any other kind of unity was meaningless. If they felt that he was destroying unity, it was only because they themselves were divided as to their national goals and the methods for achieving them.

Saudi Arabia and Inter-Arab Relations

Besides Syria, Iraq, and Jordan, Arabian Peninsula states were apprehensive about Egypt's role in the Arab world. In Saudi Arabia, Abd al-Aziz died in 1953 and was succeeded by his son Sa'ud who tried to increase the country's independence by arranging for separate oil transport. Sa'ud decided later that his future lay in intermittent agreements with the United States. Belatedly, the Americans had to admit that Sa'ud was accumulating debts not for national development but for his own personal pleasure. Instead of becoming financially secure, the Saudis were heading for disaster. The United States pressured the Saudi royal family first to give more power to Crown Prince Faysal and later to depose Sa'ud. Another significant factor was the accusation in 1958 that Saud had concocted an assassination plot against Abd al-Nasir. Sa'ud's brothers sought to reduce tension with Egypt.

Saudi Arabia also became involved in a dispute with Oman and the Gulf emirates over the Buraymi oasis. Although Musqat and Abu Dhabi had controlled this interior oasis, the Saudis were pressured by A.R.A.M.C.O. to take it over in order to obtain a concession. In 1952, Saudi forces moved in, but in 1955 the British (on behalf of the Gulf emirates and Oman) gained back the nine villages involved in the takeover. Abu Dhabi and Musqat divided the area in 1955, with the former taking six villages and the latter, three. The dispute showed the impact of petroleum on inter-Arab relations.

Moreover, A.R.A.M.C.O. furthered strengthening of U.S.-Saudi defense ties. The Saudis maintained both an army and a national guard. The United States aided the establishment of both groups. While the national guard focused on safeguarding the oil fields and urban areas, the army's task involved defense against external attacks and internal disorders. In 1962, the U.S.-built military base at Dhahran reverted to Saudi ownership because the Saudis terminated the lease. In the mid-1960s, the Saudis purchased arms and defense systems from Britian and France as well as from the United States. These arms enabled the Saudi-U.A.R. rivalry to erupt in a proxy war in Yemen, but the Saudi army remained small.

Conflict in the Yemen and Oman

The Yemeni regime of Imam Ahmad loosely federated with the U.A.R. between 1958 and 1961 before Abd al-Nasir abrogated the arrangement. During that time, Egypt introduced new technology and progressive reforms. Within a month after the 1962 Arab League debates, Egypt, Saudi Arabia, and Yemen became embroiled in a conflict provoked by Imam Ahmad's death. His weak son Muhammad al-Badr could not rally the Yemeni armed forces to his side when pro-Nasirite officers revolted. Saudi Arabia began to back the royalists while Egypt took sides with the republicans.

Egypt's experience in Yemen proved to be not unlike that of the United States in Vietnam. Egyptian troops, as many as 50,000 at one time, could not woo the Shi'i tribesmen away from the imam, nor could they give the largely Sunni officers a military victory. Although Soviet and Chinese economic aid supplemented that of Egypt, the war nullified economic gains. Besides Yemen's famous coffee (*mokha*), fruit and vegetable cultivation provided potential exports. Yemenis also grew *qat*, a plant drug widely used within the country.

The more widespread impact of the Yemeni war was revealed when the Saudis, in a move designed to counter criticism of the monarchy, announced the abolition of slavery. To the south of Yemen, nationalists in Britain's colony at Aden resisted a British-sponsored federation with tribal leaders of the Aden protectorate in the Hadhramaut. Aden port was a major stop for oil tankers; it maintained its own refinery. A British base provided jobs and revenues. In the Hadhramaut, 75 percent of the population tried to eke out a living from the 1 percent of the cultivable land. The Arab world grew increasingly polarized between "progressive" and "reactionary" regimes exemplified respectively by Egypt and Saudi Arabia. In the Arabian peninsula, the "reactionaries" were clearly on the defensive.

The war in Yemen lingered on even after Saudi Arabia and Egypt reached the Jidda Agreement of August 1965. In November 1966, Egyptian planes dropped bombs on villages in Saudi-claimed territory. In the following January, Egypt's air force attacked royalist strongholds. It was not until after the June 1967 Middle East war that Egypt and Saudi Arabia agreed to withdraw finally from Yemen. Even then, Egyptian troops did not finally begin to pull out until December. Although the royalists were defeated, republican squabbles brought in a pro-Saudi faction in 1970.

In southern Arabia and the Gulf, Britain had longstanding agreements to provide military protection to rulers. When Kuwayt acquired full independence in 1961, revoking the 1899 Anglo-Kuwayt treaty, Iraq attempted to move into the vacuum left by the British withdrawal. Kuwayt, however, appealed to Britain to send troops to end the Iraqi threat. Although Britain responded, its troops were soon replaced by an Arab League force. This event represented one instance in which the Arab League was able to take concerted action to preserve the status quo. The British were able to move their forces to Kuwayt quickly because of the military and naval base located in Bahrayn and the even more crucial base at Aden. While Gulf rulers generally approved of Britain's role as protectors against more powerful neighbors—Iran, Iraq, and Saudi Arabia—the situation differed in Yemen.

Elsewhere in Arabia, Sultan Sa'id ibn

Taymur from 1932 to 1970 operated a repressive regime in Oman. A follower of Ibadi Kharijism, Sa'id used his authority to keep the country isolated. Even in the petroleum era, the sultan managed to persuade the oil companies to minimize improvements in workers' health or welfare. The revenues, which began rising in 1967, were used for his own benefit. Not surprisingly, Omanis revolted in 1957–59, and in 1966 an assassination attempt failed to eliminate the sultan. His regime survived because the British continued to subsidize his government and serve as officials. Britain also represented the country in foreign affairs, even while claiming publicly that Oman was fully independent.

The Omanis came into conflict with their western neighbor during the revolt in Dhufar province next to the boundary of southern Yemen. The guerrilla war began in 1965. By 1969, it had resulted in the sultan's losing control of most of the province except for Salala where he was living. In 1970, the rebels attacked areas near petroleum concessionary outposts. The Dhufar war could disrupt the entire Gulf region if not checked. It was only at this point that the British decided to support the overthrow of Sa'id, who was permitted to go into exile in England. His son Qabus (1970–) was freed from his four-year imprisonment in his father's palace and placed on the throne. The British denied complicity in the coup, but their role was obvious.

Qabus embarked on a measure of modernization, but could suppress the revolt in Dhufar only by force. The Dhufari region differs from areas to the east and west in its much higher rainfall and tropical climate. Coastal and mountain peoples interacted over the years through trade. Many Dhufaris are Sunni Shafi'is

(like coastal Yemenis) and therefore from the ruling Ibadiyya. On the whole, however, people remained relatively isolated from formal religions; they followed indigenous practices. Oman did not annex the area until the 1870s and thereafter treated it like a colony. The territory might have continued to be just a remote province had it not been for petroleum exploration and a British air base built during World War II. Nevertheless, the territory under Sa'id maintained no health care facilities, no utilities in either town or country, only one school, and widespread slavery and poverty. High taxation prevented escape from this oppression.

Dhufaris traveled abroad for work in the Gulf petroleum industries and in Gulf military forces. Revolution in the nearby Yemens could not be completely isolated from Omanis. Gamal Abd al-Nasir encouraged the Dhufar Liberation Front. The early phase of the guerrilla war resulted in the sealing off of the territory. The Dhufari organization changed its name to the Popular Front for the Liberation of the Occupied Arab Gulf (P.F.L.O.A.G.) and benefited from the existence of the new revolutionary regime in South Yemen. Britain claimed that the petroleum channels were threatened by Chinese intervention, allegedly because Communist Chinese were thought to be advising the Dhufaris. It was a fact that many Dhufari militants had visited the People's Republic of China. The Dhufar rebellion was eventually crushed by intervention of British and Iranian forces in the mid-1970s, after which many Dhufaris escaped west. Potential for future conflict remained, though, unless Qabus could extend substantial social and economic reform.

The Tripartite Union Talks

The thrust toward Arab union revived briefly in 1963 when Abd al-Karim Qasim's popular regime in Iraq was overthrown by Ba'thists connected with his former colleague Arif. Qasim had won mass support by expropriating in 1961 most of the I.P.C.'s concession and trying to invest in national development. Ongoing revolt in the Kurdish north, however, contributed to the undermining of his regime among the military elites. The Ba'thists killed Qasim in the February coup. One month later, Ba'thi forces returned to power in Syria. The stage was set for tripartite union talks that opened in March 1963 in Cairo. The Syrians and Iraqis hoped that they could achieve preeminence in the Arab unity movement. Nasirite forces in Syria backed the unity talks.

Well-documented in the A.U.B. publication *Arab Political Documents*[1], conversations between Gamal Abd al-Nasir and the Ba'this revealed the essential weakness of the union plans despite the federation agreement concluded on 17 April. Abd al-Nasir's remarks displayed his bitterness of the failure of the first union. He mistrusted the Ba'th and doubted its ability to implement an effective union in either Iraq or Syria. His comments also show that he suspected the two Ba'thi blocs of trying to use a union with him to strengthen their hands at home.

His suspicions appeared to have been fulfilled when the Syrians in May and June put down Nasirite demonstrations. Factional fighting between Nasirites and Ba'thists continued in July, prompting Abd al-Nasir to condemn the Ba'th. The union died before it could be established.

Ba'thi Rivalry in Iraq under the Arifs

Between the Ba'thi coup of February 1963 and the anti-Ba'th coup of November, the Iraqi Ba'thi leaders showed themselves to be more nationalist than unionist. They turned to a more vigorous prosecution of the war with the Iraqi Kurds, and ruled by force rather than by democracy. Arif as president continued to favor the idea of union with Egypt and can therefore be characterized as a Nasirite. In October 1963, a Ba'thi conference in Damascus announced the immediate union of Syria and Iraq, thereby promoting a dispute between Arif and the Ba'th and between Iraqi and Syrian Ba'thists. Their joint defense pact lasted only two months, because in November Arif staged his anti-Ba'th coup, rooting out of the government and army supporters of the civilian Ba'thi faction in Iraq.

Abd al-Salam Arif died in 1966. He was succeeded by his brother Abd al-Rahman. Ongoing efforts of Iraq's technocrats and civilians to end the Kurdish war failed. In July 1968, Ba'thi officers, led by Ahmad Hasan al-Bakr, collaborated with other nationalists in overthrowing the regime. Iraq has since been ruled by officers largely from the town of Tikrit in the northwestern Sunni Arab Iraqi countryside.

The Early Ba'th in Syria

The anti-Ba'th coup of November 1963 in Iraq ended Syrian hopes for a Syrian-Iraqi union. With the earlier suppression of the Nasirites in Syria, the Ba'thists were free to govern in their own right. The regime's leading figure was General Amin al-Hafiz, a Sunni Muslim from Aleppo. Because he had not been part of the Ba'thi military

---

[1] Walid Khalidi and Yusuf Ibish, eds., *Arab Political Documents, 1963.* (Beirut: American University of Beirut, 1963).

committee that had outsted the former government, Hafiz proved able for a few years to balance opposing forces in the country. Officers who had hoped to manipulate him were disappointed, but they managed to build up support in the army. The most prominent officers were Alawis: Salah Jadid, Hafiz al-Asad, and Muhammad Umran. Druze and Isma'ili officers also played an active role in Ba'thi military indoctrination programs.

The opportunity to govern led to disputes within the Ba'th about the meaning of freedom, unity, and socialism. Older civilian Ba'this, including ideologues Aflaq and Bitar, continued to emphasize unity while a new generation (including some Alawi officers) felt that a balance should be struck to give greater importance to socialism. Civilians such as doctors Nur al-Din Atasi, Yusuf Zu'ayyin, and Ibrahim Makhus were also significant in forming this more leftist neo-Ba'th ideology. Hafiz brought them into his government but concentrated more and more power in his own hands.

The inter-Ba'thi squabbles impeded the formulation of an economic policy that would lend confidence to business and industry. Instead, investment declined and, with decreasing revenues, the government cut back on employment and wages in the public sector. Because the government feared alienating rural elites, land reforms that had been approved were neglected and led to demonstrations by peasants demanding their rights.

A religious-oriented opposition reappeared to challenge Ba'thi rule, centered on majority Sunnis belonging to the Muslim Brothers and Nasirites. In April 1964, religious leaders in Hurani's stronghold of Hama announced that people could choose between Islam or the Ba'th. Government troops shelled a mosque when opposition forces fired on them from its environs. General Umran blamed Hurani for opposition activities more clearly associated with the Muslim Brothers.

In fact, however, Hurani represented the civilian forces who opposed the government because of its antidemocratic, increasingly centralized character. Urban businesspeople, professionals, and students supported the protests for this reason, not out of religious motivation. Although Hafiz refused to support Umran's effort to discredit Hurani, the outcome was the creation of a more active military opposition within the Ba'th. Conciliatory measures introduced by Hafiz toward the bourgeoisie and socialists failed to attract support. Bitar served as premier in a union government, but Hurani continued to call for a more leftist orientation—nationalizing oil or seeking aid from the U.S.S.R. to build a dam on the Euphrates. The dam would stabilize agricultural production (previously at the mercy of irregular rainfall). By October 1964, Bitar was ousted and the neo-Ba'th increased its role in decision-making.

The government nationalized Syria's modest petroleum industry, including refining and transit facilities. Since the West Germans wanted to build the Euphrates Dam but only in conjunction with an oil concession for a West German firm, nationalization meant that the Syrians were now most likely to secure aid for the dam from the Soviet Union. Further nationalizations took place in domestic industry in January 1965. Even small workshops were taken over, although the government later rescinded this aspect of the measure. The government also assumed control of some 70 percent of the import and export trade. The government imposed martial law to discourage demonstrations on the part of discontented urban bourgeoisie, but the Muslim Brothers still organized protests in collaboration with merchants. The increasingly neo-Ba'thist government implemented many reforms initially imposed during the U.A.R. era.

From that time on, rival Ba'thists within the military attempted to strengthen their positions. General Jadid presented a strong challenge to General Hafiz through his control of the Ba'th's Regional Command. Still hoping to salvage his position, Hafiz announced the disbanding of the Regional Command and the appointment of a new government under Bitar. But on 23 February 1966, the neo-Ba'th officers struck in yet another coup d'etat. The key figure who insured the success of the bloody coup was air force commander Hafiz al-Asad, but the new regime was dominated by the doctors and General Jadid. Bitar, Hafiz, and Umran were jailed and later banished. The old Ba'th under Aflaq's leadership resurfaced in Beirut and cooperated with Iraq's Ba'thi leadership off and on.

In Syria, the neo-Ba'th, generally of minority rural middle-class peasant origins, directed its attention toward undermining the urban bourgeoisie (as it had been doing before) but did not enact rural reform that would appreciably alter land ownership. It also attempted to patch up Syria's foreign relations with Egypt which finally recognized an independent Syria. The regime's premier Yusuf Zu'ayyin used the good offices of the Soviet Union to achieve the reconciliation after having accepted the offer of the U.S.S.R. to build the Euphrates (now Tabqa) Dam. For their part, the Soviets made an international commitment to uphold the regime. Although the neo-Ba'th brought one Communist minister into the government and allowed Baqdash to return from exile, Communist newspapers remained banned. Soviet economic and political aid did not translate into a pro-Communist policy in Syria.

One Druze officer, Major Salim Hatum, however, first sought Communist support and then accused the government of being Communist-controlled. He had been a key figure in the February coup. His coup attempt from the Jabal Druze failed because the government rallied its own troops. Hatum further eroded his position by enlisting Jordanian support for his revolt. This event of September 1966 eliminated one of the major minority factions that had supported the neo-Ba'th: the Druze officers. Hatum was executed in June 1967 when he returned to Syria during the June war.

The neo-Ba'th leaders were blamed for the defeat in 1967. Even Syrian support for Palestinian nationalism, exemplified by its creation of the Palestinian liberation group al-Sa'iqa and support for Fatah, did not translate into a postwar anti-Israeli campaign. Syrian officers were reluctant to involve the regular army in military action against Israel. Moreover, the government safeguarded the interests of most Jewish Syrians during and after the 1967 War.

Conclusion

The pan-Arab era did not end with the 1967 war, but the challenge of a greater Israel made the Arab-Israeli conflict more pressing than inter-Arab squabbles. With portions of Syria and Egypt as well as Gaza and Palestinian portions of Jordan under Israeli occupation, attention shifted to bringing about an Israeli withdrawal. Although leaders embarked on new efforts to unite Arab countries, the 1970s was largely a decade of stability and retrenchment. With the death of Gamal Abd al-Nasir and Egypt's reorientation under Sadat (September 1970–October 1981), Libya's Mu'ammar al-Qadhdhafi became the region's principal proponent of Arab unity.

CHAPTER NINETEEN

Palestine and the Arab-Israeli Conflict from 1967

The 1967 War brought new Palestinian territory under Israeli occupation and further complicated prospects for peace. The question of Palestine—how to resolve two mutually exclusive claims to the land—remained the outstanding fundamental issue. To the Arab-Israeli conflict was added the new dimension of occupied territory. As long as the Arab-Israeli conflict (and the occupation of parts of Syria, Egypt, and Jordan) continued, both the Arab states and Israel could avoid directly addressing the Palestinian question. At times, the Arab-Israeli dispute also distracted both Israel and various Arab countries from domestic problems. The Palestinian resistance that evolved in the diaspora in the wake of the 1967 War showed that Palestinians could and would try to obstruct any settlement pertaining to them that excluded P.L.O. participation and self-determination. Jordan's initial annexation of the West Bank made its status an even greater question mark, with Palestinians, Jordanians, and Israelis all claiming the right to decide its future and that of its Palestinian population.

Consequences of the 1967 War: Local and International

The 1967 War added other new dimensions to the conflict. It created between 150,000 and 200,000 new Palestinian refugees who fled the West Bank for presumed safety in Jordan. A further 100,000 Syrians left the Julan (Golan) Heights while some 300,000 Egyptians evacuated Sinai and the canal cities. Jordan suffered further hardship from the closure of the Suez Canal; this brought about the decline of port traffic to Aqaba. Moreover, the holy places for Christians (notably Bethlehem, the Jordan River, Qumran, Jericho, and Jerusalem) and for Muslims (al-Aqsa Mosque and the Dome of the Rock in Jerusalem and tombs of the patriarchs in Khalil) came under Israeli authority. Jordan's largely unknown treasures at Jerash, Petra, Kerak, and Madaba could hardly make up the difference in lost revenues from pilgrimages and tourism. West Bank farmland production was also lost to the Jordanians.

For Egypt's Abd al-Nasir, the humiliation was such that on 9 June, he proffered his resignation as president to the Egyptian people. Widespread demonstrations throughout the Arab world and the support of the Egyptian National Assembly, however, convinced him to stay in office. Abd al-Nasir seemed to recognize that he had overplayed his hand. Had he fully anticipated war, he should have recalled his best troops stationed in Yemen, but he had not done so. Instead, he had left Egypt vulnerable to attack, trusting in the promises of the United States and the Soviet Union while provoking Israel with statements the Israelis interpreted as threatening their statehood and the lives of their people.

Britain and the United States, accused by Egypt and Jordan during the war of having participated in the fighting on the Israeli side, suffered a decline in prestige. Despite the lack of concrete proof, Britain's unacknowledged collusion of 1956 lent credence to the accusation. Although the U.S. defense leadership had viewed Israel as a strategic liability, administrations after 1967 began considering it an asset. The idea that Israel served as a radicalizing force in the region lost ground to the view that it helped deter Soviet aggression.

Between 1969 and 1979, Israel received in all some $20 billion in U.S. military supplies, mostly provided by low-cost loans and/or grants-in-aid. In 1980, Israel possessed the world's seventh-largest military inventory, including both sophisticated U.S.-made and Israeli-developed equipment. Moreover, the 1967 war aroused profound sympathy for Israel among Western, especially American, Jews. Within one week some $500 million in donations was raised in the United States alone. Promises of increased investment in Israel were soon forthcoming. From these foreign commitments, the Israeli economy secured a much needed boost.

From Khartum to the War of Attrition

But the war did not bring peace to Israel. The Arab failure to prevent the catastrophe fueled the Palestinian national movement. Palestinians decided that only on their own initiative would they achieve self-determination and national recognition. Arab leaders met in Khartum in August 1967 and adopted the seemingly inflexible position of what Israel called the "three noes": no to negotiation, no to recognition, and no to peace. These noes, however, would be rescinded if Israel recognized Palestinian rights and withdrew

from all territories occupied during the war. The door, then, had been left open for Israel to acknowledge the national rights of Palestinians. The Arabs felt that their only bargaining chip was recognition of Israel. If they conceded it at the outset, without securing mutual recognition for the Palestinians, they risked gaining nothing. In retrospect, they might have achieved territorial concessions from Israel by negotiating immediately instead of allowing the Israelis to consolidate their hold over the territories.

The Khartum meeting produced other important decisions. Kuwayt and Saudi Arabia assured Egypt and Jordan of financial aid to offset their losses in the war and the cost of continuing the struggle. Kuwayt promised $50 million per year; Libya and Saudi Arabia made commitments of $30 million and $50 million respectively. In order to pay these subsidies, an embargo on oil shipments to Britain, the United States, and West Germany would have to be dropped. France escaped these sanctions because of neutrality during the war.

U.N. Resolution 242 and the Jarring Mission

As a final consequence to the war, the United Nations attempted to set up a framework for peace by the passage of Security Council Resolution 242 on 22 November 1967. It called for the following:

1. Israeli withdrawal from territories occupied during the recent conflict.
2. An end to belligerency and respect for and acknowledgment of sovereignty, territorial integrity, and the political independence of every state in the region.
3. The right of all states to live in peace within secure and recognized boundaries free from threats of acts of force.
4. Freedom of navigation through international waterways.
5. A just settlement to the refugee problem.

What exactly did these provisions mean? To the Israelis, the phrase "secure and recognized boundaries" meant that some boundary adjustment would take place. "Withdrawal from territories" meant some, not all, territories occupied. Arab parties to the dispute viewed the resolution differently. They too were interested in secure and recognized boundaries because their own had proved vulnerable to Israeli attack. They re-garded Israeli withdrawal from all territories occupied as a precondition for establishing peace. As for the Palestinians, the statement about a settlement of the refugee problem only reaffirmed resolutions the UN General Assembly had been passing for years. These stated that Palestinians ought to be allowed to return to their homes from which they had fled during the wars. Nothing was said about their national rights.

Because of the ambiguity of Resolution 242, it did not promote regional peace. Palestinian resentment at the omission of their rights grew during the following years. Although Israel insisted that not all territories were included in "withdrawal from territories," it interpreted "freedom of navigation through international waterways" as meaning *all* waterways. Concern over passage through the Straits of Tiran, though, proved superfluous during the 1973 war when Egypt blocked the southern end of the Red Sea (the Bab al-Mandab Straits).

The fact that Resolution 242 represented a compromise offered by Britain to the Security Council meant that not all parties would gain full satisfaction. Yet, U.N. members agreed that the resolution contained useful principles and that the United Nations should play a key role in furthering a settlement. Perhaps the most important provision of Resolution 242 required U.N. Secretary General U Thant to appoint a mediator to encourage negotiations.

One day after the passage of Resolution 242, Swedish ambassador to Moscow, Dr. Gunnar Jarring, a diplomat with Middle East experience, took up a new supplementary assignment as U.N. special representative. Jarring spent some six years trying to resolve the ongoing conflict peacefully. Both superpowers, though perceived by some as partisans in the dispute, supported his efforts, but they also kept arming the disputants. The break in diplomatic relations between the Soviet Union and Israel and between the United States and a number of Arab states limited superpower effectiveness in promoting a settlement.

International efforts to resolve the issues of the 1967 War were both numerous and persistent, although they failed in the end. In 1968 and 1969, Jarring held many meetings with the disputants. Because both Egypt and Jordan had accepted Resolution 242, Jarring hoped that he could bring them together with Israel. After nearly one and a half years of talks, both Egypt and Jordan stated their willingness to accept a phased Israeli withdrawal in conjunction with enforcing the other provisions of the resolution. Israel, however, continued to insist on direct talks with individual Arab countries and on the necessity for boundary alterations. While Egypt and Jordan desired a comprehensive settlement on all issues simultaneously, Israel felt that the refugee question required international agreement that would not necessarily follow U.N. resolutions on the subject.

The combined acceleration of establishing Israeli settlement on occupied territory and the escalation in Palestinian resistance hindered the promotion of an atmosphere of mutual trust. Palestinians, especially Fatah leader Yasir Arafat, gained enhanced pride when in March 1968 the Karameh refugee camp in Jordan put up a spirited fight against a full-scale Israeli attack before Jordan's army could reach the scene. Egypt and Jordan could hardly accept direct negotiations with Israel when it was carrying the war against the Palestinians into their own countries. Neither could they effectively curtail Palestinian resistance activities.

Because of the impasse of March 1969, Jarring returned to Moscow. U Thant turned instead to the major powers. Beginning in April 1969, Britain, France, the United States, and the Soviet Union met in hopes of finding a solution that would give security to all disputants so that Israel would withdraw. Having cooperated with Jarring, Egypt and Jordan regarded big-power intervention as crucial to progress. Bolstered by the fact of military superiority, Israel continued to insist on face-to-face negotiations and advance territorial concessions.

War of Attrition

Instead of awaiting the results of the big power efforts, Egypt in spring 1969 launched the war of attrition. Supposedly by initiating periodic military barrages across the canal, Egypt would remind the powers of the urgency of resolving the crisis. What happened instead was that Israel responded by heavily shelling Egypt's canal cities. In December 1969, U.S. Secretary of State William Rogers made two policy statements: one in which he disavowed expansionism and unilateral alterations in the status of Jerusalem, and a second in which he called on Israel and Jordan to accept an agreement negotiated by Jarring that would require Israeli withdrawal from the West Bank. The Israeli reply involved not only public denunciation but also an expansion of the war of attrition. In January 1970, Israel struck deep into the heart of Egypt in raids which resulted in civilian casualties. Egypt's defenses were inadequate against the superior Phantom jets the United States had supplied to Israel the preceding fall. When the Soviet Union brought SAM-3 missiles to protect the interior, Israel concentrated its attacks on the canal cities. Israeli Chief of Staff Chaim Bar-Lev affirmed Israel's intention to continue the war along the canal.

The escalation of the war of attrition brought on a new U.S. effort to end the fighting. In June 1970, Rogers introduced a new plan to bring about a ceasefire. Both Abd al-Nasir and King Husayn accepted in July. By August, Israel agreed to cooperate as well. The ceasefire began and Jarring renewed his contracts. Jordanian and Egyptian participation involved implicit recognition of Israel. After one session of indirect negotiations, however, Israel withdrew alledgedly because Egypt was continuing to move defensive missiles into the canal area. Egypt insisted that it was merely completing moves underway prior to the ceasefire's conclusion and refused to remove them. Apparently, Israel hoped by its withdrawal from the talks to pressure the United States into supplying more sophisticated aircraft and military credits. Once these had been granted, however, the Israelis were less willing to continue negotiating.

Palestinians in the Occupied Territories: An Overview

During the course of these discussions, Israel set the tone for subsequent policies in the occupied territories. The population of Gaza prior to 1967 consisted of refugees, whereas the West Bankers were both natives and refugees. The most well-known expulsions and demolitions of homes after the war took place in East Jerusalem, in Qalqiliya, and in the Latrun Salient.

The 1967 War brought the whole of League of Nations-mandated Palestine, as well as Julan and Sinai, under Israeli rule. Israelis rejoiced in the reunification of Jerusalem that restored access to the Western Wall. Arab houses next to the wall were demolished to make room for large congregations, and partitions were set up to create a large prayer area for men and a smaller area for women. The Israelis set about assuring that the old and new cities would never again be separated. On the hills surrounding East Jerusalem, the Israeli government constructed large apartment blocks which aroused aesthetic concern in some international quarters. Arab and Armenian residents who could not afford new high taxes were forced out of business. Deprived of a livelihood, many left. New apartments were filled not by Arabs whose Old City residences had been destroyed but by new Jewish immigrants.

In a move not recognized internationally, Israel annexed the Old City and proclaimed the unified entity as Israel's capital. The former mayor of the old city, Rouhi Khatib, was deported in March 1968. His wife was denied re-entry after going to Jordan to visit him. Under Israeli occupation, the Arab-owned electric company, which had served Jerusalem since 1928, became the subject of Israeli government takeover. Unionized workers protested the proposed action in July 1979, viewing it as an effort to bring Palestinians more fully under Israeli control.

The Allon Plan

In one sense, Israeli rule meant that the Palestinians traded one foreign government for another. But the Israeli military government represented more than an occupation. The demand of many Israelis for the incorporation of Judea and Samaria led to a policy of gradual but steady colonization by both the Labor and Likud governments. The Labor government set up a line of settlements along the Jordan River; around Jerusalem, Bethlehem, and Khalil; and in scattered areas in the west. These were in addition to those built on the Julan (Golan) Heights and in occupied Sinai. Moshe Dayan insisted that individual Israelis should be allowed to buy land in the occupied territories instead of relying on government and military expropriations. Deputy Prime Minister Allon proposed a chain of military settlements in what became known as the Allon Plan for sharing the West Bank with Jordan. The Begin government embarked on construction of a new line of Jewish settlements in the western and central portions of the West Bank. Construction of Israeli settlements was accompanied by an infrastructure of utilities and roads of a permanent nature. Illegal settlements like that of Gush Emunim at Elon Moreh in the Nablus area won eventual approval despite early setbacks. By late 1982, 104 West Bank and 11 Gaza settlements had been founded with a total estimated population of 25,000 Jews. The Israelis also planned to build a Jewish quarter in such West Bank cities as Khalil (Hebron) and Nablus, the area's largest town. Shechem (the ancient Biblical name) replaced the latter name on Israeli maps. While an estimated 80 percent of the Jordan Valley's farmland had been seized by the Israeli government by 1978, remaining Arab settlements were endangered most often by policies intended to cut off their water supply.[1]

Human Rights in the Occupied Territories

The Fourth Geneva Convention, adopted on 12 August 1949 and ratified by Israel on 10 April 1951, addressed the issue of policy in occupied territories. Article 49 forbade transfer by the occupying power of part of its own civilian population in territory occupied, as well as transfer of the territory's population. Article 53 banned destruction of real or personal property, whether belonging to private individuals, organizations, or the public. Hospitals could be requisitioned for temporary medical use only, not for use as police stations (Article 57). The status of public officials was to remain the same, and under Article 4, people who fled in wartime were to be given re-entry. Under Article 68, only internment or imprisonment—not deportation—were accept-

able means of dealing with offenders. Moreover, Article 78 barred internment or detention without trial except for reasons of security, and Article 72 safeguarded the right to counsel of choice for any accused person. Articles 31 and 32 debarred physical or moral coercion as well as brutality by civil or military agents.

Throughout the period from 1967 to at least 1983, Israel and Israeli authorities violated all of these provisions, thereby fueling sustained protest and the radicalization of Palestinians in Gaza and the West Bank. Israeli civilian transfers, expropriation of lands as security zones, deportation of the territories' elites—medical personnel, judges, women's groups leaders, student leaders, lawyers, journalists, mayors, labor, and religious leaders—were condemned by the International Committee of the Red Cross, the U.S. State Department, the U.N. Commission of Human Rights, and many outspoken Jewish Israelis. Israeli governments demolished many homes, usually on the grounds that someone living there had collaborated through association or actual assistance with occupation opponents.

In the area of detention and imprisonment, Israel was often accused by international bodies of inappropriate practices. After Amnesty International, a human rights watchdog organization, reported strong evidence of civil rights violations in 1970, Israel barred it from further investigations in both Israel and the occupied territories. The International Committee of the Red Cross complained repeatedly about its exclusion from interrogation centers and about conditions in prisons to which it was allowed access. A number of Palestinians died in detention. In 1977, the London *Sunday Times* substantiated serious accusations against Israel about policies in the occupied territories.[3] The U.S. State Department in February 1979 came up with similar conclusions.

---

[1] On settlements and water policy, see articles by Larry Ekin, Uri Davis, and Hayim Shibim in *Merip Reports* No. 78 (June 1979), pp. 12–21.

[2] "Insight Report," *Sunday Times* (London), 19 June 1977.

Economic Integration with Israel

More and more Israelis came to accept annexationist viewpoints over the years. Israel viewed its economic policies as having improved conditions in Gaza and the West Bank. Gazans and West Bankers, like Arab Israelis, were gradually transformed into a proletariat dependent on the Israeli economy. The young and the increasingly landless West Bankers and Gazans sought employment in Israel as a means of improving material welfare. Indeed, Palestinians acquired more consumer goods than before. Palestinians worked in Israel, however, because West Bank employers could not pay equally high wages. Israeli inflation, imported into the West Bank and Gaza, meant that former wages no longer sufficed. After 1973, more construction workers were employed in Israel than on the West Bank; the number of Palestinian agricultural workers in Israel also increased throughout the period. With land alienation, the decline of those employed or self-employed in agriculture was precipitous on the West Bank. Moreover, crop retention was influenced by Israeli restriction of some imports and encouragement of others, often for re-export to other countries. Although Israel allowed farmers in the occupied territories to sell their products to the Arab world via Jordan, Israel's share soon exceeded that going to the Arab countries.

In the area of industry, the occupied territories exchanged light industrial goods for more capital-intensive Israeli products. Israel's occupation and trade policies eventually produced a huge balance-of-trade deficit for the territories. Palestinians there were dependent on Israel for 90 percent of their imports by 1973, and the occupied lands had become Israel's second largest export market. In fall 1981, Arab countries protested Israel's plan to cut a Mediterranean to Dead Sea energy canal, saying that it would dilute the Dead Sea's minerals and reduce phosphate production so important to Jordan. Transportation of West Bank water into Israel was a point of contention in the 1980s.

Although the Israelis pointed out that their occupation, in contrast to Egyptian administration and Jordanian rule, improved health and general welfare, the standard of living in capital-rich Middle Eastern countries experienced even greater improvement during the same period. Palestinians under Israeli occupation consistently resisted Israeli rule. No improvement in living standards could compensate for loss of freedom and denial of cultural and national expression. Strikes and demonstrations were the most persistent form of protest; they occurred so often that Israel accused various American private voluntary organizations of having encouraged them. American efforts to help Palestinians develop their institutional framework were cited as examples of U.S.-based provocation. In particular, Israeli governments objected to development projects aimed at improving water resources.

Evolution of Resistance in the Palestinian Diaspora

The Palestinian national movement began seriously debating three major issues during the Middle East impasse between 1967 and the fall of 1970. The first question related to the territorial objective. Should the movement redefine Palestine as the West Bank and Gaza, or should it aim to acquire all of Palestine? Secondly, what ideology should be emphasized in striving for a nation: unity or liberation? Was it necessary to adhere to a particular doctrinal stance in inter-Palestinian debates, or should individuals or groups with different opinions work to achieve consensus? Finally, what role would the tactic of terrorism play in moving toward realization of the political goal in light of apparent international indifference? These are questions to keep in mind while examining more closely the Palestinian resistance groups that proliferated and grew, with frequently intense rivalries, during this period.

After Yasir Arafat was thrust into the international spotlight at Karameh, Fatah became the most important champion of a democratic, secular state; eventually, its leadership seemed to acquiesce to the idea of a truncated Palestinian state in the West Bank and Gaza. Like other Palestinian organizations, Fatah used youth groups and schools to instill in young dispersed Palestinians a patriotic attitude toward their Palestinian homeland. Fatah tended to represent moderation in the Palestinian national movement, although it carried out periodic attacks against civilian targets in Israel. Despite strong challenges from less conciliatory groups, Fatah remained the largest military and most important political organization within the P.L.O. Its regular forces consisted of about 8,000–10,000 fighters late in the 1970s.

The next largest group was generally the Syrian-backed Sa'iqa. The number in its army probably never exceeded 2,000, but some estimates placed the figure as high as 5,000. Three other movements arising from the old Arab National Movement (A.N.M.) loosely divided over strategies: liberation through Arab unity or Arab unity through liberation of Palestine. The Popular Front for the Liberation of Palestine (P.F.L.P.), led by a Beirut-educated doctor of Christian origins, George Habash, was the first of these to achieve notoriety. Membership in the P.F.L.P. forces varied between 1,000 and 1,500. In ideology, the P.F.L.P. believed in leadership of the masses by a small, dedicated vanguard. Like Fatah, it objected to U.N. Resolution 242 because it referred to Palestinians only as refugees, but the P.F.L.P. spurned the idea of a peaceful political solution increasingly favored by Fatah. Moreover, it rejected cooperation with Arab regimes not fully committed to the Palestinian cause.

The P.F.L.P. received publicity from a series of hijackings of civilian aircraft in 1969–70. Mainly protesting the exclusion of Palestinians from peacemaking efforts, the hijackers also aimed to liberate their comrades in European jails and to strike at U.S. interests aiding Israel. Novelist Ghassan Kanafani, who was later assassinated, defended the hijackings as a legitimate way of protesting Jordanian cooperation with the U.S.-sponsored Rogers Plan.

In 1974, the P.F.L.P. left the executive committee of the P.L.O., rejecting the acceptance of a step-by-step plan to liberate Palestine. The P.F.L.P., supported by two other groups—the Popular Front-General Command led by Ahmad Jibril and the Iraqi-backed Arab Liberation Front led by Abd al-Rahim Ahmad—emerged later as the leader of these "rejectionists." Jibril's group was among the successors of the A.N.M.

The third group that owed its origins to the A.N.M. was Nayyif Hawatmah's Democratic Popular Front for the Liberation of Palestine (D.P.F.L.P.). In 1969, its members split with the P.F.L.P. over collaboration with bourgeois elements in the Arab world. The D.P.F.L.P. (now D.F.L.P.) favored emphasizing progress for dispossessed peasants and workers. In its policy statements, the D.P.F.L.P. criticized both Palestinian and other Arab leaders. It also advocated an alliance with anti-imperialist and anti-Zionist groups within Israel. It rejected chauvinistic solutions like Israeli expansion or expelling Jews from Palestine. Nevertheless, it accepted armed struggle as one means of achieving international recognition of the P.L.O. as sole representative of the Palestinians. Though an offshoot of the P.F.L.P., the D.F.L.P. generally controlled military forces larger than those of the P.F.L.P., and did not always agree with the rejectionists. All of these groups derived their strength from the Palestinian diaspora.

With the passage of time, the P.L.O. as an umbrella group for guerrillas devoted huge amounts of money to setting up institutions to serve dispersed Palestinians. Schools, hospitals, and other social services were placed at the disposal of Palestinians, especially those in camps. The P.L.O. also sponsored workshops and industries. The camps themselves acquired permanent structures and in fact became towns. Recent studies have shown that camp life strengthened Palestinian nationalism through indoctrination of new generations, but this education was more than equalled in effectiveness by negative experiences with Israel and the Arab states.

Despite the independent policies of Palestinian guerrilla groups, Israel adopted the policy of treating all Palestinian attacks as excuses for retaliating against any neighboring Arab country with a Palestinian population. For example, when in 1968 a Palestinian group attacked an El Al plane in Athens, the Israelis responded by launching a retaliatory raid on Beirut airport in which over ten planes were destroyed. In September 1969 and May 1970, Israel again sent troops into Lebanon against alleged Palestinian positions. With only a tiny national army, Lebanon pressured the Palestinians to curtail their activities.

Having found their Lebanese base restricted, groups shifted their operations to Jordan. When Jordan accepted the cease-fire, Palestinian guerrillas felt their efforts were being jeopardized. In early September 1970, the P.F.L.P. forced four airliners to land in the Jordanian desert, thereby convincing Husayn that his throne and control over his kingdom were in danger. He accordingly sent his army against Palestinian concentrations in refugee camps and towns. During ten days of battles between 17 and 26 September, the Jordanian army not only inflicted a stunning defeat on the Palestinian forces but also killed many noncombatants. Syrian intervention on behalf of the Palestinians threatened to provoke Israeli entry into the fighting. The repression by Jordan later gave rise to the name of a previously unknown group that emerged at the 1972 Munich Olympics: Black September.

Relying on his prestige, Egyptian president Gamal Abd al-Nasir convinced the warring parties to come to Cairo for negotiations. He succeeded in arranging for the cessation of hostilities, but the strain of discussions had taken its toll. On 28 September, Abd al-Nasir died of a heart attack. His successor Anwar al-Sadat defied predictions of his own early demise as Egypt's president and proceeded to extend Egypt's cooperation in the Rogers and Jarring program of continued talks.

Sadat, Israel, and the Palestinians: Failure of Peace Plans

Considering Sadat's cooperative attitude toward U.N. and U.S. peace efforts from the outset, why did the desired peace fail to materialize in the early 1970s? What factors favored or obstructed resolution of ongoing differences? In the short run, willingness of the disputants to accept continuation of the U.N.-sponsored ceasefire promoted an atmosphere conducive to negotiations. The U.N. General Assembly, by passage of Resolution 2628 on 4 November 1970, looked toward a comprehensive peace by calling respect for Palestinian rights "an indispensable element in the establishment of a just and lasting peace." Although both the United

States and Israel voted against this resolution, its encouragement of the Jarring mission helped to bring Israel back to the negotiating table in January 1971. The displacement of the radical Ba'th in Syria by General Hafiz al-Asad in November 1970 also contributed to the reduction in tensions.

Sadat's "Year of Decision" and the Expulsion of Soviet Military Advisors

Seeking an early resolution to the conflict, Sadat in 1971 offered to open the Suez Canal if Israel would withdraw its forces some distance from the canal's east bank. The United States sent Rogers to the Middle East in May 1971 to promote a canal agreement. Israel rejected the idea that its withdrawal would represent the first stage in a general pullback from Sinai and reoccupation of the east bank by Egyptian forces. Sadat, however, was so anxious to settle Egyptian-Israeli differences that he called 1971 "the year of decision."

Although Sadat renewed the Soviet-Egyptian friendship treaty in May 1971, he made no secret of the fact that he was looking to the United States to break the impasse; only the Americans could pressure Israel. The United States, however, while sending its representatives to negotiate steps leading to peace, furthered Israeli intransigence by continuing to assure Israel of military superiority over any combination of possible opponents. The Israeli authorities could pursue their settlement policy without fear of reduced U.S. backing. Sadat's "year of decision" was a bluff which failed.

Little progress could be expected in 1972. Because it was a presidential election year in the United States, President Nixon told the Soviet Union in June 1972 that the United States would initiate no new proposals until after the election. Sadat looked again to the United Nations for support while shopping for arms to counter the most recent U.S. deliveries to

Israel. When his efforts to obtain more sophisticated equipment from the U.S.S.R. failed, Sadat in July 1972 expelled the Soviet military advisors stationed in Egypt.

Sadat's action was critical. It must be seen in the context of the Nixon Doctrine, generated out of U.S. involvement in Vietnam, which anticipated that American interests abroad would in the future be protected by U.S.-armed local or regional surrogates. In the Middle East, that policy between 1967–72 led to the emergence of Iran and Israel in regional preeminence tacitly accepted by Saudi Arabia. In addition, the Saudis' concern over Communism in the area brought them to see in Sadat's Egypt a potential U.S. ally that U.S. arms would liberate from dependence on the Soviet Union. Sadat, for his own anti-Communist reasons, accommodated the Saudis by expelling the Russians; the United States did not effectively respond and thus rebuffed both nations.

Sadat's frustration mounted as the United States accelerated arms deliveries to Israel and allocated funds for settlement of Soviet Jews in Israel and, by extension, in Israeli-occupied territory. Israel, for its part, was conscious of its new importance to U.S. strategies in the Middle East after the 1967 victory; it was also euphoric over its territorial gains that gave it both enhanced security and bargaining chips in future negotiations with its Arab neighbors.

Palestinian and Israeli Terrorism

The Palestinians were not even part of the Israeli equation as Israeli leaders publicly denied their existence. The Palestinian sense of isolation regionally and internationally grew. These respective Israeli and Palestinian moods were reflected in the acceleration of acts of violence— Palestinian individual and group terrorism and Israeli state terrorism.

On 8 September 1972 Israeli athletes at the Munich Olympic Games were kidnapped by hitherto unknown Palestinian group called Black September. The subsequent deaths of the athletes prompted the Israeli bombing of refugee camps in Syria and Lebanon and was a contributory factor in the Israeli invasion of Lebanon a few days later (which resulted in many civilian deaths.) Subsequently, a few Palestinian groups staged intermittent attacks in Israel and abroad while the Israeli government launched severe actions against Palestinians and Arabs in general. International sympathizers with the Palestinian cause also carried out acts of terrorism. In June 1972 three Japanese attacked Lod Airport; twenty-eight people were killed and over eighty wounded, most of them tourists.

Among the incidents in 1972–73 were the massive Israeli attack of January 1973, in which 125 civilians in the Julan (Golan) Heights were killed, and the February raids on two refugee camps in northern Lebanon, in which another thirty Arabs lost their lives. Israel in February 1973 also shot down a Libyan civilian airliner over occupied Sinai. Over 100 people, most of them Egyptians, died. No Arab country or group took any reprisal action. In April 1973, three moderate Palestinian leaders were killed by Israeli commandos in their Beirut homes. On the same day, Israelis entered two refugee camps in Lebanon and destroyed the main headquarters of the P.D.F.L.P. Lebanon's inability to protect the Palestinians led to further clashes (the first major ones occurred in April 1969) between Palestinians and the Lebanese Army. Although Israel was condemned by the United Nations for these acts, such disapproval was ignored. A more covert battle took place in Europe between Mossad and Palestinian leaders. By mid-1973, five Israelis and five Palestinians had been killed in mutual executions.

Incidents of Palestinian terrorism or of acts committed on behalf of the Palestinians by others tended to be glossed over by the United Nations. The fact that the Palestinians were a stateless people and that attacks were made by an assortment of groups made international action far more difficult in their case. Moreover, the Palestinians were regarded by many as fighting a war of liberation just as the Jews had felt that they were fighting for freedom in the Palestine of the 1940s.

Whether they were freedom fighters or terrorists, the results for the victims were the same. Israeli actions were easier to condemn than attacks by Palestinians because Israel was a United Nations member obliged to adhere to internationally-accepted behavior. Neither the Israeli settlement policy nor attacks on neighboring countries were likely to be met with international approbation when such acts violated United Nations principles and the Geneva convention. Israel could not be persuaded that its actions furthered rather than halted Palestinian terrorism.

The postelection policies of the Nixon administration in the United States appeared to condone Israeli actions. Oil shortages in the United States during the first half of 1973 inspired Nixon's government to portray Israel in a new light as a force of coercion to be used against Arab oil producers. He stated publicly that these Arabs might find themselves in a position analogous to that of Iran's government in the early 1950s should they raise petroleum prices. Sadat could hardly keep looking to such a government for assistance in achieving peace. There was ample forewarning of more concerted action in summer 1973 when Arab leaders were still hoping for a negotiated Middle East peace.

In mid-September 1973, Egypt, Syria, and Jordan restored their diplomatic relations, broken over a year before. The Israeli response was to send its jets into battle with Syria in which Israel claimed to have shot down a total of thirteen Syrian jets. Syria claimed that the battle was more even, but the Israeli message seemed to be that the new spirit of unity among its Arab neighbors should not lead to war, as it did in 1967.

The October War

The combined Syrian-Egyptian attack on 6 October 1973 on Israeli-occupied Egypt and Syria represented the first time that Israel's Arab neighbors launched an unprovoked attack against Israeli forces. Historians have now determined that Israeli leaders were alerted to the possibility of an attack. Indeed, as early as May they had mobilized for one but did not believe themselves to be in imminent danger of it. Since the attack took place on the Jewish Day of Atonement (Yom Kippur) and during Ramadan, it came as an even greater surprise, a fact that delayed the response.

Egypt and Syria clarified their objectives at the outset. They wanted to break the impasse in negotiations, especially since the superpowers seemed committed to the status quo. The element of surprise and careful planning allowed both Syrian and Egyptian forces to make headway during the first few days of the war. Egyptian troops constructed pontoon bridges across the Suez Canal and quickly overran the supposedly impregnable Bar Lev Line built by Israel. The air defense system Sadat had insisted on maintaining near the canal served Egypt well. Israeli jets could not establish their accustomed air superiority. Egyptian successes created a feeling of elation and pride in Egypt, so badly humiliated during the 1967 surprise Israeli attack. The subsequent behavior of Egypt's armed forces gave the impression that they had not expected to cross the canal so easily and had no concrete plans about what to do next. In fact, instead of pushing ahead, the Egyptians stood ground near the canal because of orders from President Sadat. This respite gave the Israeli forces time to counterattack effectively.

Syria's forces also achieved early success in the war. But like the Egyptians, they focused on regaining part of the territory lost in the 1967 war to alter the status quo. They had no plans for invading Israel. In contrast to the 1967 war, broadcasting by the Egyptians and Syrians in 1973 avoided inflammatory rhetoric and exaggeration.

Yet the war proved to be very costly to the Israelis. Their proportionately high casualties demonstrated that the carefully nurtured idea of Israeli invincibility was a myth. Success in 1967 had given Israeli leaders a false notion of superiority and security. Egypt and Syria in 1973 showed that territorial expansion could not bring future guarantees of peace. With a small population, Israel could not assume that future military encounters against regular armies would be less costly. The 1973 war enabled Egypt, Syria, and Israel to reopen negotiations.

Who won the 1973 war? Politically, Syria and Egypt achieved their objectives. They broke the diplomatic stalemate and demonstrated that Arab forces were capable of fighting. Jordan did not participate in the war, but Moroccan troops contributed to early Syrian successes on the Julan (Golan) Heights. Militarily, the Israeli forces regained the initiative with the massive airlift of war material from the United States (which began during the war's second week). Although the Egyptians were resupplied by the U.S.S.R., failure to follow up their initial successes allowed the Israelis to pinpoint weaknesses in Egypt's Sinai positions. Israeli forces separated Egypt's armies in a series of huge tank battles that enabled them to break through to the canal. At Deversoir, north of the Great Bitter Lake, the Israelis established a bridgehead and crossed into Africa. They penetrated the interior of Egypt, with a huge bulge of territory nearly surrounding the city of Suez.

Although U.S. Secretary of State Henry Kissinger later stated that the United States had desired the "most massive Arab defeat,"[3] the Israelis did not undo all of Egypt's initial gains. What Kissinger had expected to take less than a week after the U.S. resupply did not transpire in full. The Arab Gulf States joined the war economically; U.S. efforts on Israel's behalf provoked the petroleum embargo. Israeli forces were sufficiently successful that they expanded the territory under their occupation both in Golan and in Egypt. By the end of the war, they had penetrated Syrian defenses to bomb the refinery in Homs and civilian areas of Damascus. Had the war gone on much longer, a decisive Israeli victory might have taken place.

Why did the war end when it did? The United States believed that the Soviet Union would not stand by if either Egypt or Syria were overrun. The Soviets, for their part, appealed to the United States (already in the midst of the Watergate crisis and unable to withstand a long oil embargo) to help arrange a ceasefire. On 22 October, U.N. Security Council Resolution 338, drawn up by the superpowers, was passed. It called for a ceasefire and the implementation of Resolution 242. Egypt and Israel accepted immediately, with Syria a day later. By 23 October, all fighting should have stopped. Israeli forces, however, continued to advance in an effort to surround Suez and isolate Egypt's Third Army east of Suez in Sinai. This action prompted the Security Council to pass Resolution 339 calling for return of all forces to positions of 22 October. Egypt appealed for help, and the U.S.S.R. seemed ready to respond. On 25 October,

U.S. Secretary of State Henry Kissinger placed its armed forces around the world on nuclear military alert for reasons which have not yet been revealed fully. The crisis passed. But Israel had achieved its objective; the Third Army was trapped.

The United Nations immediately sent an Emergency Force into the area to monitor the ceasefire. Israel allowed the sending of medical and other nonmilitary supplies to the Third Army. Meetings between Egyptian and Israel commanders at Kilometer 101 on the Suez-Cairo road began. However, troops were so entangled that sporadic fighting kept recurring. The United States, with Soviet support, organized a new Geneva conference to discuss the disengagement of forces. The prominent role the United States had envisaged for the U.N. failed to materialize because of Israeli objections, but Egyptian and Israeli representatives nevertheless went to Geneva in December. Disengagement discussions ensued in which Kissinger assumed the major role, and on 18 January and 31 May 1974, Egypt and Israel and then Syria and Israel agreed to disengage their forces. Both agreements affirmed the importance of implementing U.N. Security Council Resolution 338 and by extension, Resolution 242. Israel withdrew from the west bank of the canal and from parts of Julan, including Qunaytra. United Nations forces created a buffer zone that has remained there. In December 1981, Israel announced annexation of Julan, an action condemned internationally and vigorously protested by its Druze Arab population. In the aftermath, Israel imposed military rule and sealed off the area from outside observers for a time.

Residents opposed in particular the regulation requiring them to carry Israeli identity cards because they did not accept the idea of permanent Israeli rule. This opposition to annexation remained an ongoing fact of life in the Julan Heights. The annexation itself was an obstacle blocking any improvement in Syrian-Israeli relations.

---

[3] Quoted in "Document: Kissinger Memorandum: "To Isolate the Palestinians, June 15, 1975," *Merip Reports* No. 96 (May 1981), p. 24.

Aftermath of the 1973 War: Consequences and Coincidences

Through his bold initiative, Sadat gained for Egypt what Gamal Abd al-Nasir had failed to achieve. He placed Egypt in a position to make peace with Israel and inspired unity in the Arabic-speaking world exemplified by the oil embargo (see Chapter 21). Yet what made the oil embargo and subsequent price rises successful was not the 1973 War but rather the preexisting international pressures for market adjustment. The coincidence of a tightening oil market allowed for its brief linkage to the Palestine question. The massive transfer of wealth to Saudi Arabia and the Gulf allowed conservative states of the region, through their new financial preeminence, to assume a paramount role in regional affairs.

Vast increases in oil revenues, as coincidence rather than consequence, accruing to big producers like non-Arab Iran (which did not observe the embargo and led the fight for higher prices at this time) fueled other developments of an equally serious nature: expanded Western and Japanese economic penetration, exacerbation of inequities between rich and poor, erosion of societal values and, eventually, the Iranian revolution of 1977–79 and the Makka mosque-occupation of 1979. Arab and non-Arab migrant labor in oil-rich states also increased, creating a much greater measure of regional economic integration despite the lack of substantial interregional trade.

In the political arena, the 1973 War brought about an alteration in the Palestinian position worldwide. Although the oil embargo in the United States tended to obscure the Palestinian problem, this was not true elsewhere. The Palestine question resurfaced as a crucial element in achieving lasting peace in the Middle East and stability in energy supplies and prices. An October 1974 meeting of Arab heads of state finally recognized the Palestine Liberation Organization as the sole representative of the Palestinian people. One month later, P.L.O. leader Yasir Arafat addressed the U.N. General Assembly. In late November, the General Assembly passed two resolutions granting U.N. observer status to the P.L.O. and affirming national independence and sovereignty as rights of the Palestinian people. Arab refugee repatriation was also reaffirmed.

But to a great extent, the P.L.O.'s moment of political recognition proved ephemeral. Instead of achieving true gains for the Palestinians, the 1973 War resulted in breaking the stalemate for Egypt and apparently, in removing Egypt from the war equation. As Sadat concerned himself with domestic issues, he turned to the United States for aid in reaching a solution to the Egyptian-Israeli impasse; Syria and the Palestinians grew increasingly isolated. The Israelis took advantage of Egypt's desire for peace to found new settlements, especially in the West Bank. Although more Israelis debated their government's policies because of the social and economic consequences, only a minority favored negotiating with the P.L.O. or even ending military rule in the occupied areas. Expansion of U.S. military support for Israel, in addition to the emergency $2.2 billion voted in the war's immediate aftermath, sustained Israel's military capabilities.

Renewed Palestinian terrorist acts in early 1974 represented an attempt to keep alive the world's awareness of the Palestine question. Within the P.L.O., Palestinians could not agree on policies and actions. The rejectionist split weakened the organization, but its representatives nevertheless talked to Israelis regarded as sympathetic to Palestinian nationalism. Some P.L.O. leaders accepted the idea of a small Palestinian state that would not aim to destroy Israel as a Zionist entity. Palestinian lawyer Sabri Jiryis, among others, suggested that the P.L.O. abandon armed struggle altogether. The political recognition in late 1974 was soon obscured by Palestinian involvement in the Lebanese Civil War which began in April 1975.

Egypt, meanwhile, proceeded on the road to further agreement with Israel. With American assistance, the Egyptians cleared the Suez Canal of debris from the 1967 and 1973 wars and reopened it in June 1975. Israeli cargoes were permitted transit through the canal. Kissinger's shuttle diplomacy succeeded in winning a further Israeli pullback in Sinai so that the Abu Rudays oilfields were returned to Egyptian control. The United States won Israeli acquiescence by guaranteeing Israel's oil supplies and stepping up economic aid. American civilians entered Sinai to help monitor the new Egyptian-Israeli agreement; they were still there in the 1980s.

Israel, because of ongoing deportations, land expropriation, and new settlements, faced protest in the occupied territories. Demonstrations swept over the area between November 1975 and June 1976. In particular, they were sparked by a speech of then Minister of Defense Shimon Peres advocating autonomy for the West Bank to be set up not by the Palestinians but by Israeli military authorities. Autonomy remained objectionable to Palestinians because water and land would remain under Israeli control. Limited powers to operate their municipalities would not change appreciably for Palestinians under autonomy. Palestinian Muslims were angered, too,

by the Israeli decision to allow Jews to worship in the Haram al-Sharif compound in Jerusalem. Within a two-month period, ten Palestinian civilians were shot by Israeli security forces, and Israeli authorities tried to pressure the West Bank's Bir Zeit University (founded as a high school in the 1920s; a college from 1972) to stop accepting Arab Israelis, all assumed to be Rakah activists.

Because its students tended to come from families with modest incomes, Bir Zeit provided an education to a group who could not easily obtain it elsewhere. During the Israeli occupation after 1967, the school experienced frequent harassment and closures. Unlike Israeli universities, the institution was not exempt from taxation and faced restrictions on importing equipment and Arabic books including books allowed in Israel. Because Bir Zeit students often protested Israeli policies, they were often detained, arrested, or denied permission to leave the West Bank. Other West Bank universities existed. While Bir Zeit received financial support from bodies such as the World Council of Churches, Bethlehem University was sponsored by the Roman Catholic Church. Al-Najah University in Nablus was associated with Jordan. While Israel permitted such universities to come into existence, then, it obstructed their continuous operation. Although demonstrations occurred on an ongoing basis, they intensified after the conclusion of the Egypt-Israel peace treaty of March 1979.

Israel's actions on the West Bank in 1976 helped P.L.O. candidates running under the National Front banner to win the municipal elections in nearly all of the West Bank cities. Traditional supporters of Jordan's King Husayn suffered heavy losses. In June 1976, however, the widespread unrest temporarily abated, partly as a consequence of the Lebanese Civil War. Nevertheless, Israel permitted no unfettered elections after 1976.

The New Lebanese Civil War, Stage One: 1975–76

American intervention helped curtail the Lebanese civil war of 1958. The New Lebanese Civil War of 1975–76 (which in its initial phase resulted in 40,000 to 60,000 deaths, primarily of unarmed civilians) was exacerbated partly because of tensions arising from the Arab-Israeli conflict and the Palestine question. Except for a general laissez faire attitude, the Lebanese had failed to establish a consensus about their government. Supporters of social and political reform had to contend with the fact of inter-Lebanese communal rivalries, some of a feudal nature. Extension of the Arab-Israeli conflict into Lebanon exacerbated this preexisting malaise. Heightened tensions led to Palestinian-Lebanese Army clashes. The Lebanese Government alternated policies of rapprochement and confrontation with the Palestinians. Early in the 1970s, Maronite Christian parties committed to their own preeminence in Lebanon stepped up arms-procurement for their individual armies. The two main groups were the Kata'ib (Phalange) Party of Pierre Jumayyil and the National Liberal Party of former President Sham'un. The Phalange was later to become central to Israeli plans.

The Palestinians strove to avoid the isolation that had led to the 1970 civil war in Jordan. After 1973, Palestinians in Lebanon tried to preserve their position in the south without antagonizing the Lebanese. This proved impossible when Israeli raids into southern Lebanon began precipitating an exodus of poor, mostly Shi'i Muslim Lebanese to the Beirut area. In over forty separate attacks, the Israelis had killed by mid-1974 some one thousand Palestinians and Lebanese residing in Lebanon. Neither the government nor the army seemed to have a policy for Lebanon's defense.

How can we best describe the disputants in the war? This was not a religious war between Christians and Muslims as has often been implied. What has been described as the Christian side consisted of the Maronite factions of Jumayyil and Sham'un. The third leg of the Maronite stool was led by then Lebanese President Sulayman Franjiyya, whose stronghold was in North Lebanon and who often looked to Syria for support. A blood feud existed between Franjiyya and Jumayyil. The Maronites were only the largest of Lebanon's Christian sects, but they were bound to pay the heaviest price politically should the status quo be changed appreciably.

Who, then, were their opponents if not Muslims? There were various Palestinian forces, well-organized but not all united under P.L.O.-Fatah leadership. Muslim and secular reformers, most of them Sunni Muslims, as well as Greek Orthodox Lebanese—two of the most prosperous urban groups—tended to sympathize and cooperate with the Palestinians. The Lebanese National Movement (L.N.M.) expressed their concerns. More politically and economically dispossessed elements in the population, including rural Shi'i Muslims and Beirut's urban poor, also supported changing the old and corrupt political, social, and economic order. The group A.M.A.L. came to represent rural Shi'is in southern Lebanon. The Christian Armenians, with an estimated 20–25 percent of Beirut's population, considered themselves neutral and were to be later attacked by Maronites for their stance.

To avoid confusion, we refer to the first group as either Maronites, Maronite nationalists, or rightists and to the other groups as either reformist, leftist, and/or Palestinian, depending on the combination of forces involved at any one time. External elements also played a significant role in the war.

When the Lebanese war actually began is open to debate. In February 1975, Lebanese fishermen in Saida demonstrated against a fishing company dominated by Sham'un interests. They were attacked by the Lebanese army while Lebanese Muslim leaders were striving to avoid an incident. The member of Parliament from Saida later died as a result of the intervention. Clearly, Lebanon's central government was not united. In events still shrouded in mystery, Pierre Jumayyil's bodyguard on 13 April 1975 was shot, an event immediately followed by an attack of Kata'ib forces on a Palestinian bus, killing twenty-seven people. Heavy fighting ensued with Palestinian and Lebanese Murabitun leftists opposing the Maronite nationalists. During the last six months of 1975, Beirut's exclusive hotel district became their main battle zone. The Lebanese National Movement of Druze leader Kemal Jumblat, seeking to establish a more just socioeconomic order in Lebanon, expanded its efforts to achieve national conciliation.

The P.L.O. leadership might have succeeded in maintaining a low profile had it not been for the siege of Tel al-Za'tar refugee camp initiated by the Kata'ib in January 1976. Because the camp was located in a predominantly Maronite area, it was fortified. Lebanese president Sulayman Franjiyya, Jumayyil, and other Maronite leaders officially proclaimed the onset of a Lebanese Christian versus Palestinian Christian and Muslim struggle, extending attacks to the Damur refugee camp south of Beirut. Lebanese leftist and Palestinian leaders viewed the Maronite moves as a prelude to the partition of Lebanon. Besides precipitating a full-blown Palestinian leftist versus Lebanese rightist conflict, the siege of Tel al-Za'tar led to Syrian intervention. In early February 1976, the Syrian-supported Palestine Liberation Army and al-Sa'iqa entered Lebanon to safeguard the Palestinian community. Syria tried to promote compromise between the rightists and leftists. Jumblat objected to Syria's political mediation as too little, too late.

A Lebanese Second Lieutenant, Anwar al-Khatib, showed his own disgruntlement with the politicians by reconstituting forces under his command (as the Lebanese Arab Army) while General Aziz Ahzab in March announced a coup d'etat that collapsed for lack of support. President Franjiyya took refuge in Juniya north of Beirut. Yasir Arafat began mediating between the Syrians and the Lebanese leftists but could not achieve consensus among Palestinians about the future of Lebanon or of Syria's role in it. The main Palestinian factions—Fatah, the P.F.L.P., and al-Sa'iqa—had very different goals. At the end of May 1976, the Syrian-backed candidate Elias Sarkis was elected to a six-year term as Lebanon's president.

In June, Syrian president Hafiz al-Asad decided to establish a Syrian presence in Lebanon by sending in regular troops, not to help the Palestinians and reformers but to fight against them. What brought about the change? Apparently, Asad had concluded that Syrian mediation without action could neither solve Lebanon's problems nor preserve Syria's interests. Asad, fearful of a leftist victory in Lebanon, now threw his support to the Maronite right. Asad's action set Palestinians against Palestinians as Syrian-backed Palestinian forces sided with Syria's army. Egypt broke diplomatic relations with Syria to show disapproval of this new turn of events.

Sympathy for the Palestinian predicament in the war was muted by the 28 June hijacking of a French airliner by terrorists of a P.F.L.P. offshoot led by the late Wadi Haddad. Forced to land at Entebbe Airport in Uganda, the plane stayed on the runway for nearly a week. A female Jewish hostage disappared and was presumed killed. Israeli paratroopers, though, effected a dramatic rescue on 4 July, thereby preventing further abuse of Jewish passengers.

In Lebanon, the Palestinians took heavy losses and despite a sustained defense were defeated. Tel al-Za'tar camp fell on 13 August 1976 after a 51-day siege, two days after another rejectionist group attacked an Israeli El Al plane in Istanbul. Syria's army in Lebanon began consolidating its hold against Muslim, Palestinian and pro-Jumblat forces.

By October 1976, Saudi Arabia organized a summit in Riyadh at which Syria, Egypt, Kuwait, Lebanon, and various Palestinian groups were represented. Egypt restored relations with Syria, and Libya decided to join the final peacekeeping arrangements. Syrian troops would still constitute 70 percent of a proposed Arab peacekeeping force. In mid-November, Syrian troops fully occupied central Beirut. The city was effectively partitioned into two sections divided by the so-called *green line*.

For Lebanon, the 1975–76 phase of the civil war confirmed that the country remained a loose alliance of traditional leaders, each with his own private army and revenues. Israel openly supplied the Maronites based in Juniya and in the South, while Libya was among those funding rejectionist elements. Other countries and their citizens channeled military aid to factions in Lebanon. The first phase of this new civil war ended without a resolution of fundamental differences among the Lebanese and between them and Palestinian factions.

Sadat's Peace Initiative

The troubles in Lebanon highlighted basic problems in the Arab-Israeli impasse. No progress had been made on the Palestinian question, and Egypt, Syria, and Jordan had not rolled back Israel's gains of 1967. The unrest of January 1977 in Egypt showed that the October War had not solved Egypt's socioeconomic problems. Sadat had to resort to antistrike and anti-demonstration legislation to suppress outward manifestations of internal opposition. In July 1977, Egyptian forces clashed with Libyan troops, supposedly to discourage Libyan agitation in Egypt.

During 1977, Egypt, Syria, and Saudi Arabia engaged in discussions aimed at reconvening the Geneva Conference. Syria sought assurances that Egypt would not abandon its Arab allies for an easy peace with Israel. Because of economic difficulties, Egypt counted on Saudi Arabia and the Gulf states to keep the regime afloat. Sadat wanted to avoid having his options limited by Syria. At the same time, he was not yet prepared to risk alienating his Arab benefactors by isolating Syria.

The victory of the Likud bloc in Israel's parliamentary elections of May 1977 created new problems for Egypt. Begin viewed the occupied territories as liberated lands, to be opened as Judea and Samaria to even greater numbers of Jewish settlers. Sadat realized that only a moderate response to the Israeli provocation could facilitate progress toward an overall resolution of both the Palestine and Arab-Israeli conflicts. While he negotiated with his Arab allies, Sadat's representatives opened direct but secret talks with the Israelis, including with Moshe Dayan. Begin seemed to imply in these talks that everything was negotiable.

Meanwhile, U.S. president Jimmy Carter had not remained aloof from these regional developments. He had met with leaders and had sent secretary of state Cyrus Vance to the Middle East for talks. Carter hoped to produce a new agreement among the Arab countries, the Palestinians, and the Israelis on the circumstances under which a negotiated settlement could be reached. Proposals sent to Carter by the P.L.O. signified implicit acceptance of coexistence between Israel and a future Palestinian state.

Based on these hopeful signs, the U.S. and the U.S.S.R. joined forces to produce a communiqué issued on 1 October 1977. They committed themselves to a resumption of the Geneva talks. Then the Americans seemed to sabotage this apparent agreement by making another, different joint statement with Israel. Carter admitted to Sadat that his efforts had failed to break the stalemate. Nevertheless, Arab foreign ministers scheduled a meeting in Tunis to take place on 12 November to discuss the U.S.-Israeli proposal in hopes of finding an acceptable course of action.

Why, then, did Sadat disrupt this opportunity for a unified stand with his allies by making a bold gesture to achieve agreement with the enemy? Sadat's move came at a time of intensified Israeli assaults on southern Lebanon. The war had dragged on throughout the year. Revenge-killings followed the assassination of Kemal Jumblat in mid-March 1977. Until September, rightist Lebanese and Israeli forces on the one hand and Lebanese reformist and P.L.O. forces on the other were battling in southern Lebanon. Much of the fighting took place near villages close to Israel's northeastern border. Israel launched a full-scale military offensive in mid-September. The ceasefire of 25 September failed to stop the fighting. Carter's apparent rapprochement with Israel could have been interpreted either as condoning this latest intervention or as attempting to put a brake on Israeli military actions by lending political support. In any case, Arab leaders still looked to the United States for leadership in the region.

Having already minimized his war option, Sadat apparently decided that a direct appeal to Israel offered better hope for a quick reopening of negotiations. Because the Israelis had assured him that not only the status of Sinai but also that of Julan, Gaza, and the West Bank would be negotiable, Sadat hoped to win the support of his allies once he had sprung his surprise. If recognition and direct negotiations were, as Israel claimed, the only obstacles to peace, then Sadat in a single stroke would remove them and place the responsibility for progress solely on Israel's leaders.

Sadat proclaimed to Egypt's National Assembly on 9 November 1977 that he would be willing to go to Jerusalem and talk directly and in public with the Israelis. When Begin responded positively, Sadat immediately accepted the invitation despite new Israeli air raids on the Lebanese coast at Sur. Ten days after his announcement in Egypt, Sadat addressed the Israeli Knesset before an international radio and television audience. In his statement, Sadat expressed his willingness to sign a peace treaty with Israel, providing that Israel agree to formation of a Palestinian state and withdraw from all territories taken in 1967. Startled and outraged by Sadat's de facto acknowledgement of Jerusalem as the Israeli capital and by his visit to occupied East Jerusalem, not to mention his open implicit recognition of the Israeli state, Sadat's Arab allies rejected his initiative. To the Palestinians and Syria, the move seemed to represent a step toward a separate peace despite Sadat's insistence on resolving just grievances as part of any settlement. He was disappointed when only the United States and Israel agreed to attend his Cairo Conference of December 1977. Nevertheless, he pressed on.

Sadat tried to ignore the consequent bomb attacks on Egyptian embassies. The assassination of P.L.O. representative Sa'id Hammami, who allegedly was meeting with Israeli moderates in London in January 1978, may have signalled an attempt of the rejectionists to disrupt diplomatic activity although responsibility for the action was undetermined. In Cyprus, assassins gunned down Yusuf al-Siba'i, editor of Cairo's al-Ahram newspaper and chair of the Afro-Asian People's Solidarity Organization; they hijacked an airliner in the process. Cypriot and Egyptian troops later clashed in a gun battle when the Egyptians tried to mount an Entebbe-type operation, with Cypriot leaders claiming that Egypt's action was unnecessary because the crisis had already been resolved. Despite these external pressures on Egypt, channels between Egypt and Israel remained open.

What circumstances impeded progress toward a settlement? Egypt could not promise Israel perpetual peace with neighbors unwilling to enter into negotiations while Israel seemed reluctant either to evacuate Egyptian territory or to concede self-determination to the Palestinians. What Begin had to offer Palestinians represented little more than what they already possessed: autonomous rule over the towns, with no political independence and no jurisdiction over land and water resources of Gaza and the West Bank. Jewish settlements in these areas and Julan would remain and expand. Neither Sadat nor Begin could break this latest impasse.

The Carter administration focused on creating a new breakthrough. In September 1978, Carter invited Sadat and Begin to his presidential retreat at Camp David in Maryland. Mediating between the two leaders, Carter finally led them to agree on two frameworks: one relating to peace in the Middle East and the other designed to produce a peace treaty between Egypt and Israel. Apparently Carter assured Sadat that Saudi Arabia would support the agreement. Other Arab parties would go along. Israel was also said to have promised to suspend establishment of new settlements in occupied territories. Contrary to Carter's expectations, Saudi Arabia rejected the deal as did Syria, Jordan, the P.L.O., and others. Not long after that, the Israelis committed themselves to return Sinai to Egypt and to dismantle Israeli settlements there.

There was no unanimous agreement in Israel about the settlements, even in Sinai, and most of the settlers protested violently the government's promise. Sadat continued to pressure the Israelis to concede some measure of Palestinian self-rule in exchange for a normal relationship with Egypt. The treaty had not been signed by the time the first deadline expired in December 1978. In time, Carter's personal diplomacy brought the two sides together again. Almost as soon as the ink on the treaty signed on 26 March 1979 was dry, the two parties disputed its terms. Begin insisted that Israel would not indefinitely suspend construction of new settlements in occupied territories.

Benefits to Egypt and Israel of a Negotiated Settlement

The Camp David accords and the treaty obviously represented a landmark in Egyptian-Israeli relations. Israel agreed to a staged withdrawal from Sinai (completed in April 1982). Egypt and Israel ended their longstanding state of war and agreed to normalize relations. Egypt's removal from enemy status greatly reduced any prospective threat of war against Israel. Israel looked forward to establishing Egyptian-Israeli cooperation in economic development and to the opening of Egyptian markets to Israeli entrepreneurs. The United States promised to provide both parties with more costly and sophisticated weapons for their arsenals. Certainly the majority of Egyptians, though not necessarily enthusiastic about Israel, appreciated an end to the wars which had cost so many Egyptian lives and had brought so much destruction of Egyptian homes and other property. Though not fully trusting the Egyptians and disliking the withdrawal from Sinai, Israelis tended to appreciate the end to Israeli isolation within the region.

Most Egyptians did not understand the relationship between the Israeli fortress-mentality and the long-term physical isolation of Israelis. Each country, to be sure, had created a good deal of mythology about the other. Stereotypes did not dissolve overnight, but the opening of the frontier allowed for sufficient human interaction that the potential for mutual appreciation existed. Jewish as well as Arab Israelis visited Egypt in growing numbers. A smaller number of Egyptians went to Israel.

Even in the most positive light, the Egyptian-Israeli rapprochement was bound to disappoint Egyptians and Israelis. Israelis saw their business opportunities in Egypt as limited. Israelis also had to develop a respect for Egyptian sensitivity about Sinai—especially regarding the question of tourism to resorts established along the Gulf of Aqaba during the occupation. Israelis had grown accustomed to thinking of Sinai as theirs, and Israeli maps rarely designated the area as anything other than part of Israel. A dispute over the border town of Taba smoldered. In the overall area of peace, it became increasingly evident that Egypt and Israel did not agree on its meaning. The Israelis desired an all-embracing marriage, whereas the Egyptians focused on restoring correct but not necessarily cordial relations.

Impact on the Arab-Israeli Conflict and the Palestine Question

There is no doubt that the 1977–79 Israeli-Egyptian dialogue altered the equation in the Arab-Israeli conflict. Egypt undertook commitments involving former allies without their approval. Concomitantly, Egypt was ostracized by other Arab countries who expelled it from the Arab League (its headquarters were subsequently moved to Tunis). Egypt's separate peace left the country politically isolated because it removed Egypt from the war equation and created an Arab power vacuum.

Palestinians, including resistance groups defeated but not destroyed during the 1975–76 war, felt that Egypt had accepted the idea of autonomy to emasculate the Palestinian national movement. They were less than convinced about the sincerity of Arab countries in advocating Palestinian independence. Having consolidated their position in southern Lebanon, the Palestinian resistance groups assumed, correctly as it turned out, that Israel would use its ability to strike at will in Lebanon in order to try to wipe them out.

The political advantage that the Palestinians failed to exploit fully was the favorable international climate created by Sadat's dramatic visit to Jerusalem. Israeli leaders were more likely to be viewed by the world as intransigent now that Sadat had broken the twin barriers of recognition and direct negotiations. If Palestinian leaders in exile and under occupation had indicated their willingness to support a gradualist approach to resolution of their statelessness, it would have been harder for Israel to justify its onslaught against Palestinians in Lebanon. In the end, some of their political goals might have been achieved.

Israeli Invasion of South Lebanon

Were Israel's invasions of Lebanon in March 1978 and June 1982 part of a long-range plan to take over the south, or did they represent acts of retribution for particular incidents? Some Zionists from early in the twentieth century defined their state's desired boundaries to include the area south of Lebanon's Litani River. This would have given the new country control of the area's water resources. There is no evidence that this objective was ever abandoned. Undoubtedly, some Lebanese believe that the Israeli bombing campaign in southern Lebanon was designed to expel the population so that Israelis could move in.

The first invasion of 15 March 1978 was preceded four days earlier by an act of terrorism within Israel by people who embarked from Tyre, Lebanon. A bus on the Tel Aviv-Haifa road was attacked, and a gun battle ensued in which over thirty

Israelis and some of the terrorists died. The Israelis claimed that the terrorists belonged to Fatah although some prominent Israelis publicly doubted that Fatah had played any part in it.

No one theory offers an adequate explanation for the expedition. The Zionist plan for Palestine represented an idea far divorced in time from the recent history of the Palestine-Arab-Israeli conflict. The idea of a reprisal raid is equally unsatisfactory because the Israeli operation evidenced a good deal of long-range planning and preparation; it was simply of too great a scale to be seen as a reaction to a specific event. More than likely, the Israelis had been looking for an excuse to neutralize south Lebanon. Apparently, the Israelis expected quickly to overrun the area's defenders. Ironically, the Israelis, through their frequent bombing raids, had prevented the Lebanese Army from occupying positions in the south by which they might have curtailed Palestinian operations from Lebanese soil.

More than 25,000 troops invaded Lebanon through five different routes, with the heaviest concentrations in southeastern Lebanon. Contrary to their expectations, they met with heavy resistance on all fronts. During the first two days, the Israelis tried to control a ten-kilometer area beyond the Israeli border. On the third day, though, they embarked on a policy of massive destruction of villages. Since the Palestinians had anticipated the attack, some of them had been evacuated, but the largely Shi'i southern Lebanese had remained at home. The Israeli invasion provoked a mass exodus from the south of an additional estimated 250,000–300,000 Lebanese.

Because of the heavy fighting, the Israelis sent in another 15,000 troops. Observers estimated that the invaders outnumbered the defenders by at least ten to one. During the four days which the Israelis took to reach the Litani, they also tried to take Sur through heavy shelling, naval bombardment, and air strikes. Israeli forces crossed the Litani for a full assault on all of the refugee camps in the area. Sur, however, did not fall, and a

U.N. ceasefire sponsored by the United States was imposed. Within a week of the invasion, the United Nations Interim Force in Lebanon (U.N.I.F.I.L.) troops from Senegal, Fiji, Norway, Ireland, Nigeria, the Netherlands, Ghana, and France began taking up positions south of the Litani and northeast of Marj Uyun (see Map 22). The French troops later withdrew. Upon their own evacuation, the Israelis assured that their client in southern Lebanon, Greek Catholic Major Sa'd Haddad, remained in control of the border areas. Prior to the invasion, the Israelis had been supplying this *cordon sanitaire* (an area in which the Palestinian resistance was banned) through their *good fence* at Metulla.

If the Israeli thrust was designed to eliminate the P.L.O. militarily and politically, did it succeed? The answer is clearly negative, as the 1982 invasion ultimately aimed to accomplish the same goal. The strong defense of the combined Palestinian-Lebanese forces inflicted heavy casualties on the Israelis despite the overwhelming Israeli superiority in numbers and weaponry. The invasion of south Lebanon in 1978 became a symbol of resistance of Palestinians against aggression. Moreover, the transformation of the campaign into a massive assault on civilian areas inhabited largely by Lebanese subjected Israel to the kind of international condemnation that might have been avoided by a more limited thrust.

In the political sphere, the Israelis also failed to curb Palestinian nationalism or to destroy the P.L.O. Because Haddad's Maronites and some Shi'i joined the Israelis in fighting the Lebanese, Israel's puppet state in the south was discredited as a representative of the rightist Lebanese Front. This latter continued to oppose a permanent Israeli presence in south Lebanon although it, too, was supplied by Israel. Lebanon's government could hardly play a decisive role in that part of the country under the circumstances.

Even after the sending of U.N. I.F.I.L., Israel's operations into the United Nations zone continued, with a major assault in January 1979. There is no

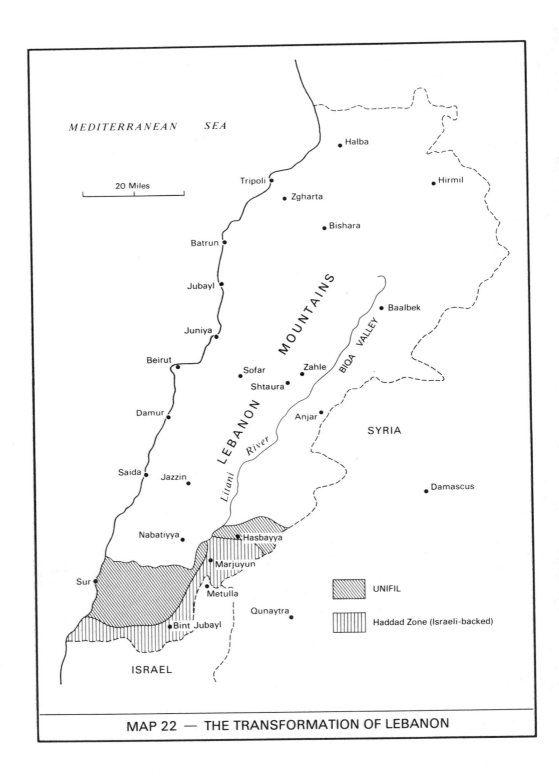

MEDITERRANEAN   SEA

20 Miles

Halba

Hirmil

Tripoli

Zgharta

Bishara

Batrun

Jubayl

Baalbek

Juniya

BIQA VALLEY

LEBANON   MOUNTAINS

Beirut

Sofar

Zahle

Shtaura

Damur

Anjar

SYRIA

Litani River

Saida

Jazzin

Damascus

Nabatiyya

Hasbayya

Marjuyun

Sur

Metulla

Bint Jubayl

Qunaytra

UNIFIL

Haddad Zone (Israeli-backed)

ISRAEL

MAP 22 — THE TRANSFORMATION OF LEBANON

evidence that President Sadat seriously considered abandoning his peace initiative because of the Israeli actions, perhaps because the pressures of Egypt's economic and political problems were too great. In all fairness to Sadat, he may not have set out in 1977 to make a separate peace, but in 1979 that is what he did.

Aftermath of the Egyptian-Israeli Treaty

Tensions in the Middle East failed to abate during the years following the Egyptian-Israeli treaty. Palestinians objected violently to its provisions, particularly to the proposed Palestinian autonomy that did not seem to represent progress toward a state. Though rejectionist groups had rejoined the P.L.O., there was little unanimity over the future course of action. The Israelis, confronted by widespread unrest on the West Bank and in Gaza, tried to suppress every expression of support for the P.L.O. Israeli attacks and bombings in Lebanon also continued.

Despite the growing publicity given to the Palestinian spokespersons on the West Bank, the Israeli military authorities continued to deport prominent West Bank leaders, and Jewish terrorists attacked Arab notables. After an effort to deport the elected mayor of Nablus, Bassam al-Shaka, failed in November 1979, all mayors and councils in twenty-four West Bank cities resigned. Shaka was accused of having supported terrorism when he stated that he could understand the feelings of those who carried out acts of violence. He did not condone such violence, though, and by early December 1979, the Israelis were forced to reinstate him.

In June 1980, Shaka was one of two West Bank mayors wounded in separate bomb attacks. The other was Ramallah mayor Karim Khalaf. Shaka lost his legs and Khalaf his foot. Ibrahim al-Tawil of al-Bireh escaped injury only because he was warned, but an Israeli demolitions expert was wounded while trying to defuse the bomb intended for Tawil.

The assassination attempts against the mayors seemed to be an inappropriate retaliation, if that is what it was, for an attack on Jewish settlers in Khalil in May by unidentified terrorists. At least two Jewish Israeli groups claimed credit for the attack on the mayors. Former American Rabbi Meir Kahane, leader of Israel's extremist Kach, consistently advocated expulsion of Palestinians through acts of intimidation. Arab governments and Israel have tended to be lenient with their respective sympathizers convicted of carrying out terrorist operations. Although unrest in the territories continued, it heated up again mainly after Israel's unilateral introduction of civilian rather than of military rule late in 1981. Palestinians viewed this move as a prelude to annexation.

In Lebanon, despite repeated ceasefires and the ongoing presence of Syrian troops, fighting continued. Although nominally part of the rejectionist camp of Arab states objecting to the whole Camp David peace process, Syria's Hafiz al-Asad had previously indicated a willingness to recognize Israel and work out a negotiated settlement that would return occupied territory and give the Palestinians a state in the West Bank and Gaza. In April 1981, the Syrians became engaged in a battle over Christian-dominated Zahle, the Biqa Valley's major city near the Damascus-Beirut highway. Their main opponents were the Kata'ib troops led by Bashir Jumayyil, Pierre's youngest son, engaged at that time in building a road from their base at Juniya to Zahle. The Syrians feared that the northern Maronites would link up with the Haddad forces in the south. The battle over Zahle spread to Beirut. The Israelis took advantage of the Syrian preoccupation with Lebanese forces to step up their bombing of Palestinians in southern Lebanon.

Considering that Syria had intervened in Lebanon in 1976 to prevent the defeat of Maronites by the reformist coalition, it is ironic that the Syrians found themselves fighting former allies. What had happened to cause the shift? During their five years in Lebanon, the Syrians proved unable to establish the authority of the Lebanese government despite the victory of their candidate Sarkis in the presidential election. The Maronites no longer needed the Syrians after the initial intervention; they received continued Israeli backing. For their part, the Syrians objected to the persistent attempts of the Maronite forces to expel the Palestinians from Lebanon and to the growing rapprochement between the Maronites and Israelis. In April and May 1981, to defend their Maronite allies, the Israelis stepped up their eighteen-month old campaign of shooting down over Lebanon planes belonging to Syria's air force.

As the conflicts intensified, Syria moved a more sophisticated air defense system into the Biqa Valley. American Special Envoy Philip Habib shuttled between various Middle East capitals trying to achieve a face-saving formula to reduce both Syria's defenses and Israel's flights in Lebanon. Military analysts seemed to agree that Israel could not threaten the SAM-6 surface-to-air missiles without mounting both a ground and air operation. Moreover, the missiles did not threaten Israel proper.

With world attention focused on the crisis in Lebanon, Israel embarked on another action that provoked international condemnation. On 7 June 1981, the Israeli air force undertook an evening raid against Iraq's French-supplied Tammuz nuclear reactor just outside Baghdad, killing a French technician in the process. Begin justified the attack based on the assumption that Iraq was intending to build nuclear bombs to kill Israeli children. Oddly enough, Iraq unlike Israel had signed the international nuclear non-proliferation treaty and had kept its nu-

clear facilities open to international inspection. Israeli general Moshe Dayan had confirmed just before the attack that Israel had already manufactured all of the components necessary to build nuclear bombs. While most analysts attributed the Israeli raid and dispute with Syria in Lebanon to the Israeli elections scheduled for 30 June (in which Begin's coalition barely won a plurality), the same actions brought on unanimous censure by the U.N. Security Council, including the United States. The greater implications of attacking nuclear energy facilities were not lost on the international community.

With criticism of Israel already mounting, the Israelis resumed bombing Lebanon once the elections were over. In almost daily raids, they hit Palestinian concentrations in Lebanon. Palestinian forces replied by shelling Israel's northern development towns like Kiryat Shimona, heavily populated by North African immigrants. By late July 1981, about 60 percent of Kiryat Shimona's population had fled to escape the shelling. Israel began sending its jets directly over Beirut. In the subsequent bombing and strafing, over three hundred Lebanese were killed and nearly one thousand injured. This occurred while Habib was still trying to achieve a breakthrough on Syrian-Israeli differences. Some U.S. officials regarded the Israeli attack as an effort to obstruct the U.S. mediation shuttle. The Reagan administration found it increasingly difficult to defend Israel in the face of so much Israeli military action.

The years had already demonstrated that Israeli raids provoked instead of diminished Palestinian shelling of northern Israel. Israeli actions promoted Jordanian-Palestinian rapprochement and suggestions of a future Palestinian-Jordanian federation. The civilian and even military fatalities caused by indiscriminate Israeli attacks did not appear to reduce the numbers willing to fight for the Palestine cause. Although both the E.E.C. and Saudi Arabia's Prince (King from 1982) Fahd made proposals in 1981 for breaking the stalemate, the main obstacles to a comprehensive peace remained unchanged. The P.L.O. initiated virtually no artillery or rocket retaliation attacks into Israel between the ceasefire in July 1981 and May 1982 when Israel attacked Palestinian positions in Lebanon by air. Although Lebanon's economy in the past showed resilience, the destruction of much of south Lebanon's tobacco, cit-rus, and olive industry meant that recovery there was a long way off even before the 1982 attack. The country's banking system and its gross national product were upheld only because the war atmosphere led to increases in home remittances of Lebanese working abroad and to illegal inputs.

The Territories and the Israeli Invasion of Lebanon in 1982

The institution of an Israeli civilian administration in the West Bank late in 1981, and the Israeli invasion of Lebanon in 1982, were two interrelated developments. Viewed as an annexationist move, the imposition of civilian rule in no way relaxed Israel's hold over the territories. Retired Israeli Brigadier General Benyamin Ben Eliezer, the West Bank's military governor until December 1981, called the civilian administration an Israeli provocation that placed Israel in a trap. Israel feared allowing a Palestinian state in the territories, assuming that it would aim to destroy Israel. But with annexation, Israel in a few decades would be a binational state of its own making.

In March 1982, armed Israeli settlers were allowed to fire submachine gun blasts into Arab homes in Bireh while Israeli soldiers stood by. Israel's army met an Arab strike by using strike-breaking tactics and a curfew in Nablus, Ramallah, and Bireh enforced from 8 A.M. to 4 P.M. Between March and May, some sixteen Arabs, mostly youths, were killed and another three hundred wounded by Israeli military forces as Palestinians resisted the firing of Tawil, Shaka, and Khalaf—all elected mayors. On Easter Sunday, an American-Israeli in military uniform attacked the Dome of the Rock, killing and wounding several people.

This was the second major attack on Jerusalem's Muslim holy places under Israeli rule, the first having been a fire set in al-Aksa Mosque in 1968 by an Australian tourist. Further demonstrations ensued. Later that month, Israeli planes bombed Lebanon, resulting in civilian deaths and injuries. Early in May 1982, Israeli defense minister Sharon said: "We are not going to give this area any sign of a Palestinian state, even a symbol of a state."[4] Meanwhile in Israeli-annexed Julan, Druze Arabs resisted Israeli attempts to give them Israeli identification cards, and Israel's troops fired on demonstrators, killing several.

Israel's actions in the occupied territories between March and May aroused Israel's *Peace Now* movement from quiescence. In April, over 20,000 Israelis demonstrated for peace in Tel Aviv, and a kibbutz movement representative, Danny Shapiro, criticized in the *Jerusalem Post* (16 May) "the utter inability of so many of us to come to grips with or even acknowledge, the profound tie which binds the Palestinian people to this land." Shapiro feared for Israel's future unless some accommodation could be reached soon.

Yet the Israeli government adopted a very different approach to its problems on the West Bank. When an Israeli army truck driving in Lebanon hit a mine, Israel accused the Palestinians of having broken the ceasefire. On 3 June, Israel's ambassador in London was severely wounded by

---

[4] *Time Magazine,* 3 May 1982, p. 29.

two Jordanians and an Iraqi. Although no evidence tied the P.L.O. to either of these incidents, the Israelis seized the event as a pretext for launching an invasion of Lebanon long threatened by Sharon.

On 6 June 1982, Israel began Operation Peace for Galilee with its objectives stated as trying to achieve an end to shelling in northern Israel, shellings which had virtually stopped until renewed Israeli attacks. The real purpose was to accomplish what the 1978 invasion had failed to achieve: an end to the P.L.O. as a military and political force so that Israel could proceed with annexation of the occupied territories. It also hoped to establish some Israeli control over South Lebanon and its waters through the reassertion of Maronite primacy in Lebanon. Over 70,000 Israeli troops again entered Lebanon. In Israel, the action was openly described as a full-scale war on land, sea, and in the air. As in previous engagements, the Palestinians offered more resistance than Arab armies had been able to muster against the Israelis. American-supplied cluster and phosphorous bombs—restricted to defensive use only by U.S.-Israeli agreements—were dropped on civilian targets in Beirut, extending even to an Armenian hospital in the Biqa Valley.

After their initial advance, Israeli forces went far beyond their stated objective and began surrounding Beirut. Relentless shelling of the city continued almost unabated despite periodic ceasefires, again used by both Israelis and Palestinian fighters to improve their offensive and defensive positions respectively. Since P.L.O. fighters were well within Beirut, the vast majority of the thousands of casualties that resulted from the bombings were of civilians. At first, Israeli tanks also surrounded the Lebanese presidential palace but pulled back in the wake of criticism. The battle for Beirut finally ended after the August 12 firebombing of the city provoked an intervention by President Reagan. It was the first determined public U.S. attempt to bring the Lebanese hostilities to an end.

Despite protest by Lebanese leftists and Muslims, a quorum was mustered in August 1982 to elect Bashir Jumayyil, the Kata'ib's military leader, as Lebanon's new president. Political opponents declared that it was inappropriate to hold an election under Israeli guns. Moreover, they opposed the election of the 34-year old Jumayyil who might use his position to strike at the Lebanese leftists.

Within and outside of Israel, the invasion and the way it had been carried out was strongly criticized although most Israelis seemed to approve. One concerned Israeli group sent thirty ambulances into southern Lebanon to help alleviate the suffering. At first, deaths in the war were estimated at 10,000, roundly condemned by Israel as an exaggerated figure. But by the time U.S. negotiator Habib had arranged a withdrawal of Palestinian fighters, accomplished by 1 September 1982, relief agencies placed the number of dead at over 18,000, with thousands more wounded and several hundred thousand left homeless. In this, Israel's longest war since 1949, Israel lost about five hundred soldiers, low relative to Lebanese and Palestinian casualties but high relative to its own population.

Subsequent to the withdrawal from Beirut of P.L.O. forces and of the multinational troops who had supervised it, a sequence of events occurred to produce the most serious moral crisis in Israeli history. On 14 September 1982, President-elect Bashir Jumayyil and some of his top advisors were killed in a bomb blast later thought to be the work of opponents within his own party. Ostensibly to maintain order, Israeli troops violated the U.S.-negotiated withdrawal of Palestinian troops by moving into West Beirut almost immediately.

Surrounding areas of Palestinian concentration, the Israelis agreed to allow Kata'ib troops into the refugee camps—in fact, towns with permanent buildings—for cleanup operations. Israeli army officials met with the Kata'ib to coordinate the operation. Within two days, Kata'ib troops killed an estimated one thousand civilians—mostly old men, women, and children—in the Sabra and Shatila camps. Although Israeli troops had not perpetrated the massacre, Israelis realized that it had taken place in an area under their control and within their view, and in violation of a U.S. promise to protect Palestinian civilians after the departure of P.L.O. forces. Arafat's worst fears had been realized.

In the aftermath, the Israelis, though not the Lebanese, conducted an inquiry into the massacre. When its conclusions were presented in 1983, both Prime Minister Begin and Defense Minister Sharon as well as several high-ranked officers were blamed for not taking appropriate precautions to prevent a massacre and for failing to act decisively when they learned about it. Sharon was removed from his post but was retained in the Israeli cabinet. The inquiry showed that Israel was willing to exercise self-criticism in the face of international condemnation, but it did not necessarily portend any changes in governmental policy in Lebanon.

In the Arab world, the massacres helped to further a rapprochement between P.L.O. leader Arafat and Jordan's King Husayn in seeking to reopen negotiations for Palestinian autonomy in Israeli-occupied territories. The entry of Jordan into the autonomy talks was a U.S. foreign policy goal likely to prove elusive unless Israeli withdrawal from Lebanon could be achieved. However, Israel seemed unwilling to withdraw entirely, even if the similar withdrawal of Syrian forces took place. Its protege in southern Lebanon, Major Sa'd Haddad, moved his own troops into the southern third of the country in accordance with Israeli plans for a security belt in the region. Lebanon's new president, Amin Jumayyil (brother of Bashir), was less charismatic than his brother and seemed insufficiently strong to assert Lebanese sovereignty over the entire country.

Meanwhile, Israel continued to harass Bir Zeit and Bethlehem universities. It fired or deported all elected mayors in major West Bank cities. The elected councils of Nablus and Dura (near Khalil) were also dismissed. In their place, the Israelis appointed persons regarded by most West Bank Palestinians as collaborators connected with the Israeli-financed Village Leagues. Even mayors such as Freij of Bethlehem and Shawa of Gaza, who previously had not been closely connected to the P.L.O., affirmed their support for it as representative of the Palestinian people.

Past and Future in the Palestine Question and Arab–Israeli Conflict

In the 1980s the main obstacles to a comprehensive peace that would resolve both the Palestine question and the Arab-Israeli conflict remain. There are mutual suspicions and fears harbored by the disputants, reluctance of both to negotiate, lack of Israeli recognition of Palestinian self-determination and the P.L.O., and ambiguity about Israel's position on the future of the West Bank, Julan, and Gaza.

The humiliation of being a stateless person was expressed most vividly by Fawaz Turki in his memoir *The Disinherited: Journal of a Palestinian Exile.*[5] Like most diaspora Palestinians of his generation, Turki felt that Palestinians, even those like himself who took advantage of educational opportunities provided by U.N.W.R.A., were viewed with contempt by Arab and Israeli leaders. More-

---

[5] Fawaz Turki, *The Disinherited: Journal of a Palestinian Exile* (New York: Modern Reader, 1972).

over, such leaders mistreated Palestinians. Turki also resented the insistence of some Arab leaders that they were only anti-Zionist even when they repressed Jews in their own countries. In working for A.R.A.M.C.O. as an English teacher, Turki lasted only a week when he protested segregation of toilet facilities for Arabs and Americans. For him, the rise of a Palestinian national movement in the 1960s and early 1970s signified a restoration of pride in being a Palestinian.

Lebanese-Syrian sociologist and novelist Halim Barakat explored dilemmas faced by Palestinian professionals in his *Days of Dust*.[6] The protagonist, a Palestinian professor in Beirut, could not seem to take any decisive action, saying "words are the only weapon we know how to use." Palestinian poets, including Mahmud Darwish, Tawfiq Zayyad, and Salma al-Jayyusi, also expressed longings for Palestine which diaspora Palestinians have retained and increasingly affirmed in public.

With the attraction of employment in Saudi Arabia and the Arab Gulf States, unskilled Palestinians as well as professionals have sought employment and new lives. The attempts of poor Palestinians to improve their lot by seeking work in Kuwayt provided the theme for Kanafani's story "Men in the Sun," which ends with the prospective workers' tragic deaths.

Palestinians in the diaspora thus heightened their nationalism in response to a world that relegated them to the status of endlessly wandering refugees. Met with the inability of their fellow Arabic-speakers to find a solution to their national dilemma, they asserted themselves as an independent people. The Palestinian resistance evolved in the Arabic-speaking world as much in opposition to various Arab leaders as to Israel.

The reality of Egypt's peace with Israel, the dispersal of the P.L.O. fighters and leadership throughout much of the Arab world, and the ongoing campaign against the Palestinians in Lebanon and the occupied territories reduced options open to the resistance. The P.L.O. itself became divided and even fought over the strategy of the leadership. Would Palestinians ever secure from Israel more than a token of self-government? Although the postwar history of Palestinian-Jewish Israeli relations did not seem to portend an optimistic future, Israel's Labor Alignment and others within Israel at least were willing to consider the possibility for negotiation. Despite President Reagan's peace initiative of Sept. 1982 American and international involvement seemed insufficient to promote a settlement which, by definition, would require both Israelis and Palestinians to compromise. The Arab plan approved at a summit in Fez resembled the earlier proposals of King Fahd. It called for Palestinian self-determination and a change in status for Jerusalem but also left room for negotiation.

Postscript

There is ample evidence in the world today that unresolved questions tend to fester and that terrorism offers one of the only means whereby dispossessed elements can attract international attention. An example much older than the Palestinian case may be found with the Armenians whose demise was discussed earlier.

After years of quiescence, Armenians began forming groups in the 1970s such as the Armenian Secret Army for the Liberation of Armenia (A.S.A.L.A.), Commandoes for the Justice of Armenian Genocide (C.J.A.G.), and the New Armenian Resistance Movement (N.A.R.M.). Between 1973 and 1982, at least eighteen attacks were made on Turkish diplomats around the world, beginning with the shooting of the Turkish consul and consul-general in Los Angeles by a 76-year old man who had been waiting since 1915 for the world to do something

---

[6] Halim Barakat, *Days of Dust* (Wilmette: Medina Press, 1974).

about the Armenian genocide. Between 1978 and 1981, bombings in European capitals accelerated and in the summers of 1982 and 1983, A.S.A.L.A. terrorist attacks in both Ankara and Paris airports killed several people. Maronite attacks against the neutral Armenians in Beirut heightened Armenian fears of renewed persecution.

The message to the world was clear. Even though the world's estimated six million Armenians were now spread over the world's continents (with two thirds in the U.S.S.R.), a few violent nationalists were going to assure that the world did not forget its failure to rectify a past injustice. Moreover, some of the Armenian terror-

ists forged links with Kurdish and leftist Turkish dissidents as well as with the Palestinian resistance. They recognized that theirs was not the Middle East's only unresolved national question.

We have tried to show that neither the U.N. nor any other great power or regional organization acting alone in the Middle East has experienced more than limited or temporary success in resolving conflicts through mediation. Military intervention has achieved little in the way of constructive action. Unless the Palestine question finds resolution through mutual acceptance, its protagonists and those involved in the Arab-Israeli conflict face long years of frustration and enmity.

CHAPTER TWENTY

Stability and Retrenchment: The Arab World in the 1970s and Beyond

The 1970s in the Arab world witnessed few violent upheavals. Relative stability characterized most regimes. In many respects, Middle East foreign and even domestic policy was far more predictable than that of the United States during the same period. Energy market forces provided Middle Eastern and North African petroleum producers with revenues to develop their economies as well as their arsenals. Many Middle Eastern blue collar and professional workers benefited materially with their families from oil wealth. The Arabian Peninsula emerged as a focus of inter-Arab affairs with new international prestige and influence.

Toward Regional Power: Saudi Arabia

Except for the Yemens, the Arabian states in the 1970s were all significant oil producers still under their traditional rulers. Until his assassination by a nephew in March 1975, King Faysal (1964–75) restored solvency and began building his regional base. Through Islamic activities, the Saudis under Faysal maintained their longstanding role as leaders in the Muslim world. Faysal and his successors King d (1975–82) and King Fahd (1982–) ̲ent̲ly supported Islamic-oriented ̲ty, regionally and internationally. Saudis took very seriously any ̲o the security of Muslim holy ̲ home and abroad. As its financial ̲w, Saudi Arabia became more ̲ its opposition to Israeli expansion ̲lteration of Jerusalem's Old City. ̲ncern was heightened late in the 1960s when an Australian tourist set fire to Islam's third holiest mosque, al-Aqsa, and again in 1982 when on Easter Sunday, a Jewish Israeli caused great destruction within the Dome of the Rock, killing several bystanders in the process.

On 29 November 1979, Muslim zealots occupied the Great Mosque in Makka, seizing an unknown number of hostages. Rumors that the United States, whose diplomats had just been taken hostage in Iran, played a role in the mosque events provoked mobs in Pakistan to burn the U.S. embassy in Islamabad, killing two Americans. Although King Khalid first had to secure permission from the country's ulama because of Shari'a proscriptions against shedding blood in holy places, Saudi troops aided by foreign advisors retook the mosque after a three-day siege.

First suspected to be the work of Shi'is inspired by Iranian leader Khumayni, the onslaught was later attributed to members of a Sunni tribe whose leader claimed to be the Mahdi. Although some of its perpetrators were later caught, tried, and executed, the rebellion seemed emblematic of the growth in religious-based opposition to Saudi rule which, despite its roots, was being viewed increasingly as corrupt and secular.

The combination of Saudi Arabia's religious preeminence and its position as the leading petroleum exporter heightened Saudi concern for regional and internal stability, both of which were threatened by the attacks. Saudi Arabia was among the major donors to confrontation states involved in the Arab-Israeli conflict following the 1967 War. During the 1973 War, the Saudis took the lead in promoting the petroleum embargo, although subsequent price increases were instigated by Iran. When as Crown Prince in 1981 King Fahd proposed a plan to resolve the Palestine question and the Arab-Israeli conflict, the world took notice, but no one, including the Israelis and Palestinians, acted on it. The Saudis recognized that continuation of conflict in the region promoted destabilization. However, Saudi intervention in the Yemens and in Oman, added to Saudi support for Iraq during the Gulf War, showed that Saudi Arabia would intervene to support the status quo against threatening reformist or revolutionary elements. Saudi Arabia joined with Bahrayn, Kuwayt Oman, Qatar, and the U.A.E. in 1981 to form the Gulf Cooperation Council.(G.C.C.), an organization that had strategic as well as economic, political, and social influence.

Because of lack of a sufficiently sizable and well-trained army, which in 1980 numbered only about 70,000, Saudi Arabia hired foreigners as officers and foreign companies as defense contractors. In 1978 alone, the Saudis spent more than $8 billion on military hardware and services. The United States and Western Europe, along with Japan, exhibited increasing concern for Saudi security following the revolution in Iran. When U.S. President Reagan decided in 1981 to sell the Saudis sophisticated surveillance planes called AWACs, he was trying to safeguard the oil lanes endangered by the Gulf War. Although Israel protested the sale as threatening to its own interests, the planes allegedly failed to detect the Israeli jets that flew through Saudi air space in June 1981 to bomb Iraq's nuclear reactor.

The Saudi state in the oil-boom era changed from an isolated Wahhabi society to a development haven in which foreign workers outnumbered indigenous workers by figures estimated at three to one. As in other such states in the Gulf area, foreign workers brought values and life styles that violated the norms of the indigenous society. Saudis themselves grew more interested in the materialism usually associated with Western societies. Having experienced labor protests among Shi'i Saudi workers in oil-rich al-Hasa, the

Saudis could expect an increase in pressures for social, economic, and political democratization. Conservative in their public behavior, as mandated by law, wealthy Saudis often splurged in neighboring countries or in the privacy of their own homes.

Education provided one of the means whereby the ruling Saudi elites, governing basically through a consensus oligarchy, co-opted less well-connected but bright men into the government. Although coeducation was shunned, the Saudis expanded educational opportunities for both male and female subjects. As a pioneer in petroleum-oriented education, Saudi Arabia devoted special attention to providing training for the new generations. Opportunities for university education, both at home and abroad, were expanded. An example of one of Saudi Arabia's most prominent technocrats was the country's petroleum minister— Shaykh Ahmad Zaki Yamani. He achieved wide recognition and respect in international circles as both an eloquent spokesman and a tough negotiator, especially in the Organization of Petroleum Exporting Countries (OPEC).

Arabia's Emirates: Independence and Social Change

After encountering opposition to its plans to unite the colony at Aden with traditional rulers of the interior, the British late in 1967 left Aden. Shortly thereafter, negotiations with the various Gulf shaykhs over the future of that region began. In 1970, Britain's new Conservative government announced that the base at Bahrayn would close the following year. Subsequently, Bahrayn and Qatar chose individual independence. The other shaykhdoms joined together in the federated state called the Union of Arab Emirates or United Arab Emirates (U.A.E.). Although Britain remained involved in defense of the Gulf and Oman, it began interfering less regularly in Gulf affairs.

As petroleum exploration in the emirates expanded in the 1970s, it helped fund welfare states in which education was a key element. Al Ain University in the U.A.E. was founded late in the 1970s to provide university training for both men and women. Bahrayn and Kuwayt were also active in advancing higher educational opportunities at home. The Gulf in the oil-boom era was one of the world's most rapidly changing regions.

Expansion of communications was utilized to further education and training. An Arabic television program based on the U.S. children's program *Sesame Street* and called *Iftah Ya Simsim* (Open Sesame!), for example, was developed in cooperation with U.S. producers by the Arabian Gulf States Joint Programme Production Institute. A magazine of the same name was printed in Saudi Arabia and distributed in G.C.C. member states. As in the American series, the program and magazine aimed to present learning as a pleasurable experience.

Scientific development was encouraged, too, in organizations such as the Kuwayt Institute for Scientific Research. From modest beginnings in the 1970s, it focused on advanced scientific research and training of Kuwaytis. Arabs trained in the West formed the backbone of its research staff. Besides studying petroleum and petrochemicals, the institute dealt with solar energy, agriculture, fisheries, building, and other areas of social and environmental concern.

Already dependent on desalinization plants for expansion of water resources, Kuwayt as well as other Gulf states planned for a future in which petroleum revenues would no longer be available. Wealthy but developing, they were generous in their foreign aid programs. (see Ch. 21). They sought to further potentials in areas such as agriculture in which their own prospects were limited.

Politically, Arabia's amirs increasingly faced pressures for democratization. Tensions arose from the high proportions of foreign workers. Kuwayt's ruler from 1978, Jabir al-Ahmad al-Sabah reopened the National Assembly in 1981 after a few years' closure imposed by his predecessor Shaykh Sabah. The assembly was allowed to vote on measures proposed by the government. One controversial measure rejected by the assembly would have given women the right to vote. Islamic influence was seen in the passage of a law restricting citizenship to Muslims. With Kuwaytis less than half of the population according the 1980 census, the government was bound to encounter more conflicting pressures despite the high standard of living available to most residents.

The Yemens in the 1970s

Social Change in the P.D.R.Y.

After the conflict over the Yemen Arab Republic (Y.A.R.) in the 1960s, the area faced new challenges arising from the independence of Aden and the Hadhramaut in 1967. Internal rivalries kept the People's Republic of South Yemen's politics in a constant state of flux, but there were considerable advances in the participation of heretofore restricted groups. Women, for example, could join the General Union of Yemeni Women founded in 1968. Within two years, women were also demonstrating against the wearing of the veil. In 1974, laws regulating divorce were changed so that polygamy was abolished. Education for both boys and girls was also expanded. Although traditional leaders often objected to the revolutionary government's progressive reforms, the leaders in South Yemen believed that the old tribal structures would have to disappear in order to forge a new society. Innovations in socially useful fields such as health, education, and agriculture might otherwise be impeded.

The modest breakup of large estates after independence created a rich peasantry but did not solve the basic inequities in agriculture. With little aid from former colonial power Britain or other outside powers, the government was easily ousted in 1969 by pro-Chinese Communist Yemenis who in 1971 changed the country's name to the People's Democratic Republic of Yemen; the new rulers hoped for the eventual unification of north and south Yemen.

In 1970–71, the government followed up antitribal measures with mass mobilization of poor peasants to rise up against landowners. After the subsequent takeovers, state farms and cooperatives were set up. The government hoped that these would somehow improve agricultural output, although results of similar experiments in other Middle Eastern countries were mixed at best.

To accommodate the loss of major government revenue-earners including the military base and port, the government instituted an austerity program, cutting salaries of employees and raising taxes. From the outset, major companies were nationalized, except for the British Petroleum refinery that provided the country's oil. The fishing industry was targeted as a growth area to supplant cotton as the primary export crop.

Because of its revolutionary posture, the P.D.R.Y. faced a rocky road initially in international relations. In 1969, it broke off relations with the United States because the latter country allowed its citizens to serve in Israel's armed forces. Of more immediate and local interest was the confrontational relationship with both Oman and Saudi Arabia, and the occasional conflict with the Y.A.R. The P.D.R.Y. aided the Dhufari liberation forces in the 1970s as Britain, Jordan, and Iran helped Sultan Qabus. In 1982, British officers continued to manage Oman's Union Armed Forces, which had originated with Britain's Trucial Oman Scouts.

During the 1970s, the P.D.R.Y.'s early aid donors—the U.S.S.R., Cuba, and the German Democratic Republic—were joined by Algeria, Kuwait, North Korea, and even Saudi Arabia which hoped to extend its influence. Although rumors about Soviet naval and air bases in the P.D.R.Y. abounded during the 1970s, it was not until 1979–80 that the Soviet Union fully developed facilities on the island of Socotra. During the late 1970s, the P.D.R.Y.'s major trading partner was not the U.S.S.R. but Japan, mainly because of petroleum-product exports. Because of its great need, the P.D.R.Y.'s efforts to establish a sound economy were bound to depend on foreign aid for the foreseeable future. The P.D.R.Y., regardless of the current government's professed ideology, was willing to accept whatever aid it could obtain.

The Y.A.R. Between Saudi Arabia and the P.D.R.Y.

In the Y.A.R., the industrialization program begun in the 1960s continued, but high wages in nearby Saudi Arabia and the Gulf sent over one million Yemenis to work in Saudi Arabia alone. With the largest population in the Arabian Peninsula, Yemen could hardly provide at home the relatively profitable employment available abroad. Yemen offset its trade imbalances with remittances from these workers. Both the United States and Saudi Arabia developed substantial aid programs for the Y.A.R. in the 1970s and 1980s.

Center-periphery differences compounded by Zaydi-Shafi'i rivalry continued to characterize politics. After the eight-year civil war, a three-man presidential council under Qadi Iryani governed the country, but in 1974, Lieutenant Colonel Ibrahim al-Hamdi—conservative, conscientious, and charismatic—was installed as president through an army coup. In 1977, Hamdi was assassinated, presumably because of his independence from tribal and pro-Saudi factions. The increasing involvement of the Saudis in both Yemens helped provoke a crisis in 1978 in which both of their presidents were killed. The new Y.A.R. president, Lieutenant Colonel Ali Abd Allah Salih, sought both internal and external tranquility. One month after a border conflict escalated into a short war in 1979, a unity agreement between the two Yemens was concluded. Despite its victory in the 1979 fighting, the P.D.R.Y. remained a poor, struggling, dependent country. The Y.A.R. tried to pursue a course more independent of Saudi Arabia despite Yemeni predominance in the Saudi work force. In the early 1980s, both the P.D.R.Y. and the Y.A.R. brought arms from the Soviet Union. Their unity agreement remained dormant.

Iraq under the Tikriti Ba'th

After the coup of 1968, despite Iraq's potential for growth in hydrocarbons and agriculture, the new regime aroused little enthusiasm. Reacting against the Arab defeat of 1967, the Iraqi leadership persecuted its opponents, accusing them of being Israeli spies. The premier of 1965–66, Abd al-Rahman al-Bazzaz, an advocate of Arab federation in his scholarly works, was among those imprisoned. In January

1969, fourteen alleged Israeli spies, nine of them Jewish Iraqis, were hanged in a public execution in Baghdad. Internationally isolated, the Iraqi regime seemed destined for an early demise.

Gradually, though, the Iraqi Ba'th, inspired by Aflaq and under the control of Vice President and later President Saddam Husayn al-Tikriti, embarked on a social-reform and national reconstruction program. The government freed political prisoners and instituted trade unions. National planning and commitment to fulfillment of goals allowed the regime to complete many projects that heretofore had lagged far behind schedule. With Iraq's mixed economy, the Ba'th encouraged not only public but also private investment, especially in communications and services. Tax incentives for industry were provided.

In agriculture, the government instituted a wide-ranging land reform program intended to keep peasants on the land by making farming more profitable for them. As with other socialist programs in the Arab world, peasants resisted collectivization. In conjunction with provisions for irrigation and drainage systems, the government also aimed at providing safe drinking water in the previously neglected villages.

The mainstay of the Iraqi export industry—petroleum—was nationalized in 1972 and continued to provide revenues for development. Because the government focused on long-term projects, results were not always visible, but the commitment remained. After Saudi Arabia, Iraq provided the Middle East's richest market in 1982. South Korean, Japanese, and West German contractors were most heavily involved in Iraqi development. Among the problems to beset the regime during the late 1960s and early 1970s was the yet-unresolved Kurdish problem and the related Iranian question.

The linkage between the two problems was established because of Iranian support, ongoing until 1975, for Iraq's Kurdish rebels. Iraqi-Iranian differences at that time focused on the greater question of which nation would control the Gulf. Iran

in April 1969 created a provocation by revoking the 1937 treaty whereby Iraq had secured control of the Shatt al-Arab waterway dividing the two countries. Then, as the U.A.E. was born in 1971, Iran seized three of its islands. Iraq protested. Realizing that the Kurdish problem was a thorn in its side, the Iraqi government in 1970 made an agreement with Kurdish nationalist Mustafa al-Barzani, which gave the Kurds a measure of autonomy in their own region and a greater role in Iraq's government. By 1974, however, the idea of autonomy was judged a failure by Barzani, who resumed the revolt. Aided by Iran, the Kurds still failed to make headway against the Iraqi regular armed forces. In March 1975, Iran and Iraq temporarily resolved their dispute.

In the settlement, Iraq conceded half the Shatt al-Arab to Iran in exchange for securing Iran's promise to cease all aid to the Kurds. The Iraqis felt that they could no longer sustain their military campaign, but they also felt pressured by Iran's military superiority that was bolstered by the latest American equipment. Barzani died in Washington, D.C. in March 1979. In the wake of the Iranian revolution of 1977–79 the Iraqis attempted to reopen negotiations over both the Shatt al-Arab and the Gulf islands. When Iranian leader Khumayni refused and called on Iraq's Shi'i majority to revolt, Saddam Husayn in August 1980 initiated the inconclusive Gulf War. After three years of fighting, over 100,000 Iraqis and Iranians lost their lives. Of longer-range significance, perhaps, was the ecological disaster, caused by oil slicks from uncapped and bombed Iranian wells, which threatened all of the Gulf states.

As in its early days, the Ba'thi regime continued its vocal support of Palestinian nationalism and its opposition to negotiations with Israel. During the 1973 War, Iraqi troops entered Syria to assist its army on the northern front but did not substantially affect the course of the fighting. Between 1960 and 1978, Iraq bought Soviet arms worth some $3 billion. After 1979, when the Iraqi Communist Party was banned, Iraq increased its purchases from France and Italy and sought closer relations with the United States. Often allied with Libya, Iraq found itself opposed by Qadhdhafi in the Gulf War and aided by such conservative Arab states as Jordan, Kuwayt, and the U.A.E. Iraq in the 1980s generally sought to strengthen its ties in the Gulf.

The Victory of the Rural Alawi Ba'th in Syria

After the 1967 War, Hafiz al-Asad spoke out on behalf of the military against the government whose purges, in his opinion, had weakened the army's fighting capacity. The focus on economic development appeared to him as secondary to the need to build up the armed forces. The popular Palestinian war would not provide for Syria's defense needs. When Egypt accepted Resolution 242, embodying a peaceful solution to the Arab-Israeli conflict, Asad wanted to go along, too. Why should the party decide military policy when it was unwilling to provide for any substantive alternatives to the strengthening of the army? If Syria was unwilling to bolster its military capabilities, it should at least mend its fences with the Iraqi Ba'th. Asad's position was rejected by the Ba'th late in 1968.

Asad secured additional influence in the regime in February 1969, however, through an attempted coup. Although he succeeded militarily, he could not completely overthrow the political regime of Jadid supporters. In a compromise, Asad retained control of the military, but the Jadid factions continued to dominate the government. To broaden his base of support, Asad influenced the regime to consider cooperating with other progressives whom it had previously persecuted. He also tried to appeal to the urban bourgeoisie. The new Eastern Command created at his suggestion brought Iraqi and Syrian forces into Syria and Jordan under the command of an Egyptian general, but it did not appreciably alter the atmosphere of mutual suspicion. Other initiatives to fellow Arabs did bring about a response, especially in terms of economic aid.

In 1969–70, Syria began to cooperate with Egypt, then engaged in the war of attrition, by reactivating its front when Israel attacked Palestinians in Lebanon. When Libyan leader Qadhdhafi appeared in Damascus in June 1970, he lent support to Asad's belief that only regular armies would be able to stand up against Israel. Asad was finally moved to displace his colleagues during the civil war of September 1970 in Jordan. During the war, the Syrian government was the only Arab government to send regular forces to help the Palestinians, combined with troops of the Syrian-supported Palestine Liberation Army. These forces helped to protect Palestinians' in northern Jordan.

Historians have debated Asad's role in the absence of air cover when American threats led him to order a retreat in which heavy casualties were suffered. Did Asad want his forces to suffer in order to discredit the government? Did he favor or oppose the intervention at the outset? Did Asad fear American intervention from the beginning? Did he feel that government had prevented his forces from securing their victory? Whatever the precise reason, Asad on 13 November 1970 staged a bloodless coup which he called a "normal development." Qadhdhafi soon arrived as a representative of the Egyptians, Libyans, and Sudanese who had concluded the Tripoli Charter leading to a tripartite federation. Asad announced his intention to bring Syria into the union, too.

Hafiz al-Asad established Syria's first longstanding postwar regime, dependent on his own rural Alawi base but enlisting sufficient support from other national groups to remain in power in 1983. How did he do it? First of all, he broadened his government to include non-Ba'thi socialists and Communists as well as members of other ethnic groups. Secondly, Asad bolstered the position of the urban bourgeoisie by relaxing trade restrictions, giving Syrians overseas inducements to return home, easing travel restrictions to Lebanon, and lowering food prices. Instead of a firm commitment to socialism and state capitalism, he emphasized a mixed economy in which private enterprise could play a role. Asad also encouraged archeological exploration, but not tourism, despite the great potential in Syria's rich heritage. Late in the 1970s, the private sector accounted for the greater part of tourism, commerce, real estate, and small manufacturing (including textiles). Artisans and small shopkeepers prospered. Encouragement of private enterprise through guarantees, facilities, and permission to contract with foreign firms for development attracted support from Syria's petite bourgeoisie.

Thirdly, he normalized relations with less radical Arab countries and conservative regimes such as those in Tunisia and Morocco. Syria also joined with Egypt in drawing closer to Saudi Arabia. Moreover, he brought al-Saiqa under his control through purging its leadership, who had been more closely associated with the old regime. Although the Federation of Arab Republics uniting Egypt, Libya, and Syria (Sudan having opted out in order to settle internal problems) was concluded in April 1971, it never became a reality. Libya and Syria continued to discuss union as late as December 1980 with no firm results.

In foreign policy, the Asad government joined with Egypt in waging the October 1973 war against Israel. It then intervened in the Lebanese civil war in June 1976. The Arab League sanctioned the Syrian presence in October 1976 as a temporary measure, but the troops were still there in June 1982 when Israel invaded Lebanon. In the years following the 1973 War, Syria feared that Egypt would conclude a separate peace with Israel. In

1976, Egypt broke relations with Syria over the intervention in Lebanon, but restored them after the October decision approving the Syrian presence. President Sadat's visit to Jerusalem in November 1977, followed by the Camp David talks of September 1978 and the Egyptian-Israeli peace treaty of March 1979, led the Syrian regime to move closer to Sadat's neighbor and sometime rival, Mu'ammar al-Qadhdhafi. Both Syria and Libya proved sympathetic to the Iranian revolution of 1977–79 and supported Iran after the Gulf War began in August 1980. The Syrians prohibited transit of Iraqi oil. This action cramped Iraq's economy. Ironically, only a few months before, Syria and Iraq had held union talks. The fact is that years of Ba'thist rule in both Syria and Iraq had led to more rivalry than unity. A Syrian-Jordanian war threatened to break out in 1981, and the two countries continued to accuse each other of subversion.

Jordan, however, was not threatened appreciably. Although the civil war of 1970 had discouraged investment, Jordan benefited from the Lebanese war of the mid-1970s by offering a more stable environment for Western financial institutions. The Arab League, bilateral aid funds of major oil producers, the United States, and various Western European countries all stepped in to aid development of Jordan's economy, especially in the areas of water resources, mining, and agriculture. Jordan in the 1970s and 1980s benefited also from remittances sent home by its citizens working elsewhere, especially in the Gulf. In fact, because of the number of overseas workers, Jordan (which formerly had an unemployment problem) suffered from a labor shortage early in the 1980s. Foreign workers had to be hired. The amount of capital sent home by these workers, however, was far smaller than the amount remitted by Jordanians working abroad. Despite political differences, Syria and Jordan cooperated in economic ventures during the late 1970s and early 1980s.

What brought on accusations of subversion? In Syria, the main complaint focused on alleged Jordanian aid for the

Muslim Brothers, a group closely associated with the Sunni Muslim opposition based in Hama, Latakia, and Aleppo. It is true that Sunnis had protested when in 1973 the new Syrian constitution dropped the statement that Islam was the state's religion, but economic factors also played a role in ongoing disturbances, especially between 1979 and 1982. One source of resentment was the development project in the Ghab Valley to the west of Hama along the Orontes River. Asad's government brought in peasants from the nearby Alawi mountain areas to farm land that had formerly belonged to Sunni landowners in Hama, thereby antagonizing them. Rural-urban migration to other cities called attention to inequities increased by the government's encouragement of the private sector, especially the businesspeople of Damascus. The Muslim Brothers, as a well-organized urban group, could channel both the religious-based and more socially-based opposition

to Alawi rule. The Syrian government proved unable to curtail or suppress the Muslim Brothers' assassination and terrorist campaign.

Disgruntlement and Brotherhood-opposition in Hama culminated in a three-week battle in February 1982 between Syrian army forces and Muslim Brotherhood cadres. Estimates of deaths varied between 5,000 and 10,000, and perhaps 25 percent of the city was leveled. In 1982, it was uncertain how much longer Asad would be able to maintain troops in Lebanon and still uphold his increasingly fragile regime at home. The Israeli invasion of June 1982 strove to expel Syria's forces. Although both the United States and France gave Syria weapons after 1973, it relied on the Soviet Union for most military aid and advice. Israel interpreted its victory over Syrian forces in Lebanon as demonstrating the superiority of American as opposed to Soviet weaponry.

Sadat's Egypt and the Era of De-Nasirization (1970–81)

Gamal Abd al-Nasir's last years were spent in the gloomy atmosphere that followed the massive defeat of 1967. His close associate Abd al-Hakim Amer, commander of Egypt's armed forces, committed suicide. Popular forces in February 1968 protested the handing down of lenient verdicts against those judged responsible for the defeat. To provide for an orderly succession, Abd al-Nasir in January 1970 designated his old associate Anwar al-Sadat as his vice-president and heir-apparent. During Jordan's *Black September,* Abd al-Nasir negotiated an end to the war and then died.

Abd al-Nasir's legacy in Egypt and the Arab world was considerable. Within eighteen years, he had made Egypt a symbol of Third World nationalism and anti-imperialism, despite Egypt's accumulation of foreign debts during his rule. He

had supported industrialization, agrarian reform, education and social responsibility. But in the 1960s, Egypt had to rely on food-aid as the economy stagnated and population growth outstripped food production. Although his efforts at political mobilization had met with only limited success, he established a reasonably stable regime with an orderly government. Despite his failures in inter-Arab politics, he also enjoyed some successes and was able to make his exit with a massive outpouring of grief throughout the Arab world. Nasirism remained a force in the region long after his death.

Sadat's Priorities

Sadat came to the presidency of Egypt in 1970 amidst predictions that he could not last long. Although he was an old R.C.C. member, an experienced politician, a former contact of the Muslim Brethren, and a publicist for the regime in its early days, observers assumed that stronger personalities such as leftist Vice President Ali Sabri would be able to supplant him. At the outset, Sadat continued the thrust of the Abd al-Nasir regime in its waning days. He moved toward a rapprochement with Saudi Arabia and Jordan as well as with Iran, and turned to reliance on the United States to achieve a solution to the Arab-Israeli conflict. He supported a more mixed economy of state and private capitalism in industry and agriculture.

In his Corrective Revolution of May 1971, Sadat arrested Sabri and his associates on the grounds that they were planning to overthrow him and were responsible for police repression in Egypt. Although Sadat signed a friendship treaty with the U.S.S.R. in May 1971, the broadening of his contacts in the Arab world showed that ideology was not likely to play an important role in foreign policy under Sadat. While continuing to rely on technocrats and the military, Sadat restored a pragmatic, Egypt-first orientation. In 1971, the country was renamed. Instead of U.A.R., it would be called the Arab Republic of Egypt (A.R.E.).

An important component of his program was the recovery of land lost to Israel in 1967. When efforts to achieve a diplomatic solution through U.S. and U.N. mediation failed, he led Egypt into the October 1973 War. With Egypt's humiliation erased, Sadat embarked on a new domestic direction while working toward a negotiated settlement with Israel. Disengagement agreements in 1974 and 1975 were followed by the surprise Jerusalem visit of 1977, the Camp David talks of 1978, and the peace treaty of 1979. Sadat was disappointed when Arab leaders failed to back up his initiatives and accused him of betraying the Palestinians. Moreover, his negative response to the Islamic revolution in Iran further antagonized his enemies. When he was assassinated in October 1981 by Muslim fundamentalists from what he had assumed to be a loyal army, few in Egypt and the Arab world mourned his death.

Social and Economic Change in the Sadat Era

How did Sadat's policies influence the course of social and economic development in Egypt? His introduction of economic liberalism (*infitah* or opening) in 1974—designed to attract foreign investment—met with limited success. Egypt acquired huge debts to international lending agencies such as the International Monetary Fund and the World Bank. Egypt's free zones, intended to encourage foreign investment, attracted Egyptian investors who had foreign currency. But foreign investment tended to replace domestic consumer industry rather than promote development. Investment in the tourist industry by foreigners—Arabs and others—as well as Egypt's state-run Misr Travel brought about increased local employment opportunities in construction and services but also demanded extensive transportation, food supply, sanitation, and communications facilities. Non-Arab investors remained cautious about taking advantage of Egypt's new incentives, mainly because of uncertainty about long-range prospects.

Future historians will probably agree that Sadat's personal style lent itself to support by the more prosperous Egyptians, some of whose wealth he helped create through government policy. A conspicuous consumer himself, Sadat encouraged expansion of private enterprise, made expropriation of private property illegal in 1974, and much later rescinded earlier expropriations. While officially pursuing an austerity program, Sadat held a lavish wedding for his daughter. Gamal Abd al-Nasir's family had stayed in the background, but Sadat's half-British wife Jihan took on an important role as spokesperson for the regime and for women's rights. A controversial new marriage and divorce law was passed in 1979.

During his presidency, Sadat acquired many villas and estates. Even old wealthy landlords made a comeback. Mechanization in agriculture did not increase yields, and agriculture remained labor-intensive, with cotton as the major export earner. Poor Egyptian farmers resisted mechanization because of the greater utility of multipurpose work animals and the high cost of purchasing and maintaining equipment. Drainage and other problems arising from the Aswan High Dam completed in 1970 continued to complicate Egyptian agricultural planning (although on balance, hydrologists in 1982 judged the dam a success). Yields of major crops increased after the dam was built. Though the sardine crop in the Delta declined, losses were more than offset by the new fishing possibilities presented by Lake Nasir, which brought several thousand new fishermen to the area. Agriculture in the Sadat era was affected by investment in low-labor agriculture, including fruit production, which furthered rural-urban migration. Egypt's agricultural growth rate of the 1970s was far lower than that of the 1950s and 1960s.

Reclamation in 1980 was still proceeding slowly in the west, but the al-Salam Canal to Sinai, completed in 1980, was expected to help in reclaiming land in the eastern Delta and Sinai. Two thirds of the amount of land reclaimed was lost, however, to industrial and urban expansion. Because of the increased water available for irrigation, Egypt also needed to expand the capacity of existing drainage systems. Poor drainage contributed to soil salinization and to waterlogging.

Perhaps the most pressing agricultural concern faced by Egypt was its dependence on food imports. These far exceeded the value of agricultural exports. The increase in the population growth rate from 2.4 percent in 1977 to 2.9 percent in 1979 meant that Egypt was adding 1.5 million people every year despite an increase in the use of contraceptives. Food subsidies provided by the government so that the poor could eat grew from $13 million in 1960 to $29 million in 1970 and $1.9 billion in 1979. Attempts to abolish food subsidies in January 1977 because of international aid donor pressure brought about food riots. Politically and socially, the country could not afford to abandon food subsidies.

The economy throughout much of the postwar period was overburdened with military expenditures. The arms race, which in the Middle East was accelerated by the Gaza raid of 1955, grew to astronomical proportions in the 1970s and early 1980s. Although Egypt's greatest military adventure was Abd al-Nasir's war in Yemen, the Egyptian-Israeli peace treaty of March 1979, signed by Sadat, resulted in a rise rather than a decrease in military spending.

Egypt in the 1970s became a significant petroleum exporter. It had equally promising prospects for development of the natural gas industry. Refineries in Cairo, Alexandria, Suez, and Tanta processed oil for domestic use. Egypt also began to develop the petrochemical industry. Although much of the population was still engaged in agriculture, Egypt's main non-petroleum foreign exchange earners in 1980 were workers' remittances from abroad, Suez Canal receipts, and tourism.

Although life in the cities improved for many Egyptians, people resented high inflation and continued government control over trade union activities. Hulwan steel workers rioted in January 1975, followed by strikes in the textile industry in August 1975 and among Cairo transport workers in January 1977. Women formed an estimated 12 percent of the labor force by the late 1970s because their families needed the income. High inflation occurred because of the disparity between imports and exports and the high debt service. Both for export and for local consumption, Egypt's textile and leather industries remained productive. As such industries like those in Turkey tended to cater to the needs of Egypt's emerging middle and upper classes, there was no guarantee that the rural and urban poor saw their lives improved. Students constituted an important segment of Sadat's opponents because they could not find suitable jobs after graduation. Sadat introduced measures encouraging Egyptians to work overseas and repatriate their hard currency to ameliorate the hardship caused by low salaries arising from the government's efforts to keep expanding the bureaucracy.

Political Liberalization and the Islamic Revival

In November 1976, Sadat allowed a return to multiparty life in Egypt. Groups such as the leftist Tagamu'a and the New Wafd appeared. When the New Wafd seemed to be winning widespread support despite its similarity to the A.S.U., Sadat became alarmed. By June 1978, the party was dissolved. To assure that the regime could maintain democratic appearances, Sadat in July 1978 created his own National Democratic Party. Although it was supposed to add to the multiparty system, most members of the A.S.U. bolted to the new group which became a rubber stamp for Sadat's policies.

Despite the veneer of democracy, Sadat imprisoned many of his opponents, including popular socialist poet Ahmad Fu'ad Nagm as well as political rivals. The Muslim Brothers led the protest against the peace treaty with Israel. Shortly before his assassination, Sadat rounded up several thousand Egyptians accused of having promoted sectarian violence. Although the vast majority were Muslims like the popular Shaykh Kishk, Sadat also arrested Copts. Moreover, he used the opportunity to accuse the old New Wafd leadership of plotting his overthrow and to jail many secular opponents, among them the Tagamu'a. His defenders insisted that he did not go far enough because he did not round up the military opposition. His successor Husni Mubarak released the detainees by early 1982 and began a dialogue to defuse the opposition. But Sadat's principal assassins were tried and executed.

The Muslim Brothers and their offshoots gained a wider following in Sadat's Egypt because he initially encouraged them to balance the forces of the secular left and the Nasirists.

After the events of the early 1950s, government repression had curbed open Muslim Brotherhood activity. The regime of Abd al-Nasir moved against the organization again in 1965–66 and hanged its ideologue and leader Sayyid Qutb for an alleged conspiracy against the state. While the Muslim Brotherhood remained the symbol of the Islamic movement in Egypt, other groups—notably Takfir wa Higra (Repentence and Deliverance) and Jihad (striving; the group which killed Sadat)—arose. While inspired by the Muslim Brothers' message, they differed in tactics, believing that they should challenge overtly and with violence if necessary the non-Islamic nature of Muslim societies, as explicated in Sayyid Qutb's famous work, *Milestones*.[1] The Brothers also insisted on the idea of a more Muslim-oriented regime. Egypt's 1973 union with Libya had collapsed because of Qadhdhafi's insistence on applying Muslim law in Egypt.

The Islamic revival in Egypt was associated with external symbols like the wearing of more conservative dress by men and women, especially by university students. But this outward expression manifested an inward reality related to the infusion of American aid, adoption of foreign styles, and a materialism judged by many to be excessive. Average urban Egyptians blamed the government's economic liberalization associated with pro-West policies not only for inflation but for straining urban public transport and public services. A return to Islamic essentials seemed to provide the answer to solving society's problem of increasing social alienation. Since sons and daughters employed in the tourist or service industries began earning, as in Iran, more money than their fathers, family relationships often became strained. Islamic societies (Jam'at al-Islamiyya) arose and grew because they focused on social and academic services as well as psychological needs.

Women have long been in the forefront of the Muslim revival. Zaynab al-Ghazali was a leader of the feminist

---

[1] Sayyid Qutb, *Milestones*. No translator given. (Beirut and Damascus: Holy Quran Publishing House for International Federation of Muslim Student Organizations, 1978.)

Muslim movement (the Muslim Sisters) in Egypt from 1936. Attracted to the thrust of the Iranian revolution, she advocated the implementation of an Islamic state in Egypt that would impose Shari'a and otherwise reflect Islamic tradition. The Muslim Brethren in Egypt maintained ongoing contacts with their counterpart in Syria whom they favored because the Alawi Asad is viewed as a heretic. These presumed relationships among Muslim Brothers have led Arab leaders to suspect the Brothers as an antigovernment force bent on displacing their regimes. Al-Ghazali is typical of Muslim-oriented opposition in rejecting the idea of great power alliances.

When Anwar al-Sadat died, the United States sent three former presidents to his funeral. Europe's heads-of-state and Israeli prime minister Menachem Begin also attended. But in the Arab world, the only head-of-state present was Sudanese president Ja'far al-Numayri who had been drawing closer to Egypt's leader in an effort to counteract Libyan subversion and opposition in Sudan.

Sudan under Numayri

British policy before Sudan's independence in 1956 limited north-south interaction, particularly any that might have promoted the Arabization of the southern Sudanese. When Britain reversed this policy prior to Sudan's independence, it left the southerners as potentially disadvantaged partners in an Arab-dominated state which might regard Arabization as vital to national integration. From 1955–72, southerners rebelled against the efforts of the Sudanese government to unify and stabilize the country. Guerrilla fighters received substantial assistance from Israel during their struggle. Ja'far al-Numayri brought about an end to the war when an autonomy plan was agreed upon. Besides north-south differences, he had to mediate between Bantu groups in Equatoria, who had constituted the rebel leadership, and the Nilotic Dinkas, the largest of the numerous tribes in the south. Bantu-Dinka differences resurfaced in 1982 to threaten the 1972 settlement. The southern issue made Numayri withdraw from the 1970 union plans with Egypt and Libya. But their joint concern over Nile water usage and old ties kept Egypt and Sudan in a close, cooperative relationship. Just as the Aswan High Dam required agreement with Sudan, so also did Sudan's four dams and the Jonglei Canal (to be completed by 1985) entail Egyptian approval. In 1981, Sadat said that Sudan could construct for its own use a Mediterranean port on Egyptian soil to supplement Port Sudan on the Red Sea. Egyptian-Sudanese relations remained strong under Sadat's successor, Husni Mubarek.

Like Egypt, Sudan received substantial aid from the Soviet Union during its independence period, but the country was generally preoccupied with is internal problems. When relations with the Soviets deteriorated, Sudan expelled Soviet experts and drew closer to the capitalist-oriented bloc in which Egypt had taken the leadership role. Sudan's conservative shift was a factor in bringing about increased Arab aid and investment as well as assistance from the United States. The United States also sought to bolster the regime against Libya which from December 1980 to November 1981 maintained troops in neighboring Chad and actually proclaimed a Libya-Chad union. In February 1983, the United States sent AWACs to Egypt because of intelligence pointing to a Libyan strike against Numayri.

Despite its vast and rich agricultural potential, Africa's largest country in territory suffered from long years of civil war.

Agricultural development and diversification required a huge capital-investment effort, though little local capital was available. Expansion of the cotton industry, especially in the Gezira area between the Blue and White Niles, made Sudan a major world producer vulnerable to changes in the international market. The Kenana sugar project, and agricultural investment in meat and vegetable oils, were among the hundred or so projects supported by Arabic-speaking countries in Sudan from the 1970s. Although the United States also invested in Sudan, the $1 billion in debt arrears accumulated by the Sudanese government in 1979 made lending bodies such as the U.S. Import-Export Bank cautious. Sudan was expected to become self-sufficient in petroleum once production from its Bentiu oil field began, probably in the mid-1980s, but development problems were likely to remain. Initially, the U.S.-based Chevron Oil Company debated constructing a refinery in the north at Kosti or in the south at Bentiu. Late in 1982, however, it abandoned the refinery plan and opted instead for a pipeline to the coast which would destine the oil for export rather than domestic use.

During Numayri's first two years as Sudan's leader, his government banned the Mahdist and Khatmiyya parties and founded the Sudanese Socialist Union (S.S.U.) based on the A.S.U. in Egypt. With the traditional leaders discredited, Numayri forged closer links with Sudanese Communists. He nationalized banks, industries, and properties, especially those of the Mahdi family. After an assassination attempt on Numayri's life, he defeated a Mahdist faction based in the White Nile region at Aba Island. Numayri's decision to unite with Egypt and Libya in November 1970 broke up his alliance with the Communists who briefly overthrew his regime in July 1971 and killed some thirty of his military supporters. Through Libya's timely action in downing a plane carrying the principal coup leaders on their way from London to Sudan, the coup had few chances of survival. Moreover, Sudanese themselves rallied in

Numayri's favor. The Communists were crushed in the aftermath, and Numayri turned away from reliance on the eastern bloc.

With the firm backing of religious elements who had feared Communist rule, Numayri was overwhelmingly elected Sudan's first president in Octrober 1971. The S.S.U. was recognized as the country's sole legal political party. Under the agreement that ended the war in southern Sudan, a regional assembly for the south was formed with an executive council whose head would be a vice-president in the Sudanese Republic. Abel Alier occupied this post for six years after conclusion of the agreement in 1972.

Numayri's suppression of Communists did not mean an immediate swing to the traditionally based rightist parties who formed a new National Front and who tried from time to time to overthrow him. Coup attempts in September 1975 and July 1976 failed. The latter effort was financed by Libya and indicated a dissolution of the friendship that had characterized relations between Qadhdhafi and Numayri. Gradually Numayri patched up his relations with the dissidents. In 1977 he became reconciled with Sadiq al-Mahdi, who had been sentenced to death but had fled into exile. Sadiq joined the S.S.U. and became an active participant in the regime. After Numayri backed Egypt's peace treaty with Israel, however, he resigned from the party. Like Mahdists in the early years of self-government and independence, Sadiq had serious reservations about Numayri's growing economic and political ties with Egypt. Meanwhile, Numayri expanded his relations with Saudi Arabia and the Gulf states and, until Libya's involvement with the Chad civil war, with Libya as well.

Economic deterioration in the early 1980s took its toll on Sudan's internal and external politics. In 1981, Numayri began to suppress dissent in the south by imprisoning many of its leaders. Like Sadat, he tried to court Muslim Brethren support by emphasizing Sudan's Islamic identity to the detriment of the southerners' culture and religion. Muslim Brother Hasan al-Turabi, Sudan's attorney general, hoped to Islamize Sudan's laws gradually. Yet, despite his conciliatory approach to the conservatives, Numayri by 1982 found the Muslim Brethren among his opponents.

Observers agreed that Numayri, by trying to accommodate his disparate opponents, had grown increasingly isolated while his economic policies had failed to transform Sudan into the eagerly anticipated Arab world breadbasket.

Assertion of Hasan II in Morocco

During the late 1960s, Hasan II discouraged democracy and arrested opposition leaders for plotting against his life. Early in the 1970s, his fears were justified. The Moroccan army attempted coups in July 1971 and August 1972. The July 1971 effort involved one thousand military cadets. One of the plotters, Colonel Ababu apparently killed his coconspirator General Madbuh for having shielded the king who then escaped with his own right-hand man General Oufkir. This initial plot showed the king that his assumption of army loyalty was a myth. Later examination of the motives of the leaders revealed discontent over widespread corruption, although Ababu himself had a record of involvement in it. In the aftermath, the government instituted corruption trials but in fact focused on rounding up the U.N.F.P. opposition. The king presented a new constitution, too, but the political parties rejected it because it gave them only an indeterminate role in government.

During the second coup attempt in 1972, the Moroccan air force attacked the king's plane, returning from France. When they ran out of ammunition, they launched an air attack on the airport followed by a machine gun barrage against the palace. Oufkir was blamed for having instigated the coup and was shot the same night. Eleven officers were executed in January 1973 for their role. Two months later, the government announced the discovery of a third plot, again used as a pretext for detaining U.N.F.P. members. In subsequent trials, more death sentences were passed and carried out. Through 1975, trials and interrogations

were conducted, characterized by secrecy and torture. Many people disappeared after having been acquitted.

In 1975, the U.N.F.P. was divided as the Rabat branch took on the name Socialist Union of Popular Forces (U.S.F.P.). This party's leaders, notably Abd al-Rahman Bouabid, were imprisoned in September 1981 when they challenged the king's decisions on the Western Sahara question. Although Morocco's socialist parties joined with similar groups from Jibuti, Gambia and Senegal (now Senegambia), Ghana, Mauritius, Somalia, Sudan, and Tunisia to form the Socialist Inter-African in 1981, they focused more on anti-Communism than on socialism. Regardless of their participation in African politics, Morocco's parties continued to take a back seat to the king in ruling their own nation.

Besides the tactics of suppression and division, Hasan II pursued popular policies as well. In 1973, he sent troops to Syria; these played a key role in initial Syrian successes on Julan. Moroccan expansion also won widespread popular approval. When Spain announced its decision to withdraw from the Spanish Sahara in 1975, it turned over the territory to Morocco and Mauritania. The indigenous Polisario Front, supported first by Algeria and periodically by Libya, proclaimed the territory's independence as the Sahrawi Arab Democratic Republic (S.A.D.R.). The subsequent war in the Western Sahara forced Mauritania to withdraw its claims in 1979, but Morocco remained in the territory. Morocco was influenced by phosphate deposits in addition to historical ties. When by 1981 the majority of Organization of African Unity members recognized the S.A.D.R., they admitted it implicitly as an O.A.U. member, too. The Western Sahara question was among the factors that prevented the assembling of a quorum in 1982 for the O.A.U. annual summit. It remained a subject of controversy in inter-African affairs.

In foreign policy, Hasan II pursued a pro-Western slant but maintained ties with the Soviet Union, too. The United States and France gave Morocco substantial military and economic aid. Relations with France were strained for some years over the kidnapping and disappearance (and presumed death) of U.N.F.P. leader Mehdi Ben Barka in 1965. Oufkir was blamed for his murder, and though he too died, questions about Ben Barka resurfaced from time to time in Moroccan politics and international relations. American support for Morocco by the Reagan administration was viewed with some apprehension by Algeria, the country that mediated the U.S. hostage crisis with Iran.

The Moroccan economy experienced a brief decline during decolonization. Moroccan agriculture suffered from drought and a gradual exodus of settlers, combined with the subdivision of large estates. The Moroccans, however, invested in successful large-scale irrigation projects. Phosphates provided for foreign exchange, and a plant at Safi produced fertilizers and phosphoric acid. Food processing was also important. Morocco profited from tourism and remittances from Moroccans working abroad. During the early 1970s, local industries were Moroccanized.

The war with the Sahrawis, though, proved a costly drain on economic resources. In June 1981, the government decreed huge price rises in the cost of basic food items; this provoked widespread rioting in Casablanca. Although the government was forced to back down, it faced severe financial problems. Prices for phosphates remained in a state of decline on the world market. The Moroccan economy in 1981 was in such great need that Morocco borrowed $1.2 billion from the I.M.F. Positive future areas of the economy included the extracting of oil from shale to provide for the country's expanding energy demands, and the modernizing of the fishing industry.

Morocco's educational structure under Hasan II faced some of the same problems found in Algeria and Tunisia. The modern educational system benefited very few Moroccans. French influence persisted through the employment of French teachers. University education emphasized law and letters rather than technical training, agriculture, or sciences. Despite the maintenance of Arabic influences in traditional schools, the Moroccan system remained alienated from local culture and manpower needs. Cultural decolonization was not a *fait accompli* even twenty-five years after independence.

Boumedienne's Algeria

In Algeria under Boumedienne, economic development received the greatest attention. Although he had acquired an Arabic education at Egypt's al-Azhar and was viewed as socially and culturally conservative, he tried to develop the country's educational system in a way to promote Arabic but in addition to meeting national needs. Algeria at independence lacked trained teachers. To promote rapid educational expansion, Boumedienne brought in teachers from other Arabic-speaking countries. By the early 1980s, primary and secondary education was conducted in Arabic but university students could study in both French and

Arabic. Arabic education was often re-sisted by Berbers, mainly in the Kabyle areas, who spoke Arabic only as a third language after Berber and French. Dem-onstrations in 1980 showed that the reten-tion of a Berber cultural identity was still important to the Kabyles.

The economy stressed petroleum pro-duction and industrial development. A small cadre of dedicated bureaucrats con-trolled these areas. Algeria nationalized its largely French-owned petroleum in-dustry in 1971. High-quality Algerian oil brought a high price on the world market, especially after the price increases of the early 1970s. Because of the vulnerability of the petroleum industry to international market conditions and the limited quan-tity of oil in Algeria, the government used revenues to build up secondary industries, including machinery and fertilizer produc-tion. An agreement with the E.E.C. in January 1976 gave Algeria preferential treatment; this helped its petroleum and wine industries. Natural gas held promise for future revenues after the projected decline in oil production and export.

The weak spot of the Algerian econ-omy was agriculture. Most Algerians earned their living from this source. De-spite land-reform measures designed to increase incentives for production, Al-geria suffered from shortages of agri-cultural products as well as of consumer goods. Several hundred thousand Alge-rians chose to work abroad, especially in France, rather than earn lower wages or grow crops at home. Despite the impor-tance of home remittances for Algeria's foreign exchange earnings, the failure to generate higher production in indigenous agriculture forced the country to spend increasingly higher percentages of its own income for food imports.

Political life proved disappointing to many Algerians during the period of inde-pendence. With the passage of time, the F.L.N.'s role in national life diminished, although the army remained instrumental in social and economic development. Stu-dent activism was generally encouraged; many went to work in the countryside during their course of studies. From June 1967 onwards, communal assemblies were elected, and governorate representatives were chosen beginning in June 1974. No national parliamentary institutions ex-isted until elections in February 1977 chose a People's Assembly.

Considering the mass participation that accompanied the revolution, the lack of progress in female emanicipation noted by Algerian feminists such as Fadela Mrabet was disappointing. Mrabet pro-tested that Algerian women have con-tinued to be treated like chattel. Instead of remaining in the revolutionary vanguard, women retreated into conservatism. Ja-mila Buhrayd, a revolutionary heroine, now has publicly stated that women should play a quieter role in building the nation through raising children with a nationalist consciousness and a sense of social responsibility. The current diverg-ence of views is reminiscent of debates that took place in Egypt around the turn of the century. At that time too, the most revolutionary of the nationalists tended to favor a more family-oriented role for women while the liberal bourgeois nationalists advocated greater female emancipation.

While President Shadhli Benjedid (1978–) toned down Algeria's revolu-tionary rhetoric, he tried to address some of the country's persistent problems: ex-cessive centralization, Arabization, and relations with North African neighbors. He implemented a more decentralized governmental structure and improved quality and productivity in industry. Al-though he kept an open mind on the Arabization question, he was unquestion-ably Arab-oriented. Often at odds with Morocco, especially in the pursuit of rival goals in Western Sahara, Algeria under Benjedid tried to negotiate a resolution of the differences. Relations with Tunisia were generally stable, and those with Libya fluctuated. The Libyans and Alge-rians competed to some extent in support-ing the S.A.D.R. and other revolutionary governments including that of Iran.

A leader in third-world politics, Algeria was in the forefront of nations calling for a New International Economic

Order (see Chapter 21). Although Algeria participated in Arab League affairs, it did not forget that it was also part of Africa. The country's leadership maintained consistent support for African political and economic liberation. Moreover, Algerian diplomats negotiated the release of U.S. diplomatic hostages held in Iran from November 1979 to January 1982. The respect Algeria achieved internationally through all of these efforts promised to give the country further significance in nonaligned affairs throughout the 1980s.

Evolution of Bourguiban Pragmatism in Tunisia

In the 1970s, Bourguiba grew less tolerant of rivals for popularity and power. He arrested and imprisoned in 1970 his principal economic planner, Ben Salah, partly because of the latter's growing following. Three years later, Ben Salah escaped prison and took refuge in Switzerland. In 1974, an assassination plot against him was discovered and averted. Ben Salah, though abroad and subject to arrest should he return home, became leader of the Movement of Popular Unity (M.U.P.) which in November 1981 was among the parties contesting Tunisia's first postindependence multiparty elections. Claiming that the government did not intend to allow the opposition to operate freely, Ben Salah was not surprised when Bourguiba's party won every seat in the 121-member national assembly.

Even after the demise of Ben Salah, Bourguiba sought symbiosis in state-private sector industrialization. Yet Tunisia's bureaucracy consumed about one quarter of the gross national product. Tunisia's experience with state capitalism was not unlike that of Iraq, Algeria, Syria, and Egypt. Smaller enterprises seemed to operate more efficiently than large, labor-intensive industries.

With its small population, Tunisia depended on good management of scarce resources for economic success. The floods of 1969, which had exacerbated the rural discontent arising from Ben Salah's reform, were followed by better agricultural years. Tunisia won protection for its olive-oil and other industries through a tariff agreement concluded with the E.E.C. in 1976. Tunisia was the world's fourth largest phosphate producer behind the United States, the Soviet Union, and Morocco. The country also developed an indigenous chemical industry. In the 1980s, petroleum and natural gas revenues outstripped those of phosphates, with promise of greater gains after 1982 when agreement with Libya was reached over offshore finds. Tunisia's single most important industry, however, remained tourism. As in Algeria, Morocco, and Egypt, remittances from Tunisians working abroad, especially in France and Libya, also contributed to foreign-exchange earnings.

Independent Tunisia was not free of labor disputes and protests. On 26 January 1978, now known as *Black Thursday,* between forty (official figures) and four hundred Tunisian workers died during government suppression of a general strike by workers (particularly by those in the phosphates industry at Gafsa). Nearly one thousand trade unionists were convicted of crimes associated with the demonstrations. Two years later, on the morning of 27 January, a hitherto unknown Tunisian group calling itself the Tunisian Resistance Army attacked the army and national guard barracks as well as the police station in Gafsa. The estimated three hundred attackers took over the buildings and were evicted only at the cost of heavy casualties. Although the attackers crossed into Tunisia from Algeria, the government tried to place the blame on Libya. The group was assumed to consist of Tunisians working there. Although

Tunisian workers no doubt were upset at this time about wages, observers also suggested that outsiders wanted to exploit the Islamic revival to help destabilize Bourguiba's regime, long associated with secularist policies. An article in *Jeune Afrique*[2] in May 1982 declared that Boumedienne instigated the attack to discredit Prime Minister Hedi Nuwayra. Libya's Qadhdhafi admitted only to having armed Tunisian commandoes.[2]

Liberalization measures followed the demonstrations. Bourguiba, elected president-for-life in 1974, in fact did replace Nuwayra (previously assumed to be his heir-apparent) with Muhammad Mzali. The government freed political detainees, legalized the Tunisian Communist Party which had been suspended in 1963, permitted free trade-union elections in the U.G.T.T., and allowed opposition groups to publish their own newspapers. The subsequent assembly elections in 1981 attracted not only Ben Salah's M.U.P. but also the Movement of the Islamic Tendency that supported a more fully Islamic Tunisia; the Movement of Socialist Democrats led by well-known national figure Ahmad Mestiri, who advocated a more liberalized democracy; and the Tunisian Communist Party which focused on criticizing economic policies but offered very little in the way of alternatives. As Bourguiba reached his eighties observers wondered who would carry on after his death.

The position of women in Tunisian society has usually been considered in the context of laws forbidding polygamy. Tunisia's Muslims, the overwhelming majority of the country's population, considered Quranic statements about marriage, and determined that husbands could never treat several wives fairly. Fathia Mzali, the prime minister's wife, became the first woman to serve in the Destour's political bureau and was also the head of the National Union of Tunisian Women in the early 1980s. She was

not unlike many modern Muslim women in believing that Muslims themselves had over the centuries taken away many rights that the Quran had given to women. As in other industrialized countries, women in Tunisia customarily received lower salaries than comparably qualified men performing the same jobs. The Arab Working Women's Committee based in Tunis and led by Tunisian Saida Agrebi was specifically dedicated to the task of improving working conditions for women in the Arab world. Founded in 1975, the committee advocated the establishment of childcare facilities and adequate but not excessive maternity leave. Agrebi believed that women sometimes jeopardized progress by making unreasonable demands related to pregnancy. Since women in 1981 constituted an estimated 14 percent of the work force, she felt that the country was in an ideal position to lead the movement of working Arab women.

Tunisia's foreign policy under Bourguiba was both pragmatic and opportunistic. Cooperation with France continued in the early years of independence, although the two countries fell out in 1959 and 1961 over the issue of the French base at Bizerte. French properties were nationalized in 1964, but in 1972, Bourguiba made his first official visit to France. In 1981, Tunisia was the first Arab country to be visited by the new French foreign minister, Claude Cheysson. French aid continued to be a mainstay of the Tunisian economy.

Tunisia also maintained cordial relations with the United States and the Soviet Union. The "Libyan threat" caused the Reagan administration in 1981 to rush military aid (already increased under Carter) to Tunisia, although U.S. aid had been expected to end in 1982. In prior administrations, the Peace Corps provided one of the most visible symbols of U.S. economic assistance to Tunisia. During the 1967 June War, the U.S. embassy became a focus for anti-American feeling in Tunisia, but the government arrested those who had sacked it.

In inter-Arab politics, Tunisia remained a maverick following its own

---

[2] "Mouammar Kaddafi révèle comment Boumedienne a preparé Gafsa," *Jeune Afrique* No. 1114 (12 Mai 1982), pp. 52–53.

independent and often erratic course. Periodically, Bourguiba broke off relations with the Arab League when it refused to follow his lead, but it was to Tunis that the League moved its offices in 1980 after Egypt concluded the peace treaty with Israel. In 1974, Tunisia signed a union agreement with Libya that lasted exactly four days, thereby promoting an ongoing uneasy relationship. Despite disputes over offshore oil and allegations over the Libyan role at Gafsa, many Tunisians viewed Libya as the best hope for capital investment despite the government-projected reliance on oil-rich Kuwayt, Saudi Arabia, and the U.A.E.

Qadhdhafi's Libya

From the inception of his regime in 1969, Mu'ammar al-Qadhdhafi aimed to further Maghribian unity. Like Abd al-Nasir, but with the additional advantage of oil wealth, Qadhdhafi aspired to leadership in both Africa and Arab states. Unions with Sudan, Egypt, and Syria in 1970–71, Egypt in 1973, Tunisia in 1974, Syria in 1981, and Chad in 1981 failed to materialize. Qadhdhafi also advocated a revolutionary federation to unite Algeria, the S.A.D.R., and Mauritania. Although Libya and Mauritania fell out in December 1980 over Libyan-incited agitation against Iraqi teachers (an extension of Libyan support for Iran in the Gulf War), the two countries drew somewhat closer in 1981 after Morocco was accused of staging a coup-attempt against the Mauritanian government. Even as the Libyans tried to improve their deteriorating relations with the United States in 1981 and 1982, the Americans enlisted King Hasan II of Morocco in their campaign against Qadhdhafi. The United States expressed its disapproval of Qadhdhafi by stationing U.S. navy ships off the Libyan coast and by overt and covert attempts to contain his activities. Ironically, the United States in 1969 and 1970 had helped to thwart coup attempts intended to oust the Libyan leader.

Even with his foreign adventures, Qadhdhafi's approach to Africa and the Arab world remained both pragmatic and Islamic-oriented. Libya emerged as a generous donor to multilateral economic aid funds as well as to its own bilateral aid program in Africa and Asia, regardless of the political ideologies or religious beliefs of the beneficiaries. Qadhdhafi also tried, however, to convert various African leaders to Islam. Moreover, his intervention in the internal affairs of countries such as Niger and Ghana often exacerbated local political rivalries, and relations within the O.A.U. His personal lifestyle was unostentatious and in line with his beliefs, but his political and socioeconomic ideology was more difficult to practice.

Making use of revolutionary committees, Qadhdhafi suppressed dissent expressed by students from time to time. The committees were also blamed by critics for overseas assassinations of Libyans (nine took place in 1980). Libya's "democracy" was regarded by many Libyans, especially those dispossessed by his policies, as an instrument of oppression rather than liberation.

Society's Mirror: Cultural Developments in the Arabic World

The Arabic language has enabled all Arabic-speaking peoples to share in cultural manifestations such as literature and cinema. Prewar Egyptian singer Umm Kulthum has remained, despite her death in 1975, the Arab world's most popular singer. In the postwar world, Egypt continues to lead in the film industry. Under the early years of the revolution, socialist realism was the dominant trend in the government-sponsored industry. During the 1960s, Egypt produced several films that won international acclaim. The film version of Sharqawi's novel *The Land,* emphasizing peasant oppression, was still in circulation in the 1980s, produced by leading film maker Yusuf Shahin. Salah Abu Sayf also represented the realist trend in films like *al-Qahira Thalathin* (*Cairo 30*), again addressing problems of the interwar period but emphasizing urban politics.

After the 1967 War, film makers criticized the factors held responsible for the defeat. The government often banned films it regarded as demoralizing. After the death of Abd al-Nasir, films disparaging his regime began to emerge as the industry was returned to the private sector. Well-known novelists, including Nagib Mahfuz and Ihsan Abd al-Quddus, wrote scripts in this vein. In the 1980s, writer Lutfi al-Khuli—a critic of the Sadat regime and a member of Tagamu'a—made an allegorical film based on Egyptian emigration.

Yusuf Shahin also continued to teach at Egypt's film institute and to make films such as *Alexandria . . . Why?,* a brilliant portrait of Egypt during World War II. The institute's new director, Hisham Abu al-Nasr, received a doctorate in the United States. His first film, *al-Aqmar,* won prizes in French, Tunisian, and Egyptian festivals. Director Abu Sayf was responsible for the Iraqi-sponsored epic film *Qadisiyya,* which appeared in 1981. In this, his thirty-eighth film, the Egyptian director resisted the temptation to turn the historical event into a propaganda piece designed to relate to the 1980–83 Gulf War between Iraq and Iran. Qadisiyya was the principal historical battle that opened Sassanian Iran to Muslim government.

Syria, another early pioneer in films, continued to produce directors. Foreign education, especially in France, was common to most of them. Salah Dahny, for example, directed and authored fifteen films, including *Heroes are Born Twice* about a Palestinian boy in Gaza who wants to join the resistance. The Palestinian theme absorbed the attentions of both Palestinian and non-Palestinian filmmakers in Syria. Although Syria, Iraq, and other Arab countries had neither the audiences nor the numerous theaters of Egypt, they too worked to expand their film industries and to participate in regional and international festivals.

In 1980, a new festival began to alternate between Carthage and Damascus. The Tunisian festival focused on Arab and African films, while in the alternate year the Damascus festival treated Asian and Arab films. The Syrians then decided to expand the event to include the third-world countries of Latin America. The fact that Asian republics of the U.S.S.R. participated indicated growing contacts between Soviet Muslims and those of Asia and Africa.

Theater and folklore also developed in the Arab world after World War II. With their rich archeological heritage, the Arab countries of Southwest Asia and North Africa began to utilize ancient theaters for contemporary purposes. An annual festival in Ba'lbek, Lebanon attracted international performers for years. Jordan inaugurated a festival in Jerash. In 1981, the Syrians founded a summer festival in the Roman amphitheatre at Busra. Most Arab countries maintained folklore troupes who toured internationally. Egypt's Rida and National troupes often traveled abroad. Cairo has remained the center for Arab drama; many theaters play to packed audiences. As with film, playwrights have not always been free to present works critical of the government. Layla Abu Sayf has been among the producer/actresses who has staged serious plays that often criticize the position of women in society.

Arabic literature is among the most noteworthy achievements of the postwar Arab world. Works are increasingly translated into Western languages. Sudanese writer Tayyib Salih has addressed the problems of identity and confrontation with British culture in *Season of Migration to the North*. Nagib Mahfuz has continued to be Egypt's leading writer of novels, commenting on dilemmas of everyday life often in a broad context of allegory. Although he did not encourage translation of his numerous works, his novels *Midaq Alley, Miramar,* and *Children of Gebelaawi* exist in English versions. Many of his novels, including *Chatter on the Nile, The Thief and the Dogs,* and *The Mirage* were made into films. Mahfuz also wrote screenplays.

In the short-story field, the best-known Egyptian writer was Yusuf Idris, a doctor who dealt with social struggle, especially that of women and oppressed people. Often his stories seemed fatalistic. In the "House of Flesh," for example, a widow marries a blind Quran-reader, encouraged by her three ugly marriage-age daughters who then exploit his condition by sharing his marital bed. Yahya Haqqi, Fathi Ghanim, and Yusuf al-Siba'i were among Egypt's more prolific short-story writers. Women in the Arab world also achieved recognition in this field. Author of the novel *I Live,* Lebanese Layla al-Ba'lbaki wrote "A Spaceship of Tenderness to the Moon," soon confiscated by the authorities for its explicit references to sensual experience. The censors also disapproved of the reservations about childbearing expressed by the story's female protagonist.

In drama, Tawfiq al-Hakim is probably the best-known writer, again because of wide circulation of his works. In *The Fate of the Cockroach,* Hakim presents two cockroaches trying to escape from a bathtub; he compares their problems with those of the human occupants of the house and society as a whole.

Among newer fiction writers are Sabri Moussa (*The Seeds of Corruption*) and Sami Bindari (*The House of Power*). Both authors deal with social dilemmas, although Moussa's novel is far more abstract. *The House of Power* is a gripping tale of Egyptian peasant life.

Poetry is of the oldest genres of Arabic literature, and writers still abound. Nazik al-Mala'ika is an Iraqi who pioneered in the free-verse movement. Writing before and after World War II, she also wrote scholarly studies of the movement. Her poetry tends toward the romantic. Badr Shakir al-Shayyib—initially a Communist who wrote romantic and then realistic poetry—and Abd al-Wahab al-Bayati, also in the socialist realist school, were also important Iraqi poets. Kurdish Iraqi poet Baland al-Haydari lived much of his life in exile in Beirut, dealing most often with the theme of oppression.

In Egypt, Salah Abd al-Sabur was one of the most productive poets. His work in literary criticism was widely circulated through newspaper columns in *al-Ahram*. He wrote many poems and plays in free verse until his death in 1981. Muhammad al-Maghut and Ali Ahmad Sa'id (Adonis) were two of the most active and well-known Syrian poets. Adonis settled in Lebanon and published not only his own poetry but also volumes of classical Arabic poetry and literary criticism. A Syrian diplomat, Nizar Qabbani (also residing in Lebanon), turned to political themes in the postwar period, with special emphasis on the theme of Palestinian resistance.

Cultural life has consistently been vigorous and responsive to modern challenges. Arab governments have helped to promote literature and the arts but have occasionally applied censorship. Because of the opportunity to publish or produce in many Arab countries, though, repressive policies have not achieved their desired aim. Authors have simply sent their work elsewhere, particularly to Beirut. With the problems created by persistent fighting in the 1970s, Beirut's publishing industry suffered. The Gulf states, however, offered new possibilities for publication.

Oil, Investment, and Aid in Southwest Asian and North African International Relations and Political Economy

The history of foreign investment and aid in the Middle East has long involved concessions, rivalry, judicial peculiarities, long negotiations, and on occasion, hostility. Egypt paid for Suez Canal and other debts until 1943 partly because its revenues had been pledged to the Ottoman debt in the nineteenth century. Collapse of the empire did not prevent creditors from placing the burden of payment on Egypt. Traditionally, foreign investment aimed for the highest possible profits. Foreign governments often used investment by nationals as a pretext for intervention in local politics.

Capital flow in the first twenty-five years after World War II most often, directly or indirectly, involved oil and foreign aid. Not by coincidence, countries lacking large petroleum industries tended to be large foreign-aid recipients. Oil producers also received aid in preproduction or low-revenue years. Some foreign-aid recipients maintained modest aid programs of their own. In the 1970s and 1980s, Southwest Asian and North African countries themselves became major donors of foreign aid, especially to other developing nations in Asia and Africa. Petroleum revenues made the big difference.

The most important economic change in postwar Southwest Asia and North Africa was its development as the world's premier regional petroleum producer and exporter. In 1982, Middle Eastern and Arab African nations produced over 36 percent of the world's oil, exceeding by more than 10 percent the output of the Soviet bloc. Offshore and onshore finds gave the region an estimated 50 percent of world reserves.

International Supply and Demand: An Overview

For some fifty years, Western companies that developed oil dominated all industrial operations because of unequal concessions. They often embraced huge tracts of land. Paying royalties but no taxes, companies could influence politics in oil-dependent countries. The U.S. State Department analysts of the 1940s noted that Southwest Asian oil would be a major source for the U.S. by the 1980s. In 1940, the United States consumed about 70 percent of the world's production. As long as petroleum elsewhere was inexpensive, the United States conserved its own oil and even let its domestic oil industry decline. When World War II ended, U.S. and Venezuelan production could not provide for demand in Europe and Japan where reconstruction needs were great. North African and Southwest Asian oil was to meet this demand. By the mid-1960s, Japan was the Middle East's largest oil importer. In the 1970s it became the largest trading partner. Developing countries began to need greater amounts of oil, too. Even by 1967 when the Middle East produced 29 percent of the world's oil, it consumed only 2 percent. Supply far exceeded local demand.

Moreover, Middle East oil was relatively cheap. In the 1960s, the average Middle Eastern well produced 4,500 barrels compared with 300 for a Venezuelan well and 15 for a U.S. well. Oil reached the surface without costly pumping. With low-cost production, companies expanded exploration. This led to new discoveries not only in prewar producers but also in Libya, Algeria, the Gulf, and Egypt. As long as companies controlled production, refining, and marketing, they ensured themselves ample supplies and generous profits. Most profits were repatriated, benefiting the home countries and permitting diversifiation of oil-company operations.

During the 1950s and 1960s, posted prices for Saudi oil dropped from the levels of the late 1940s. While oil prices remained stagnant, the cost to producers of goods manufactured abroad more than doubled. Concessional arrangements in the 1950s allowed more revenues to accrue to producing nations through fifty-fifty profit-sharing agreements. In the 1970s, oil companies undertook joint ventures with government companies set up for that purpose. During the 1970s, the petroleum industry began to undergo nationalization (with compensation), but downstream operations, especially transportation and marketing, remained under the oil majors' control. Map 23 depicts Middle East hydrocarbons in the early 1980s (see Map 21). Because of company-control over supply and the excess of supply over demand, proportionately minimal benefits went to the Middle Eastern and Southwest Asia countries. The oil industry in the 1950s and 1960s employed few indigenous workers. Those that were hired were heavily concentrated in non-managerial positions. To the mid-1970s, oil-power existed but it was mainly in corporate hands.

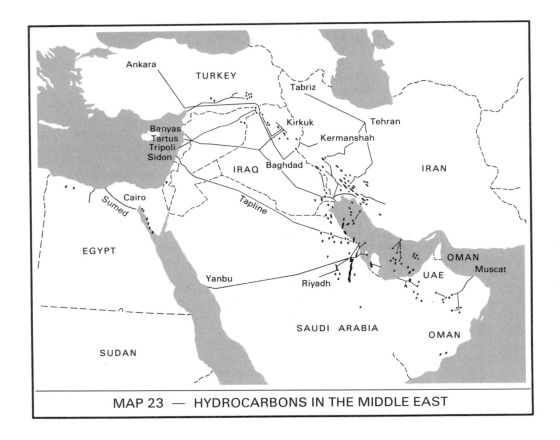

MAP 23 — HYDROCARBONS IN THE MIDDLE EAST

Exploration, Discoveries, and Production: Mutual Accommodation

There are three main categories of postwar North African and Southwest Asian producers. The production giants—Saudi Arabia and Kuwayt—along with Libya, the U.A.E., Qatar, and Oman (all four beginning after 1960) were overwhelmingly dependent on petroleum as a source of national wealth but had proportionately tiny populations and, therefore, high per-capita incomes.

Development took place initially under single companies or consortia which, like the old I.P.C. group, included companies from different countries. The old U.S., French, Dutch, and British in-

terests predominated, though Italian, Japanese, and German companies won new concessions. Small U.S. firms such as Getty Oil (earlier Pacific Western) and Aminoil (American Independent) gained a share, too, making it more difficult for the majors to control the industry. Production expanded by leaps and bounds. From 1945–1955, daily output in Kuwayt zoomed from a few thousand to over one million barrels. In Saudi Arabia, annual production between 1945 and 1974 grew by 150 times from 21 million barrels to 3.2 billion barrels. Saudi output still came from its eastern Arabian, Shi'i province of al-Hasa. In 1982, Saudi Arabia was the world's second largest producer after the Soviet Union. Though far below the level of these six, Bahrayn, a prewar oil producer, still enjoyed a per-capita income in the late 1970s higher than that of Israel but one-third the size of that in Kuwayt. The small local demands on their energy made all seven countries exporters of high percentages of their oil.

The mutual profitability and dependency between governments and countries led to reasonably cordial relations because both wanted to maximize their profits with minimal effort. Saudi Arabia's King Sa'ud (1953–64) ignored government budgets and piled up debts through personal extravagance and foreign intervention in neighboring countries. After the Saudis replaced him with his brother Faysal (1964–75), the government repaid the debts, balanced the budget, and reduced the royal family's share of government revenues. Yet the economy remained closely integrated with international markets. In the 1960s and 1970s, Saudi defense-spending rose. Technical expertise, machinery, building material, and consumer goods were imported from abroad, principally from the United States, Japan, Western Europe, and South Asia. Individual wealthy Saudis also invested overseas. Whether for national development, defense, or personal pleasure, Saudis and the Saudi government recycled their money outside the country. Diversifying companies could expand their business interests in the kingdom.

The Kuwaytis used their revenues for urban development in the 1950s and 1960s, especially in education, health, sanitation, and other social services. Because of this investment in human resources, Kuwayt achieved by the mid-1970s higher life expectancy and lower infant mortality rates than any other North African or Southwest Asian country except Cyprus and Israel. Both boys and girls benefited from educational opportunities at all levels. Without oil revenues, this comprehensive program would have been impossible. Similar programs

were developed in more recent producers such as Libya and Abu Dhabi.

Countries and companies worked hard to accommodate each other. Ruling elites and companies needed stability if revenues were to keep pouring in. Labor unrest—for example, a strike against A.R.A.M.C.O. in 1953—brought about improved working conditions but it also led to a strike ban. The impact of oil in low population-high production countries was regional as well as international. Besides foreign aid, oil states provided jobs for workers from poorer Arab countries, for Palestinians, and for South Asians. Remittances provided significant foreign exchange for the workers' home countries. While Palestinians and Egyptians often held skilled and managerial positions, other foreign workers, especially Yemenis, were likely to get lower-level work.

The Gulf city-states employed foreigners in social services, the tourist and hotel trades, general clerical positions, construction, education, and skilled and unskilled labor. While the oil industry itself employed few workers, the revenues it generated opened up new employment opportunities. For the workers, the hope of earning a better living in the oil countries usually materialized, though occasionally it did not, especially for illegal entrants. Recruits discovered that living and working conditions could be less than ideal. Governments and oil companies did not have to provide guest workers with the same benefits given to their own nationals. This work force could easily be expelled. Nevertheless, labor migration spread oil wealth to citizens of poorer countries in the region, expanding the lower middle classes but also increasing aspirations and expectations.

At the other end of the production spectrum are Israel, Morocco, Turkey, and Tunisia. These states produced small quantities of oil insufficient for domestic needs, and were import-dependent. Only Tunisia, with its offshore finds of the late 1970s and early 1980s, could hope for future self-sufficiency though Morocco in

1981 considered developing shale oil to meet its needs. Syria, though a larger producer, also absorbed its domestic production. In none of these countries did oil contribute over 10 percent to the gross national product.

Until the 1980s, Egypt was on the same list but between 1974 and 1980 (excluding recovery of fields occupied by Israel in 1967), oil production quadrupled, thus increasing the share of oil in total government revenues by 28 percent and in export earnings to 50 percent. In 1980, foreign petroleum sales, even with domestic subsidies, brought in $2.65 billion. By 1981, Egypt's production exceeded that of Ecuador, Gabon, and Qatar—all members of the Organization of Petroleum Exporting Countries (OPEC). With its diversified industry and agriculture, Egypt could hardly be characterized as oil-dependent, but its problems more nearly approximated those of big producers with large populations—Algeria, Iraq, and Iran.

In much of the postwar period, Iraq and Iran rivalled Saudi Arabia and Kuwayt in production. Governments in both countries suffered production declines in the 1950s because of attempts to nationalize or gain greater control over their oil. They set up national companies of their own in the process. Algeria also suffered briefly in the 1970s after handing over French-controlled oil to its own national company, Sonatrach. Both Iran and Algeria were expecting to experience production declines in the 1990s but still could look to natural gas and petrochemical development as potential major income earners of the future. Algeria, Iraq, and Iran invested oil revenues in long-term projects in agriculture and industry, moving toward economic diversification (the greatest potential for which was in Iraq). Iran under Shah Muhammad Reza also indulged in conspicuous consumption to glorify the Pahlevi dynasty. In all three countries, efforts to promote agricultural growth for food production achieved mixed results. As a result of discoveries between 1978 and 1981 near Bentiu in the south, Sudan was expected to be self-sufficient in petroleum by the mid-1980s.

Transportation and Marketing

The task of bringing Middle Eastern oil to market led companies to invest in pipelines, offshore terminals, and tankers. I.P.C.'s first pipelines—12 inches in diameter—took oil from Kirkuk to Tripoli, Lebanon and Haifa, Palestine. After World War II, two more lines were added, but the company abandoned the Haifa lines in the wake of the establishment of Israel and the Palestine War of 1947–49. In 1952 and 1961, new 30-inch lines were built, terminating at Banyas in Syria. Jordan, Syria, and Lebanon all received transit revenues. All three also profited when A.R.A.M.C.O. built TAPLINE, opened in 1950, a 1000-mile long 30-inch pipeline from eastern Arabia to the Lebanese port of Saida. The road built alongside the line to connect pumping stations developed into a main Mediterranean Gulf artery. These pipelines proved valuable when the 1967 War closed the Suez Canal. Disputes with Syria over transit fees in the 1970s led Iraq to plan two new lines, through Turkey and to the Gulf. Iraq's two terminals, at Khur al-Amaya and Mina al-Bakr, were badly damaged during the Gulf War in September 1980. In August 1981, Iraq and Saudi Arabia announced construction of a new Iraqi line from Basra to Yanbu, to follow the route of Saudi Arabia's own PETROLINE from Ghawar in Eastern Arabia to Yanbu. Egypt sponsored construction of SUMED to connect Suez with the Mediterranean. Because Iranian oil was already located near the sea in Khuzistan, most of its pipelines carried oil to northern cities. But Iran also built large terminals at Kharg Island, Bushire, and Bandar Mashur along the Gulf. Pipelines were also important for transporting oil to the Gulf from Qatar's interior fields. This concentration of oil terminals made the channel from the Gulf to the Gulf of Oman and Indian Ocean one of the world's most strategic locations, especially for Japan, Western Europe, and the United States.

Most oil exporters sent oil abroad unrefined. In the late 1940s, tankers of 25,000 deadweight tons (dwt) were viewed as large. As sizes increased, the Suez Canal was deepened. Its closure from 1967–75 led to construction of supertankers of over 300,000 dwt. From 1975 to 1980, Egypt renewed an earlier project to allow fully laden tankers of 150,000 dwt. Larger ships could use the canal after having offloaded their cargoes. By 1988, Egyptian and Japanese companies expected to prepare the canal for fully laden ships of 250,000 dwt. By reducing fees for large tankers, Egypt hoped to regain traffic lost during the canal's closure though export declines of 1981–82 arising from the Gulf War and the oil glut also lowered canal revenues.

OPEC: Myth and Reality

In the 1950s, the fifty-fifty sharing of net profits increased revenues to producing nations (although royalties were deducted from gross rather than net profits) by companies, thereby reducing the amounts. Saudi Arabia and A.R.A.M.C.O. pioneered this arrangement, followed by Iran, Iraq, and Kuwayt. Saudi Arabia's revenues grew enough to enable it to join the International Bank for Reconstruction and Development or World Bank (I.B.R.D.) in 1957. Management of revenues became a question of social, political, and economic importance in all four countries. When the companies reduced prices in 1959 and 1960, the producers concluded that concerted action was required.

In 1960, the four producers joined the world's third largest producer at the time (after the United States and the Soviet Union) Venezuela, to form OPEC. Its first job was to secure restoration of prices to their former level and to pressure companies to consult with it when changes in price were anticipated. OPEC's ultimate goal was to secure control for producers over their petroleum industries, but the organization did not expect to achieve this overnight. In the 1960s, OPEC's members could not agree on pricing because the companies coordinated production and marketing. The only concession won by OPEC from the companies was to have royalties deducted from gross earnings rather than from profits. The Iran settlement of 1954 which sustained the National Iranian Oil Company (N.I.O.C.) founded in 1951, paved the way for it to embark on joint exploration and exploitation ventures. Although the international consortium continued to control over 95 percent of Iran's production, the initiation of partnership brought more Iranians responsible positions. Producing countries also inaugurated training programs. The Saudi government in 1963 founded the College of Petroleum and Minerals at Dhahran; it has become one of the Middle East's premier educational institutions. A.R.A.M.C.O., too, initiated training programs that gradually gave Saudis supervisory positions, though in the 1960s top management remained predominantly American. In other oil-producing countries, government efforts and joint ventures (more than company plans) accounted for increased numbers of nationals trained to advance their nation's oil industry.

The idea of national control received a boost in November 1966 when the United

Nations General Assembly affirmed the right of every country to hold permanent sovereignty over national resource development. OPEC in a 1968 statement recognized that only when countries exploited their petroleum resources themselves would they be able to derive full benefit from them. While the step-by-step approach brought gradual improvement to long-range prospects for national control, little progress was made in altering company-producer relationships. National companies and joint ventures lacked sufficient strength to challenge the big foreign companies that could often look to their countries for diplomatic support.

Because of the reduced prices of the late 1960s, OPEC again tried to settle pricing with the oil companies. OPEC members observed that Egypt, Libya, and Iran had won concessions in new agreements contracted with various small companies. As an OPEC member, Iran was also committed to working with other producers. A negotiating team from Iran, Iraq, and Saudi Arabia achieved agreement with the companies for guaranteed increases to take place between 1971 and 1975. This prevented unilateral price reductions on the part of companies. The Gulf states agreed to uphold these prices. International pressures, though, altered the situation. Because prices were posted in dollars, devaluations of 1971 and 1973 cut into the revenues of Middle Eastern governments. Companies viewed the subsequent demands for increased prices as justified. Even then, the posted price for a barrel of oil had risen by only $1.10 between 1947 and 1973.

Countries also renewed efforts to win a greater role in production decisions. Algeria and Libya nationalized their oil operations in 1971, obtaining participation agreements in the aftermath. Though individual arrangements varied, Algeria won 50 percent participation in operations. The successes of Algeria and Libya helped Abu Dhabi, Qatar, Kuwayt, and Saudi Arabia reach similar agreements in 1972. In every case, a government firm would receive an annually increasing share in local operations. By 1983, the government would own 51 percent. All countries acknowledged that the companies would be compensated, but specific amounts were left open for negotiation. Having won concessions over pricing and ownership of oil, producing nations decided to abandon the gradualist approach to achieving greater control. Iran acquired majority ownership in the foreign consortium by promising to continue to supply the company partners. The 1973 Middle East War gave other Gulf producers the same opportunity.

The picture that emerges from the impact of OPEC and the oil producers in general is still one of a tacit alliance between rulers and governments, on the one hand, and companies, on the other. Nationalization in its varying degrees did not, in itself, translate into fundamental social change. That depended on the ruling elites, whether elected, appointed, hereditary, or self-proclaimed. The cheap energy provided by Southwest Asian and North African output was taken for granted by consumers in the industrialized world. Perhaps the ensuing energy crisis meant simply the realization on the part of giant consumers that foreign sources could no longer be counted on to supply cheap energy. Poor countries that lacked petroleum faced the same reality, albeit with few resources available to fund their desired development.

The Oil Embargo of 1973 and its Aftermath

Before countries had acquired some control over their oil industries, an oil embargo could not have achieved success.

Companies in the 1970s made the necessary concessions based on the realization that security of supply was more important than ownership of local operations. Pressure succeeded because of the exponential increase in international oil consumption. Even with new discoveries of the 1950s and 1960s, the oil industry could not come up with new finds quickly enough to meet the quantum leap in demand. Middle Eastern rulers and governments recognized that the buyer's market had become a seller's market. Western Europe and Japan were especially dependent on Middle East oil, and the United States could expect to rely on foreign imports because of depletion of U.S. reserves.

Participation and nationalization agreements, by the time of the embargo, had made Middle Eastern countries partners in the oil industry. In 1970–71 Libya had demonstrated through slashing production that a high-revenue low-population country could afford to pressure companies because local demand for funds was relatively low. Early in the 1970s, countries were already accumulating huge reserves, even with price stagnation and dollar devaluation losses. The combination of 1) being able to manage with less, and 2) recycling problems created by excessive production placed these countries in an ideal position to cut production.

In 1973, Arab oil producers warned Western nations that they would use the oil weapon to pressure Israel into a settlement if no action was forthcoming. Israeli intransigence in negotiating a return of territories occupied in 1967, and expressed Israeli intentions to further colonize occupied Sinai, made Egyptian President Anwar al-Sadat especially apprehensive. In summer 1973, Sadat traveled to Arab capitals to rally support. Saudi Arabia and Gulf states warned that continuation of the cordial U.S.-Saudi relationship in petroleum would require changes in the long-standing U.S. bias in the Middle East. During 1972–73, both Libya and Iraq recommended an embargo. These hints were not entirely ignored. The chairman of the U.S. Senate Foreign Relations Committee, William Fulbright, told his colleagues that the

United States was bound to pay for its overriding commitment to Israel. Although Egypt and Syria failed to disrupt oil in 1956 (and various Arab countries threatened in 1967), this did not mean that a future attempt would fail, too.

Announcement of the oil embargo and of the first production cuts came on 17 October 1973, when the United States began airlifting military supplies to Israel. The Organization of Arab Petroleum Exporting Countries (O.A.P.E.C.) began with 5 percent reductions but promised further cutbacks unless Israel agreed to withdraw from Arab territory occupied in 1967 and to recognize the rights of the Palestinians. Oil prices were raised, too, with non-Arab Iran taking the lead. Since reduced production harmed Europe and Japan much more than the United States, the oil producers beginning with the U.A.E. also imposed an embargo on oil shipments to the United States. The Netherlands and Denmark were also included in the embargo. Iraq objected to the idea, preferring to nationalize on 21 October the Dutch share in the Basra Petroleum Company. The Arab blockade of the Bab al-Mandab Straits at the southern end of the Red Sea cut off potential Iranian deliveries to Israel but not elsewhere.

How effective were the embargo and production cuts? The quantity of oil leaving the Middle East actually rose slightly as Iran stepped up production. Companies continued to receive their oil supplies, making record profits in 1973–74 because price increases were passed to western consumers—old oil was sold at new prices. (Only a small fraction of the extra amount paid by consumers for the oil reached the producing nations.) Because of control over marketing, oil companies could manipulate supplies.

Producer nations derived great benefit from the price increases that accompanied the embargo. The price of an average barrel of oil jumped from $3.28 in 1973 to $10.46 in 1974. Spot market prices reached much higher levels. When Iran's oil revenues jumped from $2.5 billion in 1970 to $18 billion in 1974, the Shah announced that within a generation, Iran would join the United States, the Soviet Union, China, and Japan as one of the world's five great powers. Because producers were receiving so much more income, those who decided to cut production could apparently afford to do so. Conservation seemed like a good idea.

In the political arena, though, the embargo demonstrated the limited potential of using petroleum to achieve political goals. While helping to promote ceasefire and disengagement agreements, the embargo against the United States and other countries was dropped in March and July 1974 respectively. Neither of the stated aims—Israeli withdrawal or recognition of the Palestinians' national rights—had been achieved. Moreover, a vicious anti-Arab campaign was launched by the U.S. media; they presented the spectre of oil-rich Arabs taking over Western economies. The question of Palestinian rights and Israeli expansion was lost as people accused the Arabs of greediness. Europeans more readily welcomed Arab and non-Arab OPEC investment in their economies.

Despite the potential of the use of oil as a political weapon, the 1973–74 embargo underscored the fact of international economic interdependence and the possibility of military intervention by a big power. As the oil companies diverted ample supplies to other countries, consumers in cold climates began to suffer because of high winter demands and escalated energy costs. Recession struck the developed world in 1974. Because oil producing nations had placed their investments overseas, they too suffered. Ambitious development plans formulated earlier in the year had to be abandoned as countries faced falling revenues and, consequently, indebtedness to Western creditors. To prevent an oil glut, production was curtailed. Although most consumers hoped that OPEC's new price structure would collapse, U.S. Secretary of State Henry Kissinger pointed to the utility of high pricing in forcing conservation and the development of alternative energy sources.

Despite the oil price increases, not all Middle Eastern and North African oil producers after 1974 reaped a windfall from the oil price increases. Only Saudi Arabia between 1974 and 1980 was able to maintain its high-cost development plan. In 1976, the Saudis initiated negotiations to purchase A.R.A.M.C.O., finally achieving success in 1980. Kuwayt nationalized its oil in 1975. However, for the five years before 1979–80, all OPEC producers lost value because of inflation and the decline of the dollar internationally. As world prices stabilized at $12–13 per barrel, Iran in 1976 suffered a balance-of-payments deficit. Meanwhile, consumer and industrial goods manufactured overseas rose in price.

Market Pressures

Why did prices rise again? Renewed high demand combined with low prices to divert undervalued oil to spot markets, especially in Iran. Foreign companies often resold at high rates oil purchased for low contract prices in the Middle East. As the uniform pricing system fell apart in 1979–80, dramatic price hikes resumed. Within two years, oil prices tripled. The highest quality oil from Nigeria, Algeria, and Libya reached an official price of $40 per barrel. Importing countries that had relaxed conservation efforts as the memory of the embargo faded, Kissinger's warning notwithstanding, renewed these efforts. Oil imports to the United States, still the greatest energy consumer, declined from a 1978 high of nearly 9 million barrels per day to 5 million by mid-1981. Besides expanding the search for alternative sources, coal reserves and natural gas began to be more heavily exploited. By 1981, the introduction of more energy-efficient machinery, long a feature of European conservation, also contributed to reducing U.S. demands.

As the high cost of energy affected poor nations disproportionately—though they consumed little when compared with the industrialized world—oil producers in 1980s faced new decisions about pricing and their own needs. Nigeria, Algeria, and Indonesia—countries with limited reserves and high population and industrial demands—regarded the maintenance of high prices as essential. In January 1981, Saudi Arabian Oil Minister Shaykh Ahmad Zaki al-Yamani told students at the University of Petroleum and Minerals: "At present Algeria sells one million barrels of oil a day. In 1985, it will be selling only one-half million and in 1990 sales will drop to zero. If I were Algerian, I would certainly want the price of oil to reach $100 a barrel this very day, even at the risk of driving the world to an economic depression. If by doing so, I drive the world to invest in alternate sources of energy, such investments will not bear fruit in less than ten years. By then, the matter would be of no concern to me." (*Newsweek International*, 1 June 1981)

Gulf producers and Saudi Arabia could afford the idea of long-term and gradual price rises, especially as a means of protecting investment abroad. In 1981, Saudi Arabia stepped up production to some 10 million barrels per day in order to force other OPEC members into a substantial price cut. Ultimately, they hoped to achieve agreement on linking prices to inflation, to the rate of the U.S. dollar, and to economic growth in industrialized countries. Saudi Arabia's effort to reduce prices was so successful that in 1982 it intervened on behalf of Nigeria to prevent further price erosion. By 1983, the OPEC-percentage of world oil production and export had shrunk in the face of an ongoing glut. Economic experts agreed that stabilization of price was a desirable goal to prevent a collapse of international finance.

The OPEC impasse showed that its members did not necessarily share the same needs and goals. If actions by one member, especially when combined with those of nonmembers such as Mexico, Britain, and Norway, could impair the long-range plans of other member states, then OPEC's utility was limited. It was up to members to decide whether OPEC and O.A.P.E.C. had outlived their usefulness.

Although Mahdi Ali, an administrator with the OPEC Fund for International Development, predicted in 1981 that Middle East oil would dry up by 2011 at 1977 pumping levels, no one could accurately assess the long-term prospects for the industry. With so many variables at work, countries could only hope that their development plans would accomplish the economic diversification necessary to sustain their people once the oil was gone.

Investment and Banking

While the price increases of the 1970s helped Saudi Arabia triple its gross domestic product and double its real per capita income between 1970 and 1980, they also raised the level of Saudi investments in and purchases from the industrialized world, not to mention the huge Saudi aid program. Foreign contractors and companies flocked to the developing oil states in the 1970s and 1980s in hopes of gaining a share of the wealth. At least in part, the Iranian revolution of 1977–79 represented a reaction to inequities and social disruption created by sudden oil wealth. Social justice was likely to persist as a crucial question until people could see tangible benefits and the end to erosion of social values.

While agricultural sectors of national economies continued to sustain low growth, governments could expect more severe economic dislocation in the future, especially with rapidly growing populations and food import bills. Finally, though investment abroad carried an element of danger, the leverage over foreign economies that it brought about reminded consuming nations of the need for ongoing dialogue and mutual support. Western countries that had grown accustomed to playing key roles in Middle Eastern and Arab African economies were confronted with new realities of partnership and power.

Increasing Middle Eastern financial power led to new developments and relationships. Initially, Middle Easterners put money into real estate and banks, often outside their own countries. The economy of Lebanon, for example, was to a great extent based on serving tourism and financial interests of Arab oil producers. Viewed as the Switzerland of the region, Lebanon also attracted Asians and Africans to its universities. Beirut was the conduit for goods from all over the world. Through the civil war and U.S. intervention in 1958 up to 1975, Lebanon sustained this position. Even early in the 1980s, Lebanon's banking system and gross national product remained strong because Lebanese refugees working abroad continued to remit money home. After the June 1982 Israeli invasion of Lebanon, however, the country's prospects for ongoing recovery grew dimmer.

Middle Easterners also began to found banks as one way of keeping financial resources under their own control. When the Arab Banking Association was set up in London in 1980, over one hundred local and another hundred overseas banks joined. Several governments established banks, including the Arab Banking Corporation (major shareholders: Kuwayt, Libya, U.A.E.) or the Gulf International Bank, both based in Bahrayn, a rapidly growing financial center. The Saudi Arabian Monetary Agency (S.A.M.A.) held 50 percent of the shares in the Saudi International Bank of London. Privately owned banks included al-Saudi Banque based in Paris. Islamic banks that neither paid nor charged interest experienced rapid growth, often focusing on development aid, in the 1970s. Overseas commercial banks, like their Western counterparts, more often invested in and lent to the industrialized world.

Development Aid in Arab Africa and the Middle East

During cold-war years—the 1950s and the 1960s—the United States and the Soviet Union contributed both economically and militarily to Middle Eastern governments in hopes of gaining political or ideological advantage. In both cases, development aid often led recipients into new dependency relationships through requirements that loans or grants be used to purchase supplies from the donor. Foreign aid boosted donor economies. Even if the recipients could have obtained more suitable products closer to home, the option was rarely given. France and Britain gave aid, too, mostly but not necessarily to lands formerly occupied by them. Japan, West Germany, and Italy maintained aid-connections closely associated with their trading interests. Excepting Japan and with the addition of the People's Republic of China, these economic aid donors also provided the bulk of weapons, general military supplies, and training in the post-war period. Because of their desire to safeguard their independence and the primacy of national interests, Southwest Asian and North African governments adopted and then discarded patrons of conflicting ideologies. Both regional and nonregional donors often refused aid to countries that rejected their ideological stance in international relations. When they could, countries—especially the poorest—kept open channels to all possible sources of aid.

How did aid-relationships evolve in

the early postwar period? Egypt, Israel, and Turkey received the greatest amounts. The poorest of the three—Egypt—was given the least aid. In the 1950s, both Eastern and Western blocs provided aid to Egypt, but U.S. cold-war politics and the Suez War pushed Egypt closer to the U.S.S.R. from the mid-1950s to the early 1970s. As the region's largest and most influential Arab country, especially under Gamal Abd al-Nasir who gained international respect in the non-aligned movement, Egypt could hardly be ignored for long.

Israel, consistently the highest per capita recipient of foreign aid in the world since its establishment, received aid which on a per capita basis exceeded that of Egypt by some thirty to forty times, at least until the 1980s (when it was reduced to perhaps fifteen times). Overall aid to Israel also exceeded that given to Turkey. Early Soviet hopes that Israel would provide a base for socialist expansion into the Middle East proved mistaken. Although Israel benefited from its perceived status as a new Western outpost of great strategic value, sympathy of the United States and Western Europe, among Jews and non-Jews alike, for Holocaust survivors played a key role in maintaining an influx of capital. The Federal Republic of Germany paid war reparations which along with foreign loans and grants, and remittances from overseas supporters, made up Israel's annual trade deficits. In the United States, public opinion kept legislators generally supportive of Israeli requests despite periodic attempts by the State Department to steer Congress on a more balanced course due to U.S. regional interests.

The United States viewed Turkey as a bulwark against Soviet Communist expansion. Soon, it became NATO's southeastern flank with U.S. bases scattered in the interior. Jordan, too, received aid from the industrialized West, but far less than Israel. Until 1956, Britain subsidized the weak Jordanian economy, but after the Suez War, the United States and Arab countries stepped in, too.

Fluidity of Foreign Aid Patterns

What factors most influenced changes in foreign-aid patterns of the 1950s and 1960s? Revolution, ongoing decolonization, continued polarization arising from the cold war, and the first fruits of oil expansion were the primary forces. The Egyptian revolutionary government, first viewed positively in the West, became increasingly regarded as a threat. Its neutrality conflicted with the cold-war idea of fixed alliances. Pan-Arabism presented an attractive alternative to external ideologies such as Communism or capitalism, or to the onset of neocolonialism. Revolutionism, coming as it did from the first Arab country to overthrow its monarchy, potentially threatened monarchies in Iraq, Jordan, Libya, Morocco, Saudi Arabia, and Yemen—all independent after the mid-1950s—as well as independent republics such as Syria and Lebanon. Western countries maintained bases in Libya, Morocco, and Tunisia.

The Suez War and French intransigence in Algeria contributed to the erosion of British and French influence in the Middle East. When its largest remaining client—Iraq—fell to revolutionaries in 1958, Britain rushed troops to Jordan to prop up King Husayn's regime, just as the United States landed troops in Lebanon. By adopting postures hostile to emerging nationalistic regimes, Britain, France, and the United States facilitated the entree of the U.S.S.R. into regional affairs. Ongoing U.S. and Western European support of Israel had the same effect. The Soviets succeeded in presenting themselves as revolutionary sympathizers despite their repression of dissidence in Hungary in 1956 and (later) in Czechoslovakia in 1968. During the Yemeni civil war of the early 1960s, Soviet and Chinese aid supplemented the Egyptian program. Syria, too, drew closer to the U.S.S.R. in the mid-1960s, through the Soviet offer to build the Tabqa Dam after nationalization of oil ended West German cooperation in the project. Though the Ba'this remained generally anti-Communist, U.S. policy makers interpreted this economic aid as a sign that Syria was in the Soviet camp.

In the People's Republic of South Yemen, independent from 1967, the British closed their military base, an important income earner, and neither they nor other countries stepped in to aid the local economy. Floundering with the closure of the Suez Canal, which cut revenues to Aden's port, and lacking clout to impose land reform throughout the country, the nationalist government was easily overthrown by more revolutionary leaders willing to undertake a detribalization program to impose its authority in the interior. The U.S.S.R., the German Democratic Republic, and Cuba gained influence through providing necessary aid. After gaining independence in 1956, the Sudan also looked more to the eastern bloc.

Historians should not ignore the regional role of international development and relief aid in the postwar period. U.N.W.R.A. maintained its program of basic services to Palestinian refugees of the 1948 and 1967 wars. Besides giving food and shelter, the United Nations encouraged establishment of local industries and self-help projects. Schools assisted by U.N.R.W.A. gave Gaza inhabitants one of the highest Arab literacy rates. Through U.N. programs, many refugees acquired new skills that enabled them to escape dependency. The U.N. Development Program operated in many Middle Eastern countries, focusing on agriculture and intermediate technology transfer programs.

In terms of Middle East foreign aid, the Egypt-Israel conflict made both countries modest foreign aid donors in the late 1950s and 1960s, especially in granting scholarships. Israeli aid focused on technical assistance—water resource development and construction—but it was often under private or semiprivate auspices like that of the Histadrut. Asians, Africans, and Latin Americans were favorably impressed that a small country would give aid, apparently with few strings attached when compared to big powers. Although Israeli programs faded away late in the 1960s, they helped Israeli corporations like Solel Boneh gain contracts in the 1970s and 1980s. Noncorporate, individual assistance of Egyptians to African countries was much less visible, though more widespread.

In the 1960s, especially during the post-1967 War period, petroleum producers embarked on their own bilateral aid programs. The Kuwayt Fund for Arab Economic Development, set up in 1971, emphasized soft loans and grants. Kuwayt, Libya, and Saudi Arabia pledged millions in compensation to Jordan for revenues lost from West Bank agriculture and tourism, and to Egypt for loss of Suez Canal and Sinai oil revenues.

The New International Economic Order (N.I.E.O.) and Middle East Aid

The 1970s brought about changes in Middle Eastern aid patterns. These were closely associated with political developments (especially the 1973 War) and the first huge transfer of capital to Middle Eastern oil producers in 1973–74. Middle Easterners could lend financial support to other developing countries with whom they shared problems of food, population growth, unemployment, urbanization, and the environment. When in May 1974, the U.N. General Assembly adopted the Declaration of the Establishment of a New International Economic Order, Middle Easterners rallied around it, envisioning a new world based on "equity, sovereign equality, interdependence, common interest and cooperation among all states, irrespective of their economic and social systems which shall correct inequalities and redress existing injustices, make it possible to eliminate the widening gap between the developed and the developing countries and ensure steadily accelerating economic and social development and peace and justice for present and future generations."[1]

Two of the most vigorous proponents of setting up a special program of emergency relief and development assistance to increasingly indebted developing nations were Muhammad Reza Pahlavi, Shah of Iran, and Houari Boumedienne, President of Algeria—leaders of major Middle Eastern petroleum producers. In N.I.E.O.'s program, industrialized nations and other potential contributors would increase multilateral and bilateral aid on concessional terms to the poorest countries. Renegotiation of debts, provision of commodity subsidies, long-term credits, arrangement for preferred I.M.F. terms, provision of goods, technical services, and investment in poor countries on favorable terms were requested of creditor nations. The special program called on the World Bank and the I.M.F. to place their expertise at the disposal of needy governments. In 1974, the U.N. Conference on Trade and Development was launched to add substance to N.I.E.O. goals, especially technology transfer, economic justice, and cooperation among developing nations.

Arab-African and Middle Eastern nations with ample resources responded to the N.I.E.O. call. Between 1974 and 1980, $36 billion was given to third-world countries. The Arab Gulf countries alone provided $26 billion between 1976 and 1980. By 1977, economic aid from the region was exceeded only by the total for NATO's European partners. Next to the United States, Saudi Arabia was the largest individual donor of economic aid in the world. Kuwayt gave more aid than Japan. Other significant donors in order of amount given were the U.A.E, Iran, Qatar, Libya, Iraq and Algeria. These countries in 1977 gave more than $5.7 billion in bilateral economic aid (the total for the entire Warsaw Pact bloc was only $440 million). On a per capita basis, the Gulf states emerged in the early 1980s as the most generous aid donors in the world, according to statistics of the O.E.C.D. Arab aid in general far exceeded minimal amounts recommended by U.N. agencies. Kuwayt, Saudi Arabia, Qatar, and the U.A.E. were giving from 3–5 percent of their gross national products. While the most generous European countries were contributing less than one percent, the U.S. donated about one-fourth of one percent. Yet, every one of the Middle East donors was a developing country, too.

Multilateral Aid and Development

Multilateral and bilateral agencies dispersed Middle East aid. Saudi Arabia, Kuwayt, Abu Dhabi, Iraq, and Qatar set up their own bilateral funds. Donors also contributed to the World Bank (emphasizing long-term lending) and the I.M.F. (providing short-term aid to countries that had balance-of-payments problems). In 1981, Saudi Arabia acquired the sixth largest share in the 140-member I.M.F., ranking after only the United States, West Germany, Britain, France, and Japan. The African Development Bank and the African Development Fund also received contributions from Arab oil producers.

Arab oil producers were also major

---

[1] *Yearbook of the United Nations 1974*, vol. 28 (New York: United Nations Office of Public Information, 1977), pp. 324–325. The full declaration and program are found on pp. 324–332.

donors to other multilateral funds dispersed to non-Arab and non-Muslim countries: the OPEC Fund for Development (the largest aid fund), the Islamic Solidarity Fund, the Islamic Development Bank, the Arab Fund for Economic and Social Development, the Special Arab Aid Fund for Africa and the Arab Bank for Economic Development in Africa (B.A.D.E.A.). Arab philanthropists—among them Prince Talal ibn Abd al-Aziz of Saudi Arabia—were active in fundraising and in donating to the U.N.D.P., UNESCO, and the F.A.O.

During the mid-1970s, most Arab aid went to needy Arabic-speaking countries, but by 1977, non-Arabs received a greater share, about 60 percent of the total, with 17 percent to Asia and 34 percent to non-Arab Africa. Both Muslim and non-Muslim countries benefited. In Sri Lanka, for example, funds from Kuwayt and the U.A.E. helped build a fertilizer plant which in the late 1970s was that country's biggest industrial project. Among other non-Arab countries helped by Arab funds were Korea, India, Malaysia, Pakistan, Afghanistan, and Papua-New Guinea. The Iraqi Fund and the Islamic Development Bank in 1980 paid for oil shipments to financially troubled Turkey and Senegal. Libya, too, gave aid to Turkey.

When prices rose in the wake of the 1973 oil embargo, Black Africa was especially hard hit. Since Black Africans had all broken diplomatic relations with Israel in sympathy with Egypt, they hoped for some reward from the Arab world. Resolutions of the November 1973 Algeria Arab summit led to the establishment in March 1975 of B.A.D.E.A. The Arab Fund for Africa, a disaster relief fund, merged with B.A.D.E.A. at that time. By 1981, the organization had committed some $383 million to thirty-six African countries, with a maximum loan ceiling $10 million. Jordan, Tunisia, Algeria, Saudi Arabia, Bahrayn, Qatar, Kuwayt, Lebanon, Morocco, Syria, and Iraq belonged to B.A.D.E.A. in 1980. A fully paid up contribution was also recorded for Palestine, thereby showing that Palestinians had joined together for donating aid despite their failure to achieve self-determination. Though B.A.D.E.A. had its headquarters in Khartum, Sudan could not fulfill its own pledge because of financial difficulties.

In giving aid, B.A.D.E.A. preferred to sponsor cooperative ventures with other multilateral donors because of high start-up costs for many projects. It addressed itself to Africa's greatest problem, the need for agricultural productivity increases in the face of annual population increments averaging 2.7 percent, and in line with N.I.E.O. objectives it emphasized projects that would provide employment as well as local resource development. Unlike most other banks, B.A.D.E.A. focused on aiding the worst rather than the best credit risks. By 1980, 70 percent of its loans had gone to developing countries, especially in Francophone Africa. Recognizing the lag between disbursements and commitments, B.A.D.E.A. hoped to accelerate its program and expand its development capital in the future.

Bilateral Development Aid to the Arabic–Speaking World in the 1970s and 1980s: Toward Regional Integration

In terms of bilateral aid from OPEC-member funds, debt-ridden Sudan was a prime recipient because of its need for access to loans on favorable terms. During the late 1970s, twelve Arabic-speaking countries pledged over $6.5 billion over a ten-year period to improve Sudan's development infrastructure and to develop agriculture in hopes that it would be the Middle East's future breadbasket. Morocco, too, received substantial assistance from the Arab world. Its largest aid donor in 1981 was Saudi Arabia, which gave over $1.3 billion to develop a new port, dams, and other projects. Kuwayt and Abu Dhabi also continued as generous bilateral aid donors to Morocco.

Syria, Jordan, Egypt, Y.A.R., and the P.D.R.Y. received huge sums in the 1970s and 1980s from Arab oil states. In 1981, Hashimite Jordan's biggest aid donor was Iraq, despite the fact that the Iraqi revolution had brought down the Hashimites in 1958. Saudi Arabia, along with Kuwait and Algeria, in the 1970s gave generously to both the Y.A.R. and the P.D.R.Y. The Lebanese secured commitments from Arab countries to help rebuild their economy damaged by the civil war and its aftermath, but Israeli invasions of 1978 and 1982 dampened prospects for long-range recovery in southern Lebanon. With several oil-rich countries ready to help, Tunisia was not harmed when a Libyan-Tunisian rift over oil in 1981 ended a Libyan offer to finance a refinery project in Tunisia designed to supply Morocco; Iraq stepped in to promise both funding and supplies until Tunisia's production might rise sufficiently.

Arab countries in the early 1980s actively sought ways of integrating their economies. Jordan and Syria in the late 1970s and early 1980s cooperated in transportation, shipping, and industrial ventures, despite the ups and downs in political relations. The Syrian-Jordanian Company for Industry, based in Amman, invested in cement, automobile assembly, and clothing manufacture.

Two formal efforts at regional economic integration were the Arab Common Market (A.C.M.) and the Gulf Cooperation Council (G.C.C.), both founded in 1981. The A.C.M. brought together Iraq, Jordan, Syria, Libya, and Mauritania in an organization focusing on unification of tariffs, unity of trade unions and federations, and expansion of joint ventures and multilateral agreements such as those already existing between Jordan and Syria. Considering the backing which Libya and Syria gave Iran in the Gulf War, it was difficult to assess the immediate prospects for their economic integration with both Iraq and Jordan. Moreover, Mauritania's location and economy did not appear to lend itself to close economic cooperation with any of its A.C.M. partners except perhaps Iraq and Libya.

The G.C.C. appeared to have a brighter future, mainly because of the greater similarity and homogeneity of its partners—Bahrayn, Kuwait, Oman, Qatar, Saudi Arabia, and the U.A.E. Aiming to strengthen not only economic and cultural but also strategic relations among its members, G.C.C. states placed billions of dollars at the disposal of Iraq during the Gulf War. They, like Iraq, feared the revolutionary ideology of the Islamic republic in Iran and sought to reassert Arab rather than Iranian power in the Gulf. Ongoing stability of the Gulf economies depended on continuing internal stability of Arab Gulf regimes. If regional integration was to be achieved in the long run, Middle Easterners, like states in the E.E.C. or West Africa's E.C.O.W.A.S., would have to find ways of burying temporary or longstanding political disputes in order to achieve economic progress for the area as a whole.

Pluses and Minuses of Foreign Aid

In the 1980s, some aspects of foreign aid were criticized as detrimental to the recipients' interests, especially in cases where donors encouraged countries to drop basic food crops in favor of export-oriented crop production. In Egypt and Iran, such policies vastly increased food dependency. It was equally clear that foreign aid, even when it benefited the recipient, rarely achieved the donor's political aims. Foreign aid also led to accusations of mismanagement, originating mainly from the industrialized West in the late 1970s and early 1980s when economic difficulties there reduced foreign-aid funding.

In what ways did Middle Eastern aid to developing countries differ from industrial world aid? Capital-rich Middle Eastern nations did not gain industrial development from foreign aid. Arab aid, like Arab investment, helped to buttress the economies and financial institutions of the industrialized world. Arab donors themselves imported finished products from Japan, the United States, and Europe's industrial giants. In addition, Kuwayt, the U.A.E., and Qatar derived no political benefits from their aid programs because most were arranged without publicity.

Like transnational investment, foreign aid in the 1980s would continue to be a debated topic. Did it increase dependence or did it promote independence? Did it promote social justice or did it alter local economies in accordance with elite interests? To what extent could intermediate technologies bridge the gap between the most and least industrialized countries? Would Southwest Asians and North Africans be able to feed their people in the future? How could foreign aid be structured so as to complement the economies of Middle Eastern donors?

Military Aid and Trade

In the cold-war context of post-World War II political and economic relations, newly independent and still-occupied Southwest Asian and North African countries found themselves pressured to ally with one or more of the victors. Stalin at the Yalta Conference had insisted on the necessity of having friendly states on its borders, including its southern boundaries with Turkey, Iran, and Afghanistan.

The United States, however, emerged from the war as the dominant world power. Its huge industrial, territorial, and demographic resources were largely intact. American firms dominated the international economy. Development of sophisticated weapons, especially through nuclear technology, maintained U.S. military superiority over the U.S.S.R. throughout most of the 1950s and 1960s. Until the Vietnam War, the United States was able to intervene successfully in Asia, Africa, and Latin America, with the Middle East of particular increasing interest.

Between the mid-1960s and 1983, some nineteen Middle Eastern and North African countries were involved in military conflicts. Arms supplied by the United States, the Soviet Union, Britain, France, Italy, the Federal Republic of Germany, and the People's Republic of China encouraged military solutions to problems. Despite arms-limitation agreements of the early postwar era, arms exportation came to be viewed favorably both as a means of offsetting energy imports and as a means of gaining leverage over the recipients (an unproved though oft-propounded argument). Arms reached the area through commercial sales, government sales, and military aid, including loans, grants, and training programs. Besides allocations for new weapons and equipment, government military budgets included military salaries, weapons maintenance and operation, and research and development—mainly of the conventional variety. Manufacturers argued that they should be allowed by their governments to market their arms freely because purchasers might otherwise turn to another supplier. As a result, the transfer of military resources to the Middle East alone generally exceeded in value on

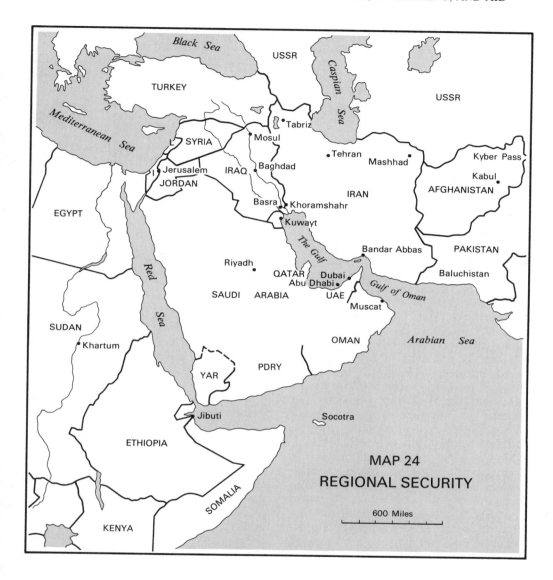

MAP 24
REGIONAL SECURITY

600 Miles

an annual basis the total amount of economic aid provided to the world by O.E.C.D. countries alone.

Sales and aid patterns illustrate the fluidity and opportunism that characterized relationships among states. The idea that arms could buy firm allies or friends proved to be largely a myth. Despite buying and receiving Soviet military equipment in the 1950s and 1960s, Egypt expelled its Soviet military advisors in 1972 and turned to the United States, Britain, and China for arms in the mid-1970s. But trade-relations with the U.S.S.R. continued. Late in the 1970s, the United States supplied not only Egypt and Israel but also Syria, Jordan, and Lebanon despite their varying degrees of animosity toward one another. The Soviets in the 1960s aided Algeria, newly independent, and wooed Jordan unsuccessfully. Although Iran in 1967 bought over $100 million worth of military equipment from the U.S.S.R., this purchase was not indicative of the general trend in Iranian-Soviet trade which focused on nonmilitary products. Iran in the 1970s was the leading arms customer of the United States. When the civil war in North Yemen began, the Soviets provided weapons to the Egyptian-aided republicans and helped the Marxist factions in the P.D.R.Y. to gain power. The Y.A.R. later won Western backing in its intermittent struggle with the P.D.R.Y. In Sudan, the U.S.S.R. backed the government of Numayri following the 1969 coup. Numayri, however, decided to expel the Soviet advisors in 1977, and looked to the United States for military aid.

Another switch seemed to occur in Libya. Under King Idris, Libya leased military facilities to Western countries. With the advent of oil money, such arrangements were no longer of use to the Libyans. Nationalists in Libya tried to avoid alliances with major blocs and criticized Iraq early in the 1970s for having signed a treaty of alliance with the Soviet Union. Weapons were bought from available suppliers: the United States, France, and increasingly, the U.S.S.R. By mid-1981, Libya was buying most of its arms from the Soviet Union, especially after France curtailed shipments following Libya's intervention of December 1980 in Chad. With the best-equipped military force in northern Africa and receipt of Soviet supplies, the Libyans were accused of being closely allied with the U.S.S.R. Although Libya provided no military bases, the Soviet navy had access to Libyan naval facilities. Mu'ammar al-Qadhdhafi's foreign policy could only be characterized as extremely independent.

The United States responded to Sudanese requests of the late 1970s and early 1980s because of fears of Libyan expansionism and security in the Horn of Africa. Likewise, the United States stepped in early in the 1980s in Somalia to fill the vacuum left by the U.S.S.R. after it shifted its support to the Marxist Mengistu government that took power in Ethiopia

in 1974. Previously, Ethiopia had received more U.S. arms and military aid than any other country in Africa! Moreover, the United States remained one of Ethiopia's major trading partners even after 1974. The U.S.S.R. in the 1970s backed the Ethiopians in the war with Somalia over the Ogaden. Although the United States won a lease from Somalia for the U.S.S.R.-built base at Berbera vacated in 1977, the base was not occupied by 1983. The United States was reluctant to back the renewed offensive in the Ogaden advocated by Somali President Siad Barre. Although the last Somali troops pulled out of the Ogaden in February 1981 after four years of war, Barre did not fully give up aspirations in the region.

Soviet-American rivalry in the Horn of Africa was amplified by the accompanying activities of states in south Arabia and the Indian Ocean along the sea lanes leading to and from the oil-rich Gulf. The U.S.S.R. moved in 1979–80 to develop the P.D.R.Y. island of Socotra as a base. In the next two years, the United States sent military supplies to Oman to use facilities on the island of Masira and along the Omani coast. The U.S. Rapid Deployment Force was formed by President Jimmy Carter as an alternative to relying on any one country (because of the experience in Iran after 1978). An agreement with Britain to lease the Indian Ocean island of Diego Garcia (formerly administered by Mauritius, which renewed its claim in 1982) was arranged in 1980. The U.S. deals with Somalia, Oman, and Britain led an Iraqi newspaper in December 1980 to accuse the United States of trying to revive the old idea of regional defense blocs with the aim of dividing the Arabs and preserving Israel's conquests. Iraq was supplied primarily by the Soviet Union before 1979.

Although the Soviet Union tried to avoid no-win situations in the Middle East, the Soviets lent considerable support to anti-Communist governments like those in Iraq, Egypt, and Sudan which periodically accused the U.S.S.R. of complicity in plots to overthrow their regimes). The Soviet intervention in Afghanistan late in December 1979 seemed to contravene this earlier policy. Afghan resistance to the Soviet presence had inflicted heavy casualties on Soviet troops by 1983. Ironically, many of the weapons used by Afghan insurgents fighting against the U.S.S.R. derived from the $4 billion in military supplies given to Egypt by the Soviets during the postwar years.

In 1982, the countries most heavily dependent on the Soviet Union militarily, though primarily through purchases and not aid, were Afghanistan, Libya, and the P.D.R.Y. As was the case with other large Middle Eastern and North African arms suppliers, the U.S.S.R. had no assurances that today's apparent allies would not be tomorrow's adversaries or that arms purchases created allies. As an instrument of foreign policy, military sales and aid at best brought short-term political and economic benefits to the supplier while aggravating the potential for war in the recipient country.

Conclusion

The Middle East and North Africa today are undergoing a process of rapid transformation. The spread of communications, introduction of computer technology, increase in rural-urban interactions, and new realities of wealth and power are creating disparities more startling than those found in highly developed regions. The discovery of new products or technologies, the onset of disease or famine, and the changes in habits and preferences—all of these are processes that in the past altered relationships and even the nature of polities in the Middle East and North Africa. The people living in the region today know that they have an opportunity, presented by a happy coincidence of geography and technology, to build a more promising future for their people. The chance of today may be lost tomorrow because of a revolutionary development in science and technology or because of circumstances of history.

History as we have revealed it is at best an inexact science, an interpretation based on concrete but limited information obtained through research. Only through continuous reappraisal can we add to our present knowledge. Each of us can be part of that process. While hoping that all of the nations of the Middle East and North Africa will resolve their current conflicts so that resources can be utilized for productive purposes, we challenge you to reexamine issues we have raised here in terms of your own country. Historians, we believe, should occupy themselves as much in asking questions as in providing answers.

On the state level, the reader should already be aware of the following operative questions. How will the Islamic experiment in Iran fare? How will Turkey's secular-religious tensions be resolved? How will Lebanon look in the future? Will the Alawi state in Syria survive? How will the Ba'th experiment in Iraq proceed? Will the Gulf states, especially Saudi Arabia, be able to transform their economic wealth and power into long-term political viability, given their current dependence on expatriate labor and management? Will Egypt be able to keep its economic house in relative order, and in what way will that process affect relationships with the region? Can the Sudan be brought to its economic potential without jeopardizing or aggravating internal stability? Will the Libyan leader preserve his revolution against domestic, regional, and international opposition? Will the North African states resolve their cultural dichotomies? How will the Western Saharan question be settled in the context of inter-Maghrib and inter-African relations? How will the two Yemens relate in the future, given their conflicting ideologies? All of these questions will be affected by three major issues in the region: the ideological ferment, the ongoing impact of Israel and Zionism, and the role of great powers.

On the most general ideological level, we shall be closely watching the fate of the idea of the nation-state. The Islamic revival, whatever else it means, is fundamentally a challenge to this concept. In addition to preaching spiritual regeneration, Muslim fundamentalists argue that the state system in the Middle East and North Africa has failed, and that the Muslim peoples of those areas are still subject in various degrees to foreign control and are impotent with regard to direct political, economic, and social developments in their countries. They even denounce as a false god the notion of Arab nationhood. They argue that such a political organization with its secular underpinnings cannot resolve their problems. The third option, other than the supranationalisms of Arabism and Islam, one equally open to all nations in the area, is the existing nation-state system, set in place in World War I, which accommodates plurality on the western model. Although the Islamic system effectively dealt with pluralism in the past, the emergence of tribal, religious, ethnic, and other local nationalisms has militated against its continued viability as historically defined. A redefinition of the imported system to reflect the Islamic heritage more fully is a very real possibility.

The developments on the ideological level in the area will be influenced by many factors not the least of which is the course of the Palestine question and the Arab-Israeli conflict. Much of the intensity of the ideological ferment ensues from the introduction of Zionism into the area, the subsequent establishment of the Jewish state, and the failure of the Arab state system, with its variety of ideologies, to prevent it. Ironically, the successful reintroduction by Israel of religion as an organizing principle of polity in the Middle East and North Africa, which on the national level offends Muslim activists, provides, in effect, a model for those Muslims seeking a religious alternative to the present state system. The overriding questions for the future in this context include the demographic evolution of the state of Israel and how the Palestinian question is addressed. The cultural division in Israel between European and Oriental Jews is reshaping the country's future. Nevertheless, the Palestinian fate seems unlikely to be resolved soon, if at all. For Palestinians, the question is not only what Israel does but also what their Arab brethren, notably Jordan (whose fate is inextricably tied up with that of the Palestinians), may do. Israel will also continue to be a factor in both internal and regional affairs of the other states in the area.

In regional terms, important questions need to be asked about the fate of monarchies and other hereditary-based states in an increasingly proletarianized and urbanized region. We should also continue to examine the relative importance of pragmatism versus ideology in both internal and external relationships. For example, how will regional integration—the Gulf Cooperation Council, the Nile Valley merger schemes, the Arab Common Market—fare, especially in the face of the ongoing interchange of capital and human resources? How long will petroleum revenues sustain this regional dynamic which will most certainly have political implications, especially in the distribution of power within the region? To what extent is a regional culture developing? The cultural factor along with the economic may be creating the *de facto* Arab unity about which ideologues and politicians have been talking for years, or it may be underscoring more localized identities. Only time will tell.

Finally, although the great powers will continue to operate in the area, the role they play will follow from their perception of both domestic and regional developments. The current primacy of the United States as the dominant Middle Eastern power will depend in large part on how threatening the Soviet Union continues to be perceived by the area countries. Apart from its use as a weapons supplier (as in Libya and Syria) and potential counterforce to the United States, the Soviet Union has no significant influence in the area outside South Yemen. Whether the secondary nature of the Soviet role will continue is the major international question in the region. A second question is the extent to which Europe and Japan will work independently of both superpowers to protect their own interests and also, in the process, help the region liberate itself from great power manipulation and polarization. However it evolves, there is no reason to doubt that the Middle East and North Africa will continue to be the object of great power rivalry. Both location and resources assure this fate.

Further Readings

We intend our bibliography to serve two purposes. The first is to provide students and general readers with up-to-date sources for further reference. The second is to acknowledge works we utilized in writing our text.

Readers will find that we have preferred recent studies over classics listed by older works in their bibliographies. Moreover, we have opted for a balanced approach in terms of both regional and topical coverage and of viewpoints on controversial issues. We do not necessarily agree with the viewpoints of all books listed. Although many books are pertinent to several chapters, we list each in the chapter in which it is deemed most relevant and useful.

Our decision to write our own historical text derived partly from our experiences in using, both as students and as teachers, the following books: Jamil M. Abun-Nasr, *A History of the Maghrib,* 2nd ed., Cambridge: Cambridge University Press, 1975; Yahya Armajani, *Middle East Past and Present,* Englewood Cliffs, N.J.: Prentice-Hall, 1970; Sydney Nettleton Fisher, *The Middle East: A History,* 3rd ed., New York: Alfred A. Knopf, 1979; Arthur Goldschmidt, Jr., *A Concise History of the Middle East,* 2nd ed., Boulder, Colo.: Westview, 1983; Philip K. Hitti, *History of the Arabs,* 10th ed., New York: St. Martin's, 1970; Marshall G. S. Hodgson, *The Venture of Islam,* 3 vols., Chicago: University of Chicago Press, 1975; P. M. Holt, A. K. S. Lambton, and Bernard Lewis (eds.), *The Cambridge History of Islam,* Vols. 1A, 1B, 2B, Cambridge: Cambridge University Press, 1970; Charles-Andre Julien, *History of North Africa from the Arab Conquest to 1830,* New York: Praeger, 1970; George Kirk, *A Short History of the Middle East,* 7th ed., New York: Praeger, 1964; Abdallah Laroui, *A History of the Maghrib: An Interpretive Essay,* Princeton: Princeton University Press, 1977; Peter Mansfield, *The Arabs,* New York: Pelican, 1978; Don Peretz, *The Middle East Today,* 3rd ed., New York: Holt, Rinehart and Winston, 1978; William R., Polk, *The Arab World,* Cambridge, Mass.: Harvard University Press, 1981 (4th ed. of *The United States and the Arab World*). In varying degrees, they helped to shape our ideas about what makes an effective text and we extend our appreciation to their authors. Students should take note of them here since they will not appear in the chapter bibliographies.

Many periodicals now treat the Middle East. For modern history and contemporary students, the most useful professional association journals are *The Middle East Journal* and *The International Journal of Middle East Studies*. Timely periodicals include *The Middle East, Middle East Research and Information Project MERIP Reports,* and *Jeune Afrique.* Two good periodical reference works are J. D. Pearson, *Index Islamicus 1906–1955,* Cambridge: Heffer and Sons, 1958 (with supplements); and Center for the Study of the Modern Arab World, St. Joseph's University, Beirut, *Arab Culture and Society in Change,* Beirut: Dar El-Mashreq, 1973.

We also recommend the following reference works: *The Encyclopaedia of Islam* Leiden: E. J. Brill, 1913–1938; 2nd ed., 1954– ; Europa Publications, *The Middle East and North Africa,* London, 1950– (annual); Michelle Raccagni, *The Modern Arab Woman: A Bibliography,* Metuchen, N. J.: Scarecrow, 1978; and Jean Sauvaget, *Introduction to the History of the Muslim East: A Bibliographical Guide,* Westport, Conn.: Greenwood, 1982 (reprint of 1965 ed.). The *Middle East Studies Association Bulletin* (1967–) helps keep students and teachers abreast of recent developments through publication of book reviews, research grants awarded, and news of professional conferences. The Area Handbook Series published by the American University and now in its 3rd edition is extremely useful for individual country studies.

Chapters 1 and 2

Adams, Michael, ed. *The Middle East: A Handbook.* London: Anthony Blond, 1971.

Bacharach, Jere. *A Near East Studies Handbook.* 2nd ed. Seattle: University of Washington Press, 1976.

Bates, Daniel G. and Rassam, Amal. *Peoples and Cultures of the Middle East.* Englewood Cliffs: Prentice-Hall Inc., 1983.

Beaumont, Peter, Blake, Gerald H., and Wagstaff, J. Malcolm. *The Middle East: A Geographical Study.* London: John Wiley & Sons, 1976.

Bergmann, Frithjof. *On Being Free.* Notre Dame: University of Notre Dame Press, 1977.

Birken, Andreas. *Die Provinzen des Osmanischen Reiches.* Wiesbaden: Dr. Ludwig Reichert Verlag, 1976.

Boulares, Habib. "Nos Ancêtres les Berbères." *Jeune Afrique,* No. 1015 (18 June 1980): 72–73.

Coon, Carleton. *Caravan: The Story of the Middle East.* Rev. ed., New York: Holt, Rinehart and Winston, 1964.

Drioton, Etienne, Georges Contenau, and J. Duchesne-Guillemin. *Religions of the Ancient East.* Translated by M. B. Loraine. London: Burns and Oates, 1959.

Eickelman, Dale F. *The Middle East: An Anthropological Approach.* Englewood Cliffs, N.J.: Prentice-Hall, 1981.

Fisher, W. B. *The Middle East: A Physical, Social, and Regional Geography.* 7th ed. New York: Barnes and Noble Books, 1978.

Frankfort, Henri. *The Birth of Civilization in the Near East.* Bloomington; Ind.: Indiana University Press, 1959.

———. ed. *Before Philosophy: The Intellectual Adventure of Ancient Man.* Baltimore: Penguin Books, 1974.

Kinder, Hermann, and Hilgemann, Werner. *The Anchor Atlas of World History.* 2 vols. Translated by Ernest A. Menze. Garden City, N.Y.: Anchor Press, 1974 and 1978.

Knapp, Wilfred. *North West Africa: A Political and Economic Survey.* 3rd ed. London: Oxford University Press, 1977.

McNeill, William H. *The Rise of the West: A History of the Human Community.* Chicago: University of Chicago Press, 1963.

Moscati, Sabatino. *The Face of the Ancient Orient: A Panorama of Near Eastern Civilizations in Pre-Classical Times.* Garden City, N.Y.: Anchor Press, 1962.

Powell, Grace L.; Geib, M. Margaret; and Spengler, Alex. *Atlas of the Middle East.* Dubuque: Kendall /Hunt Publishing Company, 1975.

Roolvink, Roelof. *Historical Atlas of the Muslim Peoples.* with Saleh A. el-Ali, Hussain Mones, Mohammed Salem. Amsterdam, Djambatan, 1957.

Chapter 3

Brand, Charles M., ed. *Icon and Mineret: Sources of Byzantine and Islamic Civilization.* Englewood Cliffs, N.J.: Prentice-Hall, Inc., 1969.

Cragg, Kenneth. *The House of Islam.* Belmont, Calif.: Dickenson Publishers, Inc., 1969.

Gilsenan, Michael. *Recognizing Islam.* London: Croom Helm; New York: Pantheon Books, 1982.

Goldziher, I. *Introduction to Islamic Theology and Law*. Princeton: Princeton University Press, 1981.

Martin, Richard C. *Islam*. Englewood Cliffs, N.J.: Prentice-Hall, 1982.

Rahman, Fazlur. *Islam*. London: Weidenfeld and Nicolson, 1966; 2nd ed., Chicago: University of Chicago Press, 1979.

Rodinson, Maxime. *Mohammed*. New York: Vintage, 1974.

Schroeder, Eric. *Muhammad's People*. Portland, Maine: Bond, Wheelwright Company, 1955.

Tabataba'i, 'Allamah Sayyid Muhammad Husayn. *Shi'ite Islam*. Translated by Sayyid Hossein Nasr. Albany, N.Y.: State University of New York Press, 1975.

Watt, W. Montgomery. *Muhammad: Prophet and Statesman*. Oxford: Galaxy, 1974.

———. *Bell's Introduction to the Qur'an*. Rev. ed. Chicago; Aldine, 1970.

Chapter 4

Cahen, Claude. *Pre-Ottoman Turkey*. New York: Taplinger, 1968.

Dols, Michael W. *The Black Death in the Middle East*. Princeton: Princeton University Press, 1977.

Donner, Fred McGraw. *The Early Islamic Conquests*. Princeton: Princeton University Press, 1981.

Gibb, H. A. R. *Studies On the Civilization of Islam*. Edited by S. J. Shaw and W. R. Polk. London: Routledge and Kegan Paul, 1962. Reprint. Princeton: Princeton University Press, 1982.

Holt, P. M. *The Eastern Mediterranean Lands in the Period of the Crusades*. Forest Grove, Oreg.: Aris and Phillips, 1978.

Lassner, Jacob. *The Shaping of Abbasid Rule*. Princeton: Princeton University Press, 1980.

Makdisi, George. *The Rise of Colleges: Institutions of Learning in Islam and the West*. Edinburgh: Edinburgh University Press, 1982.

Nizam al-Mulk, *The Book of Government or Rules for Kings*. Translated by Hubert Dark. London: Routledge and Kegan Paul, 1978.

Rice, David Talbot. *Islamic Art*. New York: Praeger, 1965.

Rogers, Michael. *The Spread of Islam*. Oxford: Elsevier, 1976.

Saunders, J. J. *A History of Medieval Islam*. London: Routledge and Kegan Paul, 1969.

Spuler, Bertold. *The Mongols in History*. Translated by Geoffrey Wheeler. London: Pall Mall, 1971.

———. *The Muslim World: a Historical Survey*. Vols. 1 & 2. Atlantic Highlands, N.J.: Humanities, 1960. Vol. 4, 1981.

Udovitch, A. L., ed. *The Islamic Middle East: 700–1900: Studies in Economic and Social History*. Princeton: Darwin Press, 1981.

Watt, W. Montgomery. *The Majesty That was Islam*. New York: Praeger, 1974.

Watt, W. Montgomery, and Cachia, Pierre. *A History of Islamic Spain*. Edinburgh: Edinburgh University Press, 1965.

Chapter 5

Barbir, Karl K. *Ottoman Rule in Damascus, 1708–1758*. Princeton: Princeton University Press, 1980.

Berque, Jacques. *L'Intérieur Du Maghreb: XVᵉ–XIXᵉ Siècle*. Paris: Gaillmard, 1978.

Braudel, Fernand. *The Mediterranean and the Mediterranean World in the Age of Philip II*. Translated by Sian Reynolds, 2 vols. New York: Harper & Row, 1973.

Hess, Andrew C. *The Forgotten Frontier: A History of the Sixteenth Century Ibero-African Frontier*. Chicago: University of Chicago Press, 1978.

Holt, P. M. *Egypt and the Fertile Crescent: 1516–1922: A Political History*. Ithaca, N.Y.: Cornell University Press, 1966.

Hurewitz, J. C., ed. and trans. *The Middle East and North Africa in World Politics*. 2nd ed. Vol. 1, *European Expansion: 1535–1914*. New Haven and London: Yale University Press, 1975.

Inalcik, Halil. *The Ottoman Empire: The Classical Age, 1300–1600*. Translated by N. Itzkowitz and Colin Imber. London: Weidenfeld and Nicolson; New York: Praeger, 1973.

Itzkowitz, Norman. *Ottoman Empire and Islamic Tradition*. New York: Alfred A. Knopf, 1972.

Julien, Charles-André. *Le Maroc Face aux Impérialismes: 1415–1956*. Paris: Editions J. A., 1978.

Keddie, Nikki R., ed. *Scholars, Saints, and Sufis: Muslim Religious Institutions Since 1500*. Berkeley: University of California Press, 1972.

Kinross, Lord. *The Ottoman Centuries: The Rise and Fall of the Turkish Empire*. New York: William Morrow, 1979.

Perry, John R. *Karim Khan Zand: A History of Iran, 1747–1779*. Chicago: University of Chicago Press, 1979.

Savory, Roger. *Iran Under the Safavids*. New York: Columbia University Press, 1980.

Shaw, Stanford. *History of the Ottoman Empire, 1280–1808*. London, New York, and Melbourne: Cambridge University Press, 1976.

Sugar, Peter. *Southeastern Europe Under Ottoman Rule 1354–1804*. Seattle: University of Washington Press, 1977.

Woods, John. *The Aqquyunlu: Clan, Confederation, and Empire*. Minneapolis and Chicago: Bibliotheca Islamica, 1976.

Chapter 6

Amin, Samir. *Imperialism and Unequal Development*. New York: Monthly Review, 1977.

Anderson, Matthew S. *The Eastern Question, 1774–1923.* New York: St. Martins, 1966.

Bayat, Mangol. *Mysticism and Dissent: Socioreligious Thought in Qajar Iran.* Syracuse; N.Y.: Syracuse University Press, 1982.

Braun, Thom. *Disraeli the Novelist.* Boston: George Allen and Unwin, 1981.

Chaliand, Gerard, ed. *People Without a Country: The Kurds and Kurdistan.* Translated by Michael Pallis. London: Zed, 1980.

Crecelius, Daniel. *The Roots of Modern Egypt: A Study of the Regimes of Ali Bey Al-Kabir and Muhammad Bey Abu Al-Dhahab, 1760–1775.* Minneapolis and Chicago: Bibliotheca Islamica, 1981.

Findlay, Carter V. *Bureaucratic Reform in The Ottoman Empire: The Sublime Porte, 1789–1922.* Princeton: Princeton University Press, 1980.

Gran, Peter. *Islamic Roots of Capitalism: Egypt, 1760–1840.* Austin: University of Texas Press, 1979.

Issawi, Charles, ed. *The Economic History of Iran: 1800–1914.* Chicago: University of Chicago Press, 1971.

———. *The Economic History of the Middle East: 1800–1914.* Chicago: University of Chicago Press, 1966.

———. *The Economic History of Turkey, 1800–1914.* Chicago and London: University of Chicago Press, 1980.

Keddie, Nikki. *Roots of Revolution: An Interpretive History of Modern Iran.* New Haven: Yale University Press, 1981.

Naff, Thomas, and Owen, Roger, eds. *Studies on Eighteenth Century Islamic History.* Carbondale and Edwardsville, Ill.: Southern Illinois University Press, 1977.

Rafeq, Abdul-Karim. *The Province of Damascus, 1723–1783.* Beirut: Khayats, 1970.

Richards, Alan. *Egypt's Agricultural Development, 1800–1980: Technical and Social Change.* Boulder, Colo.: Westview, 1982.

Shaw, Stanford J., and Shaw, Ezel Kural. *History of the Ottoman Empire and Modern Turkey: 1808–1975.* London, New York, and Melbourne: Cambridge University Press, 1977.

Thornton, A. P. *Doctrines of Imperialism.* New York: John Wiley & Sons, 1965.

Valensi, Lucette. *Fellahs Tunisiens: L'Économie Rurale et la Vie des Campagnes Aux 18ᵉ et 19ᵉ Siècles.* Civilisations et Sociétés 45. Paris and the Hague; Mouton, 1977.

Vatikiotis, P. J. *The Modern History of Egypt.* 2nd ed. Baltimore: The Johns Hopkins University Press, 1980.

Walz, Terence. *Trade Between Egypt and Bilad As-Sudan, 1700–1820.* Cairo: Institut Français d'Etudes d'Archéologie du Caire, 1978.

Wallerstein, Immanuel. *The Capitalist World-Economy.* London: Cambridge University Press, 1979.

Chapter 7

Algar, Hamid. *Religion and State in Iran: The Role of the Ulama in the Qajar Period.* Berkeley: University of California Press, 1970.

Armajani, Yahya. *Iran.* Englewood Cliffs, N.J.: Prentice-Hall, 1972.

Aroian, Lois A. *The Nationalization of Arabic and Islamic Education in Egypt: Dar Al-Ulum and Al-Azhar* (Cairo Papers in Social Science, Vol. VI, Monograph 4). Cairo, 1983.

Berkeş, Niyazi. *The Development of Secularism in Modern Turkey.* Montreal: McGill University Press, 1964.

Davison, Roderic H. *Reform in The Ottoman Empire, 1856–1876.* Princeton: Princeton University Press, 1963.

De Jong, F. *Turuq and Turuq-Linked Institutions in Nineteenth-Century Egypt.* Leiden: E. J. Brill, 1976.

Holt, P. M., ed. *Political and Social Change in Modern Egypt.* London: Oxford University Press, 1968.

Kazemzadeh, F. *Russia and Britain in Persia, 1864–1914: A Study in Imperialism.* New Haven: Yale University Press, 1968.

Landen, Robert G., (comp.) *The Emergence of the Modern Middle East: Selected Readings.* New York: D. Van Nostrand, 1970.

Landes, David S. *Bankers and Pashas: International Finance and Economic Imperialism in Egypt.* Cambridge, Mass.: Harvard University Press, 1958.

Lewis, Bernard. *The Emergence of Modern Turkey.* 2nd. ed. London and New York: Oxford University Press, 1968.

Maoz, Moshe, ed., *Studies in Palestine During The Ottoman Period.* Jerusalem: The Magnes Press, 1975.

Mardin, Şerif. *The Genesis of Young Ottoman Thought: A Study in Modernization of Turkish Political Ideas.* Princeton: Princeton University Press, 1962.

Nashat, Guity. *The Origins of Modern Reform in Iran.* Champaign: University of Illinois Press, 1982.

Wilbur, Donald. *Iran, Past and Present: From Monarchy to Islamic Republic.* 9th ed. Princeton: Princeton University Press, 1982.

Chapter 8 and 10

Ahmad, Feroz. *The Young Turks: The Committee of Union and Progress in Turkish Politics, 1908–1914.* Oxford: Clarendon Press, 1969.

Antonius, George. *The Arab Awakening.* New York: J. B. Lippincott, 1939.

Avineri, Shlomo. *The Making of Modern Zionism: The Intellectual Origins of a Jewish State.* New York: Basic Books, 1981.

Berque, Jacques. *Egypt: Imperialism and Revolution.* Translated by Jean Stewart. London: Faber and Faber, 1972.

Buheiry, Marwan, ed. *Intellectual Life in the Arab East, 1890–1939.* Beirut: American University of Beirut Center for Arab and Middle East Studies, 1981.

Busch, Briton Cooper. *Britain, India, and the Arabs, 1914–1921.* Berkeley: University of California Press, 1971.

Cohen, Israel. *The Zionist Movement.* London: Frederick Muller, 1945.

Hourani, Albert. *Arabic Thought in the Liberal Age.* London, New York, and Toronto: Oxford University Press, 1962.

Hovannisian, Richard G., ed. *The Armenian Image in History and Literature.* Malibu, Calif.: Undena Publications, 1981.

Kayyali, Abdel-Wahhab Said. *Palestine: A Modern History.* London: Croom Helm, 1978.

Krikorian, Mesrob K. *Armenians in the Service of the Ottoman Empire, 1860–1908.* London: Routledge and Kegan Paul, 1977.

Kushner, David. *The Rise of Turkish Nationalism, 1876–1908.* London: Frank Cass, 1977.

Laqueur, Walter Z. *A History of Zionism.* New York: Holt, Rinehart, and Winston, 1972.

Levin, N. Gordon, comp. *The Zionist Movement in Palestine and World Politics, 1880–1918.* London and Lexington, Mass.: Heath, 1974.

Nalbandian, Louise. *The Armenian Revolutionary Movement: The Development of Armenian Political Parties Through the Nineteenth Century.* Berkeley: University of California Press, 1963.

Reid, Donald M. *Lawyers and Politics in the Arab World, 1880–1960.* Minneapolis and Chicago: Bibliotheca Islamica, 1981.

Robinson, Ronald; Gallagher, John; and Denny, Alice. *Africa and the Victorians: The Official Mind of Imperialism.* 2nd ed. London: Macmillan & Co., 1981.

Sati al-Husri, Abu Khaldun. *The Day of Maysalun.* Translated by Sidney Glazer. Washington, D.C.: The Middle East Institute, 1966.

Scham, Alan. *Lyautey in Morocco.* Berkeley: University of California Press, 1970.

Sharabi, Hisham. *Arab Intellectuals and the West: The Formative Years, 1875–1914.* Baltimore: The Johns Hopkins University Press, 1970.

Tignor, Robert. *Modernization and British Colonial Rule in Egypt: 1882–1914.* Princeton: Princeton University Press, 1966.

Waines, David. *A Sentence of Exile: The Palestine/Israel Conflict, 1897–1977.* Wilmette, Ill.: Medina Press, 1977.

Walker, Christopher J. *Armenia: Survival of a Nation.* New York: St. Martin's, 1980.

Winder, R. Bayly. *Saudi Arabia in the Nineteenth Century.* New York: St. Martin's, 1965.

Winks, Robin, ed. *British Imperialism: Gold, God, Glory.* New York: Holt, Rinehart, and Winston, 1963.

Zeine, Zeine N. *Arab-Turkish Relations and the Emergence of Arab Nationalism.* Beirut: Khayats, 1958.

Chapter 9

Ageron, Charles-Robert. *Les Algériens Musulmans et la France (1871–1919).* 2 vols. Paris; Presses Universitaires de France, 1968.

Baroudi, Abdallah. *Maroc: Impérialisme et Émigration.* Paris: Sycomore, 1981.

Brown, Leon Carl. *The Tunisia of Ahmed Bey, 1837–1855.* Princeton: Princeton University Press, 1974.

Danziger, Raphael. *Abd Al-Qadir and the Algerians: Resistance to the French and Internal Consolidation.* New York: Holmes and Meier, 1977.

Green, Arnold H. *The Tunisian Ulama, 1873–1915: Social Structure and Response to Ideological Currents.* Leiden: E. J. Brill, 1978.

Perkins, Kenneth. *Qaids, Captains, and Colons: French Military Administration in the Colonial Maghrib, 1844–1934.* New York: Africana, 1981.

Sullivan, Antony T. *Thomas-Robert Bugeaud, France, and Algeria, 1784–1849: Politics, Power, and the Good Society.* Hamden, Conn.: Shoe String Press, 1983.

Temimi, Abdeljelil. *Le Beylik de Constantine et Hadj Ahmed Bey (1830–1837).* Tunis: Publications de la Revue d'Histoire Maghrebine, 1978.

Chapters 11 and 12

Abrahamian, Ervand. *Iran Between Two Revolutions.* Princeton: Princeton University Press, 1982.

Anderson, Irvine H. *ARAMCO, The United States, and Saudi Arabia: A Study of the Dynamics of Foreign Oil Policy, 1933–1950.* Princeton: Princeton University Press, 1981.

Batatu, Hanna. *The Old Social Classes and the Revolutionary Movements of Iraq.* Princeton: Princeton University Press, 1978.

Beshir, Mohamed Omer. *Revolution and Nationalism in the Sudan.* London: Rex Collings, 1974.

Bonine, Michael E., and Keddie, Nikki, eds. *Modern Iran: The Dialectics of Continuity and Change.* Albany, N.Y.: State University of New York Press, 1981.

Holt, P. M. *A Modern History of the Sudan.* London: Weidenfeld and Nicolson, 1961.

Hurewitz, Jacob Coleman, ed. *The Middle East and North Africa in World Politics: A Documentary*

Record. Vol. 2, *British-French Supremacy, 1914–1945*. 2nd ed., New Haven; Yale University Press, 1975.

Husry, Khaldun S. "The Assyrian Affair of 1933." *International Journal of Middle East Studies* 5, pt. 1 (April 1974): 161–76; 5, pt. 2 (June 1974): 344–60.

Istanbul Boy: The Autobiography of Aziz Nesin. Translated by Joseph S. Jacobson. Austin: University of Texas at Austin, Center for Middle Eastern Studies. Part I, 1977. Part II, 1979.

Jankowski, James P. *Egypt's Young Rebels: "Young Egypt": 1933–1952*. Stanford: Hoover Institution Press, 1975.

Karpat, Kemal, ed. *Political and Social Thought in the Contemporary Middle East*. Rev. ed. New York: Praeger, 1982.

Katouzian, Homa. *The Political Economy of Modern Iran: Despotism and Pseudo-Modernism, 1926–1979*. London: Macmillan, 1981.

Kazancigil, Ali, and Özbüdün, Ergun, eds. *Atatürk: Founder of a Modern State*. Hamden, Conn.: Arehon; London: Croom Helm, 1981.

Kemal, Yashar, *Memed My Hawk*. Translated by Edward Roditi. London: Collins and Harvil Press, 1961.

Kinross, Lord. *Atatürk*. New York: William Morrow, 1965.

Longrigg, Stephen Hemsley. *Iraq: 1900–1950: A Political, Social, and Economic History*. London: Oxford University Press, 1956.

———. *Syria and Lebanon Under the French Mandate*. London: Oxford University Press, 1958.

Mahfouz, Neguib. *Midaq Alley*. Translated by Trevor Le Gassick. London: Heinemann, 1975.

Marsot, Afaf Lutfi al-Sayyid. *Egypt's Liberal Experiment, 1922–1936*. Berkeley, Los Angeles, and London: University of California Press, 1977.

Mitchell, Richard P. *The Society of the Muslim Brothers*. London: Oxford University Press, 1969.

Monroe, Elizabeth. *Britain's Moment in the Moment in the Middle East, 1914–1971*. Rev. ed. Baltimore: The Johns Hopkins University Press, 1981.

Petran, Tabitha. *Syria: A Modern History*. London: Benn, 1978.

Robinson, Richard D. *The First Turkish Republic: A Study in National Development*. Cambridge: Harvard University Press, 1963.

Woodward, Peter. *Condominium and Sudanese Nationalism*. London: Rex Collings, 1979.

Chapter 13

Allon, Yigal. *Shield of David: The Story of Israel's Armed Forces*. London: Weidenfeld and Nicolson, 1970.

Bauer, Yehuda. *From Diplomacy to Resistance: A History of Jewish Palestine, 1939–1945*. New York: Atheneum, 1973.

Begin, Menachem. *The Revolt: The Story of the Irgun*. New York: Schuman, 1951.

Elon, Amos. *The Israelis: Founders and Sons*. New York: Holt, Rinehart, and Winston, 1971.

Hadawi, Sami. *Bitter Harvest: Palestine Between 1914–1967*. New York: The New World Press, 1967.

Lesch, Ann M. *Arab Politics in Palestine, 1917–1939*. Ithaca, N.Y.: Cornell University Press, 1979.

Migdal, Joel S., ed. *Palestinian Society and Politics*. Princeton: Princeton University Press, 1980.

Moore, John Norton, ed. *The Arab-Israeli Conflict: Readings and Documents*. Princeton: Princeton University Press, 1977.

Porath, Yehoshua. *The Emergence of the Palestinian Arab National Movement, 1918–1929*. London: Frank Cass, 1974.

———. *The Palestinian Arab National Movement, 1929–1939*. London: Frank Cass, 1977.

Sachar, Howard M. *A History of Israel: From the Rise of Zionism to Our Time*. New York: Alfred A. Knopf, 1979.

Sykes, Christopher. *Cross Roads to Israel*. Bloomington, Ind.: Indiana University Press, 1967.

Weinstock, Nathan. *Zionism: False Messiah*. Translated and edited by Alan Adler. London: Ink Links, 1979.

Willner, Dorothy. *Nation-Building and Community in Israel*. Princeton: Princeton University Press, 1969.

Chapter 14

Abbas, Farhat. *La Nuit Coloniale*. Paris: R. Julliard, 1962.

Ageron, Charles-Robert. *L'Algérie Algérienne de Napoléon III Á De Gaulle*. Paris: Sindbad, 1980.

Al-Fasi, 'Allal. *The Independence Movements in North Africa*. Translated by H. Z. Nuseibeh. Washington, D.C.: The Middle East Institute, 1954.

Berque, Jacques. *Le Maghreb Entre Deux Guerres*. Rev. ed. Paris: Seuil, 1979.

Bidwell, Robin. *Morocco Under Colonial Rule: French Administration of Tribal Areas, 1912–1956*. London: Frank Cass, 1973.

Grimal, Henri. *Decolonisation: The British, French, Dutch, and Belgian Empires, 1919–1963*. Translated by Stephan DeVos. Boulder, Colo.: Westview Press, 1978.

Halstead, John P. *Rebirth of a Nation: Origins and Rise of Moroccan Nationalism, 1912–1944*. Cambridge, Mass.: Harvard University Press, 1967.

Sivan, Emmanuel. *Communisme et Nationalisme en Algérie, 1920–1962*. Paris: Presses de la FNSP, 1976.

Stora, Benjamin. *Messali Hadj.* Paris: Éditions Le Sycomore, 1982.

Waterbury, John. *North for the Trade: The Life and Times of a Berber Merchant;* Berkeley: University of California Press, 1972.

Contemporary Thought in Southwest Asia and North Africa (spans several chapters)

Abdel-Malik, Anouar, ed. *Contemporary Arab Political Thought.* London: Zed Press, 1982.

Ajami, Fouad. *The Arab Predicament: Arab Political Thought and Practice since 1967.* Cambridge: Cambridge University Press, 1981.

Amin, Samir. *The Arab Nation: Nationalism and Class Struggle.* London: Zed Press, 1978.

Cudsi, Alex and Dessouki, Ali E. Hilal, eds. *Islam and Power in the Contemporary Muslim World.* Baltimore: The Johns Hopkins University Press, 1981.

Enayat, Hamid. *Modern Islamic Political Thought.* London: Macmillan & Co.; Austin, Tex.: University of Texas Press, 1982.

Esposito, John, ed. *Islam and Development: Religion and Sociopolitical Change.* Syracuse, N.Y.: Syracuse University Press, 1980.

Ismael, Tareq. *The Arab Left.* Syracuse, N.Y.: Syracuse University Press, 1976.

Jansen, G. H. *Militant Islam.* New York: Harper Colophon Books, 1979.

Laroui, Abdallah. *The Crisis of the Arab Intellectual: Traditionalism or Historicism?* Translated by Diarmed Cammell. Berkeley: University of California Press, 1976.

Mortimer, Edward. *Faith and Power: The Politics of Islam.* New York: Vintage Books; London: Faber, 1982.

Qutb, Sayyid. *Milestones.* No translator given. Beirut and Damascus: Holy Quran Publishing House for International Federation of Muslim Student Organizations, 1978.

———. *Social Justice in Islam.* Translated by John B. Hardie. New York: Octagon, 1970.

Said, Edward. *Orientalism.* New York: Pantheon Books, 1978.

Shari'ati, Ali. *Marxism and Other Fallacies: An Islamic Critique.* Berkeley: Mizan Press, 1980.

———. *On the Sociology of Islam: Lectures.* Berkeley: Mizan Press, 1979.

Voll, John Obert. *Islam: Continuity and Change in the Modern World.* Boulder, Colo.: Westview, 1982.

Akhavi, Shahrough. *Religion and Politics in Contemporary Iran: Clergy-State Relations in the Pahlevi Period.* Albany, N.Y.: State University of New York Press, 1980.

Baraheni, Reza. *The Crowned Cannibals: Writings on Repression in Iran.* New York: Vintage, 1977.

Behrangi, Samad. *The Little Black Fish and Other Short Stories.* Translated by Mary and Eric Hoogland, Washington, D.C.: Three Continents, 1976.

Berberoğlu, Berch. *Turkey in Crisis: From State Capitalism to Neo-Colonialism.* London: Zed Press, 1982.

Cottam, Richard W. *Nationalism in Iran.* Pittsburgh: University of Pittsburgh Press, 1979.

Fischer, Michael M. J. *Iran: From Religious Dispute to Revolution.* Cambridge, Mass.: Harvard University Press, 1980.

Frey, Frederick W. *The Turkish Political Elite.* Cambridge, Mass.: The M.I.T. Press, 1965.

Graham, Robert. *Iran: The Illusion of Power.* New York: St. Martin's, 1979.

Halliday, Fred. *Iran: Dictatorship and Development.* New York: Penguin, 1979.

Hoogland, Eric J. *Land and Revolution in Iran, 1960–1980.* Austin, Tex.: University of Texas Press, 1982.

Karpat, Kemal. *Turkey's Politics: The Transition to a Multiparty System.* Princeton: Princeton University Press, 1959.

Lenczowski, George, ed. *Iran Under the Pahlevis.* Stanford: Hoover Institution, 1978.

Lewis, Geoffrey. *Modern Turkey.* 4th ed. New York: Praeger, 1974.

McLaurin, R. D., ed. *The Political Role of Minority Groups in the Middle East.* New York: Praeger, 1979.

Nobari, Ali Reza. *Iran Erupts: Independence: News and Analysis of the Iranian National Movement.* Stanford: Iran-America Documentation Group, 1978.

Roosevelt, Kermit. *Countercoup: The Struggle for Control of Iran.* New York: McGraw-Hill, 1979.

Rubin, Barry. *Paved with Good Intentions: The American Experience and Iran.* New York: Oxford University Press, 1980.

Weiker, Walter F. *The Modernization of Turkey from Ataturk to the Present Day.* New York: Holmes and Meier, 1981.

Yalman, A. E., *The Development of Modern Turkey.* New York: AS Press, 1968.

Zabih, Sepehr. *Iran Since the Revolution.* London: Croom Helm, 1982; Baltimore: Johns Hopkins University Press, 1982.

Chapter 15

Ahmad, Feroz. *The Turkish Experiment in Democracy, 1950–1975.* Boulder, Colorado: Westview, 1977.

Chapters 16 and 19

Abu-Lughod, Ibrahim, ed. *Palestinian Rights: Affirmation and Denial.* Wilmette: Medina Press, 1982.

American Friends Service Committee. *A Compassionate Peace: A Future for the Middle East.* New York: Hill and Wang, 1982.

Amos, John W., Ill. *Palestinian Resistance: Organization of a Nationalist Movement.* New York: Pergamon Press, 1980.

Ben-Ner, Isaac (Yitzhak). *The Man from There,* Translated by Dorothea Shefer. New York: Sabra Books, 1970.

Bulloch, John. *Death of a Country: The Civil War in Lebanon.* London: Weidenfeld and Nicolson, 1977.

Curtiss, Richard H. *A Changing Image: American Perceptions of the Arab-Israeli Dispute.* Washington, D.C.: American Educational Trust. 1982.

Davis, Uri. *Israel: Utopia Incorporated.* London: Zed Press, 1977.

El-Asmar, Fouzi. *To Be an Arab in Israel.* Beirut: Institute for Palestine Studies, 1978.

Ennes, James M., Jr. *Assault on the Liberty: The True Story of an Israeli Attack on an American Intelligence Ship.* New York: Random House, 1979.

Hazleton, Lesley. *Israeli Women: The Reality Behind the Myths.* New York: Simon & Schuster, 1977.

Hurewitz, Jacob Coleman. *Middle East Politics: The Military Dimension.* 2nd ed., Boulder, Colo.: Westview, 1983.

"Insight Report," *Sunday Times* (London), 19 June 1977.

Isaac, Rael Jean. *Israel Divided: Ideological Politics in the Jewish State.* New York: Longman, 1981.

Jiryis, Sabri. *The Arabs in Israel: 1948–1966.* Translated by Meric Dobson. New York: Monthly Review, 1977, and Translated by Inea Bushnaq. New York and London: Monthly Review, 1976.

Kanafani, Ghassan. *Men in the Sun.* Washington, D.C.: Three Continents, 1978.

Kerr, Malcolm, ed. *The Elusive Peace in the Middle East.* Albany, N.Y.: State University of New York Press, 1975.

Khalidi, Walid. *Conflict and Violence in Lebanon: Confrontation in the Middle East.* Cambridge, Mass.: Harvard Center for International Affairs, 1979.

Khouri, Fred. J. *The Arab-Israeli Dilemma.* 2nd ed. Syracuse, N.Y.: Syracuse University Press, 1976.

Krammer, Arnold. *The Forgotten Friendship: Israel and the Soviet Bloc, 1947–53.* Urbana, Chicago, and London: University of Illinois Press, 1974.

Lustick, Ian. *Arabs in the Jewish State: Israel's Control of a National Minority;* Austin, Tex.: University of Texas Press, 1980.

Oz, Amos. *Elsewhere Perhaps.* Translated by Nicholas de Lange and the author. London: Secker and Warburg, 1974.

———. *My Michael.* Translated by Nicholas de Lange with the author. New York: Knopf, 1972.

Peretz, Don. *The Government and Politics of Israel.* Boulder, Colo.: Westview Press, 1979.

Rabikowitz, Dalia, ed. *The New Israeli Writers.* New York: Sabra Books, 1969.

Rodinson, Maxime. *Israel: A Colonial–Settler State?* Translated by David Thorstad, New York: Monad Press, 1973.

———. *Israel and the Arabs.* Translated by Michael Perl. 2nd ed. London: Penguin, 1982.

Said, Edward. *The Question of Palestine.* New York: Times Books, 1979.

Salibi, Kemal S. *Crossroads to Civil War: Lebanon, 1958–1976.* Delmar, N.Y.: Caravan Books, 1976.

Sayigh, Rosemary. *Palestinians: From Peasants to Revolutionaries.* New York: Monthly Review Press, 1979.

Sid-Ahmed, Mohamed. *After the Guns Fall Silent: Peace or Armageddon in the Middle-East.* New York: St. Martin's, 1977. London: Croom Helm, 1976.

Smooha, Sammy. *Israel: Pluralism and Conflict.* Berkeley: University of California Press, 1978.

Tillman, Seth P. *The United States in the Middle East: Interests and Obstacles.* Bloomington, Ind.: Indiana University Press, 1982.

Turki, Fawaz. *The Disinherited: Journal of a Palestinian Exile.* New York: Modern Reader, 1972.

Zucker, Norman L. *The Coming Crisis in Israel: Private Faith and Public Policy.* Cambridge, Mass.: The M.I.T. Press, 1973.

Chapters 17, 18, and 20

Abdel Nasser, Gamal. *The Philosophy of the Revolution: Egypt's Liberation.* Introduction by Dorothy Thompson. Washington, D.C.: Public Affairs Press, 1955.

Ageron, Charles-Robert. *Histoire de L'Algérie Contemporaine.* 2 vols. Paris: Presses Universitaires de France, 1979.

Allan, J. A., ed. *Libya Since Independence: Economic and Social Development.* London: Croom Helm. New York: St. Martin's, 1982.

Awwad, Tawfiq Yusuf. *Death in Beirut.* Translated by Leslie McLoughlin. London: Heinemann, 1976.

Baker, Raymond William. *Egypt's Uncertain Revolution Under Nasser and Sadat;* Cambridge, Mass.: Harvard University Press, 1978.

Barakat, Halim. *Days of Dust.* Wilmette: Medina Press, 1974.

Beck, Lois and Keddie, Nikki, eds. *Women in the Muslim World.* Cambridge, Mass.: Harvard University Press, 1978.

Berque, Jacques. *Cultural Expression in Arab Society Today.* Translated by Robert W. Stookey. Austin: University of Texas Press, 1978.

Bidwell, Robin. *The Two Yemens.* Boulder, Colo.: Westview, 1983.

Bindari, Sami. *The House of Power.* Translated by Sami Bindari and Mona St. Leger. Boston: Houghton Mifflin Company, 1980.

Boulatta, Issa J., trans. and ed. *Modern Arab Poets, 1950–1975.* Washington, D.C.: Three Continents, 1975.

El Saadawi, Nawal. *The Hidden Face of Eve: Women in the Arab World.* Translated and edited by Sherif Hetata. London: Zed Press, 1980; Boston: Beacon Press, 1982.

First, Ruth. *Libya: The Elusive Revolution.* New York: Africana, 1975.

Ghareeb, Edmund. *The Kurdish Question in Iraq.* Syracuse, N.Y.: Syracuse University Press, 1981.

Halliday, Fred. *Arabia Without Sultans.* 1974. Reprint. New York: Penguin, 1979.

Hamalian, Leo, and Yohannen, John, eds. *New Writings from the Middle East.* New York: Mentor, 1978.

Haykal, Muhammad Hasanayn. *The Cairo Documents: The Inside Story of Nasser and His Relationship with World Leaders, Rebels, and Statesmen.* New York: Doubleday & Company, 1973.

Heikal, Mohamed. *The Sphinx and the Commissar: The Rise and Fall of Soviet Influence in the Arab World.* New York: Harper and Row, 1979.

Helms, Christine Moss. *The Cohesion of Saudi Arabia.* London: Croom Helm, 1981; Baltimore: The Johns Hopkins University Press, 1980.

Hodges, Tony. *Historical Dictionary of Western Sahara.* Metuchen, N.J.: Scarecrow, 1982.

Hopwood, Derek. *Egypt: Politics and Society, 1945–1981.* Winchester, Mass.: Allen and Unwin, Inc. 1982.

Hudson, Michael C. *Arab Politics: The Search for Legitimacy.* New Haven: Yale University Press, 1977.

Hussein, Mahmoud [pseud.] *Class Conflict in Egypt: 1945–1970.* Translated by Michel and Susanne Chirman, Alfred Ehrenfeld, and Kathy Brown. New York: Monthly Review, 1973.

Kerr, Malcolm. *The Arab Cold War: Gamal Abd Al-Nasir and His Rivals, 1958–1970.* London and New York: Oxford University Press, 1971.

Johnson-Davies, Denys trans. *Modern Arabic Short Stories.* London: Oxford University Press, 1967; London: Heinemann, 1976.

Khadduri, Majid. *Socialist Iraq: A Study in Iraqi Politics Since 1968.* Washington, D.C.: Middle East Institute, 1978.

Khalidi, Walid, and Ibish, Yusuf, eds. *Arab Political Documents, 1963.* Beirut: American University of Beirut, 1963.

Khalifa, Ali Muhammed. *The United Arab Emirates: Unity in Fragmentation.* Boulder, Colo.: Westview Press, 1979.

Lackner, Helen. *A House Built on Sand—A Political Economy of Saudi Arabia.* New York: Monthly Review; London: Ithaca, 1978.

Love, Kennett. *Suez: The Twice-Fought War: A History.* London: Longman, 1970.

Mabro, Robert, and Radwan, Samir. *The Industrialization of Egypt: 1939–1973: Policy and Performance.* London: Oxford University Press, 1976.

Manzalaoui, Mahmoud, comp. *Arabic Writing Today: The Short Story.* Cairo, Egypt: American Research Center in Egypt, 1968.

———. comp. *Arabic Writing Today: Drama.* Cairo, Egypt: American Research Center in Egypt, 1977.

Mikhail, Mona A. *Images of Women.* Washington, D.C.: Three Continents Press, 1981.

Moussa, Sabri. *The Seeds of Corruption.* translated by Mona N. Mikhail. Boston: Houghton Mifflin Company. 1980.

Niblock, T., ed. *Iraq: The Contemporary State.* London: Croom Helm; New York: St. Martin's, 1982.

Ottoway, David and Marina. *Algeria: The Politics of a Socialist Revolution.* Berkeley: University of California Press, 1970.

Penrose, Edith, and E. F. *Iraq: International Relations and National Development.* Boulder, Colo.: Westview Press, 1979.

Peterson, John E. *Oman in the Twentieth Century.* New York: Barnes & Noble, 1978.

———. *Yemen: The Search for a Modern State.* London: Croom Helm; Baltimore: The Johns Hopkins University Press, 1982.

Raymond, André, ed. *La Syrie D'Aujourd'hui.* Paris: Centre National de la Recherche Scientifique, 1980.

Seale, Patrick. *The Struggle for Syria: A Study of Postwar Arab Politics, 1945–1958.* London: Oxford University Press, 1965.

Taylor, Alan R. *The Arab Balance of Power.* Syracuse, N.Y.: Syracuse University Press, 1982.

Van Dam, Nikolaos. *The Struggle for Power in Syria: Sectarianism, Regionalism, and Tribalism in Politics, 1961–1978.* New York: St. Martin's, 1979.

Vatin, Jean-Claude. *L'Algérie Politique: Histoires et Societe.* Paris: Presse de la Fondation Nationale des Sciences Politiques, 1974.

Waterbury, John. *The Commander of the Faithful: The Moroccan Political Elite—A Study in Segmented Politics.* London: Weidenfeld and Nicolson, 1970.

———. *Egypt: Burdens of the Past, Options for the Future.* Bloomington, Ind.: Indiana University Press, 1978.

———. *The Egypt of Nasser and Sadat: The Political Economy of Two Regimes.* Princeton: Princeton University Press, 1983.

Zartman, I. William et al. *Political Elites in Arab North Africa: Morocco, Algeria, Tunisia, Libya, and Egypt.* New York: Longman, 1982.

Chapter 21

Chibwe, Ephraim Chipampe. *Afro-Arab Relations in the New World Order.* New York: St. Martin's, 1978.

Hallwood, Paul, and Sinclair, Stewart. *Oil, Debt, and Development: OPEC in the Third World.* London: George Allen and Unwin, 1981.

Ibrahim, I., ed. *Arab Resources: The Transformation of a Society.* Washington, D.C.: Georgetown University Center for Contemporary Arab Studies; London: Croom Helm, 1983.

Jabber, Paul. *Not by War Alone: Security and Arms Control in the Middle East.* Berkeley: University of California Press, 1981.

Johany, Ali D. *The Myth of the OPEC Cartel.* Chichester, Sussex and New York: John Wiley, 1980.

Kerr, Malcolm H., and Yassin, El Sayed, eds. *Rich and Poor Nations in the Middle East.* Boulder, Colo.: Westview Press, 1982.

Nelson, Joan M. *Access to Power: Politics and the Urban Poor in Developing Nations.* Princeton: Princeton University Press, 1979.

Rothstein, Robert L. *Global Bargaining: UNCTAD and the Quest for a New International Economic Order.* Princeton: Princeton University Press, 1979.

Sayigh, Yusuf. *The Economies of the Arab World: Development Since 1945.* New York: St. Martin's, 1978.

Selassie, Bereket Habte. *Conflict and Intervention in the Horn of Africa.* New York: Monthly Review, 1980.

Shihata, Ibrahim F. I. *The Other Face of OPEC: Financial Assistance to the Third World.* London and New York: Longman, 1981.

Sivard, Ruth Leger. *World Military and Social Expenditures 1980.* Leesburg, Va.: World Priorities, 1980 (New editions issued periodically).

Stork, Joe. *Middle East Oil and the Energy Crisis.* New York: Monthly Review, 1975.

Waterbury, John and El Mallakh, Ragaei. *The Middle East in the Coming Decade: From Wellhead to Well-Being?* New York: McGraw-Hill, 1978.

Index